Monographs of the Hebrew Union College
Number 32

———

Exile in Amsterdam

Saul Levi Morteira's Sermons
to a Congregation of "New Jews"

I. Edward Kiev Foundation Volumes

Benny Kraut, *From Reform Judaism to Ethical Culture: The Religious Evolution of Felix Adler*

Alan Mendelson, *Secular Education in Philo of Alexandria.*

Raphael Jospe, *Torah and Sophia: The Life and Thought of Shem Tov ibn Falaquera*

Richard Kalmin, *The Redaction of the Babylonian Talmud*

Shuly Rubin Schwartz, *The Emergence of Jewish Scholarship in America: The Publication of the Jewish Encyclopedia*

Philip Miller, *Karaite Separatism in Nineteenth-Century Russia*

Warren Bargad, *To Write the Lips of Sleepers: The Poetry of Amir Gilboa*

Marc Saperstein, *Your Voice LIke a Ram's Horn: Themes and Texts in Traditional Jewish Preaching*

Eric L. Friedland, *"Were Our Mouths Filled with Song": Studies in Liberal Jewish Liturgy*

Edward Fram, *Ideals Face Reality: Jewish Law and Life in Poland, 1550-1665*

Ruth Langer, *To Worship God Properly: Tensions Between Liturgical Custom and Halakhah in Judaism*

Carole Balin, *To Reveal Our Hearts: Jewish Women Writers in Tsarist Russia*

Shaul Bar, *A Letter That Has Not Been Read: Dreams in the Hebrew Bible*

Eric Caplan, *From Ideology to Liturgy: Reconstructionist Worship and American Liberal Judaism*

Zafrira Lidovsky Cohen, *"Loosen the Fetters of Thy Tongue, Woman": The Poetry and Poetics of Yona Wallach*

Marc Saperstein, *Exile in Amsterdam: Saul Levi Morteira's Sermons to a Congregation of "New Jews"*

EXILE IN AMSTERDAM

Saul Levi Morteira's Sermons to a Congregation of "New Jews"

MARC SAPERSTEIN

Hebrew Union College Press
Cincinnati

© Copyright 2005 by the Hebrew Union College Press
Hebrew Union College-Jewish Institute of Religion

This paperback edition, 2015

ISBN 13: 978-0-8229-6373-8
ISBN 10: 0-8229-6373-6

Printed on acid free paper in the United States of America
Typeset by Posner and Sons Ltd., Jerusalem, Israel

In memory of my parents

Rabbi Harold I. Saperstein and Marcia B. Saperstein
1910–2001   *1920–2004*

and of my teacher

Isadore Twersky
1930–1997

שלי ושלכם שלהם הוא

Contents

The I. Edward Kiev Library Foundation

In loving memory of Dr. I. Edward Kiev, distinguished Rabbi, Chaplain, and Librarian of the Hebrew Union College–Jewish Institute of Religion in New York, his family and friends established a Library Foundation in September 1976 to support and encourage scholarship in Judaica and Hebraica. The Hebrew Union College Press is proud to add this work by Marc Saperstein to the growing list of scholarly works supported by the Kiev Foundation.

Preface: A Tale of Three Sabbaticals

This study is the fruit of almost fifteen years of living with the sermons of the Amsterdam rabbi Saul Levi Morteira (1596?–1660).* A brief review of my engagement with this material may be appropriate.

After my first book—based on my doctoral dissertation analyzing medieval philosophical exegesis of non-legal rabbinic texts—went to press, I decided to turn to a different body of literature as a focal point for future research: the sermons delivered by Jews in Europe in the Middle Ages and Early Modern period. Midway through my reading for the book that eventually became *Jewish Preaching, 1200–1800*, I found in the attic of my parents' house a box of books that had belonged to my father's grandfather, Rabbi Hyman Lasker of Troy, New York. Most of them were exegetical and legal *novellae* of various sorts sent out by their authors to a mailing list of colleagues, asking for contributions. But among them was *Giv'at Sha'ul*, a book of sermons by Saul Levi Morteira, published at Warsaw in 1912. I had never heard of the author before; my sense of the canon of Jewish preachers from this period was informed by Israel Bettan's *Studies in Jewish Preaching* and Joseph Dan's *Sifrut ha-Derush ve-ha-Musar*, neither of which mentions Morteira. (In his encyclopedic review of Jewish preaching, Leopold Zunz includes Morteira's name in a long list with no further information than the title of his book.) As I read the Hebrew texts from one *parashah* to the next, I began to sense that this was the work not of an ordinary preacher, but of a homiletical master.

I selected one of the sermons to translate and annotate for *Jewish Preaching*—"The People's Envy," which still strikes me as one of the pinnacles

---

* In the scholarly literature, the name is spelled both "Mortera" and "Morteira." H. P. Salomon, editor of the preacher's polemical *magnum opus*, insists that the first spelling is correct and the second is a Portuguese adaptation of the original Italian-Ashkenazi name. Nevertheless, I use "Morteira" for the following reasons: 1) this is the spelling I have consistently employed in publications beginning in 1981, 2) I have generally used the *Encyclopedia Judaica* as a standard for the spelling of names, and 3) the fact that the spelling "Morteira" (though apparently not the way the preacher signed his own name) appears in official contemporary documents published by Salomon, including the last will and testament, establishes its legitimacy. Occasionally, the two different spellings appear in the same document.

of Jewish homiletical literature, masterfully integrating biblical exegesis and powerful rebuke. Before that book was completed, I published my first article on Jewish preaching, which addressed not its historical but its aesthetic dimensions: "The Sermon as Art Form: Structure in Morteira's *Giv'at Sha'ul.*" There I argued that, working with what had become a standard structure of the classical Sephardic sermon, Morteira had expanded its capacity for flexibility, complexity, and surprising innovation, much like other authors working with and transcending the conventions of their genre, or composers testing the limits of the sonata form.

During a conference at Harvard in the fall of 1988, when *Jewish Preaching* was already in press, a chance conversation with my Jerusalem colleague Yosef Kaplan, one of the pre-eminent experts on the Portuguese Jewish community of Amsterdam, influenced the course of my research and publication from then until now. Noting that Morteira's disciples wrote in their introduction to the original 1645 edition of *Giv'at Sha'ul* that they knew of 1400 sermon texts by Morteira to that date, I asked Kaplan whether he thought that any of these manuscripts might some day be discovered. To my astonishment, he replied that a microfilm of Morteira's sermon manuscripts from the Rabbinical Seminary in Budapest had recently been received by the Institute for Microfilmed Hebrew Manuscripts in Jerusalem. Since I had been invited to be a research fellow of the Hebrew University's Institute for Advanced Studies in Jerusalem during my spring 1989 sabbatical leave from Washington University in St. Louis, I decided that those manuscripts would be the focus of my research.

Settled in Jerusalem, I requested the new microfilm in the National and University Library and found myself looking at a text with unnumbered pages, which I later determined ran to some 385 folios, counting both sides of the page as one. A quick perusal led to dismay: I could barely read a single word of the Hebrew. My doctoral dissertation had been based on medieval Hebrew manuscripts, but those were written by professional scribes, whose letters were clear and consistent. The writing before me turned out to be from the author's own hand—what Morteira actually wrote each week in preparing his sermons for delivery (see chapter two). His letters were not at all clear or consistent. He might form the same one two different ways; his *beit* and *kaf* were usually indistinguishable except by context, and sometimes also his *vav* and his *yod.* It was like reading a hand-written Hebrew letter from an Israeli friend, written in a hurry. Indeed, on a number of occasions during the following months, Israeli visitors to the microfilm reading room would look over my shoulder at the text on the screen and ask me "What language is that?" I quickly realized that working through this text was going to be a long-term project.

I began to decipher the letters using the biblical verses cited at the beginning of each sermon as a key. Although I never reached the point where I could readily skim the material—and some words have remained puzzles—eventually I was able to read the texts with some fluency. But there were other problems. Morteira wrote on both sides of the page. If he happened to be using a heavy ink, it showed through from the opposite side, making the microfilm photograph all but illegible. Furthermore, he frequently wrote all the way to the edge of the page; with the pages bound together, the last few letters of each line were missing in the photograph. When I got to the point of publishing my first article based on the manuscripts—Morteira's previously unknown eulogy for his younger colleague Menasseh ben Israel—I realized that I would need to travel to Budapest to check my transcription from the microfilm against the original.

That visit, in April of 1989, was the first of three to the Budapest Rabbinical Seminary. Rabbi Jozsef Schweitzer, its director, ushered me into a room with a long table piled high with books, and opened the door to a closet where manuscripts were kept. He then removed not one but five volumes: the microfilm on which I had been working full-time for several months was of the largest, volume three, but there were four other volumes containing material I had never seen before. I counted about 550 different sermons in all, the largest extant collection by any Jewish preacher before the second half of the nineteenth century. For the better part of a week, I sat alone in the room from nine to five, reading and copying as much as I could. Among my discoveries that week was a major eulogy for Dr. David Farar, one of the pioneers of the Portuguese community in Amsterdam, which supplemented a short eulogy Morteira had delivered in the cemetery and which was found in volume three. In addition, as I had suspected, many passages from the third volume that were indecipherable in the microfilm were indeed legible in the original text. The Seminary had no facilities for microfilming, but Rabbi Schweitzer graciously arranged for the other four volumes to be microfilmed for me at the Hungarian Academy of Sciences.

I returned to St. Louis from my sabbatical semester with a massive amount of material. My first task was to convert the microfilms into pages of text that I could work on without recourse to a reading machine. Then came the arduous task of identifying and dating the sermons contained in the five volumes, reading through the material systematically, deciding which sermons were of unusual significance, finding material that enhanced our understanding of this special community, and noting the themes that Morteira addressed frequently in his preaching and that appeared to be central to his worldview and his message. I published a few preliminary studies in the following years, including the newly discovered eulogies of David Farar and Menasseh ben Israel, which were included in the original Hebrew with annotated translation in *"Your Voice Like a Ram's Horn."* But it was not until my next sabbatical, in 1995–1996, at the University of Pennsylvania's Center for Advanced Judaic Studies, that I was able to devote extended, uninterrupted time to writing about the texts. Several articles published in the following years were written during that period, including one in a volume that emerged from the colloquium in which I participated: *Transmitting Jewish Traditions: Orality, Textuality, and Cultural Diffusion.*

While my work on Morteira continued, publication of a comprehensive treatment of his manuscripts was delayed by an academic detour that turned out to be not entirely unrelated to the Amsterdam preacher. My father, Harold I. Saperstein, was rabbi of a congregation in Lynbrook, New York from 1933, when he was a student at the Jewish Institute of Religion, until his retirement in June of 1980. Hearing his Friday evening sermons as a teenager had a formative influence on me and undoubtedly contributed to my decision to devote a substantial part of my academic career to the study of Jewish preachers. I knew that my father typed out a full text of each sermon before delivery, but I had never looked at any of these texts. In the process of clearing out his office at the synagogue, I discovered in the filing cabinets typescripts of sermons dating back to 1933. Many of them were homiletical responses to important twentieth-century events and movements: the destruction of European Jewry, the birth of the State of Israel, the oppression of Soviet Jewry, the civil rights movement, the war in Vietnam.

I recalled having heard some of these sermons delivered; others were totally new to me. Convinced that this material had considerable historical significance as a reflection of American rabbinic leadership in turbulent times, I decided to select fifty-two samples from the forty-seven year span. Brief introductions placed them in historical context, and annotations explained references and allusions to events that would have been familiar to his congregants but were largely opaque today. The resulting book, *Witness from the Pulpit: Topical Sermons 1933–1980,* was, as far as I know, the first publication in English of Jewish sermons by a single preacher with full historical annotation.

In my introduction to the book, I noted a number of similarities between the seventeenth-century preacher from Amsterdam and the twentieth-century preacher from a suburb of New York (pp. 6–15). Both considered the weekly sermon an important component of their rabbinical work. Both wrote out their texts fully before delivery, so that what remains for us are the products of their own hands. Both organized their material carefully so that the listener would have a clear sense of the sermon's structure. Both preached to congregants who were not steeped in traditional Jewish learning and who looked to the rabbi's sermon as a major source of information about Jewish issues. And both spent their entire rabbinic careers in only one congregation, with all the implications this had for the preaching enterprise: most of the listeners had a positive relationship with the preacher, whose authority derived not just from his title, or his reputation among scholars, but also from his having officiated at the most important events in their lives (wedding, *brit milah* for a son, funeral for a parent), perhaps over two generations. The preacher knew the listeners; they trusted him. This bond was especially significant when the preacher resorted to what I have called "the rhetoric of rebuke," criticizing the behavior of those who sat before him.

In addition, this stable and enduring relationship with a congregation ensured a continuity of discourse. Here is how I formulated this principle:

As a genre, a sermon is a discrete entity, complete in itself—like a short story, a poem, a one-act play—and it should be analyzed as such. But for a rabbi who addresses the same congregation week after week and year after year, the individual sermon also becomes part of a larger cumulative message. Just as there is an expectation of novelty, so there is an expectation of consistency and continuity. Not the consistency of a philosophical treatise; it is understood that different occasions may require different emphases. But blatant contradictions between one sermon and another or fundamental shifts in position are problematic and need to be explained. The advantage of this situation is that not everything need be covered on any one occasion. The preacher knows that most of the listeners have heard him before, and he can refer back to an earlier communication. He also expects that his audience will return in the future to hear more, and he can promise to address a topic in further detail on another occasion.

This common situation leads to a striking degree of "self-referentiality" in the sermons of both preachers. Almost every sermon by Morteira after the first few years refers back to earlier ones, which he paraphrases, summarizes, or recapitulates, in order to lay the foundation for the current discourse. Sometimes he will begin by referring to a sermon he delivered the previous year on the same Torah lesson, or on a different lesson several years in the past. This way of introducing a topic saves time; there is no need for a full discussion of a particular point at present, and the preacher can, after a brief summary, go on to a new aspect assuming that the foundation is in place (p. 8).

In short, despite all the substantial differences between the historical contexts, the congregations, the content of the sermons, and the stature of the rabbis, my work on each of these two large collections of sermons enhanced my understanding of the other.

The work on my father's sermons led me to further investigation of other Jewish sermons in the twentieth century, especially those by American and British rabbis responding to Nazism and the annihilation of European Jewry during the Second World War. But when yet another sabbatical leave came up in the fall of 2002, this time from George Washington University in Washington D.C., I decided to focus on Morteira. Among my projects during an appointment as Rabbi Hugo Gryn Visiting Fellow in Religious Tolerance at the Centre for Jewish-Christian Relations in Cambridge, England, was an effort to bring together all I had written on Morteira's sermons, to fill in topics that had not been covered, to establish the Hebrew texts, and to translate a selection of his most important sermons. The present book is the product of this third sabbatical leave.

* * *

I believe that this study has significance in several different areas of Jewish Studies. First, of course, is the broad topic that has been a central focus of my academic research and publication over the past twenty-five years: the history of Jewish preaching, and the sermon as a primary source for Jewish history, literature, and thought. I therefore begin in Section One with the preacher and the evidence for his homiletical enterprise. After reviewing the broad outlines of his biography, his treatment by scholars, and his image in several literary works, I turn to the extant manuscripts of his 550 sermons, which supplement the 50 sermons in the printed edition (Amsterdam 1645, reprinted at Warsaw in 1902 and 1912). In the absence of video-tapes or detailed reports from his listeners, his texts must be the starting point for any consideration of the man. First, then, I describe the typical text of a discrete sermon intended for a specific Sabbath, analyzing its various components, including what was added to it after the delivery. I then move on to the entire collection of these discrete sermons in the five bound volumes of the Budapest Rabbinical Seminary, and finally I consider the even larger collection of sermons, many of which are no longer extant, that served as Morteira's ever-expanding data base.

Having established this foundation, I move back in time to the "preacher's workshop" in order to reconstruct the process by which Morteira produced his texts. First I consider the various decisions he had to make each week: whether to write a new sermon or revise an old one, which biblical verse and rabbinic dictum would serve as its fundamental building blocks, what central theme or problem it would address, and how the material should be structured and organized. Then I turn to the resources at his disposal, especially the books in his library from which he drew much of the traditional substance of his sermons, before he supplemented it with his own original approach.

Having considered the completed written text, I then move forward to the next critical stage: the sermon's oral delivery. In my work on Jewish preaching, I have insisted that the text is only our best evidence for the sermon; it is not the sermon itself. The actual sermon is what the preacher says to the congregation, an event of oral communication, or performance. An integral part of this event is the "delivery," with all that this word implies: tempo, pitch, emphasis, intensity, and quality of voice, as well as hand gestures, facial expression, level of animation, even interaction between preacher and listeners. After a preliminary discussion of this performance event in comparison with other art forms, I focus on the text of one particularly powerful sermon by Morteira—one delivered under dramatic circumstances, containing some purple passages of finely-crafted rhetoric. I analyze not just the homiletical challenges the preacher faced in this sermon, but how the listeners may have responded to what they heard and experienced.

This book is not just about Morteira, however. It is also about a community, indeed one of the most dynamic communities in early modern Jewish history. In this respect as well, the sermon is different from most other literary texts. The author of a book may believe that he is responding to issues of concern, but once the book is completed it is dispatched into a darkened space. The author has no knowledge or control over whom (if anyone) it will reach, where they may be, and how much time will elapse before its audience considers what he has to say. Both positive and negative response to his message will reach the author, if at all, only indirectly. If it is too controversial, the author has the option of concealing his identity with a pseudonym or anonymity.

The preacher, by contrast, delivers his words facing the listeners for whom they are intended. Knowing the audience, he is able to craft his message to their needs, pitch its content to their level of knowledge. If the sermon is too long, if the point is too abstruse, if the rebuke strikes too deeply and angers or offends, the preacher can see the audience's reaction in "real time." Listeners may fall asleep, start talking to their neighbors, get up and walk out, even challenge the speaker before the sermon has ended. In Amsterdam, each preacher spoke in the imposing presence of the regents, members of the *Mahamad*, a wealthy lay oligarchy that exercised authority and discipline not only over the ordinary members of the community but to some extent over the rabbis as well. A respected rabbi and preacher like Morteira was capable of communicating a message that he knew would arouse displeasure in at least some of the listeners, but he certainly could not be indifferent to their responses.

Consequently, the sermons Morteira delivered over more than a forty-year period can teach us something about the community he addressed. To be sure, there are serious methodological challenges inherent in drawing conclusions about the audience from the texts of what was said to them each Sabbath morning. But certain kinds of information are accessible from the sermons, and they supplement and complement the data in the abundant archival sources preserved by the community. I begin Section Two, "The Community," with information about individuals in Morteira's Amsterdam, preserved in eulogies he delivered over a period of forty years for such respected leaders as Jacob Tirado, David Farar, and Menasseh ben Israel, and for lesser known figures, including Morteira's own students. I then discuss the evidence in the sermons for a dramatic event in the early (1618) life of the community, and for the community's institutions, especially the *Bikkur Ḥolim* confraternity, one of its most important voluntary associations.

A critical component of any preacher's homiletical activity is his need on occasion to criticize what he considers to be the shortcomings and failures of his congregants when they are measured against the standards of traditional Jewish behavior and belief. The unique character of this community—in its first generation composed almost entirely of immigrants who had lived as Christians in Portugal and who were assuming a Jewish identity with minimal prior knowledge or experience—makes this component especially important as a historical source. What aspects of behavior did the leadership judge to be beyond the boundary lines of toleration? What beliefs were considered to be most dangerous, necessary to condemn and, if possible, suppress? How did the preacher mobilize the resources of the classical texts to present his rebuke in a manner intended to produce maximum effectiveness and inspire general assent? And how do the violations he attacks from the pulpit compare with those that generated archival evidence of sanctions imposed by the lay leadership of the community?

Important as this material is, the central purpose of the sermons was certainly not to preserve information about individuals or institutions. Nor was the preacher's primary goal in the pulpit to criticize his audience. This was a congregation composed of sophisticated individuals, many of them educated in the Portuguese universities of Coimbra or Evora, highly accomplished physicians and successful international merchants. They knew that they wanted to be Jews. But they had come to Amsterdam with little solid grounding in traditional Jewish texts, and lacking the linguistic tools to read them in their original language. The substance and content of the Jewish tradition had to be communicated to them in a manner that was aesthetically appealing and appropriate for their level. This is what Morteira and his rabbinic colleagues undertook in their sermons week after week. Cumulatively, their homiletical works provide evidence for an ongoing program of adult education that mediated and transmitted a tradition, on a consistently high yet accessible level, to a congregation of "new Jews."*

Section Three, "From Past to Future," therefore focuses on some of the ideas Morteira thought to be crucial to communicate to his people. I begin with his incorporation of historical material in the sermons; he used it, not to turn his listeners into historians, but to draw lessons from the past for a homiletical purpose in the present. A central aspect of that history, with bearing on the experience of virtually all in the audience, was a confrontation with Christianity. Most of Morteira's listeners had been exposed to a barrage of Christian claims intended to heap ridicule upon the Jewish religion, attack with contempt the "judaizers," and trivialize or even demonize the Jews. This discourse of disdain remained resonant enough in the memories of some congregants that it had to be confronted and contested. Morteira apparently concluded that in order to construct a new Jewish identity, it was necessary to dismantle the relics of the older Christian identity. I therefore analyze what Morteira said in many passages of his sermons about Christianity, especially its manifestation in the Catholic Church. He also devoted considerable attention to the "New Christians" who had elected to remain in Portugal; he explains the reasons for their decision, the rationalizations they used to justify remaining in the "lands of idolatry," and the ultimate punishment that he felt awaited those who erroneously assume that they can distance themselves from the fate of their people. Again, he apparently concluded that at least some of his congregants were—like Jews who left the Soviet Union for Israel in the 1990s—ambivalent about their decision and in need of reinforcement from the pulpit.

One of the critical polarities of classical Jewish thought and consciousness is that of exile and messianic redemption. Many members of the Amsterdam

---

* This term, a neologism parallel to the term "New Christians" invented in Spanish and Portuguese society to characterize recent converts to Christianity and their descendants, has been used by Yosef Kaplan (e.g., in his article, "Wayward New Christians and Stubborn New Jews," and in his book *Les nouveaux-Juifs d'Amsterdam* [see Bibliography]), although I am not certain whether he was the first modern scholar to use it in this context. (The term actually appears in a front quotation from an Inquisitional document of 1687, reproduced in Kaplan's book.)

Portuguese community had undergone a transformative experience analogous to the Exodus from Egypt. Living now in an environment that was unparalleled for its religious toleration and lack of discrimination, and with some flourishing economically on a competitive basis with their Christian neighbors, they may have found the traditional model of exile irrelevant to their experience. Though recognizing the uniqueness of the Jewish status in Amsterdam and the good fortune of the Jews who lived there, Morteira insisted that they were still at one with their fellow Jews with regard to *galut*. His sermons elucidate the negative aspects of the exilic condition, but at the same time they emphasize that God protects the Jewish people from its most serious dangers. The theme of messianic redemption also pulsates in many of his sermons. In evaluating Morteira's treatment of this topic, I pose the question: Might his preaching have contributed to the kind of "messianic tension" that could generate the enthusiastic response in the community to the claims of Sabbatai Zevi a few years after Morteira's death?

With the publication by H. P. Salomon in its Portuguese original of Morteira's *magnum opus*, the "Treatise on [God's Providence over Israel and] the Eternity of the Law of Moses," a work completed in 1659 near the end of his life, we can draw some conclusions about the relationship between this comprehensive work and Morteira's preaching. In our discussion of ideas about history, Christianity, exile and redemption in the sermons, we shall see many examples of exegetical and conceptual motifs that appear many years, even decades, before they were recast for his Treatise. Perhaps the most important and pervasive motif in Morteira's message is his insistence on "God's Providence over Israel": that the vicissitudes of Jewish historical experience were not the result of chance or the product of power politics, but rather an unfolding of an overarching plan that reflects God's unique relationship with and enduring commitment to the Jews. A related principle is reiterated in many of his sermons: that the events of the Bible were not just occurrences in the distant past, but rather types, pre-figurations, and emblems that encode information about patterns that will be reenacted in subsequent generations, in the more recent past, the present, and the future.

The approach in this discursive part of the book is synthetic, analyzing specific passages in the sermons but then weaving them together with similar passages to construct a fuller picture. Throughout my study of Jewish preaching, however, I have insisted that the fundamental unit for analysis must be the individual sermon. Therefore, in order to illustrate and concretize, I have selected eight previously untranslated sermons for analysis and annotation: three for ordinary Sabbaths, one for a specific community occasion, two long sermons for the Sabbath of Repentance, and two eulogies. I hope that, together with the Sabbath sermon included in *Jewish Preaching* and the three eulogies included in *"Your Voice Like a Ram's Horn,"* this substantial corpus of Morteira's preaching, now accessible to the English reader, will establish his position in the canon of the outstanding practitioners of Jewish homiletical art.

* * *

For some time I have wondered about the unsung hero of the academic profession who first made the ingenious proposal to take an agricultural institution of the Bible—allowing fields to remain fallow and to "rest" for one year out of every seven—and apply it to faculty members who would take a year out of every seven from their teaching and administrative responsibilities, with pay (generally half-salary), to devote full time to research and writing. Certainly this is a person whose statue should adorn the grounds of the American Association of University Professors headquarters. Yet none of the many colleagues I have asked about this have had the foggiest idea when, where, or how this institution began and became accepted by university administrations. And there is surprisingly little written about it. After some hunting, I discovered that it was initiated by President Charles W. Eliot of Harvard in 1880 (reportedly as part of an effort to woo a faculty member from Johns Hopkins), followed in the next decade by Cornell, Wellesley, and Columbia.* This is therefore another reason to express my gratitude to the university of my undergraduate and doctoral studies, for having facilitated through this institution opportunities for research without which this book would never have been written.

The Gloria M. Goldstein Chair of Jewish History and Thought at Washington University in St. Louis, and the Charles E. Smith Chair of Jewish History at The George Washington University, provided funding for my academic positions during the entire period when I was working on this project. My indebtedness to the donors of these chairs and to the respective universities that have provided supportive environments for my teaching and research should be obvious.

---

* For the first evidence of the institution (though the word is not used here), see "Annual Reports of the President and Treasurer of Harvard College, 1879–80, The President's Report for 1879–80," pp. 19–20 (*http://pds.harvard.edu:8080/pds/servlet/PageDeliveryService?id=1589 83&type=leaf&seqno=20*). The term was already apparently well accepted by 1886, as seen by its use at Wellesley (*OED* ad verbum). For discussion, see Walter Crosby Eells, "The Origin and Early History of Sabbatical Leave," *AAUP Bulletin*, Autumn 1962, pp. 253–56; Eells and Ernest V. Hollis, *Sabbatical Leave in American Higher Education: Origin, Early History, and Current Practices* (Washington, 1962).

As indicated earlier, during the three sabbaticals when I was working on the Morteira manuscripts, I was hosted and funded by three institutions. The Institute of Advanced Studies in Jerusalem provided my first opportunity to work in an environment entirely devoted to individual research, supported by a talented staff and challenged by colleagues of various areas of expertise, brought together by Moshe Idel to interact on a broad common topic, in this case, biblical exegesis. My second sabbatical host, the Center for Advanced Jewish Studies at the University of Pennsylvania, under the inspired leadership of David Ruderman, provided a very similar environment in the United States. This time the theme was "Orality, Literacy, and the Transmission of Knowledge in Jewish Culture"—a topic for which the sermons of Morteira were obviously relevant. My two presentations to the scholars in this group elicited important critical feedback midway through my project. My host during the third sabbatical—the Centre for Jewish-Christian Relations in Cambridge, England, an institution created by my former student Edward Kessler—and the larger context of the University with its library and its Faculty of Divinity—provided the perfect environment in which to fill in lacunae in my material as I was starting on a new research project. My gratitude to all three institutions for their generosity and hospitality is abundant.

Several libraries have been crucial to my research. The Institute of Microfilmed Hebrew Manuscripts in the National and University Library of Giv'at Ram, Jerusalem was where I first encountered the manuscripts of Morteira's sermons, and spent many long days reading them from microfilms. Benjamin Richler and Abraham David have throughout the years been extraordinarily responsive to my every request. This project would have been stymied near its beginning were it not for the cooperation of Rabbi Jozsef Schweitzer, until 1997 the director of the Rabbinical Seminary of Budapest, who first made the actual manuscripts available to me and gave me permission to publish Hebrew texts and translations from them. During my last visit, in November 2002, the Librarian of the Seminary, Dr. Ferenc Borsanyi-Schmidt, made the manuscripts available to me even during an inconvenient period of transition for the library. The Harvard University Library, with its Judaica Librarian Charles Berlin, has continued to be the place where I could track down those unusual sources not accessible in my own university libraries (the Olin Library of Washington University in St. Louis and the Gelman Library of The George Washington University, with its wonderful Kiev Collection). I have also benefited greatly from access to the libraries of the University of Cambridge, the Jewish Theological Seminary, and Yeshiva University.

Over the years, I have been enriched by frequent consultations with experts on various aspects of the Portuguese Jewish Community of Amsterdam, especially Miriam Bodian, Yosef Kaplan, Richard Popkin, H. P. Salomon, Odette Vlessing. For help on specific conundra (indicated in the footnotes), I am grateful to Howard Adelman, James Aitken, Nicholas de Lange, Arthur Eckstein, Talya Fishman, Barry Freundel, Avraham Gross, William Horbury, Julia Lieberman, Ronald Mellor, Richard Menkis, Miri Rubin, David Ruderman, Jacob Schacter, James Shapiro, Haim Soloveitchik, Shaul Stampfer, Krister Stendhal, and Thomas Worcester. Kimmy Caplan's review of my annotation of the Hebrew texts of several of the sermons elucidated many details.

My Washington University colleagues Nancy Berg and David Hadas made helpful comments on several chapters of the book. Hava Tirosh-Samuelson gave a sympathetic and insightful reading to the entire text; my formulation of several chapter titles is indebted to her. H. P. Salomon read through the typescript with painstaking care and enabled me to correct many technical typographical errors and technical inaccuracies (especially in Portuguese transcriptions), as well as imprecisions in formulation, infelicities in translation, and oversights in bibliography.

Among those who have studied the sermon texts with me in the original Hebrew or in translation, and often provided perceptive feedback, were students in the Doctor of Jewish Studies Program at Chicago's Spertus Institute of Jewish Studies during the summers of 1999 and 2003, graduate students at the Revel School of Yeshiva University in the spring of 2002, and colleagues of the University of Cambridge's Faculty of Divinity and at the Leo Baeck School in London during the fall of 2002 and at a conference on "Religion and the State: Community and Identity," sponsored by the Centre for History and Economics at the University of Cambridge, in July 2003. I have discussed topics in Morteira's preaching with colleagues at the Hebrew Union College-Jewish Institute of Religion in the spring of 1999 and in a Colloquium led by James Shapiro at the Folger Institute in the spring of 2001.

Earlier versions of some of the chapters have been published as follows, and I am grateful for permission to use revised versions of this material:

- Chapter 2: *Studies in Jewish Manuscripts*, ed. Joseph Dan and Klaus Herrmann (Tübingen: Mohr Siebeck, 1999), pp. 171–98.
- Chapter 4: *Transmitting Jewish Traditions: Orality, Textuality, and Cultural Diffusion*, ed. Yaakov Elman and Israel Gershoni (New Haven: Yale University Press, 2000), pp. 248–78
- Part of chapter 6: "The Rhetoric and Substance of Rebuke: Social and Religious Criticism in the Sermons of Hakham Saul Levi Morteira," *Studia Rosenthaliana* 34 (2000): 131–52.

- Chapter 7: *Jewish History and Jewish Memory: Essays in Honor of Yosef Hayim Yerushalmi*, ed. Elisheva Carlebach, John M. Efron, and David Myers (Hanover, NH: Brandeis University Press, 1998), pp. 113–33.
- Chapter 8: *Hebrew Union College Annual*, 70–71 (1999–2000): 329–84.
- Part of Chapter 9: *Me'ah She'arim: Studies in Medieval Jewish Spiritual Life in Memory of Isadore Twersky* (Jerusalem: The Hebrew University Magnes Press, 2001), pp. 208–49.

In all cases, the articles contain in the notes the Hebrew texts from the original manuscripts translated in the body of the texts (though the Hebrew in the Yerushalmi *Festschrift* was for technical reasons badly mangled). I decided that there was no reason to replicate the Hebrew in the present publication; readers who are interested may consult the publications above. The Hebrew texts of sermons 1 and 2 will appear in a Memorial Volume for Prof. Isadore Twersky, to be published by Harvard University Press.

I would like to express my enduring gratitude to the Hebrew Union College Press, and especially to Michael Meyer, Chair of the Publications Committee, Barbara Selya, a wonderfully perceptive and helpful copy editor, and Ari and Phyllis Kiev, benefactors of the I. Edward Kiev Library Foundation, which has generously supported the publication of this book.

Marc Saperstein
Washington, DC,
July 2004

The Preacher

1
Morteira's Historical Image

Consider the following characterizations. Saul Levi Morteira was "a fanatic of the Law, a ruthless inquisitor" (Kayser); "a doughty controversialist" (Roth); "the leading opponent of Jewish tolerance of Christianity and its adherents" (Melnick); "rationalistic" (Nadler). He was "not even a distinguished preacher" (Graetz); he was "a renowned preacher" (Popkin). He was "one of the dominant personalities of Sephardic Jewry in Western Europe during the seventeenth century" (Kaplan).[1] To some extent, these statements reflect differences in perspective, like the proverbial six blind men examining different parts of the elephant. But beyond this, they indicate the changing attitudes toward Morteira as more and more of his work has become part of the scholarly domain. Before we analyze Morteira as leader and educator of the Portuguese Jewish community of Amsterdam through his sermons, it will be useful to survey some of our shifting images of this multi-faceted man.

Life
This is not the place for a full biographical sketch of Morteira. Nor is there need for a comprehensive characterization of the community he served as rabbi for more than forty years. That community has itself has been the study of several recent monographs and dozens of articles.[2] While there is no adequate biographical treatment of Morteira in English, his life and some of his

---

1. The statements by Kayser, Roth, and Graetz are quoted in a fuller form further in this chapter. "Leading opponent" is from Ralph Melnick, *From Polemics to Apologetics* (Assen, 1981), p. 23; "rationalistic" is from Steven Nadler, *Spinoza's Heresy* (Oxford, 2001), p. 178; "renowned preacher" is from Richard Popkin, "The Historical Significance of Sephardic Judaism in 17th-Century Amsterdam," *The American Sephardi* 5 (1971): 22; "one of the dominant personalities" is from Yosef Kaplan, "Rabbi Saul Levi Morteira's Treatise" (below, n. 3), p. 95.

2. See Miriam Bodian, *Hebrews of the Portuguese Nation* (Bloomington, 1997); Daniel M. Swetschinski, *Reluctant Cosmopolitans* (London, 2000); J. C. H. Blom, R. G. Fuks-Mansfeld, and I. Schöffer, eds., *The History of the Jews in the Netherlands* (Oxford, 2002), esp. the articles by Swetschinski, Jonathan I. Israel, and Yosef Kaplan (pp. 44–163), all with extensive

works have been recently discussed in Hebrew articles by Yosef Kaplan and in the massive introduction to his Portuguese and Dutch editions of Morteira's *Tratado* by H. P. Salomon.[3] I will therefore present only the bare outlines of his life before I survey the presentation of Morteira in scholarly literature, his image in several literary renderings, and the academic investigation of his various writings.

The major source of early published information about Morteira's life is the introduction to *Giv'at Sha'ul,* the collection of fifty of his sermons published at Amsterdam in 1645, during his lifetime. The introduction was written by two of his students, who gathered the sermons, one on each of the weekly scriptural lessons from the Torah, and brought them to press with their mentor's acquiescence. In their introduction, the students report the following information: Morteira was born in Venice; when he was about 20 years old, he passed through Amsterdam on his way back to Venice; at that time the leaders of the Beth Jacob congregation urged him to remain with them and to deliver a sermon every Sabbath, and later they made him head of their yeshivah. Other documents fill in the background of Morteira's arrival. He had accompanied the distinguished *converso* physician Elijah Montalto, recently converted to Judaism, to Paris, where Montalto served in the court of Queen Marie de Médicis, a position that required a special waiver of the prohibition against professed Jews residing in France. When Montalto died suddenly in 1616, his body was brought to the nearest Jewish burial ground: the Ouderkerk cemetery of the Portuguese community in Amsterdam. It was as a member of this entourage that Morteira first came to Amsterdam; in one of his manuscript sermons, he refers to the eulogy he delivered for Montalto (no text of the actual eulogy is extant).[4] The following year, in the summer of 1617, he

---

bibliographies, including references to many important articles by Kaplan, Israel, Popkin, and I. S. Révah, and H. P. Salomon.

3. Yosef Kaplan, "R. Sha'ul Levi Morteira ve-Ḥibburo 'Ta'anot ve-Hasagot Neged ha-Dat he-Notsrit,'" *Meḥqarim al Toledot Yahadut Holland* 1 (1975): 9–31, with abridged English version, "Rabbi Saul Levi Morteira's Treatise 'Arguments Against the Christian Religion,'" *Immanuel* 11 (1980): 95–112. H. P. Salomon, introduction to Morteira's *Tratado da verdade da lei de Moisés* (Coimbra, 1988), pp. ix–cxxvii, with documents pp. cxxxv–cxliv. The Dutch edition of this work, *Traktaat betreffende de waarheid van de wet van Mozes,* was published at Braga in 1988.

4. Montalto's date of death is inscribed on his tombstone as 29 Shevat 5376 (February 19, 1616); see David Henriques de Castro, *Keur van grafsteenen* (Ouderkerk aan de Amstel 1999), pp. 60–62. The reference to the eulogy is in Budapest Rabbinical Seminary MS 12, 1:71r, *Naso,* Num. 6:24–26, Morteira's earliest dated sermon, from the spring of 1617 (all subsequent references to this manuscript are identified simply by MS followed by the volume and folio number, scriptural lesson and theme-verse; on the manuscript itself, see below,

preached at the occasion of the marriage of Montalto's son Moses to Esther Curiel; in this sermon, he refers enigmatically to having been "saved" in Paris—an allusion to an event that most of the listeners would undoubtedly have understood, but which remains tantalizingly vague today.[5]

This information notwithstanding, much remains uncertain about this early period in Morteira's life, and his sermons unfortunately divulge little. Until fairly recently, the scholarly literature about Morteira has been divided over whether he was of Ashkenazi or Portuguese Sephardi background. Discovery of a new document in the community archives finally established that he was an Ashkenazi, and passages in the manuscript sermons reveal that he was from one of the most distinguished Ashkenazi families: the Katzenellenbogens.[6] Virtually all of the discussions of Morteira have set his year of birth at 1596, derived from the statement by his students that he arrived in Amsterdam (in 1616) at age 20. Yet this makes the chronology problematic: Montalto assumed his responsibilities in Paris in 1612, which would make Morteira sixteen years old, hardly mature enough to have completed his education and to serve as Montalto's private rabbi. It seems likely, therefore, that he was born a few years earlier.[7]

Virtually nothing is known about Morteira's upbringing or education in

---

chapter 2). On Montalto, see most recently, S. W. Baron, *SRHJ* 15:101–3; Melnick, *From Polemics to Apologetics,* pp. 24–29; H. P. Salomon, "Une letter inédite du Docteur Felipe Rodrigues Montalto," in *Les rapports culturels et littéraires entre le Portugal et la France* (Paris: 1983), pp. 151–63, and the Introduction to his edition of Morteira's *Tratado,* pp. xl–xliii; Bernard Cooperman, "Eliahu Montalto's 'Suitable and Incontrovertible Propositions': A Seventeenth-Century Anti-Christian Polemic," in *Jewish Thought in the Seventeenth Century,* ed. I. Twersky and B. Septimus (Cambridge, 1987), pp. 469–97; Jonathan Israel, *European Jewry in the Age of Mercantilism 1550–1750* (Oxford, 1985), p. 70.

5. MS 2:129r, *Eqev,* Deut. 7:13, 1617. (A possible context for the allusion is the royal decree of April 23, 1615, ten months before Montalto's death, ordering all people practicing Judaism to leave the country under penalty of death: see Baron, *SRHJ* 15: 102). Esther Montalto lived until 1692—75 years after her wedding—and was buried under the same tombstone as her deceased husband's father Elijah (Castro, *Keur van grafsteenen,* pp. 60–61).

6. On the debate in recent years, see further in this chapter; in a 1989 publication, Menahem Dorman wrote that "scholars are divided about his family origin, and it cannot be settled," although he tended toward the Sephardic *converso* theory: Dorman, *Menasheh Ben-Isra'el* (Tel Aviv, 1989), p. 15. For Morteira's reference to his grandfather, R. Judah Katzenellenbogen, see the Exordium to "The Dust of the Earth," below, p. 381.

7. This would be confirmed by a document cited by Isaac Emmanuel, stating that on August 10, 1654, the rabbis and *parnasim* of the Portuguese nation went to the Amsterdam Notary to testify in proceedings involving Jacob Moreno, his wife, and Daniel Castiel. Required to list their ages, Saul Levi Morteira stated that he was "about 60" years old, yielding a birth date of 1594. See Isaac Emmanuel, "Yedi'ot Ḥadashot al ha-Qehillah ha-Portugesit be-Amsterdam," *Otsar Yehudei Sefarad* 6 (1963): 166. In a personal communication, H. P.

Venice. Most accounts describe him as the disciple of the great Venetian Rabbi Leon Modena, and indeed a cordial if occasionally strained relationship between them is attested in later correspondence. But in all of Morteira's sermons, I have not been able to find a single explicit reference to Modena.[8] Nor have I found any clear evidence that Morteira used or was directly influenced by the book of Modena's sermons, *Midbar Yehudah*, which was published at Venice in 1602. This does not necessarily mean that Morteira was not influenced by Modena's preaching. *Midbar Yehudah* is a very limited selection of Modena's homiletical output, encompassing only twenty-two sermons for holidays and life-cycle events. We do not have any of the ordinary Sabbath sermons that Modena preached week after week for many years, sermons that Morteira probably heard while growing up and may indeed have remembered. Where Morteira does refer to "my master and teacher," he is invoking not Modena but the distinguished physician whom he accompanied to France, Elijah Montalto. In a single sermon on the theme of Esau as a typological prefiguration of Christianity during the period of Jewish exile, Morteira cites four different interpretations by Montalto, in one place identifying him as "*ha-Rav*" (Rabbi).[9] Richard Popkin asserted that Morteira was "educated at the University of Padua," but provided no reference for this information, and I have been unable to discover any confirmation.[10]

Once in Amsterdam, Morteira established a binding relationship with a figure in some ways quite similar to Montalto: a charismatic Portuguese *converso* physician named David Farar. Dr. Farar left Portugal, joined a Jew-

---

Salomon has provided a more accurate summary of the text; he doubts that it requires modifying the traditional 1596 birthdate for Morteira.

8. While the authors of the historical notes to Modena's *Autobiography* refer to Morteira as "one of Modena's most distinguished students" from the early period of his career, Modena does not mention Morteira in his autobiography (*The Autobiography of a Seventeenth-Century Venetian Rabbi* (Princeton: 1988), p. 214, cf. p. 244). In June 1618, Modena addressed a letter to Morteira that begins with the statement that "Your father and your brother have come to me," refers to his having heard complaints about Morteira, and says he is speaking to him "as a father to a son" (*Iggerot R. Yehudah Aryeh mi-Modena*, ed. Jacob Boksenboim (Tel Aviv, 1984), p. 162.This letter clearly indicates a relationship, quite possibly of teacher and disciple, but it is strange that Morteira does not seem to refer to Modena at all.

9. See below, p. 110, n. 116; this title also appears on Montalto's tombstone (הרב הכולל כמוהר"ר אליהו , *o rab rabi eliav Montalto*); see Castro, *Keur van grafsteenen*, pp. 60–61. This suggests that Jonathan Israel's characterization of Morteira in Paris as Montalto's "young disciple" (*European Jewry*, p. 70), or Salomoñ's characterization as his "religious secretary" (*Tratado*), p. lxii, is more accurate than the notion that Montalto took Morteira along so that he would have a rabbi and teacher in Paris.

10. Popkin, "Historical Significance," p. 22.

ish community, and became a staunch defender of Judaism both in speech and in writing. Although he commanded the respect of Christian scholars as well as of those in his own congregation, Farar was attacked in 1618 by Joseph Pardo, the *Ḥakham* of the Beth Jacob congregation, in a controversy that was submitted to rabbinical authorities in Venice and Salonika for adjudication. The bitter split led to the formation of a break-away congregation, Ets Ḥaim, and to Morteira's appointment as rabbi of Beth Jacob. Morteira traveled to Venice with two other representatives of the Beth Jacob congregation and two representatives of the new Ets Ḥaim congregation in an attempt to reach a mutually acceptable solution to the conflict. When the Beth Jacob congregation was vindicated following an appeal to the Dutch authorities, Morteira delivered a celebratory sermon emphasizing reconciliation.[11] In his eulogy for Farar six years later, Morteira paid the physician impressive tribute, saying, "From his deeds, I learned to serve God properly."[12]

Morteira's relationships with his rabbinic colleagues in the Portuguese community were not always cordial. In the mid-1630s, he was involved in another controversy involving his younger colleague Isaac Aboab da Fonseca over a theological issue—whether eternal punishment is given to unrepentant sinners—as we shall see below. Later, his relationship with Menasseh ben Israel, whose reputation in the Christian world was spreading far beyond the Dutch republic, became so strained that the Regents of the community had to intervene to settle what was becoming a public scandal.[13] In the merger agreement for the three Portuguese synagogues in 1639, it was stipulated that Morteira would preach on three consecutive Sabbaths or holidays and then Menasseh ben Israel would preach on the fourth. Aboab was not even included in the rotation, and was actually designated as the fourth of the four *ḥakhamim* in the community at a salary less than three-fourths of Morteira's (David Pardo, whose son would later marry Morteira's daughter, was in second place). This slight may have impelled Aboab to leave Amsterdam in 1642 to become the first rabbi in the "New World" at Recife.[14]

---

11. For the events and the sermon, see below, pp. 166–72.

12. For the relationship with Farar and the texts of both eulogies, see Marc Saperstein, *"Your Voice Like a Ram's Horn"* (Cincinnati, 1996), pp. 367–98.

13. See Salomon, in Morteira, *Tratado*, pp. lxxiv, xcii, cxli–cxlii, and Morteira's eulogy for Menasseh, Saperstein, *"Your Voice Like a Ram's Horn,"* pp. 411–44.

14. For a summary of the provision in the merger agreement, see Daniel Swetchinski, *Reluctant Cosmpolitans*, pp. 204–5; for a fuller discussion, see Arnold Wiznitzer, "The Merger Agreement and Regulations of Congregation Talmud Torah of Amsterdam (1638–1639)," *Historia Judaica* 20 (1958): 109–20, esp. pp. 117–18. On Aboab in Recife, see M. Kayserling, "Isaac Aboab, The First Jewish Author in America," in Martin A. Cohen, ed., *The Jewish Experience in Latin America*, 2 vols. (New York, 1971), 2:193–204, and Wiznitzer, "The Mi-

Although endowed with a sometimes combative disposition, Morteira did apparently develop close relationships not only with older mentors such as Montalto and Farar, but also with his students. The introduction to *Giv'at Sha'ul* reveals the considerable devotion of the two disciples who wrote it. They report having borrowed the text of Morteira's sermons on various Torah lessons. Apparently they told their teacher that they wanted to copy them and send them to other Jewish communities—their real intention being to prepare the book for publication. Indeed, Morteira seems to have been rather dedicated to his students (several of whom he eulogized, as we shall see). In his introduction to the commentaries on Ecclesiastes and Psalms written by his disciple Moses Mercado and published in 1652 a few months after the young student's death,[15] Morteira summarized his current position in Amsterdam:

> Now, God be praised, about forty "armed soldiers" in the war of Torah regularly eat at my table, some of them masters in Mishnah and Talmud, some in the legendary and rhetorical texts, some of them eloquent preachers, some focus on the simple meaning of Bible, some are poets,[16] some experts in books of metaphysics. For all of them, reverence for God is their treasure (cf. Isa. 33:6). All of the scholars who have visited us observed this with astonishment (Ps. 48:6); they examined these students and said, "God's blessing is upon you, and we bless you in God's name."[17]

This passage emphasizes the diversity of interests and talents among Morteira's students, all assembled at his table under the banner of the "war of Torah." One imagines that in the category of "experts in books of metaphysics," he would have included the twenty-year old Baruch Espinosa,

---

nute Book of Congregations Zur Israel of Recife and Magen Abraham of Mauricia, Brazil," in ibid., 2:245, showing that his salary increased by 350% when he assumed the position in Recife.

15. Morteira's eulogy for Mercado is translated below.

16. One of his students, Abraham Pimentel contributed a poem of praise printed at the end of *Giv'at Sha'ul* (1645: p. 92b). The Warsaw edition includes a second poem (1912: p. 311) by Josiah Pardo (son of the *Ḥakham* David, and Morteira's son-in-law), who became a rabbi in Rotterdam, Curaçao, and Jamaica, and left a manuscript of his own sermons, some of which bear close resemblance to those of his mentor (Ets Ḥaim MS 51 (47 B 21). (H. P. Salomon's genealogical chart following the Introduction to his edition of Morteira's *Tratado* reveals that Josiah Pardo's son Saul, born in 1652 and named after his maternal grandfather, became *Ḥazan* of the She'erit Israel Congregation in New York.)

17. Moses Israel Mercado, *Perush Sefer Qohelet u-Tehillim* (Amsterdam, 1653), Morteira's Introduction, column 4. To my knowledge, this text has never been cited in any discussion of Morteira or the community.

whose father Michael had been a leader of Morteira's congregation before the 1639 unification.[18] There is certainly no hint in the passage of the tensions that would erupt a few years later leading to the severing of all relations with Spinoza. In this regard, we might compare another description of Morteira's school, written a generation later by Daniel Levi de Barrios, and reflecting problems that may not have been apparent to Morteira in 1652:

> The Crown of the Law [*Corona de la ley*, i.e., *Keter Torah*] ever since the year of its joyous foundation, never ceased burning in the academic bush, thanks to the doctrinal leaves written by the most wise Saul Levi Morteira, lending his intellect to the counsel of Wisdom and his pen to the hand of Speculation, in the defense of religion and against atheism. *Thorns* [*Espinos*] are they that, in the *Fields* [*Prados*] of impiety, aim to shine with the fire that consumes them, and the zeal of Morteira is a flame that burns in the bush of Religion, never to be extinguished.[19]

Although the number of texts of new weekly sermons diminished considerably in Morteira's later years, he apparently remained productive throughout his life. His magnum opus, the *Tratado*, completed in 1659, the year before his death, not only brought together themes he had treated from the pulpit years earlier, but also included a new apologetic and polemical thrust: against the great Reformation theologian and preacher John Calvin. Morteira's last will and testament was notarized on February 4, 1660, three

---

18. For example, Morteira records at the end of one of his manuscript sermons that Michael de Espinosa was honored as *ḥatan bereshit* on the holiday of Simḥat Torah in 1624 (MS 3:314v, *Berakhah*, Deut. 33:5) and the following Sabbath when the first lesson in Genesis was read (MS 3:317v, *Bereshit*, Gen. 1:6); further, that he was among those whose term as Regent of the *Biqqur Ḥolim* Society began on Hanukkah 1624 (MS 3:328v, *Va-Yeshev*, Gen. 37:6) and a sermon for the following year records that the term ended on Hanukkah, 1625 (MS 5:112v, *Mi-Qets*, Gen. 41:2). (Morteira sometimes writes in Hebrew "Espinosa," and sometimes "Despinosa.") On Michael Espinosa's role in the congregation, see most recently Steven Nadler, *Spinoza: A Life* (Cambridge, 1999), pp. 37–39, which deals primarily with the 1630s. Morteira's references provide explicit evidence for Michael's presence in Amsterdam (indeed for his recognition by the Beth Jacob congregation) a year earlier than the earliest notarial record cited by Nadler, p. 31; cf. Salomon in *Tratado*, p. xcv. In addition, a postscript to a sermon on *Va-Yaqhel*, states "The sermon I delivered in the year 5391 on the day of celebration of the son of the honorable Michael Espinosa" (MS 2: 177v, Exod. 35:21). This places the birth of Michael's first son, Isaac, in February 1631, some 21 months before the birth of Baruch on November 24, 1632 and establishes him as the full brother of Baruch (cf. the uncertainties in Nadler, *Spinoza*, pp. 36, 359 n. 20).

19. The passage has been frequently cited because of its allusions to Baruch Spinoza and Juan de Prado; see, most recently, Nadler, *Spinoza: A Life*, pp. 90, 145–46.

days before his death.[20] The main eulogy at his funeral was delivered by his protégé and younger rabbinical colleague, Samuel de Caceres, who chose for his rabbinic dictum, "When does fire break out? When thorns are found nearby" (b. *Baba Qamma* 60a), and applied the qualities of fire to Morteira, culminating in the motif of Elijah's ascent to heaven in a fiery chariot. One has to wonder whether the dictum about "thorns" might have been intended as an allusion to Spinoza—which would have been particularly poignant since de Caceres was married to Spinoza's sister, Miriam! It is quite possible that de Barrios might have been consciously echoing this eulogy in the passage cited above.[21]

Image

To the limited extent that Morteira is known beyond a small circle of scholars concerned with the Portuguese Jewish community of Amsterdam, it is as the rabbi of Baruch Spinoza's family and as the teacher of the young Spinoza. Morteira eventually played a role in the mature Spinoza's excommunication. The earliest biography of Spinoza, written by Jean-Maximilien Lucas within a generation of Spinoza's death, presents Morteira as "the least ignorant of all the rabbis of his time," albeit highly regarded by the Jews. Morteira is not the villain of the story, at least at first: this role is played by two young men from the community who, pretending to be his friends, elicit Spinoza's true, radical theological views, and denounce him to the leadership of the community. Morteira, who had "found nothing to criticize both in his morals and in the fineness of his mind," and who had devoted considerable energy to Spinoza's education, was initially skeptical of the charges made. But he interrogates Spinoza in the presence of the other judges, implores him to repent, and warns him of the dire consequences of his rebellious contempt for the Law. Spinoza holds his ground, facing the prospect of the ban with equanimity.

At this point, "the Rabbi in a passion vented all his spleen against him." Morteira, "irritated by the contempt which his disciple had shown for him and his Law, changed his friendship to hatred, and in launching his thunder-

---

20. The text of the will was published by Salomon, *Tratado*, p. cxliii.

21. The manuscript Portuguese text of the eulogy is in the Ets Ḥaim Library 48 E 12. On de Caceres's marriage to Spinoza's sister, see Nadler, *Spinoza: A Life*, p. 85. In 1644, Samuel had copied the Portuguese text of seven of Morteira's sermons that remain in manuscript, and two years later the text of Rehuel Jessurun's "Dialogo dos Montes," containing seven mini-sermons by Morteira (Salomon, *Tratado*, p. xcvii, n. 24); see also Philip Polack, ed., *Dialogo dos Montes* (London, 1975), pp. xviixix. Samuel later became a *ḥakham*. Cf. also David Kaufmann, "L'élégie de Mose Zacout sur Saul Levi Morteira," *REJ* 37 (1898): 111–19.

bolt at him tasted the pleasure which base souls find in revenge." After the *ḥerem* is pronounced, he goes with another rabbi to the authorities and accuses Spinoza of "execrable blasphemies against Moses and against God. He exaggerated the falsehood by all such arguments as holy hatred suggests to an irreconcilable heart, and demanded in conclusion that the accused should be banished from Amsterdam. From the behavior of the Rabbi ... it was easy to judge that it was personal wrath rather than pious zeal that incited him to vengeance."[22] No source is provided for the behavior of Morteira, including his initiative in seeking out the Amsterdam authorities to arrange for Spinoza's banishment, let alone for the personal vindictiveness that allegedly impelled Morteira to act.

The legacy of this image, though considerably transformed, can be seen in a fictional rendering of the event by a Haskalah writer in the 1870s. The story, called "Ha-Perud" ("The Separation"), begins with a description of "R. Moses Morteira" sitting in his study. The characterization is not at all unsympathetic: the rabbi is said to be God-fearing and pious, self-abnegating to the point of asceticism, devoted to the study of Kabbalah and to traditional faith, as well as to his only daughter, whose mother died in childbirth. His servant announces the arrival of Baruch, a handsome young man, whom the rabbi confronts about reports that he has abandoned faith in God and openly repudiated traditional Jewish observance of the Sabbath and the dietary laws. This is expressed with considerable pain, for the young man was the rabbi's student, for whom he had a deep affection. Indeed, he considered this student to be a worthy candidate to succeed him in the rabbinate of Amsterdam, as well as to marry his daughter. Baruch defends himself, emphasizing the inner struggle that he has experienced, insisting that he cannot abandon his new conception of God, explaining his renunciation of traditional Sabbath and dietary regulations, yet proclaiming that he will never leave his religion. Morteira pleads with him to keep his theological views to himself, but when Baruch is unwilling to back down, the rabbi responds in anger: "Go then on the way you have chosen, that will lead you to eternal perdition." The following day, Morteira pronounces the "great *ḥerem*" in the presence of the entire congregation, including his daughter, who weeps in the balcony. At the end we are told, "In

---

22. A. Wolf, *The Oldest Biography of Spinoza* (London, 1927), pp. 44–55. The work was first published 1719 in the *Nouvelles littéraires*, x, 40–74, under the title: *La vie de Spinosa*. See on this Richard Popkin, "Skepticism About Religion and Millenarian Dogmatism," in. *Beyond the Persecuting Society*, ed. John Christian Laursen and Cary J. Nederman (Philadelphia, 1998), p. 237, and Popkin's doubts about the historicity of the account in "Spinoza's Excommunication," in *Jewish Themes in Spinoza's Philosophy*, ed. Heidi M. Ravven and Lenn E. Goodman (Albany, 2002), pp. 272–73.

such dreadful circumstances, Baruch Spinoza, the sage who conceived a new philosophical system, left the city of his birth in 1660."[23]

This is certainly not the historical Saul Levi Morteira. While not opposed in principle to Kabbalistic doctrine, he could by no means be described as a Kabbalist; while critical of ostentatious display and conspicuous consumption, he was also opposed to ascetic mortification of the flesh. His wife (named Esther) did not die in childbirth; he had two sons and three daughters, the last of whom married in 1648, eight years before Spinoza's excommunication.[24] Yet the story is important for the image of the rabbi it presents. One might have expected that a Haskalah author would have trivialized or demonized the rabbi as a rigid, tyrannical, close-minded and heartless representative of a repressive society.[25] Yet the character is drawn with a measure of sympathy, as someone who is willing to allow his disciple to harbor heretical thoughts if he will only avoid expressing his dissent openly. Similarly, the character of Baruch is shown to have a genuine respect for his teacher, although he cannot accept the rabbi's faith. The relationship between Baruch and the rabbi's daughter adds an element of pathos, but it is clearly the relationship between master and wayward disciple that lies at the heart of the story.[26]

In his chapter on "The Maker of Lenses" from the literary vignettes in *Dreamers of the Ghetto*, Israel Zangwill refers briefly to Morteira with a measure of empathy: "Poor Saul Morteira! How his [Spinoza's] ancient master must have been pained to pronounce the Great Ban, though nothing should have

---

23. Tuviah Pesach Schapiro, *Beit ha-Otsar: Sippurim* (Warsaw, 1876), pp. 50–61 (my translation, MS). I learned of this text from Shmuel Feiner's *Haskalah and History* (Oxford, 2002), p. 237.

24. Biographical information from H. P. Salomon, introduction to Morteira's *Tratado*, pp. xi–xiii. The manuscripts include a sermon delivered on the lesson *Va-Yishlah* in the fall of 1639 "on the day I arranged the marriage (*shidakhti*) of my oldest daughter Malkah" (MS 4:62v, Gen. 32:19) and another "sermon that I delivered at the banquet for the wedding of my daughter Malkah, *blessed among women in tents* (Jud. 5:24), on 15 Shevat 5400 (Wednesday, February 8, 1640; MS 4:82v, *Yitro*, Exod. 20:20: this latter sermon refers to the occasion, but does not provide biographical details). The name of this daughter, Morteira's first-born, in the Portuguese sources was "Reina": see Salomon, *Tratado*, p. xci.

25. Cf. for example, the image of Vofsi ha-Kuzari, the rabbi in J. L. Gordon's "Al Kotso shel Yod," apparently a blatant distortion of the rabbi from Shavli on whom the character was based (Abraham Rhine, *Leon Gordon* [Philadelphia, 1910], pp. 173–74, n. 98.

26. I am baffled by Feiner's reading of the story, in which "The fundamental problem in this fictional story is not the charge of heresy or ideological deviation, but the dissolution of the bonds of love between Spinoza and the rabbi's daughter." Not a word is said in the actual story about Spinoza's feelings for the daughter, or about any pain he may have suffered in renouncing the possibility of a future with her. In the story, this element is marginal to the relationship between the two men.

surprised him in a pupil so daring of question, even at fifteen."[27] Even more suffused with pathos is the formulation by Joseph Shein, author of the biographical sketch at the beginning of the 1902 edition of *Giv'at Sha'ul*: "The sorrowful incident of his student Spinoza, as beloved to Morteira as his own life, crushed him to the ground" (cf. Ps. 143:3).[28] Far less interested in Morteira's own feelings is the characterization in a biography of Spinoza published in 1946, written by the German biographer Rudolf Kayser: "[H]e knew his pupils and trained them for their studies. He also recognized the unusual talent of the student, Baruch Despinoza. But this rabbi could never understand the painful depth of Baruch's spiritual yearning and the nobility of his character."[29]

A considerably fuller depiction of Morteira is in the 1991 drama "Solo" by the Israeli playwright Yehoshua Sobol. Here the troublesome views are not theological (from the *Ethics*), but political (from the *Theological-Political Treatise*): in the play, Spinoza holds that the laws of the Torah were not revealed by God but made by human beings as the laws of the first Jewish commonwealth; when the commonwealth ceased to exist, the laws lost their authority. As in the story by Schapiro, a close personal relationship between the rabbi and Spinoza is asserted: "My son, Baruch. I venture to call you 'my son.' You were just a young child when I accepted you as a trust from your father, of blessed memory. I gave you everything I had to give." The continuation goes beyond asserting facts for which there is no historical evidence; it attributes to Morteira words and thoughts that are most improbable:

> Now you have outstripped me in Torah and philosophy. Don't turn your back on me. *Don't cast me off in old age* (Ps. 71:9). ... Stay with me. Work with me. Baruch, we can lead the community together.... I'll make sure you have no worry about a livelihood. Your time will be free for the study of Torah. Do you want to study external subjects? You'll be the rabbi; who will tell you what you can do? ... You can be the head of the yeshivah; its fame will be known wherever Jews live. Listen to me, give me your hand, and together we can transform Amsterdam into Sura and Pumbedita, into a second Jerusalem. You can write your own commentary on the Bible, I will support you. We will publish it and distribute it among Jewish communities far and wide. You can make emendations, you can come up with great new insights, you can write a new *Guide for the Perplexed.* You have the capacity to do this. Just say

27. Israel Zangwill, *Dreamers of the Ghetto* (Philadelphia, 1898), p. 188.

28. *Giv'at Sha'ul* (Warsaw, 1902), p. 16.

29. Rudolf Kayser, *Spinoza: Portrait of a Spiritual Hero* (New York, 1946), pp. 51–52.

yes…. Do you want to go to a different community? I will ordain you,
I will send you to Venice, a wealthy, flourishing community. You will
be its rabbi…. You are strengthening my worst enemies. I am
surrounded by poisonous snakes that want to bring me down. I can't
sleep at night, I can't close my eyes! … Have mercy on me.[30]

In the Haskalah story, Morteira, who had thought of his disciple as a potential
successor, implored him to keep his heretical views to himself. But this was
for the sake of Spinoza, to spare him the ordeal of anathema. Here Morteira
is pitifully pleading for his own sake. That a rabbi some sixty years old would
tell a twenty-four year old student who had proclaimed that the laws of the
Torah were not divine and had lost their force that he had outstripped him in
Torah, offer to make him the head of the yeshivah, or to send him to Venice
with rabbinic ordination and a recommendation for a rabbinical post stretches
the border of dramatic license. The final words, "have mercy on me," seem as
unlikely as the cruel, vindictive motivation attributed in the early biography.

Less implausible is another passage in Morteira's address to his student:

I have given my strength, the best of my days, to raise this community
from shattered vessels, from refugees fleeing fire and sword, from pale
shadows of human beings. Now this community is beginning to flourish.
… And a second generation arises, people like you, born and raised in
freedom…. We have invested in them everything we can…. The
moment has come when the tree is bearing magnificent fruit, like you.
But strangers are coming and picking the fruit![31]

Such words may well have reflected the anguish of the elderly founders of the
Portuguese community, who perceived their work challenged by a new
generation, much as the founding generation of the state of Israel reacts with
dismay at the critiques of the "post-Zionists."

In the last few years, Morteira has appeared once again as a subject of
interest because of his connection with Spinoza and the physician Juan de
Prado, a recent arrival from the Iberian peninsula also accused of heresy and
excommunicated. De Prado may have met Spinoza in the yeshiva where
Morteira taught the advanced class. H. P. Salomon showed that the text of
the ban promulgated by the leadership of the Amsterdam community against
Spinoza on July 27, 1656 was brought by Morteira from Venice in 1618 for
use in the inter-communal conflict of that year, but never actually employed

---

30. Yehoshuʻa Sobol, *Solo* (Tel Aviv, 1991), pp. 72–73 (my translation, MS). I am grateful
to my colleague Nancy Berg for directing my attention to Sobol's plays.
31. Ibid., p. 72.

then or in the intervening years. After noting the unique use of this excommunication text, Salomon continues:

> It therefore would seem that *Ḥaham* Morteira was especially implacable (*acharné*) against Spinoza, and that in this case he resorted specifically to a text of anathema that had a ferocity without precedent or equivalent in the history of Portuguese Jewry in Holland. This can be explained only if one concedes that Morteira had already in 1656 understood that the issue of Spinoza (who had not yet published anything) involved someone who denied the divine character of the Bible, and consequently someone who was undermining the foundations of Christianity as well as of Judaism.[32]

In this reconstruction, the relations with the host community in Amsterdam become a critical consideration, driving Morteira to greater vigor than would have been necessary in a purely internal Jewish challenge.

Yirmiyahu Yovel focuses more on Morteira's role in the proceedings against Juan de Prado, recounting reports of Prado's bitter hatred for Morteira who, as Yovel put it, "did not shrink from employing a spy (Monsanto) and setting a trap" for Prado. According to the records of the investigation, Morteira encouraged Jacob Monsanto to study with Prado in order to draw out his true views, and Monsanto reported a conversation in which Prado denied the doctrines of creation and resurrection and generally repudiated the authority of rabbinic tradition. These arguments, Yovel reports, "are specifically, and relentlessly, aimed against Morteira." Defending himself, Prado accused Morteira of a bias and hatred that perverted his judgment. Yet, although Yovel refers to the proceedings as "the Jewish 'Inquisition,'" he does not portray Morteira as an obscurantist fanatic desperately trying to suppress freedom of thought, but rather, as Salomon does, as one of "the great rabbis" of the community, defending tradition against someone who foreshadowed the later emergence of a non-orthodox Judaism but who was incapable of articulating his principles compellingly.[33]

In his recent biography of Spinoza, Steven Nadler provides a sympathetic sketch of Morteira's life, drawn from H. P. Salomon's lengthy introduction to the *Tratado*. In recounting the events leading to the excommunication of Juan

---

32. H. P. Salomon, "La vraie excommunication de Spinoza," *Forum Litterarum* (Amsterdam, 1984), p. 188.

33. Yirmiyahu Yovel, *Spinoza and Other Heretics* (Princeton, 1989), pp. 71–73. Note that the account of the "trap" set for Prado is quite similar to the narrative of the purported friends who drew out Spinoza's true beliefs and then denounced him to the community leaders in the early biography of Spinoza cited above.

de Prado, Nadler, unlike Yovel, does not place Morteira in a central position. As for the younger heretic, Nadler concludes, "It is impossible to say with any certainty how active a role Mortera took in the excommunication of Spinoza or what his personal feelings about Spinoza's apostasy were. Perhaps it was, after all, at his request that the extraordinarily harsh *ḥerem* text that he himself had brought back from Venice almost forty years earlier should be dusted off and used against Spinoza."[34]

I have found no specific references to Spinoza in the sermons, although, as we shall see, more than a few deal with heretical challenges to traditional doctrines such as the divine revelation of the oral law and the immortality of the soul. There do seem to be examples, however, of ideas expressed in the sermons that may have influenced Spinoza, who transformed and secularized them. That he was Morteira's favorite student cannot be demonstrated.[35] But that he listened to some of Morteira's sermons while he was growing up seems beyond any reasonable doubt.

Yet whatever the drama of Morteira's position as a mentor and perhaps a foil for one of the greatest minds and most independent personalities of the seventeenth century, Morteira's life's work touched the religious lives of many other Jews in Amsterdam besides Spinoza, who was, after all, part of the third generation to whom Morteira addressed his sermons. The first was composed of those who, educated as Christians in Portugal and having established careers there, came to Amsterdam as mature adults and were already leaders of the congregation when Morteira arrived in 1616; these were people for whom one religious identity had to be dismantled and another constructed. The second generation included those, like Menasseh ben Israel, who came as children to Amsterdam with their parents; they may have had memories of living as Christians in Portugal, but their identities were largely formed in the synagogue and schools of their new home.[36] The third generation was those born in Amsterdam during the 1620s and 1630s; its religious identity was entirely

---

34. Nadler, *Spinoza: A Life*, pp. 91–93 (biographical sketch), 138 (role in Spinoza excommunication).

35. H. P. Salomon asks, "Was Spinoza Morteira's student in the school attached to the synagogue? No document proves it, but the contrary would be surprising." "La vraie excommunication," p. 188. Cf. the formulation by Joseph Shein, author of the biographical sketch at the beginning of the 1902 edition of *Giv'at Sha'ul*: "the sorrowful incident of his student Spinoza, as beloved to Morteira as his own life, crushed him to the ground" (cf. Ps. 143:3). *Giv'at Sha'ul* (Warsaw, 1902), p. 16.

36. Marriage records for the years 1598 to 1630 reveal that of 124 Jews married in Amsterdam, 111 had been born in places where Judaism was not permitted (95 in Portugal, 10 in Antwerp, 3 in Spain, 3 in France), and only 9 in Amsterdam. Henry Méchoulan, *Être juif à Amsterdam au temps de Spinoza* (Paris, 1991), p. 28.

intertwined with Morteira's rabbinic leadership. Since this Jewish community quickly became one of the most dynamic in the world, it is worth looking carefully at the full corpus of Morteira's writings to assess his role in mediating a tradition to congregants with varying religious needs.

Works

In their Introduction to the 1645 edition of *Giv'at Sha'ul*, after discussing Morteira's method of preaching and their selection of sermons for the present book, his students mention three other works by their mentor: a treatise on the immortality of the soul, a treatise responding to the attack on the *aggadot* of the Talmud by Sixtus of Siena, and a collection of responsa. Let us consider these in turn.

Morteira's Hebrew treatise on the immortality of the soul (*She'erut ha-Nefesh* [The Survival of the Soul] cited in his Portuguese treatise as *Libro da Imortalidade dAlma*) was reported by the bibliographer Johann Christophe Wolf to be part of the library of Rabbi David Oppenheim of Prague. Although subsequent scholars have claimed that it was present in the Bodleian Library (which acquired Oppenheim's collection) and among the manuscripts of the Ets Ḥaim Library in Amsterdam, there is no record of this text in either of these collections, and it has apparently been lost. There are two references to the book in the printed sermons of 1645. The manuscript sermons contain thirteen further references to it, and the Portuguese *Tratado* an additional one. From these references, we can conclude that the book was an extensive (at least nine chapters with subsections), discursive, perhaps encyclopedic treatment of a full range of questions pertaining to the soul. It was completed in 1624, at a time when the issue of immortality was generating considerable controversy in the community.[37]

The Spanish treatise responding to the attacks by Sixtus of Siena on the aggadic literature of the Sages, written in the middle of Morteira's career, around 1644, exists in a number of manuscripts in the Ets Ḥaim Library of Amsterdam and the *Stadtbibliothek* of Hamburg. Sixtus (1520–1569) was a prominent Jewish convert to Christianity who (following the path of many other apostates, both earlier and later) agitated against his former co-religionists and wrote a work, called *Bibliotheca sancta*, containing attacks on rabbinic Judaism. Most of his criticisms were focused on the non-legal

---

37. For a full discussion of the problems relating to this work, including title, dating and content, and the text of all the references to it in Morteira's extant writings, see Saperstein, "Saul Levi Morteira's Treatise on the Immortality of the Soul," *StRos* 25 (1991): 131–48. For the context of other works on a similar topic at the time, see Nadler, *Spinoza's Heresy*, pp. 165–81.

content of the rabbinic literature, the aggadah, although some mocked rabbinic law as well. After an important methodological introduction, Morteira responded in kind, ridiculing the author for his literalistic interpretation of passages that were not intended to be taken literally, and condemning him for taking words out of context, citing inaccurately, and occasional fabricating. In doing so, sometimes Morteira suggests novel interpretations of aggadic and even halakhic statements.[38]

The third work mentioned by the disciples was "a composition of [legal] questions and awe-inspiring answers" (*ḥibbur she'elot u-teshuvot nora'ot*). There is no evidence that such a collection is extant today. However, several of his responsa have been cited by other rabbinic scholars. Moses Rivkes, who emigrated to Amsterdam from Lithuania after the violence of 1655 and may have known Morteira, summarized a "long legal decision" by Morteira on the subject of licentious sexual relations with an "idolatrous" (Christian?) woman, concluding, "May God make us worthy of seeing this in print, together with his other compositions, for they are numerous."[39] At least two of Morteira's responsa on important contemporary issues are extant in manuscript. One pertains to a Jew from Amsterdam who was offered a significant honorarium for using his friendship with a Portuguese Gentile who could ask another Gentile acquaintance in Rome to urge the Pope to issue instructions that would facilitate the acceptance of Portuguese New Christians as priests,

---

38. Morteira, "Declaracîon de los Mahamarim del Talmud," Ets Ḥaim MS 48C5; on the manuscripts, with variant titles, see Kaplan, "R. Sha'ul Levi Morteira," p. 14, n. 22. On Sixtus, see Cecil Roth, *A History of the Jews in Italy* (Philadelphia, 1946), pp. 302–4; Clemente Ancona, "Attache contro il Talmud di Fra Sisto da Siena," *Bolletino dell'Istituto di Storia della Società e dello Stato Veneziano* 5–6 (1963–64): 297–323 (I am grateful to Talya Fishman for this reference); Howard Adelman, "Success and Failure in the Seventeenth-Century Ghetto of Venice: The Life and Thought of Leon Modena, 1571–1648," Brandeis University Ph.D. Dissertation, 1985, pp. 665–69 (including a discussion of Modena's unpublished response to Sixtus). (The widely repeated view that Sixtus was a convert from Judaism has been recently challenged by Fausto Parente and H. P. Salomon; see Salomon, *Tratado*, p. 1228 n. to l. 203). Morteira's novel response to Sixtus's attack on a perennially problematic rabbinic law is discussed by Shalom Rosenberg, "Emunat Hakhamim," in *Jewish Thought in the Seventeenth Century*, ed. by Isadore Twersky and Bernard Septimus (Cambridge, 1987), pp. 301, 324–27, and cf. **Abraham Gross, "Demuto shel Rabbi Ya'aqov Sasportas Mi-Tokh Sefer ha-She'elot u-Teshuvot *Ohel Ya'aqov*," *Sinai* 97 (1983): 133–34.** On the beginning of this work, see Salomon in *Tratado*, pp. xxxvii–xxxviii. Some of Morteira's arguments in this work were later incorporated into his *Tratado*.

39. See *Be'er ha-Golah* to *Shulḥan Arukh, Even ha-Ezer* 16,1, n. א. This reference was cited in R. Hayyim Soloveitchik's approbation to the Warsaw 1902 edition of *Giv'at Sha'ul*, and mentioned in the publisher's Preface to the 1912 reprinting of this volume.

monks and nuns. Reviewing the possible grounds for prohibition of this act, Morteira refutes them and concludes that there is no reason to prevent it.[40] The other, noted by H. P. Salomon, is a responsum on the very practical issue of whether it is permissible for Jews to keep paintings and sculptures in their homes (his answer was affirmative).[41]

As far as I know, the existence of yet another apparently lost treatise, on the "*qeri*" and "*ketiv*" readings of the Masoretic text of the Bible, has never before been noted. Morteira refers explicitly to this work in one of his manuscript sermons: "I have on this a long discussion in my 'Sefer ha-Qeri ve-ha-Ketiv.'"[42] Since this sermon is from the second cycle, on the second verse of the *para-shah*, it would have been delivered around 1620 or 1621, which would mean that the book or treatise cited was one of his earliest writings. Furthermore, in a sermon delivered around 1640, Morteira refers to his commentary on the Book of Joshua, yet another of his works that is apparently lost.[43]

Morteira's extensive Hebrew discussion of the doctrine of eternal punishment for unrepentant sinners will be treated presently (see below, pp. 25–26). His other manuscript works are of a polemical nature, which may well be the reason they were not published during his lifetime, although other scholars knew of them. One, preserved in an Ets Ḥaim manuscript, was entitled, "Preguntas que hizo un Clérigo de Ruan de Francia, a las quales respondió el Exelente y Eminentísimo Senor H. H. Saul Levy Mortera." (Questions Posed by a Priest of Rouen in France and Answered by … Saul Levi Morteira). In addition to Morteira's Portuguese responses to the twenty-three Spanish ques-

---

40. See the discussion of this text (from the manuscript collection of the Jewish National and University Library) by Kaplan, "R. Sha'ul Levi Morteira," pp. 23–26 (English version pp. 105–8).

41. Salomon in Morteira, *Tratado*, p. lxi, n. 19; this responsum, written in Portuguese and entitled "Tratado sobre as figuras," is identified by Salomon as being in the Biblioteca Nacional de Madrid, codex 18292, folios 132–135. Cf. the reference to this responsum by Nadler, *Spinoza: A Life*, pp. 91–92, and Nadler's documentation of the large number of paintings in Amsterdam Jewish homes, *Rembrandt's Jews* (Chicago, 2003), pp. 72–84.

42. Budapest MS 12, 3:8r, *Va-Yetse*, Gen. 28:11, ca. 1620. The sentence comes immediately after the passage cited in Saperstein, "*Your Voice Like a Ram's Horn*," p. 31. Based on this explicit reference, we may conclude that the statement in *Giv'at Sha'ul, Va-Yeshev* (1645, p. 17c, 1912, p. 44), "as I have written on the *qeri* and *ketiv* of Je'ish [in Gen. 36:5], which is read 'Je'ush,' that he was the first born of Oholibamah" also refers to this treatise.

43. MS 4:102r, *Yitro*, Exod. 18:15, ca. 1640, 7 lines from the end: "This provides a fine answer to the question raised by the commentators why Joshua is never seen to consult [the High Priest] Elazar, and never had need of the Urim and Thummim; we raised this question in our commentary on the Book of Joshua and gave a different solution, but the answer that is appropriate to our subject is…" Note also Morteira's reference to yet another treatise dealing with the right to rebel: *Tratado*, p. 613, and 1231 (note ad loc.).

tions by the Christian cleric, he added some forty-six counter-questions of his own and a series of problems challenging the coherence of the New Testament.[44] In 1644, the Mennonite theologian Daniel de Breen (1594–1664) published a book entitled *Amica Disputatio adversus Iudaeos continens Examen scripti judaici e lusitanico in latinum versi et responsum ad quaestiones inibi christianis propositas* (A Friendly Disputation Against the Jews, Containing an Analysis of Jewish Texts Translated from Portuguese into Latin, and a Response to the Questions Therein Posed to the Christians), continuing the polemical dialogue in response to Morteira's treatise. A further development, published some twenty years later, was a Latin commentary on de Breen's work by the Protestant theologian and Hebraist Johannes Coccejus (Coch) called *Judaicarum Responsionum et Quaestionum Consideratio* (A Consideration of the Jewish Answers and Questions).[45] Coccejus did not know the name of the Jewish author on whose work he was writing. Morteira's answers to the twenty-three questions were subsequently published in an English translation by J. R. Paynado of Hackney, England, in the nineteenth-century American Jewish periodical *Occident* 3:3 (June 1845): 17; 3:8 (November 1845), 813; 3:9 (December 1845), 1419), 3:10 (January 1846): 2023.[46] A second polemical manuscript, bound together with the previous one, is the "Obsfaculos y oposiciones de la Religion Christiana en Amsterdam" (Arguments Against the Christian Religion). It has been analyzed at length by Yosef Kaplan; we shall discuss it below.

Morteira's most important single manuscript text is the massive treatise written near the end of his life on "God's Providence over Israel and the Truth of the Law of Moses" (hereafter, "Tratado"). Despite its length, many manuscripts of the Spanish translation have survived, as well as the Portuguese original. Though published only in 1988 by H. P. Salomon, it was known to earlier scholars. One of the most extensive treatments of Morteira by any writer, Jewish or Christian, before the past generation, is by the French Huguenot minister Jacques Basnage, whose multi-volume post-biblical his-

---

44. Morteira refers to this work (his answer to the sixth question)—"this entire matter [i.e., the eternal validity of the Torah] is as written in one of the topics I addressed in my written response to the questions that a Christian asked me"—in a sermon for the second day of Shavu'ot dated in 1620, indicating that this, like the treatise on *qeri* and *ketiv*, was one of Morteira's early works. This problematizes Salomon's dating of the text in 1631 ("Haham Saul Levi Morteira," pp. 135–36, *Tratado*, p. lv).

45. On Morteira's treatise and the two Protestant responses to it, see H. P. Salomon in *Tratado*, pp. lv–lviii. On Coccejus's knowledge of Hebrew and rabbinics, see Aaron Katchen, *Christian Hebraists and Dutch Rabbis* (Cambridge, 1984), pp. 65–75.

46. This translation is now available at the website *www.jewish-history.com* under "The Occident" (see Bibliography).

tory of the Jewish people—a continuation of Josephus, as he put it—was unprecedented.[47] Basnage devotes some eight quarto pages to a discussion of the *Tratado*, which he carefully read in a Spanish recension.[48] His presentation of Morteira's argument is remarkably dispassionate. Morteira's general purpose, he notes, is "to prove that the Law of Moses is perfect, sufficient, and that the Christians are wrong by adding new precepts under the pretext that they add new degrees of perfection."[49] A second strand of Morteira's argument, for Basnage, is to prove God's ongoing providential love for the Jewish people, as revealed in two ways: the flourishing of the Land of Israel while the Jewish people lived on it, its desolation under every subsequent conquering power, and the survival of the Jewish people during all the centuries of oppression in exile outside the land.[50] Morteira's critique of Christianity is summarized without editorial comment:

> The Christians invented the miracles of their Messiah, but none of them is new. They invented precepts, but they did this for the sole purpose of accommodating the laws of God to the taste of the Gentile nations. Finally, they attracted people to accept their religion through vague hopes and rewards, the truth of which no one could recognize, because they are hidden in the future…. As this author has read several Christian authors, among others Sixtus of Siena, he draws on their authority to show that the Christians themselves do not agree about the authenticity and reliability of their Sacred Scriptures.[51]

47. *Histoire du peuple Juif depuis Jésus Christ jusqu'a présent, pour servir de continuation à l'histoire de Joseph,* 9 vols. in 15 pts. (The Hague, 1716–1721). See Yosef Yerushalmi, *Zakhor: Jewish History and Jewish Memory* (Seattle, 1982), pp. 81–82; Lester A. Segal, "Jacques Basnage de Beauval's *L'Histoire des Juifs*: Christian historiographical perception of Jewry and Judaism on the Eve of the Enlightenment," *HUCA* 54 (1983): 303–324; Adam Sutcliffe, *Judaism and Enlightenment* (Cambridge, 2003), pp. 81–89.

48. Comparing the precise form of the title given (Basnage, *Histoire* 9:1018 n. [a]) with the list of manuscripts provided by H. P. Salomon, *Tratado,* pp. xix–xx, it would appear that he consulted either Codex Ets Ḥaim LM 48 C 10 [Fuks 224] or Codex Ets Ḥaim LM 48 C 11 [Fuks 278].

49. Basnage, p. 1018. This Christian claim to add new degrees of perfection is the central theme of *Tratado,* chaps. 47–51 and 59, pp. 225–63, 322–29, as well as of Morteira's earlier sermon, "Do Not Add To His Words," translated below, pp. 408 ff.

50. Basnage, pp. 1018–20; see *Tratado,* chaps. 9–14, pp. 21–39, on the providential care of God for the Jewish people in exile (also a central theme in Morteira's sermons), and chaps. 22–24, pp. 68–85, on the flourishing of the Land of Israel and its later desolation under all foreign rule.

51. Basnage, p. 1021. On the invention of miracles and the accommodation to the taste of the Gentiles in order to attract converts, see *Tratado,* chaps. 35–38, pp. 145–70; cf. below, p. 256 and the *Ha'azinu* sermon on Deut. 32:21 pp. 501–2, n. 31. On the hopes hidden in

The nature of Morteira's critique of the discrepancies between the Vulgate and the original Greek, among Greek manuscripts, and among the different Gospels, as well as the strong attacks against the Eucharist and the cult of images, is set out in a manner that would have to arouse either fury or confusion in a Catholic reader.[52] Basnage seems a little less comfortable about Morteira's disputes with what Calvin says against Judaism, but he does not flinch even here. "He does not spare Calvin or the Reformation, for he maintains that the same objections that the Reformers use against visual images apply to spiritual images;"[53] "Without sparing the name of Calvin, whom Morteira criticizes like the others, [he was] unable to pardon what Calvin said against the efficacy of the law and the possibility of fulfilling it."[54] It would be a long time before Morteira was again to receive such thorough and balanced treatment.

He was not ignored by later Christian savants. John Locke's friend Anthony Collins (1676–1729), a self-proclaimed apostle of "freethinking," apparently went out of his way to gain access to Morteira's *Tratado* when he was in Holland, after stressing how difficult it was to procure a copy of this work. From this fact, Jonathan Israel described Morteira as one of the "Dutch Sephardic writers whose work appealed to radical deists in the eighteenth century,"[55] although it is difficult to see why, as the theology of the *Tratado*, with its emphasis on divine providence, is if anything antithetical to the deistic worldview.

Study of Morteira From the Late Nineteenth Century

The great German Jewish historian Heinrich Graetz, who shows no sign of having consulted Basnage on Morteira's polemical *magnum opus* let alone the manuscript itself, speaks of Morteira with considerable disdain.

It was a misfortune for the Amsterdam community that its first spiritual

---

the future, see *Tratado*, pp. 68 and 167–68, and the sermon cited below, p. 271, at n. 46.

52. Basnage, pp. 1022–1023; see *Tratado*, chaps. 43–45, pp. 203–19, on Sixtus of Siena and internal Christian criticisms of New Testament material; chaps. 53–57, pp. 273–317, for Morteira's attack on the Eucharist.

53. Basnage, p. 1024; see *Tratado*, chaps. 40–42, pp. 185–203. By "spiritual images" is meant the typological interpretation of matters pertaining to the Jews in the "Old Testament" as figures of the spiritual Christian truth, a technique used extensively by Calvin in his *Institutes*.

54. Basnage, p. 1025; see *Tratado,* chaps. 67–69, pp. 388–410, for Calvin on the Law.

55. Jonathan I. Israel, *Radical Enlightenment* (Oxford, 2001), p. 615 and n. 124. On Collins's reference to Morteira's magnum opus, cf. H. P. Salomon, *Tratado*, p. cxix.

guides, who exercised remarkable influence, were possessed of only mediocre talents, in some degree lacked mental poise. With the vast resources which this first Dutch community had at command, with the fund of culture characterizing its members, and their devotion to Judaism, its leaders might have brought about remarkable results, if they had possessed more independence, profounder intellect, and greater genius. The first Amsterdam rabbinical college had nothing of all this. David Pardo appears to have been of very little importance. Saul Levi Morteira ... was not even a distinguished preacher; his colleagues, Aboab and Manasseh ben Israel, far outshone him. His sermons, the only printed productions of his literary activity, have a philosophical complexion, but no depth of thought. Morteira followed the broad, beaten paths, repeating what had been thought and pointed out before him. Even in rabbinical learning he had no mastery, and was not even considered an authority by contemporary Talmudists.[56]

Morteira appears again in Graetz as the rabbi who probably imposed the penitential scourging upon Uriel da Costa and the teacher of Spinoza. Indeed, Spinoza is identified as "a favorite of his teacher," who was reluctant to judge the rebellious youth worthy of excommunication.[57] If Graetz spoke of Morteira with disparagement, Simon Dubnow gave him little more than a fleeting mention. He lists the three leading rabbis of Amsterdam as "Saul Mortara [sic in the English translation] of Venice; the versatile writer and political figure Manasseh ben Israel; and the gifted preacher Isaac Aboab da Fonseca." He then devotes four paragraphs to Menasseh and a paragraph to Aboab, but hardly a further word to the rabbi designated by the community as senior to them both.[58]

56. Heinrich Graetz, *History of the Jews,* 6 vols. (Philadelphia, 1891–1898), 4: 682; Graetz of course did not have any sermons by Aboab or Menasseh ben Israel as a basis for comparison. See the defense of Morteira in the note to the Hebrew translation by Saul Phinehas Rabbinowitz, Graetz, *Divrei Yemei Yisrael,* 8 vols. (Warsaw, 1890–1899), 8:14. Rabbinowitz emphasizes the role of Morteira and his colleagues in constructing an informed Jewish congregation from the Portuguese immigrants, and he mentions especially the sermon "The People's Envy" (translated in Saperstein, *Jewish Preaching,* pp. 270–85) and "Do Not Add To His Words" (translated below). Cf. also the criticism of Graetz for his treatment of Morteira in the publisher's biographical introduction to the Warsaw 1902 edition of *Giv'at Sha'ul,* p. 4.

57. Graetz, *History,* 5: 63, 87, 92–93.

58. Simon Dubnow, *History of the Jews From the Later Middle Ages to the Renaissance,* 5 vols. (South Brunswick, N.J.: 1967–1973), 3:631, 633–35. Morteira later is mentioned in passing as an "eminent" teacher at the school in which Spinoza studied, and then as the "old teacher" of Spinoza, who repudiated his former teacher's appeal before the excommunication (pp. 640–41).

In this tradition of denigrating Morteira's abilities and significance is the following passage from a biography of Spinoza published in 1946 with an introduction by Albert Einstein. The work was written by the German scholar Rudolf Kayser, who also wrote biographies of Kant, Stendhal, Saint Simon, and Judah Halevi:

> He [Morteira] was not one of the Marranos, being neither Spanish nor Portuguese; he was an Ashkenazic Jew, and had been born in Venice. He knew nothing of the sufferings endured under the Inquisition nor of the aristocracy created by these sufferings. His features were coarse and less spiritual than those of most of the others in the congregation.... Precious little did this mentor and preacher know about the Spanish soul and the Catholic memories of his congregation; and he knew just as little of the deep religious yearning and the humanitarian spirit of the century. Rabbi Morteira was no sage; he wasn't even a persuasive conveyor of God's holy Word. But he was a preacher who dominated his congregation. He was an ecclesiastical functionary of the Talmudic tradition, and certainly no great scholar. A fanatic of the Law, a ruthless inquisitor, he was the leader of the rabbinate and took his stand in opposition to the times. His eyes never strayed beyond the walls of the Synagogue. And his erudition was limited to a knowledge of the Talmud and the Bible. But he knew his pupils and trained them for their studies. He also recognized the unusual talent of the student, Baruch Despinoza. But this rabbi could never understand the painful depth of Baruch's spiritual yearning and the nobility of his character.[59]

It is indeed remarkable how much an author can assert about what his subject knew and did not know, the limits of his erudition, his persuasiveness, and what he could understand in his students, without showing the slightest evidence that he has read a single word the man wrote.[60]

More sympathetic to the stature of Morteira and the significance of his

---

59. Rudolf Kayser, *Spinoza: Portrait of a Spiritual Hero* (New York, 1946), pp. 51–52.

60. For example, the author knows that "As Rabbi Morteira was intoning the funeral service [for Isaac de Castra Tartas], a radiance streamed out of this gloomy man, such as Baruch never saw in him again" (ibid., p. 53). There are no notes in the book, but this is apparently imagined from the statement by Isaac Cardoso that "when [Tartas's] parents and brothers received the news that he had been burned alive in Lisbon, on the first Sabbath of his funerary honors, the *Ḥaham* Rabbi Saul Levi Morteira, peace be unto him, devoted his sermon to the blessed martyr" (Yosef Hayyim Yerushalmi, *From Spanish Court to Italian Ghetto* [New York, 1971]: p. 398).

preaching is the characterization by Cecil Roth in his biography of Morteira's younger (and more famous) colleague, Menasseh ben Israel:

> For nearly half a century, [Morteira] was one of the dominant figures in Amsterdam Jewry. He thus influenced Menasseh ben Israel both as teacher and, later, as colleague: ultimately surviving him by a couple of years. He was famous as a preacher, the volume of his sermons issued by his pupils throwing many vivid sidelights upon local conditions. But above all he was a doughty controversialist; and the series of works which he composed, to champion Judaism against Christianity and to encourage doubting Marranos to remain true to the faith of their fathers, long remained classical.[61]

More recent scholarship has focused on specific previously unpublished works by Morteira. In 1973, Alexander Altmann published a substantial article entitled "Eternality of Punishment: A Theological Controversy Within the Amsterdam Rabbinate in the Thirties of the Seventeenth Century."[62] At issue was whether the most egregious, unrepentant sinners of the Jewish people, including those apostates who died without abandoning their idolatrous worship, would be punished by eternal damnation (the view of Morteira), or whether all Jews, no matter how grave their sins, including the unrepentant *conversos*, were, after a finite punishment, guaranteed a share in the world to come (the view of Morteira's younger colleague Isaac Aboab). Altmann identified a Hebrew manuscript text (published in the article) as a letter written by Morteira around 1635 that describes the outbreak of the controversy, which erupted in response to one of his sermons. In the letter, Morteira defends his position, which he asserts is the view espoused in classical Jewish texts, as contrasted with the newer view supported by kabbalistic doctrine.[63]

In addition to the textual argument, Morteira insisted that the new doctrine of universal salvation for all those of Jewish descent would undermine the willingness of *conversos* to leave the Iberian peninsula and return to their Jewish roots. He further claimed that his opponents tried in vain to convince the Regents of the *Mahamad* to forbid him to preach the doctrine of eternal punishment, lest this "strengthen the faith of the Christians who say that

---

61. Cecil Roth, *A Life of Menasseh ben Israel: Rabbi, Printer, and Diplomat* (Philadelphia, 1934), p. 25. On the relationship between the two rabbis, see Saperstein, *"Your Voice Like a Ram's Horn,"* pp. 412–13, with reference to documents published and discussed by H. P. Salomon.

62. *PAAJR* 40 (1973): 1–88.

63. Altmann, "Eternality of Punishment," pp. 41–51.

Adam's sin was eternal." To this he replied that the Christians will indeed think badly of the Jews if the liberal, tolerant theology allowing the good and the evil to enjoy the same ultimate reward were to prevail.[64] The polemical response by Aboab, entitled "Nishmat Ḥayyim," also published by Altmann, reveals the depth of the fissure in the Amsterdam rabbinate, with Aboab trying "to break the spell of the traditional eschatology of hell by publicly embracing the Lurianic doctrine of *tikkun.*"[65] Morteira is presented here as an accomplished polemicist, a traditionalist suspicious of Kabbalah, vehement in his antipathy toward Iberian Catholicism and hostility toward those of Jewish ancestry who choose to remain Christians. We will see some of these same attitudes articulated emphatically in his sermons.

Among the articles in the first volume of the Hebrew *Studies on the History of Dutch Jewry* was an essay by Yosef Kaplan based on a unique Spanish manuscript in the Ets Ḥaim Library.[66] Kaplan, who has written extensively on many aspects of the history of the Amsterdam community and the broader western Sephardic diaspora, presented Morteira as "in his time one of the dominant personalities of Sephardic Jewry in seventeenth-century Western Europe." After reviewing biographical data and some of Morteira's other works, Kaplan analyzed the manuscript text and its historical background. It is constructed as a record of an encounter in France between two Portuguese men of "New Christian" background. One of them was returning from Rome after a futile attempt to be accepted in the Jesuit order, and the other was an émigré to Holland, where he embraced Judaism. The work contains a harsh critique of Christian doctrine, especially the doctrine of the Trinity and the belief that the Messiah has already come.[67]

The following year, in 1976, H. P. Salomon published an article on Morteira in Dutch.[68] In it he cited important passages from Morteira's other anti-Christian polemical treatise, "Questions Posed by a Priest of Rouen, which—as noted above—contains answers to twenty-three theological questions. Salomon was especially interested in this text because it reflected Morteira's attitude toward the New Christians who remained in Portugal; he

---

64. Ibid., pp. 50–51.

65. Ibid., p. 22. This entire debate was reviewed recently by Steven Nadler in *Spinoza's Heresy*, pp. 160–65 as part of his broader discussion of the importance of the doctrine of immortality of the soul for the Amsterdam Jewish community in this period.

66. Yosef Kaplan, articles cited above, n. 3.

67. Kaplan, "R. Sha'ul Levi Morteira ve-Ḥibburo," pp. 24–25; "Rabbi Saul Levi Morteira's Treatise," pp. 105–7.

68. Salomon, "Haham Saul Levi Morteira en de Portugese Nieuw-Christenen," *StRos* 10 (1976): 127–41.

maintains that Morteira "is the first Sephardic rabbi who considers the New Christians no longer as Jews."[69] We will have an opportunity to see how the themes of both these treatises—Christianity, Christians, and New Christians— are discussed at length in the homiletical context of his sermons (chap. 8, below). Morteira refers several times in his monumental *Tratado* to a work entitled "Tratado das Controuersias dos Euangelios" (Treatise of Disputations Over the Gospels), and he may also allude to that treatise in one of his sermons.[70] It is apparently the same as the *Argumentos contra los Evangelicos, Actos, y Epistolas* (Arguments Against the Gospels, Acts, and Epistles), bound together with the *"Preguntas"* in a manuscript at the Jewish Theological Seminary. It was cited, along with Morteira's other polemical treatises, by Ralph Melnick in his 1981 study.[71]

In his Dutch article, Salomon followed a suggestion by Kaplan and argued that Morteira was himself of a Portuguese New Christian family.[72] Later, Salomon abandoned this Portuguese origin theory after he discovered a stunning document from 1640: in it, the Sacred Society for the Dowering (*Dotar*) of Orphans and [Impoverished] Young Women declared a variance from its rule of accepting only those of the Hebrew Portuguese or Castilian nation or their descendants, and accepted Morteira as a member because of his marriage to a Portuguese wife, his residence in Amsterdam for thirteen years, and his great distinction as a rabbi.[73] As noted above on p. 5, we shall see in one of his sermons evidence not just for Morteira's Ashkenazic ancestry, which has been widely accepted, but that he belonged to one of the most distinguished families of Ashkenazic Jewry.

Over the past generation, considerable attention has been devoted to

---

69. Salomon, p. 136, n. 48 end; the English summary modifies the formulation and makes it more accurate: "He appears to be the first Amsterdam Sephardic rabbi to refer to a category of New Christians who were sincere and pious Catholics."

70. Morteira, *Tratado*, pp. 827 and 1039, cf. p. 5, and see Salomon's notes on pp. 1242 and 1249. For the sermon, see below, p. 531.

71. Melnick, *From Polemics to Apologetics*, pp. 30–31, 66, 83 n. 22; Jewish Theological Seminary Library MS 2526 (SHF 1511:7); see Alexander Marx, "Polemical Manuscripts from the Library of the Jewish Theological Seminary of America" (Vienna, 1929), p. 263.

72. Kaplan made this assertion on the basis of a passage in the introduction to Morteira's "Declaracion de los Mahamarim del Talmud contra las calumnias del Seniense" (op. cit., p. 10); the passage is discussed by Salomon in his Introduction to the *Tratado*, pp. xxxvii–xxxviii. Salomon took this further by identifying Morteira with the Portuguese *peregrino* who was returning from Rome in the *Obstáculos* treatise, a claim that Kaplan never made.

73. Salomon, "La vraie excommunication," p. 182; cf. *Tratado*, p. xxvii–xxxix, and p. cxxxxvii for the text.

Morteira's last work, the "Treatise (*Tratado*) on God's Providence Over Israel and the Truth of the Law of Moses." Although, as we have seen above, an early Spanish translation of this work was read in manuscript and described with admirable objectivity by the French scholar Jacques Basnage, subsequently it was largely ignored. Since the mid-twentieth century, however, a passage from the treatise has been cited by scholars investigating the early Jewish presence in the western hemisphere. In it, Morteira makes dramatic reference to contemporary events: the Portuguese conquest of the Dutch colony of Recife in 1654, the decision of the Portuguese governor Francisco Barreto de Menizes to allow the Jews to leave in sixteen ships for Holland; the capture of one of these ships by Spaniards who wanted to turn the Jews over to the Inquisition; and the appearance of the French, who freed the Jews and allowed them to continue to "New Netherland." Morteira thus provided the historical context for the first settlement of twenty-three refugees in New Amsterdam, although the circumstances of their arrival remain murky. Morteira's passage ends with the return of the people he describes to Amsterdam. Nevertheless the story has been frequently retold, usually without awareness of its source, and has become part of the foundation myth of American Jewry. For our purposes, what is crucial is Morteira's emphasis at every turn of events that the outcome was the result of God's providential care for His people, a central theme in the *Tratado* as well as in his sermons. We shall note a passage in a 1656 sermon where Morteira refers to these events.[74].

In the 1973 article cited above, Alexander Altmann had noted the appearance in the 1630s of at least ten Dutch translations of Socinian texts, expressing a "trend toward the liberalization of the rigorous Calvinist dogma of predeterminism and its corollary, the doctrine of eternal damnation."[75] This theme was taken up a few years later by Henry Méchoulan in his study of the relationship of Morteira and Spinoza with the Socinians in Amsterdam. The "Polish Brethren," as they were sometimes called, were those Protestants who repudiated the doctrine of the Trinity and refused to recognize Jesus as divine, considering him to be a human being endowed with consummate wisdom. Méchoulan focused on the explicitly polemical thrust of the *Tratado* manuscript. He showed how Morteira—while welcoming the Unitarian theology of the Socinians—deplored their insistence on the divine authority of the Gospels and attacked traditional Catholic doctrines, institutions, and practices (veneration of crosses and images, temporal power of the pope, the Inquisition,

---

74. For a translation of the passage, see Baron, *SRHJ* 15:349–50; the original Portuguese is in *Tratado*, pp. 75–77; for further references, see below, pp. 103–4, n. 105.

75. Ibid., p. 20.

ascetic mortification of the body), sometimes citing Calvin's critique for support, but then attacking Calvin with comparable vigor. Finally, Méchoulan cited a passage from Morteira's *Tratado* that insists that God's presence is manifest in joy, not in the melancholy of self-abnegation (we shall see a similar passage in the earlier eulogy for David Masiah) alongside a passage from Spinoza's *Ethics* that reflects a similar outlook.[76] A few years later, Ralph Melnick's study of polemical and apologetical literature included several similarly strong anti-Christian passages from the *Tratado*.[77]

H. P. Salomon's monumental edition of the *Tratado* appeared in 1988: it contains 146 pages of introductory material, followed by 1,277 pages of text. The core of the book is a facsimile of Morteira's autograph manuscript in Portuguese—71 chapters, 419 pages—with Salomon's Portuguese transcription on facing pages. This is followed by notes that identify biblical and other citations, address textual and linguistic issues, and (to a lesser extent) comment on matters of content. Indices of biblical verses and of proper names follow. All this is preceded by the most thorough biographical treatment of Morteira ever published, supplemented by twelve documents, mostly from archives, that shed light on his life.[78] For the first time, a major work by Morteira is made available in a scholarly form—although unfortunately it is still inaccessible to non-readers of Portuguese or Dutch.[79]

But what about the historical response to the texts of Morteira's sermons? We cannot determine how many copies of the 1645 edition of *Giv'at Sha'ul* were printed, how many were sold, and how many were read, but it seems clear that this book was not commonly cited by later Jewish authors. The first

---

76. Henry Méchoulan, "Morteira et Spinoza au carrefour du Socianisme" *REJ* 135 (1976): 51–65. See the eulogy for Masiah below, p. 530, n. 10.

77. Melnick, *From Polemics to Apologetics*, pp. 31–32.

78. Saul Levi Mortera, *Tratado da verdade da lei de Moisés*, introduction and commentary by H. P. Salomon (Coimbra, 1988): Salomon's translation into Dutch was published in the same year (see above, n. 3). It should be noted that, as Salomon's Bibliography reveals, some 28 manuscripts of the work exist in Spanish translation, of which fifteen are entitled something like "Providencia de Dios con Ysrael y verdad de la Ley de Mosse." Ten others reverse the two elements: "Tratado de la verdad de la Ley de Moseh y providencia de Dios con Su pueblo." Only three have a title containing only the element of "truth of the law of Moses" without reference to providence. As Salomon notes (p. cxxiii), divine providence is the central theme of the first part of the book. It is therefore unfortunate that this theme—which we shall see at the heart of many of the sermons translated below—is missing from the title in the authoritative edition of the text.

79. A Dutch study of one aspect of the *Tratado* is Pieter Cohen, "Saul Levi Mortera's historische opvattingen in zijn 'Traktaat Betreffende de Waarheid van de Wet van Mozes,'" in *Een gulden Kleinood*, ed. H. den Boer, J. Brombacher, and P. Cohen (Appeldoorn, 1991), pp. 106–20 (I am grateful to Jenneke Oosterhof for translating this article for me).

evidence of thorough study of the work pertains to a Christian, the eighteenth-century Hebraist Paul Theodor Carpov, who published one of Morteira's sermons in Latin translation at Leipzig, 1740.[80] He chose the final sermon in the Amsterdam 1645 *Giv'at Sha'ul*, on the lesson *"Berakhah,"* entitled *Otsar Neḥmad* (rendered *Thesaurus pretiosus*), which takes Deuteronomy 33:4 as its theme-verse. The translator seems to have been totally at home in all the levels of Hebrew that Morteira uses, including not only the references to the terminology of Jewish life, but also the linguistic and literary subtleties and ambiguities that are mastered only with deep learning.[81] He cites not only such Christian scholars as Pico, Buxtorf, Wolf, Selden, Leusden, and Carpov, but also a multitude of Hebrew sources, including Moses of Coucy, Jacob ben Asher, the *Shulhan Arukh*, Meir Aldabi, and Tobias Cohen's medical encyclopedia *Ma'aseh Tuviah* (e.g. p. 158 n. [q]). Nor was this the only sermon by Morteira that Carpov had read, as he cites others in the collection as well (pp. 160–61, n. [x], 165 n. [m]). Only once is he apparently stymied: by Morteira's citation of "the author of *Tehillah le-David*" (a reference to David ben Judah Messer Leon's encyclopedic summary of Jewish theology published at Constantinople in 1576), where he notes that "this book is not accessible to me" (p. 153, n. [d]). It would be difficult to find any sermon by Morteira, or indeed by any other Jewish preacher, that was subjected to such an exhaustive, intensive, and sympathetic analysis until quite recently.[82]

---

80. Carpov, *Animadversiones philologico-critico-sacrae* (Leipzig, 1740), pp. 141–72.

81. For example, discussing the first word of the theme-verse, *Torah*, Morteira cites R. Simlai's statement about the 613 commandments and juxtaposes it with R. Hamnuna's linking of the number 613 with the numerical equivalent of "Torah," 611, with the first two of the Ten Commandments, heard by the entire people making 613 (b. *Makkot* 24a). He concludes, "the majority agree that [the Israelites] heard *all* the [Ten] Commandments directly from God, and they did not contradict the statement of R. Simlai, for it is a *davar mekubbal ve-amiti*." Carpov renders this last phrase, *id enim pro vero agnoscitur omnino*, "for it is acknowledged by all to be true." But he adds a note, giving the Hebrew (in Hebrew letters) and continuing, "Yet it can be rendered otherwise, for קבל is "to accept by tradition," and אמיתי among other things can be "Kabbalistically," whose adepts are said to be חכמי האמת ." He concludes by providing justification for his own translation, appealing to the great Hebraist of the previous century: "Buxtorf, in *Cosri* [the younger Johann Buxtorf's translation of the *Kuzari*, published at Basel in 1660], p. 397, renders the phrase from Abravanel קיימו וקבלו תורת משה לאמיתית , They acknowledged the Teaching of Moses to be true" (agnoscunt legem Moisis esse veram), p. 153 n. (c). And this is one of the less learned of the notes, which contain citations in Greek, Arabic (see p. 154 n. (f)—the appearance of a midrash in the Quran), and Yiddish (see p. 148 n. (u)—a long and learned discussion of the Sabbath of Repentance (*Sabbato poenitentiae*), including the information that the "current" one is on the sixth day of Tishri 5499, corresponding to 20 September 1738).

82. One passage that does not ring quite true in the Latin translation comes at the very

A different kind of tribute was paid to Morteira by several subsequent rabbis. As we shall see in the following chapter, Morteira's manuscript sermons came into the possession of an Italian rabbi, who recorded that he delivered some of them in Ancona (presumably in Italian, and without giving credit to the author) more than a century after Morteira's death; as the texts were in his possession, he could do so without fear that anyone would discover his source. A greater degree of effrontery was exhibited by Rabbi Moses Edrehi. Born in Morocco in 1774, Edrehi spent several years in the Sephardi community of London before coming to Amsterdam, where he often preached in the large Portuguese synagogue. In 1809, he published at Amsterdam, with the enthusiastic approbations of the Regents of the community, a volume of fourteen sermons delivered in Morocco, London, and Amsterdam itself entitled *Yad Moshe.*[83] To my knowledge, it has until now never been noticed that several sermons in this book contain long passages from the 1645 edition of Morteira's *Giv'at Sha'ul,* incorporated almost verbatim, and without attribution, into the texture of Edrehi's sermons.[84] To use this material in sermons delivered in Morocco might have seemed not to be much of a risk. But to come to Morteira's own city and *publish* a book there with passages from the 1645 edition, sometimes introducing the passage with "in my humble opinion"—that takes a certain amount of gall.[85] It is a rather sad comment on the lack of ongoing knowledge of Morteira's homiletical opus in his own city, although it might also reflect an ironic measure of ongoing if limited influence.

Similarly, on the Sabbath preceding Pesach, March 26, 1831, David Aaron de Sola, minister of the Spanish and Portuguese "Shaar Ashamayim" Congregation in London, delivered a sermon that he described as the first "ever

---

end, where Morteira's characteristic invocation of "the advent of our righteous Messiah (*mashiah tsidqenu*)" is rendered, *sub adventum Christi justitiae nostrae!*

83. See Abraham Yaari, "R. Moshe Edrehi u-Sefarav," *Qiryat Sefer* 33 (1957–58): 521–28; Moshe Hallamish, *Ha-Qabbalah bi-Tsefon Afriqah le-min ha-Me'ah ha-Tet Zayin* (Tel Aviv, 2001), p. 48; Daniel J. Schroeter, *The Sultan's Jew* (Stanford, 2002), pp. 73–74.

84. For examples, see below, pp. 191 n. 22, 310 n.4, 319 n. 31, 487 n. 98.

85. On the expectation that the sermon delivered is the original creation of the preacher, see below, p. 120 and n. 14. Compare Benjamin Franklin's account of an Irish Presbyterian preacher who came to Philadelphia in 1734 and impressed many listeners, until it was discovered that part of his sermon had been written by another and appeared in a British periodical. He later admitted that none of the sermons he delivered were his own. His supporters abandoned him, except for Franklin, who wrote that "I rather approv'd his giving us good sermons compos'd by others, than bad ones of his own manufacture, tho' the latter was the practice of our common teachers." *The Autobiography of Benjamin Franklin* (New York, 1944), pp. 110–11. This, of course, is not quite the same as publishing sermons with passages plagiarized from another.

pronounced within this holy place in the language of this country." Discussing the "excellence of the Holy Law," he begins by noting,

> Every possessor of a worldly treasure is subject to a partial or total loss thereof, from a variety of causes: either if he be not fully acquainted with the full amount and importance of this treasure, ... or that the proprietor of the treasure should neglect to give it the necessary attention and care, [or] in case the possessor ... should withdraw his attention and transfer it to some object of more importance, or ... he may be deprived of it by events which no human wisdom could foresee, nor any human power resist, [or because] such is the instability of all the objects of human pursuit and desire of a worldly nature that they all, as it were, carry within themselves the seeds of their own destruction.... Now it is the peculiar excellence of the treasure we possess in our holy law, that none of the causes of diminution or loss, to which all human possessions and worldly treasures are subject, can affect it.

This entire passage from the first section of de Sola's discourse is based, without attribution, on Morteira's sermon on the lesson *Ve-zot ha-Berakhah*, published in the Amsterdam 1645 edition of *Giv'at Sha'ul* (and translated into Latin, as noted above, by Paul Theodor Carpov). The same five causes for the loss of a treasure are given, and the rest of the sermon is an argument that none of them apply to the Torah. Born and educated in Amsterdam, de Sola undoubtedly had access to the book of Morteira's sermons, which he used to good avail on this historic occasion, apparently assuming that no one in the "large and admiring audience" would recognize his source.[86]

After 1645, *Giv'at Sha'ul* was never republished until the 1902 edition in Warsaw, with a brief statement of approbation by R. Hayyim Soloveitchik of Brisk. In his brief Preface, the publisher of this book, Joseph Shein, noted its rarity and praised its content, affirming that "these things that the consummate rabbi Saul Morteira said then to the *conversos* of Spain and Portugal who had returned to their people and to the Torah of their ancestors are worthy of being said now in our own time to our children and our brethren who, inspired from on high, have returned to their home territory and abandoned the idols of assimilation and begun to work and toil for the welfare of their

---

86. David Aaron de Sola, "A Sermon on the Excellence of the Holy Law" (London, 1831), pp. 6–7. The description of the audience on this occasion is taken from Abraham de Sola (his son), *Biography of David Aaron de Sola* (Philadelphia, 1864), p. 17, and cf. the encomium by a listener, p. 18. I am grateful to Richard Menkis for making available to me copies of both of these texts.

people and their land."[87] This publication, which includes a fairly extensive biographical introduction (written, as Shein conceded, despite the paucity of source material), and its reprinting ten years later, shows an interest in the sermons and an appreciation of their quality. And apparently there was a community of readers willing enough to support the publication of the text (somewhat truncated by censorship, as we shall see below).[88]

The one other printed text providing evidence of Morteira's homiletical prowess is the *Dialogo dos montes*, the Portuguese text of which was first printed at Amsterdam in 1767, reprinted in the 1930s, and then republished with an English translation in 1975. The work was actually presented in "performance" in the Beth Jacob synagogue on Shavu'ot 1624. Students played the roles of seven biblical mountains, and their presentations were linked by seven mini-sermons delivered by Morteira. The production seems to have been an adaptation of the contemporary plays performed in Spanish and Portuguese churches. Eight years later the leadership of the Jewish community prohibited any further dramatic presentations in the synagogues.[89] The text thus exemplifies the close links between homiletics and theatre, a theme we shall address in chapter four.

In the nineteenth and twentieth centuries, Morteira's printed sermons were largely ignored by those doing research on the history of both Jewish preaching and the Jewish community in Amsterdam. In his monumental survey, Leopold Zunz mentioned Morteira only in a long list of early-modern Jewish preachers, with the bibliographical reference to the 1645 edition of *Giv'at Sha'ul*,[90] but without a word on the form, content, or homiletical techniques of the sermons. Israel Bettan, whose *HUCA* articles and subsequent *Studies in Jewish Preaching* virtually established a canon of important Jewish preachers,

---

87. Morteira, *GS* 1902, publisher's Preface. A new Preface was written for the 1912 edition, in which the publisher noted that Morteira was cited with respect by several leading rabbinic scholars, including Moses Rivkes (see above). On the original Warsaw edition, see Hayyim Lieberman, "Sefer *Giv'at Sha'ul*," *Sinai* 72 (1973): 389–93 (I am grateful to Rabbi Jacob Schacter for this reference).

88. I am not competent to determine whether the book had significant influence on preachers in eastern Europe. An example would be the celebrated Warsaw preacher Isaac Nissenbaum; I have not found any reference to Morteira in the collection of his sermons I have read (*Mo'adim: Derashot la-Ḥaggim ve-la-Mo'adim* [Jerusalem, 1967].

89. Rehuel Jessurun, *Dialogo dos montes*, ed. Philip Polack (London, 1975); Swetschinski, *Reluctant Cosmopolitans*, p. 286. Two of the four manuscripts identify Morteira as the sole author; the attribution to Rehuel Jessurun follows de Barrios and the first printed edition (Polack, p. xvii–xx).

90. Leopold Zunz, *Ha-Derashot Be-Yisra'el* (Jerusalem, 1974), pp. 199, 524 n. 37.

at least for readers limited to English publications, never referred to Morteira in print. (He did, however, direct a rabbinic thesis on "The Sermons of Saul Levi Morteira" by Hirschel Levin.)[91] Joseph Dan's *Sifrut ha-Derush ve-ha-Musar*—not intended as a complete survey of Jewish homiletical literature, but the best academic treatment of the topic available in Hebrew—does not mention Morteira. Only in the more popular survey by Hyman Reuven Rabinowitz, *Diyokna'ot shel Darshanim*, is there a brief chapter on Morteira's *Giv'at Sha'ul*, in which the author focuses on the specific nature of the congregation and their needs (he makes Morteira himself into "one of the *conversos* from Spain"), and cites several passages of ethical rebuke that he finds "sharp and penetrating."[92]

Despite all that has been written about the Jewish community of Amsterdam and about Spinoza, it is rare to find any indication that someone has actually consulted the sermons as evidence. We noted above that Graetz did not think highly of Morteira, describing him as "not even a distinguished preacher; his colleagues, Aboab and Manasseh ben Israel, far outshone him. His sermons, the only printed productions of his literary activity, have a philosophical complexion, but no depth of thought. Morteira followed the broad, beaten paths, repeating what had been thought and pointed out before him." (The editor for the Hebrew edition, Saul Phinehas Rabbinowitz, by contrast, showed not only that he had read the sermons but that he had a better sense of the preacher's purpose than did the great historian: "His intention," said Rabinowitz, "was not to innovate but to fortify" the beliefs of his listeners.[93]) Cecil Roth, biographer of Menasseh ben Israel, tempered some of Graetz's negative characterization, stating that Morteira "was famous as a preacher, the volume of his sermons issued by his pupils throwing many vivid sidelights upon local conditions," though providing no illustrations of this.[94] In his study of Spinoza's philosophy, Harry Wolfson cited the opening statement of Morteira's printed sermon on *Mishpatim* to illustrate the principle of the natural

91. Hirschel Levin, "The Sermons of Saul Levi Morteira," Rabbinical and MHL Thesis submitted to Hebrew Union College, February 1942. This is written on the model of Bettan's essays, with two short bio-bibliographical chapters (13 pages) followed by an extensive treatment of the "ideas" (64 pages); these are discussed thematically, with paraphrases and quotations from various sermons juxtaposed, but very little analysis. The result is that the reader never receives any sense of what an individual sermon was like. The situation of the congregation and the element of social and religious criticism are barely addressed. For a discussion of Bettan's methodology, see Saperstein, *Jewish Preaching*, pp. 3–4.

92. Hyman Reuven Rabinowitz, *Diyokna'ot shel Darshanim* (Jerusalem, 1967), pp. 192–97.

93. See above, n. 56.

94. Roth, *A Life of Menasseh ben Israel*, p. 24.

impulse toward self-preservation, relevant for the explication of a passage in the *Ethics.*[95] The Zionist historian B. Z. Dinur wrote that "the impassioned homilies of Rabbi Saul Morteira" were an "important factor" explaining the "wildly enthusiastic participation of the Sephardi communities in this [Sabbatian] movement."[96] And Alexander Altmann briefly discussed philosophical and mystical references in *Giv'at Sha'ul* in his article on the conflict over the eternality of punishment.[97]

But with these relatively minor exceptions, the scholarship both on Morteira himself and on the community he led, the people who listened to his sermons every week for four decades, has all but ignored *Giv'at Sha'ul.* And if this is true for the printed texts that have been readily accessible, it is all the more true for the manuscripts that came to light outside of Budapest only in 1989, and have been cited in print only since 1991. I hope to demonstrate in this book that it is time to integrate a full knowledge of Morteira's extant homiletical oeuvre into the literature about Morteira himself and the community he served. This will enable scholars to determine, for example, how polemical claims attested in early treatises and fully developed in his late *Tratado* were an ongoing part of his preaching in the intervening years. And how themes attested in the community archives as preoccupations of the lay leadership—which they addressed in their ordinances—were also emphasized by the rabbi in his sermons. And how an enlightened yet traditional exposition of Judaism was structured and communicated to listeners who depended on the sermons for the content of their new identity as Jews. And how a rabbi with many obligations devoted a considerable amount of his time to the preparation of a weekly homiletical discourse. The first step in this process is to look at the material evidence: the extant manuscripts that Morteira himself wrote each week.

---

95. Harry Wolfson, *The Philosophy of Spinoza,* 2 vols. in 1 (New York, 1958), 2: 196.

96. B. Z. Dinur, *Israel and the Diaspora* (Philadelphia, 1969), p. 42. I have no idea to which printed sermons accessible to Dinur when this was written he could have been referring. On Morteira's messianism, see below, chapter 9.

97. Altmann, "Eternality of Punishment," p. 3. n. 13.

2

The Manuscript/s

Our access to the sermons delivered by Morteira—or any preacher before the age of videotapes or tape recordings—is indirect, for the preaching is oral communication, while the evidence that remains for it is written. At best, we possess a full Hebrew text of a sermon he wrote, supplemented by external sources that reveal the circumstances in which he delivered it and the issues he was addressing. Yet even with this evidence, we can only imagine the appearance of the preacher, the sound of his voice, and the reactions he evoked in his listeners. Despite these limitations, the texts of Morteira's sermons provide abundant information about the content and manner of his preaching, his role as a leader and teacher of Judaism to a unique community, and—somewhat less directly—the nature of the congregation that he was addressing. Indeed, Morteira has left us a fuller record of his homiletical career than we have for any other Jewish preacher before the late-nineteenth century.[1] We must therefore begin with the texts that provide our best evidence for what happened in the pulpit during the more than forty years of Morteira's rabbinate.

As noted in the preceding chapter, a collection of Morteira's Hebrew sermons was published in Amsterdam in 1645. Its compilers, Moses ben Benjamin Belmonte and Benjamin ben Jacob Dias Fatto, inform us in the book's introduction that they, not their teacher, were responsible for initiating the publication. As we have seen, they provide some biographical background about Morteira, including his preaching responsibilities. After describing his distinctive homiletical method, they note, "As of this day, the number of his sermons has reached 1400, each one different." To this massive accumulation of texts they gave the name *Giv'at Sha'ul,* (Saul's Hill) (1 Sam. 11:4): "This is its name because it is a mound of great and lofty stones."

---

1. There are some 550 sermons in the Hebrew manuscripts and six additional sermons in Portuguese manuscripts, plus twenty printed sermons not in the manuscripts. This record of Morteira's weekly preaching is, of course, considerably smaller than, let us say, the extant sermons of John Calvin, who preached in Geneva a major sermon each day, leaving texts of 200 different sermons on Deuteronomy alone.

Yet—the students attribute this to Morteira's modesty—he never sought to publish any part of this corpus. Together with his unpublished polemical writings and his treatise on the immortality of the soul,[2] the sermons remained unknown beyond the city. "The light of his learning was left in a corner, Saul's hill in his home." Finally, the students decided that the world beyond Amsterdam should have some benefit from their teacher. "For a number of years, without his knowledge [of our true intentions], we determined and set our minds to ask him from time to time, as if with no ulterior motive, just for our own enjoyment and benefit, [for the text of a specific sermon] in order to [copy it and] send it to other Jewish communities." In this way they gathered material, in the hope that their collection would impel Morteira to consent to publication. Eventually he decided to support the project. In addition to the fifty sermons printed, one on each weekly lesson from the Torah, a table of contents for 500 of Morteira's sermons (including the 50 published) was included at the end.

The disciples' introduction informs us that Morteira kept the texts of all of his sermons, that the sermons accumulated over the years into a large collection, that Morteira made them available for students to consult, and that the published *Giv'at Sha'ul* represents a selection of at most ten per cent (and possibly only about 3.5 per cent) of the Morteira sermons available in 1645. What happened to the others? With the exception of seven unpublished ones in Portuguese,[3] there is no reference to sermon manuscripts by Morteira in any of the published catalogues of the great libraries; nor did any of the scholarly literature on Morteira or Amsterdam before the 1990s mention their existence. It was a natural assumption that they had simply been lost.[4] As I indicated in my preface, that assumption was, happily, erroneous.

To the extreme good fortune of all who are interested in Morteira, the Portuguese community of Amsterdam during its first two or three generations, and the history of Jewish preaching, a monumental collection of Morteira's manuscript sermons, written in Hebrew and bound in five large

---

2. On Morteira's unpublished polemical texts, see above, pp. 19–22, 26–27.

3. "Sete Derashot Compostos pelo doctimissimo è carissimi Sinhor Haham asalem Morenu a Rab Saul Levi Morteira em Amsterdam Anno 5404," Ets Ḥaim MS 48 C 7. This contains six sermons for which there is no extant Hebrew counterpart, and one, for Sukkot, for which a Hebrew version exists among the manuscripts.

4. This indeed was my assumption in my first published study about Morteira ("The Sermon as Art Form: Structure in Morteira's *Giv'at Sha'ul, Prooftexts* 3 [1981]: 243–61), and when I included a sermon by Morteira in *Jewish Preaching.* See also p. 6 of that book for evidence of substantial numbers of sermons by other Jewish preachers that apparently have not been preserved.

volumes, turned up in the Rabbinical Seminary of Budapest.[5] It contains more than ten times the number of sermons included in the 1645 book, a uniquely important and hitherto untapped source for the history of Jewish preaching and of the fascinating community of former Portuguese "New Christians" that Morteira served.

We begin our analysis with the texts themselves. I maintain that the recently discovered Budapest "Giv'at Sha'ul" challenges us to expand our ordinary understanding of what a manuscript is. As I trust will become clear from the following discussion, there can be no question that what we have here is a collection of "autographs," the writing not of a later scribe but of the author himself. Yet the term "manuscript" can be applied to the material in three different ways, representing different entities and different stages in a process.

First, the term refers to the text of a single sermon written by Morteira in Hebrew, usually during the days immediately preceding its public delivery before the Beth Jacob Congregation of Amsterdam. Most of these manuscripts were written on two sheets of paper, one significant exception being the substantially longer sermons for the Sabbath of Repentance. A second use of the term refers to the larger collection, the five volumes on the shelf of the Rabbinical Seminary in Budapest identified as its MS 12, containing some 550 "manuscripts" of the first kind, put together in a particular order, which we shall describe. The third sense of the term represents an intermediate stage between the first and the second meanings. It refers to something that no longer exists and is now just a theoretical construct: the "mound of great and lofty stones," namely, the ever-expanding corpus of individual sermon manuscripts that accumulated in Morteira's own library. This corpus is not at all identical with the five volumes of the Budapest manuscript; many sermons written by Morteira, delivered from the pulpit, and subsequently cited by the preacher, are not to be found in that collection and apparently have been lost. Distinctive about this entity is that it was constantly growing, It can be reconstructed to a considerable extent from the "table of contents" in the 1645 edition of *Giv'at Sha'ul,* and from cross references in the extant manuscript

---

5. "Giv'at Sha'ul," Hebrew Manuscript 12 of the Rabbinical Seminary, Budapest (henceforth simply, "MS"). All subsequent references to the five volumes of this collection will be cited by volume and folio (unnumbered in the original when the microfilms were made and when I first consulted them, but subsequently numbered in pencil), *parashah,* theme- verse, and usually the precise or approximate year of delivery. (Some of the sermons were given a precise date by the author; in other cases their dating is approximate. On the problem of dating, see Saperstein, "Saul Levi Morteira's Treatise on the Immortality of the Soul," *StRos* 25 [1991]: 136.) I first learned of the arrival of a microfilm in the Institute for Microfilmed Hebrew Manuscripts from Yosef Kaplan in the fall of 1988.

texts. We might conceive of this third "manuscript" as the equivalent of a filing cabinet, to which new material was constantly being added (and, as we shall see below, to which updates to the current material occasionally made). It was intended primarily for the use of the preacher, but it was also available to serious students. We shall now consider each of these categories separately.

The Individual Sermon

The manuscript of a discrete Morteira sermon is visually quite distinctive. It is written in a characteristic Italian Hebrew cursive hand. The letters are generally rather small and everything is squeezed together, up to twenty words in a line, between sixty and seventy lines on a page, with virtually no margins at top or bottom and very small margins at the side. The author wrote on both sides of the page, and the text usually ends about two thirds of the way down on the first side of the second sheet. There is indeed a striking consistency of length—approximately 3,000 words. While some sermons go only half way down the third side, and others extend to the top of the fourth side, it is clear that Morteira had an ideal length in mind and did not vary from it by much.

There are Budapest manuscripts for twenty-six of the fifty sermons published in 1645, and by comparing them with the printed versions we can see what was changed. Textually, there are no important differences; it appears as if these were the actual texts used by the printer. In a few cases there are corrections in the manuscript;[6] in others, passages appear at the end, marked for insertion in the text.[7] In these cases, the printed version reflects the additions. It is not always clear whether these corrections were made at the time of the original writing or whether Morteira polished his material when he

---

6. There are relatively minor corrections added between the lines on MS 3:175v, *Va-Yetse,* Gen. 28:13. One is an additional example for the point being made, one emends a misquotation from aggadah. The only example I have found with substantial stylistic revisions—again through words crossed out or inserted between the lines—is the sermon on *Shemot* (MS 3:187r–188v, on Exod. 1:7), which I published in translation. This appears to have been one of Morteira's favorite sermons, and he seems to have worked on the style before releasing it to the printer.

7. For example, in MS 3:182v, at the end of the sermon on *Mi-Qets* (Gen. 41:4), there are two insertions that were incorporated into the 1645 edition, as well as additions between the lines. These may therefore have been added as the text was going to the printer. However, other texts not included in the book also have passages appended for incorporation into the body of the sermon. At the end of MS 3:6v (*Toledot,* Gen. 25:19), a wedding sermon from 1619, there are two such additional passages. As they pertain to the circumstances of the occasion—involving an orphan married with a dowry provided by the *Biqqur Ḥolim* Society—the inserts were intended for the original delivery.

knew it would be printed, but there is no evidence of substantial rewriting for publication.

The most important difference between the manuscripts and the printed texts is material appended to the end of many manuscripts pertaining to the date and circumstances in which the sermon was delivered—which usually appears on the second side of the second sheet. I will give several examples from manuscripts of sermons that were printed in *Giv'at Sha'ul,* and then refer to other examples of unprinted manuscripts.

First, the sermon on *Mi-Qets* is devoted to a seemingly barren discussion of the source of dreams. But it ends with a surprising shift and applies the subject to the institutions of the community. There are three purposes of a valid dream at this time, the preacher maintains.

> And if we look at them closely, we see that they are the activities of this sacred congregation. The first is to open people's ears to wisdom: is this not the goal of the Talmud Torah Society, to impart knowledge of God's word? The second is to divert people from doing something specific: this the activity of the regents (*parnasim*) of the sacred congregation—to guide everyone in the good path. The third is to make people aware of the punishment [for sin] so that they will change their way and it will not come: this is the sacred society whose meritorious activity is [honored] this very day. For its entire agenda is bound up with the "wretched poor" (Isa. 58:7); upon seeing them, they think, *Did not the One who made me in my mother's belly make him too?* (Job 31:15); I am just as eligible for sorrow as he is," opening their ears to an ethical message, so that they repent. This applies to the sick, to those who lack clothing, to those who die.[8]

There follows an explication of Isaiah 58:7 in light of these three categories, containing a rather powerful and moving call for empathy with the disadvantaged. But the identity of "this sacred society" is not specified; indeed, there was no need to do so in the body of the sermon, for everyone in the audience knew exactly what was meant.

At the end of the manuscript version (following two insertions that appear in the body of the printed text), we find the following notation, which was not printed:

The sermon I delivered on the Sabbath of Hanukkah in the year 5389

---

8. *GS* 1645, p. 19d–20a, 1912, p. 96.

[December, 1628], on the day when the following gentlemen ended their term as regents (*parnasim*): Mr. Abraham de la Costa, Mr. Abraham Preto, Mr. Jacob Burgos, and Mr. Isaac Israel Mendes. May God protect and defend them.

The following gentlemen began their terms: Mr. David Judah Rodrigues, Mr. Isaac de Aguilar, Mr. Moses Cardozo, and Mr. Tobiau Israel da Silva. May God protect and defend them.[9]

This notation gives us valuable information. The date situates this text at a specific point in time that can be related to other information known from the abundant documentation about the Portuguese community. The circumstances of delivery also become clearer: this was a Sabbath on which a particular confraternity of the community celebrated the installation of its officers. The names recorded are known from other community records: this note names the officers during two separate terms. The name of the society is not specified. But when we look at other sermon manuscripts from the lesson *Mi-Qets*, of which fifteen have been preserved, we find a regular pattern. All of them are dated, ranging from December 1625 to December 1644. All of them until the year 1640 record the outgoing and incoming regents, making possible a fairly complete reconstruction of the leadership of the confraternity over a sixteen-year period. And most of the other notices specifically identify the confraternity in question: it is the *Biqqur Ḥolim* (Visiting the Sick) Society.[10] We learn from the manuscripts that each year, on the Sabbath of the lesson *Mi-Qets*, the Sabbath of Hanukkah, the *Biqqur Ḥolim* Society was honored in the Beth Jacob synagogue; Morteira's sermons on this occasion often included references to the Society's activities as well as the names of its current officers.[11] The manuscripts, then, reveal the sermons not as abstract disquisitions, but reflections of a specific occasion.

In another example, at the end of the manuscript sermon on Genesis 28:13, we find the following notation that does not appear in the printed *Giv'at Sha'ul*: "The sermon I delivered on the lesson *Va-Yetse* on the day of the cel-

---

9. MS 3:182v, *Mi-Qets*, Gen. 41:4.

10. E.g. MS 5:112v, *Mi-Qets*, Gen. 41:2: "The sermon I delivered in the year 5386 [Dec. 1625] on the day when the following end their terms as regents of the sacred society of *Biqqur Ḥolim*..."

11. For further discussion of this material, see below, pp. 174–80. Similarly, a manuscript sermon delivered on the first day of Shavu'ot, 1621, and referring to the occasion as "this day of the giving of the Torah and the festival of the sacred Talmud Torah Society and the election of its regents," lists the outgoing and incoming regents of the Talmud Torah Society (MS 2:63r and 64v, Deut. 16:10; cf. a similar list from 1626 in MS 3:40v, Lev. 1:1).

ebration [*shurah*][12] of Mr. Samuel Duarte with his relative, the modest orphan Ms. Clara Benveniste, who was married through the sponsorship of the sacred *Biqqur Holim* Society in the year 5382 [1621]."[13] Here again these few words provide a date, a life cycle occasion, the names of the principles and a detail of their background, and the fact that one of the undertakings of the *Biqqur Holim* Society was to provide for the marriage of orphaned girls.[14] Situated on this occasion of a marriage, certain themes in the sermon pertaining to the importance of future generations—for example, "God will save Israel even if they have no merit because of the future offspring who will sanctify God and serve Him"[15]—take on heightened significance.

At the end of the manuscript sermon on Genesis 1:10, Morteira wrote, "The sermon I delivered on the Sabbath of *Bereshit* in the year 5394 [1633] on the day when the *Hatan Bereshit* was Mr. David de Solis." Underneath this is another line: "And I delivered it a second time in the year 5400 [1639] when the *Hatan Bereshit* was Mr. Jacob del Sotto."[16] There is a third notation, with the title of the sermon ("Which were Designated by Name," cf. 1 Chron. 12:32),[17] and a short characterization of its content: "Its content is to explain how by means of the [Hebrew] names God used for six products of the creation week—day, night, heaven, earth, sea and human being—they became eternal; it explains how God granted a similar eternity to Israel, and indeed that the eternity of Israel is even stronger than the eternity of these things." This title and epitome appear in the 1645 edition at the top of the page, before the theme-verse, which was the first thing the preacher actually uttered.[18]

---

12. The Hebrew word means literally "line," and in the idiosyncratic usage of the Sephardim refers apparently to the line of individuals honored by being called to the Torah on special celebratory occasions, especially the Sabbath before a wedding or following the birth of a child. See Wiznitzer, "The Minute Book of Congregations Zur Israel of Recife and Magen Abraham of Mauricia, Brazil," in Cohen, *The Jewish Experience in Latin America*, 2:31011.

13. MS 3:176r, *Va-Yetse*, Gen. 28:13.

14. This is generally associated exclusively with the *Santa Companhia de dotar orfans e donzelas pobres*, founded in 1615, on which see Miriam Bodian, "The 'Portuguese' Dowry Societies in Venice and Amsterdam," *Italia* 6 (1987): 30–61.

15. *GS* 1645, p. 15b, 1912, p. 80.

16. MS 5:6v, *Bereshit*, Gen. 1:10. *Hatan bereshit* (literally: "bridegroom of [the lesson] 'in the beginning')," refers to the person honored by being called to the Torah for the reading of the first verses, either on the holiday of Simhat Torah or on the following Sabbath. Cf. Pieterse, *de Barrios*, p. 161.

17. Morteira's practice of giving each sermon a title, almost always a biblical phrase related to the sermon's content, aided in his system of cross-reference, which will be discussed below.

18. GS 1645, p. 3a. The epitome was not used in the 1902/1912 edition.

Here again, these notations appended to the final page of the sermon manuscript provide us with a date and the name of an individual, in this case a person granted a major honor in the congregation by being called to the Torah for the beginning of the annual cycle.[19] We also see that Morteira sometimes reused his sermons, in this case only six years after the original delivery. These notations of re-use are fairly common and added to the text years after the original composition.[20]

Thus we see that the individual sermon manuscript is more complex than might be imagined. While it appears as if it is the work of a few days—that is, the days just before it was first delivered[21]—we see that Morteira sometimes returned to earlier manuscripts to write something more. The notations about the date and circumstances of the original delivery were presumably added soon after the Sabbath, before Morteira filed the text away. But the notations about re-use would have been added years later, at the time of re-use. In some cases Morteira records four or five different occasions of delivery, each notation added at a different time. Occasionally he recorded material added to the sermon on the occasion of re-use.[22] In the case of the Genesis 1:10 sermon, there is the epitome, material that must have been added by the author sometime between the fall of 1639 and the publication in 1645—undoubtedly with the printing of *Giv'at Sha'ul* in mind. Thus there was a process of moderate

---

19. According to Emmanuel, this was a "very expensive mitsvah," reserved for the individual elected as *gabbai* of the *ma'amad* (Emmanuel, "Yedi'ot Hadashot al ha-Qehilah ha-Portugezit me-Amsterdam," p. 166. Jacob del Sotto's name appears in a list of regents for the community in 1645, 1654, 1659, 1664, and 1668 (ibid., pp. 175–179). He was extremely wealthy; at his death in 1670, his will was contested, creating a scandalous conflict in the community: ibid., pp. 164–65; Yosef Kaplan, *From Christianity to Judaism: The Story of Isaac Orobio de Castro* (Oxford, 1989), pp. 196–99.

20. Another example of such a notation appended to a manuscript sermon that was not included when the sermon was printed in 1645 is at the end of *Va-Yiggash* on Genesis 44:20 (3:105v): "I preached it a second time in the sacred congregation 'Beth Israel' in the year 5391 [1630] on the day of the celebration of the marriage of Mr. Moses Cohen Henriques (may God bless and preserve him) with his relative Miss Rachel Espinosa (may she be blessed among women in the homes): may it be a good omen." The much lighter ink and thinner pen clearly indicate that this was added at a later time.

21. The argument justifying this conclusion that the text was written before delivery will be made below.

22. For one example: MS 5:96r *Mi-Qets*, Gen. 41:10, 1634: "I preached it a second time in the year 1654 and I added to each part of the sermon the verse, *The steps of a man are made firm by the Eternal, when He delights in his way* (Ps. 37:23).... I also added in Psalm 66 an interpretation of the verses...." Other significant examples of material added for a new occasion will be discussed below.

accretion (in addition to the moderate editing noted above) in the manuscripts. In this way some of the texts grew through the years.

Morteira recorded the dates of delivery for almost all his sermons on *Bereshit,* which provide the names of the individuals honored, and on *Mi-Qets,* which list the outgoing and incoming officers of the *Biqqur Ḥolim* Society. Most of the others provide dates of delivery only when there was a special circumstance—a minority of cases. Nevertheless, the dates that do appear provide a framework that facilitates at least an approximate dating of the other sermons.

It should also be noted that while the manuscript of the individual sermon constitutes the building block for the composite "manuscript" we will discuss later, the individual text itself is the end result of a composition process that will be discussed in detail in the following chapter. It is difficult to believe that anyone, no matter how accomplished and experienced a preacher, could sit down and compose a text like those that appear before us without previous written preparation—notes, an outline, a rough draft. If such written evidence for the process of preparation existed, it is unsurprising that Morteira did not think it important to preserve it. Yet among the manuscripts are some that look as if they are not finished products,[23] and there are other indications of the process by which the preacher produced his weekly sermons.

To illustrate, each sermon begins in the traditional Sephardi pattern with a

---

23. For example, MS 1:25r, *Shemini,* Lev. 9:16, contains three paragraphs of text, (two after the introduction), extending to 8 lines on back of the first sheet. There is then a small slip of paper, with the words: "To complete the sermon, you need to bring up that in the incident of the [golden] calf there were all four reasons that cause evil beliefs, and all of them are hinted in the *Baraita*... [four are then listed].... And for each one, you need to find that they caused the sin of the calf, and in this way the sermon will be completed." Apparently he was interrupted and unable to finish writing the sermon. As a note to himself, he recorded how he intended to complete it. It is unclear whether the sermon was ever delivered. An interesting parallel and contrast is found in a powerful sermon of social and religious rebuke, which I shall analyze in detail and then translate below. The assertion that "God has dealt more beneficently with us than with any [other] Jews in the exile" is followed by the words, "here this matter should be discussed at length" (*u-ve-khan ye'arekh al ha-'inyan ha-zeh*), which concludes the paragraph. Beneath it, written with a slightly finer pen point, is a passage that makes precisely this point at length, mentioning the great Jewish communities of Italy, Germany, Poland, the Ottoman Empire, and North Africa, and specifying the persecutions suffered by the Jews there that are not present in Amsterdam. Apparently, Morteira wrote the words "more beneficently with us than with any [other] Jews in the exile," and then had to interrupt his writing. As in the previous example, he wrote a note to himself, certainly not included in the oral delivery, about how he intended to continue, but he returned to his writing soon afterward and completed the task (MS 2:96r, *Mishpatim,* Exod. 21:8, 1627; see below, p. 135 n. 44 and p. 402.

verse from the weekly Torah lesson (the "*nosei,*" theme, or "text"), a rabbinic dictum, and then an introduction.[24] Morteira's selection of theme-verse was determined by his self-imposed discipline, described in the Introduction to *Giv'at Sha'ul,* of starting with the first verse of each *parashah* and progressing verse after verse through the scriptural lesson. But how did he select the rabbinic statement? The physical layout of many of the sermon manuscripts gives us a clue. As already noted, Morteira was not one to waste space on a page; he squeezed his lines together and wrote all the way to the margin. Yet in many of the manuscripts, there is a blank space equivalent to four or five lines between the end of the dictum and the beginning of the introduction. In some cases, the theme-verse and the body of the sermon are written in a small script, while the dictum is written in much larger letters.[25] The explanation is obvious. Frequently, after writing the theme-verse, Morteira left an empty space and began with the introduction and the body of the sermon. He did not decide upon a rabbinic dictum until the sermon was almost completed, at which point he went back and wrote it in the space he had left. Sometimes the dictum was much too short to fill up all the space, even if written in larger letters. In each one of these instances, we find that the dictum is discussed only near the end of the sermon. In other words, not everything had been planned out before the first words were set on paper. The manuscripts sometimes reveal a process of ongoing creativity.

As we have seen, the statements about the circumstances for the sermons on *Bereshit* and *Mi-Qets,* containing dates and names of the *Ḥatan Bereshit* or the outgoing and incoming regents of the *Biqqur Ḥolim* Society, were separated from the body of the sermon and written on the back side of the second sheet of paper. A number of less formal notations immediately follow the conclusion of the sermon. For example, on the back of the second page, following the end of the sermon for *Mi-Qets* on Genesis 41:3, we find the words "I have not preached it yet" crossed out.[26] As we have seen, all other sermons on *Mi-Qets* are dated by the preacher. The one on Genesis 41:2 is dated 5386

---

24. On the background of this structure, see Marc Saperstein, *Jewish Preaching 1200–1800* (New Haven, 1989), pp. 66–69. Morteira's introductions, usually one or two large paragraphs, all conclude with an invocation of help from God, and were not at all conventional; cf. ibid., pp. 76–77.

25. E.g., MS 2:150r, *Va-Yeshev,* Gen. 37:9; 2:188r, Num. 4:30; 3:5r, *Toledot,* Gen. 25:19, *1619;* 3:13r, *Mi-Qets,* Gen. 41:12; 3:33r, *Tetsaveh,* Exod. 27:21; 3:41r, *Tsav,* Lev. 6:3, 1620; 3:45r, *Tazria,* Lev. 12:3. Many other examples could be given. Occasionally, the dictum appears to be squeezed into the allotted space, written in smaller letters than the rest, as if Morteira chose a longer statement than he had expected: 3:29r, *Mishpatim,* Exod. 21:2.

26. MS 3:103v, *Mi-Qets,* Gen. 41:3: *lo derashtiv 'adayin* (crossed out).

(December, 1625) and the one on Genesis 41:4 is dated 5389 (December, 1628).[27] This enables us to reconstruct the following scenario: in accordance with his pattern, Morteira prepared a sermon on Genesis 41:3 for December of 1626, when the regents of the *Biqqur Ḥolim* Society would be installed. Indeed, the final paragraph of the sermon mentions five major funds of the Portuguese community, including "the fund of the confraternity that saves from afflictions," an allusion to the *Biqqur Ḥolim* Society.[28] For reasons unspecified, Morteira put it away, noting for his records that it had not been delivered, and used it the following year, December, 1627, continuing in 1628 with a sermon on Genesis 41:4.

Other notations give more specific reasons why a prepared sermon would not have been delivered. Immediately following the end of the sermon for *Be-Shallaḥ* on Exodus 14:9, Morteira wrote, "I did not preach it yet because of the cold." Then, on the other side of the page, we read, "The sermon I delivered in the year 1636 on the day of the celebration of Mr. Aaron Senior with his relative Sarah Senior, may it be under a good sign for them."[29] This shows that sometimes the preacher came to the synagogue with a sermon all prepared, but decided, for his listeners' comfort, not to deliver it. That would, of course, save him the need for preparing a new sermon the following year. Or sometimes even sooner: another sermon on the same lesson, this one on Exodus 13:18, has the following notation appended: "The sermon I prepared for the Sabbath of *Be-Shallaḥ,* the fifteenth of Shevat 5381 [February 6, 1621], but I did not deliver it publicly because of the intensity of the cold on that day, unprecedented." These words were written with the same ink and pen as the rest of the sermon. Immediately after but written with a thinner pen point, we find the words, "and afterward I delivered it on the Sabbath of the Pesach week that same year."[30]

Winter cold was not the only climatic influence on the congregation; the heat of the summer could be just as oppressive. We see this in an appended notation written on the overleaf of a sermon for *Be-Ha'alotekha:* "I preached

---

27. MS 5:112v, 3:182v.

28. MS 3:103r, *Mi-Qets*, Gen. 41:3. This fits Morteira's descriptions, in other *Mi-Qets* sermons, of the activities of the *Biqqur Ḥolim* Society as focused on the needs of the poor. (These will be discussed in the chapter on the community, below pp. 172–80.)

29. MS 4:76r, *Be-Shallaḥ*, Exod. 14:9: *lo derashtiv 'adayin mipnei ha-qor* (crossed out); reference to Aaron and Sarah Senior on 4:76v. The sermon on Exod. 14:6 is dated 1632 (4:74r). This suggests that a sermon on Exod. 14:7 was delivered in 1633 (not extant), a sermon on Exod. 14:8 in 1634, and the sermon on Exod. 14:9 was originally prepared for 1635 but not delivered until 1636.

30. MS 3:26v, *Be-Shallaḥ*, Exod. 13:18.

this sermon in the year 5389 [1629] on the day of celebration for the son of the honorable Mr. Isaac Masiah; however, because of the heat I did not deliver it in its entirety—only the introduction and the interpretation of the first rabbinic dictum. In the year 5390 [1630] I delivered it in its entirety."[31]

Occasionally the circumstances that prevented delivery of the sermon were of a personal nature. A rather poignant example can be found at the end of a sermon for *Naso*:

> Half of this sermon was prepared in the year 5391 [1631], but I was unable to complete it because I got sick. The second half was prepared in the year 5392 [1632], but I did not deliver it publicly because I again took sick in that very week. Blessed is the Healer of all flesh who has made me sick and healed me; may He in His mercies make me whole in two days and on the third day raise me up (cf. Hos. 6:2), so that I may deliver it before Him next year at this time.

Beneath this is the statement, "Blessed is the Eternal who has kept me alive and raised me up and brought me to the third year, when I delivered it publicly. May God make me worthy of many years, Amen, be this His will."[32] A quick glance at the overleaf of the first page of the manuscript reveals immediately where Morteira stopped writing because of his illness the first year: there is a clear shift from a thicker pen point to a thinner one, occurring in the middle of a sentence.[33] Had this text been included in the 1645 edition and not preserved in manuscript, none of this personal drama would have been revealed.

I have mentioned these notations by the author not only because they shed light on the preacher's work, but because they reveal one of the most important facts about the nature of these manuscripts. Every extant sermon text raises the question of its relationship to a sermon that was actually delivered. Most extant texts from the medieval and early modern periods seem to have been written *after* the delivery. In the Christian community, this was some-

---

31. MS 2:117r, *Be-Ha'alotekha*, Num. 8:9.

32. MS 2:189r, *Naso*, Num. 4:30. Morteira uses the root *'asah* to refer to writing the text of the sermon, and the root *amar* (or in other instances *darash*) for delivering it in public. Cf. *Jewish Preaching*, p. 25, on Joseph Garçon. Morteira's older British contemporary Lancelot Andrewes prepared a sermon on repentance to be delivered at the royal Court on Ash Wednesday, 1624, but was prevented by illness from delivering it (he died two years later); the text, written in advance, was published under the title "A Sermon Prepared to be Preached." See G. M. Story, Introduction to Lancelot Andrewes, *Sermons* (Oxford, 1967), pp. xlxxx–xliv.

33. In addition, one can see several places where Morteira went back and corrected his text from the previous year with the finer pen.

times the product of stenographic transcriptions taken in shorthand during
the delivery of distinguished preachers.[34] For Jews, this was precluded by the
prohibition of writing on most occasions when sermons would have been
delivered; rather the preacher himself decided at some later point to reconstruct what he had said and prepare it for circulation or publication.[35] The
text I have just cited, written in part but not completed the first year, completed but not delivered the second year, and finally delivered the third,
shows beyond any doubt that Morteira wrote these texts *before* he delivered
them.[36] The manuscript of the discrete sermon is, at first instance, a record of
what the preacher *planned* to say; after the fact, it became a record of what he
had said.[37] Indeed, occasionally we find that the preacher added at the end of
the text some material that was not originally written but that was included
in the sermon when delivered.

Let us look at one of many examples. At the end of a sermon on Exodus
18:3, we find the following statement:

> And I added, pertaining to the wedding, that if it is so that first God
> saved Moses from the sword of Pharaoh and afterward he lived in a
> foreign land, why did he name his first son Gershom and his second
> Eliezer? The answer is that first he lived [in a foreign land] and then

---

34. For the earlier period, see the references in *Jewish Preaching*, p. 11 n. 16. A striking
example from a time closer to Morteira is the sermons of John Calvin, recorded in shorthand by professional stenographers, who then transcribed the notations into a long-hand
manuscript. See T. H. L. Parker, *Calvin's Preaching* (Louisville, 1992), pp. 65–67.

35. For a clear example, see Leon Modena, who tells us that he wrote the sermons that
he published "from the outline notes [*rimzei rashei peraqim*]" that he had written before the
delivery (*Midbar Yehudah*, Venice, 1602, introd. p. 4b; 2001, p. 50); cf. the general discussion
in *Jewish Preaching*, pp. 20–26. See also Israel of Belzyce's "Tiferet Yisra'el" (Oxford Bodleian Hebrew MS 989), a manuscript of over 400 folios put together near the end of the
preacher's career, apparently for publication, from individual sermons he had delivered
between 1632 and 1653 (*Jewish Preaching*, pp. 286–87). Also Benjamin ben Eliezer ha-Kohen
Vital, *Gevul Binyamin* (Amsterdam, 1727), a massive collection of 190 sermons delivered
throughout a 48-year career of continuous preaching in Alessandria and Reggio, edited and
written for publication in the preacher's old age (Introduction).

36. Indeed, it is all but inconceivable that a preacher who had to deliver a sermon each
week for many years would devote substantial time and energy to producing a finished
product in Hebrew *after* the sermon had been delivered and he already had to start thinking
about the following week's address. For similar statements in other manuscripts and printed
texts indicating that the preacher wrote out his material in advance, see *Jewish Preaching*, pp.
25–26.

37. Not, of course, a stenographic transcript. Although the texts are in Hebrew, Morteira
delivered them in Portuguese, the only language his congregants would have understood.
See the discussion below.

Jethro gave him his daughter for a wife. Therefore he named his first Gershom, alluding to his living as a foreigner [*ger*] and the second Eliezer, for *The God of my father was my help* (Exod 18:4), referring to his marriage, for the Bible says that God made *a fitting helper* [*ezer*] *for him* (Gen. 2:18). The verse means that the God of my father, who is the father of orphans, arranged my marriage here and became my helper, and that is why he saved me from the sword of Pharaoh.

On the overleaf, the preacher noted the circumstances of delivery: "The sermon I delivered on the lesson *Yitro* on the day of the celebration for the marriage of the honorable Mr. Isaac Frances with the modest maiden Miss Rachel Perez, *blessed among women in tents* (Jud. 5:24). She was married with the sponsorship of the Holy Society of *Biqqur Ḥolim* in the year 1622."[38] The thicker nub and darker ink used for these two sections show that they were not written at the same time as the sermon text. The most plausible reconstruction is that the sermon was prepared for this week without any reference to the forthcoming marriage. Then, at the last minute, Morteira incorporated a homiletical allusion to the life cycle event, which he subsequently recorded after the time of delivery.[39]

How did Morteira use these manuscripts in the pulpit? Did he read to his congregation the texts he had written word for word? On the one hand, the sermons are carefully composed, with many passages revealing impressive rhetorical flair. It may therefore seem unlikely that a preacher would put so much effort into writing and polishing a complete text if he were not going to follow it closely. Nevertheless, several considerations militate against the assumption that these texts were simply read from the pulpit. First of all, as noted above, the writing is usually quite small, and the lines are long and squeezed together. It would be easy to lose one's place when moving from the end of one line to the beginning of the next. Second, Morteira wrote on both sides of the

38. MS 3:196r, Yitro, Exod. 18:3, 1622: *ve-hosafti le 'inyan ha-nisu'in...*; reference to circumstances on 3:196v.

39. The passage actually seems like an allusion to biographical facts about the bridegroom and/or bride that people in the congregation would have known. The language would be particularly appropriate if the bride (and possibly both parties) had suffered the loss of parents in Portugal, escaped, and come as a stranger to Holland, where—like Moses in Midian—she was now getting married. Once again we see the role of the *Biqqur Ḥolim* Society in sponsoring marriages, apparently of orphans. On the addition of material at the last minute later recorded in brief, cf. the passage from Josiah Pardo quoted in Saperstein, *Jewish Preaching*, p. 26.

page, and the ink sometimes showed through from one side to the other. This is not to say that it could not be done, but it is difficult to imagine an effective delivery if one had to read from a text with these technical drawbacks.

More decisive is the consideration of language. The manuscripts, of course, are written in Hebrew, but there is little evidence to suggest that Jewish preachers in Europe ever delivered sermons in the holy tongue to a general audience.[40] For this particular congregation of immigrants from Portugal, whose capacity to understand the Hebrew of even the basic texts of the Jewish tradition—prayerbook, Haggadah, Bible—was extremely limited, regular preaching in Hebrew would be particularly implausible.[41] If Morteira had read from his original manuscript texts, he simply would not have been understood. The sermons must have been delivered in the language of the community, Portuguese.

How should we imagine this was done? Could he have used a translator? The first religious leader of the Portuguese community was Moses Uri Halevi of Emden, who came to Amsterdam in 1602. In the year 1673, a respected scholar named Ḥakham David Cohen de Lara gave a testimonial stating that as a youth, he had heard Halevi preach with an interpreter.[42] Although at least fifty years had passed, this detail remained vivid enough for Cohen de Lara to emphasize it. Theoretically Morteira could have used the same technique, reading the texts phrase by phrase in Hebrew and waiting for each few words to be translated, but it seems extremely unlikely. Such a cumbersome mode

---

40. For a review of this matter, see Saperstein, *Jewish Preaching*, pp. 39–43.

41. See, Yosef Yerushalmi, "The Re-Education of Marranos in the Seventeenth Century," Rabbi Louis Feinberg Memorial Lecture in Judaic Studies, University of Cincinnati, March 26, 1980, pp. 7–11, on translations of classical texts and basic works written in Spanish and Portuguese; also H. P. Salomon, *Portrait of a New Christian* (Paris, 1982), pp. 144–45; Harm den Boer and H. P. Salomon, "Another 'Lost' Book Found: The Melo Haggadah, Amsterdam 1622," *StRos* 29 (1995): 119–20. Note the statement by David Abenatar Melo in the dedication to a Spanish version of Pslams published in 1626: "for in that land [Spain, probably encompassing the entire Iberian peninsula, as Melo came from Portugal], for our sins, our elders did not teach us the holy tongue and allowed it to be lost, so that not one word of it is spoken over there" (ibid., p. 167). Cf. also Cecil Roth, "The Religion of the Marranos," *JQR*, n.s. 12 (1931): 12–13. A recent scholar concludes, "Some knowledge of Hebrew was undoubtedly acquired by adult immigrants. It is doubtful, however, whether many of them ever really attained much more than prayerbook proficiency." Daniel Swetschinski, "The Portuguese Jews of Seventeenth-Century Amsterdam: Cultural Continuity and Adaptation," in *Essays in Modern Jewish History*, ed. Frances Malino and Phyllis Albert (Rutherford: N.J, 1982), p. 57.

42. See H. P. Salomon, "Myth or Anti-Myth?" *LIAS* 16 (1989): 291–93, 313–14, citing Daniel Levi de Barrios, *Triumpho del Govierno Popular*: "e o ouvi darsar com interprete diversas vezes" (p. 314).

of communication may be tolerated by a congregation as an emergency method, but it is inconceivable that they would choose to listen to broken discourse week after week for more than forty years, and unimaginable that a speaker with such a keen rhetorical sense as Morteira would tolerate this arrangement. Morteira knew Portuguese, although it was not his native tongue; he married a woman from the Portuguese nation, and he later wrote his magnum opus, the *Tratado*, in that language. Morteira wrote his sermons in Hebrew, but he himself must have then delivered them in the vernacular of his congregants.[43]

We can refine this technique still further. Reading a prepared text verbatim was not considered a sophisticated method of communication in either the Jewish or the Christian community. A modern scholar has described the technique of Morteira's London contemporary, John Donne: "He never read his sermons, but neither did he preach extempore. He prepared his sermons very carefully, made voluminous notes, and then committed the whole discourse to memory."[44] The most plausible conclusion about Morteira's sermons, then, is that after having written one, he mastered his material to the point where he could transmit it in Portuguese, either entirely by memory, or possibly from an outline or brief notes.[45] The manuscript remains, therefore, the most accurate record of what he said, if not always of the way he said it.

One other significant feature of the Budapest manuscripts reveals a fasci-

---

43. Indeed, a record from the Portuguese Inquisition containing the statement of a New Christian who returned from Amsterdam in 1641 reports that Morteira preached regularly in Portuguese: "E que aos sabbados pella menħa pregava sempre o sobreditto Mortera, explicando paços da Ley em portuguez" (H. P. Salomon, in Morteira, *Tratado,* p. lxxviii). Another argument is that Menasseh ben Israel referred to the texts of hundreds of his sermons, written in Portuguese, which he had delivered in Amsterdam and hoped some day to publish (see *Jewish Preaching,* p. 6). It is absurd to think that Morteira would have preached in the Beth Jacob congregation in Hebrew while Menasseh was delivering sermons down the road in Neveh Shalom, to a very similar kind of congregation, in Portuguese. This would be even more implausible during the period after 1639, when Morteira and Menasseh alternated as preachers in the combined Talmud Torah.

44. See *John Donne's Sermons on the Psalms and Gospels,* ed. Evelyn Simpson (Berkeley, 1963), pp. 6–7, and below, p. 124, n. 25. Cf. also the description of John Angell James, one of the leading British pulpit orators in the first half of the nineteenth century. He wrote out a full text of important sermons and then memorized it; his brother sat with the text in hand to prompt if necessary, but reported that James hardly every forgot a single word. G. Holden Pike, *The Life and Work of Charles Hadden Spurgeon* (Edinburgh, 1991), 1:105.

45. An analogy to this is the report that when, in 1948, Leo Baeck went on a speaking tour in the United States, he wrote out his remarks in German and then prepared his delivery in English, "searching the dictionary to be certain of the precise meaning of every English word that he wanted to use, and then pacing up and down in his room until he had his text

nating sidelight about their history. As we pointed out above, Morteira frequently noted his subsequent uses of the same sermon, sometimes indicating the special circumstances and recording the material he added at the later date. At the end of several of the manuscripts, there is yet another notation, in a different hand. The statements, culled from seven different sermons, are as follows:

1.   I preached it here in Ancona for the Sabbath of Repentance, 5525 [fall 1764].
2..   I myself preached it, exactly as it is, on the Day of Rejoicing in the Torah, here in Ancona, 5525 [fall 1764].
3..   And I preached it in the year 5525 [fall 1764].
4..   This was preached in the year 5525 [winter 1764–65]
5..   I copied it [possibly: translated it: *he'etaqtiv*] in the year 5527 [fall 1766].
6..   I copied it to preach before a large congregation in the year 5530 [fall 1769]
7..   Already preached in the year 5530 [winter 1770][46]

Clearly, a rabbi or preacher in Ancona not only possessed the manuscripts but delivered the sermons to his own congregation between the fall of 1764 and the winter of 1770, presumably without acknowledging the identity of their real author. As none of these sermons had been printed in 1645, the preacher could be confident that his lack of originality would not be detected.

Can the Italian owner of the manuscripts be identified? Studies published by Cecil Roth and Mordecai Wilensky provide us with detailed information about the rabbis of Ancona in the second half of the eighteenth century.[47]

---

by heart." Marianne C. Dreyfus, "Remembering My Grandfather, Leo Baeck," *CCAR Journal* (Winter 1999), p. 52.

46. 1. MS 3:80v, *Shabbat Teshuvah, Va-Yelekh,* Deut. 31:2; 2. MS 1:130v, *Berakhah,* Deut. 33:18; 3. MS 2:215v, *Va-Yishlaḥ,* Gen. 32:13; 4. MS 5:134v, *Va-Yeḥi,* Gen. 48:3; 5. MS 3:93r, *Ḥayyei Sarah,* Gen. 23:14–15; 6. MS 3:4r, *Ḥayyei Sarah,* Gen. 23:13; 7. MS 3:36r, *Ki Tissa,* Exod. 30:13.

47. Bezalel (Cecil) Roth, "Rabbanei Ancona," *Sinai* 11, (1947): 323–26; Mordecai Wilensky, "Al Rabbanei Ancona," *Sinai* 13 (1949): 64–82. Among them were Yehiel ben Jacob ha-Kohen, whom Hayyim Azulai heard preach on his visit in the fall of 1753 (*Sefer Ma'agal Tov ha-Shalem* [Berlin, 1921], p. 6) but who would have been in his 90s in the 1760s, Isaac Fiano, who served as rabbi from 1752–1770 and Samuel Shemaiah Papo, *dayyan* of Ancona from 1756 to 1761 (but possibly no longer in the 1760s) (Wilensky, pp. 75–76, 80–81). Hayyim ben Moses Volterra, described by Wilensky at length (pp. 77–80), left sermon epitomes in manuscript, but he apparently left Ancona in 1733 and was rabbi in Venice in the 1760s.

None of this material is sufficient to identify the plagiarist. Yet the seven notations supplement the information recorded by Morteira himself. They inform us that, in a manner that remains unknown at present, the manuscripts traveled from Amsterdam to Ancona, on their eventual journey to Budapest. Second, the decision of the Italian preacher to record the occasions of his use of the sermons suggests he did not think there was anything wrong with such appropriation. Third, and perhaps most important, the Ancona rabbi's own style of composing a sermon could not have been so dramatically different from Morteira's; otherwise the sermons would have been immediately recognizable as someone else's works. Thus homiletical tastes and intellectual preoccupations among the listeners must have remained stable enough in the seventeenth and eighteenth centuries that a sermon written 130 to 140 years before could be given "just as it was," in a different country, without seeming hopelessly dated. The manuscript of an individual sermon might seem to be a paradigm of ephemera, but it could have an interesting afterlife.

Budapest Rabbinical Seminary Hebrew Manuscript 12

In the collection of the Budapest Rabbinical Seminary is a work labelled "Giv'at Sha'ul."[48] Our task now is to describe *this* "manuscript" and characterize its relationship to the first sense in which I have used the word.

The Budapest "manuscript" comprises five bound volumes, each one of which contains the manuscripts of individual sermons by Morteira. Volume 1 contains 68 sermons, volume 2 has 132, volume 3 has 178, volume 4 has 100, volume 5 has 71, yielding a total of some 550 different sermons. A quick examination of any one volume reveals that while the sermons are all the work of the same man, they were produced at different times. Not all the pages are the same size, and there is variation from one sermon to the next in the darkness of the ink, the thickness of the pen, the size of the writing, the number of lines on a page. The variations in handwriting are, on the whole, consistent with material written over a period of more than forty years.[49] The

---

48. I was informed by the current librarian, Dr. Ferenc Bersanyi-Schmidt, that around 1875, the Budapest Seminary purchased the library of Rabbi Lelio della Torre of Padua (d. 1871). It is possible that the manuscripts, which (as we have seen) were in Ancona in the second half of the eighteenth century, came to Budapest in this collection.

49. There are a few significant variations in writing. In Ms 1:71r–72v, we have a sermon on *Naso* dated in the spring of 1617, the earliest date in the collection (see following note). This is written in a print totally different from the Italian cursive of almost all the other texts. Yet this seems to be the work of Morteira. Not only is the structure and homiletical style similar to the other sermons, but the author refers to what he said in his "eulogy for our esteemed rabbi and teacher, Elijah Montalto, his soul in Eden." As Morteira, a close companion of Montalto, accompanied his body from France to Amsterdam in order to provide

Exile in Amsterdam

earliest date in the collection is the spring of 1617; the latest is the early winter of 1659–1660.[50]

There is no indication of who collected the sermons and who was responsible for arranging them in the present order and binding them, but it is obvious that neither task was accomplished with professional skill. Some of the sermons were actually bound upside down and backward, and some of the longer ones appear with their pages in the wrong order.[51] More important,

---

for proper Jewish burial, it stands to reason that he would have delivered the eulogy. Unfortunately, that text is apparently no longer extant. If indeed the early *Naso* was written by Morteira, then he had two different writing styles, one in print (which he may have used earlier, to make the text more readily legible), and the other a freer cursive.

One sermon, for the holiday of Sukkot, is written entirely in very different and larger cursive script (MS 3:73r–75r). The explanation is as follows: In a different volume of the collection, the same sermon appears in Morteira's characteristic hand (MS 2:67v–r; bound backwards). The following page contains the statement, "The sermon delivered by my student, Joseph de Paro, on the second day of the holiday of Sukkot in the year 5785 [September 29, 1624]." Comparison of these two texts reveals that the student copied over Morteira's sermon for his own use, introducing minor editorial changes, and both copies were eventually included in the collection.

Finally, a sermon on *Tetsavveh* (MS 2:31r–32r) is written in yet another small cursive style. At the end of this sermon, there appears in Morteira's characteristic hand the words, "the sermon I preached at the celebration of the weddings of Mr. Jacob Judah Leon and Joshua Katniel in the year 5378 [1618]." To further complicate the issue, there is a sermon on the second verse in the lesson *Va-Yiggash* (MS 5:127r–128v) which begins in Morteira's hand, but after the theme-verse, dictum, and two-paragraph introduction, contains two paragraphs in the writing of the *Tetsavveh* sermon, before shifting back to Morteira's hand for the rest of the sermon. The uncharacteristic empty spaces above, beneath, and between these two paragraphs suggest that Morteira left a space that was filled in by someone else who crammed his words together even more than Morteira. The only explanation I can suggest for this is that on rare occasions, Morteira may have used an amanuensis.

50. MS 1:72v, *Naso,* Num. 6:24–26: "The sermon I delivered on the lesson *Naso* in the year 5377 on the day when there were three bridegrooms together in the synagogue, namely, the gentleman [*ha-gevir*] David Curiel, the gentleman Daniel Testa, and the gentleman Bezalel Coronel." MS 5:82v, *Va-Yeshev,* Gen. 37:13: "And I preached it a second time in the year 5420."

51. Upside down and backward: the sermon on *Tazria,* Lev. 13:29, beginning on 1:44v and ending on 1: 43r; it was written on smaller pages than the surrounding material. Similarly, the eulogy for Jacob Tirado was bound upside and backward, beginning on 1:78v and ending on 1:77r. The page that records the additional material for Morteira's eulogy for Menasseh ben Israel is bound backward between the first and second pages of the original sermon that provided its framework (3:169r–172r with insert 171r–v, *Hayyei Sarah,* Gen. 23:17; see Marc Saperstein, *"Your Voice Like a Ram's Horn"* (Cincinnati, 1996), pp. 414–15. For an example of pages in the wrong order, see 3:307r, *Ha'azinu,* Deut. 32:21, 1641; the first two pages to appear in the bound manuscript are actually the third and fourth pages of the sermon.

the efforts to impose some order on the material were not successful, as can be seen by a review of the contents of each of the five volumes. Even the numbering of the volumes makes absolutely no sense, and we must describe them in a different order to understand how they were composed.

The third volume was obviously put together first. The initial 82 folios of this volume contain sermons on successive Torah lessons, beginning with *Bereshit* (on Gen. 1:2), and continuing with *Hayyei Sarah* through all the lessons in Exodus and the Leviticus lessons through *Tazria*. After a sermon for Pesach and a eulogy on *Be-Har*, all the lessons in Numbers are represented in the proper order. The cycle is completed with sermons on *Re'eh* and *'Eqev*, a Sukkot sermon on Lev. 23:43 (obviously out of place), a sermon on *Va-Yelekh* for the Sabbath of Repentance, and two on *Ve-Zot ha-Berakhah*. At this point, a new cycle begins, with sermons on *Bereshit* (Gen. 1:3) through *Tazria* (except for *Lekh Lekha*), all the lessons in Numbers, *Ha'azinu* for the Sabbath of Repentance, and *Ve-Zot ha-Berakhah*. The third cycle begins on folio 167r with *Bereshit* (Gen. 1:4) through *Tazria* (missing *Noah* and *Lekh Lekha*), the lessons on Numbers, and again, *Ha'azinu* for the Sabbath of Repentance and *Ve-Zot ha-Berakhah*. A fourth cycle, beginning on folio 243r with a sermon on Gen. 1:5, follows precisely the same pattern. The last cycle, beginning on folio 316r, starting with a sermon on Gen. 1:6, has several sermons misplaced (e.g. the sermons on *Va-Yehi* and *Tetsavveh* are switched, and a Shavu'ot sermon on Deut. 15:23 comes between *Va-Yeshev* and *Va-Yiggash* where the sermon on *Mi-Qets* should come. Thus the organizer's principle was to follow the order of the sermons as they were delivered week after week, and year after year, starting with the second year Morteira was preaching and including five years of sermons.

The volume numbered 2 continues the same pattern from the point left off. It begins with two holiday sermons, then *Hayyei Sarah* through *Tazria* and the lessons in Numbers. A new cycle begins on folio 63r with two more holiday sermons, and again *Hayyei Sarah* through *Tazria* and the lessons in Numbers. This time there are sermons on *Eqev, Ha'azinu,* and *Zot ha-Berakhah*. The third cycle, beginning on folio 140r, starts with *Bereshit* (on Gen. 1:7), and follows the same pattern once again, with no sermons on Deuteronomy. The final cycle begins with a sermon on Gen. 1:8, continues with *Hayyei Sarah* through *Shemini,* and after seven sermons on lessons from Numbers concludes with *Ve-Zot ha-Berakhah*. When we put these two volumes together, we see an effort to represent the second through the tenth cycle of sermons written by Morteira in the proper order.

The next volume to be put together must have been the fifth. But the organizing principle was different from that of the two discussed above; instead

of placing the sermons in the order they might have been delivered over a
period of several years, this volume is devoted entirely to the book of Genesis,
grouping the sermons lesson by lesson. As noted above, the first two volumes
(numbered 3 and 2), contains sermons on Genesis 1:2 through 1:8, in the
proper order, at the beginning of six different cycles. The present volume
begins with six additional sermons on *Bereshit* in the following order: Gen.
1:11. 1:12, 1:10, 1:15, 1:9, 1:16. Then eleven sermons on *Toledot*, ten on
Va-Yetse (two of which are misplaced), nine on *Va-Yishlah* (one misplaced),
ten on *Va-Yeshev*, nine on *Mi-Qets*, nine on *Va-Yiggash*, one misplaced), and
seven on *Va-Yehi*. In all these cases, as we have seen for the sermons on
Bereshit, the order of the sermons for each lesson is random; no effort was
made to place them in the order of the verses, the order in which they would
have been written and preached.

The next volume, numbered 4, follows the same principle for the book of
Exodus. All the lessons are well represented. It begins with twelve sermons
on *Shemot*, followed by eleven on *Va-Era*, ten on *Bo* (in the middle of these is
a misplaced sermon on *Be-Ha'alotekha*), six on *Be-Shallah*, twelve on *Yitro* (and
two occasional sermons), twelve on *Mishpatim* (and one occasional), nine on
Terumah (one misplaced), six on *Tetsavveh*, six on *Ki Tissa*, eight on *Va-Yaqhel*
(two misplaced), and five on *Pequdei*. The final sermon, on *Va-Yiqra* (Lev.
1:13), should have been bound in a different volume. As with the volume on
Genesis, within each lesson the sermons are arranged in a haphazard order.

Finally, the volume numbered 1 is composed for the most part of sermons
on lessons from Leviticus and Numbers. There are five on *Va-Yiqra*, six on
Tsav, three on *Shemini*, and eight on *Tazria*. Next comes a sermon on *Pinhas*
(Num. 26:6), clearly out of place, followed by nine sermons on *Be-Midbar*, four
on *Naso*, and two on *Be-Ha'alotekha*. There follow two out-of-place sermons
on *Tetsavveh* and one on *Ki Tetse*, also out of place. In the middle of six sermons on *Korah* comes another sermon on *Pinhas*. Then seven sermons on
Balaq, followed by an out-of-place sermon on *Va-Era*. After three more sermons on *Pinhas* and one on *Mattot*, the volume concludes with eight sermons
on *Ve-Zot ha-Berakhah*. Once again, the order of the sermons within each
lesson seems to be completely random (e.g., the sermons on *Va-Yiqra* appear
as Lev. 1:15, 1:10, 1:14, 1:12, 1:16), rather than following the obvious progression that reflects the order in which Morteira wrote and delivered them.

To summarize from this detailed presentation, the volumes numbered 3
and 2 respectively present sermons that follow the weekly progression
through nine cycles of verses, beginning with the second. The volumes numbered 5, 4, and 1 are for the most part composed of sermons on verses after
the tenth verse of the lesson; the sermons are grouped together by lesson, in

volume 5 from Genesis, in 4 Exodus, in 1 from Leviticus and Numbers, with a few from Deuteronomy. While the two organizational schemes are clear, the implementation appears to be rather sloppy. As Morteira reveals himself to have been meticulous in his retrieval system for earlier sermons, we must conclude that the grouping of these sermons for the bound volumes was done by someone else.

A comparable collection of sermons that gives a clear sense of a regular preaching agenda is Solomon Levi's *Divrei Shelomoh*, printed at Venice in 1596. Morteira may well have owned the book, though I have not found a direct citation from it.[52] The Levi volume is not a selection from sermons he delivered over an entire career, but rather a record of sermons preached during a specified period in different congregations of Salonika, from the spring of 1571 through the late autumn of 1574. It contains three complete cycles, beginning with Rosh Hashanah of 1571, 1572 and 1573,[53] in addition to the earlier sermons on *Va-Yiqra* through the book of Deuteronomy in 1571 and the fall holy days and the book of Genesis in 1574. A typical cycle includes sermons for the first and second day of Rosh Hashanah, the Sabbath of Repentance, Yom Kippur evening and morning, the first and second day of Sukkot, the Sabbath in the middle of the Sukkot week, Hoshanah Rabbah, Shemini Atseret, and Simhat Torah, followed by the weekly cycle beginning with *Bereshit*.[54] In some cases the written text is less than what the preacher actually said ("The second day of Sukkot, I preached this at length, praise be to God"); in some cases more ("Yom Kippur, 5332 [1571]: I preached some of this sermon, praise be to God, for there was no time to deliver all of it, as I had to pray before a large congregation all the prayers of this great and holy day").[55] Yet these texts appear to be a fair representation of the sustained effort required to fulfill the expectations of a congregation during a terribly demanding period of the fall, and then, at a less frenzied pace, throughout the rest of the year.

Morteira's manuscripts are not as rich in holiday sermons as is *Divrei Shelomoh*—he did not preach on Rosh Hashanah and Yom Kippur but instead delivered an especially lengthy sermon on the intermediate Sabbath of Repentance—and the extant manuscripts do not allow us to reconstruct with certainty an entire year of Morteira's preaching. On the other hand, while

---

52. See on this Saperstein, *Jewish Preaching*, pp. 240–52, with references to the illuminating studies of Joseph Hacker (p. 240, n. 1, p. 244, n. 11), who first called my attention to this extremely important preacher.

53. Solomon Levi, *Divrei Shelomoh* (Venice, 1596), pp. 59c, 151c, 218d respectively.

54. Ibid., pp. 59c–69c.

55. Ibid., pp. 66a, 63c.

Solomon Levi's book provides a fuller picture of one period (some three and three-quarters years) of a preaching career, Morteira's work reflects the output of decades. It also contains occasional comments about the preacher's role that illuminate aspects of a sophisticated homiletical craft.

When we review all of Morteira's manuscripts in the Budapest Rabbinical Seminary collection, certain lacunae are obvious. Some of the lessons are abundantly represented—twenty-one on *Shemot*, twenty on *Va-Yeshev* and *Va-Era*, nineteen on *Yitro*. But *Noaḥ* is represented by only two eulogies, and there is not a single manuscript sermon on *Lekh Lekha* or *Va-Yera*. Nor is there a single sermon for the last four lessons in Leviticus: *Aḥarei Mot, Qedoshim, Emor,* and *Be-Har*. There are seventeen sermons on *Ve-Zot ha-Berakhah,* five on *Ha'azinu,* and one on *Va-Yelekh,* but the rest of Deuteronomy (except for two incomplete texts and one occasional sermon) is entirely absent.. There is no basis for assuming that the sermons on these lessons from the beginning of Genesis, the end of Leviticus, and most of Deuteronomy would have been grouped together in a sixth volume that was lost. We must conclude that they must not have been available at the time when the individual manuscripts were grouped and bound.

Can we determine if they ever existed? The lessons without manuscript sermons group into three clusters: three weeks in the fall, three to four weeks in the spring, nine weeks in the summer. One might surmise that perhaps Morteira had an arrangement whereby he simply did not preach every week, and regularly took these weeks off.

But that was not likely. In the 1645 edition of *Giv'at Sha'ul,* with its table of contents for the first ten cycles of sermons, not only is a sermon printed for each lesson, including those not represented in the manuscripts, but the table of contents shows that sermons existed for all of the missing lessons. For example, it describes a sermon on each of the first ten verses of *Noaḥ and Lekh Lekha,* and the first nine verses of *Va-Yera,*[56] none of which is included among the Budapest manuscripts. Moreover, many of the sermons refer back to sermons delivered at an earlier date. Some of these can be found in the Budapest manuscript, but others cannot, including many on lessons for which the Budapest manuscript has no representation.

Thus between the individual sermon manuscript of two pages and the five-volume Budapest manuscript of 550 sermons, there was a third entity: the collection of sermon texts Morteira stored in his study for future use. Already in the first year, it contained sermons that do not appear in the Budapest

---

56. In the eighth cycle, the sermon described where *Va-Yera* should come is actually a Pesach sermon, using Song of Songs and Exodus 12:17. See *GS* 1645, p. 109b.

manuscript. Growing year after year, it eventually became considerably larger than the 550 sermons preserved, totaling some 1400 sermons by 1645. The first and second kinds of "manuscript" refer to documents we can see today; the third kind refers to something that once existed, but that we can now only attempt to reconstruct.

Morteira's Burgeoning Collection

Let us look at an example of the kind of evidence that reveals Morteira's use of manuscripts that have not been preserved. He begins a sermon on Genesis 23:19 from the lesson *Ḥayyei Sarah* by emphasizing the problem of preaching on a particular verse when so many previous verses deal with the topic of Sarah's burial. In order to exemplify the *topos* that there is nothing left to discuss (before he indeed goes ahead to define his subject), he provides a capsule review of sermons he has delivered in previous years on this *parashah*. The passage is worth citing at length:

> The Torah expended many verses from the beginning of the lesson to this point on the narrative of the burial of our righteous mother Sarah, peace be upon her. Following our practice to investigate a single verse each Sabbath, nothing remains for us to investigate about this verse [Gen. 23:19] that comes upon us at present that we have not [previously] discussed, inasmuch it has already arisen in prior verses.
>
> If we thought of asking the reason why the Bible mentions the length of our mother Sarah's life at the time of her decease—something never done in the entire Bible for any other woman, not even the [other] Matriarchs–why, we asked and answered this on the verse, *Sarah's lifetime* (Gen. 23:1).
>
> If we should desire to preach about matters pertaining to burial, its importance, its various categories, its special character, and how much a person should seek it, to the point where the Sages said (b. *Berakhot* 8a), "*Therefore let every faithful person pray to You in a time of finding* (Ps. 32:6): this refers to burial, as proven by the verse, *Who rejoice to exultation, and are glad to find the grave* (Job 3:22)—why, we have spoken about this at length in all its aspects on the verse, *Sarah died in Kiriath Arba— now Ḥebron* (Gen. 23:2).
>
> And if we should seek to preach about the subject of mourning, its levels and its categories—why, we have already preached about it on the verse, *Abraham rose from beside his dead* (Gen. 23:3), for there we explained the rabbinic statement, "Whoever mourns excessively will weep over yet another dead person," for we took as a sign the word *midai* [excessively], which stands for fifteen [in the numerical equivalent

of its last three letters] to say that the sages took the fifteen components of mourning as a sign of the fifteen [?] things than can occur in conjunction with death to increase and intensify grief, so that through them the mourner can find a place to mourn properly over his sorrow and not to weep any more.

And if we should desire to speak about how one should behave regarding the burial of the dead, how this is a fundamental and important matter not to allow them to be buried naked, and how in every respect one should behave with them as they behaved in their lifetime close to their death—why, we have already spoken about this on the verse, *I am a resident alien with you; give me a burial site with you* (Gen. 23:4).

And if we should choose to make our subject the eminence and merit of the land in which the righteous are buried, and thus the great eminence achieved by the children of Ḥeth by giving a burial site on their land to the holy Patriarchs who are [buried] there—why, we have already spoken about this on the verse, *The Hittites replied to Abraham, saying to him* (Gen. 23:5).

And if we should agree to investigate the eminence of the cave of Machpelah, and why it is so called, and the special qualities of the person who prays on the graves of the righteous—for these are ancient things—why, we have already spoken about it on the verse, *Let him give me the cave of Machpelah that he owns* (Gen. 23:9).

And if we should desire to tease out of this all of the guarantees and conditions necessary to sustain a negotiation, and how the Sages derived them from our father Abraham's purchase of this burial site—why, we have already derived them beautifully from the verse, *"No, my lord, hear me,* etc." (Gen. 23:11).

And if we should desire to ask why our father Abraham, peace be upon him, insisted so adamantly not to receive this field except at the full price, so that he buried his wife Sarah [only] after having paid out the money, while from Pharaoh and Abimelech he accepted gifts—why, we have already asked and answered this on the verse, *If you would only hear me out! Let me pay the price of the land; accept it from me* (Gen. 23:13).

And if we determined to investigate the rabbinic dictum that the Torah emphasized with precision three places, so that the nations would not be able to press Israel by saying that these places were stolen, namely, the cave of Machpelah, as the Bible says, *Abraham paid out to Ephron* (Gen. 23:16), the Temple, as it says, *David paid Ornan for the site six hundred shekels' worth of gold* (I Chron. 21:25), and the burial place of Joseph, as it says, *He purchased the parcel of land* (Gen. 33:19). But there is a problem here: why did it not emphasize the entire land of Israel? For, as the Sages noted [elsewhere], the nations could say, "You are thieves, for you conquered it from the seven nations," and an adequate answer would be, "The entire earth belongs to God; He created it and gave it to those He saw fit; He disposed of it in accordance with His will, and now He has taken it from you and given it to us in accordance with His will." But we have already spoken of this sensibly on the verse, *Abraham paid out to Ephron* (Gen. 23:16).

And if we should desire to speak about the matter of monuments and tombstones [?] for the righteous, and what their nature is, and the rabbinic statement, "we do not build monuments over the graves of the righteous, for their words are their memorial"—why, we have already spoken about this substantively [on the verse], *Ephron's field in Machpelah was transferred* (Gen. 23:17).

And if we should desire to teach several valuable lessons concerning the proper behavior of forbearance for one whose beloved dead lies before him unburied, deriving these lessons from our father Abraham, peace be upon him, whose wife, unburied before him, was like his own body, and he did all of this with deliberation, in the best possible manner—why, we have already taught them well from the verse, *to Abraham as a possession, in the presence of the Hittites* (Gen. 23:18).

Therefore, nothing remains for us from this verse to provide us with a new theme to investigate different from these earlier ones.[57]

We shall turn to the continuation of this passage in the following chapter. Of the sermons mentioned above, those on Genesis 23:13, 16, 17, and 18 have been preserved in the Budapest collection. But those on Genesis 23:1, 2, 3, 4, 5, 9, and 11 have not (though the one on Genesis 23:2 was included in the printed *Giv'at Sha'ul*). To write a passage like this, someone needs to have either detailed notes on each sermon delivered or the manuscripts of his sermons spread out before him. It is likely that Morteira had both: a filing system organized according to each scriptural lesson, and notes that allowed him to make cross references by subject to sermons on different pericopes. By these capsule reviews of sermons delivered over a period of some twenty years, the preacher established his own claim of thoroughness and demonstrated his ingenuity in being able, after all, to find a new subject despite all he had already said. But beyond this, he appealed to the audience as a community of listeners, reminding them of sermons they had heard in the past, and recapitulating what they might already have learned.

57. MS 2:69r, *Ḥayyei Sarah*, Gen. 23:19, mid 1640s?

The above passage cites many sermons in a single later text. By contrast, a single sermon, no longer extant, can be partially reconstructed through references in several different manuscripts. The listing of 500 sermons in the 1645 edition of *Giv'at Sha'ul* describes a lost sermon on the first verse of the lesson *Va-Yeshev*, Genesis 37:1, entitled "The Hand of the Resident Alien" (*Yad Ger ve-Toshav*, Lev. 25:47) as follows: "It explains the definition of *ger* and the definition of *toshav*, and *ger ve-toshav*, together, which is a matter of dispute for the commentators...."[58] Since this was in the first cycle of sermons delivered by Morteira, and since the sermon on Genesis 37:3 is dated 1621, the missing one was probably delivered in the fall of 1619. The description does not provide much substantive information about the content.

An extant manuscript, however, reveals that a little more than two years after the original 1619 sermon, Morteira referred back to it, reiterating a point he had made. He describes three kinds of alien (*ger*), based on two criteria: living outside one's homeland, and owning no land, either one of which is enough to place an individual in this category. He then applies this to Moses:

> In naming his son this way [Gershom], he taught something great and important. For as we have already explained in the lesson *Va-Yeshev*, the thirty years added to God's promise to Abraham when He said *four hundred years* (Gen. 15:13; cf. Exod. 13:40) were the thirty years when Jacob was not an alien, for he was in the land of his birth and on his own patrimony.[59]

The passage continues with the preacher's assertion, based on no apparent source but his own reconstruction, that Moses could have purchased property in Midian but did not do so. As Jacob delayed the time of redemption by purchasing his own land, so Moses knew that he would have added to the period of enslavement if he had become a land-owner in Midian. The implications for the audience—that land ownership is not appropriate for Jews in exile and will serve to delay the redemption—are not made explicit, but are clearly implied.

A second manuscript, written about ten years later, shows that Morteira returned to this theme in another sermon on the original lesson of *Va-Yeshev*. Speaking about Jacob's acquisition of land, mentioned in Genesis 33:19, he maintains:

---

58. *GS* 1645, p. 93a.

59. MS 3:195v, *Yitro*, Exod. 18:3, 1622. For a fuller explanation of Jacob's status based on Morteira's definition of *ger* see below.

And in this act [i.e., the purchase] he harmed his descendants considerably, as we already explained on the first verse of this lesson [*Va-Yeshev*,
Gen. 37:1], for the Holy One, blessed be He, decreed upon Abraham,
that your offspring shall be aliens in a land not theirs (Gen. 15:13). In His
great mercy He hastened the end by beginning to count the [400] years
from the time he first had offspring, as the Sages said.[60] But when Jacob
purchased a portion of real estate in the land [at Shechem, Gen. 33:19],
he left the category of "alien," and he had to depart from that place and
to abandon[?] his property, so that the subjugation in Egypt would not
be prolonged. When he came to the land of his fathers' sojournings and
settled there and purchased real estate [at Hebron], Joseph's troubles
sprung upon him, [causing him to move to Egypt and] to dwell in a
country not his, so that the decree would be fulfilled, *that your offspring
shall be aliens ...* (Gen. 15:13).[61]

Again, the assertion that Jacob was required to leave the vicinity of Shechem
because of the land he bought there, and the purchase of additional land in
the Hebron region where this fathers had dwelled caused new problems,
would have conveyed an implicit message to many of the listeners.

Finally, a third manuscript from a year or two later contains yet another
reference to the early sermon on *Va-Yeshev*:

In this regard too the Torah was precise in calculating the thirty years
in addition to the 400, so that it would be known that their time had
come to an end in every respect: namely, what we have already
explained in the lesson *Va-Yeshev Ya'aqov*. There I explained the
definition of the word alien (*ger*) as depending on two factors: [it can
refer] either to one who has no patrimony even if he is in the land of his
birth, or to one who is outside the land of his birth even if he has a
patrimony there. I will not dwell at length on the proofs that I brought
there; we shall assume that the matter is agreed upon, and **whoever has
doubts about it may look it up in its place.** From this conclusion it
follows that once Jacob acquired a portion of real estate in the land of

---

60. See Gen. Rabbah 44,18 and Rashi and David Kimhi on Gen. 15:13, and below, sermon on Deut. 32:12, pp. 484–85.

61. MS 5:75v, *Va-Yeshev*, Gen. 37:12, ca. 1632–1633. With this passage, cf. *Derashot R.
Yehoshu'a ibn Shu'eib*, 2 vols. (Jerusalem, 1992), 1:74 (*Va-Yeshev*). Ibn Shu'eib draws the distinction between Jacob's attempt to settle in the land and the temporary sojournings of his
father and grandfather, and he links this with the beginning of the Joseph story that would
impel Jacob to leave the land. But he does not connect this theme with the prophecy of
Genesis 15:13 or with the purchase of real estate in Gen. 33:19.

his birth, the land of Canaan, he became a resident, and it was no longer "the land of his temporary abodes."[62]

Several conclusions can be drawn from Morteira's pattern of frequent reference to an idea in an earlier sermon. First, we learn considerably more about the early sermon than is conveyed by its brief characterization in the 1645 edition's table of contents. The references also provide us with some of the substance of Morteira's understanding of the concept of alien, *ger,* an extremely important theme in his sermons with implications for his position on Jewish life in contemporary Amsterdam.[63] In addition, we get a sense of Morteira's educational goals for his congregation: he understood the sermons not just as self-contained entities, as might be suggested from the review of his discourses on *Ḥayyei Sarah,* but as part of an ongoing disquisition, building upon points made earlier. These were reiterated in summary form to remind listeners who had heard the original sermon and provide others with just enough information to make the current argument intelligible. We shall see many examples of this approach in the sermons translated below.

The earlier sermons thus remained for the audience as memories of oral communication that could be activated by the preacher's reference. As manuscript texts, they also existed in a form to which Morteira could easily refer when he was preparing a new homily. But more than that, the above passage suggests they were accessible to members of the congregation, or advanced students, who were capable of reading them in the original Hebrew and had the inclination to seek them out: "Whoever has doubts about it may look it up in its place."

That this was not just a rhetorical flourish can be established from other similar statements in the manuscripts. A sermon on the lesson *Ḥuqqat,* delivered in 1630, proclaims somewhat immodestly that "With God's help, I myself have, during the years preceding this, investigated and probed into various aspects of this subject [i.e., the red heifer], and I have delivered fine sermons, with new insights, **as anyone who looks at my sermons can see.**"[64] In the sermon on Genesis 1:10 printed in *Giv 'at Sha'ul,* Morteira refers to his manuscript sermon on Genesis 1:5, which discussed the question why God gave the things He created names before any human beings existed to use

---

62. GS 1645, p. 29a; 1912, p. 127, *Be-Shallaḥ,* Exod. 14:8, MS 4:77r (ca. 1634).

63. See, for example, Saperstein, *Jewish Preaching,* pp. 273–74, and the full discussion of his concept of exile in chapter 9 below. One of Morteira's Portuguese sermons in manuscript indicates that he rendered the Hebrew *ger* by the Portuguese *peregrino,* linked with our word "pilgrim."

64. MS 2:123r, *Ḥuqqat,* Num 19:9, 1630.

them, citing the answers of various commentators, and concluding, "**[You] can see them in the aforementioned place,** for this is not the place to dwell at length."[65] And there are other such invitations in the sermons to look up material that existed only in his manuscripts.[66]

As noted above, in the introduction to the 1645 edition of *Giv'at Sha'ul,* Morteira's students wrote that from time to time they asked to borrow the manuscripts of his sermons, an indication that the preacher was serious about making his material accessible. All of this indicates that Morteira's collection of manuscripts served as more than the content of his own personal filing cabinet. It seems also to have been part of a private library open to a small circle of the intellectual elite in his community.[67] The five volumes in the Budapest Rabbinical Seminary are a remnant of this collection, which was once considerably larger and undoubtedly better organized. It was also constantly in a state of flux. New manuscripts were added week by week, existing manuscripts were consulted in the process of preparing new ones, borrowed and returned, re-labeled and sometimes updated when used on a different occasion from the pulpit. Morteira's disciples described the totality of Morteira's manuscript homiletical oeuvre as it grew between 1617 and 1645

---

65. *GS* 1645, p. 3a, 1912, p. 40. Virtually the same language is used in a sermon on *Ki Tissa* (MS 4:177v, on Exod. 31:13), referring to a discussion given in an earlier sermon on *Va-Yaqhel,* Exod 35:3.

66. E.g. MS 1:27r, *Shemini,* Lev. 9:14, referring to sermons on Lev. 1:9 (MS 2:244r–245, and 1:13 (printed, manuscript not exant): "And we solved the problems in a beautiful manner; **it can be seen in its place.**" MS 1:45r, *Pinḥas,* Num. 26:6, reviewing several sermons on the eternity of Jewish people.

67. For evidence of such a private library and the benefit it provided to students of the collector, see Meir Benayahu, "Rabbi Avraham Skandari," in *Sefer Zikkaron le-ha-Rav Yitsḥaq Nissim,* vol. 2 (Jerusalem, 1985), especially pages 291–92, citing Joseph Sambari and David Conforte. See also references to private libraries in several articles in *Cultures of the Jews,* edited by David Biale (New York, 2002), pp. 445 n. 73 (Spain), 533 and 536–38 (Poland), 592 and 602–3 (Italy), 665 (Amsterdam). Note the recent formulation of Shlomo Berger: "[S]ince the Sephardi community was small, one may assume that the role of the private library was far more important than generally considered. Moreover, since the synagogue was an important centre of daily life, and located in the middle of the Jewish quarter, there were more opportunities to exchange ideas and lend books.... This in turn enhanced the importance of the private library. Secondly,... the Chief Rabbi's library most probably operated as a middle point [i.e., an intellectual center] among Sephardi intellectuals, so that his collection served a wider circle of readers." "Codices Gentium: Rabbi Isaac Aboab's Collection of Classical Literature," *StRos* 29 (1995): 10–11. On private libraries in the Christian environment, see Roger Chartier, *The Order of Books* (Stanford, 1994), esp. pp. 64, 82, 85; idem, *Forms and Meanings* (Philadelphia, 1995), pp. 26–28.

as "a mound of great and lofty stones." We might prefer a different metaphor: the "manuscript" as an active data base that served both the preacher and his listeners in many ways.

3

In the Preacher's Workshop

How did these manuscripts get written? In this chapter, I will attempt to reconstruct the creative process by which they were produced—from the time the preacher first focused on the sermon to be delivered on a fixed occasion of the liturgical calendar until he completed the text we have in hand. The extant manuscript cannot definitively answer all of the questions we might want to ask: for example, how many hours did it take to write? How much additional time did Morteira devote to preparing its delivery? On what day did he began his preparation for a Shabbat sermon? How much effort did he devote to research? Nevertheless, there are clues in these texts that shed light on the process by which Morteira was able to plan and implement his ongoing homiletical tasks.

One reason the manuscripts are so useful is that they enable us to appreciate the schedule by which Morteira prepared and delivered his sermons, week after week, and year after year. A printed collection containing one sermon on each scriptural lesson—such as the 1645 edition of *Giv'at Sha'ul*—provides examples of individual efforts, but little insight into how representative each text would have been of the average weekly sermon. Looking at a single text on a particular scriptural lesson, we have no way of determining whether this was the only sermon the preacher ever wrote on that lesson, whether he selected for publication the one to which he devoted the most effort or that he considered his very best, whether it was unusual or representative of his homiletical output. The prodigious number of extant manuscripts and the consistently high level of the writing reveal an achievement sustained regularly throughout the year over many decades of a public career.

How much time went into the preparation of the ordinary Sabbath sermon? For much of his career, Morteira was preaching every week. Thus it is apparent that he would not have begun serious preparation until the week the sermon was to be delivered. But did he begin on Saturday night after the Sabbath ended, or first thing Sunday morning, or did he wait until later in the week? In 1693, a Jesuit professor of theology and Hebrew at the University of Prague accused Jewish preachers of blasphemies against Christianity and instigated a campaign demanding that every sermon be submitted in writing for review by the authorities three days before its delivery. The Jews responded that this was impossible. First, they did not know what they would be preaching until Thursday or Friday of a given week; second, they did not have time to write out a complete manuscript of the weekly sermon, and the community could not afford to hire scribes for them.[1]

Intriguing as this historical account appears, it provides little solid information relevant to Morteira, for several reasons. First, we cannot know whether the Jewish response to the Jesuit was an honest reflection of the preachers' actual work habits or merely a tactical reply to a disturbing threat. And second, we know that Morteira did indeed write out the full texts of his sermons in advance of delivery. He may well have begun, at least with preliminaries, before "Thursday or Friday."

Be that as it may, once Morteira began work, his first decision had to be whether to compose a new sermon or repeat one that he had already delivered. That his preferred pattern was to prepare a new sermon for each Sabbath can be seen in the large number of different sermons on various scriptural lessons preserved in the manuscripts, including twenty-one on the lesson *Shemot*, twenty each on *Va-Yeshev* and *Va-Era*, nineteen on *Yitro*. But as we have seen, Morteira did re-use some of his sermons, carefully noting each subsequent occasion at the end: "I preached this a second time in the year x," "I preached this a third time in the year y." Sometimes a special circumstance would make a particular sermon from the past especially appropriate. For example, a sermon on Gen. 32:10, the beginning of Jacob's prayer before confronting Esau, originally delivered in late 1625 or 1626, was appropriately devoted to the subject of those prayers that request something from God. Some twenty years later, Morteira chose to re-use this sermon under dramatic conditions noted at the end: "I preached it a second time in the year 5406, on the ninth day of the month of Kislev [Sunday, November 27, 1645], a day on which the congregation decreed a public fast because the entire community Tsur Yisrael in Brazil was being besieged. May the Holy One, blessed be He, deliver them from suffering to relief..."[2] For this special occasion, he proba-

---

1. S. Schweinburg-Eibenschitz, "*Une confiscation des livres hébreux à Prague*," *REJ* 29 (1894): 266–71, esp. p. 268.

2. MS 2:14v, *Va-Yishlaḥ*, Gen. 32:10. On the siege of Recife by the Portuguese army in late 1645 and early 1646 in support of Portuguese rebels against the Dutch, see *The Jewish Experience in Latin America*, ed. Martin Cohen, 2 vols. (Waltham, 1971), 2:122–27, 194–97; Günter Böhm, *Los sefardíes en los dominios holandeses de América del Sur y del Caribe, 1630–1750* (Frankfurt am-Main, 1992), pp. 52–56.

bly looked through all his sermons on the week's *parashah* and chose one that was thematically appropriate: its earlier abstract discussion had acquired deep resonance.

Not infrequently, when using a previously written sermon, Morteira would add new material, which he recorded after the report of re-use. A dramatic example of this is reflected in material appended to a sermon entitled "His Voice in Weeping," on Genesis 45:2 in the lesson *Va-Yiggash.* The similarity between this verse and Genesis 27:39 describing Esau's weeping suggested a discussion of various types of tears: of supplication, compassion, pain and joy. The events of early 1656 impelled Morteira to return to this sermon, adding an extensive coda that I shall discuss at some length later in this chapter (pp. 101–6)—a stunning example of how a preacher can transform an earlier text in light of contemporary events, while still retaining its homiletical integrity.

In addition to just adding something new at the end of a sermon being re-used, occasionally Morteira would recast it in a more fundamental way. In his 1657 eulogy for Menasseh ben Israel, he adapted a sermon delivered many years before, using whole sections from the original text and interspersing new material, including an ending totally devoted to the deceased. By contrast, his long eulogy for David Farar in 1624 is a totally new creation, although it mentions an earlier sermon and incorporates small segments of it.[3]

What prompted Morteira to re-use old material? For most preachers, the introduction of novelty becomes more difficult as the years elapse, both because of the waning of intellectual powers and because so much has already been incorporated into earlier sermons; thus the temptation to resort to an ever-burgeoning collection of prior writings grows naturally stronger. While younger preachers often depend on ideas from the published works of older colleagues, established preachers generally feel more comfortable drawing from their own archives. Listeners in the pews may come expecting novelty from the pulpit, but rabbis, in turn, expect a measure of forgetfulness from their congregants. They may desperately—often futilely—want their listeners to remember what they say, but they do not want them to remember everything forever.

Moreover, there is turnover in the membership of every congregation. In Morteira's case, every year new immigrants were arriving in Amsterdam. Children were growing old enough to listen attentively to the sermons; after seven to ten years, enough new people would have been present to justify a

---

3. On the Manasseh ben Israel eulogy, see Saperstein, *"Your Voice Like a Ram's Horn,"* pp. 414–15, with text and translation pp. 424–44; on the Farar eulogy, see ibid., p. 389, n. 13.

decision to bring an old sermon back to life. Finally, in any specific week, Morteira's other rabbinic responsibilities may have left him insufficient time to prepare a new offering. Only rarely does he indicate the actual circumstances of his decision, as in the following poignant appendage: "I preached it a second time in the year 5391 on the 18th day of Kislev [November 24, 1630], at the time of the plague in Venice. I was emotionally incapable of composing a new sermon because of [or: about] the news that terrified me."[4]

Once having decided to prepare a new sermon, the next step for Morteira, as for most preachers in the Sephardi tradition beginning in the late fifteenth century, would have been the selection of a biblical verse to serve as the "theme" or "Text" (נושא) of the sermon.[5] Unlike in the thirteenth and fourteenth centuries, when the opening biblical verse was usually taken from the Hagiographa, the later Sephardi tradition was to begin with a verse from the weekly Torah lesson. This still left considerable choice and flexibility for the preacher, who could usually select a verse from the lesson that would accommodate the subject he wanted to address. Morteira's selection was much more constrained because of a practice that he imposed upon himself: to begin his regular preaching career in Amsterdam by using the first significant verse in each scriptural lesson, and then to progress systematically, verse after verse, in subsequent years. I know of no other Jewish preacher who followed this discipline, though some Christian preachers delivered series of sermons on successive biblical verses.[6]

---

4. MS 3:178b, *Va-Yishlaḥ*, Gen. 32:6. On this plague in Venice, which killed more than 46,000 of its citizens (almost one-third of the population) between June of 1630 and November of 1631, see *The Autobiography of a Seventeenth-Century Venetian Rabbi: Leon Modena's Life of Judah*, ed. Mark Cohen (Princeton, 1988), pp. 134–37. The editor notes that the plague was at its worst during October 1630, when 101 Jews died, and November, when 102 Jews died (p. 244 n. j); these are the reports that must have reached Amsterdam and left Morteira, with his close ties of family and friendship to Venice, so distraught.

5. See Saperstein, *Jewish Preaching*, pp. 66–69. In all previous writings, I have used "theme" or "theme-verse" as the translation for *nosei*, a term derived from the medieval Latin technical term *thema*. However, I have recently discovered that when Sephardi preachers in England began to publish translations of their Spanish sermons in the eighteenth and nineteenth centuries, they referred to this opening verse (as did Christian preachers) as their "Text" (see below, p. 382, n. 7). I therefore use this term in my translations of the preacher's own use of *nosei* in quotations below and especially in the sermons translated in Section 4.

6. Larissa Taylor, *Soldiers of Christ: Preaching in Late Medieval and Reformation France* (New York, 1992), p. 195: Calvin "usually followed the texts sequentially from day to day, or Sunday to Sunday, a practice copied by many other reformers." This, however, is rather different from Morteira's practice of following the texts sequentially from year to year.

Morteira often reminds his listeners of this procedure, usually at the beginning of a sermon:

> It has always been our practice, which we began some years ago, to preach every Sabbath on one verse from the weekly lesson in the order in which they were written.[7]
>
> According to the order to which we have been drawn up to now—year after year always to base our sermon on the order of verses that come in the weekly lesson—our sermon today should be on the verse..[8]

This practice eliminated an important decision, but at the same time it limited some of the preacher's flexibility in choice of subject. It also presented problems when the verse in line did not look especially promising. Yet this was the kind of challenge in which the master homiletician apparently reveled.

Committed as Morteira was to his system, there were exceptions, to which he himself often called attention. There was repetition within the liturgical calendar, as the Torah readings for Sabbaths coming in the middle of the Sukkot and Pesach weeks replicate material from other weeks. Morteira made his listeners aware of the problem and his solution:

> Although it has always been our practice to base our sermon on the lesson of the week, today—the Sabbath during the week of Sukkot—has no Torah lesson of its own, but only a repetition of the passage beginning *See, You say to me* (Exod. 33:12), which is from the lesson *Tissa*. Therefore it seemed a good opportunity to investigate as the basis for our sermon a topic from the prophetic lesson (*Haftarah*) used throughout Israel, as it is an ordinance of the Talmud and a tradition of our ancestors from the ancient past.[9]

There is no indication that Morteira ever preached on the verses from *Ki Tissa* used in the scriptural reading for that day, as they come quite late in the *parashah*. Apparently he decided that the eschatalogical content of the Ezekiel verses was more appealing than the theological conundra of the holiday Torah lesson.

Morteira's initial sermon on *Ki Tissa* used the first substantive verse (Exod. 33:12); this sermon, not included in the extant manuscripts, is listed in the 1645 edition of *Giv'at Sha'ul* (p. 94a) and mentioned in a later sermon.[10] Each

---

7. MS 3:217r, *Naso*, Num 4:26 (mid 1620s).

8. MS 4:177r, *Ki Tissa*, Exod. 31:13.

9. MS 2:1r, *Hol ha-Mo'ed* Sukkot, on Haftarah, Ezek 38.

10. MS 1:49v, *Be-Midbar* Num. 1:22, 1632.

subsequent year, until the early 1640s, he worked his way systematically through the rest of the verses in chapter 30; the extant manuscripts include a total of 14 sermons on the 21 verses between Exodus 30:13 and 30:33. But then he decided to jump over a group of verses at the beginning of chapter 31; the following sermon is on Exodus 31:13. Morteira explained his decision to the listeners as he began to speak. According to the established order,

> our sermon today should be on the verse, *See I have singled out by name Bezalel son of Uri...* (Exod. 31:2), and then on the verse, *I have endowed him with a divine spirit* (Exod. 31:3), and then on the verse, *to make designs for work in gold, silver, and copper* (Exod. 31:4). But we have already fulfilled out obligation to all these verses in the lesson *Va-Yaqhel.*[11]

And indeed, in the manuscripts on *Va-Yaqhel* we find sermons on Exodus 35:30–32, Moses' repetition of the verses, which Morteira would later skip over when preaching on *Ki Tissa.* When Torah verses were almost identical, Morteira felt no obligation to preach on them twice.

Even without explicit explanations, other instances in which the preacher departed from his formal practice and skipped over verses near the beginning of the lesson can be determined from the extant manuscripts and the listing of sermons at the end of the 1645 edition of *Giv'at Sha'ul.* When the first verse of the lesson was formulaic—e.g., *God spoke to Moses, saying*—he began to preach on the first substantive verse, the one that provides the traditional name for the *parashah.*[12] When the beginning of the lesson included a list of names, Morteira did not include these verses as themes for his sermons. In *Shemot,* there is a sermon on Exodus 1:1, but he skipped 1:2 through 1:4—the names of eleven of Jacob's sons—and preached the following year on Exodus 1:5. Similarly with the lesson *Shallah*: the 1645 *Giv'at Sha'ul* lists sermons on Numbers 13:2, 13:3, and 13:4, but the next eleven verses, naming the representatives of eleven tribes, were skipped, and the following year's sermon was on Number. 13:16.[13] Although Morteira was obviously committed to his project, he was not compulsive about it.

Following the theme-verse from the weekly lesson, the next decision for

---

11. MS 4:177r, *Ki Tissa,* Exod. 31:13.

12. Thus there are no sermons for the following first verses: Exod. 25:1, *Terumah;* Exod. 30:11, *Ki Tissa*; Lev. 6:1, *Tsav*; Lev. 12:1, *Tazria;* Lev. 19:1, *Qedoshim*; Lev. 25:1, *Be-Har*, Num. 4:21, *Naso*; Num. 8:1, *Be-Ha'alotekha*; Num. 13:1, *Shalah*; Num 19:1, *Huqqat*; Num. 25:10, *Pinhas.*

13. This sermon, MS 3:221r, was printed in *Giv'at Sha'ul.* At the beginning he refers to the previous year's sermon on Num. 13:4 and reiterates its discussion of the significance of name change, before turning to his the new subject.

the preacher was about the second building block of the Sephardi sermon, the rabbinic dictum or *ma'amar.* Unlike the scriptural text for Morteira, this choice was entirely open-ended: it could come from anywhere in the rabbinic literature, and it could have an obvious connection with the verse (e.g., a midrash in which the verse was used) or no obvious connection at all. Almost all of the dicta were taken from the aggadic sections of the Babylonian Talmud and from the Midrash Rabbah, and these texts must have been among the most frequently used in his library. As noted in our discussion of the manuscripts (see above, p. 45), the empty space left for the dictum reveals that Morteira often did not choose one until the sermon was almost completed, at which point he went back and wrote it in the space he had left. In such instances, we find that the dictum is discussed only near the end of the sermon. Morteira apparently often began to write before he had planned out every detail of the sermon he was in the process of creating.

However, the dictum was not always selected as a kind of afterthought. In some sermons, the structure was actually determined by the dictum, which obviously had to have been chosen at the outset. In these instances, the manuscript shows that it was written before the introduction, with no extra space left over.[14] Occasionally, the dictum would be selected well in advance as worthy of sermonic investigation when the opportunity arose. Explicit reference to this process can be seen in a passage in which the preacher reveals advance planning:

> In the course of our sermon of last year on this lesson, we explained with compelling proofs the greatness of the comparison between the soul of the righteous human being and the lamp in its form…. For the lamp itself alludes to the soul, and the oil to the Torah, and the fire to God, as we explained at length in its place. This topic provided us an opening to understand our rabbinic dictum [*"This is how the lamp was made* (Num. 8:4): it teaches that he saw it four times…" from *Sifre*], small in quantity but great in quality. From that day on, I determined to

---

14. An example would be Morteira's second eulogy for David Farar (Saperstein, *"Your Voice,"* pp. 387–410). The manuscript (5:27r) shows no space between the end of the dictum and the following line, beginning the introduction. Similarly, the sermon on *Va-Yeshev,* Gen. 37:11, starts, "When we look at the words of the Sages in our opening dictum [Gen. Rab. 84,12), we find…." The manuscript (5:79r) shows no space between the end of the dictum and the beginning of the introduction. Clearly in this case, the rabbinic statement, which discusses the theme-verse, was chosen by the preacher from the outset. Also, MS 5:11r, *Bereshit,* Gen. 1:16, which begins, "I am not unaware that the listeners will be surprised at our taking for the topic of today our initial dictum…." There is no space between the end of the dictum and the introduction.

construct upon this dictum a separate investigation and sermon of its own, for that sermon could not encompass it. Now that God has brought me to this point, I will explain it as best as God gives me to do in accordance with this principle, for it certainly needs explanation.[15]

Apparently, the decision to share with his listeners the fact that he had decided long ago to devote a sermon to this dictum was a technique of emphasizing its importance.

One additional task relating to the theme-verse and dictum and not re-flected in the Hebrew manuscripts was to translate them into Portuguese, the only language intelligible to most of the listeners. Morteira's use of the Bible in the vernacular can be seen in four different texts: (a) the manuscript collection of seven sermons in Portuguese, one of which is the same sermon as a Hebrew text preserved in our manuscripts; (b) the eulogy for Moses Mercado, published at Amsterdam in 1652, for which there is also a Hebrew equivalent in the manuscripts; (c) the seven sermonettes incorporated into Rehuel Jessurun's *Dialogo dos Montes*; and (most important) (d) Morteira's re-cently published *Tratado*, a massive work filled with biblical quotations.[16] These texts show how Morteira must have cited his biblical verses when he preached, probably after quoting the Hebrew originals A detailed analysis, which cannot be documented here, reveals that, since no Portuguese Bible translation was available to him, the Portuguese verses in Morteira's writings indicate a close dependence on the 1553 Ferrara Spanish translation—a classic for Sephardi Jews—modified at times in accordance with the Christian version of Cipriano de Valera or the Hebrew text, and occasionally in accordance with the rabbinic tradition.[17] When it came to the translation of the rabbinic

15. GS 1645 p. 56a, 1912 p. 213, MS 3:140r, *Be-Ha'alotekha*, Num 8:4, beginning. In the manuscript, however, there is a large empty space left after the end of the rabbinic dictum, even though this dictum was obviously chosen in advance. I am not certain how to explain this exception to the general pattern.

16. "Sete Derashot compostos pelo doctissimo è carissimo Senhor Haham asalem Morenu à Rab Saul Levi Morteira," Ets Haim MS 48 C 7; "Sermão funeral feito em bet aHaim pelo excelentissimo Moreno Arab o H. r. Saul Levi Morteyra" (Amsterdam, 5412 [1652]); Rehuel Jessurun, *Dialogo dos montes*; *Tratado da verdade da lei de Moisés* (Coimbra, 1988).

17. On the Ferrara Bible, see Mayer Kayserling, *Biblioteca Española-Portugueza-Judaica*, re-print edition with Prolegomenon by Yosef Yerushalmi (New York, 1971), pp. 50–51. Yerushalmi noted elsewhere that "the Bible and the liturgy were always printed in Spanish, never in Portuguese, even though from the end of the sixteenth century most of the Marra-nos were of Portuguese rather than of Spanish extraction." "The Re-Education of Marra-nos," p. 7. For an example of Morteira's use of Cipriano, see p. 417 below, n. 33. In her recent study of thirty Portuguese sermons published at Hamburg in 1629, Julia Lieberman concludes that the "biblical quotations in the sermons are from the Ferrara Spanish Bible

dicta, however, Morteira had no such basic reference as a starting point. He may well have owned a copy of the Spanish translation of the Mishnah with Maimonides' commentary, published at Venice in 1606,[18] but few of the dicta are taken from the Mishnah. In rendering passages from the Talmud and Midrashim into Portuguese, he was essentially on his own.

Either before or immediately after the rabbinic dictum had been selected, the preacher had to move from his biblical theme-verse to an actual subject for the sermon. This topic to be investigated, whether exegetical or conceptual, directly emerging from the verse, implicit in it, or only tangentially connected, was invariably set forth at the end of the preacher's introduction, the first non-textual component of the sermon. Morteira often began his introductions in ways that had no obvious connection with either the theme-verse or the dictum. Occasionally, he used a description of the challenges of developing a sermon from the verse as a way of opening his discourse, thereby, as it were, inviting his listeners into his study where the sermon was being prepared.

We have already seen that Morteira sometimes decided to skip over repetitive verses when he had already preached on a verse quite similar to it. A well-known repetition is in the accounts of Pharaoh's dreams at the beginning of *Mi-Qets*, first told as a third person narrative, then in the first person. Arriving in 1644 at Genesis 41:17, *Then Pharaoh said to Joseph, "In my dream, I was standing on the bank of the Nile,"* which repeats the content of the first verse of the lesson, *After two years' time, Pharaoh dreamed that he was standing by the Nile* (Gen. 41:1), Morteira had to decide whether to skip over this and the following verses and move to the interpretation of the dreams. In this case, he chose not to skip ahead, and he describes his dilemma at the beginning of his introduction:

> It is not an insignificant challenge to probe, investigate, and prepare a complete sermon on a verse that is nothing more than a repetition and reiteration of something already said. That is the case with our text, which is nothing more than a repetition of matters already said above....
> We have already explained all these matters pertaining to the topic of the dream in the sermons mentioned, except for what we have seen fit to investigate today, namely, the change introduced into Pharaoh's narration of his dream compared to what was told the first time.[19]

---

translated word for word into Portuguese." Julia R. Lieberman, "Sermons and the Construct of a Jewish Identity: The Hamburg Sephardic Community in the 1620s," *Jewish Studies Quarterly* 10 (2003): 52.

18. Kayserling, *Biblioteca*, pp. 27–28, 93.

19. MS 5:99r *Mi-Qets*, Gen 41:17 (1644).

Thus the decision was to follow the practice of preaching on successive verses, even when there was a case of repetition, and to create a sermon out of the apparently minor differences between the new formulation and the old.

In other instances too, Morteira begins by sharing with his congregation the difficulties he encountered in building the sermon—in this case, on the foundation of what appeared to be an unpromising theme-verse. When he came to Numbers 13:17 in *Shallaḥ*, he apparently had a temporary mental block, for his sermon on this verse begins:

> I will not conceal from my listeners that it took me a great deal of diligent work and more time than usual to extract a theme and a topic from this verse, for its content is not readily expandable as a proper foundation for a sermon. Nevertheless, knowing the rabbinic maxim, "Work and you shall find the truth" [cf. b. *Megillah* 6b], I did not abandon it until I found what I was looking for. I discovered it in the word "this": *Go up this into the Negev* (Num. 13:17). It did not say, "Go up into the Negev and go up into the hill country," but *Go up this*, the meaning of which is always "this time," or "now."[20]

Morteira here provides a glimpse of the preacher's modus operandi, taking the verse mandated by his own disciplined progression, examining it for possibilities as the basis of a sermon, feeling the frustration of not finding in the verse any obvious opening for homiletical expansion until he finds a peg—a small word unexpected in context—that suggests both an exegetical problem and an overall theme.

A similar process is reflected in his remarks at the beginning of a sermon on *Naso*. The verse is Numbers 4:26: *the hangings of the enclosure, the screen at the entrance of the gate of the enclosure that surrounds the Tabernacle, the cords thereof, and the altar, and all their service equipment and all their accessories; and they shall perform the service.* After reminding his listeners of the practice that produced this verse for his biblical text, he continues,

> Now, this year, in reaching our text, it is clear to anyone who looks at it that it has some measure of [aridity?], and it does not provide an opportunity to expand a message upon. For it is merely a narrative recounting that the sons of Gershon carried the hangings of the enclosure, etc. However, in order not to pass over it, thereby denying it a place with its companions, I lingered over it until [I found] some

---

20. MS 3:295r, *Shalaḥ*, Num. 13:17 (1624?). The examples given for "this" meaning "now" are Genesis 45:6 and Numbers 22:28.

issue that the commentators were stirred by, and especially Rashi.[21]

Here too, the preacher deemed it important to communicate that the process of producing a sermon from a biblical verse sometimes took considerable effort and prolonged study.

As we have seen in our discussion of the manuscripts, sometimes a verse was troublesome because of its relationship to the preceding verses in the lesson and to sermons already delivered upon them. This was particularly pronounced in the lesson *Ḥayyei Sarah*. Reaching Genesis 23:19, *After this Abraham buried his wife Sarah in the cave of the field of Machpeleh, facing Mamre—now Ḥebron—in the land of Canaan*, Morteira realized that this essentially recapitulated information already recounted in the preceding narrative, which had provided occasion for sermons on every aspect of death and burial. What could be left to discuss? This is the challenge the preacher conveys:

> The Torah expended many verses from the beginning of the lesson to this point on the narrative of the burial of our righteous mother Sarah, peace be upon her. Following our practice to investigate a single verse each Sabbath, nothing remains for us to investigate about this verse that comes upon us at present, that we have not [previously] discussed, inasmuch as it has already arisen in prior verses.

An exhaustive review of all the different subjects he has covered on this lesson in previous years follows, each connected with its appropriate verse.[22] The introduction concludes,

> Therefore, nothing remains for us from this verse to provide us with a new theme to investigate different from these earlier ones. If so, what shall we do *after this*—if not to build our sermon on these two words, *After this* (Gen. 23:19)? For they are problematic. If *Abraham rose from beside his dead and spoke to the Hittites* (Gen. 23:3), and did not want to accept the field without paying full price, and then paid it out, it is simple and obvious that *after this he buried* (Gen. 23:19). The Bible should have said merely, "Abraham buried his wife Sarah," as part of a continuous narrative. What is the purpose of *After this*? The understanding of this matter and the lesson we shall derive from it will be our sermon today, which we shall begin with the help of God, who, "after this," will *call us City of Righteousness, Faithful Metropolis* (Isa. 1:26).[23]

---

21. MS 3:217r, Naso, Num 4:26 (mid 1620s).
22. For the full passage, see above, pp. 59–61.
23. MS 2:69, *Ḥayyei Sarah*, Gen. 23:19.

This multivalent passage points in several directions. Directly related to our present topic, it may reveal something of Morteira's process of working: actually opening up his file on the lesson *Ḥayyei Sarah*, reviewing all the sermons he had delivered in chronological order, perhaps making notes on the content, and then trying to find a new slant. In deciding to incorporate this material into the new sermon, he provides a recapitulation of the themes of previous sermons, thus reminding his listeners of what they have already heard, and how much material their rabbi has already covered. At the same time, he is taking care of the required introduction, perhaps twenty percent of the entire sermon. In addition, we see here something of a rhetorical game, in which the problem of finding a subject becomes itself a homiletical *topos*. Morteira emphasizes the difficulty of his task, challenges the listeners to think of a subject not already covered, heightens the suspense with a rhetorical question ("what shall we do *after this*?"). Then, perhaps after a tension-heightening pause, he triumphantly emerges with a solution couched in a play on words—as if the ending of the question itself—"after this"—provided the answer, for these are the first two words of the theme-verse, the only ones that raise a new exegetical problem. It also shows that on occasion, the very process of thinking through a sermon topic could become a significant part of the sermon itself.

In the above passage, the review of previous sermons delivered on the same lesson reveals Morteira beginning to spread out his working materials, the written resources from which he could draw to expand his topic. In beginning to prepare a new sermon, Morteira was creating an independent work that would stand on its own and be fully intelligible to any listener coming to the synagogue for the first time. But, unlike a new painting, or a sonata, or a play, more like a short story that shares certain characters with other stories by the same author, the sermon was also part of a larger corpus of work that was available in written form to the preacher in his study and, much more diffusely, as part of the shared memory of his listeners. Thus while each sermon was self-contained, its relationship to other components of the preacher's oeuvre was important, as can be seen in his constant cross-referencing to other sermons.

Sometimes the preacher intended to continue a discussion begun on earlier verses of the week's lesson. Here the problem for the audience is obvious. We can put the manuscripts of successive sermons from a particular lesson in order and follow the preacher's progression year after year. But the listeners did not have this opportunity. When they heard a scriptural text read at the beginning of a sermon, they may well have recalled the previous verses; but the sermons that discussed them had been delivered not a week or two ago, but a year or two earlier. Looking over his previous efforts, Morteira sometimes felt the need for recapitulation, not (as in the above passage) to demonstrate that he was selecting something new, but rather to link the present discussion with what had been said in prior years.

Awareness of this need is expressed to the congregation in the opening words of a sermon on Genesis 29:7 from the lesson *Va-Yetse: He said, "It is still broad daylight, too early to round up the animals; water the flock and take them to pasture."* After the verse and the rabbinic dictum, Morteira begins,

> If these words [from the theme-verse] had been read from a book, there would be no need to review what was already established in the preceding verses, which are linked together with those that follow them. However, since they have been said orally, and a year or two passes between one verse and its predecessor, it is absolutely essential to review briefly what we have already said about them, for they are an introduction to the verse we shall examine today, and it is impossible to understand what is meant without first presenting what came before.[24]

This passage is an important reminder that while Morteira was writing, even with his manuscripts from previous years spread before him, he was thinking of an oral medium, aware that the memory of his listeners was imperfect. He therefore continues with a recapitulation of previous sermons on this *parashah*, an indication that his own process of review was an integral part of his preparation.

The very next week, Morteira was preaching on Genesis 32:21 from the lesson *Va-Yishlah: And you shall add, "And your servant Jacob himself is right behind us."* He begins his introduction as if the words from the beginning of the previous week's sermons, cited above, were fresh in his listeners' ears:

> In this sermon too, we need to return briefly to what we have said about the previous verses, as we did with other matters. This is because the verses are connected with each other, and it is impossible to understand what comes after without recalling what came before in detail, as we pointed out last Shabbat in our sermon on the verse, *"It is still broad daylight,* etc." (Gen. 29:7).[25]

He then continues at some length to review the content of previous sermons on the preceding verses—all of which describe Jacob's relationship with Esau,

---

24. MS 5:46r *Va-Yetse*, Gen. 29:7, ca. 1645.
25. MS 5:57r, *Va-Yishlah*, Gen. 32:21, ca. 1645.

which Morteira then applies to the relationship between Christians and Jews in past, present, and future. For the listeners, he provides a full review and an opportunity to catch up on what may have been missed. One can almost envision Morteira skimming over these earlier manuscripts to determine precisely what needed to be summarized to enable the congregation to follow his current discussion.

Yet Morteira must have done more than skim through the texts of his earlier sermons on the same lesson. His references to earlier sermons, found on almost every page of his manuscripts, are often on lessons from totally different books of the Torah and on verses that have no obvious connection at all to the present discourse. In some cases the reference to the earlier sermon is no more than a sentence long; in others—and we shall see examples in the sermons translated below—the content is repeated at length and in detail, suggesting that he actually had the older text in front of him and copied over many lines into the new text. Either Morteira had a phenomenal memory or he developed a retrieval system containing some sort of indexing of topics, verses, and rabbinic statements discussed in the hundreds of sermons that he cited at a later date. Other than the list of titles, topics, and verses included at the end of the 1645 *Giv'at Sha'ul,* however, we have no documentary evidence of such indices. Without something more detailed and arranged topically, his ability to retrieve passages from sermons written many years—even decades—before, seems uncanny.

In addition to his own previous sermons, Morteira also used works written by others. If, up to now, we have been talking about Morteira's filing cabinet where he stored his manuscripts after each sermon was delivered, now we need to talk about his library, the collection of books that he had available for use. In the absence of an inventory,[26] we must depend upon the evidence from the sermons themselves.

We have already noted that Morteira almost certainly owned a copy of the Ferrara 1553 Spanish translation of the Bible, probably in the Amsterdam 1611 re-publication, and used it extensively for his Portuguese citation of biblical verses. What other books comprised his working library? They fall into three different categories: biblical commentaries, philosophical and kabbalistic literature, and halakhic and miscellaneous texts. By analyzing several representative sermons, we can demonstrate his incorporation of these texts into his homiletical works.

---

26. Such as the inventory of the library of his younger colleague, Isaac Aboab: *Luaḥ sefarim: Catalogus variorum ... librorum, praecipue theologicorum ... clarissimi doctissimique viri D. Jsaaci Abuab ...* (Amsterdam, 1693). See Alexander Marx, *Studies in Jewish History and Booklore* (New York, 1944), p. 209; Katchen, *Christian Hebraists and Dutch Rabbis,* pp. 114–16.

1. Biblical commentaries

Morteira refers to and discusses standard Jewish biblical commentaries in virtually every sermon. Sometimes he begins directly by raising an exegetical problem pertaining to the theme-verse, thereby showing that he must have gathered the available commentaries even before he began writing.[27] For example, in a sermon delivered in the early 1630s, the theme-verse from the lesson *Va-Yishlah* is Genesis 32:14. Immediately after the rabbinic dictum from Genesis Rabbah, Morteira's introduction raises the exegetical problem: "No one from among the commentators fails to sense that the manner of expression in this verse—*He took from what came into his hand (va-yikah min ha-ba be-yado)*—indicates randomness and chance, namely, that he took from what happened to come into his hand. Yet according to the context, this cannot be...."

The preacher then proceeds to problematize the passage for the listeners by explaining why randomness does not fit the narrative, both according to the "apparent" meaning—the rest of the narrative indicates the inordinate care taken by Jacob in his choice and arrangement of gifts—and according to the "inner" meaning, the esoteric significance of the offering to Esau. This esoteric meaning is illustrated by a long quotation from Eliezer Elijah Ashkenazi's *Sefer Ma'aseh ha-Shem*, published at Venice in 1583, introduced by Ashkenazi's statement that "as for the matter of the gift, some years ago I have seen in one of the books written in the science of Kabbalah that this offering contained 580 animals... equivalent to the numerical value of the word Se'ir...."[28] Note that Morteira has raised one central problem with the verse, and it is not the only one that commentators would address. Having established this exegetical conundrum—that the phrase cannot indicate the randomness it seems to

---

27. E.g., "R. Moses ben Nahman showed beautiful and profound insight in his comment on this verse [Gen. 44:31] when he said ..." (MS 5:115r, *Va-Yiggash*); "It is worth raising an appropriate subtle point about this verse [Gen. 45:3]" (MS 5:121r, *Va-Yiggash*). In both cases, references to "this verse" without any other identification indicate the theme-verse read at the beginning of the sermon.

28. See Ashkenazi, *Ma'aseh ha-Shem* (New York, 1962), p. 118c. Morteira's direct quotation actually contains material that does not appear in this reprint edition; I have not been able to consult the 1583 edition that Morteira would have used. On this author, see Jacob Elbaum, *Petihut ve-Histagrut* (Jerusalem, 1990) according to index, especially pp. 166–69, and André Neher, *Jewish Thought and the Scientific Revolution of the Sixteenth Century* (New York, 1986), pp. 44–45. Morteira referred to this book frequently in his sermons. Compare the Kabbalistic interpretation of the number 580 with Menahem Kasher, *Torah Shelemah* (New York, 1949), p. 1276 on the verse, citing the same interpretation from *Sefer Hemdat Yamim*. Clearly there was an earlier source.

imply—he brings his introduction to its conclusion: "Therefore many answers to this problem have been given, some of them quite strained. Now the ones I have seen in the books that I have seen—that will be our sermonic investigation today, and afterward what seems most likely in my own humble opinion."[29] In this way he invites his listeners to accompany him through his exegetical library.

Morteira begins with "the chief of commentators, Rashi," whose commentary would have been available either in a *Miqra'ot Gedolot* edition of the Torah or in a separate volume.[30] Morteira notes that Rashi brings three interpretations: 1. *his hand* means "his possession," 2. the phrase refers to gems and precious stones actually held in the hand, 3. it refers to possessions left after a tithe had been taken in fulfillment of Jacob's earlier pledge to God. Immediately after, Morteira proceeds to report the discussion of Elijah Mizrahi's super-commentary on Rashi, first published at Venice in 1527: "Rabbi Elijah Mizrahi, desiring to give a reason for the aggadic explanation [i.e., the second one cited] contradicted the first interpretation and rebutted it"; as Mizrahi points out, who would imagine that Jacob sent Esau something that was *not* in his possession?[31] Yet the second interpretation, based on the aggadic Midrash, is refuted by Nahmanides, who insists that the phrase referred to the flocks and herds Jacob had with him, as the exigencies of travel made it impossible to carry gold, silver, or precious stones. Therefore because of the weakness of the first two interpretations, Rashi included a third.

This comment, linked with Jacob's fulfillment of the vow he made following his dream (Gen. 28:20–22), leads Morteira to a discussion of the delay in its fulfillment. He brings in a passage from the Midrash, a reference to another

---

29. MS 5:51r, *Va-Yishlaḥ*, Gen. 32:14.

30. See Shifra Baruchson, *Sefarim ve-Qor'im* (Ramat-Gan, 1993), pp. 125–26, indicating the presence of Rashi's commentary in over 27% of late sixteenth-century Italian Jewish households, not including the 12% that owned at least partial editions of *Miqra'ot Gedolot.*

31. Morteira cites Mizrahi's super-commentary frequently. Another example: discussing the phrase in Exodus 31:13, *akh et shabbetotai tishmoru,* he begins, "It is known how Rashi interpreted this," going on to quote Rashi's comment. He then continues, "The difficulty RaMBaN raised with this is also known," and summarizes RaMBaN's point. The next step is a bit of a surprise: "It is also known what Rabbi Mizrahi responded to this—there is no need to dwell upon it at length—and also the problem we ourselves raised about this matter." Now it is extremely unlikely that Mizrahi's response to Nahmanides could be assumed as common knowledge in a congregation of Portuguese Jews even after Morteira had been preaching and teaching for a generation. But the name may well have been familiar, some may have owned his book, or Morteira may have discussed it in a sermon not too much earlier, and his formulation is a way of saying that he does not want to go into too much detail at the present (MS 4:177v, *Ki Tissa,* Exod. 31:13).

sermon, and a statement from Maimonides' legal code. Eventually he returns to the verse, turning now to Bahya ben Asher,[32] who gives an explanation similar to Rashi's first: it was what he earned himself, not what was stolen. After explaining this, Morteira cites Bahya's second explanation: "There are those who explain *from what came in his hand* as referring to a bird called *falcon.* "Esau, the hunter, used the falcon to hunt; *his hand* refers back to Esau. Morteira dismisses this rather caustically: "This proposal is extremely far-fetched, totally implausible."[33]

The preacher's survey of exegetical literature is not yet completed. He now turns to more recent commentators, citing Abravanel's reference to discourse of the court: "Such is the manner of those who send a gift: they say that what they send does not fit the dignity of the noble to whom the gift is brought; it is only what was at hand at present."[34] Morteira quickly rejects this view: "But this does not fit, for the verse does not say that this is what he instructed the emissaries to say. This is what the Bible tells actually happened." Next, he returns to Ashkenazi's *Ma'aseh ha-Shem*, which cites, expands, and para-phrases the point that Jacob was explaining: that he could send only animals, which he possessed, not servants, whom he could not transfer to the realm of idolatry. Then comes the comment of Ephraim Luntshitz, "the author of *Keli Yaqar*" (published at Lublin in 1602 and at Prague in 1608), who explains the phrase with reference to Isaac's blessings: the gift of animals, movable property, "not of the heaven or of the earth," was intended to avoid arousing Esau's anger by showing that the blessing of Genesis 27:28 had not been fulfilled.[35]

By now one might expect the listeners to be approaching a saturation point. Yet before he turns to his own explanation, Morteira cites two more books from his library. First is the preacher from the generation of the expulsion, Joel ibn Shu'eib, "the author of *'Olat Shabbat*," whose collection of sermons

---

32. His Torah commentary, first published at Naples in 1492 and in at least eight other Italian editions of the sixteenth century, was second only to Rashi's commentary in popularity. See Baruchson, p. 125.

33. MS 5:51v. This interpretation is attributed in the exegetical literature to Rabbenu Tam. See *Hadar Zeqenim* on this verse, Kasher, *Torah Shelemah* on Genesis 32, section 85, Joshua ibn Shu'eib, *Derashot al ha-Torah*, (Jerusalem, 1992), 1:68.

34. Abravanel's *Commentary on the Torah*, published at Venice in 1579, was found in 9% of Italian Jewish households in the late sixteenth century: Baruchson, p. 126. Morteira, who cites Abravanel frequently, undoubtedly had a copy.

35. When news of Luntshitz's death reached Amsterdam in late spring, 1619, Morteira concluded a sermon with a eulogistic tribute, mentioning *Keli Yaqar* and three other works of the renowned preacher (the first four of Luntshitz's works to be published): MS 1:47r, *Be-Midbar*, Num. 1:2, 1619.

was published at Venice in 1577. Morteira cites a brief passage from a long
sermon on *Va-Yishlaḥ* and explains ibn Shu'eib's understanding of the phrase:
that it shows the effort invested by Jacob in arranging the gift in a manner that
would make the finest aesthetic impression on his brother.[36] Finally, he cites
"The *ḥakham* R. Moses Alsheikh," whose *Torat Mosheh* was published at Venice in 1601; according to this commentator, the phrase indicates that Jacob
chose the best of his herd, what he himself would lead by the hand, not what
he turned over to the care of others.

At this point, having ransacked much of his exegetical collection and exposed his listeners to a plethora of differing views, Morteira moves on to his
own interpretation of the apparently simple yet tantalizingly elusive phrase:
the words indicate that Jacob's wealth came providentially, despite the obstacles of arriving as a penniless alien in a strange land, and not as a result of his
own hard work and initiative. It has typological significance, intended as a
message to his descendants, and Morteira makes the application to his audience in Amsterdam quite clear.[37] This climactic moment in the sermon has
been prepared for by his lengthy, indeed rather exhaustive review of the earlier exegetical literature, which (at least for some of the listeners) may have
built up suspense regarding how their own preacher could indeed come up
with something new. In this exercise, we have seen Morteira referring to eight
different commentators, from seven or eight different books (depending on
whether he consulted Rashi and RaMBaN in separate volumes or in *Miqra'ot
Gedolot*), all published within the generation or two before the sermon, most
of them at Venice, and almost certainly in his library at Amsterdam.

Another example of Morteira's incorporation of biblical commentaries
may be seen in his sermon on Genesis 48:5 from the lesson *Va-Yeḥi*, delivered
in the early 1630s. It begins by referring to a major exegetical-conceptual
problem: "On the matter of the blessings given by Isaac to Jacob and by Jacob
to his sons, the great commentators have posed an enormous problem. The
first to raise it was R. Abraham ibn Ezra."[38] He proceeds to summarize Ibn
Ezra's question about the nature of the blessings: whether they are a pronouncement of future events, or a prayer to God about the future. Once the
alternatives have been established, the preacher devotes considerable time to
explaining the problem with each interpretation, before revealing the solution given by Ibn Ezra—that the blessings are indeed a form of prayer—and

36. See ibn Shu'eib, *Olat Shabbat* (Venice, 1577, offset edition Jerusalem, 1973), p. 31d
bottom. On ownership of this book, see Baruchson, p. 170.

37. See the citations below, pp. 327–29.

38. MS 5:131r, *Va-Yeḥi*, G. 48:5, early 1630s.

his response to the difficulties with it.[39] The next step is to cite Levi ben Ger-shom (Gersonides) and his attempt to mediate between the two positions, maintaining that the blessing contains elements of both foretelling the future and prayer.[40] This is not allowed to stand, however, as the preacher raises a difficulty he finds with Gersonides' solution. He then proceeds to Isaac Arama's classic work of homiletical exegesis, *'Aqedat Yitshaq*, in which Arama cites Gersonides and moves on from there.[41] Eventually, Morteira turns to Abravanel's lengthy discussion of the blessings in his commentary on Genesis 27. Finally, near the very end of the sermon, the preacher reaches a conclusion and applies it to the theme-verse pertaining to Jacob's blessing of Menasseh and Ephraim.

Morteira's purpose in drawing so extensively on the views of others in this and other similar sermons is to expose his listeners to the problematics of biblical passages and the philosophical issues they raise. In this case, does the person proclaiming the blessing actually know what the future holds in store? What if he speaks of something that violates the nature of the individual being blessed or the astrological constraints upon that person's life? Do the words have power to influence or change the forces of nature, or God's will? If so, does this power depend upon the piety of the one who blesses, his intention at the moment? The preacher obviously believes that something is to be gained by encouraging his listeners to confront issues they may not have thought through before, what I have called the "problematizing" of the biblical text.[42] In order to accomplish this, he roams through his own library of commentators. Perhaps he began with the later ones (Abravanel, Arama) and moved back to the authors they cited. But he obviously consulted the earlier commentators directly, as he includes quotations that do not appear in the later discussions.

---

39. See ibn Ezra on Genesis 27:40. Actually, the formulation of the two clear alternatives is not in Ibn Ezra's comment here, but taken from Gersonides, whom the preacher proceeds to cite.

40. Levi ben Gershom (RaLBaG), *Perush al ha-Torah*, p. 35d–36a: a long passage is cited directly from RaLBaG. This was published at Venice in 1547; on ownership, see Baruchson, p. 126. Morteira also cites RaLBaG's introduction to his Torah commentary on the various categories of material in the Torah (MS 5:125r, *Va-Yiggash*, Gen. 25:1, 1643) saying, "I have already cited this in other sermons'). Cf. also MS 5:139r, *Va-Yehi*, Gen. 48:6, citing RaLBaG on the question whether Joseph had children other than Menasseh and Ephraim, an issue discussed in the "disputed question" form.

41. Arama, *'Aqedat Yitshaq*, chapter 24 (Warsaw, 1883, 1:140a–b).

42. See on this Marc Saperstein, "The Method of Doubts: The Problematizing of Scripture in Late Medieval Jewish Culture," in *With Reverence for the Word*, ed. by Jane McAuliffe et al. (New York, 2003), pp. 133–56.

Few of the classic Jewish commentators fail to appear in his sermons. With the exception of Rashi (who, as noted above, is often cited with the accompanying super-commentary of Elijah Mizrahi), the Sephardi commentators predominate. A quick review to supplement the above examples must suffice. David Kimhi's commentary on Isaiah is cited, as are several of his etymological interpretations from his *Book of Roots* (both among the earliest Hebrew books printed, and quite popular).[43] Nahmanides' commentary on the Torah appears frequently in the sermons, often in a discussion of his critique of Rashi's comment. Jacob ben Asher (identified as "the author of the *Turim*") is cited for matters of orthography, e.g. the *ketiv* and *qeri* in Genesis 25:23 and 25:24. From the later period, in addition to Arama and Abravanel, we should note Isaac Aboab's supercommentary on RaMBaN, from which a long passage is quoted and criticized,[44] and Abraham Saba's homiletical-exegetical work *Tseror ha-Mor*.[45] Occasionally, Morteira cites an interpretation without giving the commentator's name.[46] For interpretation of the aggadic texts he used as his opening rabbinic dicta and elsewhere in his sermons, he resorted

---

43. In MS 5:95r, *Mi-Qets*, Gen. 41:10, 1634, commenting on Ps. 121:4, *The guardian of Israel neither slumbers* (yanum) *nor sleeps* (yishan), he states: "R. David Kimhi wrote under the root *n-u-m* that the word *tenumah* is not as deep a sleep as *sheinah*." Discussing the key word *shamar* in Genesis 37:11 and the midrash on that verse, Morteira notes that one of three possible meanings refers to *waiting*, "As R. David Kimhi explained on the root *sh-m-r*, interpreting the verse *lo tishmor al ḥatati* (Job 14:16)" (MS 5:79r, *Va-Yeshev* (Gen. 37:11). He also invokes Kimhi while discussing Lam. 2:6 in a Sukkot sermon: "Now it would seem that the meaning of *va-yaḥmos* is removal of something from its proper place. That is what R. David Kimhi wrote under the root *ḥamas*: 'R. Jonah [ibn Janah] wrote that the meaning of *ḥamas* in the Arabic language is removal of something from its proper place'" (MS 2:67v: Lev. 23:43, 1625). For other examples, see below, pp. 351, n. 114; 387, n. 23; 388, n. 27; 456. On the popularity of *Sefer ha-Shorashim,* see Baruchson, p. 140; for the references, see *Sefer ha-Shorashim* (Berlin, 1847), pp. 422, 791, 216.

44. MS 5:115r, *Va-Yiggash*, Gen. 44:31, beginning, citing Aboab on RaMBaN's comment on the beginning of Gen. 44:32. The work was first published in Constantinople in 1525. See Aboab, in *Otsar Mefarshei ha-Torah*, 2 vols. (Jerusalem, 1973), Genesis, p. 17b.

45. MS 2:123r, *Ḥuqqat*, Num. 19:9, cites Saba's interpretation of Ecclesiastes 7:23 with regard to the enigmatic "red heifer," indicating that the claim to have understood such mysteries is itself a sign that one is far from the truth. See Saba, *Tseror ha-Mor* (Tel Aviv, 1975), *Be-Midbar*, p. 15b.

46. In his discussion of Genesis 45:3, *I am Joseph your brother; is my father still alive*, he notes, "There is one who explains that this utterance was not a question to his brothers, but rather an expression of wonder about himself, as if speaking to himself, as if to say, 'Is this good fortune truly possible that my father is still alive!'—not as one who doubts and asks, but in amazement." The reference is probably to Obadiah Sforno, author of another Torah commentary, first printed at Venice in 1567, which was quite popular in Italy (Baruchson, p. 125).

to Jacob ibn Habib's popular *'Ein Ya'aqov* (which he called *'Ein Yisra'el*): "The author of *'Ein Yisra'el* gave a beautiful esoteric interpretation [of R. Yose's entering a ruin, b. *Berakhot* 3a] which we will sweeten even more with our words, and it is worth remembering it here."[47] Morteira obviously had a good collection of exegetical literature and used his books to good effect.

We might expect to find a special emphasis on the works of other Jewish preachers, but although some are cited, their work is not given prominence. As we have seen above, Morteira cites homiletical-ethical works such as Arama's *Aqedat Yitshaq* and Abraham Saba's *Tseror ha-Mor*, alongside books of strict biblical commentary, as a source for various interpretations of biblical verses, though Arama is also engaged on broader conceptual issues, as we shall see. The great Polish preacher Ephraim Luntshitz is represented by his exegetical work, *Keli Yaqar.* Joel ibn Shu'eib, a pre-eminent preacher from the generation of the expulsion, is cited sparingly in an exegetical context (see above on Genesis 32:14). Morteira refers in passing to the *Sermons* of Nissim ben Reuben Gerundi (*Derashot ha-RaN*), but the passage does not show clearly that he used the work (see below).[48] He also cites a passage from "the author of *Qohelet Ya'aqov*," apparently Barukh ben Barukh ibn Jedaiah (or ibn Yiziah), whose commentary on Ecclesiastes and collection of sermons by that title was published at Venice in 1598.[49] Morteira apparently owned the text of the *Twelve Sermons* of his grandfather Judah Katzenellenbogen, which he cited at least twice in the extant manuscripts. But I have found no explicit references to the earlier Joshua ibn Shu'eib, or to Joel's contemporary Shem Tov ibn Shem Tov, to Ottoman preachers such as Solomon Levi, Moses Almosnino, Moses Alfalas or Moses Albelda, to Italian preachers such as Judah Moscato or Morteira's own purported mentor, Leon Modena, all of whose collections of sermons were readily available in print.[50] Nearer at hand

---

47. MS 3:289v, *Be-Midbar*, Num 1:4, mid-1620s. On the popularity of this work and the reason for the change in its name, see Israel Zinberg, *A History of Jewish Literature: The Jewish Center of Culture in the Ottoman Empire* (Cincinnati, 1974), pp. 26–27.

48. MS 2:63r, Shavu'ot, 1621, Deut. 16:10. Here Rabbenu Nissim is cited in passing among a series of discursive writers, including Maimonides, Albo, and Abravanel.

49. *GS Va-Era* 1645, p. 25b–c; 1912, p. 115. Cf. the citation from this work by Menasseh ben Israel, *De la fragilité humaine et de l'inclination de l'homme au péché,* Introd., transl., and notes by Henry Méchoulan (Paris, 1996), pp. 168–69.

50. Many sermon collections were published at Venice around the turn of the seventeenth century, including Moses Almosnino's *Me'ammets Koah* (1588), Solomon Levi's *Divrei Shelomoh* (1596), Moses Alfalas's *Va-Yaqhel Moshe* (1597), the afore-mentioned *Qohelet Ya'aqov* (1598), Leon Modena's *Midbar Yehudah* (1602), Moses Albelda's *Darash Moshe* and Jacob di Alba's *Toledot Ya'aqov* (1603). This bespeaks an enormous interest in sermons on the part of a reading public in precisely the environment in which Morteira grew up, and it

was the *Trinta discursos o darazes* by Samuel Yahya, published at Hamburg in 1629, the first collection of Jewish sermons printed in Portuguese; I have found no mention of this work, although Morteira may have used it.[51] Unlike the exegetical literature, there is no indication that Morteira made a systematic effort to collect books by Jewish preachers and to use them regularly in his preparation of the weekly sermon. He rarely refers to homiletical conventions—except for his own—and there is little evidence that he saw himself working as part of a tradition. A complete comparison of his sermons with these homiletical texts may yet produce evidence that he consulted them (I suspect this is so especially with *Divrei Shelomoh*),[52] but if he owned and used these works, he does not identify his sources, as he does with so many other texts.

2. Philosophical and Kabbalistic Literature

Another way to begin a sermon was by raising not an exegetical problem with the verse, but a broader conceptual problem not connected with it in an obvious way. When this was the approach, Morteira needed the more discursive philosophical texts in his library. For example, in a sermon delivered on the holiday of Shavu'ot, 1621, following the theme-verse and rabbinic dictum, the preacher begins, "A fitting question has been investigated by our scholars of recent generations concerning the reward for the commandments, namely, whether the acquisition of perfection and felicity and reward in the world to come requires the observance of *all* the commandments of the Torah, or whether *some* of them will suffice, or one of them alone." The preacher turns first to Joseph Albo, citing his *Sefer ha-'Iqqarim*, book 3, chapter 29, where Albo argued both sides of this issue in the form of a disputed question. He then informs the listeners that "Abravanel cited this question in his *Commentary on Avot*, chapter 2, on the statement, 'If you have studied much Torah, they will give you a good reward,' and similarly Rabbenu Nissim in his

---

seems reasonable that Morteira could have had these books in his library when he started to preach regularly at Amsterdam in 1619. But none of these seems to me to provide a clear model for his homiletical style. The same is true of Joel ibn Shu'eib's *Olat Shabbat* (Venice, 1577), which he cites and may have owned. Cf. the list of printed sermons recommended by Menasseh ben Israel in 1642 (*De la Fragilité humaine*, p. 217), including Nissim Gerundi, Joel ibn Shu'eib, Judah Moscato, Solomon Levi, Samuel Laniado, and Judah Modena.

51. On this work, see Salomon, *Portrait of a New Christian*, pp. 49–51, and the recent study by Lieberman, "Sermons and the Construct of a Jewish Identity." For the possible use, see below, pp. 110, n. 116; 529, n. 6.

52. Compare, for example, their use of typological interpretation for the Patriarchal narratives: *"Your Voice Like a Ram's Horn,"* pp. 28–33.

Sermons."[53] Subsequently he turns to two statements of Maimonides: one from his *Commentary on the Mishnah*, on the last statement of *Makkot*, discussing the reward for observing even one commandment with full devotion, and another from *Hilkhot Teshuvah* 3,6, on those who are denied a portion on the world to come and are condemned to all eternity because of their evil. We have seen above how Morteira considered it to be part of his homiletical task to problematize biblical passages for his listeners. In a passage such as this, we see him problematizing a basic issue of Jewish doctrine: informing his listeners of a complexity they were probably unaware of, exposing them to arguments on both sides, and working through the process of resolving the tensions within the authoritative texts before coming to a resolution.

We similarly see Morteira searching through his library to explore a knotty conceptual problem with his listeners in the sermon on *Mi-Qets* (Genesis 41:4), published in *Giv'at Sha'ul.* The introduction defines the problem: What is the source of the dream that provides correct information about the future? Does it come directly from God, or from God through an intermediary, or from an intermediary in accordance with God's will? After raising problems with each one of these positions, he undertakes to resolve the issues in the body of the sermon:

> I will not conceal from all my listeners that this matter that I am addressing is lengthy and profound; it is worth writing a separate book in itself.[54] Maimonides has dealt with this at length in chapter 36 of Part II [of the *Guide*], and similarly Gersonides in Book II of *The Wars of the Lord*, and [Abraham Shalom,] the author of *Neveh Shalom* in chapter 4 of Book VI, and Abravanel [in his commentary] on this lesson,[55] and [Samuel Jaffe,] the author of *Yefeh To'ar* on Genesis Rabbah chapter 17.[56] To cite even briefly the conclusions in their writings would take

---

53. See Abravanel, *Naḥalat Avot* (New York, 1953), pp. 127–31. Abravanel writes there, "And R. Nissim, *z"l,* in his *Sermons*, cited the aforementioned position of Maimonides," and Morteira may have taken his reference to Nissim from there without having used the *Sermons* directly. Abravanel's commentary, published at Venice in 1545, was one of the most popular commentaries on *Avot* (Baruchson, p. 135).

54. Compare Menasseh ben Israel, *Nishmat Ḥayyim*, section 3, chapter 5, on the levels of dreams—a chapter filled with personal pathos about his own dreams. At the end, he says, "Know that Artimedoro Daldiano wrote five books on dreams and their interpretation—all of which are filled with nonsense and contain nothing substantive."

55. See Abravanel, *Perush al ha-Torah*, 3 vols. (Jerusalem, 1964), 1:384–86. Although he does not actually cite Abravanel in the sermon, Morteira seems to have used this passage in his subsequent classification of dreams, although he adds a category—dreams emanating from a demon—that Abravanel did not use.

56. See Samuel Jaffe, *Sefer Yefeh To'ar*, vol. 1 (*Bereshit*) (Jerusalem, 1989), p. 118d.

much time, and far more to bring the problems that emerge from them, and what has not been satisfactorily resolved as yet. Even to set forth the fundamental problem, and the arguments that have been brought on all of the sides. Yet I shall act like a dwarf on the shoulders of giants; having seen all their words, I shall express my own view and attempt to resolve all the difficulties, in accordance with my humble opinion.[57]

Clearly there is a rhetorical function in this passage, setting out the complexity and difficulty of the challenge set by the preacher for himself. But Morteira's purpose is also to expose his listeners to some of the richness of Jewish literature, as well as, perhaps, to communicate his mastery of these texts. No one would expect a listener to remember the precise references to the discussions in five different works, but the impression left is of a rabbi with his books (or at least the detailed notes in his extensive files) spread out before him as he undertakes to prepare his sermon.

One might conclude from this passage that the preacher was indulging in pedantic exhibitionism, citing bibliography just for effect. But the sermon reveals this is not the case. He had already cited a passage from Maimonides' discussion in the introduction; he later goes on to cite a passage from Gersonides and from Abraham Shalom's *Neveh Shalom*, as well as Nahmanides' "*Sha'ar ha-Gemul*," with passing references to Eliezer Ashkenazi's *Sefer Ma'aseh ha-Shem*, Zedekiah ben Abraham's halakhic work *Shibbolei ha-Leqet* and Moses of Coucy's *Sefer Mitsvot Qatan*, not to mention passages from the Talmud with Rashi's interpretation. All of this material is incorporated into a clear structure encompassing the various sources for dreams. The sermon ends with a rather powerful application of the material to the occasion of its delivery: the Sabbath during Hanukkah, celebrating the *Biqqur Ḥolim* Society and the installation of its new slate of officers (see below, chap. 5, pp. 175–80). This text points to a considerable amount of preparation—gathering of materials, studying, planning, organizing—before the words were set down on paper.

Listening to or reading the sermons, we generally encounter the sources in chronological order. We should not assume, however, that a preacher setting out to attack a large topic like this would start from scratch. Sometimes the preparation might begin in reverse: with the latest treatment, one that already surveys earlier discussions. Abravanel was a fine resource for this approach,

---

57. *GS* 1645, p. 18b; 1912, p. 92; MS 3:181r (1628). The image of "dwarfs on the shoulders of giants" was, of course, a common medieval motif used by Jewish as well as Christian writers. See on this, most recently, Eric Lawee, *Isaac Abarbanel's Stance Toward Tradition: Defense, Dissent, and Dialogue* (Albany, 2001), pp. 64 and 242 nn. 26–28.

as he frequently outlines a series of earlier positions and explains their inadequacy before stating his own. In addition, Morteira used Jaffe's *Yefeh To'ar* for this purpose, as he indicates in a sermon given ten years later on Genesis 41:13. There he returned to the theme of dreams, once again emphasizing the enormity of the literature on it, and again stating, "This subject is worth writing a separate book on." This time he praised Jaffe's work as a useful compendium of earlier discussions, which often saved him the need to hunt for them himself.[58] Jaffe's work was published at Venice between 1597 and 1606, and Morteira obviously had access to a copy and used it to good effect.

As can be seen in the above example, the problems Morteira raised from philosophical books were usually not abstract, technical philosophy but rather issues arising from exegetical conundra. Thus from Maimonides' *Guide for the Perplexed*, in addition to the references we have noted to *Guide* 2:36 on dreams, we find discussions of amphibolous terms: "Maimonides, in the *Guide*, Part One, chapter 37, explained the homonymous meanings of the word *panim*, citing various examples. After a few of them, our text (Gen. 32:22) becomes clear."[59] Or the rule, enunciated by Maimonides in *Guide* 2:30, that wherever in the Genesis account we read that God called a certain thing by a particular name, this is intended to distinguish that thing from another with which it shares an amphibolous noun.[60] Or the statement that "If we find that biblical verses attribute vengeance to God, it is in accordance with what Maimonides wrote in chapter 54 of Part One of the *Guide*," going on to cite an extended passage.[61] Or Maimonides' statement in *Guide* 3:27 that one of the purposes of the story of the Binding of Isaac is to show that the prophets believed totally in the truth of the messages they received from God.[62]

Sometimes, however, Morteira disagreed vehemently with Maimonides.

---

58. MS 5:105r, *Mi-Qets*, Gen. 41:13, 1638. Morteira clearly had the text of the earlier sermon before him when writing the later one, and summarized some of the material he had said. Morteira begins a wedding sermon from late 1627 by citing *Yefeh To'ar* on Genesis Rabbah chap. 69 on the theme-verse, Gen. 28:16 (2:73r); cf. also the beginning of the sermon on Numbers 26:9 citing *Yefeh To'ar* on the rabbinic dictum from Genesis Rabbah chap. 37 (1:115r), and the beginning of the sermon on Genesis 1:7, citing *Yefeh To'ar* on different interpretations of Genesis Rabbah, 4,6, including Abraham Bibago's *Zeh Yenahmennu*).

59. MS 5:59r, *Va-Yishlah*, Gen. 32:22; the theme-verse contains the phrase *al panav.*

60. MS 3:243r, *Bereshit*, Gen. 1:5, 1623. Morteira continues to critique this position, using Abravanel on Gen. 1:5, and then discusses Abravanel's view and the view of other commentators. Cf. the review of this sermon in *GS Bereshit*, 1645 p. 3a-b, 1912, p. 40.

61. MS 5:125v, *Va-Yiggash*, Gen. 25:1, 1643.

62. MS 5:79v, *Va-Yeshev*, Gen. 37:121. The problem is, how can this be reconciled with the theme-verse, as interpreted by the rabbinic dictum that the truth of Joseph's dream was

To take one example, Morteira's insistence that the complete human being was the final cause or purpose of all creation put him at odds with Maimonides' view (in *Guide* 3:13) that "the Universe does not exist for man's sake, but that each being exists for its own sake." Aware of the strong philosophical tradition against him, Morteira confronts it directly. His discussion of the assertion in Genesis 1:15 that the heavenly lights were intended *to illuminate the earth* leads him to a strong rebuttal of Maimonides' analogy between this verse and Genesis 1:28, which claims man's dominion over all of nature. Morteira also criticizes Maimonides' analogy between human beings who think that the heavenly bodies were created for their sake and citizens who mistakenly conclude that the ultimate purpose of the king is to protect them. In this passage, Morteira does not cite Maimonides by name, but it is clear that he had the page of the *Guide* before him as he prepared his sermon.[63]

This is philosophy mobilized in the service of homiletical exegesis, not at all beyond the capacity of a congregation of laymen to assimilate. Without being able to provide a complete statistical basis, my impression is that the total number of Morteira's citations of Jewish philosophical works is much smaller than his frequent references to philosophical conceptual issues in Abravanel's Commentaries and Arama's *Aqedat Yitshaq*. On the other hand, references to non-Jewish philosophical texts, such as the Aristotelian corpus that was quite frequently cited by Jewish preachers in fifteenth- century Spain and the sixteenth-century Ottoman Empire,[64] are relatively unusual in Morteira's sermons. Issues of ethical theory are addressed from Maimonides' *Commentary on Avot* or from his "Eight Chapters,"[65] not from Aristotle's *Ethics,* so widely known by Jews two centuries earlier. Only rarely will he refer to "the Philosopher," i.e., Aristotle, as he does in a sermon structured on the ten

---

confirmed to Jacob by the holy spirit. How then could Jacob later believe that Joseph had been killed?

63. MS 5:7r, *Bereshit,* Gen. 1:15. A separate study of Morteira's thirteen sermons on the opening verses of *Bereshit* will appear in *Creation and Re-Creation in Jewish Thought,* a Festschrift for Joseph Dan (Tübingen, 2005). To anticipate one of the conclusions, in these sermons Morteira distances himself from mainstream positions of the Jewish philosophers, insisting on a radical break between natural causation and divine creation, and maintaining that the world would immediately revert to chaos without God's constant providential attention, as a ship that has sprung a leak would rapidly sink if the sailors were to be diverted from their task of bailing out the incoming water: MS 5:9r, *Bereshit,* Gen. 1:9. These are positions that the mature Spinoza would certainly have found indefensible.

64. See Saperstein, *"Your Voice Like a Ram's Horn,"* pp. 79, 180.

65. E.g., Maimonides' comment on Avot 1:6, "judge every person according to merit," cited in MS 5:87v, *Va-Yeshev,* Gen. 37:18; or his argument in the fourth chapter of *Shemonah Peraqim* that extreme asceticism and mortification is not God's will: MS 3:153v bot., *Mattot,* Num 30:11.

Aristotelian categories (see below), and this conception, which was common-place, Morteira may well have taken from an earlier Jewish work such as Maimonides' *Millot ha-Higayon.* Muslim philosophers are even less frequently encountered in Morteira's sermons. Whether the preacher himself had sim-ply not mastered the Aristotelian corpus, or whether he had made a conscious decision to cite in his sermons only Jewish thinkers, is as yet unclear to me.

References to Kabbalistic works in the sermons are few and usually rather general; it is doubtful that Morteira consulted any of them regularly. Al-though earlier preachers cited the Zohar as a work of midrash from which they derived rabbinic dicta used at the beginning of their sermons,[66] Morteira does not appear to do so. Occasionally he will refer to the Zohar in passing, as in the statement, "They said in the Zohar, pericope *Toledot,* 'In the sixth millennium the Messiah will come;' if so why is he hidden from us?"[67] More commonly, he will refer to Kabbalistic authorities or doctrines in general terms. Discussing the lamps of the tabernacle, he gives various interpretations of their significance, before referring to the doctrine of the "Sages of truth:"

that the "ten *sefirot* of the void" are those through which the Holy One performs His acts in this world. They are called *sefirot* because of their luminous transparency (*sapir[iy]utam*). Through them God's greatness is revealed. That is why there were ten lights always burning in the sanctuary: three atop the altar—for there were always three configurations of [wood] on fire, as we see in tractate Yoma, chapter 4[68]—and seven lamps of the candelabrum, making ten. Since the first three are pre-eminent, and are called *Keter, Ḥokhmah,* and *Binah,* they were atop the altar, the greatest of them all. And as the seven other [*sefirot*] emanated from them, so did they light the candelabrum from the fire of the altar. And as all of them were emanated from the *ein sof*

---

66. See Saperstein, *Jewish Preaching,* p. 216, n. 57.

67. *GS* 1645, p. 22d; 1912, p. 106. This statement is not in the common printed text of *Toledot,* it appears in *Sefer ha-Zohar* (Jerusalem, 1970), *Hashmatot le-Ḥeleq Rishon,* p. 257a (2:513). Compare *Zohar, Va-Yera* 119a where, after specifying the sixth millennium as the time of redemption, it goes on to say that "In the sixty-sixth year the Messiah will appear in the land of the Galilee," a specificity of date necessary for Morteira's question about the Messiah remaining hidden. It seems as if Morteira probably took the quotation from an intermediate source; cf. above, at p. 81, where he cites a Kabbalistic work in a quotation from Ashkenazi's *Ma'aseh ha-Shem.*

68. See b. *Yoma* 45a; the formulation *shalosh ma'arakhot shel eish* does not appear in the Talmud, but is apparently taken from Maimonides, *Code, Hil. Temidin u-Musafin* 2, 4.

(blessed be He), so did the fire descend from the heaven, such that the light alludes to God and His qualities."[69]

Although this passage does not prove expertise, it was written by someone who was clearly not ignorant about Kabbalah and its mysteries. The preacher knows of one tradition explaining the strange word *sefirot* (though there were indeed others), knows of the special status of the first three, the function of the *sefirot* in mediating between the transcendent God (*ein sof*) and our world, the doctrine of emanation, and the Kabbalistic interpretation of the candelabrum in the sanctuary. He takes a stance on some of the significant issues of internal debate: on the nature of the *sefirot*, and the relationship between the highest of the *sefirot* and the *ein sof*. He pays homage to the tradition, and exploits it for a homiletical purpose without embarrassment at disclosing an esoteric doctrine, and without insisting that it must be believed. In another sermon, discussing divine providence in this world, he mentions God's "fingers, which are the channels that the Sages of truth called *sefirot*, within which God emanates His providence." He then proceeds to discuss each one in turn and what comes into the world through it, so that the ten *sefirot* actually provide a ten-part structure to the body of the sermon.[70] He also resorts to the Kabbalistic association of the Patriarchs and other great figures of the Bible with the *sefirot*, though here too without providing a specific source.[71]

Morteira uses a second text that is understood by many to be mystical: the *Sefer Yetsirah*. One of his early sermons on the lesson *Bereshit* discusses the problematics of God's giving names to the various things created. The rabbinic dictum, citing verses from Psalms, introduces the idea that each star has an individual name known to God, which leads the preacher to the number of different stars, and the much larger number of their various interactions, producing the infinite variety of occurrences in the sub-lunar realm. In order to illustrate this number, he cites the *Sefer Yetsirah,* leading his audience through a bit of mathematical calculation exploring the enormous number of permutations of the letters of the alphabet:

A similar matter is written in the fourth chapter of *Sefer Yetsirah*: "Two stones [i.e. letters] build two houses [words], three build six, four [build] twenty-four, five [build] 120, six [build] 720, seven [build] 5040 houses. From this point on, you may calculate yourself what the mouth cannot pronounce, what the eye cannot see, and what the ears cannot hear."

---

69. MS 3:55r, *Be-Ha'alotekha*, Num 8:3, ca. 1621.
70. MS 2:73v, *Va-Yetse* (Gen. 28:16), 1627, a wedding sermon.
71. *GS* 1645, pp. 8b, 14a; 1912, pp. 57, 76.

Rabbi Eleazar of Worms wrote in his commentary on *Sefer Yetsirah* that the eleven letters of the longest word in the Bible, *ve-ha-aḥashdarpanim* (Esth. 9:3), produce a total of 9,916,420 words. How much more is the magnitude of number of the stars, each interacting with the others with their uniquely different appearance and composition: it is truly awe-inspiring![72]

Since these are direct quotations, it does appear as if Morteira either consulted the books in question or another from which he drew the entire precise passage.[73]

Morteira's other references to Kabbalah are fairly general. Discussing the question why God did not allow one group of Levites to assist in any task assigned to other Levites (unlike the priests), he turns to the "Sages of truth, who taught that the quality of Levi is the quality of judgment (*din*)," using this concept to explain the reason for the commandment.[74] In a sermon from 1620 culminating in a eulogy for two distinguished Kabbalists—Hayyim Vital and Menahem Azariah of Fano—news of whose deaths reached Amsterdam at about the same time, he appropriately introduces a doctrine from the Zohar. After a protracted discussion of the question whether the souls in eternity will recognize each other or have a relationship only with God, he concludes that the loves of this world endure with the soul in the next, and that souls of the righteous will derive pleasure from the company of their spouses and friends. He then proceeds to explain how the souls can recognize each other without their bodies. "We can say that it is indeed the truth that when a person performs *mitzvot* in this world, he makes for himself a new garment in the image of his body. This garment is spiritual, composed of light; in it he will clothe his soul when it rises to God. It has the image and form of his material body. This garment they called *ḥaluqah de-rabbanan*."[75] This term, not found in the classical rabbinic literature, is a characteristic doctrine of the Zoharic tradition that became part of a wide Jewish consciousness.[76] The

---

72. MS 3:243v, *Bereshit*, Gen 1:5. 1623. (The proper number should be not 9,916,420 but 39,916,800.)

73. *Sefer Yetsirah* was published with several commentaries, including that of Eleazar of Worms, at Mantua in 1563.

74. MS 2, 248r, *Shemini*, Lev. 9:9. On the law regarding Levites, see Maimonides, *Code, Hil. Kllei ha-Miqdash* 3, 10, based on Num. 4:49.

75. MS 2, 239r, *Ki Tetsei*, Deut. 21:17, 1620. A notation appended to the end reports that he delivered the same sermon again in 1622 on the lesson *Metsora* at the death of Isaac Uziel, the first rabbi of the community.

76. Zohar I (*Noaḥ*) 65b–66a; MS *Va-Yeḥi* 224a–b.

words of tribute to the deceased scholars reveal an attitude toward Kabbalah that was quite positive.

A different kind of Kabbalistic material is mentioned in the midst of one of the discussions of dreams cited above: "The purpose of these dreams is to expedite sin and to make man enthusiastic about it, which is why the Talmud says '[let me not be terrified by evil dreams] and evil thoughts' (b. *Berakhot* 60b). This agrees with what I have heard from the experts in Kabbalah: that the verse *No evil will befall you* (Ps. 91:10) refers to Lilith, whose governance is at night, as her name indicates."[77] This reveals a different kind of preparation from the preacher: not merely looking through books, but drawing from his memory (or his notes) relevant interpretations of specific verses heard from adepts whose expertise in the esoteric doctrine far exceeded his own.

On the whole, while Morteira seems to have been temperamentally open to Kabbalah, it is not a central part of the tradition he sought to communicate to his listeners; nor do Kabbalistic texts seem to have been a significant part of his library. In this respect, he differs dramatically from the polemical opposition to Kabbalah of his teacher Leon Modena. While there is no evidence that Morteira was adept at technical philosophy, the sermons give the impression that he felt far more at home in the philosophical texts of the medieval tradition, much more comfortable with Maimonides' *Guide* than with the Zohar. Applying a Midrashic formulation to himself, he concluded a reference to the Kabbalistic doctrine of the *sefirot* as emanated from God in a unity like flame and coal by proclaiming, "But as for me, I have no business with [such] esoteric matters."[78]

3. Halakhic and Miscellaneous Texts

Our discussion of the halakhic texts in Morteira's library will be briefer. Only a small portion of Morteira's sermons is devoted to discussion of issues in Jewish law. This was not the kind of audience for which a detailed probing of the intricacies of halakhic debate would have been appropriate from the pulpit. For those who grew up in a Christian environment, the most important need was to know what they must and must not do, a need fulfilled by such manuals of Jewish practice as the *Declaração das 613 Encomendanças de nossa Sancta Ley* (Declaration of the 613 Commandments of Our Law) (Amsterdam 1627) by Abraham Farar "The Younger" (with Morteira's assistance) and the *Thesouro dos Dinim* (Treasury of the Laws) (Amsterdam 1645–1647) by

---

77. *GS*, 1645, p. 19a; 1912, p. 93. The link between the Talmudic statement about evil dreams and evil thoughts and Lilith whose governance is at night suggests that the "evil" here is a nocturnal emission, a central preoccupation of Kabbalistic ethics.

78. MS 5: 3v *Bereshit*, Gen. 1:12 (ולי אין לי עסק בנסתרות); cf. Gen. Rabbah 8,2.

Menasseh ben Israel. Nevertheless, Morteira does occasionally refer to hala-khic works, and some of his sermons, prompted by the theme-verse of the scriptural lesson, do engage halakhic topics.

The halakhic work most commonly cited by Morteira is the *Mishneh Torah* of Maimonides. Some of the passages referred to deal with legal issues,[79] others—from *Hilkhot Yesodei ha-Torah, Hilkhot Teshuvah* and *Hilkhot Melakhim*—are of a more theological nature.[80] Especially interesting is a long citation from *Hilkhot Melakhim* concerning the providential nature of the exile under Christendom and Islam, which he says he will copy out "because these words are not in all the printed editions." The passage, read from the pulpit, states that Jesus "imagined that he was the Messiah, but was put to death by the court," and that instead of redeeming the Jewish people in the manner expected of the Messiah, he "caused Israel to be destroyed by the sword, their remnant to be dispersed and humiliated, and changed the Torah, and caused most of the world to err by serving one who is not God."[81] The text in the manuscript is almost identical to that in the edition of Constantinople, 1509. This passage had been published in Christian polemical works beginning in the late sixteenth-century,[82] but had been removed by Christian censors from Hebrew editions published in Italy between 1550 and 1614. It is therefore quite striking that Morteira had access to an uncensored text, and apparently saw no problem in proclaiming the passage to his listeners in the synagogue. Elsewhere he cites *Hilkhot ʿAvodah Zarah* 4,6, defending the justice of a judicial decree to slay innocent women and children of idolaters in a "seduced city," a matter that was also discussed by Christian scholars, though this entire sec-tion of the *Mishneh Torah* was subjected to censorship.[83]

Other halakhic works are utilized primarily in a non-legal context. Al-though Morteira himself preferred a different explanation for the restrictions during the period between Pesach and Shavuʿot, he cites "the author of the *Levushim*," Mordecai Jaffe, who states that it is permissible, customary practice throughout the communities of Poland to shave and to marry on the thirty-

---

79. E.g. *Hilkhot Klei ha-Miqdash,* 4, 20 in the context of an extensive discussion of laws of first born (5:33v, *Toledot,* Gen. 25:31); *Hil. Bekhorot* 7, 7: applying the laws of tithes in the Code to his discussion of Jacob's gift to Esau (5:51v, *Va-Yishlaḥ,* Gen. 32:14).

80. *Hil. Yesodei ha-Torah* 6:9 on the names of God occurring in the Abraham narrative, especially Gen. 18:3 (the theme-verse of the sermon) (*GS Va-Yera* 1645, p.8c; 1912, p. 58); *Hil. Teshuvah* 7,7, in a discussion of the efficacy of the *ḥerem,* showing that it is not the words of the pronouncement but the actual sin that separates the sinner from God (5:123v, *Va-Yiggash,* Gen. 44:32).

81. MS 1:39v, *Tazria* Lev. 13:13, early 1640s.

82. Katchen, *Christian Hebraists,* p. 5.

83. MS 5:120r, *Va-Yiggash,* Gen. 44:30. Cf. Katchen, *Christian Hebraists,* p. 204.

third day of the 'Omer season because despite the plague, none of Akiba's disciples died on that day.[84] In his discussion of demons as a possible source of dreams, Morteira makes brief references to the introduction of the *Sefer Mitzvot ha-Gadol* and to the Italian Code *Shibbolei ha-Leqet*, both of which appear as if they might have been taken from another source.[85] I have not found any reference in the sermons to Joseph Karo's *Shulḥan Arukh*, though Morteira does refer to Karo's *Beit Yosef* on *Tur Yoreh De'ah* 276, citing a responsum of Simeon bar Zemah on the holiness of the divine names in the Torah.[86] Other responsa are also invoked primarily for extra-legal content—for example, the responsa of Moses Alashqar (no. 74), brought in a discussion of the writing of the Hebrew letters in the Samaritan Pentateuch,[87] or even as historical evidence in the context of ethical rebuke.[88] That Morteira attempted to keep up with more current halakhic literature can be seen in his citation, at the very beginning of a sermon, from *Qorban Aharon,* an edition of *Sifra* with the commentary of Aaron ibn Hayyim, published at Venice, in 1609–1611.[89] There is little basis in the sermons for determining Morteira's stature as a Talmudic scholar or halakhist, though he taught the most advanced Talmud class and wrote responsa of his own. In the synagogue, neither the audience nor the context presented an opportunity for a display of casuistical virtuosity. When occasionally his sermons contain discussions of legal issues, Morteira generally begins from the formulation in the *Mishneh Torah.* On the whole, however, when the preacher spoke from the pulpit, his heart was primarily in the realm of aggadah.

In chapter 7, we shall discuss Morteira's homiletical use of historical material and themes. As we shall see, his sermons do not reveal extensive knowledge of Jewish historians. His favorite post-rabbinic source seems to have been Yosippon, and he was well acquainted with Azariah de' Rossi: Morteira provided an extensive discussion and re-interpretation of a controversial passage in de' Rossi's work.[90] Benjamin of Tudela's *Itinerary* was Morteira's

84. *GS Va-Yelekh*, 1645, p. 84b; 1912, p. 299. For sources on the background of Lag be-'Omer and the observances permitted on it, see Y. L. Barukh, *Sefer ha-Mo'adim*, 8 vols. (Tel Aviv, 1946–1965, 6:355–57.

85. *GS Mi-Qets*, 1645, p. 19a; 1912, p. 93.

86. *GS Va-Yera*, 1645, p. 8c, 1912, p. 59.

87. *GS Shalaḥ* 1645, p. 58b, cd; 1912, p. 220, 222 (these references may have been taken from Azariah de' Rossi's *Me'or 'Einayim*; de' Rossi, *The Light of the Eyes*, translated and annotated by Joanna Weinberg (New Haven, 2001), pp. 696–97). Cf. on this matter Louis Jacobs, *Theology in the Responsa* [London, 1975], p. 132).

88. See below, pp. 133, 401.

89. MS 2:41, *Shemini*, Lev. 9:7; *GS* 1645, p. 43c; 1912, p. 175.

90. See below, pp. 243–47.

source for information about what he considered to be the extremely high number of Jews scattered throughout the world.[91] Another noteworthy citation is his use, in a long sermon for the Sabbath of Repentance of "the Rabbi Don Judah Abravanel in his *Dialoghi d'Amore*"; the passage provides six reasons why light is associated with the soul and not the body.[92]

Note may be taken of books apparently *not* cited in the sermons. As mentioned above, Morteira rarely refers to collections of sermons by other preachers. Another work that surprisingly is not identified in the sermons is Solomon ibn Verga's *Shevet Yehudah*, a book that was widely reprinted after its initial publication at Adrianople in 1553, even if most later readers ignored its most original message.[93] As I have noted elsewhere, the two-fold explanation of the sinfulness of Jewish conspicuous consumption—theologically, it is conduct inappropriate for a people in exile, which arouses God's anger; sociologically, it produces hostility among Gentile neighbors in the host country, leading to expulsion—in Morteira's sermon "The People's Envy" seems to me to be inspired by ibn Verga's work, which uses the same dual model of causality.[94] There is no evidence that this idea had passed into the popular consciousness and become commonplace by this time. Why Morteira conceals his source is not clear, especially as he cites the work later in his *Tratado*.[95]

Perhaps more significant is the fact that Morteira does not seem to cite a single Christian author by name in his sermons. Yet his *Tratado* reveals that he read Christian texts extensively, citing some two dozen different works by

---

91. MS 3:249v, *Va-Yetse*, Gen. 29:14, ca. 1623; for the full context, see below, pp. 385–86.

92. MS 3:238v–239r, *Ha'azinu*, Deut. 32:22, ca. 1642.

93. See Michael Stanislawski, "The Yiddish *Shevet Yehudah*: A Study in the 'Ashkenization' of a Spanish-Jewish Classic," in *Jewish History and Jewish Memory*, ed. by Elisheva Carlebach et al., (Hanover:, 1998), pp. 134–49. A Spanish translation of the book (*Vara de Iuda*) was published in Amsterdam by Imanuel Benbeniste in 1640.

94. See Saperstein, *Jewish Preaching*, pp. 271 n. 5, 278 n. 14, 279 n. 16. A key passage in *Shevet Yehudah* is accessible in translation in Michael A. Meyer, *Ideas of Jewish History* (Detroit, 1987), pp. 113–14; cf. *Shevet Yehudah* (Jerusalem, 1947), pp. 30–31, 47. And see the extraordinary text by an anonymous chronicler of 1660, cited in Léon Poliakov, *Jewish Bankers and the Holy See* (London, 1977), pp. 145–46, which mentions the author of *Shevet Yehudah* while citing Exodus 1:7 as a paradigm for Jewish economic prosperity arousing the envy of the host population, in a manner quite similar to Morteira's sermon.

95. *Tratado*, pp. 61, 81, 87. *Shevet Yehudah* was not published at Amsterdam until 1640, after "The People's Envy" had been delivered (see Salomon in *Tratado*, p. 1188), but it was not a rare book in the early 1620s. On other occasions, Morteira shows a conscientious effort to document, even reporting that an idea that he thought to be his own original conception he later found in Isaac Arama (MS 1:39v, *Tazria*, Lev. 13:13).

Christian authors in Latin, Italian, Spanish and Portuguese.[96] In addition, he occasionally refers to works by a Christian author without identifying them. Discussing Christian arguments about the imperfections of the Torah, he adds "as is found in their books"; in a different sermon on a similar topic, he says "as is found at length in their books."[97] A more detailed reference is found in a sermon containing a long polemical passage against Christian misinterpretation of the Bible. Here, however, he finds something complimentary to quote: "This matter is so well known that just a few days ago I saw in one of the books of the Gentiles the teaching, without any embarrassment, that there is no other sovereign people whose religion and faith was not destroyed when their sovereign power was destroyed, except for the Jewish people. This is a decisive proof that the Torah of the Jews is divine."[98] Similarly, in a different sermon:

> Not only this: I have seen in one of the books of the Christians the teaching, without any embarrassment, that only among the Jews are the words of the Torah and Prophets fluent and familiar. This is not the case with any other nation. The author gave a valid reason for this: namely, that the words of the Bible are for Jews learning acquired in childhood, which becomes fluent and natural because they are constantly with it, while the Gentiles' learning and preoccupation is with other matters. All this is God's doing.[99]

Clearly it served a rhetorical function for Morteira to cite such works, in which Christian writers, perhaps in the context of self-criticism, point to the Jews' survival and dedication to Torah learning as a model from which their own readers might learn.[100] Apparently, he decided that no further purpose would be served by identifying the book to his listeners.

The most extensive example of use of a Christian text is a sermon structured upon a Christian polemical argument. We will return to this sermon later. Here I will just cite the beginning of the main section:

> Now I have found in one of the Gentiles' books the assertion that four things were changed when their Messiah came, bringing improvements over the originals. The Gentiles wax eloquent in their praise of these

----

96. Salomon, introduction to *Tratado*, pp. xxii–xxvi.

97. MS 5:62r, *Va-Yishlaḥ*, Gen. 32:19, 1639; MS 63v, *Va-Yishlaḥ,* Gen. 32:18.

98. MS 1:94r, *Pinḥas*, Num. 26:10. For the full context, see the translation below, p. 435.

99. MS 1:42r, *Tazria*, Lev. 13:10 (1640).

100. For examples of this as a rhetorical trope in both communities, see Saperstein, *"Your Voice,"* pp. 45–54.

changes, exalting them in their sermons with parables and exempla, and thereby deceiving those who are not sufficiently alert and intelligent. We must therefore warn about them, so that all will know how to guard their hearts from being ensnared, and they will also know how our holy Torah warned about these matters to keep us from stumbling.

The first pertains to the wealth that God has given to human beings as a gift or as a reward for observing His commandments.[101]

The sermon proceeds to take up each of the additional three claims in turn, but once again Morteira fails to identify the source to the refutation of which he devotes an entire sermon. It may have been a matter of principle not to mention the name of a Christian author from the pulpit of the synagogue, while there was no problem citing it in a polemical treatise. In any case, such material indicates that reading Christian books as well as studying Jewish texts could serve as a significant component of Morteira's sermon preparation.

4. Non-Textual Material

In addition to the material culled, arranged, and integrated into the sermon from the preacher's own file of earlier sermons and from his collection of books, the sermons contain material derived not from any text but from his own store of general information, his memories, his imagination. Like most pre-modern Jewish preachers, Morteira talks very little about himself and his own experiences, and relatively little about contemporary events. But his sermons occasionally respond to what is happening to Jews both at home and at a greater distance. In the following chapter we shall analyze in detail his sermon at the community gathering to generate support for the persecuted Jewish community of Jerusalem in early 1627; later, in our treatment of the community, we shall note his sermon delivered at a dramatic occasion in the life of his own congregation. A striking example of a sermon that combines both elements is an older text on the lesson *Va-Yiggash*, to which he added substantial new content when he re-used it (although the scriptural lesson was now different) in 1656. Its title is "Esau's Weeping," and the new material is dramatic and significant enough to justify citation at some length:

I delivered it a second time on the 11th of Tevet in the year 5416 [January 8, 1656], adding all that is written below, because of the events that were occurring at that time. I said, it is indeed true that at present

101. *GS Va-Ethanan*, 1645, p. 70a; for the full context, see below, pp. 413–14.

these four kinds of weeping were taking place amongst us, two of them primary and two of them secondary.

The first is the weeping of pain and anguish from the terrible events that have confronted the glorious holy community of Lublin. Cruel enemies have destroyed it, and the weeping is profuse. It is as Jeremiah said, *Do not weep for the dead and do not lament for him; weep rather for the one who is leaving, for he shall never come back to see the land of his birth* (Jer. 22:10). This means that from this point on, weeping over the dead does not seem painful in comparison with the weeping over the captives—the men killed, their wives and small children taken into captivity. This is the greatest evil. On the biblical verse, *Those destined for the plague, to the plague; those destined for the sword, to the sword; those destined for famine, to famine; those destined for captivity, to captivity* (Jer. 15:2), the Sages said, "Whatever comes later in this verse is worse than what precedes it, and captivity is worst of all" (b. *Baba Batra* 8b).

Recent scholarly discussion has emphasized the strong ethnic identity of the Portuguese "nation" in Amsterdam, and the very limited solidarity they felt with Jews from Germany and Poland.[102] Here, however, we sense a preacher—perhaps because of his own Ashkenazi roots—impelled to express grief over the destruction of a glorious Jewish community in Poland and the plight of Ashkenazi Jews taken captive, possibly never to be redeemed.[103] This calamity represents the first kind of weeping.

The second cause of weeping brings the message somewhat closer to home for his listeners:

From this is derived the second weeping, that of compassion, as Job said, *Did I not weep for the hard-pressed, did I not grieve for the destitute?* (Job 30:25). This applies when you think about the considerable number of notables who yesterday were wealthy, but for whom today fate has set up an ambush, when they were driven out of their domicile of pleasure,

---

102. Richard Popkin, "Rabbi Nathan Shapira's Visit to Amsterdam in 1657," *Dutch Jewish History* (1984): 186; Yosef Kaplan, "The Portuguese Community in 17th Century Amsterdam and the Ashkenazi World," *Dutch Jewish History* 2 (1989): 23–45; Bodian, *Hebrews of the Portuguese Nation*, esp. pp. 125–31.

103. Lublin was devastated by Russians and Cossacks in 1655. Contemporary Jewish chronicles claim that thousands of Jews were killed in that year, though that may well be an exaggeration. See Bernard Weinryb, *The Jews of Poland* (Philadelphia, 1973), pp. 194–95, and p. 363 n. 32 on a German account of the destruction of Lublin published in 1656. For a quotation from this account describing the fate of the Jews, see Joel Raba, *Between Remembrance and Denial* (Boulder, Colorado, 1995), pp. 103–104.

out of the land of Brazil. They are indeed hard-pressed and destitute; they are in anguish because of their previous good fortune, while now they have no covering against the cold (cf. Job 24:7) as they arrive from that warm land. As for you, living in your well-roofed houses (cf. Hag. 1:4), think that God in His great strength has saved them from enemies more cruel than the first ones, and while they were traveling, with all the misfortunes they encountered, He did not give them into captivity at the hands of their enemies, who had already said they would swallow them up. All this was in order to bring them into the midst of their brothers, that we might have compassion upon them, so that God would have compassion on the compassionate, as the Bible says, *He will show you compassion and be compassionate toward you* (Deut. 13:18).[104]

Everyone in the congregation would have known of the events to which the preacher alluded in this passage. The Dutch community in Recife fell to the Portuguese in January 1654, two years before the sermon was delivered. Those who chose not to remain in Brazil were given three months to liquidate their affairs and be gone. The adverse economic consequences of this situation should be obvious. Today, we associate this evacuation with the arrival of twenty-three refugees in New Amsterdam in September of 1654, the beginning of an overt Jewish presence in North America. But other Jews experienced significant tribulations and potential dangers before making their way back to Amsterdam, as Morteira himself described in his Portuguese *Tratado*. The allusion to having been saved from enemies "worse than the first ones" is explained by the details in the vernacular text already mentioned in chapter one: one ship containing refugees from Recife was captured by Spaniards, who intended to turn them over to the Inquisition, but these captives were rescued by a French battleship, and eventually reached Holland. Jewish passengers on a second ship, blown off its course to the island of Jamaica, under Spanish rule, were also in danger, but were released because of pressure by the Dutch government urged on by the Jewish community of Amsterdam. The Spanish are therefore described here as worse than the Portuguese, who protected from harm those Jewish inhabitants of Recife who had never lived as Catholics, allowed them to sell their merchandise, and permitted them to embark for Holland.[105] While the

104. Alluding to the rabbinic comment in b. *Shabbat* 151b, "Whoever is compassionate toward others receives compassion from Heaven."

105. Saul Levi Mortera, *Tratado da verdade da lei de Moisés*, ed. H. P. Salomon (Coimbra, 1988), pp. 75–77; Baron, *SRHJ* 15:349–50; Arnold Wiznitzer, "The Number of Jews in Dutch Brazil, 1630–1654," *JSS* 16 (1954): 112–14; idem, "The Exodus from Brazil and

destitute refugees had arrived in Amsterdam some time before the sermon was delivered—and it is not at all unlikely that Morteira had already spoken about these events in the context of divine providence months earlier—the ongoing problem occasioned a pointed lesson to the listeners about reversals of fortune and the need for compassion.

The next kind of weeping, however, applied directly to all in the congregation:

> At this same time, we experience a third weeping, of joy. This is because of the great miracle of abundant deliverance by which God has saved us from the plague that prevailed in this city for six months. Yet among all the Jews, no one died except for two infants; they were like the two perfect lambs, an atonement sacrifice for the entire community. This was while the number of dead each week was close to nine hundred! God in His mercy saved our household. Therefore, *Cry out in joy for Jacob, shout at the crossroads of the nations* (Jer. 31:2)... Thus we have seen that thousands and myriads have fallen from our right side, but God has not afflicted us, He has saved our homes.

Like the previous passage, this one should be compared with a parallel treatment in the *Tratado*, apparently written about the same time. There Morteira exemplifies God's providential care for the lives of Jews by noting that during the great plague that ravaged the city of Amsterdam for six months, "when the number of dead reached almost 1000 each week, during this entire period no Jew died."[106] The ethical question of rejoicing at a time of such massive loss of life among Gentile neighbors does not arise directly

---

Arrival in New Amsterdam of the Jewish Pilgrim Fathers, 1654," in Cohen, ed. *The Jewish Experience in Latin America*, 2:313–30, Böhm, *Los sefardíes en los dominios holandeses de América del Sur y del Caribe, 1630–1750*, pp. 95–99.

106. *Tratado*, p. 77: "hauendo hum contagio na cidade de Amstradama, e foj tão grande que durando algus seis meses do verão cheg[a]rão a morir perto de mil cada semana, em todo este tempo não moreo nihu judeo, com hauer na ditta cidade nuitas casas delles." Salomon, in his note, refers to the plague of 1635. But this passage from the sermon makes it clear that Morteira was referring to the plague of 1655; cf. Simon Schama, *The Embarrassment of Riches* (Berkeley, 1988), pp. 171, 186. As for the numbers of dead, an authoritative figure given for Amsterdam in 1655 is 16,727, suggesting that 900 per week for six months is exaggerated; in 1664, when the plague was as bad or worse, the peak figure was 1041 burials in a week (Schama, p. 643 n. 64; cf. Jonathan Israel, *The Dutch Republic* [Oxford, 1995], p. 625). Returning to the *Tratado*, it should be noted that chapter 11, in which the reference to the refugees from Brazil and the plague in Amsterdam are juxtaposed as expressions of divine providence, is quite sermonic in structure and may have been based either on the passage under discussion or on a different sermon that has not survived.

either in the sermon or in the "Treatise," though it is clearly appropriate to the theme of different kinds of weeping. It was apparently the abatement of the plague, the beginning of return to normalcy, and the realization that his own community had largely been spared that impelled the preacher to return to a sermon on Joseph's tears of joy, and to bring in other examples, from the recent past, for the different kinds of weeping.

Finally, the fourth part of the new material deals with weeping and prayer and builds on the previous application to the audience and the institutions of their community:

> From this is derived the fourth weeping, that of supplication, as it says of Esther, *She wept and made supplication* (Esth. 8:3). This means to weep and implore God to continue His providential beneficence with us. It is not that we must be always indebted because of favor He has shown for us, but we should always be aware of it, eternally. For several years now, the epidemic has been in this land, yet it has afflicted few from the midst of our people. As atonement for our lives, the *Ḥonen Dalim* Society established the great mitzvah of lending money to the poor ... *Then God yielded to his prayer for the land, and the plague stopped* (2 Sam. 24:25).
>
> Therefore, at this time, those who still have no part in it should enroll, and not lose such a great merit, as this was the original reason for which it was established. Now it is God's will that we appear before Him with gifts that relate to the benefits we seek from Him... How then shall we come before the Eternal, how shall we bow down before God on high (cf. Mic. 6:6) with regard to this wonder? With our gifts to the *Ets Ḥaim* Society. God has preserved our sustenance and kept us alive (cf. Ps. 66:9), so shall we preserve His sustenance, for it is our life and the length of our days (cf. Deut. 30:20): life for life. As this is the banner of our community—for so it is called: the Talmud Torah Congregation—if God has raised our banner, let us raise the banner of the Torah.[107]
>
> Now every one of you should know that while some of the members of our congregation fled from the city because of the plague, I do not criticize their decision to leave. However, it is a source of shame and a serious shortcoming if they relied on this effort alone. This was the sin of Asa, as the Bible tells us, *He did not seek the Eternal, but physicians* (2 Chron. 16:12). To the contrary, one must seek God first, and then the physicians. Thus God's love and kindness was with us, all of us are alive—those who left the city and those who remained. Think [... ?] how

---

107. For another reference to the "banner" of the congregation, see below, pp. 221, 432.

much expense there would have been, how much money would have been wasted, if God forbid, the plague had reached one small part of them. Our hair stands on end just to mention it! How much money was expended in their journey! And even though they did not refrain from giving charity where they went, the *Ets Ḥaim* Society became extremely impoverished during this entire period. Therefore, set your minds and eat from the Tree of Life; soften your hearts in weeping tears of compassion to water the Tree of Life. For then God will bestow life upon you, as the Bible says, *They shall come with weeping, and with compassion will I guide them* (Jer. 31:9)."

In short, Morteira's excursus on "Esau's Weeping" illustrates a mode of preparation that did not require books or special study, but flowed more directly from the heart.[108]

In addition, Morteira occasionally brings in illustrative material to introduce an idea in a manner intended to capture the listeners' attention more fully, to make a point in a particularly vivid way. While his use of parables and analogies is not frequent, the ones he does use are sometimes quite illuminating. The most extensive example, which he apparently created himself for this purpose, is the parable in the introduction to his sermon "Guarded Him as the Pupil of His Eye," on the lesson *Ha'azinu* for the Sabbath of Repentance, published in *Giv'at Sha'ul* and translated on pp. 451–52 below. Here we shall look at several other vivid illustrations in which Morteira taps into the knowledge and experience of his listeners.

A striking example comes at the beginning of a sermon from the year 1623 on Numbers 19:6, part of the description of the perennially problematic red heifer ritual. The introduction begins with a simple analogy: "Just as every people and every state uses its language and idioms of speech that are quite different from others, so that only those accustomed to them can understand them, so every discipline and body of knowledge has its own distinctive content and patterns and characteristics that differentiate it from the others. No one can begin the serious study of such a discipline without prior knowledge of these characteristics." The analogy is from something familiar—especially to a congregation of listeners most of whom had moved from one cultural and linguistic environment to a very different one—to a somewhat more abstract

---

108. MS 5, 118r–v, *Va-Yiggash*, Gen 45:2, additions from 1656. On the *Honen Dalim* Society (established in 1625), see Swetschinski, *Reluctant Cosmpolitans*, p. 200; on the *Ets Ḥaim* Society, founded in 1616 to support needy students, see Bodian, *Hebrews of the Portuguese Nation*, pp. 109–10. "Talmud Torah" was the name of the congregation formed by the merger of the three separate synagogues in 1639.

idea, going back to Aristotle: each branch of knowledge has its own rules and conventions, and there is serious danger of erring if these are not understood (cf. *Metaphysics* 2:3, *Ethics*, 1:3).

The preacher then concretizes his point by discussing a discipline that might surprise us in the twenty-first century, but was not so exotic to his listeners:

> Let us say that an individual were to do some reading in the science of alchemy, which deals with the mixing of metals. In one of its books, he reads, "Take a certain amount of the sun, and a certain amount of the moon, and a certain amount of the star, and mix them together; then you will get such and such a result." If the reader understands these words literally, he will be dealing with absurdities. However, if he is given an introduction to the ways of this science, he will easily understand that it is their convention to refer to effects by the name of the cause. They therefore call gold "sun," as it is caused by the sun. Similarly, they call silver "moon," and quicksilver "Mercury" [*kokhav*, lit. "star"], and iron "Mars," and tin "Jupiter," and copper "Venus," and lead "Saturn." Whoever does not know their convention simply will not understand. The same is true for all the arts and sciences: those who conceive their vocabulary literally will understand erroneous, impossible things.

The principle that each discipline must be understood by mastering its own distinctive ground rules and vocabulary is thus exemplified in a vivid appeal to alchemy, which must have been familiar enough to the listeners for this passage to gain assent.[109] For this in turn becomes the analogy by which the preacher illustrates his main topic: the proper way to understand the sacred literature of the Jewish people, and the errors made by those who approach it without prior mastery of the ground rules:

---

109. On the continued popularity of alchemy in early seventeenth cent, Lynn Thorndike, *A History of Magic and Experimental Science*, 8 vols.(New York, 1929–1958), 7:154; on correlation between seven metals of alchemy and the known "planets," see *Dictionary of the Middle Ages*, ed. Joseph Stayer, 13 vols. (New York, 1982–1989), 1:139, Raphael Patai, *The Jewish Alchemists* (Princeton, 1994), pp. 5–6, and especially the text cited on pp. 104–5: "The appearance of metals is in accordance with the determining powers that work on them and bestow power upon them by means of the elements, for the appearance of gold is due to the sun and its sparks, and the whiteness of silver is due to the moon, and similarly the appearance of each kind is due to one of the moving stars." Patai notes the interest in alchemy on the part of Leon Modena (Morteira's purported teacher) and Spinoza (Morteira's purported student): pp. 395–401.

So it is with the books of our Torah. Whoever attempts to investigate them without knowing their mode of discourse will commit very serious errors. The parable must be understood as a parable, the figure of speech as a figure of speech, the enigma as an enigma. They must not be confused with one another, for if they are, the correct meaning will not emerge. That is why Solomon said, *To know wisdom and instruction, to comprehend the discourse of understanding* (Prov. 1:2). He did not say "To comprehend understanding," but rather *to comprehend the discourse of understanding,* referring to the technical terms and mode of expression.[110]

The passage continues with a polemical barb—"From this arises the evil of our enemy to attribute to the Sages matters that they never wanted to say and to interpret literally what they never intended."[111] Another example comes from the Bible itself: "What shall we say to a man who wants to understand the words of Song of Songs literally: *Your nose is like the Lebanon tower ... your head upon you is like Carmel* (Song 7:5–6)? Finally, the application is made to the matter at hand: "So it is with today's scriptural lesson, the commandments of the red heifer, for all of them are intended to teach matters of fundamental principle; the words should not be understood simplistically: that the red heifer and the cedar tree and the hyssop have some magic power to purify."[112] Here the preacher has arrived at the point he intended for the conclusion of his introduction; he will use the rest of the sermon to exemplify this thesis. But the extended analogy with alchemy was critical: it allowed him to gain assent for the proposition that one must know the proper ways to read any kind of text in order to avoid foolish errors.

Another example of Morteira's use of such material, this time from the

---

110. MS 3:299a, *Ḥuqqat,* Num. 19:6, ca. 1623.

111. Ibid. The reference to "our enemy" (or possibly, "our enemies") is intriguing. Morteira sometimes uses this term to refer to Christian polemical arguments against Judaism. In his defense of the rabbinic aggadot against the attacks of Sixtus of Siena, he uses the term ("este enemigo" for Sixtus), and this passage from his sermon is very similar to the methodological introduction to his treatise ("Declaracíon de los Mahamarim del Talmud," Ets Ḥaim MS 48C5, fol. 9, "este enemigo" on fols. 107, 197). However, it is also conceivable that he was referring to Uriel da Costa's attacks on rabbinic tradition. Da Costa was in Amsterdam in May, 1623, and on May 15, not long before this sermon would have been delivered, leaders of the community gathered to discuss his heretical views (Uriel da Costa, *Examination of Pharisaic Traditions,* ed. H. P. Salomon and I. S. D. Sassoon [Leiden, 1993], p. 15). The main issue, however, was that da Costa's rejected the authority of rabbinic interpretation, not that he understood rabbinic statements literally when they were intended in a different way. Thus the precise resonance of the passage remains to be determined.

112. MS 3:299a, *Ḥuqqat,* Num. 19:6, ca. 1623.

middle of a sermon: the lesson is *Bo*, and the verse, Exodus 10:12, giving Moses instructions to hold out his arm and thereby bring locusts upon Egypt, leads the preacher to a discussion of intermediate forces in the performance of miracles. The problem is the nature of God's involvement in these events. After developing his position, he turns to an analogy:

> It is exactly like the pattern of the master craftsman printer. He arranges the plates that are composed of tiny elements in the letters, places them in the press, moves the wheel, and prints the pages. Now he can give over the wheel to whomever he wants to do the printing, and working just from the different colors, [print] what the master wants from the letters already composed. However, if the master wants to change that plate, to recompose, add, or change the letters on it, then certainly he must handle it himself. Correcting the plate is something only he can do. So it is when God performs great miracles, like all the miracles in Egypt.[113]

The preacher then proceeds to review all ten plagues to determine precisely which ones could be left to intermediate forces, and in which ones God had to get directly involved in order to fine-tune the details. The congregation's familiarity with the printing press—perhaps with the Hebrew press established in late 1626 under the initiative of Menasseh ben Israel—helped concretize the theoretical and exegetical points being made.[114]

In several cases, parable-like analogies are applied to overtly polemical passages concerning Christianity. A perennial problem of both Christian polemics and Jewish self-image throughout the Middle Ages was the issue of Jewish suffering in exile. Did not the historical experience of Jews—their loss of Temple, state, land and army, their subjection to foreign rule, confiscatory taxes, expulsions and massacres—prove that God had abandoned them for a "New Israel"? Although we may not associate such phenomena with the Amsterdam community, many congregants had been uprooted from their Portuguese homes after pressures from the Inquisition, and the burdens of exile with its insecurities may have weighed heavily upon many of the members of the "Nation." Here is Morteira's response:

> My *mashal*: think of a woman who nurses her infant, playing with him and speaking to him with joy. If that baby should die, or become gravely

113. MS 4:63v, *Bo*, Exod. 10:12, mid 1630s.

114. See Cecil Roth, *Menasseh ben Israel* (Philadelphia, 1934), pp. 73–83, Leo and Rena Fuks, "The First Hebrew Types of Menasseh Ben Israel," *Studies in Bibliography and Booklore* 12 (1979): 3–8.

ill, or be kidnapped, the woman might take her servant's baby in order to ease the pressure of the milk that naturally wells up in her breasts each day that she does not nurse. Thus the milk intended for her own child would be given to the child of her servant. But her playfulness in facial expression and speech, the delightful words with which she frolicked with her child… these would be totally absent, for the woman would sit in silent anguish over the loss of her son.[115]

The parable seems quite unusual and far removed from conventional rabbinic images of God as king. Jewish writers, even in Kabbalistic texts, rarely used such blatantly feminine discourse about God. Although it may been derived from an earlier text or something he heard,[116] it seems more likely that it is taken from shared experience: many of those buried in the Ouderkerk cemetery during those years were infants. It was certainly an analogy with which many of the women in the congregation could identify.[117]

Structure

At some point in the planning process, whether before or after the introduction was completed, Morteira would have had to plan out the structure of the rest of his sermon. Structure was obviously important to him; his preaching style had little in common with what I have called the "catenary" mode, characterized by an interlocking chain of exegetical insights, in which the interpretation of one passage leads by association to another verse or dictum,

---

115. *GS* 1645, p. 87d; for the full context, see below, p. 464.

116. Cf. Nahmanides' "Prayer on the Ruins of Jerusalem:" "I compare you, my mother, to a woman whose child has died on her lap; the milk in her breasts is so painful that she suckles the pups of dogs" (*Kitvei Rabbenu Mosheh ben Naḥman*, 2 vols., ed. Charles Chavel [Jerusalem, 1971], 1:428; cf. Joshua Prawer, *The History of the Jews in the Latin Kingdom of Jerusalem* [Oxford, 1988], p. 160). There, however, the nursing mother represents Jerusalem, not God. Closer at hand is an interpretation Morteira invoked in the name of his "master and teacher," Elijah Montalto. Discussing of the Christian propensity "to appear godlike," Morteira cites several phrases from Daniel (7:20 and 7:25) and continues, "and this is what the Sages said [b. *Berakhot* 3a], '[In the third watch, …] the infant nurses at its mother's breast,' according to the interpretation of my master and teacher" (MS 3: 321v, *Toledot*, Gen. 25:25). As the context of this discussion is the length of the exile and the flourishing Christians' claim to be favored by God, it may have been the source for Morteira' *mashal* in this sermon. The motif of the infant sucking its mother's breast as representing the exile of Edom (Christianity) also appears in a Portuguese sermon delivered at Hamburg in the 1620s: see Lieberman, "Sermons and the Construct of a Jewish Identity," p. 58.

117. For another example of an illustration from experience, see the use of "the practice of those who guard the walls" to provide a watchword to identify enemy infiltrators, cited below, pp. 256–57.

which is discussed and associated with a third, and the listener has little clue as to where it is all leading and whether the preacher at any point is near the end or near the beginning of his message. Whether it was a brief eulogy that would take only a few minutes or a Sabbath of Repentance sermon that took the better part of an hour (like the two translated below), Morteira wanted his listeners to follow not only the specific point under discussion, but the way in which it fit into the sermon as a whole. Especially in the longer discourses, he frequently gave his listeners signals and cues so that they would know where he was, where he had been, and where he was going. He probably hoped—and had good reason to expect—that the attentive listener would be able to outline the sermon after hearing it.

As I have written elsewhere about the aesthetic dimensions of this formal principle in Morteira's *Giv'at Sha'ul* sermons,[118] and as I shall provide a structural analysis for each of the sermons translated below—ranging from relatively simple and straightforward structures to marvelously complex contrapuntal creations—I will not do a thorough review here of this aspect of the preacher's preparation. Instead, I will merely recapitulate some fundamental points and supplement them with a few new examples from the manuscripts.

The most natural way of dividing the sermon is in accordance with a biblical verse, either the theme-verse cited at the very beginning, or another verse introduced at a later point. An example of the first is the sermon "The People's Envy" from the printed *Giv'at Sha'ul.* The theme-verse for this sermon is Exodus 1:7, describing the prosperity of the Israelites in Egypt, and the preacher takes three consecutive verbs from this verse, suitably reinterpreted, for the three major divisions of his sermon, each dealing with a different kind of sinful behavior that arouses the envy of a host country.[119] An example of the second is the sermon "The Land Shudders," translated below. There Morteira takes a new verse (from which the title is derived), Proverbs 30:21–23, recounting four phenomena that make the land (of Israel) shudder, which the preacher uses as rubrics for four causes of disasters to the Jewish community of Palestine.[120] In these cases, the subject matter is explicitly anchored in a biblical verse that will become quite familiar to the listeners by the time the sermon has ended. In sermons such as these, the preacher's purpose is not just to explore an exegetical problem, but to communicate important content. The integration of substance (in these cases, substantive rebuke) and homiletical exegesis seems fairly natural.

---

118. See Saperstein, *"Your Voice Like a Ram's Horn,"* pp. 107–26.
119. See the full translation and annotation in Saperstein, *Jewish Preaching,* pp. 272–85.
120. See following chapter and below, pp. 393–407, for the full text in translation.

The same structural principle can be seen when the division is based on a rabbinic dictum. A straightforward example for this is the eulogy for Moses Mercado, translated below. Here Morteira takes the dictum cited at the beginning of the sermon, recounting four elders who visited R. Ishmael upon the death of his sons, each one in turn citing a biblical verse and applying it to one of four reasons why young scholars may die prematurely. In this sense it is analogous to the structure of "The Land Shudders," except that the purpose of the preacher here is not to rebuke but to comfort. Somewhat more complex use of division based on rabbinic dictum can be seen in the longer eulogy for David Farar[121] and in the sermon "Dust of the Earth" translated below. The first of these is three rhetorical questions eulogizing Rav Ashi (b. *Mo'ed Qatan* 25b), the second, four explanations of the comparisons between the Jewish people and dust (Gen. Rabbah 41,9). But in both cases, there are subdivisions, yielding three or four major sections but a larger number of smaller units.

More unexpected is the preacher's decision to divide his sermon based on some principle external to biblical verse or rabbinic statement. One sermon translated below, on the lesson *Va-Ethanan*, is divided into four parts on the basis of a polemical passage in an unnamed Christian text that the preacher had read. Another sermon published in *Giv'at Sha'ul*, entitled "Like the Stars of Heaven," is divided in accordance with four reasons given by the preacher that explain why at times the stars, though still shining, cannot be seen.[122] A manuscript sermon on the first lesson, *Bereshit*, discussing the "firmament" mentioned in Genesis 1:6, is structured in accordance with a combination of external and internal principles: the Aristotelian four causes, and the four Biblical Hebrew synonyms for "heavens." These are introduced immediately with the body of the sermon:

> We have already explained many times that the causes of any subject are four, namely, matter, form, agent, and purpose. These encompass all the characteristics of anything. Now when we apply these four causes to the "firmament," we find them explained by the four names used for it in the Hebrew language.[123]

He then continues, point by point. The name that teaches about its matter is the name God gave it (in Genesis 1:8): *shamayim*. After an extensive

---

121. See Saperstein, *"Your Voice Like a Ram's Horn,"* pp. 387–98.
122. See on this ibid., pp. 117–18.
123. MS 3:316r, *Bereshit*, Gen. 1:6 (1624).

discussion of the material component of the heavens,[124] the next section begins, "Now the heavens have a second name in the Sacred Scripture, and that is *raqi'ah*.... This name teaches about its form," as it is derived from the verb meaning "to beat something flat." Then, "the heavens are called by a third name, teaching about the agent, and that is *shaḥaq*," which Morteira interprets as a compound of *she-ḥaq,* "the one who ordains." Finally, "the fourth name by which the heavens are called pertains to its purpose, and that is the name *aravot*," meaning "pleasantness," for the ultimate goal of all creation is the joy that can come to the human soul.

Occasionally, the sermon is divided into so many parts that it would tax the memory of most listeners to recall them. I have already mentioned above the sermon in which the ten Kabbalistic *sefirot* provide the structure.[125] Another is divided into component parts based on Aristotle's ten "categories." In a sermon on Leviticus 1:1 discussing the unique relationship between God and Moses, the preacher states, "God graciously endowed Moses from His own goodness to such an extent that He elevated him above all the [other] prophets in all ten of his categories, as explained by the Philosopher, namely, substance, where, position, acting, being affected, when, quantity, quality, relation, and having."[126] After explaining Moses' uniqueness in each of these respects, he then links the ten categories with the rabbinic "ten names by which Moses was called." The Aristotelian categories are used again, more extensively, in a sermon for the Sabbath preceding Pesach, in which—referring back to the earlier sermon—he now sets out to demonstrate the similarity between Pesach and circumcision with regard to each of the ten categories. The introduction establishes the thesis: "Now the substances and accidents are ten, as the Philosopher discussed, and as we have already explained on the lesson *Va-Yiqra,* showing the stature of Moses above all the other prophets with regard to all ten of these categories, and his ten names alluded to this. Now we shall explain how Pesach and circumcision are similar one to the other in all ten categories."[127] In this case, a full paragraph is devoted to each, and the body of the sermon is thereby divided into ten sections.

The most extensive division of the body of the sermon I have found is in

---

124. It is worth noting that this discussion is based on rabbinic midrash, not on current or medieval scientific cosmology.

125. MS 2: 73v–74r, *Va-Yetse,* Gen 28:16, mid 1620s.

126. MS 39v, *Va-Yiqra,* Lev. 1:1 (ca. 1620). The order of the categories specified does not follow anything in Aristotle or Maimonides's *Millot ha-Higayon,* and there is no clear homiletical reason why they should have been changed.

127. MS 3:45r, *Tazria,* Lev. 12:3, *Shabbat ha-Gadol.* Here the order is slightly different from in the previous sermon.

the sermon on *'Eqev* from the printed *Giv'at Sha'ul.* The preacher maintains that there are certain verses in the Torah where the word *mitzvah* means not one specific commandment but rather all the commandments together. "When we have reviewed all these places, we found that, in number and in nature, they teach precisely about all the fundamental principles of the divine Torah, neither more nor less." That there are precisely thirteen verses in which the word *mitzvah* is used in this generalized sense (as in the theme-verse for the sermon, Deut. 8:1) was probably not something discovered by the preacher when he sat down to prepare that week's sermon. It required either an entire re-reading of the Pentateuch with this one point in mind, or a reference work that already made the point. The integral linking of each of these thirteen verses with one of Maimonides' fundamental principles is a rather stunning challenge that the preacher set out for himself. Having a written text in front of him for his delivery, he knew that he had succeeded in the task he had set for himself, but the listeners had to await the implementation to see how it would work. Ordinarily, a thirteen-part sermon is far too complex for people to follow, but hanging the parts on the pegs of the thirteen principles—here presented in the familiar formulation of the *Yigdal* hymn—provided a mnemonic that was manageable for the audience.[128]

How did Morteira plot out the structure of his sermon? Which was chosen first in the preacher's workshop—the verse, dictum or other principle for division, or the substance of the message that he wanted to place in appropriate positions under the rubrics? Did he make an outline of the sermon before he began to write it out in full, an outline that he eventually threw away? Was it difficult to keep the various components in balance, to restrain himself from expounding excessively on any one part? In the absence of explicit statements by the author, such questions about the intricacies of the creative process for artists who work under constraints of both form and time may never yield fully satisfying answers.

Needless to say, the completed manuscript of the sermon represented the culmination of a great deal of effort in the process of preparation. But Morteira had additional work to do before the Shabbat service. As I have argued in the previous chapter, having finished his writing, he had to review the material, perhaps memorizing it, but certainly internalizing it to the point where he could deliver it fluently in Portuguese. It is to the sermon not as written on a page but as delivered from the pulpit that we now turn.

---

128. *GS 'Eqev*, 1645, pp. 71c–73b; 1912, pp. 257–63.

4

The Sermon as Oral Performance

In his inaugural sermon, delivered at the Great Synagogue of Venice on August 14, 1593, the talented prodigy Leon Modena compared the art of public speaking to two of the plastic arts so popular in contemporary Italy: painting and sculpture. The painter who makes a mistake has an opportunity to correct it and touch up his work by painting over the careless stroke, or incorporating it into a new design. Sculpture, by contrast, does not tolerate such error. One false blow with hammer and chisel changes the material permanently, in a way that cannot be undone. Writing is therefore analogous to painting. The author in his study may correct what he has written by crossing out a line and reformulating it. Preaching, however, is analogous to sculpture. An erroneous, ill-conceived, or poorly worded statement, once uttered, cannot be recalled. It is in the public domain and the speaker may be held accountable.[1]

Continuing our discussion of Saul Levi Morteira as preacher, I would like to expand upon Modena's comparison between the sermon and the arts, as it seems to me a helpful way of understanding the special qualities of the sermon as oral communication in the context of a written culture. While Modena's comparisons may apply to the *act* of producing a painting or sculpture, it is less apt for the finished product. Conventionally speaking, the visual arts, including painting, sculpture, and architecture, depend upon space, not upon time. The entire work can be perceived instantaneously. Of course, continued viewing will usually enhance appreciation of the work, through attention paid to details and nuances, and through observation from different angles. But it is the viewer, not the artist, who controls this process and determines its chronological unfolding. Except for paintings that depict a narrative, and which are therefore dependent upon other art forms, a work of visual art has no beginning, middle or end.[2] It is all there for the viewer at once.

---

1. Leon Modena, *Midbar Yehudah* (Venice, 1602), pp. 8a–9a, translated in Saperstein, *Jewish Preaching*, pp. 408–409, cf. p. 406. This introduction draws on *topoi* of Jewish pulpit oratory: the difficulty of pleasing everyone, and the claim that it would really be better to remain silent than to speak.

2. The application of the concept of beginning, middle and end to the causal movement

The sermon is therefore in the same category as works of literature, music, dance, and theatre that unfold over time. Here there is a further crucial distinction. Written literature—the poem, the short story, the novel—is delivered by an author to communities of readers. As in the case of the visual arts, the artist is ordinarily not present at all when the work is being experienced. The implications of this absence go beyond problems of interpretation and meaning. With rare exceptions, authors intend and expect their works to be read from beginning to end. But once the text is in the reader's hands, the author no longer controls the presentation of material. Readers may turn to the final lines of a poem immediately after the first lines, or they may start in the middle; they may flip to the end of a mystery novel before reading the intermediate chapters. By contrast, oral literature and the performance arts—music, dance, drama—depend upon the physical presence of one or more artists whose role is decisive: it is they, not the audience, who control the temporal presentation of the artistic creation.[3]

The sermon shares this quality of the performance arts, for there is no way for the listener to reach the end of the sermon before the preacher is ready for this to happen. We must conceive of the sermon not as a text that frequently is the only record we have of it, but as an oral communication between preacher and listeners that is scripted or recorded in writing.[4] Morteira's autograph manuscripts therefore bear a relationship to the actual sermon analogous to the relationship of a script to a drama, or a musical score to a piano sonata, chorale, or symphony. Those who know the conventions of a particular art form can read the script and envision the play, with its sights

---

in time of literary plot goes back, of course, to Aristotle's *Poetics,* Book 7, 1450b; cf. C. S. Baldwin, *Ancient Rhetoric and Poetic* (Gloucestor, MA, 1959), p. 149.

3. On the need for the artist's presence as a defining characteristic of performance art, see RoseLee Goldberg, *Performance Art: From Futurism to the Present* (New York, 1988), p. 8. The obvious corollary about controlling the presentation in time is, as far as I know, my own. On the fundamental distinction (often not appreciated in classical theory) between theatre and the poem or novel as art forms, see Marvin Carlson, *Performance: A Critical Introduction* (London, 1996), p. 82.

4. This means that the analysis of the effect of the sermon should be, insofar as possible, in terms of listener response, not reader response. Stanley Fish, after a precise unpacking of thwarted expectations aroused by a single sentence in a sermon by Lancelot Andrewes, concedes that "my analysis of the sentence is more tortuous and torturing than the reader's experience of it" (*Is There A Text in the Class?* [Cambridge, Mass., 1980], p. 186). No matter how fastidiously that sentence was delivered by Andrewes, it is even more unlikely that a listener would have reacted in the way described by Fish. Later in the essay, he does talk about listener reaction (p. 188).

and sounds; they can analyze the score and "hear" the music. But the performance itself is an artistic entity vastly different from its encoded denotations.[5]

The same is true of the sermon. Even assuming, for the moment, that the written text through which the sermon becomes accessible to us is a verbatim recording of the words that were spoken—which with Morteira is certainly not the case—it contains only one component of the totality. Missing is everything encompassed in the word "delivery": elements such as variations of tempo, pitch, emphasis and intensity, gestures and facial expressions, level of animation, occasionally even interaction between preacher and audience.[6] The text of the sermon therefore corresponds to a dramatic script without stage directions, or to an orchestral score without indications of tempo or musical dynamics. No conventional system of notation has been devised that corresponds to the marks for tempo, forte and piano, crescendo and diminuendo, accent and fermata, which might indicate how the preacher intended to deliver the written words, or, after the fact, how the delivery occurred. That is why so many texts of sermons by individuals renowned for their preaching prowess seem flat and totally unexciting.[7]

In a suggestive exploration of the origins of medieval lyric poetry, Maria

---

5. Compare the statement in the foreword to the printed edition of Molière's *L'Amour médecin* (quoted from the London, 1714 translation of John Ozell): 'Tis generally known that Comedies are only writ to be Acted; and I wou'd have no Body read this but such as have Eyes to discover the Acting in the Reading of it." Cited by Chartier, *Forms and Meanings*, p. 52.

6. For recognition of the importance of this element by Jewish writers, with their recommendations for appropriate use of voice, gesture, and and body language, see Judah Messer Leon, *The Book of the Honeycomb's Flow*, transl. and ed. by Isaac Rabinowitz (Ithaca and London, 1983), pp. 116–31; Henry Sosland, *A Guide for Preachers on Composing and Delivering Sermons: The Or ha-Darshanim of Jacob Zahalon* (New York, 1987), pp. 138–44. On the importance of delivery (*pronuntiatio* or *actio*) in classical rhetorical theory, see Brian Vickers, *In Defence of Rhetoric* (Oxford, 1988), pp. 65–67. On Christian preachers, see (among many possible examples) the treatments by Th.-M. Charland, *Artes praedicandi*, in *Publications de l'Institute d'Etudes Mediévales d'Ottawa* 7 (1936): 219–26, 332, and Hilary Dansey Smith, *Preaching in the Spanish Golden Age* (Oxford, 1978), pp. 60–69. Cf. the contemporary description of John Donne's pulpit manner and delivery cited in Gale Carruthers, *Donne at Sermons* (Albany, 1972), pp. 16–17.

7. It was reported that the great seventeenth-century preacher Bossuet, when shown the printed text of his funeral oration for Nicolas Cornet (delivered in 1663, published in Amsterdam by the heirs of the deceased in 1698), said that he did not recognize in it his own work. *Ouevres de Bossuet*, 4 vols. (Paris, 1862), 2:1a. Cf. also Patricia Tracy, *Jonathan Edwards, Pastor* (New York, 1979), p. 83: "The printed page cannot adequately convey the emotional impact which Edwards's revival sermons had on his flock."

Rosa Menocal uses modern rock music to make this point forcefully, present-ing the lyrics of "Layla" while describing Eric Clapton's rendition of the song:

> To sit and look and read the lyrics of a song is a baffling enterprise and a distorting one, particularly if we do know, and know well, what the song sounds like and what the lyrics sing like; when we can hear, for example, the desperate passion in Clapton's voice as he sings this song—the tune is in F but in the middle of her name, Layla, there is a shocking transition to the remote key of E flat minor, driving the name right through the heart—and the way that [Duane] Allman's inimitable riffs fill the gaps in between those pained "Layla's." Yet it is precisely this we do, as medievalists, if we study and work with the lyrics of the considerable corpus of songs that we have ended up with, prominent among them the lyrics of the troubadours, on both sides of the Pyrenees.[8]

And it is also precisely this that we also do, if we study and work with the texts of preachers from the long stretch of history preceding videotapes or tape recordings.

Although the performance of music or drama provides the closest analogy for the sermon,[9] the analogy is not accurate in every respect. One difference

---

8. Maria Rosa Menocal, *Shards of Love: Exile and the Origins of the Lyric* (Durham, NC and London, 1994), p. 151. She continues, later, to make a general point: "The paradox, then, is that the song lyric is a composition keyed to and written for an aesthetic, that of music, that is dramatically different from the aesthetics of writing which is meant to be read; on the other hand, we often are limited to the discourse and the aesthetics of the written and read text both to convey the essency of the song (as in the setting out of the lyrics of "Layla") and to do anything critical with it" (ibid., pp. 152–53). The same paradox applies to study of the aesthetics of the sermon. Cf. also the statement of a leading historian of performance art: "The history of performance, like a history of theatre, can only be constructed from scripts, texts, photographs and descriptions from onlookers. What was once to be seen, or to be heard, must now be reconstructed in the imagination," RoseLee Goldberg, *Performance: Live Art, 1909 to the Present* (New York, 1979), p. 6.

9. Cf. Smith, *Preaching in the Spanish Golden Age*, p. 63: "The sermon may, therefore, be considered not only as a conceptual but also as a musical structure. The preacher must be able to perform with the control of an actor, fitting words, tone, expression, and gesture together appropriately, yet without seeming in the least theatrical." For Renaissance appli-cation of rhetorical conceptions and terms to music, see Vickers, *In Defense of Rhetoric*, pp. 360–72. The most effective use of the analogy between sermon and dramatic performance I know is by Harry Stout: "To appreciate [George] Whitefield's printed sermons fully, we have to read them less as lectures or treatises than as dramatic scripts, each with a series of verbal cues that released improvised body language and pathos," *The Divine Dramatist* (Grand Rapids, 1991), p. 40, and see his full discussion, pp. xix–xxi and 40–43. And cf.

is the expectation that the sermon will be written and delivered by the same person. To be sure, there is evidence both of "ghost-writing"—distinguished rabbis writing a sermon to be given by someone else as if it were his own[10]—and "plagiarism"—delivering the sermon of another without acknowledgment or permission.[11] But the dominant model in the Jewish community throughout the ages was that of preachers publicly communicating their own material. There never developed a differentiation of roles analogous to that of the cantor and composer, the former singing music composed and words written by the latter.[12] A similar specialization developed in other performance arts. Of course, Shakespeare played minor roles in his own dramas, and great composers have often conducted and performed their own works. But this is certainly not necessary, or even expected; it is understood that composition and performance are separate endeavors, and that a differentiation of roles will produce the highest artistic achievement.[13]

Beverly Mayne Kienzle, "Medieval Sermons and Their Performance," in *Preacher, Sermon, and Audience in the Middle Ages*, ed. by Carolyn Muessig (Leiden, 2002), p. 93, and Manuel Ambrosio Sanchez Sanchez, "Vernacular Preaching in Spanish, Portuguese and Catalan," in *The Sermon*, ed. by Beverly Mayne Kienzle (Turnhout-Belgium, 2000), pp. 807–9 on Vicente Ferrer's "dramatization."

10. One of the sermons printed in Leon Modena's book of sermons is labelled, "Sermon for a Bar Mitzvah: I composed it for a youth when he reached the age of 13... that is why it is very short" (*Midbar Yehudah*, [Venice, 1602], p. 94b; for a second such sermon see p. 96b). Also preserved in manuscript are sermons he wrote for his eldest son to use on his Bar Mitzvah, and a "Sermon for Sukkot, delivered by my son R. Mordecai of blessed memory in Florence, and later also by Mr. Barukh Luzzato, my student, in Venice, and also by my grandson, Isaac, in 1637." See *Ziqnei Yehudah*, ed. Shlomo Simonsohn (Jerusalem, 1956), p. 16 n. 36. In the long list of his occupations, he includes "[writing] sermons for others;" see Modena, *The Autobiography of a Seventeenth-Century Venetian Rabbi*, p. 162. Moses Alfalas writes that he composed several of the sermons in his *Va-Yaqhel Moshe* (Venice, 1597, reprint edition Brooklyn, 1992) for someone else to preach (see beginning of sermons 3, 4, 12).

11. The most blatant example I have encountered involves Moses Edrehi; see p. 31 above. Anecdotes about preachers who pretended to be the Maggid of Dubno or who passed off the Maggid's parables as their own—anecdotes in which the true Maggid vindicates himself—show the continued expectation that the sermon *should* be the preacher's own creation.

12. For a contrast between preachers and cantors regarding originality in the period of late antiquity, see Ezra Fleischer, *Shirat ha-Qodesh ha-Ivrit bi-Ymei ha-Beinayim* (Jerusalem, 1975), pp. 266–67. At first, the cantor who led communal worship actually composed his own innovative poems on the themes of the fixed liturgy (ibid., pp. 49–51), but the separation of function between poet and "performer" became quickly established.

13. Alternative models, in which the differentiation between author/composer and performer is blurred or non-existent, include bards of oral poetry, medieval troubadours and jesters, modern comedians and other improvizational performers. Cf. Carlson, *Performance*,

With the sermon the assumption was different. Indeed, the personality of the preacher was inseparable from the message being delivered. Congregations felt entitled to assume that the preacher fully understood, believed in, and lived by what he was saying, not merely reading what another had written—an expectation similar to that of an undergraduate audience for their professors' lectures.[14] And if the sermon contained a condemnation of inappropriate, sinful behavior, the reputation of the preacher was crucial in giving the message the best chance of being heeded rather than cynically dismissed.[15]

There is a second distinction between the sermon and the other performing arts. The sermon is generally prepared for delivery to a specific audience at a specific time. To be sure, this may be true of the other categories: a play may be commissioned for performance at a festive event of the royal court; a symphony or opera may be written for a special occasion. However, it is usually expected that the play or the musical work will be performed on subsequent occasions, for different audiences, and that it will retain its power,

---

p. 83. These figures share a characteristic of the preacher that traditional actors or musicians do not.

14. Note the complaints cited in Saperstein *Jewish Preaching*, p. 55 (with n. 31). This expectation tests Walter Ong's generalization that "in all oral performance, the question of originality as a virtue does not even arise. The oral traffics in the already known." (*Rhetoric, Romance, and Technology* [Ithaca and London,1971], p. 37. Medieval theorists insisted that the preacher should not speak "like a magpie," without understanding the words he utters; see, e.g. Thomas Waleys, cited by Kienzle, "Medieval Sermons and Their Performance," p. 100. Even a forceful delivery would not always shield the preacher from the accusation of improperly using the work of others. (For a contemporary example, see the front page article in the *Washington Post*, August 16, 2003, A1 and A4, with follow-up August 18, B1 and B2. At first the preacher accused of delivering the sermon of a colleague tried the defence that "We don't say we're presenting our word but the word of God. It's better to give attribution, but we all borrow." But he then asked forgiveness from his congregants for "borrowing liberally" from other pastors' sermons.) For a parallel scandal in eighteenth-century Philadelphia, see p. 31 above, n. 85.

15. For the problematic relationship between preacher and congregation in the sermon of rebuke, see *Jewish Preaching*, pp. 46–50, with illustrative texts pp. 416–24. An English divine, Cornelius Burges, preaching to the House of Commons on a fast day in 1640, complained, "If the Preacher come home to convince the Conscience of particulars that need reformation, (which yet was the old course, and should be so still) the Preacher is either derided as worthy of nothing but contempt, or else censured as indiscrete, rash, factious, and seditious." John Chandos, editor, *In God's Name: Examples of Preaching in England 1534–1662* (Indianapolis and New York, 1971), p. 349. Chandos, however, condemns the opposite tendency, "the promiscuous amplifying of every common theologaster and loud-mouthed malcontent with a taste for haranguing his equals, or for that matter, his superiors" (ibid., p. xxv).

though perhaps shift its meaning, when the artist who composed it is no longer present, and when the occasion for which it was written has been forgotten by all but historians.[16] This is not true for the sermon. Not only is it assumed that later preachers will not ordinarily deliver the sermons written by their predecessors; it is also assumed that the same preacher will not deliver his own sermon more than once. Again there is a striking contrast with the cantor, who would never be criticized for singing the same rendition of *Kol Nidre* two years in a row. The sermon is understood to be an artistic creation for a single performance—as if Mozart would be permitted to present a new piano concerto only once, and neither he nor any other pianist would ever repeat it!

Needless to say, this understanding created an extremely pressured environment for the preacher, especially in those communities where the rabbi was expected to deliver a sermon every week—as was the case in the communities of the Mediterranean basin (Spain, Italy, the Ottoman Empire) and later in Holland. The liturgical calendar thus presented a set of severe constraints. At best, six days were available for the composition of a sermon, between the conclusion of the Sabbath and the morning of the following Sabbath. During the period of the holidays of the fall and spring, or when special events occurred in the community—including deaths requiring a eulogy, sometimes with only several hours notice—the amount of time between preaching occasions was considerably less than a week. Once the sermon was delivered, it was to be set aside, filed away, and a new deadline would loom. And of course, the rabbi had many responsibilities beyond the preparation and delivery of sermons.

Here too an analogy may be helpful. From 1733 until his death in 1750, J. S. Bach served as cantor of the Thomasshule in Leipzig. At each Sunday service, a cantata was performed, its theme connected with the liturgical and scriptural readings. Bach was often expected to compose a new cantata for the occasion, writing the music, rehearsing the musicians, and conducting the performance—and then proceeding to the next assignment. He created under constant deadlines, pouring his energy into a work that would be performed and then (temporarily) forgotten, knowing that no matter how good the new work had been, the following Sunday people would expect something different. Nonetheless, though working within the confines of a highly structured, conventional form, he managed to produce music that pulsates with vitality.

---

16. On the shifts of meaning concommitant with a play's transition from its original performance at the court of Louis XIV to an urban audience in Paris, see Chartier, *Forms and Meanings,* chap. 3, pp. 43–82.

Returning to the same mode time after time, he regularly found something new to express, so that each piece takes on an identity of its own.[17] Much of the same holds true for the best of those called upon to deliver a new sermon every week.

Of course, the conception of the sermon as a unique one-time performance was not a hard and fast rule. Later preachers, as we have noted, did sometimes use the works of their predecessors without proper attribution.[18] And preachers—including Morteira—did repeat their own material, sometimes revising and adding new content, sometimes without any significant change.[19] There was one kind of sermon, however, that could not readily be re-used. This was the occasional sermon that responded to a specific situation. In it, the preacher used the traditional forms and structures, the classical texts, the standard ideas, to articulate a reaction to and interpretation of a significant event facing the community. In this context, yet another component of the sermon requires consideration: the audience. A playwright or a composer may or may not compose with a specific audience in mind, although some-times the displeasure of the audience might actually intrude upon the perfor-mance. A sermon is much more clearly an act of direct communication. The audience is present not merely to observe or to listen; it is an integral part of the preacher's function to address, educate, inspire, console, even to chal-lenge, motivate behavior, or change the lives of those to whom he speaks. Therefore, the prior knowledge, presuppositions, perceived needs, and antic-ipated reactions of the audience at the time of delivery should be a significant component of what the preacher brings to the process of preparing what will be said.[20]

---

17. See *Grove's Dictionary of Music and Musicians*, 10 vols. (New York, 1959–61), 1:305. Five annual cycles of cantatas, totalling 295, were written, of which 265 were composed between the years 1723 and 1744; see ibid., pp. 310–15. A similarly frenetic schedule of composition and performance under a deadline was sometimes applied to playwrights. In the foreword to *L'Amour médicin* cited above (n. 5), Molière wrote that "It was Proposed, Written, Learn'd, and Acted in Five Days" (Chartier, *Forms and Meanings*, p. 52).

18. In addition to the case of Moses Edrehi, cited above, see p. 52 for evidence in Morteira's manuscripts that a rabbi in Ancona delivered some of Morteira's sermons in the 1760s, some 140 years after they were first written. Presumably, he did not announce that he was presenting an earlier rabbi's work.

19. Here too, Morteira's manuscripts provide abundant evidence, for, as we have shown in chapter 2, he regularly noted at the end all subsequent occasions when he used the same sermon, occasionally recording the new material he added. During his 40 year tenure, he may have given the same sermon as many as five times. (See above, pp. 42–43, 68–69.

20. Here too, performance art theory is helpful. See the recent formulation of Carlson, *Performance*, p. 197: "The audience's expected 'role' changes from a passive hermeneutic

I propose to concretize and illustrate these generalizations with reference to a specific sermon delivered by Saul Levi Morteira.[21] I focus on this one sermon as a reminder that my central concern is with his preaching as an activity of communication between rabbi and congregation over more than a forty-year period. When this sermon was delivered in the winter of 1627, Morteira had been preaching to his congregation every week for some seven years, a pattern that would continue (with some modification of schedule) until his death in 1660. His was thus a very different kind of preaching from that of a visitor who comes to a community to deliver a single sermon.[22] Familiarity and trust had been established; his congregation had become a slowly-changing yet coherent community of listeners. Morteira could therefore expect a level of knowledge based on previous sermons. Indeed, as we have noted, his sermons are often self-referential,[23] and sometimes—as we shall see near the end of the sermon below—reprise an earlier sermon without explicitly identifying it. Listeners learned what to expect about the sermon's length, structure, and substance; allusions not made explicit were readily understood. Morteira usually fulfilled, but occasionally decided to subvert, these expectations. Moreover, with his relationship to his listeners, he could express certain criticisms that would be highly problematic for a newcomer or a stranger.[24]

---

process of decoding the performer's articulation, embodiment, or challenge of particular cultural material, to become something much more active, entering into a praxis, a context in which meanings are not so much communicated as created, questioned, or negotiated. The 'audience' is invited and expected to operate as a co-creator of whatever meanings and experience the event generates." Compare the recent statement by a historian of music in antiquity: "The acoustic restoration of historical events is impossible not only because the source material is absent in the first place, but primarily because the historical situation, the social circumstances, and the listeners' psychological disposition and corresponding reaction to this music are forever beyond our reach." Joachim Braun, *Music in Ancient Israel/Palestine* (Grand Rapids: 2002), p. xii. For the sermon, the historian's role is to try to reconstruct this dynamic insofar as possible.

21. A full, annotated translation of the sermon can be found below, pp. 393–407. Here I shall attempt to provide a more detailed analysis of the dynamics of this one preaching event.

22. For example, the great Christian revivalist preachers, such as Vicente Ferrer in the fifteenth century and George Whitefield in the eighteenth, or the itinerant Jewish *maggidim* of eastern Europe.

23. Virtually every sermon, including those in the printed *Giv'at Sha'ul*, contains at least one reference to a previous sermon. See the justification cited above, p. 79.

24. There are, however, certain advantages of an outside preacher with an established reputation. See the formulation by Harry Stout in *The New England Soul: Preaching and Religious Culture in Colonial New England* (New York, 1986), p. 193, about the unique dynamic of Whitefield's career as "itinerant evangelist": "The itinerant speaker—neither employed

Morteira's manuscripts are particularly appropriate for the model suggested above of a script or score for a performance. He could not read word for word from the pulpit what he had written—he wrote the texts in Hebrew but delivered the sermons in Portuguese. The dense writing—in small letters, cramped lines, on boths sides of the page—could hardly have been intended to be read from the pulpit, and certainly not as the basis for a simultaneous translation. As the actor learns the script, then sets it aside, as the pianist (and often the conductor) masters and internalizes the music to the point where the score is no longer necessary, so the preacher no longer depended upon the text he had written by the time he ascended the pulpit.[25] However much time it took for Morteira to write the extant manuscript for each sermon, it certainly took additional time for him to fix it in his mind in the language he would actually speak.[26] As we have noted, there is no guarantee that the texts before us reveal precisely what Morteira actually said in Portuguese; even well-prepared preachers may occasionally improvise. However, the specific sermon that I shall now analyze in some depth strikes me as illustrating the rhetorical strategies and performative possibilities of Jewish preaching at its best.[27]

As with many of the texts for which there was a specific occasion, Morteira appended a note at the end indicating not only the date but the circumstances: "The sermon I delivered on the lesson *Mishpatim* [Exod. 21–24] at the time when written reports arrived concerning the great tribulations that were in

---

by nor in authority over a particular congregation—was freed to establish a special rapport with his audience that dramatically altered the flow of authority in public communications."

25. Note the statement made by Evelyn Simpson about Morteira's London contemporary, John Donne, cited above, p. 51. A similar statement is made by John Chamberlain, in *Increase and Multiply: Arts-of-Discourse Procedure in the Preaching of Donne* (Chapel Hill, N.C., 1976), pp. 115–16. On Puritan preachers in New England, see *Salvation in New England*, ed. by Phyllis Jones and Nicholas Jones (Austin and London, 1977), p. 17: "The use of manuscript in the pulpit was strongly discouraged by both Puritan and courtly audiences.... Such a formal degree of preparation—writing an exact copy and memorizing it for delivery—was in general reserved for infrequent and important state occasions.... Ordinarily, the preacher memorized not a fully written copy of his sermon but a much briefer outline of its major arguments, topics, and texts, which he called notes." Morteira's manuscripts show that what was unusual for the Puritan preachers was his regular pattern.

26. Harry Stout cites an early eighteenth-century New England preacher's report that after his initial preparation of the basic structure for his sermon, he could, "being a swift penman," write out a 75-minute discourse in about four hours. Then he worked on the text so that he could deliver it "memoriter." *The New England Soul*, p. 153.

27. Much of the manuscript's first page is illegible from the microfilm because of ink showing through from the other side. I was able to decipher the page from the actual manuscript in the Rabbinical Seminary of Budapest.

Jerusalem, may it speedily be rebuilt, in the year 5387 [1627].[28] This sets the sermon in a specific historical context, about which a great deal is known.

In 1625, Mehmed ibn Farukh was appointed governor of Jerusalem. He immediately imposed a harsh, anti-Jewish policy, extorting huge sums of money and imprisoning leaders of the community, including the revered Rabbi Isaiah Halevi Horowitz, for ransom. The Jews of Jerusalem were compelled to borrow 50,000 aspers from Muslim neighbors at a high rate of interest, a situation leading to the bankruptcy of the community and its economic subjugation to the Muslim population.[29] Under these emergency conditions, the Jerusalem leadership sent out emissaries to gather funds in Italy. Even after ibn Farukh was deposed in December of 1626 following prodigious efforts by Jews to intercede with higher levels of the government in Damascus and Istanbul, the economic crisis remained. Emissaries and epistles were again sent to various Jewish communities of the Diaspora in order to describe the wretched condition of the Jerusalem community and to appeal for funds. The arrival of such a letter in Amsterdam moved the leadership to action. At a special gathering of the three congregations, the calamitous conditions of the Jerusalem community were communicated to the audience (probably through a Portuguese translation of the Hebrew letters), and Morteira responded to the devastating news in a sermon.[30] It was not his task to make a direct appeal for funds; his purpose was to interpret and explain

---

28. All references to the sermon are to Budapest Rabbinical Seminary Hebrew MS 12, vol. 2, folios 91r–92v, on Exodus 21:8 of *Mishpatim.*

29. The major source for these events is the account in the anonymous *Ḥorvot Yerushalayim*, published at Venice, which had become a center for the gathering of financial aid, in 1631. See the recent edition edited and annotated by Minna Rozen (Tel Aviv, 1981), pp. 50–67, for the editor's review of the events, including a table of all exactions paid by the community and its leaders. See also Avraham Yaari, *Sheluḥei Erets Yisra'el* (Jerusalem, 1977), pp. 263–70; idem. *A Goodly Heritage* (Jerusalem, 1958), pp. 11–17; Yitzhak Ben-Zvi, *Eretz Yisra'el ve-Yishuvah bi-Ymei ha-Shilton ha-Ottomanit* (Jerusalem, 1975), pp. 220–25; S. W. Baron, *SRHJ*, 18 (New York and Philadelphia, 1983): 157.

30. The circumstances of the setting are surmised from internal evidence in the manuscript. That it was a gathering of the three congregations is implied by Morteira's reference to "the leaders of these congregations" (below). That a report had previously been read is suggested by Morteira's reference near the beginning of his sermon to "these tribulations that befell [the inhabitants of] Jerusalem," without specifying any. A few moments later, he speaks of tailoring his message to the limited time he has available at the present occasion. From external sources, we know that the decision by the representatives of the three congregations was taken on February 7, 1627 (below, n. 49), a Sunday, the beginning of the week in which the lesson *Mishpatim* would have been read. The special gathering could have been held any day of that week, including on the Sabbath, February 13.

what had happened, to address questions raised in the minds of the congregants, and to generate support for a substantial community response.

Under such circumstances, a preacher needs to make some tactical decisions. How much time will actually be devoted to the need for money? How much will be an appeal to the emotions, how much to the intellect? What traditional sources will be used, and how will they be interpreted and applied? How will the connection be established between the oppressed and impoverished Jews of Jerusalem and the community in Amsterdam. Will the mood be uplifting and inspirational or condemnatory and frightening, optimistic or lugubrious? Would he speak on behalf of his audience, attempting to articulate their feelings, or would he confront and rebuke them? In this case Morteira decided to use the occasion to expound his views of recent Jewish history, the special character of the land of Israel, and the distinctiveness of the Amsterdam community within the contemporary Diaspora—and to include some powerful condemnations of Jewish shortcomings, past and present, abroad and at home.

As with all of his sermons, Morteira follows the traditional Sephardi style of beginning with a verse from the scriptural lesson (the *nosei*: theme-verse or "Text") and a rabbinic dictum (the *ma'amar*).[31] The Torah verse was dictated by his self-imposed constraint of moving progressively verse by verse through the scriptural lesson, beginning in 1619. This year, 1627, he used a part of the eighth verse as his Text: *he shall not rule over her to sell her to outsiders* (Exod. 21:8). In context, this pertains to the law of the Hebrew slave woman and has no obvious connection to the occasion of this sermon. The chosen rabbinic dictum, however, was dramatically relevant to the circumstances, especially in its concluding prooftext: "So the Sages said, A person who is covering his house with plaster should leave a small space uncovered. A person who is preparing what is needed for a feast should leave out some small ingredient. A person who is putting on all her ornaments should omit one of them, For it is said, *If I forget you O Jerusalem, let my right hand wither* (Ps. 137:5)" (b. *Baba Batra* 60b).

Morteira's introduction or exordium to the sermon begins with a general proposition that is both jarring and reassuring. It often happens, he proclaims, that "because of the weakness of human reason, a person will utter insolent words out of the great anguish of pains he cannot bear, and say things that are not true." The examples he gives from the Bible—Joshua, Jeremiah, and Job's wife—illustrate the point that even respected leaders of the people may

---

31. On the background of this form, see *Jewish Preaching*, pp. 66–69; on Morteira's use of these in his sermons, see *"Your Voice Like a Ram's Horn,"* chap. 9, pp. 107–26.

be driven temporarily to irresponsible utterance. Then the application is made:

> Because of the distress of hearts hearing these tribulations which occurred to [the inhabitants of?] Jerusalem, may it be speedily rebuilt, they have said, "Surely it is not God's will that our people dwell in the Holy Land, for the oppressor's rod has fallen upon them to remove them from upon it." For God has said, *And you I will scatter among the nations* (Lev. 26:33), *And He cast them into another land, as is still this day* (Deut. 29:27)... I myself have heard some distinguished men, because of their zeal and their pain, saying such things and expressing this idea, out of the anguish of their hearts.

We sense here that the preacher has set for himself a delicate task. He has heard a first level of response to the news, a response that he feels constrained to reject at this important public occasion, though it is not a "heretical" position of the kind that he would attack in many other sermons. It accepts the providential view of God as responsible for the events of history; it is grounded in biblical verses; and it has been maintained by respected leaders of the community, some of whom were probably sitting in direct view of the preacher. Yet Morteira insists that one plausible conclusion—that God does not want Jews to dwell in the land of Israel at present—is the wrong lesson to draw.[32] He therefore ascribes the highest motive for this mistaken

---

32. Note that the introduction to *Ḥorvot Yerushalayim* is devoted to a detailed defense of the community leaders' decision to remain in Jerusalem during the period of oppression, against "those who say it would have been better to leave Jerusalem" (p. 78). Minna Rozen, the editor, wrote, "there are grounds to assume that after ibn Farukh was deposed, powerful voices from the Diaspora continued to complain about the continuation of the settlement in Jerusalem," impelling the author to his response (p. 69). Morteira's sermon provides evidence for, and an initial response to, such questions raised in the Diaspora. While most of the arguments in *Ḥorvot Yerushalayim* explain the decision to remain in practical terms, some of them are more ideological (pp. 68–70, 79–86).

Here I can only raise an issue that deserves fuller exploration: the relationship between the position attested by Morteira, and his refutation of it, and the little book entitled *Sefat Emet* published at Amsterdam in 1707 by Moses Hagiz. Hagiz sets out to refute very similar views that he has heard in Amsterdam: "These verses teach, in their view, that it is not God's will that the Jewish people dwell in those 'lands of the living' until He gathers in our dispersed," or even more extreme, "Now that God has abandoned that good land, the people that dwell in it are prostrate under the burden of their sins, and God considers their dwelling in that land to be a sin" (*Sefat Emet,* Jerusalem, 1881, pp. 10b, 6b; Jerusalem, 1987, pp. 30, 22). Hagiz cites additional statements indicating a full ideology of Diaspora living, rejecting any essential difference between the land of Israel and the Diaspora at present, considering any city in which Jews are well-treated and allowed to prosper as equivalent to Jerusalem,

conclusion—anguish because of the suffering of fellow Jews—and puts those who hold this view in exalted biblical company. But he then sets out to refute it, promising a full argument at some future occasion, contenting himself at present with one proof each from the Torah, the Prophets, the Writings, and the Sages.

Having dealt with that mistaken view, Morteira confronts the thorny theological question: If the suffering of the Jerusalem community was not God's way of removing a Jewish presence from the land of Israel in pre-messianic times, why did it occur? Here we begin to follow the preacher's message step by step. The structure for the second half of the sermon is derived from a verse in Proverbs, *The land shudders at three things, at four which it cannot bear: a slave who becomes king, a scoundrel* [naval] *sated with food, a loathsome woman who gets married, a slave-girl who supplants her mistress* (Prov. 30:21–23). By informing his listeners that this passage, homiletically interpreted, suggests four causes of the disasters in the land of Israel, the preacher achieves several goals. He provides an alternative explanation to the one he has rejected. He similarly roots the contemporary reality in Scripture, so that while still troubling it is no longer bewildering. He orients the listeners in advance about the structure of the material to come. And he arouses an element of curiosity: how do these phrases apply to the suffering of Jews in the Holy Land?

The verse from Proverbs is woven together with other verses in a complex pattern. As in several other sermons, Morteira invokes a threat from the lesson *Ha'azinu*, *They provoked My jealousy with a non-god, vexed Me with their trivialities; I'll provoke their jealousy with a non-people, with an ignorant nation* [am naval] *I'll vex them* (Deut. 32:21) to introduce the theme of the people's sinful ingratitude to God--making their suffering a punishment measure for measure—and to convey the humiliation of the Jews' subjugation to a people of no stature or dignity. Elsewhere he applies this same verse to the dominance of Christianity;[33] here it is to Islam and the Arabs. He interprets the

---

and rejecting any need for concern over the suffering of Jerusalem. In response, he denounces those who hold such views as ignorant or heretical, claiming their true motivation is to justify a life free from the yoke of Torah. Like Morteira later in his sermon, he not only refutes the biblical argument, but explains why those living in the land of Israel suffer so greatly. Did the views cited by Morteira become radicalized over the following eighty years, or did he decide on this occasion to respond only to the moderate form, and to present them in the most charitable way? For the context of Hagiz's book, see Elisheva Carlebach, *The Pursuit of Heresy* (New York, 1990), pp. 58–63.

33. A sermon delivered on Sabbath of Repentance in 1641 is based upon this verse; see below, pp. 491ff. Listeners may have remembered a similar theme from a sermon delivered in 1623 entitled "Despicable and Vile," stating, "it is a severe punishment to be given over

lamentation over *Mount Zion, which lies desolate; jackals prowl over it* (Lam. 5:18) as a reaction to the infamy of Arab rule:

> All kingdoms are represented by animals, the "Egyptians" by jackals.[34] *Jackals prowl over it,* a lowly, scoundrel people, without religion or law, as we see with our own eyes this very day. *Because of this our hearts are sick, ... Because of Mount Zion, which lies desolate; jackals prowl over it* (Lam. 5:17–18).

This is one of the things at which *the land* [i.e., the land of Israel] *shudders..: a slave who becomes king* (Prov. 30:21–22) reflects Morteira's contempt for the oppressors of Jerusalem, their base lineage, their inferior legal system and faith.[35] This point leads to a contrast between the inhabitants of Jerusalem and of Amsterdam and a connection between the two communities: the Jews of Amsterdam, who live under a highly respected people, bear responsibility for those Jews who suffer from humiliation as well as persecution: "If so, it is proper for us, whom God has placed in a land of princes, of religion and law—even though we are all caught up in sin—to help and aid them, so that in their prosperity we may prosper (cf. Jer. 29:7), for whoever says, 'I'll be all right, etc.' (cf. Deut. 29:18), *the Eternal will never forgive him* (Deut. 29:19)." Here he is speaking on behalf of his audience, in solidarity with them, sharing their perspective.

The parenthetical clause "even though we are all caught up in sin" provides a hint that the preacher's message is about to contain a rebuke of the congregation he is addressing. The next section, while not yet speaking specifically about Amsterdam, brings the condemnation much closer to home. The sec-

---

into the hands of a person who is vile and despicable" (MS 4:65v, *Bo*, Exod. 10:4). Both of them treat Christianity with the discourse of contempt.

34. For the association between "jackals" (or perhaps "foxes": *shu'alim*) and Egyptians, see Song of Songs Rabbah 2,42 and Rashi on Song 2:15. Morteira applies the rabbinic reference to the Egyptians of antiquity to the contemporary Muslims.

35. For a similar view of the Egyptians, cf. Judah Ayyash, an early eighteenth-century rabbi from Algiers: "There is... a big difference between exile nowadays and exile under the Egyptians—who were a contemptible and lowly nation—along the lines of the rabbinic saying, 'Better under Edom than under Ishmael'" (commentary on the Pesach Haggadah, cited by Bernard Septimus, "Hispano-Jewish Views of Christendom and Islam," in *In Iberia and Beyond,* ed. by Bernard Dov Cooperman [Newark: 1998], p. 54). It is not clear from the two parts of this statement (one of which contrasts past and present, the other Christendom and Islam) to what extent the author applies "contemptible and lowly nation" to contemporary Muslims. The source of this and Morteira's statement may be Zohar *Shemot* 2:16b–17a, applying Prov. 30:22 to Egypt and Ishmael: "There is no nation so despised of the Holy One as Egypt, and yet he gave her dominion over Israel..."

ond phrase from Proverbs, *a scoundrel* [naval] *sated with food,* picking up a word from the *Ha'azinu* verse, is applied to the paradigmatic "scoundrel": "it is Satan, it is the evil impulse, it is the angel of death, the accuser" (cf. b. *Baba Batra* 16a). This archetypal enemy is "sated with food" when it is fed the "food of vipers": the sins and transgressions of the Jewish people. The following passage must have been a moment of high intensity in the delivery, for Morteira plays with the personification of Satan gorging himself on the sins of the Jews, and he provides the menu in exuberant detail. The cumulative impact of the long list must have been troubling to at least some of the listeners:

> Alas, how sated he is with hatred between Jews! How sated with slanderous speech. How sated with vengeful hearts and nurturing enmities. How sated with robbery and violence. How sated with failure to study Torah. How sated with laxity in performance of the commandments. How sated with those who do them for improper reasons, *a commandment of men, learned by rote* (Isa. 29:13). [How sated with those who swear an oath falsely; with those who utter the Divine Name for no good purpose; with those who make vows they do not fulfill. How sated with those who have sexual relations with Gentile women].[36] How sated with the informers, and the apostates. How sated with the arrogant and the haughty. How sated with those who offer up their sons to Molech. How sated with those who mock God's words, with those who behave defiantly. How sated is this scoundrel! Divine Justice cannot annul his wish.

This is a passage in which the voice of the orator can almost be heard despite the dislocation in time. On the hand-written or printed page, the eighteen repetitions of the Hebrew word *kamah* ("how") in five lines produce clutter and make most readers think of a need for the editor's pencil. Spoken by a skilled orator—pausing just long enough for the effect to sink in but not so long that the continuity will be broken, emphasizing the sins he considered most important, perhaps even glancing at specific individuals to whom the phrases applied,[37] piling up example after example until the listeners themselves must have been sated yet terrified at the thought of Satan's surfeit—the effect of this litany must have been electrifying.

---

36. The material in brackets was written by the author between the lines as a later addition, though presumably part of what he intended to say.

37. Jacob Zahalon, in his Preacher's Manual, wrote that "if the preacher is reproving the people, he should lower his head, [focusing] his eyes directly at the people themselves" (*A Guide for Preachers,* p. 144).

Was this passage intended to be heard as describing the behavior of the Jews in Jerusalem? Or those in Amsterdam? Many of the sins specified could apply to Jews in any community. "Informing"—denouncing fellow Jews to government officials—was a major problem in the Jerusalem community, while it was not for Amsterdam. Yet other transgressions would have been familiar to the listeners from sermons in which Morteira had been explicitly talking about his own community. Particularly sensitive were the references to sexual relations with Gentile women, a familiar theme in Morteira's rebukes, as we shall see, and to "apostates," those former New Christians who abandoned the Jewish community and tried to gain acceptance once again in the Christian world. It is likely, therefore, that many listeners would have heard Morteira as recounting at uncomfortable length the religious failings of those whom he addressed.

But why then was the Jerusalem community being punished? Why was the learned and pious Rabbi Horowitz, esteemed author of *Shenei Luḥot ha-Berit,* imprisoned and humiliated? This is addressed in the continuation of the passage. Once permission is given for Satan to act, he does not distinguish between the righteous and the sinners. Indeed, he actually begins with the righteous, as biblical verses reveal (citing Ezekiel 21:8 and 9:6), for "they are the heroes, they are the walls, they are the towers for those who would not implore God." The section ends with a summons to repentance, clearly addressed to the listeners: "Be men, take it to heart, prepare and set things right, give help against the enemy, for God will be merciful; be established through righteousness (cf. Isa. 54:14), and return to God, for He is gracious and merciful, and He will feel regret about the evil."

At this point, the listeners might have drawn a deep breath and taken stock. The litany to which they had just been subjected may have hit close to home, but there was no explicit warning that they themselves would be punished for their failures. Yet they would have known that the preacher had not concluded; there were two more phrases from the Proverbs verse to be applied. Unwilling to continue at the same level of intensity, Morteira returned to the verse. But the listeners, about to be treated to a quick discourse on the deep structure of Jewish historical experience, would not have long to relax.

The third phrase from the Proverbs passage, *a loathsome woman who becomes married,* is not explained at first. The preacher begins his discussion by reasserting a traditional national theodicy:

This is what experience has shown us from the day when God chose us and took us as His people. *So Jeshurun grew fat and unruly, you grew fat and gross and coarse, he forsook the God who made him and spurned his supporting Rock* (Deut. 32:15). But we have not opened our eyes, nor have we learned a lesson from the many times when this was the cause that brought us so much misfortune, for when things were good, we have always turned to evil. To this very day in the long and bitter exile, we have not turned back from this way. Whenever God is generous to us, giving our remnant a respite, instead of this beneficence from God leading us to cling more closely to Him and strengthening us in His service, the beneficence becomes the cause of increasing sin and transgression: conflicts and sins and battles, envy and hatred for each other, until God afflicted us, so that we sought Him in distress, and chastisement brought [us] to anguished whispered prayer (cf. Isa. 26:16).

Starting in the distant biblical past, with the establishment of the covenantal relationship between God and the people of Israel, a single verse from *Ha'azinu* is summoned as the paradigm of Jewish experience made more tragic because it has been repeated so many times. The words "we have not opened our eyes" and "to this very day" prepare the listener for something unpleasant that will be applied to the preacher's own community. They may indeed have reminded listeners of a powerful sermon of rebuke entitled "The People's Envy" that Morteira delivered about five years before, bearing an extremely pessimistic message about failing to learn from past mistakes; there the application to contemporary Amsterdam was unmistakable.[38] But for the time being, the offenses remain in the past.

At this point, Morteira applies the Proverbs verse, using the "loathsome woman" to refer to the Jewish people, despised in exile, and her "marriage" to having reached a status of success and prosperity through its unique relationship with God, thereby creating an intolerable situation. He then returns to the motif of learning from history with greater specificity and, we may imagine, with increased intensity of voice:

Whoever is wise would understand this and learn from earlier times: from the greatness and glory, the affluence and wisdom that were long ago in the [Jewish communities of the] kingdoms of Spain and France. Let him see now: all is destroyed and abandoned, nothing remains. He may cry out, "Aha! O Eternal our God, what is this all about? Will You totally destroy the remnant of Your estate?" (cf. Ezek. 11:13). If he had any insight, he would turn his words back against himself. *The judgments*

---

38. *Giv'at Sha'ul*, sermon on *Shemot*; see annotated translation and introduction in Saperstein, *Jewish Preaching*, pp. 270–85.

of the Eternal are true, they are just in their entirety (Ps. 19:10). Let him read the matters in the judicial questions and responsa left by these sages: the abundance of violence, the lust, the envy, the conflicts, the informers [about Jews to the government], the most serious sexual offenses, sexual congress with Gentile women, the neglect of Torah, the eager pursuit of money, and similar things that can be found in these books by anyone who would read them.

The passage is remarkable in several ways, not the least of which is Morteira's invocation of the responsa literature not as a repository of legal precedent but as a historical source for material of ethical, homiletical value. There is almost a mockery of traditional Jewish lament, expressed in the rhetorical outcry to God following the destruction of great Jewish communities. The reasons for their downfall are obvious in the literature of past centuries. Here we encounter a powerful ambivalence toward the communities of France and of Spain. On the one hand, "greatness and glory, affluence and wisdom." But Morteira implies that this is not the full truth; there is a darker reality beneath the surface, accessible (to those who read Hebrew) in the dense pages of legal texts. These reveal the lives not just of the spiritual and intellectual leaders but of the entire population of Jews, and the resulting picture, Morteira insists as he reiterates many of the sins from his earlier litany, is dismal indeed.

By this time, listeners would have been quite certain that the preacher was not going to limit himself to a history lesson, that application to the present was certain to come. And he does not disappoint, invoking the recent history both of Amsterdam and of Jerusalem:

Still, we have not learned! Even today, we are worse than our ancestors. Did we not see during the good days that confronted us in this city how many conflicts occurred and how many bans were enacted, until war and loss of money and pestilence came, Heaven protect us! And so in Jerusalem, the holy city, may it be quickly rebuilt: for the past three years there was peace and tranquility in the land. But we knew the bewildering and chaotic conflicts among the Jews, until the anger of Satan boiled over against them and destroyed them, as our eyes see this very day. Truly, experience teaches the truthfulness of the rabbinic statement, "poverty is fitting for Israel like a red rose upon a white horse" (b. *Ḥagigah* 9b). Even a minor sin committed in that land is much greater than in another place, for it is done in God's presence. We see this in the verse, *The people who provoke My anger continually, in My very presence* [Isa. 65:3], and in the verse, *My eyes and My heart will be there always* [1 Kings 9:3]. How much greater is the transgression committed in the king's palace, in the king's very presence, than that committed in one's own house!

The reference to Amsterdam, though fleeting and allusive, is unmistakable. Few in the audience would not have had vivid memories of the conflict surrounding Morteira's friend, the now deceased Dr. David Farar,[39] the bitter split surrounding the formation of a break-away congregation from "Beth Jacob." When his own congregation was vindicated following an appeal to the Dutch authorities, Morteira delivered a celebratory sermon emphasizing reconciliation.[40] Here the mood is quite different, as he points to the conflict as a cause of upheavals in the subsequent years and suggests that its legacy of divisiveness has not yet ended. The "war and loss of money" following in the wake of the conflicts similarly alludes to realities everyone well knew: the termination of the Twelve Years' Truce between Spain and Holland in April 1621, the imposition of new embargoes against Dutch ships and merchandise in all Spanish territories, and the rapid reversal of fortune for the Jewish merchants, from vigorous economic expansion to severe economic slump.[41]

The events in the Jewish community of Jerusalem could not have been nearly as familiar to the audience, which had to accept Morteira's authority on this matter. The early 1620s, after the arrival in Jerusalem of R. Isaiah Halevi Horowitz, were considered to be years of tranquility, prosperity, and even messianic promise.[42] As for the "bewildering and chaotic conflicts among the Jews," Morteira may be referring to the collaboration of Jews as informers to government officials about Jews who settled in Jerusalem without government authorization.[43] The point he is making is that the contrast between external tranquility and internal strife in Jerusalem created an unstable situation that had to change. As in so much of traditional historiography, the political events involving the Muslim governor ibn Farukh are only the epiphenomena of a deeper reality, the structures of which are encoded in the Bible. It is as if the Muslim authorities were not protagonists at all.

Amsterdam and Jerusalem are thus set up in ambiguous juxtaposition. First

---

39. See the review of events with bibliography in Saperstein, *"Your Voice Like a Ram's Horn,"* pp. 373–74.

40. See below, pp. 168–72.

41. See Jonathan Israel, "The Changing Role of the Dutch Sephardim in International Trade, 1595–1715," in *Dutch Jewish History* 1 (1984): 35–37, summarizing his more detailed earlier studies (see footnotes 6 and 12).

42. See Yaari, *Sheluḥei Eretz Yisra'el,* p. 262; cf. *A Goodly Heritage,* p. 12: "It was reported in all countries that we were dwelling in peace and security."

43. Cf. Baron, *SRHJ* 18:161–62. Baron twice uses the phrase "chaotic conditions" to describe the circumstances in Jerusalem (pp. 162, 163).

a parallel is made: contentious behavior has within the past few years led to loss of prosperity and to suffering in both. Then the distinctiveness of the Holy Land is emphasized. Earlier in the sermon Morteira emphasized one fundamental difference between the two communities: Jerusalem subjugated to "a scoundrel people," Dutch Jewry living in "a royal land, of religion and law." Now a different contrast is drawn: the unique closeness of the divine presence to the land of Israel makes it especially sensitive to the smallest sin, incapable of tolerating even a minor transgression. In other words, the listeners should not conclude that the greater intensity of suffering in Jerusalem proves that its inhabitants must have sinned more than the present company. The juxtaposition of the two cities would have the effect upon the listeners both of dignifying Amsterdam and sounding the jeremiad warning that more suffering is in store at home unless things improve.

Morteira then turns back to the implications for his own community. "Why then are we irresolute in our actions? Why do we undermine our preparations to accept all God's kindnesses, while we anger Him over the good things He gives us? *I lavished silver on her, and gold, which they used for Baal* (Hos. 2:10). Indeed, how great is the obligation of the leaders of these congregations to bestir themselves to improve our way of serving God, in that He has favored us more than any other Jews in the Diaspora."[44] To concretize this point, the preacher continues with an extremely powerful and interesting passage ranging through the great Jewish communities of the world and succinctly specifying the humiliations and persecutions distinctive of each.

> Where here are the taxes of Venice? The censorship of books that is all over Italy? The seizing of children for forced conversions? The sign of the [Jewish] hat that is there? The Ghettos? The need to receive permission [to remain] every so often? Being shut in at the evil time [Holy Week]? Where is the derision shown toward the Jews of Rome, [forced to] go out naked on their holidays, forced to attend their services, forced to bow down to the Pope? Where are the blood libels of Poland? Where are the humiliations of Germany? Where are the hours when they prevent us from attending the [commercial] fairs? The entrances through which we may not walk, the wells from we may not

44. The reference to "these congregations" indicates that all three congregations met together for the special occasion on which this sermon was delivered. The last five Hebrew words of this section translate, "Here this matter should be discussed at length;" they were probably written by Morteira when he temporarily left off writing the text of his sermon as a reminder to himself of how he intended to continue. Indeed, the following paragraph, which appears to be written with a somewhat finer pen point, goes on to specify the uniqueness of Amsterdam.

drink? Where is the harsh oppression of Turkey? The poll tax that is levied there? The cruelty of the Gentiles? The fire thrown into houses? The deadly tortures connected with the manufacturing of their clothes? Where is the degradation of Barbary? Where is the youngster who will strike an old man? Where are the animal carcasses which they compel us to remove from their paths?[45]

Like the earlier litany of sins in Satan's feast, this series of rhetorical questions was clearly intended not for the written page but for the modulations of the preacher's voice, though its power remains palpable in its written form, even without the voice to enhance it. He begins with his own native city of Venice, which Amsterdam Jews looked upon as a model: older, larger, more established, more cosmopolitan than their own, the city to which they turned for guidance and leadership when problems arose. Yet it could not be denied that the Jews of Venice, and Rome, and the rest of Italy, suffered from disabilities and humiliations that were simply not present in Amsterdam. And if that was true of Italy, how much more was it true for other great Jewish communities of the Diaspora: Poland, Germany, Turkey, North Africa. As in the previous passage of rebuke, timing in delivery was crucial. With each clipped phrase, the preacher must have paused long enough to allow the verbal picture to register in the minds of his listeners.

After piling up his evidence, and suggesting that he could add even more, Morteira reaches his conclusion with the appropriate lesson: "And much more of the like, that our brothers, the entire house of Israel, suffer throughout their dispersion in exile. But God has brought us out from there. Why then are we ungrateful? Why do we not wake up and open our eyes [to see] that just as God has favored us more than all our brothers, so should we surpass them all in our conduct, serving as an example, a model of goodness and decency, especially by helping the Holy City at a time like this?" In addition to the general conclusion of reforming behavior, the practical application to the specific situation has now been made.

The final section of the sermon is introduced by the last phrase in the Proverbs verse, *a slave-girl who supplants her mistress* (Prov. 30:23). Citing verses to establish that the "mistress" is Jerusalem and the "slave-girl" any other land, Morteira draws a harsh lesson, shifting the spotlight entirely to the Jews of the Diaspora: the greatest disgrace of all for Jerusalem is that "her children give all its goodness and its glory to her slave-girl. They forget her [the mistress], giving every kind of joy and honor to slave-girls in the land of their enemies, in their exile, in a land not theirs." After having dramatically emphasized the

45. For fuller annotation of this rich passage, see below, pp. 402–4.

uniqueness of Amsterdam in the Diaspora, the preacher now shifts his ground, placing Amsterdam in the traditional bleak, undifferentiated category of "exile" and "land of your enemies" (cf. Lev. 26:41). Compared with Italy, Poland, and Morocco, the situation in Amsterdam was vastly better, but it was still exile, a "land not theirs."

For the alert listener, the use of the term "they forget her" would have raised the association with the Psalmist's pledge never to forget (Ps. 137:5), and perhaps even with Morteira's use of this verse in the rabbinic dictum cited at the beginning of the sermon. It is precisely this dictum that he now takes up to signal the sermon's approaching dénouement, though not that the final words will all be pleasant to hear. The rabbinic statement, which specifies ways for Jews living in the land of Israel after the destruction to remember Jerusalem properly, allows the preacher to draw a contrast between the behavior of those Jews and the behavior of his congregants. The three elements of the dictum are used to refer to three examples of conspicuous consumption. "They did not say 'covering his house with paintings,' but 'A person who is covering his house with *plaster,'* yet still a small space should be left as a reminder of the destruction... Why then should the Jews of the Diaspora seek *spacious upper chambers* (Jer. 22:14)?"[46] The rabbinic statement continues, "A person who is preparing what is needed for a feast," speaking about what is necessary; even from this, he should leave out something as a reminder of the destruction. They were not even thinking of "those banquets that destroy people's savings"; of this, the prophet said, *They lie on ivory beds, stretched upon their couches, feasting on lambs from the flock, and on calves from the stall ... They drink from the wine bowls and anoint themselves with the choicest oils, but they are not concerned about the ruin of Joseph* (Amos 6:4,6).[47] Here the prophetic verse has specific resonance for those whose lack of response to the community relief effort shows indifference to the sufferings of Jews in the Holy Land. Finally, the rabbis speak of "A person who is putting on her ornaments," namely,

> those ornaments appropriate to a woman in exile, who would not transgress the words of the prophet who cries out against them when in abundance. "She should omit one of them" as a reminder of the destruction. But they do not act this way; rather, they see how they can

---

46. The reference to "paintings" alludes to the use of artwork to decorate the homes, a practice about which Morteira seems to have felt some ambivalence. Cf. Saperstein, *"Your Voice Like a Ram's Horn,"* p. 416, including n. 20.

47. Cf. the use of this verse in the same context in the earlier sermon, "The People's Envy," *Jewish Preaching,* p. 282.

outdo the ones who preceded them, so that *a slave-girl supplants her mistress* (Prov. 30:23) by acting this way in their exile.

In this section, Morteira gives a succinct reprise of the central theme and the tripartite division in "The People's Envy"—condemnation of expenditures on unnecessarily large and beautiful houses, sumptuous banquets, and lavish clothing and jewelry. This time there is no reference to the arousal of envy and hostility in the host population. In accordance with the occasion, the preacher emphasizes the failure to follow the tradition of abnegation in memory of the destruction of the Temple, the failure to remember Jerusalem and its suffering inhabitants.

The rabbinic dictum having been interpreted and applied, the listeners would know they were nearing the end. At this point the preacher shifts to a climactic peroration, recapitulating the three areas of offensive behavior just outlined, transposing the negatives into positive ideals:

> How good and how fine it would be for every person to take pride and to compete with his neighbor:
>   •not in the great size of his house but in the greatness of his soul, which is the house of ethical virtues and intellectual attainments;
>   •not in foods but in feeding the poor and abundant charity;
>   •not in clothes, but in a good name and serenity and in imitation of God's ways and in the mystical garment of good deeds.[48]

This would be the "remembering of Jerusalem," this would be the shortening of our exile. And now that we fail to do this, the plagues of Jerusalem mount. Perhaps we may open our eyes from preoccupation with ourselves to see whether the way we are following is good, so that these afflictions will no longer come upon it…. That is why the members of the *Va'ad* passed the ordinances they did to help in its redemption, so that the feet of Israel will not move from upon it.

With this allusion to a decisive act by the lay leadership that everyone in the audience must have known,[49] the preacher has accomplished everything of substance on his agenda. Only the conventional obligations of the genre re-

---

48. *Ḥaluqa de-rabbanan,* literally: "robe of the sages." This refers to the garment worn by the righteous in the world to come (see Zohar 1:66a). Morteira referred to this kabbalistic term on other occasions in his sermons: cf. the passage cited above, chap. 3, p. 95.

49. The decision made by fifteen lay leaders on February 7, 1627 was to borrow 1800 florins from the Dowry Fund in order to send a total of 2400 florins to "our brothers dwelling in Jerusalem." Yaari, *Sheluḥei Eretz Yisra'el,* p. 265, citing Brugmans and Frank, *Geschiedenis der Joden in Nederland* (Amsterdam, 1940), p. 254. Cf. Isaac Emmanuel, "Siyyu'an shel Qehillot ha-Sefaradim be-Amsterdam u-ve-Curaçao la-Aretz ha-Qedoshah u-li-Tsefat,"

main. His insistence upon a continued Jewish presence in the land of Israel—picking up his refutation of the view expressed in the introduction (God does not want our people to dwell in the Holy Land at present)—is now connected with the theme-verse from the scriptural lesson, cited at the beginning of the sermon: *He shall not rule over her to sell her to outsiders* (Exod. 21:8). It returns, near the very end, as a framing device.[50] In a characteristic homiletical inversion, the phrase is removed from the simple meaning of its original reference—the Hebrew slave woman—and applied to the land that is currently under the power of aliens. "*And which of My creditors was it to whom I sold you off?* (Isa. 50:1). For it is not sold, only given for temporary keeping, and therefore Israel will not lose her presumptive rights, she will forever remain upon it." Not surprisingly, after a long passage of criticism, set on the broad canvas of Jewish history and geography, the preacher ends by prescribing a positive course of action linked with the traditional messianic hope.

What would the assembled congregation have remembered from this sermon? They would not have learned much about the details of the persecution in Jerusalem; that was not the preacher's purpose. Perhaps the four-part verse from Proverbs and its interpretation, or the three-part rabbinic dictum as applied by Morteira, would have remained with them. Some listeners may have been impressed by the point about the corruption of the earlier Jewish communities of Europe, as revealed in the responsa literature. Some would perhaps have been moved by Morteira's stress on the link between dissension and rupture in the community and the economic reversals that followed soon after, or the comparison between Amsterdam and Jerusalem, the claim that inner communal tensions led to external calamity in both. But perhaps more than any substantive argument, they would have recalled the rhythms and cadences and modulations of the preacher's voice at the climactic moments in the sermon: the litany of sins evoking a picture of Satan cramming his maw to the point where he could eat no more ("How sated...!"), and the globe-hopping tour of world Jewish centers, each community with its distinctive disabilities from which Amsterdam is free ("Where are...?"). These are the kind of high points that remain fixed in the acoustic memory even after

Sefunot 6 (1962): 413, n. 2, providing the reference in "Libro dos Termos da Ymposta da Naçao," fol. 19b.

50. This recourse to the theme-verse at the very end of the discourse, rather than as a structuring element, seems to be characteristic especially of Morteira's eulogies. See Saperstein, *"Your Voice Like a Ram's Horn,"* pp. 385, 397, 433. The sermon is thus framed through the rhetorical device of *chiasmus*: theme-verse, then rabbinic dictum at the beginning; dictum, then theme-verse at the end.

the structure of the sermon has been forgotten.[51] The Hebrew text written by Morteira is a rather impressive script for this special occasion. If his abilities as a speaker were comparable to his abilities as an author, the audience may well have experienced an unforgettable performance. Whether the listeners were inspired to repent and change their ways, as the preacher called upon them to do, is—one must confess—somewhat less likely.[52]

51. Cf. the report of a young man's memory of Ezekiel Landau's voice at the beginning of a eulogy, cited in *Jewish Preaching*, p. 360; or Zalman Shazar's recollection of the Maggid of Minsk in *Morning Stars* (Philadelphia, 1967), pp. 67–68; or Vladimir Jabotinsky's statement that, after many years, he "could still hear [Herzl's] voice ringing in my ears as he took the oath [at the Sixth World Zionist Congress], *im eshkahekh Yerushalayim tishkah yemini*" (cited in Shmuel Katz, *Lone Wolf,* 2 vols. [New York, 1996], p. 53). An analogy from American experience would be the memory of Martin Luther King's "I have a dream" peroration.

52. On the efficacy of Jewish preaching to affect behavior and change lives, see Saperstein, *Jewish Preaching,* pp. 61–63; on medieval Christian preaching, see Kienzle, "Medieval Sermons and Their Performance," pp. 115–22.

The Community

5

Reflecting Life:
Individuals, Events, Institutions

Up to this point, we have mined Morteira's sermons primarily for evidence about the preacher: the literary resources he had at his disposal, his style and method of composition, the rhythm of his weekly homiletical production over a period of some forty years, the drama of his delivery, especially at an occasion of special significance. But sermons are also an important historical source for reconstructing the community of listeners, the people to whom they were addressed. In the case of Morteira's unusual congregation, the historical value of this component of his texts is especially significant.

To be sure, using the texts to move from the preacher to the audience raises some challenging methodological questions. Perhaps the most significant might be termed the problem of identification and distance between preacher and audience. To what extent does the traditional preacher reflect the values of his listeners, to what extent does he try to modify values of the congregation that he recognizes to be different from his? When may we assume that a preacher is articulating thoughts, feelings, questions shared by many in the congregation, and when should we conclude that he is trying to convince them of a position that is not widely accepted, even unpopular? When he uses his sermons to communicate information and insight from the shared tradition, should we use this as evidence of what the congregation knows, or of what it does not know? When he rebukes the congregation for what he considers to be their failures to meet appropriate standards of ritual observance or ethical behavior, may we deduce that most in the audience agreed with what he was saying, or disagreed? How efficacious was the sermon of rebuke in changing the behavior of the listeners? There are no simple answers to such questions; specific texts and circumstances must be carefully analyzed for clues in each case.[1]

---

1. An intriguing example from the following century is Ezekiel Landau's eulogy for the blatantly anti-Jewish Empress Maria Theresa in 1780 (see Saperstein, *"Your Voice Like a*

In previous chapters, we have already noted references in the manuscripts to the names of individuals married under the auspices of the *Biqqur Ḥolim* society (above, pp. 41–46). We have also seen reference to a view about the desirability of Jewish settlement in the holy land during the current period of exile that Morteira decides to rebut (above, pp. 127–128). And we have seen examples of his strong condemnation of Jewish behavior in his own community and abroad. In the current chapter, we will highlight such material more systematically to demonstrate the importance of the sermons as a reflection of the Portuguese community in Amsterdam.

INDIVIDUALS

The most important information about individuals comes in Mortiera's eulogies, which comprised a significant component of his homiletical output, although they appear to be underrepresented in the extant texts. Nevertheless, those that have survived are of significant artistic merit and value.[2] We have every reason to believe that he was called upon to engage in this type of preaching on a regular basis, throughout his career. Most of the relatively small number of eulogy texts present among the manuscripts are dated from the periods 1619–1624 and the 1650s, and some of the most important eulogies may well have been lost. For example, in what seems to be his earliest dated sermon, from the spring of 1617, Morteira refers to four reasons why a person may fail to fulfill his promise, "as we said in the eulogy for the distinguished rabbi R. Elijah Montalto, his soul in Eden."[3] That eulogy must have been delivered by the young Morteira when his mentor, Montalto, was brought from France for burial in the Jewish cemetery; indeed, it may have been the first public discourse Morteira delivered in Amsterdam, but the text does not exist among the Budapest manuscripts. Much later in his career, in the winter of 1649, Morteira re-used an earlier sermon "on the day

---

Ram's Horn," pp. 445–84). Assuming the validity of my analysis (pp. 447–53) that Landau's praises for the deceased empress were sincere, the question remains whether he was expressing the sentiments of his listeners or speaking against those sentiments.

2. See chapters 16 and 17 in *"Your Voice Like a Ram's Horn,"* pp. 367–444, for Morteira's eulogies at the deaths of David Farar and Menasseh ben Israel, with general introductory remarks on the genre, pp. 367–70. For background on the genre, see Elliott Horowitz, "Speaking of the Dead," in *Preachers of the Italian Ghetto,* ed. David Ruderman (Berkeley, 1992), pp. 129–62; for the funeral sermon in the contemporary Christian world, see Ralph Houlbrooke, *Death, Religion, and the Family in England, 1480–1750* (Oxford, 1998), pp. 295–330.

3. MS 1:71r, *Naso,* Num. 6:24–26, 1617. On Montalto, see above, pp. 4–5, n. 4.

of the completion of a year from the death of the young martyr Isaac Tartas, who was killed for the sanctification of God's name in the city of Lisbon, may it be destroyed in our days, and may God avenge His servant!"[4] Morteira reportedly delivered a eulogy for Tartas on the Sabbath after the news of his execution at the hands of the Inquisition reached Amsterdam.[5] The historical value of each of these eulogies, had they been preserved, would be immense. Nevertheless, the extant texts contain significant passages about some of the distinguished members of the community, and it is worth reviewing this material.

Abraham and Sarah Farar

The earliest dated eulogy is for Dr. Abraham Farar, one of the first leaders of the Amsterdam community. Records of Farar's trading activities, under the name Dr. Simon Lopes Rosa, date from 1606. He served as *parnas* of the Beth Jacob congregation in 1614 and 1616, and was instrumental in the purchase of the Ouderkerk cemetery. According to the records of the cemetery, he died and was buried there on December 14, 1618.[6] Morteira may have delivered a short address at the cemetery on the day of Farar's burial, but this text has not been preserved. Instead, we have the text of the eulogy he delivered on the thirtieth day following the death. Within this period, Farar's wife, Sarah had also died and been buried at Ouderkerk. Thus at the conclusion of the text, Morteira wrote, "The eulogy I delivered at the passing of the outstanding elderly physician, the distinguished gentleman Abraham Ferrar,[7] of blessed memory, who departed to the house of eternity in the company of his wife, Mrs. Sarah Ferrar, and this is what I composed on their gravestone, which covers them both."[8] Next to the year [5]379, an eight line inscription in the classical style of Spanish Hebrew poetry follows. At the conclusion of the introduction to the eulogy, the preacher wrote that he was speaking "today, the thirtieth day from their passing."[9]

Morteira's eulogy follows the structural pattern of his other sermons,

---

4. MS 4:198v, *Pequdei*, Exod. 38:22, 1649.

5. See Isaac Cardoso, cited by Yerushalmi, *From Spanish Court to Italian Ghetto*, p. 398.

6. Wilhelmina C. Pieterse, *Livro de Bet Haim do Kahal Kados de Bet Yahacob* (Assen, 1970), pp. 185, 93.

7. I use this spelling here to represent Morteira's Hebrew: פירר, although in my own text I use the more conventional spelling. In other eulogies, Morteira wrote the name inconsistently (see *"Your Voice Like a Ram's Horn,"* pp. 401 l. 58 and 410 l. 245).

8. MS 4:44r, Exod. 10:1, *Bo*, 1619.

9. Ibid., *"...ha-yom be-yom tashlum sheloshim li-fetiratam."*

beginning with a verse from the current scriptural lesson (Exod. 10:1)[10] and a rabbinic dictum, which provides the structure for the body of the discourse: "If a man dies smiling, it is a good omen for him, if weeping it is a bad omen…" (b. *Ketubot* 103b). Thus there was considerable material of a general nature pertaining to death and mourning. Indeed, on the back of the second sheet of paper, Morteira noted that he repeated the eulogy at the Neveh Shalom congregation on the 14th of Av, 5383 [August 10, 1623], at the death of Jacob da Fonseca, presumably with appropriate adaptations made. In our analysis we shall concentrate not on the homiletical material but on the specific references to Dr. Farar.

If one reason a dying person feels anguish is that he is abandoning his loved ones, this did not apply in the present case, for "they went together and were not separated." Morteira applies here the verse *Saul and Jonathan, beloved and cherished, never parted in life or in death! They were swifter than eagles, they were stronger than lions* (2 Sam. 1:23):

> So with this distinguished couple, beloved and cherished, in their lives and their deaths, they were not separated because of the constancy of their righteousness. *They were swifter than eagles,* eager to do the will of their Heavenly Father with great alacrity. And although the esteemed doctor was old and heavy, nevertheless he was swifter than an eagle, strong as a lion to go to the synagogue in the morning…. And so in their death, they were swift to follow each other.[11]

The reference to the age and apparent obesity of the deceased comes in response to the preacher's realization that his listeners may well have had an image of the physician that conflicted with the biblical image of swift eagles. A deft shift from the biblical to the rabbinic use of the phrase undercuts the potentially comic impact of this tension with a serious message: even though it may have been physically difficult for Dr. Farar to get to the synagogue each morning, he went there with more regularity than many younger, more agile Jews. Later in the eulogy, the preacher states explicitly that the deceased was 70 years old, making the date of his birth 1548.

---

10. Note that a different sermon on the same verse—the first verse in the *parashah*—is printed in *Giv'at Sha'ul.* Since the sermon on Exodus 10:3 is dated 1621 (MS 4:66v), the *Giv'at Sha'ul* sermon must have also been given in 1619. Apparently the eulogy was delivered on a Sunday, 30 days after the death on a Friday (see below), and the *Giv'at Sha'ul* sermon the following Saturday. In the eulogy, Morteira uses the last phrase of the verse, *that I may display these My signs upon him,* to recapitulate the "signs" of a good death specified in the rabbinic dictum and fulfilled in the deceased.

11. MS 4:43r. Exod. 10:1, *Bo,* 1619.

A second reason for anguish is the dying person's realization that he will no longer be able to attain greater merit through his own achievements. This also does not apply if the deceased has left behind a son like himself: such a son can increase his father's merit even after the father's death. In this case, Farar has "left a son who fills his place"—a reference to the outstanding younger Dr. David Farar, whom Morteira would eulogize less than six years later.[12] The attainments of his son also allowed him to face death with equanimity.

The third reason for anguish is the fear that one will not be worthy of eternal reward. This issue was a very real one for the ex-New Christian membership of the congregation: How severely would the transgressions of the Torah they committed while in Portugal count against them before the seat of divine judgment? Many in the congregation must have been in need of reassurance on this matter:

> This too would not have made him afraid. For if he looked into his deeds from the day he was circumcised, he would have found that he had committed no sin. Since all his sins were forgiven on the day of circumcision, it is certain that from that day on he never left off observing God's Torah with all his might and with all his soul, going to the synagogue early in the morning and in the evening. This is in addition to the sacrifice of his blood that he offered before God. Indeed it is true that on the day of circumcision, a person is considered to be a new creature…[13]

Morteira wanted to be unambiguously understood. Circumcision in the context of conversion serves as a sacrifice bringing atonement for past transgressions. It therefore has the effect of wiping the slate clean. No "sins" committed while living as a Christian in Portugal will be counted against the person who returns to Judaism; only behavior from the critical moment on is relevant. This certainly would have reassured listeners concerned about their own fate. To be sure, there was a paradoxical danger in this doctrine, for the realization that they would not be held accountable for anything done before circumcision might lead some to want to delay this ritual as long as possible.[14]

---

12. On the relationship between Abraham the Elder and David, see Saperstein, *"Your Voice,"* pp. 377, 396.

13. MS 4:43v.

14. On this issue, see the fascinating text published anonymously ca. 1650 in Italy, apparently by Rabbi Samuel Aboab (Yerushalmi, *From Spanish Court to Italian Ghetto,* pp. 198–202). The author decries "the vain idea that has spread among almost all the [*conversos*] that so long as a man is not circumcised he is not a part of Israel, that his sins are no sins…. And some claim that the day of their circumcision is, according to them, the first day on

That was a problem Morteira would address in other circumstances (see below, pp. 299–301), as we shall see later on. Here the message of the eulogy is one of comfort and support.

One final point applies to the circumstances of death in the case of the Farars. The rabbinic dictum states that it is a good sign when one dies on Friday. After explaining the reasons for this assertion, Morteira notes that this good sign applied "to both of these departed, miraculously, and on days that are so short, and that there was enough time to bury them before the Sabbath." And indeed, the records of the cemetery reveal that Sarah Farar died on Friday, December 28, 1618, exactly two weeks after her husband.[15] Thirty days after *her* death, Morteira delivered another, somewhat briefer discourse, which he labeled, "The eulogy I made over the honored and humble woman, Mrs. Sarah Ferrar, in the year [5]379."[16] Near the beginning he alludes to the speech he had delivered two weeks before: "It is especially appropriate to do in this regard what I did at the conclusion of the doctor's thirty-day period, his soul in Eden; I must also do this at the end of the thirty day period for his wife, for as they were equal in every respect, we should not set them apart."[17] This, unfortunately, adds little to our knowledge about the biography or personality of Sarah Farar. The two sermons together, however, provide a rather poignant glimpse of a New Christian couple that successfully made the transition to life in Amsterdam, probably while in their fifties, established themselves as respected members of the new community, accommodated themselves to a new religious lifestyle, and died within two weeks of one another. For many in the community, the couple may well have been viewed as a model of the older generation.[18]

---

which their sins begin to count, and so no one regrets his past evils.... But this opinion is erroneous and against the principles of our holy faith" (p. 200). The author appears to be responding to precisely the position expounded by Morteira here, although the main purpose of the passage is to condemn those who delay circumcision after coming to a land of freedom. Compare also the view expressed in an epistle circulated by an Amsterdam Jew in Bayonne, according to which even the commandments observed by emigrants from Portugal before circumcision have no merit: "Those members of the Nation who keep the commandments of the Torah before being circumcised have no part in divine grace, and they are condemned to eternal damnation." Yosef Kaplan, "Wayward New Christians and Stubborn New Jews," *Jewish History* 8 (1994): 32.

15. Pieterse, *Livro de Bet Haim*, p. 93.

16. MS 4:92r, *Yitro,* Exod. 19:4, 1619.

17. Ibid.

18. Contrast the muddled formulation by Henry Méchoulan: "Abraham Farrar, a Portuguese physician, was the first to challenge openly the orthodoxy of the young community when he refused to comply with the regulations for ritual slaughter. He went as far as to

Jacob Tirado

The next eulogy for a local figure was devoted to one of the giants of the founding generation; at its conclusion, Morteira wrote, "The eulogy I delivered on the lesson *Tetsavveh* in the year [5]380 at the demise of the noble, the fortunate, the honorable R. Jacob Tirado."[19] Unlike the Farar eulogies, this one was not delivered in conjunction with a death and burial that occurred in Amsterdam. Several years before, Tirado had departed for the land of Israel, where he died. His eulogy was therefore delivered when news of his death reached his former home. Much of it is a discussion of arguments relating to the immortality of the soul. For our purposes the important passages begin with a citation of the rabbinic statement, "Our father Jacob did not die" (b. *Ta'anit* 5b).

> Now we can apply this very same rabbinic dictum to the deceased, of blessed memory. The honorable R. Tirado, may his memory be for blessing, was called "Jacob." He was called "our father," for he was the father of this Jewish community and this synagogue. May God remember to his credit how he nurtured it as a father does a son, at considerable risk to life and fortune, and how he sustained it with his financial resources, sending abroad for scholars, purchasing a Torah scroll out of his own pocket. Indeed, he paid all the expenses of the synagogue from his own resources, without help from any others. Thus it is appropriate to call him "our father Jacob." Happy is he and happy his lot, having performed the acts of the three patriarchs: of Abraham, who built the first altar, where he invoked God by name (cf. Gen. 12:8), of Isaac, who placed his body in grave danger in order to observe the instruction of his God, of Jacob, who sustained and magnified that instruction despite the trouble he had with his children.[20]

Tirado's crucial role in the establishment and sustenance of the Beth Jacob synagogue is introduced as a powerful leitmotif of the eulogy. Indeed, Morteira describes that house of prayer as if it were a personal institution, financed almost entirely by a single individual. According to the eulogist,

---

secede and create a new synagogue, *Bet Israel*, in 1618:" "Hispanicity in Seventeenth-Century Amsterdam," in *In Iberia and Beyond*, ed. by Bernard Dov Cooperman, p. 365. For a correct version of this event, which applies to Abraham's son David, see Daniel Swetschinski in *The History of the Jews in the Netherlands*, p. 69 and, at greater length, Saperstein, *"Your Voice Like a Ram's Horn,"* pp. 373–74.

19. MS 1:77r, *Tetsavveh*, Exod. 27:20, 1620. For background on Tirado in Portugal, see H. P. Salomon, *Os primeiros Portugueses de Amesterdão* (Braga, 1983), pp. 18–19.

20. MS 1:77v.

Tirado was instrumental in three areas: providing for rabbinic leadership to come from abroad to Amsterdam, purchasing the synagogue's first Torah scroll, and underwriting the ongoing expenses after its establishment. Tantalizingly ambiguous is his reference to the "risk to life" incurred by Tirado as a result of his commitment to Jewish life in Amsterdam. He reiterates that risk in the reference to Isaac, "who placed his body in grave danger." Moreover, Tirado is described as one of the very few who was willing to do so at a time when most of the others hid their Judaism out of fear. The historical validity of these assertions will be discussed below.

First, however, we will consider Morteira's reference to another event, within the more recent memory of the listeners:

> Who will deny that during the period of the "tidings," the synagogues were closed in order to show that it was because of his merit that they were reopened.... God took away our synagogues during this period in order to show that they were opened because of the merit of this *tsaddiq*. It was virtually at the time of his death that they were confiscated.... May God preserve it because of his merit until the coming of our Messiah. Thus it is appropriate for us to call him "our father Jacob."[21]

Here the eulogist alludes to a recent painful experience in the life of the community, to which we shall also return. While the incident was quite immediate to the listeners, Tirado was geographically far removed from it, and Morteira felt it necessary to connect him to it in some way. The aggadic dictum brings the preacher back to further details of Tirado's biography, with language building to a rhetorical climax through anaphora:

> And we may say that "our father Jacob has not died" in any way. He has not died because in this synagogue, the House of Jacob, his name will endure forever. He has not died in the Society for Orphan Girls of Venice, where he donated 400 ducats when he passed through that city. He has not died in the speech of the poor in the land of Israel, where his absence will be remembered every day. He has not died in the many marriages he made possible for orphan girls in the Holy Land. He has not died in the memory of all who know his reputation.[22]

After rehearsing the extraordinary charitable commitments of Tirado in

---

21. Ibid. I have translated *ha-besorah* as "tidings" and *ne'esafu* as "confiscated," although the precise resonance of these terms in this context is uncertain.

22. Ibid.

Amsterdam, Venice, and the land of Israel, Morteira puts them in a more spiritual context:

> When God saw his goodness, he attained the merit of going to the Holy Land and being buried there. About him we may say, *O God, who may sojourn in Your tent, who may dwell on Your holy mountain? He who lives without blame, who does what is right, and speaks the truth with his heart* (Ps. 15:1-2).... As the Sages called Jacob "first among the blameless,"[23] so he was in this city first among the blameless, for he was the one who began to invoke God by name in this city. *Who does what is right* refers to the manifest righteousness of his abundant charitable disbursements, as is known to all his acquaintances. He was astounding in his generosity. *And speaks the truth with his heart* refers to the truth in his heart that he proclaimed publicly, unlike those who concealed it out of fear.[24]

What historical information can be distilled from this discourse? As a literary genre, of course, eulogies entail praise of the deceased rather than detached assessments of their strengths and weaknesses. Nevertheless, some of Tirado's qualities here are confirmed by specific sources and others help to fill in the blanks in the record.

To start at the end of the man's life, Odette Vlessing's study of the "earliest history of Amsterdam Portuguese Jews" states that "The place where [Tirado] died is unknown.... It seems likely that he died in the Holy Land, but we do not know for sure." Morteira's eulogy confirms the location of death and burial beyond question. Vlessing found in the archives of the Amsterdam community a record stating that on 4 Adar I, 5380 [February 8, 1620], sixteen members of the community said "*Menuha veascaba*" for Tirado. This date corresponds to the Saturday on which the lesson *Terumah* would have been read, while the lesson for our sermon is the following one, *Tetsavveh;* the memorial was apparently held as soon as the news arrived. Morteira already had a sermon ready for that auspicious Sabbath of *Terumah* (see below), so he prepared his eulogy for the following week. Another archival document described by Vlessing records that on 27 Nissan 5374 [March 27, 1614], Tirado donated 400 ducats to the Society For Marrying Orphans of Venice; the purpose of his gift was "for supporting orphan girls in the Holy Land."[25] This document provides perfect confirmation of two details in the eulogy:

---

23. Esther Rabbah, Proem 10.

24. MS 1:77v.

25. All references to Odette Vlessing, ""New Light on the Earliest History of the Amsterdam Portuguese Jews," *Dutch Jewish History* 3 (1993): 68, n. 36.

Morteira's specification of the 400 ducat contribution, and his reference to the "many marriages he made possible for orphan girls in the Holy Land."[26] In 1616, the year Morteira arrived in Amsterdam, the leadership of Beth Jacob sent 712 florins to Tirado to distribute among the poor of Jerusalem.[27] Thus the eulogist could say that Tirado "has not died in the speech of the poor in the land of Israel, where his absence will be remembered every day."

We have cited the reference in the eulogy to the time of the "tidings," when the synagogues were closed. This event is chronologically juxtaposed by Morteira with the death of Tirado so that a homiletical-theological interpretation can be given: God brought about the temporary loss of the synagogues in order to show the great merit of Tirado, in accordance with the rabbinic statement, "At Aaron's death the clouds [of glory] disappeared, at Miriam's death the well, at Moses's death the mannah."[28] But in a sermon bound in a totally different part of the manuscript collection, the event is referred to in less spiritual terms. Morteira records that this sermon was preached "on the Sabbath when the synagogue was opened after it had been closed by order of the authorities for two weeks."[29] Here is the description of the event by a modern historian: "In January 1620, representatives of the three congregations met together in order to direct a common struggle against dangers that threatened the Jews. Among others, the municipality, under pressure from the church consistory, prohibited public prayer. The Jewish initiative achieved its goal, for in March of the same year, the Calvinist church consistory again complained that the public prayers had not been stopped."[30] The sermon delivered by Morteira on the reopening of the synagogue is dated 1620, and it is on the lesson *Terumah,* the lesson immediately preceding

---

26. The standard amount made available by the Society for the daughter of a member was 300 ducats; a worthy girl not related to a member would be given 100 ducats. See Bodian, "The 'Portuguese' Dowry Societies in Venice and Amsterdam," p. 33. For support by this Society of candidates outside of Venice, including Jerusalem and Safed, see ibid., p. 38.

27. Yaari, *Sheluḥei Eretz Yisra'el,* p. 266 n. 10, citing Brugmans-Frank, *Geschiedenis der Joden in Nederland,* p. 226.

28. Cf. Num. Rabbah 1,2.

29. MS 3:32v, *Terumah,* Exod. 25:3, 1620.

30. Jozeph Michman, "Introduction," in *Pinqas ha-Qehillot: Holland* (Jerusalem, 1985), pp. 3–4. The complaint of the Dutch Reformed Church to the Burgomasters of Amsterdam concerning the liberal General Regulation pertaining to the Jews of December 1619 is recorded in the protocols of the church council; see E. M. Koen, "The Earliest Sources Relating to the Portuguese Jews in the Municipal Archives of Amsterdam up to 1620," *StRos* 4 (1970): 36. I have not found a record of the temporary action taken by the municipal authorities in response to this complaint.

Tetsavveh, when the Tirado eulogy was delivered. The juxtaposition of these two sermons suggests the powerful resonance Morteira's remark about the closing of the synagogues would have had for those listening to the eulogy.

When Morteira speaks about the role of Tirado in the early days of the Portuguese settlement, he was obviously dependent upon reports from others. Yet the importance of this homiletical testimony is major, because the next evidence of Tirado's role was written several generations later: the narrative of Daniel Levi de Barrios characterizes Tirado, a merchant from Portugal, and Uri Halevi of Emden, as the two founders of Judaism in Amsterdam.[31] De Barrios tells of a secret prayer meeting held by Portuguese Jews on the Day of Atonement, probably in September of 1596. It was raided by the Dutch authorities, who had been apprised of an illicit Catholic rite. Uri Halevi and his son Aaron were arrested, and their lives were in jeopardy until Tirado successfully intervened and convinced the authorities to grant permission for the Jews to establish a congregation.[32]

This tradition has been questioned by recent scholarship for various reasons: its provenance is late—the work of a writer who arrived in Amsterdam only in 1662—and it seems to have an obvious mythic quality. In another source, written by the grandson of Uri Halevi and printed in 1711, no role is granted to Tirado at all, and the death penalty is threatened not because of illicit worship but because of circumcising Portuguese men living in Amsterdam.[33] Testimonials from 1673 and 1674 mention only Uri Halevi (or Uri and his son Aaron), and not Tirado, as "founder of Judaism in Amsterdam."[34] Based on these considerations, Salomon has suggested that the entire tradition of the dramatic Yom Kippur raid may have been a transformation of a raid on an actual Catholic observance of a Christmas mass, recorded in the archives for 1596.[35] Moreover, Vlessing has questioned whether the Beth Jacob congregation was indeed the oldest in Amsterdam, citing the absence of historical evidence for de Barrios's claim of primacy for that synagogue.[36]

The passage in the eulogy speaking of the mortal risks taken by Tirado for his observance of Judaism at an early stage requires us to consider the de

31. H. P. Salomon, "Myth or Anti-Myth?," p. 308 n. 64.

32. Ibid., p. 277. On the 1596 date, see Carsten Lorenz Wilke, review of H. P. Salomon, *Deux études portugaises*, in *REJ* 151 (1992): 392. Cf. also the account in Bodian, *Hebrews of the Portuguese Nation*, p. 22.

33. Ibid., p. 280.

34. Ibid., p. 292; original on p. 314: "fundador do judesmo nesta vila de Amsterdam," "primeiras pedras do judaismo."

35. Ibid., pp. 302–3.

36. Vlessing, pp. 47, 52.

Barrios tradition more seriously: other elements of that description do seem to fit what is known from archival records of Tirado's role. Religious worship was held in the house of Tirado in 1610.[37] It stands to reason that Tirado would have been instrumental in bringing Joseph Pardo and his son David to Amsterdam from Venice in late 1608 or early 1609, for Joseph to serve as rabbi of the Beth Jacob congregation. When the Pardos were arrested because of a bad debt, it was Tirado who intervened and secured their release by agreeing to guarantee repayment.[38] And when Beth Jacob split into two congregations in 1618 and their dispute over communal property was brought to an Amsterdam court, the parties turned to Jacob Tirado far away in the land of Israel to verify the circumstances of donation of a disputed Torah scroll.[39] Morteira's remarks about Tirado—sending abroad to bring scholars, purchasing a Torah scroll from his own funds, paying the expenses of the synagogue out of his own pocket—are not at all in the realm of legend. And if these activities were well known, the danger Tirado once faced must have also been known at least to some in the audience. Thus his pioneering courage in worshiping as a Jew at a time when most others continued to live openly as Christians fits what we know of the realities of the community, even in the first years of the new century.[40]

David Farar

Remarkably similar themes appear in Morteira's two eulogies for Dr. David Farar,[41] son of Abraham and Sarah. There were obvious differences in the circumstances. Unlike Tirado, whom Morteira may never have met, David

---

37. Ibid. p. 48, Bodian, *Hebrews of the Portuguese* Nation, pp. 44–45; cf. J. d'Ancona, "Komst der Marranen in Noord-Nederland," in H. Brugmans and A. Frank, eds. *Geschiedenis der Joden in Nederland* I (Amsterdam, 1940), p. 213.

38. Vlessing, p. 47.

39. Ibid., p. 50. Bodian reports that the Torah scroll was donated to the congregation by Uri Halevi, while Tirado and his wife Rachel "donated a silver Torah breastplate decorated with the crown of the Amsterdam coat of arms" (p. 45). If this is accurate, Morteira may have slightly misstated the fact, but not distorted the underlying reality.

40. Cf. Salomon, "Myth or Anti-Myth," p. 303: "The majority of Portuguese New Christians who lived in Amsterdam at the end of the 16th and the beginning of the 17th century were 'marranos,' in the sense that they openly professed protestantism and secretly observed catholicism."

41. For a full analysis of these texts, with the original Hebrew and annotated translation, see Saperstein, *"Your Voice Like a Ram's Horn,"* pp. 367–410. My discussion here summarizes the material most relevant to the current subject. Morteira also reports a eulogy he delivered at the death of Rabbi Isaac Uziel, his older colleague in the Amsterdam rabbinate, in the early spring of 1622, but this was just a repetition of what he preached two years earlier (on

Farar was a leader of the community with whom Morteira had a close personal relationship. Moreover, this was not a eulogy for a notable who died far away. Farar died in Amsterdam, at a relatively young age, after a brief illness. The first, shorter text was delivered in the cemetery at the time of the burial, while the second—as with David Farar's parents—was given at the end of the thirty-day period of mourning. A personal voice can be heard behind the written words of these manuscripts, a voice not commonly evident in Morteira's preaching. Yet beyond the human dimension of a eulogizer compelled to speak out of his own intense pain, there is material important for an understanding of the early leadership of the Portuguese community.

As in the case of Tirado, Farar is described as having "loved God to the point of endangering his body." That elliptical phrase from the first eulogy, delivered at the cemetery, is clarified a bit in the second, delivered after thirty days:

> Wherever he went, God's name was invoked upon him. During the first years in this land, when people used to conceal their [Jewish] names, he would proclaim his in public, as occasions frequently presented themselves.... Even in Spain [here meaning the Iberian peninsula, and specifically Portugal] in a place of danger, he did not conceal it, but identified himself as a "Jew," a word in which the name of God is contained.[42]

Here Morteira evokes the communal memory—all but suppressed in the late-seventeenth-century historiography—of a period when most of the Portuguese immigrants lived as Christians, and only a few heroic figures openly professed a Jewish identity. The passage suggests that if there was indeed a clandestine observance of Yom Kippur in which Uri Halevi and Tirado were leaders, Farar, and perhaps his parents, may well have participated as well. The precise circumstances of Farar's self-endangerment on the Iberian peninsula may have been familiar to some of the listeners, but they cannot be established today. His wide recognition as a spokesman for Judaism, stemming from his public debate with the British scholar Hugh

---

a different lesson) at the death of the Kabbalists Hayim Vital and Menahem Azariah of Fano, and there is no specific content about Uziel. MS 2:239v, *Ki Tetse,* Deut. 21:17.

42. Ibid., p. 378. Compare the passage in the preface to a 1675 Amsterdam sermon cited by Miriam Bodian, in which the author praises an ex-*converso* for having observed the Divine Law "fearless of the cruel dangers perpetrated by our adversaries' malice." Bodian, *Hebrews of the Portuguese Nation,* p. 91.

Broughton in 1608, continued to the point where "many Gentiles came from far away to seek him out."[43]

In addition to his defiant role as exemplar of and spokesman for Judaism in the early years of the community, and despite the public conflict in which he became embroiled, Farar maintained a position of leadership and prestige to the end of his life. Morteira states in both eulogies that he held the office of *parnas u-memmuneh* in the year of his death. He was also "physician of the *Biqqur Holim* Society," one of the most important confraternities of the community (see below); in this capacity, he "healed the poor cheerfully, going up to their houses, and giving them charity." We learn from the eulogy that Farar had the honor of standing to the right of the cantor on the Days of Awe, and that he regularly delivered sermons in the synagogue, some of which may have gotten him into trouble with listeners of a more conservative intellectual bent.[44] In addition to his work as a physician, he had commercial interests in international trade, and he used his financial resources for charitable ends: "When his ships arrived [in port], the poor, the orphan and the widow would rejoice when they went forth from his house. People entered and left carrying many gifts."

Farar is also described as having established an academy (*yeshivah*).[45] The background to this fact may be found in a short sermon on the lesson *Bo*, to which Morteira appended the remark, "The sermon I delivered on the first day of Shevat 5380 [Monday, January 6, 1620], in the house of the physician, the honorable R. David Ferrar, may God protect and preserve him, at the end of the first year of our school (*beit midrashenu*). May it be God's will that such may grow and spread."[46] We recall that the eulogy delivered at the end of the thirty-day mourning period for Farar's father, Abraham the Elder, was on the lesson *Bo* in 1619, just one year before. This suggests that David Farar decided to establish an academy, possibly to meet in his house, on precisely that occasion, in honor of his recently deceased parents, marking the humble beginnings of higher Torah learning in Amsterdam. Perhaps the most moving passage in the eulogies is that in which Morteira describes his own personal indebtedness to Farar: "Physically, for he was so diligent regarding my recuperation and the healing of those in my household without taking any pay-

---

43. Ibid. On the debate with Broughton, see ibid., pp. 371–73.

44. Ibid., pp. 379–80.

45. Ibid., p. 380.

46. MS 4:62v, *Bo,* Exod. 10:9, 1620. The sermon concludes with the prayer that God will favor the owner of the house "and give him children and make him prosper in his possessions, as is promised to all who engage in Torah." According to the eulogies, the second wish was apparently fulfilled, but the first was not, as Farar died childless.

ment.... Financially, inasmuch as he is the reason why I am in the situation I am in today. Spiritually, for from his deeds I learned to serve God properly."[47] Such a proclamation is not lightly made by a rabbi in public, and it bespeaks the powerful impact on the young Morteira of this charismatic physician.

David Masiah

Similar themes to those found in the eulogies for Jacob Tirado and David Farar appear in a later eulogy for David Masiah (Mexia), the full text of which is translated below. As in the case of the elder Farar eulogies, this one was delivered not at the funeral itself but thirty days later: "The eulogy I delivered at the conclusion of the thirty days from the passing of the pious and humble doctor, the honorable David Masiah, may the memory of a *tsaddiq* and saint be for blessing, on Wednesday, the twelfth of Adar, 5412 [February 22, 1652]."[48] (This accords with the records of the community and the grave in the Ouderkerk cemetery, which record the date of Masiah's death as 13 Shevat, 5412 [January 23, 1652].)[49]

The rabbinic dictum is the statement from *Berakhot*, "In the future world, there is no eating, no drinking, no procreation, no commercial activity, no jealousy, no hatred, no competition. Rather, the righteous sit with their diadems on their heads, delighting in the radiance of the divine presence" (b. *Berakhot* 17a). After a discussion of theoretical matters relating to body and soul in the world to come, the "diadems" lead, in the second part of the eulogy, to the rabbinic statement from *Avot*, "There are three crowns, the crown of Torah, the crown of priesthood, and the crown of royalty, but the crown of a good name is superior to them all" (M. *Avot* 4:13). The preacher insists that these are not to be taken literally as applying only to distinguished scholars, kings from the line of David, or priests from the descendants of Aaron. Rather, they can pertain to any Jew. This is shown by correlating the statement about the crowns with another statement from *Avot*: "Who is wise? He that learns from every person.... Who is mighty? He who conquers his [evil] impulse.... Who is wealthy? He who is content with his lot.... Who is honored? He that honors all creatures" (M. *Avot* 4:1). Each principle is then applied to

---

47. Saperstein, *"Your Voice Like a Ram's Horn,"* p. 376.

48. MS 1:81v, *Tetsavveh,* Exod. 27:20.

49. I am grateful to Odette Vlessing for providing me information about Masiah from the community archives. The inscription on the tombstone reads: "The grave in which rests one free of the world [Li vre do mundo], who knew how to despise it; the help of the poor, the aid of the widows, who in his life was called Dr David Masiah, whom the Blessed God summoned on the 13th day of Shevat, in the year 5412."

the deceased. After this homiletical beginning, the concluding section contains some of the most detailed personal material in any of Morteira's eulogies.

The first unit about the crown of Torah and the wise person learning from everyone tells us about Masiah's commitment to study. In the "Gentile lands," he attempted to learn and memorize some of the commandments; he sought out books or pamphlets that would clarify difficult points, both for his own benefit and "in order to teach sinners God's way and bring them close to Torah." In Amsterdam, he made the rounds of the yeshivas at night, yet was present for morning study and prayer even before daybreak. Yet despite his devotion to Torah learning, Masiah was not a scholar. His special qualities are revealed in the following sections, worth quoting at length:

> As for the crown of priesthood, [he wears this as well,] for he was a hero, conquering his impulses, and sanctifying himself in what is permitted to him. Did he not, in the sight of everyone, set aside his own affairs and tend to the poor? He did not refrain even from matters that arouse disgust in most people. He was thoughtful toward the wretched (cf. Ps. 41:2), both emotionally and physically. Those in pain, covered with scabs—he would wash them himself and cut their hair. Every Friday he would leave aside his own work and go to the jail to bring the prisoners meat, so that they would not do work on the Sabbath. He would take the bread from his own mouth, being himself poor and hard pressed, and divide it among the poor, as I myself have seen on a number of occasions. When he was arrested because some accused him of speaking against their beliefs, when Friday came he would banish from his heart all sadness and worry, adorning himself and cutting his own hair in order to receive the Sabbath with joy, for he always conquered his impulses and his emotions for the love of his Creator. How he afflicted himself here among us with fasts and ascetic discipline! And even in Portugal, for many years no meat crossed his lips, so as not to defile himself with something forbidden. Is he not a hero who conquers his impulse? He is a priest of the most high God..[50]

These words of praise, vivid, specific and detailed, are worlds apart from the conventional and generalized praises that fill so many eulogies. Masiah's life is not presented chronologically, and it is not always clear how the pieces fit together, but patterns do emerge. While he was in Portugal, he refrained from eating meat, as no kosher meat was available. If this refers to a time while he

---

50. Ibid., 1:81r. For more detailed annotation, see the full text translated below (pp. 527–35).

was living as a New Christian, it would have been a dangerous risk; if to a time when he had already been denounced to the Inquisition, it would have been open and reckless defiance. His arrest following an accusation of blasphemous attacks on Christian beliefs could have occurred in Portugal, but it seems more likely to have taken place in Amsterdam. Despite the relative freedom for Jews there, the ground rules of toleration prohibited expressions of blatant contempt for Christian doctrine. Morteira's reference to Masiah's observance of the Sabbath in prison seems to reflect a personal knowledge.

In either case, having been imprisoned, Masiah remembered what it was like, and brought meat to Jewish prisoners to safeguard against infringement of the dietary laws and the Sabbath. This detail reflects an issue of concern to the leadership of the Portuguese community. In the late sixteenth century, the governing council of Amsterdam had established a "house where all vagabonds, evildoers, rascals and the like could be imprisoned." Later known as the "Rasphuis" (Saw-House), it was intended to transform idlers and beggars into productive members of society.[51] Especially after the immigration of impoverished East European refugees to Amsterdam following 1648, the problem of Ashkenazic Jews imprisoned in the Rasphuis spurred the Portuguese leadership to action. Yosef Kaplan lists a number of edicts preserved in the community archives concerning aid given to these Ashkenazim. Especially noteworthy is a regulation of 1658 expressing both exasperation and distress: "This city has become a place of refuge for empty and idle people, so that every day many of them are imprisoned for loitering, and they are forced to violate the holy Torah and the blessed Lord, both in eating the forbidden foods given to them in prison and violating the Sabbath and other holy days."[52] Morteira's eulogy for Masiah provides evidence of how a member of the Portuguese community acted to address this religious and humanitarian problem.

The other themes similarly pertain to Masiah's selfless concern for the most wretched and downtrodden members of Jewish society. He personally tended and cared for those so sick they aroused disgust in others. Unlike Tirado and Farar, this was not a wealthy man. Yet, we are told by the preacher, he was "wealthy" in being contented with his lot: "Although he lacked everything, he never asked for anything from anyone, neither as a gift, nor as a loan. Nor did he complain. It was as if he lacked nothing."[53] Because of his own limited means, his sacrifice in caring for the poor was significant.

---

51. Schama, *The Embarrassment of Riches*, pp. 17–20.

52. Kaplan, "The Portuguese Community in 17th-Century Amsterdam and the Ashkenazi World," p. 37.

53. MS 1:81v, *Tetsavveh*, Exod. 27:20, 1:81r.

He would share his own food with them—Morteira vividly claims to have seen him take bread "from his own mouth" to do so. This theme is taken up in the following paragraph:

> Who was unaware of this: that all his fulfillment and all his desire was in honoring every person, especially the destitute widows and the modest maidens, who did not have enough to get by. Why, he used to serve them joyfully, like a servant, always going to their doors to ask if they needed anything. And he used to buy them meat and bread and vegetables, and whatever they needed. Is there a single person, old or young, in this sacred congregation, who ever had even a minor exchange with him that was not in love and affection?[54]

Finally, the preacher reminds his listeners of the element of personal piety: "How he afflicted himself here among us with fasts and ascetic discipline." This is a rather different model from that of the better-known former New Christian physicians and international merchants. While he was indeed apparently well known within the community—and Morteira notes that "no one failed to volunteer to provide for his medical needs while he was alive, and to provide for his burial after he died"—this kind of piety was not usually manifest in positions of communal leadership. Yet the eulogist conveys a powerful assurance that this life style merited the highest possible reward.

Some time after January 5, 1617, a "New Christian" named Francisco Rodrigues de Olivença, who had joined the Portuguese community in Amsterdam under the name David Mexia, left Amsterdam to make a journey back to Portugal. Knowing that he would have to conceal his Jewish identity, yet wishing to continue his Jewish observance in secret, he took with him a paper with the dates of the major Jewish holidays for 1617 through 1619 and several pages of a recently printed Spanish translation of the Sabbath liturgy. On March 12, 1618, Mexia was arrested and imprisoned by the Portuguese Inquisition in Lisbon, and the incriminating pages, which he had attempted to conceal, became part of the docket of evidence against him.[55]

Could these details correspond to what we learn in Masiah's eulogy? Given the notorious irregularity of spelling for names in communal records, Masiah is a plausible Hebraization of the Portuguese surname Mexia. The eulogist's

---

54. Ibid. Odette Vlessing reports from the records of the community that Masiah paid the very low annual contribution (*finta*) of 4 guilders, and that his free-will offerings (*promessas*) were also low, indicating that he was indeed poor, though not himself dependent on charity (private communication of 17 June 1998).

55. I. S. Révah, "*Fragments retrouvés de quelques éditions amstelodamoises de la version espagnole du rituel juif*," *StRos* 2 (1968): 108–10.

reference to Masiah's refusal to eat meat for several years in Portugal fits the circumstances of his journey after a return to Judaism. What is not clear is how he would have been able to get out of the Inquisition's prison, leave Portugal, and return to the Jewish community in Amsterdam.[56]

Students

Not all of the extant eulogies are for leaders or major figures of the community. As we have seen in chapter one, in an introduction to the commentaries on Ecclesiastes and Psalms written by his disciple, Moses Mercado, and published in 1652 a few months after the young student's death, Morteira summarized his current position in Amsterdam:

> Now, God be praised, about forty "armed soldiers" in the war of Torah regularly eat at my table, some of them masters Mishnah and Talmud, some in the legendary and rhetorical texts, some of them eloquent preachers, some focus on the simple meaning of Bible, some are poets, some experts in books of metaphysics. For all of them, reverence for God is their treasure (cf. Isa. 33:6). All of the scholars who have visited us observed this with astonishment (Ps. 48:6); they examined these students and said, "God's blessing is upon you, and we bless you in God's name."[57]

As the years of Morteira's tenure in Amsterdam progressed, he developed a relationship with students, some of whom he was unfortunately called upon to eulogize. One is identified as "the sermon I made at the conclusion of seven days from the death of my esteemed and highly intelligent student, Samuel Valverde, may his soul rest in peace. It was on Monday, the 29th day of the month of Tishri in the year 5414 [20 October, 1653]."[58] We should note that this was an additional preaching obligation, on a weekday, at the conclusion of a full month of the heaviest responsibilities in the calendar. Most of the

---

56. The last will and testament of Ilona Gomes, the wife of Francisco Rodrigues d'Olivença, was recorded on May 31, 1621. At that time she was living at the house of a Thomas Fernandes. Yet her husband was still alive, as she bequeathed to him a large cup, while dividing most of her estate among her three sisters. These provisions might be explained on the assumption that her husband was at this time still in prison in Portugal. Wilhelmina C. Pieterse and E. M. Koen, "Notarial Records Relating to the Portuguese Jews in Amsterdam up to 1639," *StRos* 19 (1985): 83. It should be noted that there may have been two different men by the name of David Masiah in Amsterdam (Vlessing, communication of 17 June, 1998).

57. Mercado, *Perush Sefer Qohelet u-Tehillim*, Morteira's Introduction, column 4.

58. MS 3:90v, *Noah*, Gen. 6:9, 1653. The year, cut off in the microfilm because it is so close to the inner edge of the page, is legible from the manuscript itself.

sermon investigates the various kinds of "rest" mentioned in the Bible and the rabbinic literature, concluding that the true scholar will not rest from his efforts to apprehend God through Torah even in the afterlife. "And this is true of this fine young man, a father in wisdom though young in years, who toiled over God's Torah with great intellectual effort: even there he will not rest from enjoying the radiant countenance of the King of life."[59] The tribute to the young scholar seems rather stereotyped and impersonal; no clues are given either to the personality of the deceased or to the circumstances of his death. It is of course possible that Morteira had already delivered a eulogy at the actual funeral a week earlier in which more personal material was included.

A little more than two years earlier, he had eulogized a former student who had left Amsterdam and served as a rabbi in Hamburg. At the end of the text, Morteira wrote: "The eulogy I made over the consummate *hakham,* our distinguished rabbi and teacher Abraham da Fonseca, who died in Hamburg. I delivered it in the year 5411 on Sunday, the 16th of the month of Iyar [May 7, 1651]."[60] After discussing the rabbinic principle of taking leave of another person with words of Torah, he applies it to the eulogy, which brings joy to the soul of the deceased. "And so as this obligation has come to us with the passing of the consummate scholar, our esteemed rabbi and teacher Abraham da Fonseca, who taught Torah in the holy community of Hamburg, as he was a branch of our school, we shall bring some satisfaction to his soul by explicating our rabbinic dictum [from b. *Berakhot* 17a], which is a prototype for him and describes him in every respect."[61] After explaining each phrase of the dictum, he returns to the deceased, "who from his youth grew up among us." Again there is little distinctive about the description, and it is difficult to evaluate da Fonseca's relationship with Morteira.[62] The eulogy does, how-

---

59. MS 3:90r.

60. MS 3:49v, *Be-Har,* Lev. 25:41, 1651. The Hebrew states, ודרשתי אותו בשנת התי"א יום א' ט"ו לחדש אייר . However, the 15th of Iyar was a Saturday, which is consistent with the date of death appearing on Fonseca's tombstone in Hamburg: Tuesday, the 4th of Iyar. Since it is more likely that Morteira erred in writing the Hebrew date in the month (writing ט"ו rather than ט"ז) than that he erred on the day of the week, I assume that the correct date is Sunday, 16 Iyar, twelve days after the death. For the Hamburg date, see Michael Studemund-Halévy, *Biographisches Lexikon der Hamburger Sefarden* (Hamburg, 2000), pp. 422–23.

61. MS 3:48r.

62. Daniel de Barrios, giving the cast of the "Dialogo dos montes," performed in 1624, in which da Fonseca played Mount Sinai, described him as "primer dicipulo del Jaxam Saul Levi Mortera." See Jessurun, *Dialogo dos montes,* p. xiv. It is somewhat surprising that Morteira does not mention in his eulogy da Fonseca's writings, such as his *'Einei Avraham,*

ever, reveal a certain pride in having been able to provide rabbinic leadership for the much older German city.

The third eulogy for a student is somewhat different in tone. Unlike all of the other eulogies, the Hebrew text (translated in full below) contains no notation of the date or circumstances of delivery. But a Portuguese version of the eulogy was printed, with important information on the title page: first, it was delivered "in the cemetery" (*em bet aHaim*), like the first eulogy for David Farar, obviously at the time of burial; second, the name of the deceased is given: "Hacham Ribi Moseh de Mercado"; and finally, the date of death is presented as the Sabbath day, 23 Tammuz, 5412 [Saturday, July 29, 1652]. David Franco Mendes recorded that Morteira delivered his eulogy on the 24th of Tammuz, 5412; since the death occurred on the Sabbath, the funeral service would have taken place on the following day.[63] The introduction to the eulogy alludes to the situation. Probably gesturing toward the coffin beneath him in the cemetery, Morteira says, "No less than this is the spectacle that is before us. When we see this flower, *who bloomed like a blossom and then withered* (Job 14:2),"[64] the normal impulse would be to remain silent for seven days, like the companions of Job. However, he continues, even though he himself is in need of comfort, he will fulfill the injunction "Let the honor of your disciple be as precious to you as your own."

After the homiletical treatment of the reasons for the death of an outstanding person at a young age, Morteira speaks in a more personal vein:

> From all of these examples, who would not know how all of us should bewail and feel pain over the loss of this wise and intelligent young man, may the memory of the righteous be for blessing, the esteemed R. Moses de Mercado. By his Torah learning, his perfection, his youthfulness, and his noble character traits, God is honored through

---

an index on the Bible and Midrash, published at Amsterdam in 1628 (Studemund-Halévy, *Biographisches Lexikon*, p. 422).

63. David Franco Mendes, *Memorias do estabelecimento e progresso dos judeos portuguezes e espanhoes nest famosa citade de Amsterdam*, ed. L. Fuks (Amsterdam, 1975), p. 62: "Le mesmo A[nn]o [5412] em 24 tamus [30.VII] darsou o H[a]H[am] Saul Levi Morteyra, prim[eir]o Rab da quehila, exequias na esnoga por seu estimado discipulo R. Mosseh de Mercado ז״ל comentador do תהלים & קהלת : esse serṁao deo o s[obr]ed[it]o J[ah]am ao prello p[ar]a perpetuar a memoria dos meritos de d[it]o seu discipulo." Franco Mendes also notes that Jacob Sasportas delivered a eulogy on the seventh day, a version of which was also published (p. 161 n. 132).

64. MS 1:119r, *Mattot*, Num. 30:17. 1652. The word I have rendered "spectacle" is *nosei*, corresponding to the Portuguese *o espectaculó*. For an annotated translation of the entire sermon, see below, pp. 537–43.

him. God found him in a state of perfection, for when he was less than twenty years old he had already written a commentary on Psalms and had almost completed his commentary on Ecclesiastes, not to mention his fine, highly rhetorical poems.[65]

Here was a student, a prodigy, in whom Morteira, now in his mid-fifties, obviously took considerable pride. His death before his full potential could be realized seems to have shocked and moved the eulogist genuinely. Indeed, he seems to have felt an obligation to give more permanent form to his memorial tribute for the young man, not only by printing a Portuguese text of the eulogy but by writing an introduction to his disciple's two commentaries, which were printed the following year. Like da Fonseca, Mercado was proof of the talent the community could produce.

Menasseh ben Israel

The most dramatic proof of that talent was Morteira's brilliant and famous younger colleague, Menasseh ben Israel. The relations between Morteira and Menasseh had been complicated, and at times quite tense.[66] Yet as senior rabbi of the community where Menasseh had been educated and then established his career, Morteira would have been expected to pay tribute when Menasseh's body was brought from Middleburg for burial in the Ouderkerk cemetery, following the apparently devastating failure of his mission to seek the readmission of Jews to Oliver Cromwell's London. Morteira did not speak at the actual burial, but a week later. For this purpose, he resorted to an earlier sermon, interspersing and adding material from a separate page with the heading:

> And I preached it again in the year 5418 [1657] at the conclusion of seven days from the burial of the Hakham Rabbi Menasseh ben Israel, may the memory of the righteous be for a blessing. He passed away in Middleburg, on his way from London. This was on the second day of the week, the 20th of the month of Kislev [Monday, November 26]. And I added what follows.[67]

As I have shown elsewhere, Morteira used the occasion to argue a controversial point on which he and Menasseh agreed: opposition to the new

---

65. MS 1:120r.

66. See *"Your Voice Like a Ram's Horn,"* pp. 412–13.

67. Ibid. English p. 424, Hebrew p. 435. For a discussion of the problems entailed in the dating, see pp. 414–15, n. 14.

tendency toward ornately sculptured tombstones.[68] Particularly relevant to the situation of Menasseh's last great endeavor—his largely unsuccessful mission on behalf of readmission of Jews to England—is Morteira's application of the rabbinic statement, "Whoever thinks of performing a mitzvah and, for reasons beyond his control, is unable to do it, is considered as if he had indeed performed it."[69] Moving closer to the situation at hand, he applies the model of Jacob and Joseph, who sought to guarantee that they would be buried in their ancestral plot at Hebron, to Menasseh's body being transported for burial in Ouderkerk.

> God has granted him the reward about which the righteous of old felt so strongly, for which they made such great exertion: to be buried in the graves of their ancestors.... Miraculously, he has arrived here, for *God will not deprive the soul of the righteous* (Prov. 10:3). He has come to his place, which he loved so much, thereby revealing his own merit, and giving us the merit that comes from burying him and from mourning him in a manner appropriate to our master and teacher.[70]

Reference to the recent death of another rabbi from the community provides an opportunity for a rather ingenious application of the theme-verse from the scriptural lesson, and leads to a climactic rehearsal of Menasseh's talents:

> This new pain of our sorrow is especially great, for only eight months ago the pious scholar Rabbi David Pardo departed from us (may the memory of the sacred pious be for blessing).[71] And *afterward, his brother* [i.e., Menasseh] *exited*, as we said at the beginning in our theme-verse, *by his hand the crimson thread* (Gen. 38:30). To understand this, recall that crimson is a metaphor for splendor of speech and eloquence, as in the verse, *Your lips are like a crimson thread, your speech is lovely* (Song 4:3). And his beautiful eloquence, his delightful words, were not in his mouth alone, but also *by his hand*, in his books, which he wrote in such an elegant style. *Therefore he was named Zerah* (Gen. 38:30), "shining," for his radiance has shone throughout the world.[72]

---

68. See the full Hebrew text, annotated translation, and introduction, ibid., pp. 411–44, especially pp. 414, 419–20. For the simple tombstones of Menasseh and Morteira, see Castro, *Keur van grafsteenen*, pp. 56–59.

69. B. *Berakhot* 6a.

70. Ibid., English p. 433, Hebrew p. 444.

71. The inscription on his tombstone shows that David Pardo died on the first day of Nisan, 1657 (15 March, 1657).

72. Ibid., pp. 433–34, 444.

This text bears the latest date of any of the eulogies preserved among the manuscripts. Less than three years later, Morteira himself would be eulogized. Facing this prospect, he may have found some comfort in the realization that, while not an old man, he had reached an age considerably beyond some of the radiant stars from the community—such as David Farar and Menasseh—at whose death he had spoken.

COMMUNITY EVENTS

A fascinating example of how a sermon can respond to events of immediate concern in the community and complement other documents pertaining to these events is an undated sermon on *Shoftim,* the only sermon on this lesson preserved in the manuscripts. The allusions to events that all in the congregation would have known, and the use of a personal voice by the preacher, make this quite different from most of the other manuscript sermons. As Morteira indicates that he is preaching "this evening," it is likely that it was not delivered on the Sabbath but rather at a special gathering, and from its content, we see it an occasional sermon. The theme-verse, a segment of Deuteronomy 18:2 (*The Eternal is their portion, as He promised them*) was selected not in accordance with the regular progression of verses in each lesson but because it obviously fit the message desired for the occasion. We shall first review what is known of the relevant events, as described in the scholarly literature based on other sources, and then analyze Morteira's response from the pulpit.

The split in the congregation crystallized around two strong figures: the Ḥakham Joseph Pardo, and the former New Christian physician, merchant, and public apologist for Judaism, Dr. David Farar. At issue was the rationalist approach to Judaism that Farar was known to espouse, and upon which he apparently based homiletical addresses he had given from the pulpit.[73] Saul Levi Morteira, who had been in Amsterdam only about two years and did not as yet hold a regular position in the congregation, supported Farar, and by June of 1618, word had reached Venice that Morteira's orthodoxy was being challenged.[74] Matters came to a head on the fast day of 17 Tammuz,

---

73. *"Your Voice Like a Ram's Horn,"* pp. 373–74 for a review of the events as they concerned David Farar; pp. 379–80 on his occasional preaching.

74. This is clear from Leon Modena's letter to Morteira, dated 22 Sivan 5378 (June 15, 1618): "I heard people complaining about you and your allies, alleging that you speak improperly against the words of the sages and against the Kabbalah. Although I write in your defense to Rabbi Isaac Uziel, in our private communication, as a father to his son, I must remind you that it is not right even for an elder and a prince, let alone for a young man who

July 10, 1618; after a forceful confrontation, the faction led by Pardo withdrew from the synagogue, taking with it ritual objects, Torah scrolls, and the community archives. This group soon established a new congregation, called at first "Ets Ḥaim," then "Beth Israel." Those who remained behind, the Farar faction, appointed Morteira to the newly vacated position of "Ḥakham" in Beth Jacob.[75]

At this point, the principals turned to two external venues to adjudicate their dispute. First, the Beth Jacob group filed a formal complaint with an Amsterdam court of aldermen, asking that the property of the congregation removed from its building by the seceding faction be restored. Pardo, in turn, apparently initiated a formal complaint against Farar to the rabbinic leadership of Salonika. They in turn passed on the dossier, with their condemnation of Farar, to Leon Modena, the celebrated rabbi in Venice, who may have been Morteira's teacher. Modena's individual response, highly supportive of Farar, has long been known.[76] The verdict of the Venetian court, recently published, indicates that Morteira had traveled to Venice with two other representatives of the Beth Jacob congregation and two representatives of the new Ets Ḥaim, in an attempt to reach a mutually acceptable reconciliation. These five emissaries signed the document, dated 2 Kislev 5379 (November 19, 1618), which included condemnation of those who fomented dissent in Amsterdam, expressions of respect and support for both Pardo and Farar, and instructions for an equitable division of property and honor between the two congregations.[77]

Morteira returned to Amsterdam with enhanced prestige: he had facilitated a resolution of the dispute in which the reputation of the principals emerged unscathed and the congregations separated without bitterness. Yet the matter was not resolved. A partisan intervention of the Salonika court, calling for the excommunication of David Farar and an even division of the property of the

---

teaches Torah, to show lack of respect for the glorious writings of our predecessors, and also to take a position in the conflict of the congregations there": *Iggerot R. Yehudah Aryeh mi-Modena*, ed. Y. Boksenboim (Tel Aviv, 1984), p. 162. This is the only document I know demonstrating a personal relationship between Modena and Morteira, who does not appear to mention or cite Modena anywhere in the extant sermons.

75. I follow here the reconstruction of H. P. Salomon, "La vraie excommunication de Spinoza," *Forum Litterarum* (Amsterdam, 1984), pp. 182–84; idem, *Tratado*, xlvi–l. Cf. also Miriam Bodian, "Amsterdam, Venice, and the Marrano Diaspora," *Dutch Jewish History* 2 (1989): 54–57.

76. See the summary in *"Your Voice Like a Ram's Horn,"* p. 373, with references in n. 23.

77. Salomon, "La vraie excommunication," pp. 183–84, 193–96; Bodian, "Amsterdam, Venice," pp. 56–57.

two congregations,[78] threatened to unravel the compromise. Then came the response of the Dutch court, which had on May 28, 1619. appointed a commission of three arbiters to rule on the division of property. The commission announced its decision on August 6.[79] Salomon informs us that Morteira, dissatisfied with one of the terms, protested to the councilors, and was arrested as a result. He was freed on August 24 upon the payment of a bond by three of his friends.[80]

There can be little question that the *Shoftim* sermon pertains to the schism leading to the formation of the new Beth Israel congregation. The first four of the five themes appearing in the sermon fit what we know of the conflict from external sources. This would, of course, require dating the sermon and the convocation in which it was delivered in the summer of 1619. As we have seen, the Amsterdam commission of arbiters gave its verdict on August 6, a Tuesday, with terms on the whole favorable to Beth Jacob. The week in which the lesson *Shoftim* would have been read began on Sunday, August 11, the first day of Elul. We must therefore imagine a festive gathering, marking the end of the conflict, held in the Beth Jacob congregation on one of the nights of that week. As we shall see below, the date can be further narrowed.

At this point, we turn to the sermon. After a general introduction in which the preacher argues that internecine warfare and internal strife are the most dangerous kinds of conflict, he continues in what is clearly a celebratory mode:

> It is therefore incumbent upon us to praise the Master of all, to exalt, glorify, and praise His great name **this evening** for the healing of the mortal disease that afflicted us: the hatred of people for each other, the

78. Bodian, "Amsterdam, Venice," p. 57 and n. 42. In response to this intervention, Modena wrote a strong defense of Farar to Salonika. In this letter, he reviewed the course of the conflict: "Concerning the conflict that occurred there in Amsterdam over the 'vessels of holiness' and other matters, in which the congregation split and became two, each one of these congregations presented its own position before the outstanding leaders of the Sephardi community [of Venice], and after thorough and exhaustive investigation they made a decision, a compromise between them based on justice and truth." *Ziqnei Yehudah* (Jerusalem, 1956), p. 49.

79. The content was summarized in "Notarial Records Relating to the Portuguese Jews in Amsterdam up to 1639," *StRos* 15 (1981): 153, no. 1816. According to the decision, all appurtenances that had been removed from the Beth Jacob synagogue had to be brought back. Books were to remain with Beth Jacob. Communal fund payments and cash were to be divided 60% to Beth Jacob, 40% to Beth Israel. Finally, "the 50 guilders fine, claimed by Beth Jacob from everyone who leaves their community, will be remitted in the hope that they will remain friends."

80. Salomon, *Tratado*, p. L.

quarrels and incessant strife that rankle within our bones and within our hearts. For this disease we tried various kinds of cures, to no avail. **We sent to foreign lands** to find medications, but we were not healed. Then God observed from heaven and provided a cure for all our pain. The Sages said, "All love that depends on some external factor ends when that factor ends."[81] How much more then is it true that all hate that depends on some external factor ends when that factor ends. Let there be among us nothing but truth and peace and fraternity, for hatreds have vanished, contentions have ended, strife is no more. For all of this, give thanks to God and call upon His name.

Praise God, for He has given us rest from the long road we have traveled **for more than a year. I myself have been traveling that road;** blessed is the Lord who has preserved me on it. Therefore, choose this rest for yourselves, and let this experience of the recent past keep you from allowing anything similar to recur. We are all children of one father, we are brothers. Sing songs of praise to His name, for we have ended the most dangerous kind of war that exists: the war within a single house. Proclaim the benediction appropriate for having been saved from danger, for God has kept you from bloodshed. The situation was very close to this, as is clear from what happened. Therefore let there be true rejoicing before God tonight.[82]

This is the allusiveness born of intimacy between speaker and audience: no details need be given because they are known to all who are present.[83] From the sermon itself, independent of other sources, the following data can be distilled: a) Morteira's congregation was rent by a severe internal conflict, with feelings so embittered that physical violence was threatened, b) the conflict lasted for more than a year, c) Jewish communities outside Amsterdam were consulted, d) Morteira was personally involved, and e) a resolution of the conflict was marked by a festive evening convocation in August at which Morteira preached.

In addition to the cessation of the conflict, Morteira specifies another major reason to rejoice: the return of the Torah to its proper house. The timing is especially appropriate, indeed providentially ordained: "God wanted that during the days of returning, the Torah too would perform an act of returning to us." As noted, the "days of returning," beginning with the first day of Elul,

---

81. M. *Avot* 5,16.

82. MS 3:155v, *Shoftim*, Deut. 18:2; emphasis added.

83. On this characteristic of the sermon and the methodological challenges it raises, see *Jewish Preaching*, pp. 81–84.

had just begun. But, after a homiletical encomium upon the Torah, when Morteira expands upon and concretizes this "return of the Torah," his discussion becomes a bit puzzling. He speaks first of "three Torah scrolls, two of the congregation, one from the honorable Mr. Abraham Jeshurun, and one from the honorable Mr. Raphael Abudiente."[84] This is the kind of statement that immediately makes one think that the writer's pen has slipped, and that he *intended* to write "four Torah scrolls." But this cannot be the case, as the number three becomes an integral part of the following discussion. The passage continues, "to teach us that these aforementioned qualities have come to us," referring to healing, rest, and victory with appropriate thanksgiving, that he has presented as attendant qualities of the Torah, "and *a three-fold cord is not easily broken* (Eccl. 4:12)." Other examples of the significance of the number three quickly follow: "In order to teach us that our rejoicing will endure, God made it begin with the number three," as with the "three pillars of the world" (M. *Avot* 1,2; 1,18), the three patriarchs, and the three-fold priestly benediction.

This benediction is then applied to the three major participants in the celebration, the congregation as a whole and the two individual donors of the Torah scrolls:

> All these blessings have been fulfilled in the three celebrants of this rejoicing for Beth Jacob. It is said, *The Eternal bless you* with all kinds of blessings, *and protect you* (Num. 6:24) from all evil. *The Eternal bless you* with [? ?][85] the investigation, *and protect you* with money. *The Eternal bless you* by enlarging the scope of your religious acts, *and protect you* with the tranquility of this day. *The Eternal bless you* in this world, *and protect you* in the world to come. *The Eternal deal kindly and graciously with you* (Num. 6:25) applies to the honorable Mr. Abraham [Jeshurun]: as a reward for this holy act, may God graciously provide him with sons. *The Eternal bestow His favor upon you and grant you peace* (Num. 6:26) applies to the honorable Mr. Raphael Abudiente. May God grant him peace so that he may in peace become the father of a son. As a special sign of the three celebrants in this rejoicing, we see that the word *ya'er* [which begins the third blessing] contains the first letters in the names Jacob, Abraham, and Raphael, indicating that for each one of these, the

---

84. MS 3:155v. Abraham Jeshurun (also known as Anfonio Gomes Alcobaça) and Raphael Abudiente appear in several lists of donors to funds of the congregation in 1619 (Pieterse, *Livro de Bet Ḥaim*, pp. 32–36. Jeshurun was later the recipient of a responsum from Morteira about the permissibility of having paintings and sculptures in one's home (Salomon, *Tratado*, p. lxi, n. 19).

85. Two Hebrew words that I cannot decipher.

Eternal will bestow *favor unto you and grant you peace.*[86]

Clearly then, the number three is integral to the passage about the Torah scrolls.

Perhaps then, the text should have read, "three Torah scrolls, *one* of the congregation," and one each from Jeshurun and Abudiente. But in the final paragraph of the sermon, Morteira states, "if two Torah scrolls departed from you, four have returned to you,"[87] indicating that the reading "two of the congregation" is correct. The only plausible explanation for the disparity in the numbers is that Morteira meant to say that there were three *categories* of Torah scrolls, the first category including the two that had belonged to the congregation and were removed by the Pardo faction, the other two categories including the scroll belonging to Jeshurun and the scroll belonging to Abudiente. Thus the congregation ended up with twice as many scrolls as it originally possessed, a significant occasion for rejoicing. The peroration, in the final paragraph, is a pastiche of biblical verses using the name of the congregation, Beth Jacob, which the preacher notes is both a reference to one of the original founders, Jacob Tirado, and a common biblical eponym for the entire Jewish people. While Morteira does express the hope that "the three congregations will be together in love, brotherhood, and trust,"[88] the rhetorical function of the concluding passage is apparently to instill a renewed sense of pride in a congregation that had gone through a period of demoralization.

There is another crux in this section of the sermon. Morteira states that the congregation "owes this assembly to God for the eight days on which the daily offering (*tamid*) was revoked from it, which you can always repay in the celebration of this night."[89] This rather ambiguous formulation is clarified by a statement in the penultimate paragraph of the sermon: the celebration is "to wipe away that which forestalled prayer in this house for eight days; in this way atonement may be made… for many evils may have possibly been born from this matter."[90] This apparently alludes to a compulsory closing of the synagogue to public worship by order of the Christian authorities. Nor was this the only occasion on which the government intervened in the internal religious activities of the Jewish community. As we have seen in our discussion of the Tirado eulogy, a sermon for the lesson *Terumah*, delivered in the late winter of 1620, records that it was preached "on the Sabbath when the

---

86. MS 3:155v, *Shoftim*, Deut. 18:2, Hebrew text at end.
87. MS 3:156r.
88. MS 3:155v.
89. Ibid.
90. MS 3:155v–156r.

synagogue was opened after it had been closed by order of the authorities for two weeks."[91] In the absence of any external information about the 1619 closing, the most plausible assumption is that it followed upon the decision of the arbiters, issued on August 6, and was perhaps intended to ensure that the stipulations of the decision would be implemented. An eight day closing would mean that the celebration marking the re-opening of the synagogue and the restoration of its Torah scrolls might have been held on Wednesday night, August 14 or Thursday night, August 15, during the first week of Elul (i.e., during the "days of repentance"), and on the week of the lesson *Shoftim*.

This, however, leaves unresolved the matter of Morteira's arrest. It is indeed difficult to imagine Morteira preaching what is in effect a victory sermon on August 14 or 15, then protesting the terms of the decision so vehemently that he would have been arrested within a few days of the public celebration; such a scenario would indicate a personality even more mercurial than has generally been thought. As the document recording a release on bail, dated August 24, 1619, says nothing about the reason for the arrest or the amount of time in detention,[92] it is possible that the arrest occurred for reasons that had nothing to do with the conflict. But whatever the reasons, the arrest would have come as an epilogue to the climactic denouement celebrated in the special gathering and triumphant sermon. Be that as it may, the text of this sermon corroborates and supplements external documents, revealing Morteira's personal involvement in turbulent events at the beginning of his official rabbinic career.

COMMUNITY INSTITUTIONS

Morteira's sermons also provide information about the institutions of his community, although much of it is sporadic and incidental. For the most part, the institutions are illuminated far more systematically in the Portuguese communal records than in anything the preacher says. Occasionally, however, Morteira does cast new light on the component groups within the larger community structure. For example, among the many sermons on the lesson *Mishpatim* contained in the manuscript, one begins with an unexpected

---

91. MS 3:32v, *Terumah*, Exod. 25:3, 1620. On the circumstances surrounding this temporary prohibition of public worship for the Jews, see above, p. 152, n. 30. Nothing in the body of the sermon, which discusses various aspects of charity, gives information about the specifics of the conflict.

92. Salomon Ullmann, "Geschichte der spanisch-portugiesischen Juden in Amsterdam im XVII, Jahrhundert," *Jahrbuch der Jüdisch-Literarischen Gesellschaft* 5 (1907): 73; for archival references, see Salomon, *Tratado*, p. L, n.37.

evocation of the setting. Following the standard initial *nosei* and *ma'amar*, the preacher continues:

> Inasmuch as my dear students are engaged during these nights in a discussion of the love between God and the community of Israel—for the word *ahavah*, love, is included among the terms beginning with *aleph* in the book *Kad ha-Qemah*, which they are studying—when my night to speak came around, I decided to investigate the subject of desire, which is the most exalted quality in the general category of love. Now in thinking about this, I realized that this is an exalted matter, extremely deep, and it is impossible to encompass very much in the limited time of fifteen minutes or less which is available [for the discourse] each night. To speak briefly about it would necessarily leave the matter incomplete, as it would be impossible to explain it properly. "Where they said to be long, one is not permitted to be short" (cf. M. *Berakhot* 1,4). Therefore I decided to keep this subject for Shabbat, when there is more freedom time to explain it fully. In addition, the theme and style of the Torah lesson will inspire us to this, as our text is *They saw the God of Israel...*" (Exod. 24:10), which is a great mystery in our discourse, which we shall explain. Yet here I am now preaching in fulfillment of my agreement. I shall begin by first asking help from God, who has known only you among all the families of the earth.[93]

This follows a standard homiletical trope of protesting the difficulty of the task at hand and the impossibility of doing it properly, before going on to engage the subject. What is important for our purpose, however, is the information about the setting that is contained in this introduction. First, Morteira has a group of his own students who meet together regularly in the evenings, at least during the winter, to engage in systematic study. Second, the topic of this study is not halakhah but ethical literature, specifically Bahya ben Asher's *Kad ha-Qemah*.[94] They are apparently near the beginning of their encounter with this book, as *ahavah* is the second topic treated by Bahya (after *emunah*). Third, the format seems to be that each of the participants, including Morteira, would take turns giving an opening presentation of a homiletical nature, no more than fifteen minutes in length, to introduce the topic in Bahya's text. For Morteira, this was a speaking occasion in addition to the regular Shabbat

---

93. MS 4:128r, *Mishpatim*, Exod. 21:10.

94. On this thirteenth-century work, see Israel Bettan, *Studies in Jewish Preaching*, chap. 3. Eighteenth-century Ashkenazi authorities recommended that every Jew (including women) spend some time each day studying a page of ethical literature: see Saperstein, *Jewish Preaching*, p. 344 and n. 53.

sermon, which provided him with a more extensive opportunity to explore a
challenging issue (although the text of the current sermon is not shorter than
his usual Sabbath texts!). The text cannot be dated; it seems to reflect a time
not near the beginning of his career but later, when Morteira had a group of
disciples (such as those who orchestrated the publication of *Giv'at Sha'ul* as
reported in its introduction) capable of studying on their own and desirous of
supplementing their more formal study with this optional further discipline,
which the rabbi clearly encouraged, but for which his presence was not
crucial. It is not clear whether we are dealing here with an institution that had
any official continuity over the years, but it reflects an aspect of the
community that is not otherwise known.[95]

Morteira refers to the lay leadership, including the regents of the *Mahamad*,
the most powerful institution in the community, only occasionally in the sermons.[96] By contrast, he devotes considerable discussion to one of the most
important confraternities in Jewish Amsterdam: the *Biqqur Ḥolim* Society,
about which the sermons provide abundant information that does not seem
otherwise to have been recorded elsewhere.

The confraternity, a voluntary association devoted to charitable acts, religious discipline, and study, also provided the late medieval and early modern
Jew with an important opportunity for socialization. As a voluntary structure
standing between the individual and the all-encompassing and mandatory
institutions of community or synagogue, it introduced an element of choice
into the life of the Jew. Considerable scholarly attention has been devoted

---

95. Cf. Swetschinski, *Reluctant Cosmopolitans*, pp. 211–12 on adult study groups, including
reference to the yeshivah "Keter Tora," which conducted disputations on subjects of Jewish
law and met each day for two hours. This was founded by Morteira in 1643 (see Pieterse,
Daniel Levi de Barrios, p. 107). If this is the group reflected in the present sermon, its subject
matter must have included Jewish ethics as well as Jewish law. Because the theme-verse
(Exod. 24:10) is not from the normal progression of verses starting from the beginning of
each *parashah*, there is no obvious way of dating this sermon.

96. Note the following references to the non-rabbinic leadership: "that is why the members of the *Va'ad* passed the ordinance they did" (below, p. 406); "how great is the obligation
of the leaders of these congregations to bestir themselves to improve our way of serving
God" (below, p. 402); "if so, you, the eyes of the community, priests of the Eternal, summon
the watches of our God to clear out the thorns from the vineyard, for a great breach has
been made. And I shall inform you so that you may know the sickness, and provide the
proper medication for it" (below, p. 203); "how much damage accrues to the regents who
have the authority to protest [about violations of the commandment pertaining to beards]
but will not" (below, p. 206).

over the past generation to Jewish confraternities in Spain[97] and in Italy.[98] Among those in Amsterdam, only the "Dotar" Society (*Santa Companhia de dotar orphas e donzelas* pobres) has been studied systematically.[99]

According to Daniel Levi de Barrios, writing considerably later, the *Biqqur Holim* society was established in 1609, very early in the history of the community; its purpose, according to de Barrios, was "to visit the sick, both rich and poor, to provide the things necessary to alleviate their difficulties of support and medicines, to watch over the dying, to wash and embalm the dead, and to accompany the mourners."[100] Later on, a proper burial society called "Gemilut Ḥasadim" took over responsibility for burial of the dead and assistance to the mourners.[101] Thus it would seem as if the *Biqqur Holim* Society, in accordance with its name, would be limited essentially to medical services and other kinds of support for the sick and dying.[102] Morteira's sermons provide significant evidence that it did much more.

What brought Morteira to speak about this confraternity in his sermons? It was an established tradition for confraternities to set one day each year for celebration and re-dedication to their purposes,[103] a practice apparently modeled after the annual celebration of the patron saint in the Christian confraternities. The *Biqqur Holim* Society of Amsterdam established their day as the Sabbath during Hanukkah, which became the occasion when the one-year term of office for the four regents (*parnasim*) of the Society ended, and four new regents were installed. When the Ets Ḥaim congregation (later

97. Yom Tov Assis, "Welfare and Mutual Aid in the Spanish Jewish Communities," in *Moreshet Sefarad: The Sephardi Legacy*, edited by Haim Beinart (Jerusalem, 1992), pp. 318–45; Saperstein, *"Your Voice Like a Ram's Horn,"* pp. 179–222;

98. Brian Pullan, *Rich and Poor in Renaissance Venice* (Cambridge, 1971), p. 563; David Ruderman, "The Founding of a *Gemilut Ḥasadim* Society in Ferrara in 1515," *AJS Review* 1 (1976): 233–67; Elliott Horowitz, "Membership and Its Rewards: The Emergence and Decline of Ferrara's *Gemilut Ḥasadim* Society (1515–1603), in *The Mediterranean and the Jews*, 2 vols., ed. Elliott Horowitz and Moises Orfali (Ramat-Gan, 2002), 2:27–65; and the encompassing survey by Bracha (Arlos) Rivlin, *'Arevim Zeh la-Zeh ba-Getto ha-Italqi: Hevrot GM"Ḥ 1516–1789* (Jerusalem, 1991). Cf. also Avigdor Farine, "Charity and Study Societies in Europe of the Sixteenth–Eighteenth Centuries," *JQR* 64 (1973): 16–47, 164–75, which treats material from central and eastern Europe as well as Italy, but not Holland.

99. Miriam Bodian, "The 'Portuguese' Dowry Societies in Venice and Amsterdam," *Italia* 6 (1987): 30–61. For the *Biqqur Holim* Society in a somewhat later period, see Yosef Kaplan, *From Christianity to Judaism*, pp. 189–91.

100. de Barrios, *Triumpho del govierno popular*, cited in Swetschinski, *Reluctant Cosmopolitans*, p. 177.

101. Swetschkinski, ibid., p. 201.

102. So in Bodian, *Hebrews of the Portuguese Nation*, p. 3.

103. Assis, "Welfare and Mutual Aid," p. 139 with references in n. 125.

Beth Israel) broke away from Beth Jacob, one point of contention was apparently where the annual ceremony of the *Biqqur Holim* Society would be held, as the reconciliation document issued by the Venetian rabbinical court on November 19, 1618 provided that it would be held in the current year at Beth Jacob, but in the following year at Ets Haim, and thereafter continue to rotate annually.[104]

It is not clear, however, whether or not this pattern continued: all of Morteira's successive sermons on the lesson *Mi-Qets*, which would be read on the Sabbath during Hanukkah, refer to the *Biqqur Holim* installation.[105] Indeed, many of the sermons provide the year in which they were delivered, and list at the end the names of the four regents whose terms ended and the four whose terms began. By correlating all this material, we can compile a fairly complete listing of the leadership of this prestigious Society from 1625 to 1638.[106] Moreover, in addition to listing the names, Morteira generally incorporates into these sermons some reference to the activities of the Society, and from this we see that its purview was far broader than ministering to the sick.

Scattered through the other sermons on other lessons are occasional remarks that also reflect on the work of the Society. Let us start with a sermon from the fall of 1619, quite early in Morteira's tenure. The theme-verse is Genesis 25:19, the first in the lesson *Toledot*, indicating that it was the first year he was preaching regularly in Beth Jacob. The rabbinic dictum, more important for our purpose, is from b. *Yebamot* 62b: "Concerning one who loves his neighbors, who befriends [lit. "brings near] his relatives, who marries his sister's daughter, and extend loans to the poor in the hour of need, Scripture

104. "E a festa que se faz em cada ano por *hanucah* em ditta *hebra* de *Bicur Holim*, seja feita hum ano no *kaal kados* de *Bet Jaacob* primeiro, e outro ano no *kaal kados* de *Es Haim*, e assi sucessivament alternatim." Salomon, "La vraie excommunication, p. 195.

105. Examples will be given below, but see the printed sermon on *Mi-Qets* in *Giv'at Sha'ul* (1645, p. 19d bottom, 1912, p. 96 bottom), referring to "this sacred Society, whose meritorious activity is [honored] this day" but not naming it. Manuscripts of other sermons on this lesson, however, do specify the confraternity being honored on that Shabbat, as well as referring to its activities, as discussed above, pp. 41–46.

106. In December 1625, for example, the term of Michael Espinosa (later the father of Baruch) came to an end together with the terms of Abraham Curiel, Jacob Israel Mendes, and Jacob Nahamjas; they were succeeded by Moses de Fonseca, Abraham de Oliveira, Imanuel Jesurun, and Abraham Farar ("the Younger") (MS 5:112v, *Mi-Qets*, Gen. 41:2). In 1639, with the reorganization and unification of the three congregations, the by-laws were changed and the number of regents for the *Biqqur Holim* was increased from four to six. See Pieterse, *Daniel Levi de Barrios*, pp. 96, 162, Franco Mendes, *Memorias*, pp. 48–49.

says, *Then, when you call, the Lord swill answer; when you cry, He will say: Here I am* (Isa. 58:9).

Toward the end of the sermon, the theme of marriage is introduced, with a statement endorsing endogamous marriage within the extended family as likely to produce fine children. This is exemplified by Amram, as is seen in the verse, *A certain man of the house of Levi went and married a Levite woman* (Exod. 2:1). The preacher then moves from theory to the actual situation at hand:

> And so it is with our bridegroom on this day, for he is a man from the house of Levi, and he has taken the daughter of a Levi, meaning a daughter of this sacred Society of *Biqqur Ḥolim,* for *levi* is also connected with the word "funeral" (*levayah*). In this way he has cleaved to his relatives from his land, from the land of his birth. The members of this society are the cause of this great honor....
>
> Now all these high achievements [in Isaiah 58:7 which is linked with the rabbinic dictum] pertain to this sacred Society. They "love their neighbors," burying their dead and visiting their sick even if they are not their "brothers," members of this Society, which is true love, for the kindness shown toward the dead is true kindness.[107] They "bring their relatives near," by teaching those of our nation a trade so that they may draw near to life and not go around begging. They "marry their sisters' daughters," meaning that they make possible the marriage of their sisters' daughters.... They "extend loans at a time of need," through the clothing they make during Hanukkah."[108]

At the conclusion of the text, the preacher appended a comment that explained the circumstances of the occasion on which the sermon was delivered: "The sermon I delivered on the day of the wedding of the honorable Mr. Moses Ha-Levi, who married an orphan girl with the dowry of the *Biqqur Ḥolim* Society, may God watch over it, in the year 5480."[109]

Morteira clearly refers to a function of the Society similar to that of the better-known *Dotar.* Nor is this the only reference in the sermons to wedding assistance.. Two years later, Morteira's sermon on Genesis 28:13 was identified by the author as "the sermon I delivered on the lesson *Va-Yetse* on the day of the celebration [*shurah*] of the honorable Mr. Samuel Duarte with his relative, the modest orphan maiden Miss Clara Benveniste, who was married

107. Rashi on Genesis 47:29.
108. MS 3:6r, *Toledot,* Gen. 25:19, 1619.
109. MS 3:6v.

by the *Biqqur Ḥolim* Society in the year 5482."[110] And a few months later, we find another similar appendage to the sermon text: "The sermon I delivered on the lesson *Yitro* on the day of the celebration of the wedding of the honorable Mr. Isaac Frances with the modest maiden Miss Rachel Perez (may she be blessed among the married women). She was married by the sacred Society of *Biqqur Ḥolim* in the year 1622."[111] Here the bride is not explicitly identified as an orphan, raising the possibility that the Society did not limit its aid to those in need, but perhaps helped defray the wedding expenses of daughters of their members as well.

The original and primary purpose of the Society, however, was apparently providing medical care for the sick. In his 1624 eulogy for Dr. David Farar, discussed above, Morteira said, "See how many years he was a physician for the *Biqqur Ḥolim* Society, gladly healing the poor, going up to their houses and giving them charity."[112] The following year, in his Sabbath of Hanukkah sermon on *Mi-Ketz,* he expanded upon this function: "The sacred Society is beneficial in this, for since its central purpose is the healing of all the sick, the poor may eat what is given to them through charity [or from the charity fund, the *sedaca*][113] without fear, for they know that if they become sick they will be healed, which would not be the case if they lacked [food].... And this Society endeavors to foster good health in those who are wanting it through the medicines which are given to them for every need.... The artisans [in the Society] pay [for the medicines] out of their own pockets, and the physicians heal without charge."[114]

But it is not only the provision of medication and expertise that Morteira praises. He also stresses the empathy for the poor that comes with ministering to them directly. In a sermon for the Sabbath of Hanukkah in 1628, he compares the *Biqqur Ḥolim* Society with two other major institutions of the community: the Talmud Torah Society[115] provided for education and edification,

---

110. MS 3:176r, *Va-Yetse,* Gen. 28:13, 1621 (printed in *Giv'at Sha'ul,* but without the following statement): דרוש שדרשתי בפרשת ויצא ביום שורת כמ"ר שמואל דורטה עם היתומה הצנועה קרובתה מרת

קלרה בינוני'סטי ונשאת ע"י חברה קדושה של בקור חולים בשנת השב"ב.

111. MS 3:196v, *Yitro,* Exod 18:3, 1622.

112. Saperstein, *"Your Voice Like a Ram's Horn,"* p. 384, Hebrew p. 400.

113. Swetschinski, *Reluctant Cosmopolitans,* p. 200.

114. MS 5:112r, *Mi-Qetz* Gen. 41:2, 1625. Cf. Pieterse, *de Barrios,* pp. 95–96. On the provision of free medical care, see also Rivlin, *"'Arevim Zeh la-Zeh,"* p. 90.

115. Reference here is to the confraternity that, beginning in 1616, undertook the responsibility for providing religious instruction for the poor; see Swetschinski, *Reluctant Cosmopolitans,* pp. 182, 210. The Talmud Torah Society had its annual celebration on the holiday of Shavu'ot, and one of Morteira's sermons refers to this, listing three regents whose term

and the wardens of the *mahamad* imposed the discipline that prevented improper behavior. But as for instilling the true motivation for the religious life,

> that is the role of the sacred Society whose meritorious activity is [honored] this day. It is entirely concerned with the impoverished, the wretched. When they see them, they think, "Did not the One who made me in my mother's belly also make him (Job 31:15)? I could be liable just like him for the misfortune he is in." This is what opens the ear to ethical insight (cf. Job 36:10) and inspires to repentance: the encounter with the sick, with the naked, and with the dead.... This is what Isaiah said (58:7), *"to share your bread with the hungry"*—not just "bread" but *your* bread, meaning the fancy bread that you yourself eat. *"And the wretched poor to take home"*—that is visiting the sick (*biqqur ḥolim*), for "out of sight, out of mind," but when you visit the impoverished sick, you "take home," meaning you will take him back to your home with you, and you will think about him, and prepare what he needs to the best of your ability. *"When you see the naked to clothe him"*—in the winter, for then you see him when you yourself need to be dressed appropriately, thinking "If it is cold for me, how must it be for those who are indigent and forlorn?" *"And not to ignore your own kin"* when he dies, but rather to be engaged in his burial. These are the essential *mitzvot* of this sacred Society.[116]

Striking in this passage is the emphasis on the benefit of the activities not just on the needy recipients, but also on the members of the Society themselves, and by extension on the community as a whole. As in previous sermons, we have reference here to yet another task taken on by the *Biqqur Ḥolim* Society: distributing warm clothing to the poor at the beginning of the winter.[117]

---

ended in 1626 (Raphael Jesurun, David Curiel, and Michael Judah Leon), and three who replaced them (Joseph Cohen, Isaac Montalto, and Solomon Judah Leon): MS 3:40v It is interesting that David Curiel and Joseph Cohen also served as regents of the *Biqqur Ḥolim* Society in different years, as did Imanuel Jesurun, likely a relative of Raphael. (Morteira wrote "Raphael," but this is probably Rehuel [Rohjel] Jessurun, author of the *Dialogo dos Montes*).

116. MS 3:182r bottom, *Mi-Qetz*, Gen. 41:4, 1628; *GS* 1645, pp. 19d–20b, 1912, pp. 96–97.

117. See Pieterse, *de Barrios*, p. 96, Kaplan, *From Christianity to Judaism*, p. 190, Swetschinski, *Reluctant Cosmopolitans*, p. 200. Morteira's sermons shows that the distribution of clothing in the winter was an undertaking of the society since at least 1619, not added, as Pieterse thought, in 1639 (cf. also Castro, *Keur van grafsteenen*, p. 29 n. 7). The Sabbath of Hanukkah was also designated as a time for collecting clothing for the poor and shrouds for

Similarly, there is emphasis on providing food for the hungry as a major priority of the Society, as we see in a sermon from two years later on the theme of hunger: "We learn friendship and loyalty that result from hunger, and how we should fear it, and have compassion for those who are oppressed by it, in accordance with the activity of the sacred Society of *Biqqur Holim*, whose public celebration is today."[118] The material in these sermons indicates that the confraternities in Amsterdam were not limited to specialized activities. While the *Biqqur Holim* Society does not seem to have undertaken any formal educational programs, it apparently engaged in a broad spectrum of humanitarian activities, some of which duplicated functions of other confraternities. The analogy would be less to departments in a municipal government, than to various fraternal associations with overlapping philanthropic projects.

In one later sermon, Morteira points with pride to the devotion of the Society, in comparison not with other confraternities of the community, but with the Gentile environment. The compassion of Jews for those in need has always been one of their outstanding qualities:

> Experience proves, for although they are in exile and do not have their own city or state, their charitableness in comparison with their position exceeds that of all other nations. We see this especially with regard to the absolute consistency of this sacred Society in fulfilling so many of its meritorious acts.[119]

All of this seems more than merely a preacher fulfilling a homiletical obligation to honor an important institution within the congregation. Morteira seemed to be genuinely impressed with the work of this confraternity and the devotion of its members. To him, they were examples of his people expressing in their behavior the very highest of Jewish and human values.

---

the dead in seventeenth-century Fez; see Eliezer Bashan, "Hevrot *Biqqur Holim* ba-Qehillot ha-Mizrah ha-Tikhon," *Daf le-Tarbut Yehudit* 213 (Sivan 5755): 8.

118. MS 2:152r, *Mi-Qets*, Gen. 41:6, 1630. When the preacher returns to the Society at the end of the sermon, however, he turns this into a metaphor: "Such will be for the members and regents of the sacred Society, for they save the poor from the great hunger, namely sickness, for 'all food is loathsome to them [the sick]' (Ps. 107:18). So may God save them from all evil" (2:153v).

119. MS 5:100v, *Mi-Qets*, Gen. 41:17, 1644.

6

Shaping Life:
The Rhetoric of Rebuke

Morteira's printed and manuscript sermons contain many passages criticizing his community for behavior that he believed to be incompatible with the laws and values of Jewish life. Quantitatively, these passages represent only a small percentage of the time he spent preaching. The central purpose of his sermons was didactic: to educate, inform, mediate a tradition, expose his listeners to classical texts with the full richness of their problematics and insights, define and defend the boundaries of acceptable doctrine against the challenges raised by spokesmen for the majority religion and by skeptics within the fold. But the preacher was also expected to serve as a moral and religious authority, and the element of rebuke for unbecoming behavior has a venerable pedigree in Jewish homiletical tradition.[1]

Criticism expressed from the pulpit in the context of public worship raises problems for both the preacher and the historian. For the preacher, the challenge is to communicate condemnation in a manner that will be efficacious. While some might relish listening to criticism they believe is directed toward others, no one enjoys being made the object of attack, especially in public, in the framework of a worship service, within an institution that one pays to support. A preacher who is respected by his congregation for his learning and piety may indeed condemn behavior he believes to violate the mandates of tradition and the norms of the community, but optimal effectiveness is lost if this is done at excessive length or on every possible occasion. Constant reiteration of a negative message dulls the barbs of attack. Listeners challenged by exposure to new ideas may "tune out" when they hear the same, familiar denunciations.

---

1. For a thirteenth-century example, see Marc Saperstein, "The Preaching of Repentance and the Reforms in Toledo of 1281," in B. Kienzle et al., eds, *Models of Holiness in Medieval Preaching*, (Louvain-la-Neuve, 1996), pp. 155–72.

In addition to limiting the quantity of castigation to a reasonably small proportion of the pulpit discourse, the effective preacher must express his criticisms in a manner that will not be counter-productive. The purpose of the rebuke is not only to reaffirm shared values but also to motivate a change in deviant behavior. A call to act in a manner that is not recognized as inherent in the tradition, or seen to be realistic and feasible, may simply turn the listeners against the preacher and the goals he proclaims. A preacher too specific in describing the offensive conduct or the guilty parties may be accused of humiliating individuals in public, but if the chiding is too general, everyone may conclude that the message applies only to someone else. A rhetorical strategy is needed that will root the criticism in the classical texts whose authority is at least theoretically accepted by all, that will inspire assent to the principle being articulated, and that will lead the listeners to recognize that improper behavior exists and to apply the criticism to those responsible, even at times to themselves.[2] We shall examine some of the rhetoric of criticism used by Morteira for these purpose.

The problems are different for the historian who seeks to use a given sermon to understand not only the values of the preacher but also the social environment in which he communicated his message. Such conclusions about a community or society, drawn from a religious leader's condemnation of its imperfections, are often of dubious value. Religious leaders, notoriously difficult to please, can always find some reason to express discontent. Moreover, some themes in the sermon of rebuke are conventional *topoi* that can be found in virtually every generation from which sermon literature has been preserved. They tell us little about the dynamics of a specific group of Jews whom the preacher is addressing. Other passages may well point to issues of considerable tension for a particular community. They help us identify those areas where the leadership believed a crisis existed and the lines needed to be unambiguously drawn, where Jews were testing the limits, exploring modes of behavior unsanctioned by the tradition.[3]

These general introductory remarks have special relevance for the Portuguese nation of Amsterdam during the first two generations of its communal existence. Because of the unique background of its members—educated and acculturated as Christians in Portugal, discovering as adults what was re-

---

2. For a fuller discussion of these problems, with relevant source material, see Saperstein, *Jewish Preaching,* pp. 58–61, 417–21.

3. For a fuller discussion of the methodological issues pertaining to the use as historical evidence of social and religious criticism in sermons and exemplification for a particular community, see Saperstein, *"Your Voice Like a Ram's Horn,"* chap. 10: "Sermons and Jewish Society: The Case of Prague," especially pp. 127–29.

quired to conform to a normative Jewish life-style—the need to define the boundaries of acceptable deviance was particularly pronounced. It is therefore crucial to distinguish between those criticisms that are little more than conventional expressions of dissatisfaction and those that expose the fault lines of the nascent community. For this, we will need to apply internal criteria and to compare the sermons with other documentary evidence, especially the ordinances promulgated by the lay leadership of the community (the *Ma'amad*). Did the rabbi and the lay leaders share a set of common values? Did they agree on the major shortcomings of behavior that needed to be addressed and controlled? Or were there fundamental differences in priorities? These are questions to bear in mind as we look at examples of Morteira's rhetoric of rebuke.

BEHAVIOR

One place where one would expect to find this homiletical element is in sermons for the Sabbath of Repentance between Rosh Hashanah and Yom Kippur. In September 1620, just a year or so after assuming responsibility for weekly preaching, Morteira devoted his Sabbath of Repentance sermon to the subject of *memento mori*, showing how thoughts of the day of death can serve as a powerful remedy to the diseases of the soul, impelling one to repent and to cultivate one's fullest spiritual potential. In his peroration, Morteira specifies the potential pitfalls that he considers particularly important for his listeners to remember:

> To be careful of meat that is out of sight, and not to send to have the slaughtering done by Gentiles, for this is a great sin. It has already occurred that a Gentile did the slaughtering and told a Jew that the meat was properly slaughtered.
>
> To watch out for those against whom a ban has been declared, for this tends to be forgotten with the passage of time. It is therefore better either to enforce these bans or to annul them.
>
> To pay off what has been vowed or pledged as a contribution, for *it is better not to make a vow at all than to vow and not fulfill it* (Eccles. 5:4).
>
> To make peace between people, for how can one seek peace from God when he clings to his private war?
>
> Not to speak during the sermon, or during the reading of the Torah, for if one refuses to hear words of Torah his prayer is an abomination.
>
> Not to speak obscenities or to utter casual oaths or vows, to be careful of speaking ill about others and causing strife between brothers.

For all of these, full repentance is possible with a sincere heart and an eager soul, accompanied by ritual immersion and lashes.[4]

Rhetorically, this passage is rather unremarkable in comparison with others we shall examine. It is essentially a list of offenses that seem to be presented in a random order. Yet it is more than just a list of warnings, for most of them are accompanied by explanatory notes. The first, about ritual slaughtering, reminds the listeners of a violation that actually occurred in the community due to laxity in supervision of the meat; the second, about the ban, emphasizes the anomalous situation and urges alternative solutions; the third, about vows, cites a biblical verse as prooftext (while most listeners may not have recognized this as a direct quote, they would probably have accepted it on its merits). The fourth is a rhetorical question based on common sense; the fifth, like the fourth, appeals to the self-interest of the listeners, asserting that their hopes for reconciliation with God and answering of prayer are futile unless their behavior changes.

Given the major challenges that members of this community of former New Christians faced, these sins may not seem to be of the highest magnitude. The complaints about obscenities and malicious gossip, about conversation during the reading of the Torah and the sermon, are commonplace and can be documented in many communities.[5] Others highlight particular problems faced by the Jews of Amsterdam. The provision of properly slaughtered meat was a challenge from the beginning. Officially, meat could be slaughtered only by members of the butcher's guild, from which Jews were excluded. It was therefore arranged for Jews to slaughter and bone the meat at the houses of non-Jewish butchers, who would then do the rest of what was needed to prepare the meat for sale. The selection of slaughterers sometimes engendered bitter controversy; Morteira's remark informs us that the Dutch butchers may occasionally have bypassed the arrangement and passed off as kosher pieces of meat from animals they themselves had slaughtered.[6]

---

4. MS 3:80r, *Va-Yelekh,* Deut. 31:2, 1620 (Sabbath of Repentance). This is the only sermon for the lesson *Va-Yelekh* preserved in the manuscripts; a different one, also for the Sabbath of Repentance, was printed in *Giv'at Sha'ul.*

5. On talking during the sermon, a matter of obvious concern to preachers, cf. Saperstein, *Jewish Preaching,* p. 53. For another criticism by Morteira of improper behavior during sermons, see MS 3:341b, *Be-Shallaḥ,* Exod. 13:22, cited below.

6. On the provision of kosher meat, see Pieterse and Koen, "Notarial Records Relating to the Portuguese Jews in Amsterdam Up to 1639," *StRos* 5 (1971): 222; S. W. Baron, *SRHJ* 15:34; Yosef Kaplan, "The Social Functions of the Ḥerem in the Portuguese Jewish Community of Amsterdam in the Seventeenth Century," in *Dutch Jewish History* 1 (1984): 122 n. 24, reprinted with revisions in Kaplan's *An Alternative Path to Modernity: The Sephardi Dias-*

Similarly, the ban (*ḥerem*) was the most important vehicle for the community to exercise and enforce social control. Unlike the Roman Catholic excommunication, which was implemented by the clergy, the *ḥerem*, primarily a call for social and economic ostracism, depended upon an entire community of Jews for enforcement. If enough members of the community were lax in carrying out the terms of the ban, whether because they disagreed with those who had proclaimed it, because contact with the individuals proscribed was important to them, or because "with the passage of time, they forget," the efficacy of the *ḥerem*, its deterrent power, and the prestige of its promulgators, would all diminish. Community registers listing those placed under the ban begin in 1622; here, two years earlier, we see that it had been already in use for a number of years, and that the problem of enforcement was one to which the leaders gave some thought.[7] It is interesting to note at the end of the passage that lashing was considered to be an integral part of the penitential process. This is confirmed by archival documents as well as the dramatic account of Uriel da Costa's autobiographical statement.[8]

About ten years later, Morteira delivered another sermon for the Sabbath of Repentance, this one based on Deut. 32:12 from the lesson *Ha'azinu*. This is a highly crafted and intricately constructed text, which will be analyzed as a literary form in conjunction with the annotated translation below. Here we shall focus on the passages of rebuke. The sermon is divided into six sections, each one linked with one element of the aggadic dictum (b. *Shabbat* 31a) cited at the beginning: "Those who are brought in to judgment are asked, 'Have you been faithful in your transactions, have you fixed times for Torah, have you engaged in procreation, have you looked hopefully toward deliverance, have you engaged in the dialectics of wisdom, have you distinguished one thing from another?'" The reprimands in the sermon come at the end of each of the six sections, in conjunction with the appropriate phrase from the dictum, as a signal that the structural unit of discourse is coming to an end. Each passage refers to several distinct patterns of behavior, and when placed together they constitute a rather lengthy list:

> We must strive to carry out God's will by remaining separate and recognizable and distinct from [the Gentiles] in every respect... [so that]

pora in Western Europe (Leiden, 2002), p. 116 n. 24. Subsequent references are to page numbers in the book.

7. Kaplan, "Social Functions," p. 108, on the earliest records. See also pp. 114 and 132–33 on problems of enforcement by the community. For the rescinding of bans, recommended by Morteira in this passage, see ibid., pp. 117–18.

8. Kaplan, "Social Functions," pp. 131–32, providing corroborating evidence for the account cited from da Costa's *Autobiography*.

whoever sees us will recognize and know and understand the difference between us and the other peoples, since in this land we have no external sign to differentiate us as is the case in all the other lands of our exile. We must therefore establish this differentiation ourselves. We must not imitate the Gentile hairstyle, we must not eat of their foods or drink of their wines at the time of their funerals. When we travel, we must pray and bring *tefillin* with us as, so that all who see us will recognize us.[9]

We must strive to uproot from within us all that is similar to idolatry and lack of faith: lies... slander... unfounded gossip and inventing things we have not seen... and profanity...[10]

We are obliged to repay God by trusting in Him and not despairing of His mercy in times of trouble, by justifying His judgments in the knowledge that all is for our good, by looking at those beneath us rather than those above us, by fulfilling our vows to Him, by never overreaching or stealing but hoping that God will fulfill our permissible needs without delay, by paying hired workers at the proper time.[11]

We must set fixed times for the study of the Torah, especially in the winter season when the nights are long, so that God's teaching will be familiar to us all.... We must also be energetic in keeping its commandments, especially on the Sabbath, by studying Torah on that day and by observing it in the best way possible.[12]

We must keep far from intermarrying with them, God forbid, for this is a terrible sin, for this caused the exile of the Jewish people from their land and disrupted their tranquility in the Gentile lands; in this way alone enemies have been able to conquer God's people and to cause strife between them and their God. For as they draw close to the nations, God removes Himself from them.[13]

We must strive to perpetuate peace and unity among ourselves, to end all quarreling and strife among us, to remove from our hearts all grudges and desires for vengeance, which are qualities of Edom... and also calumny, and envy, and baseless hate, which destroyed our Temple.[14]

Stylistically, it is worth noting that as in the first few elements of the previous list, almost all of formulations here are expressed positively: goals that should

9. *GS Ha'azinu*, 1645, p. 87b.
10. Ibid., p. 88b.
11. Ibid., p. 88c.
12. Ibid., p. 89b.
13. Ibid., p. 90a.
14. Ibid., p. 90d.

be achieved, things that should be done. The negatives, the failures of behavior, the acts being criticized, are left unstated (e.g., with regard to the Sabbath), made syntactically subordinate to the positive statement (e.g., to maintain our distinctiveness "we must not imitate their hairstyles"), or expressed as a positive act (e.g., "keep far from intermarrying," "end all quarreling and strife"). While strong criticism is implied for certain acts, the overall impression left is upbeat, in accordance with the central theme of the sermon itself: God's providential protection of the Jewish people in their exile.

There is considerable overlap between this list and the 1620 Sabbath of Repentance list, especially with regard to some of the more conventional themes (fulfilling of vows, avoidance of obscenity and slanderous gossip, seeking peace and avoiding strife). Among the new themes, that of assimilation is especially pronounced. Morteira notes that Holland is unique in not requiring an external sign identifying Jews, and indeed the ordinances promulgated by the Provincial States in December of 1619 contained a proviso that the towns may not compel the Jews to wear any distinguishing marks.[15] By the early 1630s, Morteira believed that the danger of erosion of Jewish distinctiveness in physical appearance and behavior was significant enough to warn against. While this danger seems exaggerated from a modern perspective—few of the members of the Portuguese-speaking Jewish community at this time would have mastered Dutch sufficiently to be mistaken for Dutch Christians—the consciousness of the preacher is worth noting. Particularly striking is his diatribe against intermarriage, arousing the strongest condemnation in the sermon. This is a theme to which we shall return.

A different kind of list of homiletical warnings for the congregation appears in one of the few documents in the manuscript collection that is not a complete sermon. It is rather an independent unit, written on a separate sheet of paper that was inserted unbound with the other material, but is clearly the work of Morteira. It contains a midrashic-style interpretation of one of the central passages of the daily liturgy, beginning with *You shall love the Eternal your God* (Deut. 6:5), applying each injunction to the actual behavior of the community. The content of the page is as follows:

> *With all your heart*: With your entire body, with matters pertaining to menstrual impurity and its characteristics.
> *With all your soul*: Applying to those who come from the Iberian peninsula, sullied in their souls, yet do not take care to purify them but only

---

15. See Arend H. Huusen Jr., "The Legal Position of Sephardi Jews in Holland, *circa* 1600," *Dutch Jewish History* 3 (1993): 27–28.

to adorn themselves, not bothering at all to rectify what they have perverted.

And with all your might: In matters of illicit interest, and not returning the fruits of violence in their possession (cf. Isa. 59:6).

These words shall be upon your heart: What great contempt they show for the word of God, by taking tobacco in the synagogue, and by sitting in front of the door and never entering during the time of the sermon and the reading from the Torah.[16]

You shall teach them diligently to your children: for the conversation of small children is either from the father or from the mother (cf. b. *Sukkah* 56b), and they teach their children obscenities and curses and swearing in God's name.

You shall speak of them when you sit in your house: Things that a person must say within his home, for many are extremely careless about things not done in public but in the home, such as the observance of the Sabbath, and *Havdalah*, and purchasing from Gentiles things [of a kind still] attached to the ground.[17]

And when you walk on the road: Such as eating with their utensils and of their foods when walking on the road.

When you lie down: How extensive is the licentiousness with Gentile women!

And when you arise: Wearing clothing of mixed fabrics.

You shall bind them as a sign on your hand: But they do not bring *tefillin* with them to put them on in an inn, as is the custom of Jews everywhere.

And you shall write them on the doorposts of your house: The immodest

---

16. Compare the following passage in another sermon, in which Morteira cites a Talmudic statement about a Jerusalem family that was uprooted because "it set its Sabbath meal at the time of the sermon." From this he derives the following lesson: "If those who set their Sabbath meal at the time of the Sabbath sermon are uprooted, even though this meal is part of the obligatory Sabbath observance, what will become of those who exit from the synagogue at the time of the sermon in order to take a walk and discuss trivial things that have nothing to do with the obligatory Sabbath observance?!" MS 3:341b, *Be-Shallah*, Exod. 13:22, 1625. On the use of tobacco in contemporary Amsterdam, which flourished because of powerful vested economic interests despite the efforts of the Calvinist moralists to suppress it, see Schama, *The Embarrassment of Riches*, pp. 193–201.

17. Cf. b. *Beitsah* 24b, Maimonides, *Hilkhot Yom Tov* 2:10, which prohibits a Jew from accepting on a festival a gift of freshly gathered fruit if some of this kind of fruit is still attached to the ground (I am grateful to Haym Soloveitchik for helping me decipher this passage and locate the reference). It is difficult to understand this as a crucial issue for the particular community Morteira is addressing.

figurines that are in all the houses as if they were their doorposts, as the prophet says, *Beside door and doorpost you have put up your sign* (Isa. 57:8).[18]

We cannot be certain how Morteira intended to use this passage. He may have wanted to incorporate it as it appears at a climactic point toward the end of a sermon, following the model of the *Va-Yelekh* passage cited above, or he may have broken it into its component units, using each at the conclusion of a separate paragraph, following the *Ha'azinu* model. Either way, the rhetorical function is clear. The biblical words are so familiar from their recurrent liturgical use that the worshipper may utter them automatically, without thinking. The preacher therefore teases out of each phrase an application to a pattern of behavior that he considers problematic for the community. His homiletical unpacking of the phrases produces meanings that are, in most cases, close enough to the language of the original to be effectively grounded. Particularly compelling are the connections of "lying down" with sexual licentiousness, and "doorposts" with immodest figurines decorating the homes. Thus the preacher has fundamentally problematized a passage universally recognized as one of the core assertions of Jewish identity—a series of phrases that may have been to these former New Christians a source of considerable pride. There can be little doubt that every member of the audience that heard this passage would have recognized at least one principle of conduct in which he had failed to live up to the ideals he espoused. And the preacher may have hoped to establish a mental association so that each time the worshipper would in the future utter a particular phrase, the offensive behavior would be recalled.

Here too, some of the condemnations are fairly conventional and widespread: the use of obscene language, curses and oaths particularly in the presence of children, the lack of proper attention to the sermon and the reading of Torah (both of these seen in the *Va-Yelekh* sermon above), the imprecise and incomplete observance of the Sabbath in the home, the violation of halakhic norms in economic transactions. That Jews of this unique background—growing up not in an organic Jewish community but in an environment hostile to anything Jewish, needing to learn the details of halakhic Judaism as adults—would appear lax to their rabbi with regard to the details regarding menstrual purity, permitted food purchases from Gentiles, Sabbath laws in the private domain, the complex laws regarding illicit interest, and permissible fabrics for clothing, is not at all surprising. Indeed we find such accusa-

---

18. Loose page in MS vol. 2, preceding fol. 140a.

tions even in communities of Jews nourished by long-standing traditions of Jewish communal life.[19]

Some of the other phrases, however, point to distinctive tensions of this community and problems addressed at greater length in other sermons. The claim that some of those who arrived in Amsterdam from the Iberian peninsula were not sufficiently attentive to the purification of their souls after their lives as "idolaters" but were absorbed in ostentatious materialism was the underlying theme for one of Morteira's most powerful sermons of rebuke, and was reiterated in frequent expressions of dissatisfaction with behavior and attitudes of those for whom their Iberian background continued to have a powerful pull.[20] The condemnation of licentious behavior with Gentile women appears with surprising frequency in the sermons, as we shall soon see. And the reference to "licentious figurines" set up in the homes—showing the special ambiance of seventeenth-century Amsterdam and the impact of its artistic creativity on its new affluent citizens—points to an issue that would preoccupy Morteira more than once in his career.[21]

One final example of a listing of condemnations will be considered. This comes at the climactic point in a sermon on the first lesson in Deuteronomy, printed in the 1645 edition of *Giv'at Sha'ul*. The passage begins with a Talmudic statement, "Their perversities you have followed, their good ways you have not followed" (b. *Sanhedrin* 39b), and then applies this principle to the present:

> Look at the Gentiles among whom we live. We learn from them styles of clothing and haughtiness, but we do not learn from them silence during prayer. We are like them in consuming their cheeses and their wine, but we are not like them with regard to justice, righteousness, and honesty. We are like them in shaving our beard or modeling it in their style, but we are not like them in their refraining from cursing or swearing in God's Name. We are like them in frequenting underground gaming rooms, but we are not like them in turning from vengeance and

---

19. See Saperstein, *"Your Voice Like a Ram's Horn,"* pp. 136–46.

20. See *Jewish Preaching*, pp. 272–85 and passages quoted below.

21. This is clearly related to the question of sculptured ornamentation on gravestones in the Jewish cemetery at Ouderkerk, a trend strongly opposed by Morteira, as reflected in a sermon from the 1630s, reused in his eulogy for Menasseh ben Israel. See *"Your Voice Like a Ram's Horn,"* pp. 414, 419–20. In a Portuguese responsum, he gave permission for Jews to have paintings and sculptures in their homes (Salomon, *Tratado*, p. lxi, n. 19). Perhaps he distinguished between different kinds of sculptures? For the impact of sculpture and painting on the external and internal decor of contemporary Dutch Christian houses, see Schama, *The Embarrassment of Riches*, pp. 311–19.

refraining from bearing hatred in our hearts. We are like them in fornicating with their daughters, but we are not like them in conducting business affairs with faithfulness and fairness.[22]

Although the content of the listing is similar to what we have seen before—pertaining to physical appearance (clothing, hair style), speech (curses, oaths), conduct in the synagogue, sexual immorality, business ethics—the rhetorical strategy is totally different from anything already encountered. The underlying theme is assimilation to the ways of the Gentiles, a stock theme in Jewish ethical literature, but here the condemnation is double, for each example of negative influence is balanced with a potentially positive influence that the Jews ignore. Jewish behavior is rebuked directly—by specifying the elements of negative influence—and indirectly—by alluding to the antithesis of the good things Gentiles do (e.g., *they* are respectfully quiet during prayer, *they* conduct business affairs honestly; *you*, by implication, fail in these respects).[23] The Gentiles of the host society serve here not merely as a danger and a threat, but as a source of positive values from whom Jews could indeed benefit. The message is: Be discerning. Distinguish between those characteristics of Christian Amsterdam that must be avoided and those for which emulation is appropriate.

What is the rhetorical function of such lists? Their advantage is that they enable the preacher to cover broad ground quickly, to catch in his verbal net as many of the listeners as possible, to raise many of the issues that concern him at one time rather than waiting for an appropriate opportunity based on

---

22. *GS Devarim* 1645, p. 69c, 1902, p. 257; Moses Edrehi incorporated this passage without attribution, adding a few explanatory phrases, into his book of sermons *Yad Mosheh*, p. 11b; see above, p. 31. The "gaming rooms" (*battei seḥoq*) reflects the Portuguese term *casas de juego*; cf. Yosef Kaplan, "The Sephardic Jews also met the local residents at … coffeehouses, taverns, gaming houses (*casas de juego*), and even brothels" (in *Cultures of the Jews*, ed. David Biale, p. 665). In his letter to Jacob Sasportas highlighting the penitential mood of the Amsterdam Jews in the wake of the Sabbatian movement, Aaron Sarphati wrote that "of their own accord, they have abandoned the gaming houses": Sasportas, *Tsitsat Novel Tsevi*, ed. Isaiah Tishby Jerusalem, 1954), p. 29; cf. Gershom Scholem, *Sabbatai Sevi* (Princeton, 1973), p. 523.

23. For other examples of this rhetorical instrument of rebuke by Jewish moralists (and analogous Christian examples, see Saperstein, *Jewish Preaching*, pp. 45–54. Cf. the passage by Menasseh ben Israel, discussing Ezekiel 5:7: the prophet reproves Israel in that "they did not even imitate the zeal of the pious heathen—their neighbours—who were strict observers of their religion; but they only imitated the wicked among them in their laxity and idolatries." *Conciliator: A Reconcilement of the Apparent Contradictions in Holy Scripture*, 2 vols. (London, 1842; reprint edition Brooklyn, 2000), 2:210.

the content of his sermon. The expectation is that while no one will feel responsible for every infraction specified, each listener will relate to at least one. The disadvantage of this approach is that no failing is explored in depth. If a congregant's attention wanders for a moment, he might miss the details that apply most directly to him. Furthermore, listeners may not be *convinced* that the behavior is wrong, for there is time only for assertion, not for argumentation; they must accept the preacher's premise as self-evident. Morteira apparently believed that this could be an effective mode of rebuke, but that it was not sufficient. He therefore supplemented it with more extensive discussion of specific shortcomings, focusing on a specific issue that emerged from the fabric of his explication of classical texts. We turn now to examples of this mode of rebuke.

1. *Materialism, ostentation*

A popular image prevalent today of the Portuguese Jewish community in seventeenth-century Amsterdam is that it was composed almost entirely of wealthy merchants. As we shall see, this is a distorted picture. Many of those who arrived from Portugal had lost most of their possessions, and poverty was a problem the community had to confront directly.[24] Yet some of the first generation of Portuguese arrivals were indeed wealthy, and an early sermon by Morteira, entitled "The People's Envy" and delivered in January of 1622, indicates that he considered the ostentatious display of this opulence to be a serious problem. I have published an annotated translation of this fascinating sermon and have shown its use of a verse (Exod. 1:7) about the Israelites in Egypt as a prototype for the kind of behavior that has always caused problems for Jews in exile—behavior that arouses both the anger of God and the hostility of the host population. I shall address here only the actual passages of censure it contains.

The tragic paradigm is stated in the introduction. "Expelled from certain countries, we have arrived in others totally destitute, and God has graciously enabled us to acquire new wealth and possessions. Those who knew at first hand the circumstances of their arrival lived in peace. But after their deaths, others have become arrogant, indulging in empty vanities, until the indige-

---

24. See, for example, Israel Bartal and Yosef Kaplan, "'Aliyat 'Aniyyim me-Amsterdam le-Eretz Yisra'el Be-Reshit ha-Me'ah ha-Sheva-'Esreh," *Shalem* 6 (1992): 175, and n. 3, referring to a Hebrew University doctoral dissertation on the poor in this community. The article shows that charitable support was sometimes made available to new arrivals from Portugal only on condition that they would leave Amsterdam for another Jewish community, preferably far away (p. 176).

nous population eventually expelled them."[25] This arrogance is displayed first in the propensity to acquire unnecessarily large houses. Those who live in exile "should be prepared to endure hardship." They should be content if they have what is necessary for subsistence living.

> But such a contented disposition is not what we see today. A man who is alone with his wife, or even a single man, lives in a large house with unnecessarily spacious rooms. Such people waste their money, which they may well need some day, by giving it to the Gentiles and receiving nothing of value in return. This is not befitting a people living outside its land, in the land of its enemies.[26]

Second is the social pressure to wear exorbitantly expensive clothes and to show disdain for all who eschew the latest costly fashions. Morteira's own personal frustration may be reflected in his formulation: "Since only those who dress ostentatiously are honored, and garments are a prime source of prestige, those who refrain from such dress will be called misers. No one will think highly of them. They will be hated and scorned."[27] Finally, there is the wasteful expenditure of money on lavish furnishings and sumptuous banquets in order to impress others. The preacher's interpretation of Amos 6:6, *they are not concerned about the ruin of Joseph*, introduces the theme of social consciousness in the face of blatant economic inequality, with obvious resonance for his own context:

> they forget that some of their brothers have no bread at all for themselves or their children. It would be better for them to spend their money inviting the poor and providing them with food and other necessities. But they curse the poor and spend their money on trivial luxuries that can do them no good, giving money again and again to men who mock them as soon as they leave their homes.

Explicit application to the present comes some moments later. "Such is our way today. All of us complain and weep about hard times, but when we get something, we spend a fortune on banquets with wine. The same is true of all

---

25. Saperstein, *Jewish Preaching*, p. 274.

26. Ibid., p. 276.

27. Ibid., p. 280. This is, of course, a common theme in both Jewish and Christian preaching and communal legislation in the late Middle Ages and early modern periods. For an example from sixteenth-century England, see the sermon "On Exces of Apparel," in Chandos, editor, *In God's Name*, pp. 63–67, including, "She doth but waste superfluously her husbandes stocke by such sumptuousnesse, and sometimes is the cause of much briberie, extortion, and deceite...." (p. 66).

the other unnecessary things."[28] The sermon ends with an expression of virtual despair at the chances of reforming the behavior of a community in which patterns of behavior are so deeply ingrained and social pressures so powerful that a preacher can hardly expect his admonition to be heeded.[29]

Almost twenty years later, Morteira returned to this theme in a powerful sermon on the lesson *Ha'azinu* for the Sabbath of Repentance. An alert listener, mindful of the occasion and hearing the sermon's theme-verse, *They vexed Me with their trivialities... with a foolish people* (am naval), *I'll vex them* (Deut. 32:21), would have expected to hear words of rebuke and warnings of proportionate punishment. Morteira did not disappoint. Following is one example, the first words of which echo a passage from "The People's Envy":

> In this category of vexation are those who do not give a penny to charity. Day and night they weep if any assessment is placed upon them for a true religious or humanitarian need, but afterward they spend a fortune on superfluous jewelry and clothing. These ones certainly *vex God with their trivialities*, for they make such trivialities into the foundation of their lives.... All who take excessive pride in their beauty for sinful purposes, whether to associate with Gentile women or to transgress God's words in any matter because of their baubles, *they have vexed Me with their trivialities.*
>
> For all of these, God ordained—measure for measure—*I'll vex them with a miserly nation.* The third meaning of the noun *naval* is "miser," as we see in the verse, *No more shall the miser be called generous* (Isa. 32:5) This means that against those who made money their main object, something fundamental, God will arouse a miserly nation, which lusts for money and will take from these people all of theirs, so that they will be left plucked absolutely clean. This nation will take all their money, their houses, and their fields—the calf they worship—and God will heap their carcasses upon their lifeless fetishes (cf. Lev. 26:30), as we see this very day.[30]

Another aspect of *I'll vex them with a miserly nation* in this sense is the

---

28. Saperstein, *Jewish Preaching*, pp. 282, 284.

29. Such a statement, of course, may be a rhetorical ploy in itself, covering the preacher if his pleas or denunciations fail to effect change, arousing sympathy for the lone guardian of moral purity with his "finger in the dike." Morteira returned to this sermon on subsequent occasions, sometimes citing it explicitly, sometimes recapitulating its themes in allusion, as in the peroration to his powerful 1627 topical sermon cited above in chap. 4 (above, pp. 137–38). See the full translation below, pp. 404–5.

30. Probably referring to the confiscation of property by the Portuguese Inquisition rather than to confiscatory taxation in Amsterdam.

losses that God will bring about for those who hold back from giving to the poor in accordance with their means.... So *I'll vex them with a miserly nation* alludes to the person whose debtor has fled with his money, leaving the uncollectable debt in his possession; thus he gives to *a miserly nation* what he did not want to give to the poor.[31]

This passage is more complex than it might seem, for there is a subtle shift in the object of criticism that might well have created confusion or tension in the minds of the listeners. The first paragraph seems clearly to be directed against those members of the Amsterdam Portuguese nation who resent and resist the community's imposition of fiscal burdens for religious and charitable needs, but who do not hesitate to spend money on themselves and are conspicuous in their display of expensive jewelry and clothing.[32] This is similar to the theme we have encountered in "The People's Envy." The problem of sexual license, especially with Gentile women, we have already encountered in Morteira's homiletical listings of sins, and we shall soon see other explicit discussions of this problem. These sentences seem to have been intended to strike close to home.

With the introduction of the punishment promised in the verse, there is a shift in ground. The preacher seems to be referring to the burden of heavy taxes. But does he really mean to characterize his Dutch neighbors as "a stingy people, lusting for wealth?" Were wealthy members of his own community being stripped bare of everything—money, houses, and lands—at the time when Morteira was speaking? Hardly. More likely this refers to the *Portuguese* policies of confiscation imposed on those condemned by the Inquisition. And that would make the sinners, those who make the accumulation of money into a paramount value, not the Jews of Amsterdam but the New Christians who remain in Portugal for fear of losing their wealth. Indeed, this is precisely how Morteira characterized the assimilating New Christians a few moments earlier in the same sermon: "Because of their money they abandon God, and they remain in the lands of their enemies serving another God in order to tend to their money, their lands, and their houses."[33] And the divine curse from Leviticus invoked in this passage, *I will heap your carcasses upon your lifeless fetishes* (Lev. 26:30), is a central motif of one of Morteira's most powerful

31. MS 3:308r, *Ha'azinu*, Deut. 32:21, Sabbath of Repentance, 1641. See the entire passage in context below, p. 522.

32. On resistance to communal taxation by wealthy merchants and the attempts by the governing board of the community to enforce compliance, see Kaplan, "Social Functions," pp. 112–13, 115–16, and Vlessing, "New Light on the Earliest History of the Amsterdam Portuguese Jews," pp. 60–61.

33. MS 3:308r, *Ha'azinu*, Deut. 32:21, Sabbath of Repentance, 1641 (below, p. 520).

condemnations of the New Christians who stubbornly refused to heed the call to return to the true God.[34] At this point, listeners might well have thought, "So he was not talking about *us* after all; it is those others, back in Portugal, whose materialism is being punished."

But then the focus shifts back again. "Those who hold back their hands from giving to the poor in accordance with their means" brings the audience back to the starting point: social tensions in Amsterdam and communal responsibility for the poor. The reference to a Jewish creditor whose borrower has fled leaving him with a non-collectable debt appears to be so specific that it might have alluded to a case the listeners would have recognized. Morteira presents it as a providential punishment: money that he *should* have given to the poor is lost to him anyway when taken by a Gentile cheater.[35] Each congregant is expected to assess whether this might apply to him. Thus the criticism of materialism goes beyond the stereotyped and the conventional. Organically emerging from the biblical text, it is intended to evoke powerful associations with issues of central concern back in Portugal and in the new home.

Let us examine one more sermon in which Morteira spends considerable time pounding home the perils inherent in the drive to accumulate wealth. The last section weaves his critique of materialism into a texture framed by three texts, "The more possessions the more worries" (M. *Avot* 2,7); "God's anger was mild, but they helped make it worse" (cf. Zech. 1:15); and *Riches are hoarded by their owner to his own misfortune* (Eccles. 5:12). People make their lot worse, compounding the intrinsic problems of the human condition derived from mortality and the punishments imposed in Eden (Gen. 3:16 and 18) by their compulsion to acquire.

> While God's curse applied to the necessities, men have heaped up the superfluous: in foods, clothing, houses, servants, and many other such things. In seeking to sustain these, worries abound, for men have to amass money that would not be needed if they were satisfied with what is necessary, rather than seeking to acquire what is superfluous. "The more possessions, the more worries" about guarding them, and the more one has to think about acquiring even more and regulating them

---

34. MS 3:154r *Mattot*, Num. 30:11, early 1630s; for the full passage, see below, p. 293.

35. In first publishing this passage, I read the ambiguous phrase (*Mi she-yivrah ba'al ḥovo ve-yisha'er be-yado 'im mamono ve-yiten le-goi naval..*) differently—the creditor has fled, and the debtor will not have to give the money to the Gentile government—but I believe the current reading makes more sense.

properly, to the point where it becomes a chain reaction driving man from evil to evil, from worry to worry: the manifold desires lead to the seeking after money and its increase, and the increase of wealth leads to the worry about guarding it.[36]

While there is nothing in this passage that would necessarily connect it with the Portuguese Jews of Amsterdam in 1635, one may well imagine the less affluent listeners nodding in approval, and the more affluent perhaps beginning to squirm.

The stakes are increased as the preacher goes on to speak of the impact of materialism on family dynamics, particularly the relationship with children. "Because of the acquisition of wealth, they keep their children at a distance while they try to amass a fortune. Fathers spend their days in worry because of money, quarrels and conflicts abound among them, enmities increase. Worst of all, because of the increase of money, the children learn pride and arrogance and disobedience and other such ignoble qualities, as the Bible says, *Jeshurun grew fat and unruly* (Deut. 32:15). All these are powerful reasons for a father's worry."[37] Still speaking in generalities, Morteira begins to touch upon more personal matters: the problems in a new generation of children born in Amsterdam and raised in an environment in which the parents' ambitions are given free rein.

The final section is based on the rabbinical exposition of the verse from Ecclesiastes, applying the harmful effects of hoarded wealth to various biblical characters (Genesis Rabbah 50,11, the opening rabbinic dictum of the sermon). Morteira takes this process a further step, relating these Biblical figures to contemporary types. Lot, said to exemplify the verse, "teaches about the death that men bring about for themselves because of money by remaining in a place of danger and a place of sins," a clear allusion to the Portuguese New Christians who stay in their old homes to avoid the risk of losing their possessions by emigration. Koraḥ represents those whose economic security leads them to think they can sin with impunity. Haman is "the prototype of men who involve themselves in great and dangerous business affairs, crossing seas and wildernesses to fulfill their desires." The tribes of Gad and Reuben represent yet another group: "those who, because of money, do not rest or repose; they find no respite for their feet or slumber for their eyes. Because of their business affairs they live a life of sorrow, toiling hard, running around and exhausting themselves until they bring death near."[38] It is not that

---

36. MS 5:85v, *Va-Yeshev*, Gen. 37:14, 1635.
37. Ibid.
38. MS 5:86r, *Va-Yeshev*, Gen. 37:14, 1635.

Morteira idealizes or even values poverty. Other sermons show that this is clearly not the case; he is aware that poverty causes even greater spiritual problems than wealth.[39] But for a community characterized by its economic dynamism and entrepreneurial energy, led by international merchants, some of whom must have been sitting in the congregation when these words were uttered, the force of this castigation must have been quite remarkable.

2. Licentious Behavior

Another theme that we have confronted several times in Morteira's lists of condemnations is licentious behavior crossing religious boundary lines, especially between Jewish men and Gentile women. Leaders of the Amsterdam community had to confront various sexual issues, in addition to the obvious sin of adultery.[40] Their first responsibility, a more internal problem, was to make certain that young women from the Portuguese nation actually underwent proper conversion before marriage to male members of the Jewish community. A second was to prevent the scandal of sexual liaisons between Jewish men and Christian women in Amsterdam. There was also the need to guard against the loss of young men and women who were prepared to convert to Christianity in order to marry desirable mates from Amsterdam's upper class. The passages in which these themes are addressed indicate the emotional baggage borne by those who had to confront such situations.

We begin with a sermon from 1624 on the lesson *Mishpatim*. Discussing the factors that promote assimilation and blur distinctions between different nations, Morteira cites a well-known dictum from the Midrash (Leviticus Rabbah 32,5): "Because of four things the Israelites were redeemed from Egypt: they did not change their names, they did not change their language, they did not speak slander, and none of their children was guilty of sexual licentiousness." Arriving at the theme of licentiousness, after referring to the incident of Shechem and Dinah, he makes a contemporary application:

> Even today we have seen God's gracious love in this matter. What has enabled the last remnant of *the exile of Jerusalem which is in Sefarad* (Obad. 20) to preserve its identity is their refusal to intermarry with the Gentiles of that land. This has preserved their lineage and their identity, so that they are not lost to the community of the Eternal. Woe to the one who mixes in with them while still in a Gentile state, before conversion, for

---

39. See, for example, his trenchant critique of the Christian idealization of poverty in the *Va-Ethanan* sermon of *Giv'at Sha'ul* (1645), p. 70a–c, translated below, pp. 414–20.

40. See Kaplan, "Social Functions," p. 126–27, on excommunication imposed for adultery. I have not found adultery to be a theme emphasized by Morteira in his sermons.

he destroys his offspring and his future remembrance.[41]

Here the preacher begins with an observation of historical sociology: that the Portuguese New Christian population maintained a separate identity through endogamy, marrying other New Christians.[42] Then in a single climactic sentence introduced by the interjection—Woe!—Morteira quickly shifts the spotlight from the Iberian Peninsula to matters close at home, apparently referring to marriages between a Jewish man and a female member of the Portuguese nation before she has been properly converted, and forcefully reminding his listeners that the offspring of this marriage will not be considered Jews.[43] We may see here what one scholar has termed a "tension between ethnic attitudes and rabbinic norms." It was reflected in statutes of the Amsterdam Dowry Society, which allowed that the illegitimate daughter of a "Portuguese" Jew born of a non-Jewish woman was eligible to apply for a dowry (to be received after conversion), while the illegitimate daughter of a "Portuguese" Jewess and a Gentile father could not.[44]

A year or two later, preaching on the following verse from the same lesson, Morteira returned to the story of Shechem and Dinah as an example of the problem of intermarriage. Here there could be no mistaking the forcefulness of his denunciation:

As for those Jews who lust to give their daughters and their sisters to

---

41. MS 3:345v, *Mishpatim*, Exod 21:6, 1624.

42. On the preponderant but not exclusive endogamy among the Spanish New Christians, see Cecil Roth, "The Religion of the Marranos," 30–31; Edward Glaser, "Invitation to Intolerance: A Study of the Portuguese Sermons Preached at Autos-da-fé," *HUCA* 27 (1956): 366; Yosef Kaplan, "Maslulei Hitbolelut u-Temi'ah be-Qerev Anusei Sefarad ba-Me'ot ha-Tet-Vav–Yod-Zayin," in *Hitbolelut u-Temi'ah*, ed. Y. Kaplan and M. Stern [Jerusalem, 1988–1989], pp. 167–68. At the conclusion of this sermon, Morteira indicates that this endogamy is not universal, and that some New Christian men who did into marry Old Christian women wanted to assimilate into Portuguese society. See also below, p. 284.

43. Unfortunately, the crucial sentence is not as clear as it might be due to its syntax. The literal translation would be "Woe to the one who mixes in with them while he is still a Gentile (*ba-goyuto*)," but the logic of the situation requires the interpretation I have given, even though the expected Hebrew word would have been *ba-goyutam*.

44. Miriam Bodian. "'Men of the Nation': The Shaping of *Converso* Identity in Early Modern Europe," *Past & Present* 143 (1994): 70. For the statute, see I. S. Révah, "Le premier règlement imprimé de la 'Santa Companhia de dotar orfans de donzelas pobres,'" *Boletim internacional de bibliografia lusobrasileira* 4 (1963): 677. A significant number of applications to the Amsterdam Society came from Portuguese New Christian girls living in France (Bodian, "The 'Portuguese' Dowry Societies," p. 59). The rabbinic leadership in Amsterdam apparently felt the need to insure that women from this population received proper conversions before marriage to Amsterdam Jews.

Gentile grandees, woe to them and woe will be their fate! We should
follow the footsteps of Jacob's sons, and not give our daughters to an
uncircumcised man: uncircumcised of heart, foolish, ignorant, and
senseless; uncircumcised of lips, who speaks indecency and slander;
uncircumcised of ear, never having heard words of learning; and worst
of all, uncircumcised of flesh, for in him is every defect and impurity.
We cannot give our sister to a man who is uncircumcised (Gen. 34:14), even
if he is a prince of the land and they are aliens in it.[45]

The rhetorical power of the passage is palpable. Jacob's sons, who said that
they could not give their sister to an uncircumcised man (Gen. 34:14), become
the models for the contemporary community to emulate. "Uncircumcised" is
presented first metaphorically ("uncircumcised of heart... lips... ears") in
accordance with its use in the Bible, to express the absence of proper moral
and intellectual virtues in a potential marriage partner; this is a point that
would apply to members of the community. But the climax returns to the
physical meaning of the word: "uncircumcised of flesh" is the worst of all. It
appears as if the point being made is precisely the reverse of that in the
previous sermon: that Jewish girls should not be permitted to marry
Portuguese New Christians who come to a Jewish community until they
undergo circumcision.[46] But the references in the first sentence to "Gentile
grandees" (*gedolei ha-goyim*), and in the last sentence to a "prince in the land,"
make it more likely that the preacher was talking about wealthy and powerful
Dutch Christian men.

What social and legal reality is being reflected here? It is difficult to imagine
these words being said without reference to an actual situation in Amsterdam.
Indeed, Christians as well as Jews frowned upon intermarriage.[47] Dutch law
prohibited marriage between Christians and Jews or Muslims throughout this
period.[48] Would female immigrants from Portugal who chose this path have
been considered by the Dutch authorities to be Christians because of their
background? Did such intermarriage occur frequently or only in an occasional case? There are indeed references in archival documents about such

45. MS 2:27v, *Mishpatim,* Exod. 21:7, 1625 or 1626.

46. The desire of some of these men to delay this procedure, often in order to avoid an
unambiguous and irreversible identification with Judaism, was a major problem within the
community, addressed by Morteira in several of his sermons.

47. The town council of Haarlem, in 1605, granted permission for Jews to settle in their
city provided "they did not publicly blaspheme the name of Christ and refrained from
marrying Christians" (Huussen, "The Legal Position," p. 23).

48. Schama, *The Embarrassment of Riches,* p. 442.

unions, although they seem to reflect anomalies rather than a trend.[49] The passage challenges us to reconstruct the problem to which Morteira was responding.

We recall that in the *Ha'azinu* sermon for the Sabbath of Repentance from the early 1630s Morteira was particularly eloquent in his denunciation of "intermarriage with the Gentiles" and its dire consequences (above, p. 186). In a later sermon on the lesson *Pinḥas,* he uses very similar words, but this time he exemplifies and illustrates each of the negative results. Discussing the biblical accounts of attempted seduction of the Israelites, he distinguishes between Moabite women, interested only in satisfying their lust, and the more dangerous Midianite women, who tried to induce idolatrous worship.[50] A linguistic nuance hints of the typological significance of the narrative:

> We must read carefully: it does not say "as they made you suffer," pertaining to something that occurred in the past, but rather *as they make you suffer* (Num. 25:18), in the present tense, meaning at all times. For this evil advice given by the Midianites has been for us a source of suffering and sorrow at all times. It is what cast us out of our land; it is what disturbs our tranquility; it is what brings about all our troubles; it is what delays [the ending of] our exile; it is what destroys our souls.
>
> It is what cast us out of our land; as we read, *King Solomon loved Gentile women... from the nations about whom God had said to the Israelites, "Do not go among them and let them not come among you, for they will entice you to serve their gods." But Solomon was devoted to them and loved them* (1 Kings 11:1–2).
>
> It is what disturbs our tranquility, for we have seen in historical chronicles how many evils this behavior has caused for us in every generation,

---

49. See Koen, "The Earliest Sources Relating to the Portuguese Jews," pp. 34, 36. These include a Portuguese Jew in Amsterdam who declared that he was a Christian at the registration of his intended marriage; after the death of his first, Christian, wife, he married a Portuguese Jewess (p. 34). Another Jew declared his willingness to convert to Christianity in order to marry a Christian woman (p. 34). Koen states that "There were undoubtedly more marriages between Christians and Jews" (p. 36), but the cases recorded point to Jewish males, rather than females.

50. MS 2:60r, *Pinḥas,* Num. 26:17, 1640s, top lines. This conclusion is based on a surprising exegesis of Numbers 25:1–3. The preacher maintains that while the first verse unambiguously speaks of the Moabites, the verb at the beginning of the second verse describes the Midianites, not explicitly mentioned until verse 6. His "proof" is that the god mentioned in Numbers 25:3, 25:5 and 25:18, "Peor," is the Midianite god, whereas the Moabite god was Chemosh. This seduction to idolatry explains the severe punishment for the Midianites in 25:17 and facilitates the homiletical point about the danger of such liaisons. Cf. Abravanel ad loc., who also blames the Midianite, not the Moabite women, though with different reasons.

and especially in the days of Ezra. In this regard, it is said, *When I heard this news, I rent my robe and mantle, and tore my hair and my beard, and I sat dumbfounded; and all who went in fear of the words of the God of Israel rallied to me because of the offense of these exiles* (Ezra 9:3–4).

It is what brings about all our troubles, for exiles and murderous riots and expulsions have resulted for us because of this.

And it destroys our souls, as the Bible says, *May the Eternal cut off any who do this... for he has married a daughter of a foreign god* (cf. Mal. 2:11–12), and become a bridegroom of idolatry, thereby destroying his soul. That is what the Bible says, *He did not yield to her by lying with her or being with her* (Gen. 39:10): by lying with her in this world, or being with her in the world to come.[51]

If so, how can we wonder at the length of our exile, seeing that this sin always remains among us? For this reason the Bible says, *as they make you suffer* (Num. 25:18), in the present tense.[52]

This is a powerful passage, with strong content expressed in a highly rhetorical style. As in the earlier sermon, the consequences of sexual dalliance are set forth in crisp, parallel phrases, undoubtedly reflecting a similar structure in the original Portuguese delivery. Then each is unpacked by providing a biblical prooftext; the preacher's affecting the style of the Midrash lends authority to his discourse. It does not much matter whether the connection between the biblical verse and the consequence is obvious, as in the verse from Malachi, or questionable, as in the proposed link between Solomon's Gentile wives and exile;[53] the listener would not have time to ponder the relevance of the verse before being drawn into the next point. The rhetorical question at the end—"How can we wonder at the length of our exile?"—raises one of the most painful questions of Jewish life; the response suggests that the answer should be obvious to all.

Thus the passage achieves one of the central goals of the classical preacher: to make a biblical narrative immediately and directly relevant to the experience of the listeners. There is no need for an explicit statement that "we are doing the same thing today, and the consequences will be the same." As in the "People's Envy," the moral, though implicit, is clear: don't think that Amsterdam is fundamentally different from other places where Jews have lived;

---

51. Cf. *Tanḥuma, Va-Yeshev,* chap. 8.

52. MS 2:60r, *Pinḥas,* Num. 26:17, 1640s.

53. The biblical narrative presents the punishment for Solomon's behavior not as exile from the land but as loss to the Davidic line of much of his kingdom in the following generation (1 Kings 11:9–13).

the same behavior that created problems in the past will create problems in the present. In the earlier sermon, it was ostentatious materialism that caused envy leading to expulsion; here it is sexual liaisons that cross forbidden boundaries. In both cases, the traditional doctrine is forcefully driven home: sinful behavior, the fundamental cause of persecution in the past, is the primary reason for the continued length of the exile at present.

In a sermon on the lesson *Tsav* delivered in the spring of 1639, Morteira returned to this problem. Conceding that sexual relations with Christian women do not constitute the most serious transgression according to Jewish law, he responds by citing an exhortation from Maimonides' *Mishneh Torah*:

> Even though this sin does not carry the death penalty imposed by a court, let it not seem trivial to you, for the loss entailed in this is unlike that in any other sexual offense. The child born of a forbidden sexual union [between Jews] is the father's son in every respect and is considered to be part of the Jewish people even though he is a *mamzer*, but the child from a Gentile woman is not his child... and this results in the man's clinging to the Gentile [*ha-kutit*], from whom the Holy One has separated us.[54]

After emphasizing the role played by the priests during biblical times, especially Pinḥas and Ezra, in fighting this sin, he reaches his peroration, addressing the leadership of the congregation with an exhortation of his own: "If so, you, the eyes of the community, priests of the Eternal, summon the watches of our God to clear out the thorns from the vineyard, for a great breach has been made. And I shall inform you so that you may know the sickness, and provide the proper medication for it."[55] Here he is calling not merely for reform on the part of the offending parties, but for action on the part of those in positions of authority, whose responsibility it is to enforce appropriate moral standards.

A final allusion to this theme comes from the last years of Morteira's tenure as rabbi, as we have seen in chapter 3. Reusing a sermon he had delivered some years before, he added a substantial section pertaining to recent events in the life of the community; the date he provides is 11 Shevat, 5416 [February 6, 1656], some four years before his death. One of the events was a "plague that prevailed in this city for the past six months. Yet among all the Jews, no one died except for two infants; they were like the two perfect lambs, an atonement sacrifice for the entire community. This at a time when the num-

---

54. *Mishneh Torah, Hilkhot Issurei Biah* 12:7–8.
55. MS 1:19r, *Tsav,* Lev. 6:16, 1639.

ber of dead each week was close to nine hundred!" The preacher maintains that God providentially distinguished the Jews from the rest of the population, and that the proper response is to preserve this distinctiveness in their daily behavior:

> In order to give thanks to God for this great favor of distinguishing us from the peoples and removing the evil from our midst, we too must praise Him.... We must not profane the covenant of our ancestors by having sexual relations with Gentile women and becoming impure through them. For if God has distinguished us for our benefit, why should we be with them for our detriment? This is indeed to praise God..., and to maintain our distinctiveness from the local population, for this is always the cause of our problems.[56]

It is indeed noteworthy how little emotional identification Morteira expresses with the Christian population of the city in which he had lived for forty years: he mentions the devastation that ravaged this population only to contrast it with the minimal Jewish losses. The spirit of this passage is one of rejoicing and gratitude for God's providential care of the Jews. Yet even in celebration, an element of rebuke intrudes: he reminds his listeners of the pitfalls of assimilation in general and of the specific, paradigmatic danger of sexual dalliance with Christian women. Whether or not this loomed large in the minds of men who had just survived six months of a deadly plague, it certainly remained fixed in the mind of the preacher.

All of this bespeaks what must have been considered a genuine problem for the Jewish community. It is worth noting that the Pilgrim historian William Bradford, explaining the reasons for the decision of his people to leave Holland for America, referred to "the great licentiousness of youth in that country" and its negative influence on the English youth, some of whom followed "courses tending to dissoluteness and the danger of their souls."[57] But in addition to the dangers to the souls of the Jews in his community, Morteira was apparently conscious of another dimension of the problem. Several of the most important legal texts discussing the toleration and status of Jews in

---

56. MS 5:118v, *Va-Yiggash* on Gen 45:2, second delivery 1656.

57. *Of Plymouth Plantation 1620–1647, by William Bradford*, ed. by S. E. Morison (New York, 1952), chapter 4, p. 25. Schama characterizes the impressions of Dutch mores held by foreign visitors as "a strikingly free and unpatrolled playfulness between the sexes, *together* with a strict attention to marital loyalty" (*The Embarrassment of Riches*, p. 438). On problems raised by maidservants in the homes, see ibid., pp. 455–61; this may well have been a source of the transgressions Morteira criticizes, although he does not specifically characterize the women as servants.

Holland explicitly prohibit sexual relations between Jewish men and Christian women.[58]

Nevertheless, other sources confirm that such relations did indeed occur. Miriam Bodian has recently identified thirteen cases appearing in the published notarial records between 1600 and 1623, and these reflect only instances where a problem arose (usually pregnancy). Some of the offenders were "pillars of the Portuguese-Jewish community." Yet, as Bodian notes, the records of the bans imposed by the lay leadership of the community, analyzed by Yosef Kaplan, provide no instance of sanctions imposed for this behavior, but only for adultery. Bodian concludes that sexual dalliance with Gentile women was "undoubtedly regarded with disapproval by the *ḥakhamim* and more pious members of the community. But no action was taken to punish it."[59] Morteira's sermons reflect this "disapproval." As we have seen, in at least one case, he openly addresses the lay leadership and calls for more decisive action.[60] But there is no evidence of public response by the leadership in the period beginning in 1622, when the extant records of bans begin. Perhaps the lay leaders thought it better not to call attention to potential scandals; perhaps this behavior was so engrained in their own ethos that they could not openly condemn it. Whatever the reason, it is an important example of the disparity between Morteira's preaching and the actions of the *Mahamad*, which did not seem convinced by Morteira's forceful claim that not only the spiritual but the political future of the community in Amsterdam was at stake.

3. Other Sins of Behavior

Any religious leader, recognizing that there are only limited opportunities for expressing criticism of a congregation, must set priorities, determining which offenses are important enough to justify expending rhetorical armament and which are not worth the effort to denounce, either because they are relatively insignificant or because there is no likelihood the problematic behavior will be changed. Sometimes, however, the hierarchy of the moralist does not coincide with the hierarchy of the halakhah, and certain transgressions are singled out for especially fierce opprobrium even though they do not merit the harshest punishment in the traditional system of Jewish law. There are times when a preacher feels it necessary to take a stand, to draw the line, when the

---

58. Huussen, "The Legal Position, pp. 24, 26–28.

59. Bodian, *"Hebrews of the Portuguese Nation,* pp. 61, 65–66, 114–15.

60. See above, p. 203.

offensive act takes on symbolic significance beyond its own status. An example of this would appear to be the shaving of the corners of the beard.[61]

We have seen reference to this practice in a passage cited above: "We are like them in shaving our beard or modeling it in their style."[62] There it seemed to be just one of many examples of unfortunate emulation of undesirable Gentile qualities. But in a late sermon devoted to this theme, it takes on a much greater significance:

> Now that we have reached this point, know that I have seen some licentious members of our nation rejecting all discipline and shaving the corners of their beard—scornfully and high-handedly—thereby transgressing God's commandments. Rebukes and appeals concerning this matter that have been spoken on various occasions have been of no avail. We shall therefore insist on this and publicly declare its seriousness and the severity of its punishment, and how much damage accrues to the regents who have the authority to protest but will not, and how great is the sin of those who see this evil act but will not speak out.[63]

Later in the sermon, he shifts from proclamation to argumentation:

> It is known that deeds are more serious than words. Now if one who says that a single verse [of the Torah] was not revealed by God rejects a great principle, the divine revelation of the Torah,[64] one who constantly transgresses a commandment—scornfully and high-handedly, deliberately, with thought and understanding—certainly shows that he does not care about that commandment, and he thereby rejects the entire Torah. That is why whoever does [?] and deliberately brings a scribe, pen and ink, and witnesses, and signs a document of illicit interest thereby shows that he has rejected the God of Israel.[65] We too shall say that whoever brings a razor and barber and cloth and soap and destroys his beard, indeed he inscribes and records publicly that he has rejected the God of Israel, since he does not believe in this commandment and thereby rejects the divine revelation of the Torah.[66]

---

61. The passage cited above (p. 303), quoting Maimonides' warning about sexual relations with a Gentile woman, would appear to be another example.

62. Above, p. 190.

63. MS 1:44r, *Tazria*, Lev. 13:29, 1640s?

64. Cf. b. *Sanhedrin* 99a and Maimonides, *Hilkhot Teshuvah* 3, 8. Cf. also below, p. 444, n. 39.

65. Cf. b. *Baba Metsia* 71a.

66. MS 1:43v, *Tazria*, Lev. 13:29 (the sermon was bound upside down and backward in the manuscript, hence the lower folio number for a passage that comes later).

Morteira is attacking two groups here. The first were those men who affected a new style of appearance, either clean-shaven or, more likely, in a mode that was fashionable among upper-class Dutch Christians. Morteira believed they were violating the biblical prohibition against destroying the side-growth of the beard (Lev. 19:27). For many of the former New Christians, however, this prohibition must have seemed like a relatively insignificant and bothersome rule. It is precisely this attitude that Morteira assaults using the full power of his rhetorical skill. He insists that a Jew may not pick and choose among the commandments: willful disobedience of any one of them is tantamount to rejecting the entire system. Furthermore, this is not the kind of violation that can remain within the private domain, a matter for the individual conscience, nor is it limited to a specific moment. By its very nature, this is an ongoing, public demonstration of defiance, obvious every moment the individual is seen by others in the community.

The second object of attack, rather more surprising, was on the lay leadership of the community, the regents (*parnasim*). It was extremely unusual for Morteira to express in his sermons explicit criticism of these powerful figures. Indeed, he spent considerable time defending their importance and legitimacy. Here, however, he claims that the communal leaders have failed to support his own campaign against this beard infraction. He has denounced the practice from the pulpit on other occasions from the past, but it has been to no avail. The regents too must take a stand and actively oppose the violation. With at least some of the "guilty" parties sitting before him in the congregation—men with the prohibited beard style and regents who had decided not to act on the matter—it must have taken some courage to proclaim these uncompromising words.[67]

---

67. The law regarding acceptable shaving of the beard reveals a complicated history of interaction among legal exegesis, local custom, Kabbalistic doctrine, and other factors. Styles of contemporary Dutch Jews may be seen in the portraits by the great artists, including Rembrandt; see F. Landsberger, *Rembrandt, The Jews and the Bible* (Philadelphia, 1972), Michael Zell, *Reframing Rembrandt* (Berkeley, 2002), and Nadler, *Rembrandt's Jews.* Many of them have full beards, covering most of the face (Landsberger, plates 7–8, 17–21; Zell, Figures 31, 34–38); others, including Menasseh ben Israel, have the more fashionable Dutch style of clean-shaven cheeks and beards at the chin (Landsberger, plates 9–13; Zell, figures 9–10, 13–15, 33). It is perhaps worth noting that in the full-figure engraving, purportedly of Morteira, in the Warsaw 1902 edition of *Giv'at Sha'ul* based on a seventeenth-century painting, the rabbi appears with a full beard (see Sid Leiman, "Temunato shel Rabbi Sha'ul Ha-Levi Morteira," *'Alei Sefer* 10 (1982): 153–55, and "'Al Diyuqano shel R. Sha'ul Levi Morteira(?)," in Daniel Sperber, *Minhagei Yisra'el,* 6 vols. (Jerusalem, 1989–2003) 6: יז–יט (reprinted at end of Giv'at Sha'ul, 1792). In this later publication, Leiman casts doubt on the authenticity of the identification of the subject as Morteira. If indeed this was a picture of

"HERESY"

Morteira's rabbinic tenure in Amsterdam spanned the excommunications of Uriel da Costa, Juan de Prado, and Baruch Spinoza. The experiences of these individuals are generally understood by most modern scholars to represent a dramatically new phenomenon: the "Marrano heresy" or "Marrano heterodoxy" that threatened to undermine the foundations of traditional Jewish life in the Sephardi Diaspora, and informed the skepticism that challenged religious doctrine in wider circles of European society.[68] But did the rabbis who were combating and trying to control these challenges recognize them as something new? Or did they understand and present them as contemporary manifestations of a familiar historical pattern in Jewish life? How did they evaluate the danger these threats posed to their communities? Where did they seek guidance in responding to them? These are some of the questions on which our sources may shed some light.

When, back in 1989, I first confronted the massive new source material, I thought that there might be hidden away in the dense and difficult writing a kind of "smoking gun": a sermon in which Morteira defended the excommunication of his former student Baruch de Micael Espinosa—who undoubtedly heard many of the sermons delivered as he was growing up—and addressed directly and explicitly the doctrines for which Spinoza was expelled from the community. I found no such sermon in the extant texts. Indeed, very few can

---

Morteira, or if it portrayed another rabbi with the same beard style, this may have been another source of tension between Morteira and his younger colleague. Cf. the recent discussion of another Rembrandt portrait identified by some as Morteira, with a beard that is "long, unruly, and gray": Nadler, *Rembrandt's Jews*, p. 122. The apparently authentic portrait of Morteira from 1686 (26 years after his death, see ibid., p. 123) does not clearly reveal the nature of his beard.

68. See I. S. Révah, *Spinoza et Dr Juan de Prado* (Paris: 1959), pp. 13ff. ("Les tendances heterodoxes dans la communauté judeo-portugaises d'Amsterdam au xviie siècle"); Révah, "L'hérésie marrane dans l'Europe catholique du 15e au 18e siècle," in Jacques le-Goff, ed., *Hérésies et sociétés dan l'Europe pre-industrielle* (Paris: 1968), pp. 327–37, with discussion pp. 338–39; Kaplan, *From Christianity to Judaism*, pp. 162–63; Richard H. Popkin, "Jewish Anti-Christian Arguments as a Source of Irreligion from the Seventeenth to the Early Nineteenth Century," in Michael Hunter and David Wooten, eds., *Atheism from the Reformation to the Enlightenment* (Oxford: 1992), pp. 159–81, esp. 176–80; Yovel, *Spinoza and Other Heretics*, pp. 40–54); Bodian, *Hebrews of the Portuguese Nation*, pp. 117–18; Swetschinski, *Reluctant Cosmopolitans*, pp. 259–74; and sources listed in Joseph Davis, "The *Ten Questions* of Eliezer Eilburg and the Problem of Jewish Unbelief in the 16th Century," *JQR* 91 (2001): 326 n. 107. Compare the suggestion of Rosenberg, "Emunat Ḥakhamim," p. 313, that in addition to the Marrano background, the Protestant context is important in explaining the spread of "heretical" thinking.

be dated to the 1650s; as Morteira grew older, he characteristically borrowed more from his own writing, repeating and revising sermons he had delivered some years before. It would have been more likely to find sermons explicitly attacking Uriel da Costa, as the texts dating from the 1620s are more numerous than for any other decade. Here too, however, the extant material may disappoint. While the names of many members of the community are recorded in the manuscripts, Uriel does not appear to be one of them.

This is certainly not because Morteira was so aloof as to take no interest in these figures or their eccentric views. His lost book on the immortality of the soul seems to have been a direct response to da Costa's arguments against this principle.[69] His signature appears on the writ of excommunication of Juan de Prado, along with that of his colleague Isaac Aboab, and we know he was directly involved in the process that led to the severe condemnations of Prado and Spinoza.[70] It is, of course, possible that among the hundreds of sermons that remain lost, there is one or more that may some day be found that addresses these individuals explicitly. But I doubt this, for several reasons.

First, while Da Costa was not officially excommunicated in Amsterdam, a meeting of the rabbinic and lay leadership of the community on May 15, 1623 decided that he be excluded on the basis of prior excommunications in Hamburg and Venice. After the publication of his *Examination of the Pharisaic Traditions,* he was banished from the city. Although he was reconciled with the community for a few years after his mother's funeral, new accusations got him in trouble once again. It may well have been that especially during the years when his ban was considered to be in effect, it was considered inappropriate even to mention his name in public. Samuel da Silva, writing a refutation of da Costa's chapters denying the immortality of the soul, never mentions the name of his adversary.[71]

---

69. On this work, see Saperstein, "Saul Levi Morteira's Treatise on the Immortality of the Soul," *StRos* 25 (1991): 131–48.

70. See Kaplan, *From Christianity to Judaism,* pp. 139–42 and Yovel, *Spinoza and Other Heretics,* pp. 71–73 on the investigation of Prado; H. P. Salomon, "La vraie excommunication de Spinoza," pp. 181–99; Uriel Da Costa, *Examination of The Pharisaic Traditions,* p. 16. For an early account of Morteira's role in the excommunication of his student, Spinoza, see Jean-Maximilien Lucas, *La Vie De Feu Monsieur De Spinosa* (written in 1673), in A. Wolf, ed., *The Oldest Biography Of Spinoza* (London, 1927), pp. 44–56, summarized in chap. 1.

71. Da Costa, *Examination of the Pharisaic Traditions,* pp. 15–22, 429 (where Da Silva says he will avoid specifying the name out of respect for other members of his family). Menasseh ben Israel, who cites the same chapters in his book on the soul, similarly refrains from writing Da Costa's name (ibid., p. 49). Indeed, it has been noted that the names of da Costa and Spinoza never appear in any of the published works of the Amsterdam rabbis, and

But beyond this sense of appropriateness, characteristics of the sermon genre would naturally reinforce reticence. Especially when delivered by a preacher who has served in the same congregation over an extended period of time, the sermon is a mode of discourse intended for a community of acquaintances. The preacher knows those who are listening to him, and he knows what they know. There is no need to state or explain a significant community event in detail; it may be assumed that all of the listeners are aware of the unarticulated reference. If there has been a notorious public scandal, it is unnecessary to mention the name or to dwell at length about the particulars; only the most obtuse in the congregation will fail to recognize a pointed yet non-explicit allusion. Indeed, allowing the members of the congregation themselves to draw this connection between what is said and what is meant may itself be an important rhetorical technique, making the listeners active participants in the condemnation rather than passive recipients of an explicit message. For a good preacher, the subtlety of allusion may be more effective than the bluntness of direct attack. This allusiveness on the verbal level may be underlined by elements of the delivery: a pause or slowing of pace, an intensification of voice, a glance directed toward the offending parties.

A second characteristic of the sermon genre, related to this allusiveness, is the convention that preachers will anchor their message in the classical texts of the tradition, especially the Pentateuch and the canonical works of the Sages. It is not enough to condemn behavior of the present; the preacher will want to make clear why it is unacceptable through recourse to the texts accepted as authoritative by at least the great majority of the community. More than this, it will frequently be useful for the preacher to demonstrate how the offensive behavior was neither unprecedented not unimagined in the past, but was itself foreshadowed or prophesied in the sacred texts.

This leaves, however, a serious methodological problem for historians who attempt to deduce allusions to contemporary events in discussions of personalities or occurrences of the distant past. That preachers and commentators will sometimes communicate a message about the present when speaking about the familiar passages from the Bible does not entitle us to conclude that this is always the case. The assumption of contemporary resonance without adequate justification can lead us astray. What markers or pointers, then, can reassure us in concluding that allusions to the present are intended, and would have been understood by the listeners? Let us see how Morteira addresses the issue of "heretical views."

Morteira's oeuvre is consistent with this practice. J. W. Wesselius, "Herman P. Salomon on Saul Levi Mortera" [a review of the Dutch edition of the *Tratado*], *StRos* 23 (1989): 97.

Morteira's sermons on this topic are clustered around two sections of the Torah. The first—perhaps somewhat surprisingly—is the lesson *Tazria*, specifically the first verses of the thirteenth chapter of Leviticus. These verses, describing in precise detail the priestly responsibilities toward handling various afflictions of the skin are, of course, a serious challenge to any preacher who wants to anchor a message of interest to his listeners in the scriptural lesson, for the verses seem totally irrelevant to the experience of most members of post-biblical Jewish communities. The homiletical challenge was even more pronounced for Morteira, who—as we have seen—followed the self-imposed discipline of using each successive verse of the weekly lesson as the text (*nosei*) for his sermon year after year. The way out of this quandary, already adumbrated by the Sages, was to transcend the literal meaning of the verses pertaining to physical affliction and instead to present a message both linked to the text and more germane to the needs of the present.

We see this approach in his sermon on Leviticus 13:10, delivered in the early spring of 1640. After his introductory paragraph, he continues,

> The path we have trodden in all the sermons we have delivered on the previous verses of this lesson is based on the accepted truth taught us by the Sages: that these blemishes and sicknesses [of the skin] allude to blemishes and sicknesses of the soul. We have seen this in several of their statements.... We will proceed on this same path in our present sermon, for it is appropriate with regard to these afflictions to learn what is unknown from what is explicit.[72]

After setting out the underlying principle for the homiletical exposition of the verses, he continues to apply them more specifically.

> Thus, in the esoteric mode (*al derekh ha-remez*), it seems to me that these three afflictions are in their names a signal for us about three kinds of affliction found in the soul: three kinds of heretics (*kofrim*) who diverge from the path of faith of God's Torah. They are the ones mentioned at the beginning of the *parashah* [in Lev. 13:2]. The first are the philosophers, who follow the path of logical deduction, deriving from it what they apprehend and nothing else.... The second are those who

---

72. MS 1:41v, *Tazria*, Lev. 13:10, 1640. The allegorical interpretation of the kinds of skin affliction in Leviticus 13 as different forms of heresy was a staple of medieval Christian preaching: see Saul Brody, *The Disease of the Soul* (Ithaca, 1974), especially pp. 126–27; cf. pp. 136–40; Katherine Ludwig Jansen, *The Making of the Magdalen:* (Princeton, 2000), pp. 173–74; Beverly Mayne Kienzle, *Cistercians, Heresy and Crusade in Occitania, 1145–1229* (York, 2001), p. 120.

accept the divine Torah, and have commandments and deeds intended for the service of God, but whose Teaching has been falsified, attributed to God although it is not [from God].... The third are those from among the children of Israel who boast that they observe the Torah of our rabbi Moses, but who diverge from some of its principles and roots, such as the Karaites and those like them.[73]

The first category clearly refers to the pagan philosophers, whom Morteira considers to be essentially atheistic, denying judgment and Judge;[74] the second refers to the Christians and Muslims (see below). It is the third category, composed of Jews who accept the Torah in principle, that will be of concern to us.

---

73. MS 1:41v, *Tazria*, Lev. 13:10, 1640. On "Karaites" as a code term for those in the contemporary Amsterdam community who denied the oral law, see Yosef Kaplan, "'Karaites' in Early-Eighteenth-Century Amsterdam," in *Sceptics, Millenarians and Jews*, ed. David S. Katz and Jonathan I. Israel (Leiden, 1990), pp. 196–236; chapter 10 of Kaplan's *An Alternative Path to Modernity*, pp. 234–79. Several years later, Morteira recapitulated the same classification: "We shall briefly review what we explained on previous verses: we said that the afflictions of the body teach about afflictions of the soul, and among these afflictions, we found three types of corrupted belief, corresponding to the three kinds of physical affliction" (MS 1:39v, *Tazria*, Lev. 13:13).

74. Morteira's attitude toward philosophy is a complex matter that cannot be discussed in detail here. Juan de Prado accused Morteira of stating that "a man who is a philosopher is wicked" (Yovel, *Spinoza and Other Heretics*, p. 73; cf. p. 84), but I have not found such a formulation in his written works. He does indeed condemn radical philosophical views in his sermons. For example, discussing the implications of the doctrine that the world existed from eternity (MS 1:3v, *Va-Yikra*, Lev. 1:10, early 1630s), he states:

> In positing (heaven forbid!) these premises one would imagine that God acts out of necessity, like the activities of the sun producing its light and its heat. This subverts all of God's exalted qualities: His wisdom, power, and will. For assuming that He acts naturalistically, where is the evidence of His wisdom? All His awesome acts would be delimited by nature, and they could not be different.... The consequence is to destroy the exalted nature of divinity, and to annul the entire Torah, for Torah follows from providence, and that which acts out of necessity does not exercise providence. It also annuls all of the miracles, for the miracle is a change in nature, and that which acts out of necessity has no power to change anything. And it annuls all worship and fear of God, for what value is there in worshipping that which acts out of necessity if it cannot give, or add, or reward or punish, since its power is annulled (heaven forbid!).

Whether this is a theoretical criticism of doctrines known from the distant past or a response to a kind of proto-Spinozist identification of God with nature actually held within the community is not at all clear. Yet even most defenders of philosophical study in Judaism condemned such radical views. Morteira is to be classified with the moderate philosophers rather than with the extreme opponents; he cites Jewish philosophers (Maimonides, Gersonides, Albo, Abraham Shalom) approvingly in his sermons.

A second cluster of sermons in which the topic of heresy arises is less surprising: they come in lessons from the Book of Numbers dealing with the uprising of Koraḥ. In a sermon on Numbers 16:17, dating from the mid-1640s, we find the same tri-partite classification, undoubtedly taken over from the Leviticus sermons:

> Now there are three categories of those who arise against the divine Torah at various times. The first are those who deny the divinity of the Torah. The second are those who accept the divinity of the Torah but who claim that their religion is superior to ours. The third are those who accept our religion but who deny one part of it. Now the first are the philosophers; the second are the new religions, such as the Christians and Ishmaelites. The third are such as the Karaites and Boethusians.[75]

In addition to this three-fold classification, Morteira employs on other occasions a distinction between two categories. In a sermon delivered in the 1640s, for example, he tells us that destructive forces can be of two kinds: external or internal, from without or within. This applies in the world of nature, but it also applies in the realm of religion:

> It has already occurred that some religions have been destroyed or have degenerated, either because of the multiplicity of opinions about their fundamental principles held by the adherents of such religions, leading to degeneration and division into many factions, or because another people rose up against the first religion and forcefully suppressed and destroyed it, compelling the adherents of the first religion to accept a new one.[76]

At this point, Morteira introduces two prominent biblical characters from the Book of Numbers whom he uses as typological prefigurations of subsequent challenges.[77] The first is Balaam, who represents "those from the outside, not from the Jewish people, who have arisen against the divine Torah and the

---

75. MS 1:87r, *Koraḥ*, Num. 16:17. Morteira goes on to comment that in all of these cases, the opponents of the Torah, through divine providence, were never united to the point where they would present a perilous challenge, but were always divided among themselves.

76. MS 1:93r, *Pinḥas*, Num. 26:10; see the full translation below, p. 434.

77. Compare his use of Balaam in the sermon on *Balaq* published in *GS* 1645, p. 64b, 1912, p. 120b (several long polemical passages were removed from the Warsaw edition without any indication by the editor). On Morteira's use of typological interpretation in his sermons, see Saperstein, *"Your Voice Like a Ram's Horn,"* chapter 3, pp. 30–33. For Christian typological interpretation applied to contemporary heresy, see Kienzle, *Cistercians, Heresy and Crusade*, pp. 67–68.

prophecies." Here Morteira is concerned with Christian polemical attacks, and he spends considerable energy in this sermon, as elsewhere in his preaching, outlining the falsifications in Christian anti-Jewish arguments. But that is not our subject here.[78] After dealing with the external threat, he moves on to the internal threat of sectarianism, which he sees as more dangerous than the challenges from without. The prototype prefiguring this challenge from within is Koraḥ and his associates.

Immortality of the Soul

When we turn to the actual substance of the heretical views discussed by Morteira in his sermons, we find two focal issues, neither of which has any more relevance to the biblical model than Christian arguments actually pertain to Balaam. The first is the immortality of the soul. Morteira had been concerned with this concept from the beginning of his career, and he wrote what was apparently a massive treatise covering all kinds of questions relating to the soul, from its origins to its eschatological destiny.[79] It was a subject central to the bitter controversy over Uriel da Costa,[80] a subject to which he kept returning in his sermons. To take just one example, here is a passage from a sermon on Koraḥ, delivered probably in the late 1640s:

> Regarding the soul, there is a false and pernicious view pertaining to its essence. Some have said that its origin is material, and that it is nothing more than potential, and that it may become divine-like as a result of human effort and wisdom. Now this is extremely destructive, radically undermining the excellence and dignity of the soul. It is also against the Torah, which states, "He breathed into his nostrils a living soul" (Gen. 2:7), testifying that it came from God, not through an intermediary.
>
> As a result of this pernicious view, they have sunk appallingly, stage by stage. First, they diminished the dignity of the human being, no longer believing that the human being is exalted above all other created things, although the Torah affirms that all others were created for his sake.... For it makes no sense that something that is in its origin totally material at its core can be the purpose of created things so precious and

---

78. For a full discussion of the citation and responses to Christian polemical attacks against Judaism in Morteira's sermons, see chapter 8, below.

79. See Saperstein, "Saul Levi Morteira's Treatise."

80. See on this, recently, Talya Fishman, *Shaking the Pillars of Exile: 'Voice of a Fool,' an Early Modern Jewish Critique of Rabbinic Culture* (Stanford, 1997), pp. 57–58; and Salomon's edition of da Costa's *Examination.*

exalted—an assertion that raises no problem at all if we assume that the soul is derived from the highest spiritual essences....

After this, from the same cause, were those who rejected God's individual providence [over human beings], for this is based on the premise of the preciousness of each human soul. That is what makes the human being more exalted than all other species, for which divine providence pertains only to the species in general. If we posit that the human soul is originally material, people would believe that the human species has nothing but general providence, like the other species.

Descending even further than this are others who rejected the immortality of the soul and the resurrection of the dead. For they cannot imagine or believe that there is a certain subject that, for some reason, changes its essence from one extreme to the other, as is the change from potential to reality, and from material to spiritual. The last sect is the cursed sect of the Sadducees, who denied all spiritual reward and punishment, as Maimonides wrote about them in his comment on the Mishnah "Antigonos of Sokho" (M. *Avot* 1:3). Because they did not dare to reveal this view to the masses, for it would have turned all against them, they rejected the [rabbinic] tradition, and also the principle of resurrection of the dead. Having rejected this principle, they tried to find arguments and support from the Torah to establish their view, as do all the heretics, who interpret the Torah illegitimately.[81]

On the surface, Morteira is speaking about events in the past—specifically about the spread of sectarianism at the beginning of the Christian era. He attributes that development to a materialistic conception of the soul, which diminishes the distinctiveness of the human being and leads inexorably to more and more extreme denials of widely accepted Jewish beliefs: individual providence, the immortality of the soul, and the resurrection of the dead. This process is linked with Maimonides' explanation of the origins of sectarianism, although that explanation relies not on the philosophical implications of a particular doctrine of the soul but on students' misunderstanding of a statement about reward by one of the early Sages. There is no explicit application in the sermon to anything in the present. But given the furor over the issue of the soul in this particular community, would those seated in the congregation not have heard an allusion to da Costa? Let us look at the points where this resonance might have been apparent to the listeners.

First, the proof text in this passage, Genesis 2:7 ("He breathed into his nostrils a living soul") was a major issue of contention between Da Costa and

81. MS 2:258r–259r, *Korah*, Num. 16:18.

Da Silva in their bitter polemic of 1623–1624. Da Silva, like Morteira, insisted that this verse meant that the soul was "insufflated into man by God Himself," and therefore of special dignity. Da Costa argued that the same verse showed that "the vital spirit breathed into Adam was the animal soul," namely, "that vital spirit which animates the individual, and which is contained in the blood."[82]

Second, Morteira's complaint that "They diminished the dignity of the human being, no longer believing that the human being is exalted above all other created things, as the Torah affirms," echoes the formulation of Da Costa, although it may not precisely report his view: Da Costa did not hold that the souls of human beings and animals were identical. Rather, he had written that "there is no difference between the soul of an animal and the soul of a human being *other than that man's soul is rational* and the beast's is devoid of reason." "Man has no pre-eminence over a beast *as regards permanence,* for all is vanity." "Beasts and man have the same *spirit.*"[83]

Third, Morteira states that this position leads to the repugnant conclusion of rejecting the immortality of the soul and the resurrection of the dead.[84] Everyone undoubtedly knew that the main thrust of Da Costa's discussion of the soul in his *Examination* was the explicit denial of its immortality. Much of this discussion was based on an analysis of biblical verses; perhaps even more controversial and offensive was his concluding section on the "false and pernicious consequences" of the traditional belief, a passage to which we shall return.

Finally, Morteira refers to the Sadducees as the "cursed sect" that was guilty of holding this heretical doctrine. At least some of the listeners may well have recalled that the image of the Sadducees was another issue in the conflict of 1623–1624. Da Silva stated that "the Sadducees were founded by that depraved individual, Sadok, who was moved by passionate hatred and insubordination to abandon his master Antigonos and who, surrounding himself with a gang of dissolutes, stirred them up by his false preaching against the Phari-

---

82. Da Costa, *Examination,* pp. 451, cf. pp. 479–82 (Da Silva); 321–22, 311 (Da Costa).

83. Da Costa, *Examination,* pp. 311, 321. Emphasis added. Some years after this sermon was delivered, Orobio de Castro cited Juan de Prado referring to a Dr. Cardoso, who maintained that the human soul is no different from that of the animal, and therefore mortal; see Yerushalmi, *From Spanish Court to Italian Ghetto,* p. 252. Yerushalmi believes that this could not have been Isaac Cardoso, who defended the traditional doctrine of immortality (pp. 253–56).

84. For a sixteenth-century Jewish challenge to resurrection, see Davis, "The *Ten Questions* of Eliezer Eilburg" (above, n. 1), pp. 313–14. For heretical denial of immortality and resurrection in the Christian context, see Carlo Ginzburg, *The Cheese and the Worm: The Cosmos of a Sixteenth-Century Miller* (New York, 1982), pp. 47, 72–76, 119, 123–24, 128.

sees." Da Costa took up the challenge, and replied by defending Sadok, with whom he seems to have identified personally: "If denying immortality was his sole malice and obstinacy, he must have been one of the most truthful men in the world. The Sadducees, far from being vile and depraved were, as Josephus says, the noblest members of the nation." He concluded by insisting that this was not just a matter of the distant past: "nor is their sect extinct, for there are many of them alive today."[85] For all these reasons, the passage seems to have been intended to resonate with memories and issues much more immediate than the early rabbinic period.

The Oral Law

The second major area of heretical challenge addressed by Morteira involved the divine origin of the Oral Law. In the sermon where he juxtaposed Balaam and Koraḥ as prototypes of external and internal challenges to the integrity of Jewish faith, he points to the Oral Law as the aspect of Judaism most vulnerable to attack. "Koraḥ and his cohorts subverted the tradition," a reading certainly not obvious from the biblical text but useful for a broader point, applying to others:

> None of those who arose from among the Jewish people to dispute the Jewish religion dared to dispute about the Written Law. Had they done this, they would have left the category of the Jewish people and would no longer have been considered as part of our nation; thus no one would have paid them any heed. Rather, when they sought to introduce contention and strife, they did so regarding the words of tradition and the interpretation of the Law that was given orally, for this is the most vulnerable part, having no support in a written record. They therefore thought they could destroy the Torah through the breach of this wall, for certainly without the Oral Law, the Written Law would be sundered into a thousand Torahs according to the large number of opinions, and everyone would make of it whatever he wanted.[86]

At this point Morteira returns to categories of heresy, resorting to the famous Mishnah from Sanhedrin that he had used as the opening dictum of his sermon:

> The breaches they wanted to make in this wall are those enumerated by the Sages in our Mishnah mentioning those who have no portion in the world to come. Now the first is the faction that says, "Resurrection of

---

85. Da Costa, *Examination,* pp. 515 (Da Silva), 347 (Da Costa).
86. MS 1:94r, *Pinḥas,* Num. 26:10; see below, p. 443.

the dead is not in the Torah." This is the group that wants to confound the Torah by minimizing its reward. Not daring to touch it directly, they tried to weaken its power by diminishing its rewards and limiting it to perishable, destructible things, that which we can actually see. They sought to make us despair of the great eternal future rewards on the truth of which many martyrs gave up their lives for the sanctification of God's name, exchanging the perishable for the eternal.

Was this not the very sect of Dathan and Abiram, who denied future things, saying, *Is it not enough that you brought us from a land flowing with milk and honey?.... You have not even brought us to a land flowing with milk and honey* (Num. 16:13–14). They meant by this, "Why should we lose the benefits we can actually see for benefits promised in the future about which we know nothing?" Now just as the Sages said that whoever denies the resurrection of the dead will have no portion in the resurrection of the dead (b. *Sanhedrin* 90a), so these went down below while still alive, and were buried while living, and did not see the goodness of [the land of] Israel.[87]

This passage could, of course, pertain to the second century with its martyrs to Roman oppression, but it certainly would not be without resonance for a congregation many of whose relatives had died at the hands of the Portuguese Inquisition. Uriel da Costa had indeed maintained that the future rewards and punishments promised by the Jewish tradition were an illusion, that the only real and assured good and evil were those of the present that we can perceive, and that these are sufficient to inspire moral behavior. Some listeners may have recalled that one of the more scandalous and offensive statements by da Costa had been that martyrdom was not desired by God, who does not reward those who accept torture or death to avoid committing idolatry; it was therefore a waste of life.[88] We cannot date this sermon precisely, but it would have been delivered fairly close to the celebrated martyrdom of Isaac de

---

87. MS 1:94r–v *Pinḥas*, Num. 26:10; below, pp. 443–44. Note the totally different homiletical use of Dathan and Abiram as a model for those Portuguese immigrants who long to return to the "lands of idolatry," below, p. 302.

88. On the illusory character of future rewards, see Da Costa, *Examination*, pp. 342–43 and cf. p. 529; on martyrdom, see pp. 409–11; cf. p. 342: "Others stupidly offered their souls to cruel martyrdom. Vainly and without cause these wasteful and foolish people surrendered and discarded that life so highly valued by the ancient patriarchs." Cf. also ibid., p. 563, from Da Costa's *Exemplar*. Immanuel Aboab identified martyrdom as one of the topics that proved the need for an oral law: *Nomologia* I, 14; *Be-Ma'avaq al 'Erkah shel Torah*, translated and edited by Moises Orfali (Jerusalem, 1997), pp. 101–4.

Castro Tartas in December 1647, to whom Morteira devoted a public eulogy.[89]
It is the second category, however, that is more pertinent to us at this point:

> The second group is the one that says, "The Torah was not [revealed]
> from Heaven." In my opinion, the underlying meaning in this statement
> is that it denies the tradition, saying that the entire Torah is what was
> written, and there is no additional Torah given orally from Heaven....
>
> Thus the Sages said there in a Beraita explaining this mishnah (Sanh.
> 99a), "Even if one says that the entire Torah is from Heaven except for
> one *a fortiore* argument or one argument from analogy, he is included
> in the verse, *because he despised the word of the Lord*" (Num. 15:31). The
> nature of this second group can be seen in the entire community which
> rose up the following day against Moses and Aaron and said, *You two
> have brought death upon the Lord's people* (Num. 17:6): on your own initia-
> tive you placed before them the obstacle of the incense test. This was
> not revealed from Heaven (cf. Num. 16:17, 35).
>
> Now their punishment was through a plague, and they saw by their
> own experience that without tradition, the Torah cannot be sustained.
> For if their working assumption is that the Torah was without tradition,
> it would multiply into a thousand torahs, as we have said; or they would
> give it fabricated interpretations that they had agreed upon. In this way,
> they learned by experience that tradition preserves the Torah.
>
> Thus they were tried through the plague that came upon them, for
> the incense, about which they said *You have brought death upon the Lord's
> people* (Num. 17:6), is what saved them, as it is written, *Take the fire pan,
> [and put on it fire from the altar; add incense and take it quickly to the commu-
> nity and make expiation for them]* (Num. 17:11); ... he stood between the
> dead and the living until the plague was checked" (Num. 17:13).[90]

The challenge to the Oral Law went back many centuries, but it became
especially contentious in the seventeenth century, when skeptics within the
Jewish community claimed that it was an invention of the rabbis—both in
antiquity and at present—not an authoritative interpretation of the Torah, and
not part of the divine revelation transmitted intact from antiquity. This view
was the critical claim of the *Kol Sakhal*, as well as of Uriel da Costa (beginning
with his 1616 *Propostas contra a tradição*), and others. Virtually every defender

---

89. Cecil Roth, *A History of the Marranos* (Philadelphia, 1959), pp. 157–58; Yerushalmi, *From
Spanish Court to Italian Ghetto*, p. 398; Bodian, *Hebrews of the Portuguese Nation*, pp. 82–83,
and more generally, "In the Cross-Currents of the Reformation: Crypto-Jewish Martyrs of
the Inquisition, 1570–1670," *Past and Present* 176 (2002): 66–104.

90. MS 1:94v, *Pinḥas*, Num. 26:10.

of Judaism felt constrained to respond to this charge; the accusation that tests imposed upon the Israelites were the invention of Moses and Aaron, as Morteira interprets Numbers 17:6, would certainly have resonated with more recent authorities.[91]

There is a third heretical category mentioned in the Mishnah: the "epikoros," defined in the Gemara as one who shows blatant disrespect for a scholar. The preacher continues:

> This sect, which would not dare to attack the Torah, shows contempt for those who study it and slander them, so that as a consequence their words will be scorned and the Torah will be scorned, for if they truly loved the Torah, they would be protective of those who study it. This was precisely the strategy of Korah: in order to wage war against the Torah, they waged war against Moses and Aaron, saying , *All in the entire the community are holy, all of them, and the Eternal is in their midst. Why then do you raise yourselves up to lord it over us?* (Num. 16:3, 13). This shows their need to degrade the tradition of these men. [We see this] also from the words of Moses, when he said, *I have not taken the ass of any one of them, nor have I wronged any one of them* (Num. 16:15). Thus we see what they said, see that they slandered Moses and Aaron, because they were greedy, with a burning passion for money. Indeed they were punished with fire (Num. 16:35), in accordance with their pride, for the highest kind of insolence of all was within them [?], burning feverishly with the lust for power, and with fire they were burnt.[92]

By the end of this sermon, Morteira's homiletical artistry has once again become clear. After dividing the challenges to religion into external and internal, and discussing the external (Christian) threats prefigured by Balaam, he divides the internal threats into three sub-categories: those who reject the immortality of the soul and the future spiritual rewards beyond death, those who reject the Oral Law as divine revelation, and those who reject the rabbis as authoritative expositors of Torah. These threats are associated with three categories of heretics specified in the rabbinic dictum cited at the beginning of the sermon: those who deny resurrection, those who deny the Oral Law, and the *epikoros,* the one who scorns the rabbinic scholar. Furthermore, each is associated with one of the groups that arose against Moses in the context of Korah's rebellion: Korah the Levite and his company of 250, the Reubenites

---

91. Fishman, *Shaking the Pillars of Exile*, p. 49, and index s.v. Oral Torah; Moises Orfali, introduction to Immanuel Aboab, *Be-Ma'avaq al Erkah shel Torah*, pp. 22–27.

92. MS 1:94v, *Pinhas*, Num. 26:10.

Dathan and Abiram, and the "entire community," which rebukes Moses following the death of the rebels. Finally, they are associated with the three kinds of death recounted in the story and recapitulated in the theme-verse of the sermon from the lesson *Pinḥas* (Num. 26:10): being swallowed alive by the earth, being burnt by fire, and being afflicted by plague, each one of which is said to fit the specific heresy it punished. The three heresies are also associated with past (tradition), present (rabbinic scholars) and future (spiritual rewards).

Yet with all this artistry, the question of contemporary resonance remains, for the entire structure could be construed as applying just to history: the Bible and subsequent events in the rabbinic period typified by the challenge of the Sadducees. Yet one component of the sermon, not as yet mentioned, provides a leitmotif connecting the various themes anchored in exegesis and history and emphasizing their ongoing relevance. This is the element expressed in the last word of the theme-verse, *le-nes*, taken up at the very beginning of the sermon:

> This word, *nes*, which in rabbinic usage always refers to the wondrous miracles that transcend the logic of nature, in biblical usage means something exalted, like this banner that is high and lofty [perhaps pointing to a banner in the synagogue?]. Its meaning is similar to "as a sign (of)" (cf. Num. 17:3, ibn Ezra), which is how Onkelos translated it here.[93]

Morteira continues, suggesting a subtle difference between the two words: *ot* is used for a visible sign, while *nes* applies to something purely intellectual. This concept is then applied, toward the end of the introduction, as a general principle pertaining to God's treatment of those who rebelled against His will:

> God visited great judgments against them, openly and publicly, so that they might be a sign for the rebellious, and an object lesson for future generations, that this is what will happen to all who are like them. Every one of these incidents was intended as a lesson about a specific aspect of the worship of God and the observance of His Torah. And this is as a paradigm of them all: *They became an emblem* (Num. 26:10), namely, in the hearts of those who followed, that this is what would happen to all

---

93. MS 1:93r, *Pinḥas*, Num. 26:10. Cf. the discussion of the semantic issues among medieval grammarians, focusing more on the verb than the noun, in Albert van der Heide, "Banner, Miracle, Trial? Medieval Hebrew Lexicography Between Facts and Faith," in *Hebrew Scholarship and the Medieval World*, edited by Nicholas de Lange (Cambridge, 2001), pp. 92–106.

who corrupt as they did.[94]

This formulation removes the discussion from an archaic past; it signals a typological reading of the biblical narrative, situating it as a warning for future generations, presumably including the present.[95]

Morteira's methodological principle is not limited to the introductory section of the sermon. He returns to it again and again, as if it were the most important message he wanted the listeners to internalize and remember. In order to feel the force of this repetition, we need to cite his formulations as they reappear. Here, for example, he is making the transition from external challenges represented by Balaam to internal challenges represented by Koraḥ:

> Just as God revealed an object lesson for this in the affair of Balaam, teaching about those who rise up against the divine Torah and prophesy from outside it, not from the Jewish people, so he showed another signal and paradigm pertaining to those who rise up against it from the people of the Torah, as did Koraḥ and all his cohort. From his affair, and our text (Num. 26:10), its context and its component parts, we may clearly see all aspects of these factions, their strategies and their final end; *and they became an emblem,* an object lesson and a paradigm, teaching that this is what happened to them and this is what will happen to all who are like them.[96]

Then, after he first explains the three categories in Koraḥ's rebellion, each one destroyed by a different punishment stated in the theme-verse, he continues, "and all of them were an emblem and an object lesson of what was to come."[97] In case the message might not be clear, after a discussion that re-emphasizes the danger of the attack against tradition from within, he states,

> We see this not only from the fate of these factions, but also from those who carry forward their dissension in every generation—those who have acted in ways similar to them, and who were punished measure for measure. And this is what will occur to *all* who are like them. *And they became an emblem* and a paradigm for others.[98]

Finally, in his characteristic recapitulation at the very end of the sermon, Morteira returns once again to this phrase:

94. MS 1:93r, *Pinḥas,* Num. 26:10.
95. See above, p. 213, n. 77.
96. MS 1:93r, *Pinḥas,* Num. 26:10.
97. Ibid., 94r.
98. Ibid.

These factions mentioned in our Mishnah are the ones mentioned in our text, who sought to destroy our Torah with regard to three times, past, present and future. Past, with regard to tradition; future, with regard to the spiritual reward; present, in delegitimizing the Sages. And all of them were punished measure for measure; they have no share in the world to come, *and they became an emblem* and a paradigm for all who are like them.[99]

On the printed page, these recurrences of the phrase ending the theme-verse ("they became an emblem") with its expansion ("and an object lesson and paradigm for the future," or "for all like them") blend into the surrounding paragraph with nothing to distinguish them. In oral delivery, however, we can be sure that these words would have been emphasized and highlighted to stand out from the rest of the discourse. From the beginning of the sermon to the end, the recurring leitmotif is intended to trumpet a message to the listeners: the biblical and rabbinic examples of heresy are not something that belong to the distant past: they are a warning for the present, and the punishments recorded or promised for expressions of heresy in the past are very much applicable, potentially, to those in the audience.

Did Morteira specifically intend to allude to Uriel da Costa's denial of the immortality of the soul and rejection of the authority of the Oral Law? Were his warnings about punishment measure for measure intended to evoke associations with the da Costa suicide in 1640, fairly close to the time when the sermon was delivered?[100] For his homiletical purpose, I maintain, the specifics of an actual individual were not critical. The text of the sermon suggests that he wanted the listeners to think not of da Costa, but of themselves. They were the ones potentially being prefigured and warned by the catastrophic end of Korah and his cohorts. If they harbored doubts about the spiritual reward and punishment of the soul, or about the divine revelation of the Oral Law, or about the authority of the rabbis in their community or elsewhere, they had better take to mind the fate of those who "became an emblem."

---

99. Ibid., 94v.

100. No date is given in the manuscript, but in this sermon Morteira refers back to and recapitulates a sermon on the lesson *Balaq* (on Num. 22:13; see the full translation below), for which he provided the date 1639. Since he does not say "the sermon I delivered last week" as he does when referring to a previous week's sermon, it could have been delivered no earlier than the summer of 1640. However, the theme-verse for this sermon (Num. 26:10) is the twentieth in the *parashah*, and Morteira's notations indicate that he repeated at least four of the earlier sermons in subsequent years before 1640. My best estimate, therefore, is that it would have been delivered in the mid-1640s, when the memory of da Costa's suicide was still fresh.

A second point in conclusion. No matter what contemporary historians may conclude, Morteira apparently did not conceive of the heretical views circulating in his community as something new or unprecedented—at least this is not the way he presented them from the pulpit. In this he differed from the rhetorical strategy of rabbis in other contexts—for example, the opponents of philosophical study in the thirteenth and early fourteenth centuries, and the opponents of Hasidism in the late eighteenth century—who spoke of the doctrines and behavior they were combating as unheard of, something their ancestors never imagined.[101] To the contrary, through his typological mode of reading and preaching about the Bible, Morteira presents the phenomenon of doctrinal challenge to tradition as an ancient and recurring threat to the Jewish people. The threat is serious—more so than that which comes from Christian polemicists. Yet it is a familiar one.

Finally, one does not detect a sense of fear that the heretical challenges are a rising tide, a wave that may succeed in undermining the foundations of traditional Jewish faith. To be sure, in some of his sermons dealing with excesses of Jewish behavior, including those using a typological model, Morteira expresses deep discouragement about the possibility of resisting successfully what he perceives as powerful social forces.[102] Here, however, the model leads to the belief that God has encoded into the structure of history these periodic challenges from within the Jewish people, and that God will providentially punish the heretics and ensure the purity of the true faith. It is this assurance with which Morteira concludes his sermon, moving on from the bleak punishment in the theme-verse to encouragement about the next generation, drawing from both the story of Korah and the metaphor of skin affliction from Leviticus: *But the children of Korah did not die* (Num. 26:11).

> This teaches that God did not allow this leprosy to spread even through one single house, for He purified it immediately. He put the sinners to

---

101. This rhetorical mode might be traced through the polemical use of the verse *new ones, who came but lately, whom your fathers did not know* (Deut. 32:17). See, for example in the context of opposition to philosophy in the thirteenth and early-fourteenth century: Judah Alfahar in "Iggerot Qena'ot" (*Qovets Teshuvot ha-Rambam ve-Iggerotav*, part 3, Leipzig, 1859, p. 3 col. a middle), and the formulation in the second *Herem* of Rashba (*Teshuvot* [B'nai B'rak, 1958] 1:152a): "Has anything like this evil thing ever been heard since the day when the earth was spread to its borders?" The Deuteronomy verse similarly became a leitmotif for the later opponents of Hasidism: see Mordecai Wilensky, *Hasidim u-Mitnagdim* 2 vols. (Jerusalem, 1970), 1: 103–4 (*Herem* of Vilna, 1781, 123, 138 (*Herem* of Cracow, 1786), and also 2:57: "new Torah," 1:45 and 2:57: "new customs," 2:145, 154: "new way."

102. See, especially, the conclusion of his 1623 sermon entitled "The People's Envy," translated in Saperstein, *Jewish Preaching*, especially p. 285.

death, but He saved those who were good, so that the Torah would always remain in its proper status, until all the peoples will acknowledge it, with the coming of our righteous Messiah, quickly and in our days. Amen.[103]

Here the biblical verse, stating that the children of Koraḥ remained uncontaminated by the heresy of their father, might seem to be in tension with the contemporary reality, where it was a younger generation causing the problems. Yet it is a conclusion of confidence in the future, promising his listeners the ultimate vindication if they will identify not with Koraḥ and his cohorts, but with the younger generation that kept the faith.

This conclusion, however, while grounded in an invocation of God's providential concern for the Jewish people (a major theme of Morteira's preaching throughout his career),[104] does not imply a quietistic acceptance of whatever may happen, relying on God to take care of matters. Just as Moses had to respond energetically to suppress the challenge initiated by Koraḥ, so Morteira recognized the need for decisive action on the part of the Amsterdam leadership—both rabbis and Mahamad—in specific cases of defiance. Allusions in sermons were not enough. Alongside this edification and reassurance, the contemporary leaders were prepared to act to bring about the punishment deserved by those who did not accept their authority, with the most powerful weapons at their disposal.

---

103. MS 1:94v, *Pinḥas*, Num. 26:10.

104. See, for example, Morteira's Sabbath of Repentance sermon on Deuteronomy 32:12, delivered in the early 1630s and included in the 1645 edition of *Giv'at Sha'ul*, translated below, pp. 447ff.

From Past to Future

7

Homiletical Uses of
Historical Memory

In his chapter on the Middle Ages in *Zakhor*, Yosef Yerushalmi wrote, "Interpretations of history, whether explicit or veiled, can be encountered in works of philosophy, homiletics, biblical exegesis, law, mysticism, most often without a single mention of actual historical events or personalities, and with no attempt to relate to them."[1] A separate book, at least as long as *Zakhor*, would be needed to substantiate this statement, even limiting the purview to works of homiletics. To be sure, one does not ordinarily turn to Jewish sermons for a record of past events. The preacher's task was understood to be the application of traditional texts to contemporary challenges, not the transmission of historical data. The sermon was expected to explore exegetical and conceptual problems, to provide encouragement or rebuke, not to probe the specificity of the past.[2] Nevertheless, sermons can serve as a resource for our efforts to understand Jewish historical memory and consciousness as mediated between an intellectual, spiritual leader and a community of listeners. Just as they provide crucial evidence for the way in which philosophical or Kabbalistic ideas were transmitted to broader circles of Jewish society,[3] so sermons reveal what from the past was deemed important to highlight and interpret. In so doing, the historical material in Morteira's sermons illuminates one aspect of what Yerushalmi has called "The Re-Education of the Marranos."[4]

In a sermon on the lesson *Bo*, delivered in the mid-1640s, Morteira drew an important contrast between sacred and secular historiography:

The purpose of the historical narratives in our holy Torah is totally

---

1. Yerushalmi, *Zakhor*, p. 31.

2. Saperstein, *Jewish Preaching*, pp. 80–82.

3. Saperstein, *"Your Voice Like a Ram's Horn,"* chapter 7. On Kabbalah, see pp. 14, 299, 318, 329.

4. Yerushalmi, "The Re-Education of Marranos in the Seventeenth Century."

different from the purpose of the narratives that appear in the books of historical chronicles. The purpose of the chroniclers is to recount each matter just as it was. The only thing they look to or care about is providing information about the specific event that occurred. But the purpose of the divine Torah in its narratives is to recount only those matters from which we may derive some ethical lesson or benefit, for the ultimate purpose of the Torah is doctrine, not the recounting of historical events. That is why the Torah eliminated from its narratives some details that must have occurred, and would have pleased those who heard them, for its purpose is not the story but the doctrine.[5]

It is unclear from this passage whether Morteira was comparing the Torah to Jewish chroniclers such as Yosippon or to Gentile historians. As we shall see, his sermons contain references to both. The operative distinction here is between genres. History writing is granted the virtue of objectivity—"recounting each matter just as it was"—but deemed to be of secondary importance to the ethical lesson or the doctrine.[6] History "as it really was" has little value in this schema. The divine revelation does indeed contain historical information, but its purpose is never simply to recount events of the past but rather to draw enduring lessons from them. This approach is particularly compatible with the role of the preacher. Morteira himself does not use historical material to provide information for antiquarian purposes. His references to the past serve to illustrate a doctrinal point, to teach a lesson, to intensify a polemical argument, to underscore a message of rebuke. We shall concretize this statement with examples from the period of antiquity (based on sources other than the Bible) and from the more recent past.

Roman History

---

5. MS 3:191r, *Bo*, Exod. 10:19. Compare the statement of Eusebius, that he would not attempt to recount all that occurred, but only "what may be of profit." There he is talking not about biblical history but about his own approach to recording the past. *History of the Church*, 8.2, cited in Ramsay MacMullen, *Christianity and Paganism in the Fourth to Eighth Centuries* (New Haven, 1997), p. 4.

6. This passage may be based on a statement by Abravanel, who wrote that the author of the books of Samuel did not intend "to provide a narrative for its own sake, as with the histories produced by all of the nations regarding their affairs, but for the purpose of teaching about the service of God." Thus there is a selective narration for didactic purposes, omitting many details (*Perush al Nevi'im Rishonim*, p. 164a). See Eric Lawee, "On the Threshold of the Renaissance: New Methods and Sensibilities in the Biblical Commentaries of Isaac Abarbanel," *Viator* 26 (1995): 297. Cf. the rather different contrast drawn by Abravanel in his comment on Joshua 8, cited by Lawee, p. 295.

Morteira's sermons provide nothing like the detailed account of Roman history available in the works of Jewish historians such as Yosippon or David Gans, or more schematically in Abraham ibn Daud, Abraham Zacuto, and Gedaliah ibn Yahya.[7] What we find, for the most part, is a number of brief references to Roman history, some of them quite general. A sermon printed in the 1645 edition of *Giv'at Sha'ul*, for example, begins with a discussion of permanence in this world. After discussing the natural antipathy toward death and the attempt to transcend it, Morteira turns to models from antiquity:

> Leaders of the Gentiles tried three ways of attaining permanence and ensuring that their name would endure in subsequent generations. The first was by making monuments and statues of wood and stone, silver and gold, which represent their physical appearance, as the Roman Caesars did, and as Alexander wanted to do in the Temple.[8] Second was by creating lofty, awe-inspiring buildings and palaces bearing their names.... Third was by fixing a holiday each year on which all would play games and speak their praises; the months perpetuate the names of two Caesars, Julius and Augustus..[9]

All of these techniques are said to be vain and futile efforts, as the only true permanence comes through association with God. Thus Morteira presents the examples from Roman antiquity as a foil to contrast with the manner in which Moses attained permanence beyond his lifetime.

In a sermon on *Korah*, a different kind of use is made of a well-known activity in ancient Rome. The preacher maintains that God used the generation of the wilderness, people who had all been condemned to death for their sins with the golden calf and the spies, to demonstrate His method of judgment and punishment. Since their lives were forfeited anyway, God brought about circumstances that publicly demonstrated that they deserved to die so that they would serve as an object lesson for others. Examples of this principle are drawn from common experience, and then from history: "From those

---

7. Cf. also the history of the Roman kingdom written in Portuguese, apparently in the 18th century, and preserved in the Ets Haim Library, described by Shlomo Berger, "Remus, Romulus and Sephardi Jews in Amsterdam," *StRos* 26 (1992): 38–45.

8. On Alexander's desire to have a statue of himself, see *Sefer Yosippon*, ed. David Flusser, 2 vols. (Jerusalem, 1978) 1:56; David Gans, *Tsemah David: A Chronicle of Jewish and World History*, ed. Mordecai Breuer (Jerusalem, 1983), p. 62. Gans, citing the German historian Heinrich Beunting, reports that Hadrian also erected a statue of himself on the site of the Holy of Holies, adding that this was "not for the sake of idolatry, but as a memorial" (p. 221).

9. *GS* 1645, pp. 33d–34a; 1912, pp. 136–37, *Mishpatim*, Exod. 21:1, 1620? On the naming of the two summer months after Julius and Augustus Caesar, see *Plutarch's Lives*, Numa 19,4, 11 vols. (Cambridge, 1932) 1:371; Gans, p. 207.

men already sentenced to death, the Roman emperors would select some to
entertain the people as gladiators. That some died did not matter, as they were
already deemed deserving of capital punishment."[10] Here too there is a contrast: in the Roman case the lives were sacrificed for frivolous entertainment,
in the Bible, so that the people would learn important lessons about God's
qualities. But the basic thrust of the example is to show an underlying similarity between apparently disparate realms.

Another example: discussing in 1621 his scenario of events leading up to
the messianic redemption, Morteira illustrates an aspect of military strategy
by reference to the distant past:

> For when the Christians see the multitude of people coming against
> Rome, and the pope fleeing from Rome, they will learn from the
> precedent of what Scipio did to Hannibal: by going to Carthage, he
> forced Hannibal to abandon Rome. So the Christians, by means of a
> great army going against the Holy Land and Egypt, will draw out the
> many Muslim peoples to leave Rome and come to the aid of their
> lands.[11]

The preacher is talking about something unfamiliar—the course of events in
the future messianic wars—and explaining it by recourse to something
familiar. As with the previous examples, Morteira seems to assume that his
audience knew about this material. Important also is the implication that
history follows a pattern. It is not just that military men will make similar
decisions under similar circumstances. Patterns recur, especially with regard
to the great protagonists of history—Jews, Christians, and Romans. We shall
return to this motif later.

In several passages from his sermons, Morteira refers to the writings of
Roman historians, though never identifying a specific work. For example,

> We find this in the chronicles of Rome: when one of the Roman

---

10. MS 2:53r, *Koraḥ*, Num 16:7. A second example from common experience is rather
revealing: a novice doctor will not gain experience by working on a king or noble, but rather
on a less important person, on whom harm will not be as serious. Some years later, Morteira
made a similar point about the wilderness period, but used an illustration from more recent
history: "Frequently a king will select from those men who have been sentenced to death,
and use them for dangerous assignments in his service. For example, the king of Portugal,
desirous of discovering places that were not yet settled, would send there such men, taking
their lives in their hands, to scout out the unknown territory. If they died, they died." See
GS 1645, p. 63a, 1912, p. 237, and cf. below, p. 433.

11. MS 3:99r, *Va-Yishlaḥ*, Gen. 32:6, 1621. See *Sefer Yosippon*, 1:93–95, and the discussion
of Morteira's eschatological doctrine below.

generals conquered a certain Gentile king, the king changed from his royal raiment and came before him in manifest submission. The general grew angry with him, saying that he had abased and diminished the general's glory in his victory.[12]

This historical detail is used to explain God's desire to build up Pharaoh's ego before bringing him to a humiliating downfall: "Similarly, when God wanted to be glorified through Pharaoh (as the verse says, *I will gain glory through Pharaoh* [Exod. 14:4]), Pharaoh had to see himself as exalted." The behavior of the Roman general serves as a model for God's own actions, thereby rationalizing a biblical passage. Discussing in 1624 the pressures brought to bear upon the Jews in the past to assimilate and the importance of language for national identity, Morteira provides another analogy with Roman policy of conquest based on Roman historians:

Similarly, the chroniclers recount that when the Romans conquered Spain, they forced the inhabitants to speak the Roman language. For as it was a vast, strong people that rebelled against them more than once, in order to bind them to Rome, he compelled them to learn their language.[13]

The resonance of this passage for a community of Jews clinging to their Portuguese tongue in the middle of Amsterdam can be imagined.[14]

In another passage, which we shall analyze in greater depth below,

12. *GS* 1645, p. 28a–b, 1912, p. 125, *Bo*, Exod 10:1, ca. 1620. This general type of reference to "Roman historical works" is characteristic of Abravanel, Gedaliah ibn Yahya, and others. Contrast Azariah de' Rossi's specification of the Roman historians whose work he consulted (below, [p. 177]). Morteira undoubtedly cites this exemplum from another source. A parallel (though not precise) can be found in Polybius's condemnation of Prusias II of Bithynia in Asia Minor as unworthy of royalty because he greeted the first Roman envoys to his court with shorn head, dressed in the cap worn by newly manumitted slaves, and addressed them in an obsequious and "contemptible" manner (*Histories*, xxx, 19; Alvin H. Bernstein, *Polybius on Roman Imperialism* (South Bend, 1980), p. 446). I am grateful to Arthur Eckstein for this reference, and to my colleagues Eric Cline and Elizabeth Fisher for helping to track it down.

13. MS 3:345v, *Mishpatim*, Exod. 21:6, 1624. Theodor Mommsen, *The Provinces of the Roman Empire from Caesar to Diocletian*, 2 vols. (London, 1909), 1:70–71: "By ordinance of Vespasian [in 74 C.E.], the native language [in Spain] was restricted *de jure* to private intercourse."

14. Note, however, the complexity of this implied message. Morteira cites here the rabbinic statement that the Israelites retained the Hebrew language while in Egypt (Lev. Rabbah 32,5); preaching in Portuguese (from a sermon text written in Hebrew) in a Dutch-speaking environment, he might have been understood as emphasizing the importance of either learning Hebrew or of preserving Portuguese.

Morteira refers to Roman historians' account of the death of the emperor Titus: his intent is to challenge the simple meaning of the Talmudic aggadah that describes a very different form of death.[15] Perhaps the most intriguing use of Roman historians, however, pertains to the figure of the emperor Hadrian. At issue is a rabbinic interpretation of Genesis 25:23: "*Two nations (goyim):* two proud nations *(ge'ei goyim),* one who took pride in his world and one who took pride in his kingdom: Hadrian among the Gentile nations, and Solomon among the Israelites."[16] The external material is used to explain the rabbinic choice of Hadrian as exemplar:

> And one who took pride in the greatness of his kingdom—in his kingdom alone, not in his world—for Hadrian had no children and died without heirs, as the chronicles of the Roman Emperors wrote about him…. Or it could be the opposite: the "one who takes pride in his world" refers to Hadrian, who [unlike Solomon who ruled only over the land of Israel, the choicest of lands] ruled over the entire world by force (though not literally, as he did not rule over the distant lands that have been discovered in our times)…. Hadrian took greater pride in his wealth than all other Roman emperors. The chroniclers who tell his story recounted that once he gave a gift to the people of ten million gold coins, and another time he gave an abundance of rare spices. And Solomon was similar…. They also took these two because they were at the pinnacle of their kingdoms' glory, for after the time of Hadrian the Roman Empire began to decline, so that he was at its high point, as was Solomon in Israel.[17]

One would scarcely know from this passage that this was the emperor who presided over the downfall of Bar Kokhba, the devastation of Judea, the

---

15. MS 4:65v, *Bo*, Exod 10:4: "All those historians who wrote about his death without any axe to grind mention nothing of this; they say that he died of ague." See below, n. 46.

16. Gen. Rabbah 63,7.

17. MS 3:247v, *Toledot*, Gen. 25:23. On Hadrian's lack of male offspring, see Dio Cassius, *Dio's Roman History,* 9 vols., translated by Earnest Cary (Cambridge, 1968), 8:459. On his generosity, see Aelius Spartianus, "De Vita Hadriani," in *Scriptores Historiae Augustae*, 3 vols., translated David Magie (Cambridge, 1922), 1:52–53: "omnes reges muneribus suis vicit." The reading "ten million gold coins" is not certain and it seems extraordinarily large. But the editor of the above text gives the amount of Hadrian's debt remission as 900,000,000 sesterces, with 100 sesterces equivalent to one *aureus,* thereby yielding 9 million gold coins (p. 22 nn. 2 and 5). On Hadrian's gift of spices to the people in honor of his mother-in-law, see pp. 58–59. Cf. also Gans, p. 221: "In the days of this emperor [Hadrian], the Roman Empire was at its pinnacle *(ba-ma'alah 'elyonah).*"

prohibition of the Jews from Jerusalem, the erection of a pagan temple on the Temple Mount. Other passages in rabbinic literature refer to him as "Hadrian the wicked," and hold him accountable for a massacre of Jews in Alexandria as well as in Judea.[18] Samuel Usque described his end with hatred and contempt: "As for Hadrian, who was responsible for the extermination of the remnants of your people in the regions of Syria and Jerusalem, he was plagued by the Lord with a painful illness for your vengeance. In desperation, he killed himself by depriving himself of food and drink."[19] Yet Morteira overlooks all of this; in order to explicate a cryptic midrashic comment, he draws from Roman historical memories of Hadrian's beneficence. The homiletical purpose to which historical allusion is harnessed may sometimes seem quite narrow.

Jewish History

Needless to say, there are references to Jewish history of antiquity in the sermons as well. We shall deal not with the many references to biblical history, but with the period of the Second Commonwealth.

One of the recurrent principles in Morteira's preaching is that the "exile in Egypt" was not merely an event of biblical history but a prefiguration or prototype for the subsequent exiles of the Jewish people. Morteira used this motif as a basis for a sermon on *Shemot* delivered in early 1622;[20] the following week he returned to the theme with more detailed historical exemplification. After discussing the exiles of Babylonia and Media as prefigured by Egypt, he continues into the Hellenistic period: "In the enslavement of Egypt there can also be found a prototype for the persecution of the exile of Greece. Their only concern was to make the Jews forget God's Torah, to make them transgress the commandments—nothing else." The two commandments that became most problematic during the Hellenistic period, according to the preacher, were circumcision and the Sabbath, for the historical records reveal that Jews

---

18. "Hadrian the wicked": Y. *Ta'anit* 4.8 (24a–b), Lam. Rabbah 2,5 on Lam. 2:2; b. *Gittin* 57b: "Hadrian Caesar who killed in Alexandria of Egypt sixty myriads, twice as many as went forth from Egypt." Cf. Abraham Zacuto, *Sefer Yuḥasin ha-Shalem*, ed. H. Filipowski (London, 1857), p. 245b: "Hadrian the wicked, the enemy of Israel…, who seized Jerusalem and destroyed it and decreed that no Jews should enter it;" similarly Gedaliah ibn Yahya, *Shalshelet ha-Qabbalah* (Warsaw, 1877) p. 146. For David Gans on Hadrian, see above, n. 9.

19. Samuel Usque, *Consolation for the Tribulations of Israel,* transl. and ed. Martin A. Cohen (Philadelphia, 1965), p. 161. On Hadrian's final illness and desire to kill himself, see *Dio's Roman History,* 8:455, 463.

20. This is the sermon on *Shemot,* translated in *Jewish Preaching,* pp. 271–85. There the lesson drawn from a verse about Egypt is applied to the recent and contemporary experience of his listeners.

who tried to observe these were actually put to death. After showing how the Israelites were forced to abandon these commandments in Egypt, Morteira turns to the later historical period:

> The very same occurred in the Greek period, when the commandments were prohibited to them, especially the Sabbath—for they put to death a thousand people in a cave who were observing the Sabbath—and the commandment of circumcision—for they hanged two women and their sons because they circumcised them. The Hasmoneans from the tribe of Levi remained firm and defeated them, restoring the crown to its original condition.[21]

Can Morteira's source for this passage be determined? The First Book of Maccabees, Josephus, and Yosippon all report the incident of a thousand Jews killed in a cave because they refused to violate the Sabbath.[22] But only Yosippon specifies the hanging of the two women. While we know that Morteira did use a Spanish translation of Josephus's *Antiquities* in his later work,[23] here his source appears to be Yosippon, which he uses in three ways:[24] to substantiate an over-arching conception of Jewish historical experience as patterned and providential, to emphasize the significance of the Sabbath and circumcision, and to present a model of Jewish loyalty leading to martyrdom. He probably includes the vivid historical details—one thousand Jews killed, two women hanged with their sons—for their emotional impact upon the listeners.

By contrast, other references to the Hasmoneans highlight negative models. Theirs was a period of rampant assimilation. Morteira notes in a sermon from the early 1630s that during the Hasmonean period, "many impudent Jews commingled with the Gentiles and informed against us, causing great harm to

---

21. MS 3:189v, *Va-Era*, Exod 6:6, 1622. The verb תלה might also be translated "crucified," in accordance with Josephus (see n. 25 below).

22. 1 Mac. 2:34–38; Josephus, *Antiquities*, 12, 276–77; *Sefer Yosippon*, p. 77.

23. Apparently the Antwerp, 1554 edition entitled *Los veynte libros de las antiquedades Judaycas*. See Morteira, *Tratado*, pp. 371, 388–89; edition identified by Salomon, p. 1218. Cf. Salomon, "Menasseh ben Israel, Saul Levi Mortera et le 'Testimonium Flavianum,'" *StRos* 25 (1991): 31–41.

24. *Sefer Yosippon*, p. 68: "At that time, **two women** were found who had circumcised their sons. They **hanged the women** by their breasts and they threw them and their children from the top of a tower" (emphasis added, MS). Cf. 1 Mac. 1:60 and Josephus, *Antiquities*, 12:256. Cf. also Usque, *Consolation for the Tribulations of Israel* p. 119: "two women were found who had secretly circumcised their sons. These Philip [the governor left by Antiochus in Jerusalem] punished with barbarous cruelty: he had them hurled down from a tower with their children at their breasts." Usque reports the killing of 1000 people in a cave on p. 124.

the Jewish people."[25] In a different sermon, Morteira uses the Hasmoneans to point to another problem: during the Greek period, "oppressed by persecution, Jews endeavored to cleave to their oppressors and intermarry with the Gentile nations, as occurred in the time of the Hasmoneans, when many of our people apostatized voluntarily and rejected God's Torah."[26] The resonance for the New Christian situation would not have been difficult to discern. Finally, the Maccabean revolt itself was problematic in that it could be taken to represent an activist challenge to authority incompatible with Morteira's understanding of appropriate Jewish behavior in exile. Therefore, he reviews the well-known background of the Hanukkah holiday with a clear distancing:

> In the Greek period, when they oppressed the Jews who were subservient to them, Mattathias, son of Johanan the High Priest, and his sons arose and rebelled against them. They defeated the Greeks and restored Jewish sovereignty and dedicated the Temple. But God made the Jews swear an oath not to act this way in the present exile, [not] to depart from it [by force], for it is not similar to the previous one.

Despite the positive and inspiring achievements of the Maccabees, the preacher is careful to emphasize that theirs is not a model to be emulated.[27]

Almost in passing is a reference to an episode of Second Commonwealth history that probably would not have been familiar to the listeners. In a discussion of miracles, Morteira draws on the distinction between open and hidden wonders, relating them to periods of time. During the biblical period, from the conquest of the land of Canaan through the Babylonian exile, God performed miracles that were blatantly opposed to nature, observable by all. "And similarly during the second Temple period, with the miracles of Hanukkah and Heliodorus, as recounted by Yosippon." This period is contrasted with the era of the long exile, when Jews were no longer worthy of public miracles, "yet God did not remove from us His great miracles; [they are] concealed from the sight of the masses but revealed to the sight of the wise." Here the listeners were expected to accept the reference to Heliodorus on faith, although the reference to the source in Yosippon provided an opportunity for further investigation. Morteira makes no attempt to defend the historicity of the miracles. Yosippon is cited as an authority; if he reports an

---

25. MS 2:200v, *Mattot*, Num 30:10, early 1630s.

26. *GS* 1645 *Ha'azinu*, p. 86c. See in the full sermon below, p. 454.

27. MS 5:47v, *Va-Yetse*, Gen. 29:7, ca. 1645; for the oath, see b. *Ketubot* 111a and below, p. 340, n. 84.

event, that is enough.[28] Elsewhere we shall see that Morteira is not always so uncritical of his sources.

Discussing the shrines built by Jeroboam at Bethel and Dan (1 Kings 12:29), Morteira draws a contrast by referring to another event of Second Commonwealth history. "Thus Onias, during the Second Temple period, seeing thousands and tens of thousands of Jews in Egypt, where they remained from earlier exiles, built for them a Temple like that in Jerusalem, so that God's people would attain wisdom in their exile. This entailed no disparagement to the Temple in Jerusalem." Onias's deed was in sharp contrast with that of Jeroboam, who built his competing shrines at a time when the entire people resided in the land of Israel. The apparent message is that Diaspora Jews have legitimate religious needs that also deserve to be met.[29] In a different context, Morteira's homiletical point about the dangers to Jews of internal conflict requires a more negative assessment of Onias's motivation: "Similarly in the matter of Onias: when he quarreled with his brother over the High Priesthood, he went away to Egypt, where he built an altar modeled after the altar of the Temple in Jerusalem, and he allied himself with the Egyptians."[30] Both references are brief, but they are self-sufficient. Each enables listeners to learn about an event they probably did not know about, although neither provides full clarity on its significance.

Of greater relevance to his listeners was a reference, again based on Yosippon, to John Hyrcanus. In a discussion of the agents of destruction, Morteira refers to an influx of proselytes dating from the conquests of Hyrcanus: "Many proselytes have become mixed in with them on their own land, as Joseph ben Gurion recounts that when Hyrcanus defeated Edom, he compelled them to be circumcised."[31] As we shall see, Morteira maintains

---

28. *GS*, 1645, p. 63b, 1912, p. 238, *Balaq*, Num. 22:13,1639. The manuscript (1:109r) has the correct reading. ואליהורו *GS* 1645, p. 63b reads ואלי נדרו, a good indication that the printers did not understand the reference. Nor did the printers of *Giv'at Sha'ul* 1902 and 1912 (p. 238), who indicated their confusion by writing ?ואלינדרו . For Morteira's source on the miracles of Heliodorus, ca. 180 BCE, see *Sefer Yosippon*, ed. Flusser, 1:61–64, based on 2 Maccabees chap. 3. Cf. Azariah de' Rossi, *Me'or 'Einayim* (Vilna, 1866), chap. 51, p. 431, *The Light of the Eyes*, p. 639, who reveals the same uncritical approach to this miracle. Morteira also summarizes Yosippon's account of miraculous wonders that occured in connection with the Temple during the year before Vespasian came. See MS 4:43r (a eulogy for Abraham Farar delivered in 1619), based on *Sefer Yosippon*, 1:413–14.

29. MS 2:15v, *Va-Yeshev*, Gen. 37:7, Hanukkah 1627.

30. MS 3:345v, *Mishpatim*, Exod. 21:6, 1624. The quarrel and jealousy is based on the Talmudic account in b. *Menaḥot* 109b. Cf. *Me'or 'Einayim*, chap. 21, p. 340.

31. MS 3:162r: *Shabbat Teshuvah*, 1645. On the forced circumcisions, see *Sefer Yosippon*, 1:116.

that this forced assimilation of non-Jews into the Jewish people would have disastrous consequences for Jewish history and implications for the experience of the *conversos*.

A typological interpretation emerges from verses in the lesson *Toledot.*[32] Herod, the powerful king who reigned at the end of the first century B.C.E., is said to have been prefigured by the story of the early years of Esau.

> *The children struggle in her womb* (Gen. 25:22) alludes to the Samaritan wars.[33] After that it says, *Two nations are in your womb* (Gen. 25:23), alluding to the Hasmoneans, who were kings and priests. *The first one went out red* (admoni) (Gen. 25:25), namely, kingship departed from them [the Hasmoneans] and was transferred to Herod, who was an Edomite, *like a hairy mantle all over* with intrigue. *They called his name Esau,* meaning "they made" (*'asu):* an outsider, that is, the Romans, summoned him and they made him king. *After this his brother went out* (Gen. 25:26), namely priesthood [departed], because he held on to the heel of Esau, namely the ways of the Romans.[34]

In this rather dense passage, based on wordplay that is not entirely clear even now and would hardly have been understood by most listeners, Herod is presented in a negative way, as the vehicle for the loss of kingship and priesthood from authentic Jews, and the channel through which Roman influence came to prevail in Jewish history.[35]

---

32. On Morteira's use of typology and its background, see Saperstein, *"Your Voice Like a Ram's Horn,"* pp. 30–33. Typological interpretation is obviously important to Morteira's use of history and his messianic doctrine, as can be seen in the passages cited in the aforementioned study. This approach to Scripture remained important for contemporary Christian preachers; see, for example, Lancelot Andrewes, *Sermons,* "Sermon 2 of the Passion" (1604), p. 145, and—with application to the experience of the listeners—Stout, *The New England Soul,* pp. 8, 45, and frequently throughout.

33. At the beginning of the Second Commonwealth period. The reference is clarified in a later sermon where Morteira recapitulates this phrase with a little more specificity: "*The children struggle in her womb* (Gen. 25:22), alludes to the time when Israel returned to the land in the days of Ezra, and the children fought within her, as recorded in the relations between Nehemiah and Sanbalat" (see Neh. 3:33–35, 4:1–17) (MS 3:174r, Gen 25:22).

34. MS 3:7v, *Va-Yetse,* Gen. 28:11.

35. The connection between Esau the *admoni,* Herod the Edomite, and Rome, called "Edom" in late rabbinic and medieval literature, is not to be found in any early sources. See Gerson Cohen, "Esau as Symbol in Early Medieval Thought," in *Jewish Medieval and Renaissance Studies,* ed. Alexander Altmann (Cambridge, 1967), p. 21 n.7. In a different sermon, Morteira blames the strife among the heirs of the Hasmonean line for bringing Rome into the arena of Israel: "In the days of the Hasmoneans, their wars resulted in alliances with the Romans, such that because of their internal strife, part of the people became allied with a

An example of Morteira's tendentious use of historical material and sources for a homiletical purpose can be seen in a reference to the origins of Jewish sectarianism. It is part of his sustained argument from the early 1640s, using historical examples, that truth wears the adornment of unity while its opponents are divided among themselves. When "at the beginning of the Second Temple [period]," certain Jews began to deny the validity of the authentic tradition, this opposition soon split into sects. "It did not constitute a separate bloc of opposition to the truth; rather from this opposition came Sadducees, Boethusians, and Essenes. All of them were divided against themselves, as the author of *Me'or 'Einayim* wrote at length in his book, chapter 3. He also added to them the sect of Gaulanites."[36] Most listeners would not have had either the linguistic tools or the inclination to check the reference in Azariah de' Rossi's work. If they had, they would have discovered that de' Rossi, following Josephus, speaks of four "sects," but includes the Pharisees as one in his discussion about the diversity of philosophical views within the Jewish people as a whole.[37] Morteira removes the Pharisees from the list, introduces the Boethusians as a separate sect (Azariah identified them with the Essenes), and recasts the entire passage as a description of inevitable disunity that befalls those who oppose the authentic Jewish tradition.

Christian History

The passages cited to this point mention incidents or personalities that serve an illustrative homiletical purpose. Perhaps with the exception of the last example, they were not crucial to a fundamental purpose of the preacher. Some of the references to Christian history, by contrast, are quite important to central issues of Morteira's agenda in communicating to his audience of former New Christians.

Above we noted his allusion to the campaign of forced proselytization by John Hyrcanus. Here is how he continues the passage about the Edomite converts:

They were like a boil for the Jewish people, like the proselytes in the

different people" (MS 3:345v, *Mishpatim*, Exod. 21:6, 1624). For the name Esau interpreted as *'asu* ('they made, compelled') in a rather different context, see the citation by Moshe Idel from "Sefer ha-Meshiv," in "The Attitude to Christianity in *Sefer ha-Meshiv*," *Immanuel* 12 (1981): 86.

36. MS 1:87v, *Koraḥ*, Num. 16:17.

37. *Me'or 'Einayim*, pp. 90–91; *Kitvei Azariah min ha-Adumim*, ed. Robert Bonfil (Jerusalem, 1991), pp. 234–35; *The Light of the Eyes*, pp. 1023. The "Gaulanites," adherents of Josephus's "Fourth Philosophy," are followers of Judah the Galilean (or the Gaulanite). From Azariah's Hebrew phrase כת יהודה הגבלנ Morteira makes כת הגבלנים.

rabbinic statement who were as a boil for Israel.[38] They were also those Jews in their exile who assimilated among the Gentiles and became lost among them. Nevertheless, even this agent of destruction was unable to destroy them. For God separated out all those who became assimilated among them during the Second Temple period, in that they were the Jews who accepted the new religion [Christianity] and were removed from the rest. Therefore, this is one of the reasons why this nation is called Edom, as R. Isaac Abravanel explained on chapter 34 of Isaiah. And those who were assimilated among the Gentiles in their exile became estranged from their brothers and alien to their mothers' children, so that they were set aside for evil from all the tribes of Israel (cf. Deut. 29:20). [39]

The first important point here relates to the origins of Christianity. Drawing from Abravanel,[40] Morteira explains the willingness of Jesus' disciples to break away from the ancient Jewish tradition and sever their ties with the Jewish people. These early Jewish Christians were descendants of the Edomite proselytes. Never content to be Jews, they were therefore particularly susceptible to heretical doctrines. Whereas other Jewish polemical writers dismissed the disciples for their intellectual limitations,[41] Morteira condemns their base lineage.

But this was not the only occasion in Jewish history where divine providence furnished a filtering mechanism to separate those Jews who did not really belong to the people. The pattern of antiquity, which occurred while the Jews were in their own land, was repeated during the long exile outside it. Once again, Jews were lost to their people through the adoption of

---

38. B. *Yebamot* 47b, *Qiddushin* 70b, and parallels.

39. MS 3:162r, *Shabbat Teshuvah*, 1645.

40. Abravanel's short treatise on the validity of calling Rome and Christianity Edom comes in his commentary on Isaiah chapter 35, not 34; Abravanel, *Nevi'im Aharonim*, p. 171a–173a (see however his comment on Isa. 34:5); Morteira provided a lengthy summary of Abravanel's arguments in an earlier sermon (MS 2:9, *Toledot*, Gen. 25:26). The assertion that the Edomites, who had been forcibly circumcised by Hyrcanus became the first to accept the Christian faith, is presented by Abravanel not as his own view but as that of Nahmanides, which he endorses as probably based on an authentic tradition (p. 173a). What Morteira adds to this is the suggestion that forced conversion produces a lack of loyalty to the new faith, and that Christianity was God's providential way to purify the Jewish people. On the earlier background of the association between Esau-Edom and Rome-Christianity in the rabbinic literature and Yosippon, see Gerson Cohen, "Esau as Symbol," pp. 19–48, with reference on p. 48 to Nahmanides, B. Netanyahu, *Don Isaac Abravanel* (Philadelphia., 1968), pp. 233–34.

41. See, for example, Saperstein, *Jewish Preaching*, p. 177 and n. 29.

Christianity—specifically alluding to those New Christians who seemed content to assimilate with their Christian neighbors. By attributing this behavior to their Edomite origins, suggesting that they were never fully Jewish to begin with, Morteira reassured his listeners that their decision was the right one.

In the sermon discussed above on the absence of unity among those who opposed the truth, Morteira draws another historical example from the period of the early Church. He asserts as well established fact that from the very beginning of its identity as a separate religion, Christianity was riven by dissent. And this dissent was an expression of divine providence:

> God did not allow them to adorn themselves with the ornament of truth or to dress in the raiment of unity. Immediately, at their beginning—a matter that is well known about them—they split into different groups and failed to agree. This was so that people would not stumble after them, thinking that they possessed the truth.[42]

Listeners who had been educated as Christians may well have been familiar with material in the "Acts of the Apostles" that would support this generalization. Having acknowledged that some Jews were indeed attracted to the new faith, Morteira explains here its limited impact within the Jewish people as another sign of God's providential care. Nor would that providence end even when Christianity emerged as the dominant world faith.

In order to see how Morteira integrated motifs pertaining to Rome, Christianity, and the Jews on a larger canvas and related them to events of more recent history, we shall look in greater detail at two sermons, delivered some 20 years apart—one on the lesson *Bo* and one on the lesson *Tazri'a*. The first, entitled "Despicable and Vile" (Mal. 2:9), dates from 1623, in the early period of Morteira's tenure; its theme verse is *Tomorrow I will bring the locusts on your territory* (Exod. 10:4). Morteira introduces his subject with a general proposition: "If it is a severe punishment to be given over into the hands of a person who is vile and despicable, how much more severe it is to be given over into the power of the beasts of the field and disgusting worms." Illustrating this proposition with a biblical verse (Isa. 14:11), he then turns to a highly problematic rabbinic aggadah (b. *Gittin* 56b) about the Emperor Titus. After Titus arrogantly challenged God, a gnat entered his nose and pounded in his brain for seven years. The aggadah ends with accounts of Titus's death: R. Phineas ben Aruba said, "I was there with the notables of Rome. When he died, they split open his brain and found there something like a sparrow two selas in

---

42. MS 1:87v, *Koraḥ*, Num. 16:17.

weight." A Tanna taught, "Like a dove two pounds in weight." Abaye said, "We have it on record that his beak was of brass and his claws of iron."

Morteira quotes the entire passage, then launches a critique of the aggadah. Formally, he follows a traditional pattern of late medieval Jewish homiletics, raising problems with a passage from the Bible or the aggadah, and then resolving them:[43]

> However, it is clear that all these words are filled with such startling assertions that they should not be understood according to their simple meaning. Rather, their words are intentionally enigmatic, following the practice of the Sages in many places. First, how is it possible that for such a long period of time the bird was pounding in his brain without his having died? And if it did not perforate the membrane, as the Tosafists wrote,[44] where is there enough space between the skull and the membrane for a creature of such size? Furthermore, its beak then became brass and its claws iron; but those metals are produced only in their proper place. Furthermore, all the historians who wrote about his death without any ax to grind mention nothing of this; they say that he died of ague. Most difficult of all, this same story is told in *Bereshit Rabbah*, chapter 10, and in *Va-Yiqra Rabbah* on the lesson "*Aḥarei Mot*" (chap. 22). Yet there is a significant divergence between them and what is told in the Talmud. But if this was an actual event, why did the Sages not recount it consistently?... All these things teach us and inform us that these matters are not as they seem, but that there is a deeper meaning. Yet I have not seen anyone discuss this problem and seek to solve it.[45]

Although most listeners would not have challenged Morteira's claim of originality, when writing this passage he must have had in front of him Azariah de' Rossi's discussion of the aggadah in *Me'or 'Einayim*.[46] De' Rossi

---

43. See Saperstein, *Jewish Preaching*, Index, s.v. *sefeqot*, and Saperstein, "The Method of Doubts."

44. See Tosafot *Gittin* 56b, *ve-niqer*. The idea is that since a beast with a perforation in the membrane is deemed to have a fatal organic disease (*treifah*), it is impossible for any creature to live with such a condition; therefore no perforation could have been made.

45. MS 4:65v, *Bo*, Exod. 10:4, 1623.

46. See *Me'or 'Einayim*, pp 215–16; *Kitvei Azariah min ha-Adumim*, pp. 308–318, from *Imrei Binah*, chap. 16; *The Light of the Eyes*, pp. 296–99. As we have seen, Morteira does refer to de' Rossi on other occasions (see above, note 37). The most charitable explanation for his statement that he has seen no one discuss this issue is that he is claiming originality here not with regard to the problems that preceded the statement but to the solution that follows: he has not seen anyone who both discussed the problem and presented a solution. One attempt

brought the same three categories of problems with the passage that Morteira does: the conflict with the laws of nature, the conflict with ancient historical sources about Titus, and the contradictions within rabbinic sources. In the first two instances, he is more detailed than Morteira. With regard to the anatomy of the nasal canal and the brain, he cites the work of a French scholar; with regard to the outside historians, he mentions more than a dozen by name. De' Rossi explained that according to science, metals are produced only within the earth by an established process, a point not entirely clear in our preacher's abbreviated summary. Morteira, by contrast, is more detailed in outlining the differences between the versions in the Talmud and the Midrash, as this is re.evant to the point he will make. Both share a critical approach to the rabbinic texts, which enables them, or requires them, to repudiate the simple meaning where it is contradicted by abundant external evidence. Both use the same phrase to express a deeper, esoteric content: *devarim be-go.*

Where Morteira differs from Azariah is in providing an esoteric interpretation of the statement, and this is what is relevant to our purpose. The story of Titus becomes an allegorical representation of the punishment visited against Rome through the emergence of Christianity. The gnat that entered Titus's nose is "the Christian faith, compared to a small gnat because of the lowliness of its beginnings."

> It pounded in his brain for seven years, referring to its having addled the brains of his people with its beliefs and its lies for a long time. His passing by a certain blacksmith and the gnat's growing silent because of the sound of the hammer is an allegory for those [Christians] who were killed by the Romans with swords—the sound of the hammer—to prevent the new faith from spreading. However, since God had decreed this in order to afflict the evil empire, "the creature got used to it." They did not see it again until it became like a dove, meaning that it appeared to be pure and clean like a baby dove, similar to the pig which spreads its cloven hoofs.[47] However, its beak was of brass, as in the verse, *a mouth*

---

to do this that Morteira could conceivably have seen but may not have was by Isaac ben Abraham Hayot of Prague, *Paḥad Yitsḥaq* (Lublin, 1573), sections 69–74. Hayot provides an allegorical interpretation of the aggadah in philosophical style, totally de-historicizing its content; it is therefore totally different from Morteira's interpretation. Reference to this interpretation is made by Gans, *Tsemaḥ David*, p. 218; on this book and the author's approach to the aggadah, see Jacob Elbaum, *Petiḥut ve-Histagrut* (Jerusalem, 1990), pp. 128–30.

47. See Midrash Tehillim 80,6.

that spoke proud words (Dan. 7:8),[48] and its claws were of iron, drawing everything to it. Finally, it brought about the death of Titus, referring to the Roman Empire, for He brought about the circumstances of Constantine, through whom He took Rome. Afterward he suppressed it under his feet; he divided the realm, giving it to a western emperor.[49] This is what the Sages meant in their first enigmatic account in the Gemara.[50]

Several themes in Morteira's presentation of early Christian history are worth noting: the lowly beginnings of Christianity, the persecution and execution of Christians by Rome, the gradual spread of the heretical doctrine, the eventual prevalence of new faith. He presents all of this as part of God's providential plan, punishing Rome for its crimes against the Jews. Christianity, represented by a gnat transformed into a dove with brass beak and iron claws, is used by God for a purpose fundamentally different from that of the triumphalist interpretation of the Christian accession to power.

What makes this passage unusual is its homiletical setting. Here, rabbinic discourse—shown to be highly problematic because of its inconsistency with the laws of nature and with unbiased independent historical authorities—is transformed into a communication of historical information serving a Jewish polemical purpose. The rabbis are revealed to be not naive fools but experts with prophetic powers, capable of understanding events that would occur after their lifetime.

If the Christianization of the Roman Empire in late antiquity was the first great providential transformation avenging the defeat of the Jews and ultimately vindicating Jewish historical experience, the second was the Protestant Reformation. As Constantine's conversion led to the division of the Empire between east and west, here was another dramatic breakdown of Christian unity. Morteira insists that this breakdown, too, was foreseen by Daniel and the Sages.

---

48. In a passage from the sermon not cited here, Morteira interprets verses from Daniel as prophesying the divisions that he presents as the meaning of the rabbinic statement.

49. The referent of the pronoun "he" is ambiguous in this sentence. If it refers to Constantine, then it cannot actually be a "western emperor" (*qeisar ma'aravi*), as the division of the empire did not occur until the death of Theodosius I in 395 CE. Cf. Gans, *Tsemah David,* p. 240: "The Emperor [Constantine] gave to the aforementioned Pope Sylvester authority and sovereignty over Rome and over the lands of Italy, Germany, France and Spain, together with all other lands of the west to the ocean, to him and to all Roman popes that succeeded him to this day." If "he" refers to God, reference could be to the Holy Roman Emperor of a later period.

50. MS 4:66r, *Bo*, Exod 10:4, 1623.

When [Daniel] envisioned [the empire] in the image of a beast, he first saw ten horns, which are the ten great emperors of Rome,[51] and he then saw a little horn sprouting up among them. Three of the older horns were uprooted to make room for it. There were eyes in this horn like those of a human being (cf. Dan. 7:7–8). These are the Lutherans and the Calvinists, who have repudiated the Pope. They have eyes like those of a human being, namely, Israel, meaning that they have come closer to the Jews and are no longer so similar to a beast. They have opened their eyes to flee from some of the rigidities that those who believe in the Pope still cling to. Yet they are "*like* the eyes of a human being," not actually human eyes.[52]

Morteira's presentation of the Protestant Reformation is not surprising. As a Jew in Protestant Amsterdam, he was constrained to walk a delicate tightrope. He wanted to present the Reformation as a negative event in Christian history, part of the divine process of vengeance against Rome, which now stood for Christianity. Yet prudence prevented him from speaking about the Protestants too harshly. As with some Jewish writers of the 1520s, he presented Luther and the movement he spearheaded as a return toward Judaism, repudiating Catholicism on issues in which the Protestants accepted the Jewish position.[53] Unlike the Jews writing a hundred years before, however, he knew that the Lutherans and Calvinists were not actually going to become Jews: their stance was similar, but not identical, to the truth. Thus Catholicism, not Protestantism, represented his main target of attack, both for reasons of prudence and because the break from Catholicism was a decision made by his listeners that had to be reaffirmed.

After his interpretation of the aggadah about Titus and the gnat as an allegory of the first "death" of Rome through the agency of Christianity, Morteira

---

51. Morteira states this as if it everyone would know the "ten great emperors" to whom he was referring. Most likely, he accepts Abravanel's suggestion that the ten horns allude to the ten emperors from Julius Caesar to Vespasian, that is, until the destruction of Jerusalem. See Abravanel, *Ma'aynei ha-Yeshu'ah* in *Perush al Nevi'im u-Khetuvim* (Tel Aviv, 1970), p. 336; Netanyahu, *Don Isaac Abravanel*, p. 214; Lawee, "On the Threshold of the Renaissance," pp. 317–18. In a sermon we have already discussed, Morteira provides a different interpretation of the "ten horns" as a symbol of the discord within the new Christian faith from its very beginnings (MS 1:87v, *Koraḥ*, Num. 16:17).

52. MS 4:65v, *Bo*, Exod. 10:4, 1623. The passage concludes, "Thus we see that the two great changes which have befallen the Roman Empire were not concealed from the prophets. They occurred through God's decree, to take vengeance against them, until the third change, which will occur through the King Messiah."

53. See Haim Hillel Ben-Sasson, "The Reformation in Contemporary Jewish Eyes," *Proceedings of the Israel Academy of Sciences and Humanities*, 4:12 (1970): 239–326.

presents a second interpretation, based this time not on the text of the Babylonian Talmud but on the text of the Midrash.

> Our Sages in *Bereshit Rabbah* and *Va-Yiqra Rabbah* applied their enigmatic imagery to the second change, in which God exacted vengeance against them through the multiplicity of beliefs among them. The results were worse than anything before this: loss of honor, intense hatred, numerous wars. They too selected Titus as the emblem for this; because he did such great evil to the Jews, they used his name to refer to the Pope, who took over in his place and does evil to us.
>
> They said that while he was in the bathhouse, referring to his [?] and to pleasures alluded to by the bathhouse, they brought before him a cup of wine. This means that the gnat came from his attendants and servants, namely, from Calvin and Luther came the gnat. This refers to something that was small at the beginning, which entered his nose and pounded in his brain and destroyed his greatness, his prestige, and his faith, until he cried out that they should open up his head and see how the God of the Jews exacts payment from them.
>
> The physicians came and split open his brain, meaning that they divided his realm into two, separating certain ones out from under their [his?] rule, and it [the new realm of Protestantism] grew and became enormous. Its beak was of brass and its claws of iron, to harm him and to destroy him. Nevertheless, Titus still remains alive, "as the one changes, so does the other," for the same thing will happen to them both: "the gnat flew away, and the soul of the wicked Titus flew away," meaning that God exacts payment from all of them, and both shall perish together, says the Lord (cf. Isa. 31:3).[54]

Here too, reflecting upon the experience from the middle of the sixteenth century, Morteira directs his barbs against the Catholics—primarily the Pope, who indulges in vain pleasures, represented by the bathhouse, and is a source of evil for the Jews. Yet the description of the state of Christendom is one that involves Protestants as well as Catholics: "intense hatred, numerous wars." According to the preacher, the history of the previous one hundred years reveals Christianity at its lowest state of fortune since the conversion of Constantine. Morteira's two versions of the story of Titus thus become two visions of a historical pattern manifest at different times: the Sages foresaw events not only close to the time they lived but close to the time of the listeners as well.

---

54. MS 4:66r, *Bo*, Exod. 10:4, 1623.

The second sermon, delivered in the mid-1640s, is on the lesson *Tazri'a*. Morteira continues an account of the fate of the new Christian religion and its relationship to the Roman Empire. Here he is explicating the rabbinic statement, "The son of David will not come before the entire empire has turned into heresy" (b. *Sanhedrin* 97a):

> In their days, when this new faith began in the midst of our people, they called them heretics (*minim*), to emphasize their total repudiation. When it began to spread among the Gentiles and the Romans, who became closer to them, the Sages said that the Romans had turned to heresy, even though they had earlier referred to [Roman religion?] as idolatry. Now the holy spirit had sparkled among our early Sages. They saw that even though the [Christians] were persecuted by "the empire"—namely the Romans, whom they referred to as "the empire" because all sovereignty was theirs and they ruled the entire world at that time—and the Romans killed Christians by the thousands and tens of thousands, as is known from their books—the Sages prophesied that the son of David would not come before the entire empire would turn into heresy, and the Romans would be transformed into those whom they used to persecute. This dictum would have been amazing to these [Romans] because of the lowliness and humiliation of their [i.e. the Christians'] beginnings.[55]

Morteira reminds his listeners of two stages in the relationship of early Christianity and the Jewish people: its beginnings as a sectarian movement within Judaism, and then its turn to the Gentile world of the Roman Empire as the primary arena for its initiative. He also reviews two stages in the relationship between early Christianity and the Romans' empire: the Christians, first persecuted and killed by the Romans in large numbers, later transformed the empire in their own image. Finally, the preacher refers to two sources of historical knowledge. There are the books of non-Jewish historians, the source for Roman persecution and Christian martyrdom;[56] as in other sermons, these are accepted as reliable for the information they provide. The second source is of a different order: the words of the Sages recorded in the Talmud. As in the previous sermon, the Sages are presented here less as historians than as prophets who spoke of events that would occur in the future.

---

55. MS 1:39r, *Tazri'a*, Lev 13:13.ÿ

56. It is not entirely clear whether "their books" refers to the works of Roman or Christian historians, but it is probably the latter. For Jewish historians on persecution of Christians, see Zacuto, *Sefer Yuḥasin ha-Shalem*, p. 245; Gans, *Tsemaḥ David* Topical Index, p. 477. s.v. "*Notsrim—nirdafim ve-neheragim*," and especially p. 237 on the persecution under Diocletian.

Their terminology requires explication—"heresy" refers to Christianity, "the empire" refers to Rome—but then their perspicacity becomes clear. One final motif introduced at the end we have already seen in our discussion of the Sermon on *Bo*: the humble beginnings of Christianity, and the humiliation of Rome in eventually being conquered by a force for which it once had such great contempt.[57]

How would such a passage resonate with its intended audience? It seems to be calculated not to provide the listener with substantial new information, but rather to integrate and interpret what was already known. The emphasis on Christianity as originally a Jewish heresy, the reminder that the early Christians were despised by the Romans, might well have resonated with an audience that had chosen Judaism instead. The conversion of Constantine and the Christianization of the Roman Empire become not the glorious flowering of Christian triumphalism but a part of the Jewish messianic scenario, known in advance; its function is not to prove the rejection of the Jews but to emphasize the humiliation of ancient Rome. Finally, there are themes that recur in many of the sermons: that history has a structure and purpose, and that the classic texts of the Jewish tradition—Bible and Talmud—are authoritative sources, not only for the details, but more importantly for the broad patterns of historical events.

Morteira has interpreted the messianic prediction as referring to an event that occurred during the fourth century. But the alert listener might have wondered: If the condition for the messianic advent was fulfilled so long ago, why the long delay? Morteira addresses this issue by turning once again to the period beginning with the Reformation. He begins with the theme-verse from *Tazri'a*, *If the priest sees that the eruption has covered the whole body, he shall pronounce the affected person clean; he is clean, for he has turned all white* (Lev. 13:13). "It is not improbable," he says, "that in this promise there is a hint of what we have seen during recent generations: the wondrous change that has come about within the [Christian] Empire.... Within a few years, their bonds of unity have come undone, so that many faiths and beliefs quite distant from each other have emerged, producing great hatred and powerful enmity."[58]

Morteira considers the loss of Christian unity, the plethora of different views on basic theological issues, to be a powerful argument against Christian claims of truth. The uniformity imposed by the Inquisitions of the Iberian

---

57. The humiliation of being conquered by what appears to be an unworthy foe is also emphasized by Morteira with regard to the experience of the Jews, in connection with Deuteronomy 32:21: *I'll provoke their jealousy with a non-people, with an ignorant nation I'll vex them.* See below, pp. 514–15.

58. MS 1:40r, *Tazri'a*, Lev. 13:13.

peninsula is not to be found in the present environment; Jews are no longer confronted with a clear and consistent alternative to Judaism but with a splintering Christianity—like that in the period of its origins—where little consensus remains. Morteira emphasized the point tellingly in a sermon on the same lesson delivered a few years earlier: "This is what we say to our neighbors: Before you dispute against us, go and resolve among yourselves the multitude of different beliefs held by those who confess your religion."[59] But beyond the loss of unity there is another point about the content of the new doctrines. The theme mentioned in passing in the 1623 sermon—that the Reformation brought many Christians closer to the truth of Judaism—is here developed in greater detail, using a rhetoric of open opprobrium for traditional Catholic belief:

> Many of them have abandoned the glaring errors their predecessors embraced.... They have abandoned the plurality that they introduced into the Godhead, they have restored the proper belief in the eternity of the Torah, they believe in the beneficence promised in the future to the Jewish people. They err only to some extent in the matter of the doctrine of the Messiah. In our time, these [Christians] have grown more numerous; every day truth points out the proper path, and their numbers increase. Books have already been written about this, public academic sessions have been devoted to this matter.[60]

This is not the occasion to evaluate the accuracy of this presentation of radical Judaizing in new Protestant denominations.[61] Clearly Morteira employed

---

59. MS 1:42r, *Tazri'a*, Lev. 13:10 (1640). In a sermon delivered a few years after this, Morteira turns this formulation around in a striking manner. He argues that it was an act of divine providence to eliminate the ancient Jewish sects that challenged rabbinic Judaism before the long exile, "for since it was God's purpose to scatter us among the nations in order to teach them the Torah, seeing the Jewish people divided among themselves over its content would have been an obstacle, for they would have said, 'Before you profess its truth to us, resolve the matter among yourselves'" (MS 5:47r, *Va-Yetse*, Gen. 29:7, ca. 1645). The open divisiveness within Christianity on fundamental theological issues was used by Jews as a polemical weapon both before Morteira (see Abraham ibn Migash, *Kevod Elohim*, cited by Ralph Melnick, *From Polemics to Apologetics*, p. 11) and after him (e.g. Orobio de Castro, in Yosef Kaplan, *From Christianity to Judaism*, p. 252. For a stunning example of this argument used against Catholic internal theological controversy (Domnicans vs. Jesuits, French vs. Italians, Jesuits vs. secular priests in England), see John Donne, *Eighty Sermons* (1640), p. 10 (a Christmas Day sermon from 1622), cited in *The Complete Poetry and Selected Prose of John Donne* (New York, 1941), p. 363.

60. MS 1:40a, *Tazri'a*, Lev. 13:13.

61. In the background of this passage may be a conversation Morteira had with a learned Socinian some 12 or 13 years before this sermon was delivered. According to his later de-

elements that were useful for his purpose and ignored others. What is important for our purposes is the conception of history he communicated to the listeners.

The preacher bestows the Reformation with eschatological significance for Jewish history: "This is an unmistakable sign indicating that the time of our redemption is drawing near." After applying to these changes a verse at the end of the book of Daniel—*Many will be purified and purged and refined; the wicked will act wickedly and none of the wicked will understand; but the knowledge-able will understand* (Dan. 12:10)—he returns to the statement that had earlier been interpreted to refer to the Christianization of the Roman Empire: "The son of David will not come before the entire empire has been changed to heresy" (b. *Sanhedrin* 97a):

> They spoke here as they usually do in such matters, referring to things not as they truly are but as they are generally purported to be.... Thus they call "heresy" not what is actually heretical, but what the Christians consider to be heretical, for throughout the empire, these [new Christian sects] and those similar to them are called heretics who have abandoned the faith.[62]

The theme-verse of the sermon (Leviticus 13:13), which serves as the prooftext for the Talmudic statement in its original context, is then reiterated in its metaphorical interpretation, and the sermon ends with a messianic prayer.

In his sermons, Morteira does not reveal himself as a historian. The only Jewish historical works he cites are Yosippon and Azariah de' Rossi. While

scription, the Socinian told Morteira that he and his co-religionists "did not believe in any manner in the Trinity, that they recognized only one God, Creator of everything, and that all except for Him were creatures" (*Respondeome que por nihum caso cria elle terenidade, se naõ que hauia hum so Deos, criador de todas as cosas, e que tudo fora dElle heraõ criaturas.*) See Morteira, *Tratado*, p. 336–37 and note p. 1214–15; Méchoulan, "Morteira et Spinoza au carrefour du Socianisme," pp. 59–60. Cf. also *Tratado*, pp. 149, 491. On the activities of antitrinitarian Socinians in Holland from the late-sixteenth through mid-seventeenth century, see Earl Wilbur, *A History of Unitarianism* (Cambridge, 1946), pp. 535–70. See also Robert Dan and Antal Pernat, editors, *Antitrinitarianism in the Second Half of the Sixteenth Century* (Leiden, 1982); G. H. Williams, *The Polish Brethren: Documentation of the History and Thought of Unitarianism in the Polish-Lithuanian Commonwealth and in the Diaspora, 1601–1685*, 2 vols. (Missoula, Mont., 1980).

62. MS 1:40r, *Tazri'a*, Lev. 13:13. Indeed, the antitrinitarians were deemed heretics, and not only by the Roman Catholic establishment. For an example of a Christian author explaining his use of the term "heretics" to refer to those whom the Catholic Church calls "heretics" without endorsing the validity of this appellation, see Williams, *The Polish Brethren*, 1:343 (from a work published in Amsterdam, 1637).

he refers to texts of Roman history, he may well have derived this material at second hand. Major events of medieval Jewish history do not seem to be mentioned at all.[63] Even events directly relevant to the experience of the community are not recounted in detail. Instead we have brief general references intended to drive home a moral lesson:

> Let us learn from earlier history, from the greatness and glory, the opulence and wisdom that were long ago in the [Jewish communities of the] kingdoms of Spain and France. Now all is destroyed and abandoned, nothing remains.[64]

As we have seen, this leads into a passage criticizing the failings of those communities as recorded in the responsa literature, and applying the same critique to the community of Amsterdam. Elsewhere, he calls up shared memories to illustrate a biblical verse pointing to policy for inter-group relations:

> *Better is open reproof* (Prov. 27:5), of the kind revealed when the king of Spain expelled the Jews from his land unless they agreed to abandon their religion, than that which came at the hands of the king of Portugal, who forced and compelled them to apostatize, covering up his fury and his evil heart and concealing his reproof in lying love by saying that he truly loved them and was having compassion on their souls.[65]

The preacher's point is that Gentiles always hate Jews, and that their pretense of "love," expressed in favorable treatment, may be more dangerous than open enmity in that it produces self-deception. For Morteira, history is subsumed to a homiletical or polemical purpose. Its importance is to provide lessons for conduct, and evidence for God's providential plan.

---

63. For example, I have found no reference to the Crusades in the sermons, although he does discuss the First Crusade in his *Tratado*: "as is recounted at length in the chronicles" (ed. Salomon, p. 101).

64. MS 2:96r, *Mishpatim*, Exod. 21:8, 1627; see above, pp. 132–33.

65. MS 4:16r, *Shemot*, Exod. 1:13. No such pretense of love or professed religious motivation is recorded in Usque's detailed account of the forced conversion (pp. 202–4), or in Joseph ha-Kohen's *'Emeq ha-Bakhah* (Cracow, 1895), p. 105. Cf. Yosef Yerushalmi, *The Lisbon Massacre of 1506 and the Royal Image in the "Shevet Yehudah"* (Cincinnati, 1976), p. 59.

8

Christianity
and the "New Christians"

The readers of Morteira's *Giv'at Sha'ul* in the Warsaw 1902 or 1912 edition would not be aware that Christianity was a particularly important theme in his preaching. Only by unpacking the somewhat cryptic editorial note that states "For a reason beyond our control, sermon 41 on the lesson *Va-Ethanan* could not be printed," and a similar statement about "sermon 49 on the lesson *Ha'azinu,*" could they surmise that material pertaining to Christianity had been suppressed by a censor.[1] And indeed, the Amsterdam 1645 edition, in which both sermons appear, reveals that they contain material of a rather forceful polemical nature. In addition, several polemical passages from the sermon on *Balaq* were removed from the Warsaw editions without any editorial indication that the original text had been changed.[2] Thus the Amsterdam edition contains three sermons out of fifty in which the anti-Christian motif is quite pronounced. The five bound volumes of Morteira's sermon manuscripts in the Budapest Rabbinical Seminary include many more such passages.

That material published at Amsterdam in 1645 could not be printed at Warsaw in 1902 does not come as a total surprise, given the respective reputations for openness and toleration of Dutch and Russian-dominated societies. Yet seventeenth-century Amsterdam was not without its ground rules for

---

1. *GS* 1912, pp. 257, 303. These two sermons from *GS* 1645 are translated below, pp. 408ff and 447ff. Scott Ury of the Hebrew University has directed my attention to a booklength study of Russian censorship: Dmitry Elyashevich, *Government Policy and Jewish Printing in Russia* [in Russian] (St. Petersburg and Jerusalem, 1999), esp. pp. 377–83 and 543–59; this does not, however deal in detail with Warsaw. In Amsterdam, the censorship would have been internal, by the *Mahamad,* which prohibited members of the community from publishing books in Spanish, Portuguese, or Hebrew without its approval. See Bodian, *Hebrews of the Portuguese Nation,* pp. 116–17.

2. Compare *GS* 1912, pp. 239–40 with *GS* 1645), pp. 63c–64d and MS 1:109v–110r, *Balaq,* Num. 22:13, 1639. This material will be discussed below.

its Jewish residents.[3] There was a difference between religious debate and toleration of "blasphemy." Members of the Jewish community were not free to express publicly statements blatantly offensive to Christian sensibilities. Although Morteira spoke in Portuguese and published in Hebrew, offensive or impertinent statements could become known and arouse strong opposition to the Jewish presence.[4] The lay leadership of the Portuguese community (the *Ma'amad*) was extremely sensitive to this matter, more than once issuing edicts that warned against making any statements insulting to Christianity.[5] It is therefore important to note that, although some of his points would apply to Dutch Calvinism as well, the main thrust of Morteira's polemic in his sermons is against the *Catholic* Church. Protestantism is rarely mentioned explicitly, and when it is, the references are relatively benign.[6] The anti-Catholic animus of the sermons is one that was shared by many of Amsterdam's Christian citizens.[7] Only later, in his unpublished Portuguese polemical work on the eternity of the Torah, did Morteira take up the cudgels against Calvin himself.[8]

Why was it important to polemicize against a form of Christianity that the members of his congregation had already left behind and that was not at all popular in their new home? Many of those who came to Jewish communities from a Portuguese New Christian background had a strong distaste for the

---

3. Their status throughout the period of our discussion remained "residents" (*ingezetenen*), not full burghers. See the recent discussion by Bodian, *Hebrews of the Portuguese Nation*, p. 60.

4. Note the statement in Hugo Grotius's *Remonstratie* (1615): "Furthermore, the Jews may possess, use and have printed here any books, with the exception of those containing words of blasphemy or defamation" (quoted in Melnick, *From Polemics to Apologetics*, p. 15); cf. the discussion by S. W. Baron, *SRHJ* 15: 27–29. This follows the wording of the privilege approved by the town council of Amsterdam in 1605 ("they must refrain from blasphemy or derision of the Christians, not only in print but also in words during their ceremonies in the synagogue"), which was reiterated in a town ordinance of 1616: Huussen, "The Legal Position of Sephardi Jews in Holland," pp. 24, 27; Schama, *The Embarrassment of Riches*, p. 591. The leadership of the Jewish community had to promise not to offend through religious disputes as a condition of their formal admission to Amsterdam, and the Jewish Communal Regulations (*Ascamot*) of 1638–39 threatened punishment by fine for anyone who insulted the Christian religion (Arnold Wiznitzer, "The Merger Agreement and Regulations of Congregation Talmud Torah of Amsterdam," p. 130).

5. See on this Yosef Kaplan, *Les nouveaux-Juifs d'Amsterdam* (Paris, 1999), pp. 137–38.

6. See, for example, the passage cited above, pp. 246, 250.

7. On the anti-Catholic animus of Morteira and others in his orbit, cf. Kaplan, *From Christianity to Judaism*, pp. 259–60. On the anti-Catholicism of the Calvinist *predikants*, see Bodian, *Hebrews of the Portuguese Nation*, p. 55.

8. Morteira, *Tratado* (see above, chap. 1); cf. Bodian, *Hebrews of the Portuguese Nation*, pp. 72–73.

faith in which they had been reared and the religious hierarchy that had manned the Inquisition. Not only did they have no need to be convinced of the inferiority of Christianity, they actually engaged in polemical activity themselves.[9] But for others, apparently, geographical displacement did not always bring about psychological distance. Perhaps the powerful polemical sermons delivered by churchmen at the *autos-da-fé* continued to resonate on some level of their consciousness.[10] Some listeners needed reassurance that their decision to break from the past was correct. It was such reassurance that Morteira's polemical passages provided.

Christianity

Let us begin with the relationship between the two religions. The theme of Christianity as an *imitation* of its parent religion has a long history in Jewish polemical writing of the Middle Ages.[11] This motif enabled Jewish polemicists to turn the Christian claim of being the "New Israel" on its head by depicting the newer religion as a pale copy of the old. Morteira emphasized this derivative character of Christianity on several occasions. His most detailed statement comes in a major sermon for the Sabbath of Repentance delivered in 1641. The homiletical context is important: here he is concretizing the fulfillment of a Biblical prophecy of punishment. God warns, *I'll provoke their jealousy with a non-people* (Deut. 32:21), by subjecting them to a people that is not God's but that claims all of the qualities that God gave to Israel.[12] The similarities between Christianity and Judaism are not accidental but providential:

> For behold, regarding the categories within the [Christian] nation, they have divided them as we do into priests and Levites with rights to tithes and a kind of High Priest patterned after us. They have invented a congregation of seventy-one, a kind of Sanhedrin. Look at the holy days

---

9. Well known examples are Elijah Montalto, Isaac Cardoso, and Isaac Orobio de Castro. Morteira's eulogies and the writings of Hugh Broughton allow us now to add the figure of David Farar: see Saperstein, "*Your Voice Like a Ram's Horn*," chap. 16, especially pp. 371–73.

10. See Glaser, "Invitation to Intolerance."

11. See, for example, Moses Maimonides, *Crisis and Leadership: Epistles of Maimonides* (Philadelphia, 1985), pp. 99–100 ("Epistle to Yemen"), and the statement by Jacob Anatoli in Saperstein, "*Your Voice Like a Ram's Horn*," p. 61 with parallels there in n. 12.

12. Morteira may well have known that Christian authors used this verse to validate supersessionist claims. For example, Martin Luther, commenting on this verse, wrote, "And to the present day the Jews are irreconcilably angry with us for denying that they are the people of God and for asserting that according to this verse we are the people of God." See his "Lectures on Deuteronomy," in *Luther's Works*, 55 vols. (St. Louis, Philadelphia, 1958–1967), 9:294–95. Compare below, p. 275.

of the year: they have made like us a kind of Sabbath and Pesach and Shavuot. They have invented a "jubilee" year. The structure of their communion is patterned after our prayer of sanctification (*Qiddush*) and blessing over bread (*Motsi*). The text of their liturgy is derived from our prophets. The "miracles" they placed in their books are precisely those that are written in our Sacred Scriptures—there is nothing else, as we have discussed at length in its proper place, showing one by one what corresponds to everything of theirs. Their baptism they took from our immersion of the ritually impure. And so with many of the things they boast were given them by God.[13]

The message seems to be quite clear: you know that Judaism is the older faith, you have the authentic, original version. Why be tempted to settle for the imitation?

This emphasis on the similarities between Christianity and Judaism has its dangers, however, as a listener might conceivably draw an unwanted conclusion: What difference does it make which was original and which was derivative? If the rituals in the two faiths are so similar, why sacrifice to choose the less powerful option? In his late *Treatise on the Truth of the Law of Moses*, Morteira frequently presents a different argument: that fundamental Christian beliefs and values reveal the influence not of Judaism but of paganism.[14] But the responsible preacher will have to communicate a positive message as well, highlighting aspects of Judaism's uniqueness. We see this in a sermon on the lesson *Pinḥas*, probably delivered in the late 1630s. At first, Morteira simply enumerates the areas of imitation in which "they attribute to themselves the stature of Israel: their prayers, their priests, their raiments, their names." But his point here is different: that God preserved the Hebrew language as the unique possession of the Jewish people to maintain its distinctiveness. For "if, God forbid, they were to praise God in the holy tongue, they would indeed boast excessively and claim that they were the children of Israel."[15]

There is another theoretical problem to be addressed. In comparing two religions that share so much, how can one be sure which is the genuine expression of God's will? Morteira addresses this issue in a sermon on Exodus 31:13, introducing the polemical point through a reference to military tactics.

An analogy is the practice of those who guard the walls to give each

---

13. MS 3:312r, *Ha'azinu*, Deut. 32:21, 1641; below, p. 501 for annotation regarding the number of cardinals, the jubilee year, and Morteira's work discussing the "miracles" recounted in the New Testament.

14. E.g. Morteira, *Tratado*, p. 387 (on the myth of a woman impregnated by a god).

15. MS 1:45v, *Pinḥas*, Num 26:6.

other signals known to no one else, so that the enemy will not trick them at night and, not being recognized, come [?] to climb the walls and seize the city.[16] That is what God said: Note that in everything I have done, the counterfeiters can fabricate and trick you by saying to you that a certain person is God, and that you should accept him, for "I, I am he." Through your naïveté, he may enter and seize the city, for he may boast of doing all the miracles that I have done, and the way is then paved before them to say that they were like mine. However, I have given you a great signal, by which you can distinguish truth from falsehood, and God from one who is not God. That is, if he should create a different world, then he may claim to be God.... But no one has ever done such a thing. Thus it is an unmistakable signal that he is not God.

Similarly, if there should arise another people that boasts that it is chosen, it is Israel, God's people, God's treasure, let not your hands be weakened, even if they boast of all the good things I did for you, saying that they possess holiness, and prophecy, and Torah, and esoteric doctrines, and divine loving kindness, and whatever else may occur to them. For I give you a great signal: so long as they cannot assert and confirm that I have redeemed them from the land of Egypt, they are not My people. This is what King David said, *Who is like Your people Israel, a unique nation on earth, whom God set out to redeem so it would be His people* (2 Sam. 7:23). This is impossible for anyone other than you. And that is why God engraved this signal almost everywhere in the Torah.[17]

In its homiletical context—as an explication of *a sign between Me and you* (Exod. 31:13)—the point of the analogy with guards giving passwords and signals to identify the loyal soldier from the enemy in disguise is to explain the signs of authenticity for the Jewish people in its relationship to God. But the deeper implication tears down the opponent as well. Through the analogy with the "enemy," Christian "imitation" of Jewish practices and institutions, leading to the Christian claim of being the "true Israel," is presented as not just

---

16. It is unclear whether Morteira derived this illustration from common knowledge or from the experience of some in the congregation. Peter Stuyvesant 's famous 1655 Resolution excluding Jews of New Amsterdam from military service claimed that "the said nation was not admitted or counted among the citizens, as regards trainbands or common citizens' guards [i.e., militia companies], neither in the illustrious City of Amsterdam nor (to our knowledge) in any city in Netherland." Morris U. Schappes, editor, *A Documentary History of the Jews in the United States, 1645–1875* (New York, 1950), pp. 5–6.

17. MS 4:178r, *Ki Tissa*, Exod. 31:13, early 1640s. On the Christian claim to be the "New Israel," see the end of the sermon on *Balaq, GS* 1645, p. 64c–d, cited below, p. 275, and the *Ha'azinu* sermon translated below, p. 514, n. 64.

misguided but also devious and subversive. And this is not merely an attack on the claims made by leaders of the Church. Jesus is not mentioned by name, but no one would have missed the allusion to one who "claims to be God." This claim, attributed by implication not to later theologians but to Jesus himself, is subsumed under the analogy of the enemy who resorts to deception for insidious purposes.

On many other occasions, Morteira felt compelled to emphasize fundamental differences between the religion his congregants had abandoned and the religion they had now chosen for their own. We see the emphasis on difference despite apparent similarity in a sermon for the lesson *Va-Yishlaḥ* delivered circa 1633. As this biblical passage is a narrative of the encounter between Jacob and Esau after a separation of many years, many of Morteira's sermons on this lesson are built upon a typological approach to the verses.[18] The aspect of typological significance which the preacher emphasizes is that Jacob and Esau, despite being twins, were absolutely different from each other in every way except for their voices:

> Thus even though they were equal in voice, from this they diverged from each other in a great and essential manner. One drew near to God and set God before him always (cf. Ps. 16:8), the other would say to God, "Leave me alone" (cf. Job 21:14). In this too there is something of a wonderful hint of their descendants. Even though in the quality of their voices they may be equivalent—for each one says that he is the chosen, the elder, the blessed—yet in substance one constantly makes mention of God's name, while the other bestows God's glory upon another. He may praise God with his mouth, but he gives his adoration to statues. Thus in truth, one is a goat and the other a sheep, which though both are in a common category of flock, yet their names are totally different.[19]

Here we see a strong assertion of Christianity, or at least Catholicism, as idolatry. Rhetorically, Morteira draws upon the New Testament motif of separating the sheep from the goats (Mt. 25:32–33) to dramatize the significance of the two kinds of animals mentioned in the sermon's theme-verse (Gen. 32:15) enumerating the animals in Jacob's offering to Esau.

More extensive treatment of this theme can be seen in another sermon for the lesson *Va-Yishlaḥ*, delivered a few years after the first. Referring to earlier

18. On Morteira's use of typology, see, Saperstein, *"Your Voice Like a Ram's Horn,"* pp. 30–32. For the use of typology in Portuguese Christian anti-Jewish preaching, see Glaser, "Invitation to Intolerance," p. 300.

19. MS 5:55v, *Va-Yishlaḥ*, Gen. 32:15, ca. 1633.

sermons on the subject, Morteira reiterates the underlying typological principle in the introduction: "It is not unlikely that what happened to our father Jacob and to Esau is a hint to his descendants, that we may thereby derive from his affairs comfort and knowledge and counsel as to how we should behave regarding what happens to us with Esau's descendants."[20] Then in the body of the sermon, after discussing the differences between the twins in the biblical context, he turns to the religions of the twins' descendants. Judaism and Christianity are "two great opposites that cannot co-exist in the same subject. This is the meaning of the phrase, *we have come into fire and water* (Ps. 66:12): we have come to a conflict like that of fire and water."[21] This antithetical character is illustrated in considerable detail with regard to fundamental beliefs pertaining to the past, present, and future.

The difference pertaining to the past—"the most fundamental difference of all"—lies at the heart of theology. It applies to the belief in God, bound up with "absolute primordial existence."

> Now we know how distant our belief is from theirs in many specifics touching upon this matter.
>
> First is the matter of the simplicity of God, the repudiation of corporeality from Him in every respect, as He emphasized in several places of His Torah.... But the descendants of Esau believe that He was incarnated in a woman's womb.
>
> Second is the matter of absolute unity that God taught us: *Hear O Israel: the Eternal our God, the Eternal is one* (Deut. 6:4).... But the children of Esau believe that He is three.
>
> Third is the matter of His eternity and primordial existence: that He is the first and the last, and He is the living God, as He taught us through His prophet. But the descendants of Esau believe that He was subject to death and that he died.
>
> Fourth is the matter of melancholy and imperfections, which are totally alien to Him. But the descendants of Esau believe that he was subject to them, that He was depressed, that he became a *man of suffering* (Isa. 53:3).
>
> Fifth is the matter of divine judgment: that God has control over forgiveness and atonement, that He is *gracious and compassionate* (Exod. 34:6), that He freely forgives. Yet the descendants of Esau believe that He has no capacity to do this without assuming something that makes

---

20. MS 5:63r, *Va-Yishlaḥ*, Gen. 32:18 (1636 or 1638).
21. Ibid., 63v.

> the hair of all who hear it bristle: namely, the death of God Himself!
> Can there be any differences greater, more enormous, than these?[22]

This passage does indeed touch upon the essential points of Jewish and Christian belief about God. Morteira is not concerned here with the subtleties of Christian theology. He reduces Christian belief to a series of simple propositions that overlook the distinctions between God the Father and God the Son with regard to the Incarnation and the ways in which Christian theologians defended the unity of the triune God. The polemicist, addressing an audience committed in principle to Judaism, need not worry about oversimplification.[23] The Christian propositions are presented in a manner that makes them seem absurd on their face and contrary to explicit statements of the Bible. Rhetorical power derives from the repeated parallelism of the refrain—"but the descendants of Esau"—building to the hyperbole drawn from Job 4:15 (*making the hair of my flesh bristle*), and the rhetorical question at the end. One can imagine the congregation nodding in satisfaction.

Morteira has imposed his own ordering upon the central theological differences between Christianity and Judaism, perhaps to make it easier for listeners to remember. After bringing his first section, the past, to a conclusion with a characteristic homiletical flourish and recapitulation, he moves on to the second, the present:

> The enormous difference between these two nations pertaining to the *present* is in the matter of the Torah and the divine commandments. With all their might and strength, they have attempted to annul and to replace the Torah with another. About this, Daniel says, *He will think of changing times and laws* (Dan. 7:25). They did not, however, succeed, for the Torah is God's [plan] and *God's plan shall endure forever* (Ps. 33:11). That is why Daniel says, *He shall devise*, meaning, he shall think, but not do. Their attempt is made in various devious ways.[24]

---

22. Ibid. On the final point, cf. the formulation in Morteira's "Argumentos contra los Evangelicos, Actos, y Epistolas" (Argument 36): According to Christian belief, God "cannot grant Divine justice, for in order to pardon an ordinary sin, committed by only one willful person, he committed one so grave, as to have His son killed by the hand of an entire people" (quoted in Melnick, *From Polemics to Apologetics*, pp. 31, 66).

23. Cf. Morteira's response to the first question put by a "clergyman of Rouen," in which after citing scriptural assertions of divine unity, he brings three "demonstrative (philosophical) arguments." (*www.jewish-history.com/Occident/volume3/jun1845/questions.html*).

24. Ibid.

That the status of the Torah and the commandments is a major issue between Judaism and Christianity would come as no surprise. The eternity of the Torah is one of the central themes of Morteira's oeuvre, to which he would later devote a substantial part of his monumental polemical treatise in Portuguese. Here he introduces in passing the claim that Christians not only deny the continuing validity of the old law, but substitute new laws that they claim are divine but are not—a theme rather different from his emphasis on the Christian imitation of Jewish practices in other sermons.[25] These changes were described by Daniel, who predicted the emergence (and even the subsequent history) of Christianity.[26]

The passage continues with a concise recounting of various Christian arguments that attempt to justify their belief that the commandments of the "Old Testament" have been abrogated:

> Sometimes they will say that the basis of all is faith, and all deeds are really superfluous, and when the Torah is in the heart, perfection has been acquired [as is written?] at length in their books. But they have not remembered God's word that states, *in your mouth and in your heart to do it* (Deut. 30:14).
>
> And sometimes they will say that the commandments are bound up with the land [of Israel], and with the exile of the Jewish people the Torah has been annulled. But they have not seen God's word, *When all these things have befallen you, the blessing and the curse which I have set before you, if you take them to heart in all the countries to which the Eternal your God has banished you, if you return to the Eternal your God and obey Him heart and soul in all that I command you this day, you and your children, then the Eternal your God will restore your fortunes* (Deut. 30:1–3).
>
> And sometimes they will say that it has already been annulled at the instruction of God, who brought charges against them. But they have not remembered what is written, *You shall faithfully keep the statutes, the judgments, the law, and the commandments which He wrote for you, and you shall not pay homage to other gods. You shall not forget the covenant which I made with you; you shall not pay homage to other gods* (2 Kings 17:37–38). And there are many such proofs for each one of these arguments....
>
> If so, there is before us a great, enormous difference between Jacob

---

25. This theme is taken up in detail in the *Va-Ethanan* sermon translated below, p. 408ff.

26. On the use of this verse, cf. the sermon on *Va-Ethanan*, p. 413, *Tratado*, pp. 599–601, 1067; Yom-Tov Lipman Mülhausen, *Sefer ha-Nizzahon* (Altdorf-Nurenberg 1644, reprinted Jerusalem, 1984), p. 180. Maimonides already found a prediction of Jesus in Daniel 11:14: see *Mishneh Torah, Hil. Melakhim*, chap. 11 (in the unexpurgated version).

and Esau, like the difference between fire and water. May God in his great power help and preserve us among them![27]

Each of these three arguments could be explicated at length in terms of Christian doctrine and polemical literature. In the present context, a few brief points will be made. The first is a reference to the doctrine of salvation by faith alone, without the necessity of works. It is formulated in a rather extreme form, suggesting that all human actions are devoid of religious consequence, a doctrine associated more with radical Protestant denominations than with mainstream Catholic piety. As we shall presently see, a similar doctrine, focusing not so much on faith as on the intention of the heart, is attributed by Morteira to New Christians who use it to justify their own failure to observe the commandments.[28] (A year or so later, when Morteira recapitulated these three arguments in a sermon on the following verse, he formulated the first claim differently: "Sometimes they say that [the commandments] have an inner meaning, and that there is no need to observe them according to their simple meaning."[29] This puts the emphasis on exegesis, not on psychology.) Morteira's response is based on the formulation of Deuteronomy 30:14, in which the infinitive "to do" follows the words that emphasize internalization, as if to say that what is in one's heart has no significance unless it is accompanied by action.

The second argument draws upon a Jewish distinction between commandments valid only in the land of Israel and those that are valid everywhere, and applies them to all the commandments of the Torah. We find this issue already in the sermons of John Chrysostom, who used it as an argument to delegitimize contemporary Judaism, insisting that observance of the biblical commandments was not only superfluous but actually a violation of God's will. The Sages felt the need to respond to this claim by explaining the func-

---

27. Ibid. In 1639, Morteira returned to this theme in a sermon on Genesis 32:19 from *Va-Yishlaḥ*, recapitulating this passage on Christian attacks against the Torah and mitzvot. There he says (MS 5:62r), "I have already responded against them at length." It is unclear to me whether reference is to the sermon we have been discussing, or to a polemical tract.

28. Cf. Morteira's reply to the twenty-first question from the "Clergyman of Rouen:" those who have left Portugal and live in places such as Bordeaux or Antwerp "think that the will being good, they have fulfilled their duty, and they do not consider that the Lord says, *But the word is very near to you, in your mouth and in your heart to do it.*" *www.jewish-history.com/Occident/volume3/nov1845/questions.html.*

29. MS 5:62r, *Va-Yishlaḥ*, Gen. 32:19, 1639: פעם יאמרו כי יש להם צורה ואין צורך לשמרם על פשוטם . This formulation is apparently based on the unexpurgated end of chapter 11 in Maimonides, *Code, Melakhim* (a passage cited by Morteira in MS 1:39v, *Tazri'a*, Lev. 13:13, ca. 1645, apparently from the Constantinople 1509 edition). For a vernacular statement of this claim, see Morteira's *Tratado*, p. 1149.

tion of the commandments outside the land, apparently setting out to refute not just Christian polemicists but Jewish sectarian positions as well. There are also references to this claim in literature closer to Morteira's time, including the polemics of Martin Luther.[30] Indeed, this was an important theme in the Portuguese auto-da-fé sermons, in which preachers argued that Jewish ceremonies were valid only in the land of Israel and were an affront to God when performed elsewhere.[31] Morteira's response is taken from the same passage in Deuteronomy 30, which indicates that observance of the commandments in exile is a prerequisite for redemption.[32]

As for God's nullification of the commandments in the context of a complaint lodged against the Jewish people, it is not clear to me what specific claim Morteira may have had in mind. It may refer to the widespread Christian assertion that although God had once ordained the Sabbath and festivals, the prophets bear witness that God now despises these Jewish observances.[33] But there also seems to be an allusion to a formal declaration by God that the covenant, with its structure of commandments, has been dissolved, which would go beyond anything found in the prophetic literature. As in the previous passage, Morteira presents the three claims with a structural parallelism,

---

30. John Chrysostom, Discourse 4.4.4–4.5.6, 5.1.5, 5.4.1, in Wayne Meeks and Robert Wilken, *Jews and Christians in Antioch in the First Centuries of the Common Era* (Missoula, 1978); cf. Martin Luther, "Against the Sabbatarians," in *Luther's Works,* 47:66, 79, 83–84. For Jewish responses to this claim, see Nahmanides on Lev. 18:25, citing Sifre; Jacob Mann, "An Early Theologico-Polemical Work," *HUCA* 12–13 (1937–1938): 412, 428–29, 452; Abraham Farissol in David Ruderman, *The World of a Renaissance Jew* (Cincinnati, 1981), pp. 43–44. For an encompassing survey of the status of the commandments outside the land of Israel, see Aviezer Ravitzky, "'*Hatzivu Lekha Tziyunim' le-Tziyon: Gilgulah shel Ra'ayon,*" in *Eretz Yisrael ba-Hagut ha-Yehudit BiYmei ha-Beinayim,* ed. Moshe Hallamish and Aviezer Ravitzky (Jerusalem, 1991), pp. 1–39.

31. Glaser, "Invitation to Intolerance," p. 353. According to Glaser, "Domingos Barata tells of a dispute with a rabbi residing in Holland whom he tried to convince that the celebration of Mosaic rites in the Low Lands countered God's prohibition. The rabbi resolved this 'dilemma' by denying that such an interdiction appeared anywhere in the Scriptures." (Barata's sermon was published in Evora, 1717: p. 331 n. 21). Cf. also *The Mirror of the New Christians of Francisco Machado,* ed. Mildred Vieira and Frank Talmage (Toronto, 1977), pp. 277–79.

32. Cf. Morteira's response to the sixth question from the "Clergyman of Rouen," where he cites more extensively this passage from the beginning of Deuteronmy 30: *www.jewish-history.com/Occident/volume3/jun1845/questions.html.*

33. See, e.g., Machado, *Mirror of the New Christians,* p. 235 (addressed to "judaizing New Christians"): "Why do you observe the Sabbath and the feasts of the Law of Moses? Do you not see that all these things are abhorrent to God? ... I tell you that this [Mal. 1:10] is nothing more than God's decision to renounce your sacrifices, as Malachi rightly proves, and to give the sacrifice of the altar to the Gentiles."

reinforced by the repetition of key words: "Sometimes they say.... But they have not remembered...." The formulation of the rebuttal implies that the Christian adversaries, ignorant of obvious biblical verses, are hardly worthy antagonists for a knowledgeable Jewish spokesman.

As is already clear to the listener from the previous two categories, the third area of antithesis between Judaism and Christianity set up by Morteira applies to the future:

> The third difference between the two religions, pertaining to the future time, is in the matter of the promised Messiah. The children of Esau have wanted to take their signs as true signs (cf. Ps. 74:4) to make us despair and lose hope, and to revile the footprints of the Messiah we hope for (cf. Ps. 89:52), by saying that he has already come and there is nothing to look forward to. To strengthen their position, they have set their hands upon all the prophecies and the good promises that together sing jubilantly of confidence and future hope. Some of them have said that these prophecies are figurative and hyperbolic language, which enables them to claim that they have already occurred. Some of them have said that they refer to spiritual matters that exist in heaven. Some of them have said that they have already been fulfilled in the redemption from the Babylonian exile. In this way they think they have pulled everything down and weakened our hands.[34]

As in the second category, a review of various positions taken by Christian thinkers suggests the preacher's mastery of the adversaries' polemical literature and their inability to reach consensus about an important doctrinal point.[35] In this case, the rebuttal is not introduced immediately but only at the

---

34. MS 5:63v-64r, *Va-Yishlah*, Gen. 32:18 (1636 or 1638).

35. On the Christians' figurative interpretation of prophecies, cf. (in a slightly different context) Isaac Orobio de Castro, cited in Glaser, "Invitation to Intolerance," p. 331, n. 21: "Mas vos dezis ... que el sentido de todas estas Prophecias, deve ser mistico, alegorico, methaphorico." An example from the New Testament is Paul's "allegorical" application of Isa. 54:1 to Sarah representing the "Jerusalem above," as opposed to the historical earthly Jerusalem, in Galatians 4:27. Jerome insisted that the kingdom envisioned in the book of Daniel would be spiritual and heavenly, not material and terrestrial: see Robert E. Lerner, "Refreshment of the Saints: The Time after Antichrist as a Station for Earthly Progress in Medieval Thought," *Traditio* 32 (1976): 102, and John O'Connell, *The Eschatology of Saint Jerome* (Mundelein, Il., 1948), pp. 64–72. Seventeenth-century Puritan writers insisted that there was no point in claiming to Jews that the prophetic promises of restoration were to be understood spiritually, for in response, "the Iewes laugh at us." See the sources cited

end of the passage, through a homiletical interpretation of Psalm 93:5.

In short, we have in this sermon a schematic treatment of the fundamental differences between Jewish and Christian faith, organized under the categories of past, present, and future, which correspond to doctrines of God, Torah, and redemption. In each, the Christian beliefs are set forth and then quickly torn down, without particularly deep or prolonged argumentation investigation. The basis of the rebuttal is primarily biblical, not philosophical. The style is that of the debater.

Many of the points of doctrine touched upon briefly in this sermon are explored in greater detail elsewhere. One issue that lies at the heart of the Pauline critique of Judaism relates to the possibility of justification in God's sight, and the mechanism of atonement for sin. Is observance of the commandments the way to fulfill the divine will? What kind of atonement will set things right with God when sin occurs? These issues are addressed in a sermon on Exodus 10:16 on the lesson *Bo,* delivered ca. 1640, much of which is devoted to the theme of repentance. The preacher first sets out the Christian position:

> The opponents of the Torah, in order to weaken the hearts of those who keep it from doing so with constancy, have fabricated the novel idea that this Torah is indeed impossible to keep, in two respects. First, *there is no one so righteous in the world as can do good without sinning* (Eccles. 7:20). But there is no remedy for such sin, for it is a sin against the infinite, and the sinner therefore deserves infinite punishment, which is impossible for him [in this life]. Thus he remains in his sin and is lost. Second, even if it should be assumed that such a sin is not by its nature infinite, as this syllogism indicates, one who sins against the Torah has no remedy because God said explicitly that such a person is accursed. We see this in the verse, *A curse upon the person who does not fulfill this law by doing all that it prescribes* (Deut. 27:26). Whoever bears such a curse has nothing with which to pay off his debt. In this way, they have tried to weaken the hands of those who keep the Torah of our teacher Moses. They have craftily devised contrivances to set these snares, as is well known.[36]

Morteira thus spells out two aspects of the Christian argument that Torah cannot serve as a means to salvation. The first is philosophical in nature: since

---

by Linda Munk, *The Devil's Mousetrap: Redemption and Colonial American Literature* (Oxford, 1997). p. 63. On fulfillment of prophecies during the Second Temple period (also an issue in internal Jewish literature), see Kaplan, *From Christianity to Judaism,* p. 283, citing Philip van Limborch.

36. MS 4:59v, *Bo,* Exod. 10:16, ca. 1640.

God is infinite, a violation of God's command is of infinite magnitude, incurring infinite debt, and there is nothing a human being can do to repay it.[37] The second argument is a paraphrase of Paul's argument in the Epistle to the Galatians (3:10), *For all who rely on the works of the law are under a curse; for it is written "A curse upon the person who does not fulfill this law by doing all that it prescribes"* (Deut. 27:26).[38] These are fair statements of the Christian position, which, we sense, has put the preacher on the defensive. Unlike the previous sermon, here his purpose will not be to attack the Christian faith but rather to defend Judaism.

Morteira responds to these arguments by using verses from the lesson *Nitsavim,* particularly appropriate in that they present first a rebuttal of alien ideas and then a positive statement of the Jewish doctrine of repentance.

> *For this commandment that I command you today* (Deut. 30:11) namely, repentance, is not under suspicion because of those reasons. *It is not too difficult for you* (Deut. 30:11), as if to say that it requires an infinite penance and you are finite and cannot achieve it. This is not the case. *It is not too difficult for you:* it is appropriate for you, it corresponds to you, it is indeed for you. Similarly, you should not say that being in your hands, it requires enormous effort, and that you can attain it only with difficulty. *Nor is it too remote* (Deut. 30:11).
>
> Concerning the first point, he said, *It is not in the heavens* (Deut. 30:12). This means, since there is no need for an infinite remedy, *It is not in the heavens.* That would indicate that as a remedy for transgression, it was

---

37. Cf. the discussion of the Christian doctrine in the polemical treatise written by Morteira's mentor, Elijah Montalto: "the sin [of the first human being], being infinite, would require infinite atonement, which no man could accomplish; and thus it became necessary that the second person of the Trinity (which they invented) become incarnate and die for man for the expiation of the sin" (cited in Melnick, *From Polemics to Apologetics,* p. 27). Morteira's formulation does not refer to the doctrine of "original sin." For earlier Jewish discussion of this doctrine, see *The Refutation of the Christian Principles by Hasdai Crescas,* transl. Daniel Lasker (Albany, 1992), pp. 29–30. The issue of infinite sin had arisen in the controversy over the doctrine of eternal punishment that erupted in the mid-1630s. Isaac Aboab da Fonseca, who repudiated the traditional doctrine, argued that Morteira's position supported the Christian doctrine: if eternal and therefore infinite punishment existed, it could be justified only by an infinite sin, which could be atoned only by the infinite sacrifice of God's Son. See Altmann, "Eternality of Punishment," pp. 51, 75, and the recent review in Steven Nadler, *Spinoza's Heresy,* pp. 157–65.

38. On the argument from Galatians using Deuteronomy 27:26, cf. David Berger, *The Jewish-Christian Debate in the High Middle Ages* (Philadelphia, 1979), pp. 79 and 265 n. to lines 9–10. Cf. Morteira's analysis of this verse in *Tratado,* p. 1149, turning it around to apply to the Christian spiritualizing of the commandments.

necessary to have a person who would ascend to the heavens and make atonement for the entire people, being as it were from the heavens rather than from the earth in order to be able to atone for an infinite matter.

Concerning the second, he said, *nor is it beyond the sea* (Deut. 30:13), as if God had established distant and difficult acts of penance and one had to travel beyond the sea to seek them out. They were precise about this: several kinds of animals live only in the wilderness or in the mountains, yet God commanded as a sacrificial penance only domesticated animals that grow up in the stalls of human beings. If so, how can there be a need for such forced contrivances?

For *it is not too difficult for you, nor is it too remote* (Deut. 30:11), but *It is a thing very near to you, in your mouth and in your heart to do it* (Deut. 30:14). For upon this depends the penance for what has been perverted, upon this depends the essence of repentance. They are three matters upon which repentance stands, namely, abandonment of the sin, confession, and contrition. They correspond to the three categories of human action: thought, speech, and deed: contrition corresponds to thought, confession to speech, and abandoning the sin to deed. This is the meaning of *in your mouth and in your heart to do it.*[39]

The use of the biblical phrase *It is not in the heavens* (Deut. 30:12) to repudiate the Christian doctrine that a sacrifice of infinite value—the atoning death of the Son—was the only way mankind could make reparation for the inevitable infinite sin against God, seems obvious, although it does not seem to have been used extensively by Jewish writers before. Note that in this context, Morteira is not attacking the Christian doctrine of atonement as impossible or absurd, as other philosophically inclined Jewish polemicists do, but only as unnecessary. Nor does he deal here with the Christian doctrine of Original Sin as requiring infinite atonement. The main thrust of his argument is to assert that, contrary to Christian claims, the Bible presents a doctrine of atonement that is readily accessible to the Jew for any sin he may commit,

---

39. MS 4:59v, *Bo,* Exod. 10:16, ca. 1640. The point in the second paragraph that God specified for sacrifices easily attainable domestic animals, not exotic wild ones, is based on Numbers Rabbah 21, 16. On the components of repentance, compare Maimonides, *Hilkhot Teshuvah* 2, 2 (where two additional components pertaining to the mind are added). Cf. Ephraim Luntshitz, *Keli Yaqar ad loc.* כי קרוב אליך הדבר. בפיך הוידוי ובלבבך החרטה ואז די לך בזה בתשובה. Unlike Morteira, however, Luntshitz interprets לעשותו not as a third component of repentance, but as an indication that the two components are sufficient to effect it. Closer, though still different, is Elijah Vidas, *Reshit Ḥokhmah, Teshuvah* 1,3: ולדעתי יישוב הפסוק בפיך – וידוי דברים, שצריך להתוודות, ובלבבך – קבלת התשובה בלבו ועזיבת החטא, לעשותו – אם גזל שישיב הגזילה וכיוצא

and fully adequate to set things right with God.[40] The discussion of this doctrine, in Jewish terms, will occupy him for the rest of the sermon.

Another example of a specific issue subsumed under the general category of the abrogation of the commandments pertains to the continuing validity of the Sabbath. The discussion arises in a sermon we have already cited, containing the analogy of passwords and signals to distinguish the enemy soldiers attempting to pass for allies. As that sermon is based on Exodus 31:13, it is little surprise that the Sabbath will be a significant theme. The instruction in the verse is introduced by the apparently superfluous conjunction *akh*. After mentioning other interpretations of its function, Morteira finds in this word a polemical meaning: God revealed in it a decisive refutation of those who reject the holiness of the Sabbath day. Characteristically he begins by citing the Christian argument justifying the abandonment of Saturday:

> They are so brazen as to have changed [the Sabbath] for a different day. In explanation, they say, "The purpose of this commandment is what God explained in the Ten Commandments: *Six days you shall do work, and on the seventh day you shall rest* (Exod. 23:12). Therefore, so long as we do work for six days, whichever they may be, and we rest on the seventh day, we have fulfilled the divine commandment. There is no need to count them from any particular day. Thus there is no need to observe your Sabbath day."

The refutation is based on the word "*akh*," understood to mean "but" in the sense of "only":

> Only, exclusively, My Sabbaths shall you observe, and no others that you may invent to replace them. Those Sabbaths which I set first from the beginning; those Sabbaths on which I Myself rested; those Sabbaths about which it was said, *For six days you may gather it, but on the seventh day, the Sabbath, there will be none* (Exod. 16:26); those Sabbaths which My people has observed from ancient days. *Only My Sabbaths shall you observe* (Exod. 31:13).[41]

Here the congregation is given a rationale that might justify shifting the Sabbath to a different day of the week, based on the purpose of the commandment. If it were intended simply to mandate a weekly day of rest,

---

40. Morteira may well have known of Paul's use of this passage (Rom. 10:5–10) to buttress his doctrine of salvation by faith; if so, it is one of numerous examples of the preacher turning a Christian polemical argument on its head for his own purpose.

41. MS 4:177v, *Ki Tissa,* Exod. 31:13, early 1640s. For a fuller discussion of the Sabbath in a polemical context, see Morteira, *Tratado,* chap. 18, pp. 137–49.

then any day in the week would do. The refutation of this claim by appeal to a Hebrew conjunction is clever, but not sufficient to outweigh the plausibility of the opponent's argument. Therefore he adds the pounding parallel phrases beginning with "those Sabbaths which," insisting that the seventh day has a special sanctity, ordained by God and confirmed throughout the Bible, that cannot be displaced to a different time.[42]

Another sermon containing an extensive and vehement attack on Christian doctrine is the one on the lesson *Balaq,* delivered in 1639 and included in the 1645 edition of *Giv'at Sha'ul.* (As we have noted, the polemical passages in the sermon were omitted without any indication in the Warsaw editions.) The theme of Christian distortion of the Bible emerges quite forcefully from a section of Psalm 119, focusing on verse 85, which provides the title of the sermon, *Siḥot Asher Lo Ke-Toratekha:* "Now after his prayer, [King David] set out before God the obstacles which his enemies concealed for him in order to weaken his commitment of faith in God's words and laws, saying *Evil men have dug pits intended for me, not in accordance with Your law* (Ps. 119:85)."[43] The interpreta-

---

42. This was not the common Christian claim about the Sabbath, as it concedes something most Christian authorities did not accept: that the commandment to cease from work one day each week was still binding. Although some early Christians did apparently observe Sunday as a day of rest (see the Council of Laodicea, Canon 29; Caesarius of Arles taught that Christians must observe the Lord's day as Jews observe the Sabbath), the classical view, expressed, for example by Thomas Aquinas, was that ceasing from manual labor was a ceremonial command, abrogated with the coming of the Messiah, while the moral aspect of the Sabbath—honor and love of God expressed through a day devoted to prayer and refraining from sin—remained valid. See Berger, *Jewish-Christian Debate,* p. 255, n. to l. 1; Crescas, *The Refutation of the Christian Principles,* pp. 75 and 127 n. 69; Machado, *The Mirror of the New Christians,* p. 235; Martin Luther, "Against the Sabbatarians," in *Luther's Works,* 47:92–93. For a Jewish attack on the practice of Christians to perform work on Sunday, see Berger, *Jewish-Christian Debate,* pp. 45, 96, 237–38. Various Protestant Sabbatarian movements, including Socinians in sixteenth-century Transylvania and Mennonite Anabaptists in Holland, required a day of rest on the seventh day of the week, not on Sunday. Perhaps Morteira was alluding to Calvin's discussion of the Sabbath in his *Institutes* (cited extensively by Morteira in his late work, *Tratado*), where, defending the need to observe one special day each week and the change from Saturday to Sunday, Calvin maintains that the commandment to "allow servants and labourers a remission from their labor" is "as proper for us as for the Jews." *Institutes of the Christian Religion,* 2 vols. (Philadelphia, 1936), 1:429 (Book II, chap. 8, sec. 32).

43. MS 1:109v, *GS* 1645, p. 63c, 1912, p. 239. The following passage does not appear in the Warsaw edition; the editor replaced it with the statement, "that is, they dug pits for me in Spain and Portugal so that I would turn away from Your law," words absent from the manuscript or the 1645 edition, that actually pervert Morteira's meaning by suggesting it was the Jews who turned away from the Torah rather than the Christians.

tion shifts the time frame from the biography of David to a prophecy of future Christian misuse of the Bible, through four categories of falsification:

In this he alluded to the first type of tactics used by the Gentiles to falsify the words of the living God. This is by telling the masses biblical passages cut, clipped, lopped, unconnected with what came before them or after them, and binding to these verses a "proof" instead. In this way they implant all kinds of falsehood in people's hearts.

Our witness for this is the verse, *The young woman is with child* (Isa. 7:14). But they fail to link it with *It was in the time of Ahaz* (Isa. 7:1) or *Before the child knows [to reject evil and choose good, desolation will come upon the land]* (Isa. 7:16). Similarly, *I called my son out of Egypt* (Hos. 11:1). But they do not cite the beginning of the verse, *When Israel was a boy I loved him.* Similarly, *For the Lord has created a new thing upon the earth, a woman shall compass a man* (Jer. 31:22). But they do not cite the beginning of the verse, *Come back O virgin Israel, come back to your cities; how long will you twist and turn, my wayward child?* (Jer. 31:21–22).[44]

Thus the forceful image in the words of the poet, *Evil men have dug pits intended for me, not in accordance with Your law* (Ps. 119:85). He called them evil men because they act maliciously with intention. For the matter is as clear as the sun, yet they perpetrate these falsifications in order to attain their desire. And he said "pits" because just as a person who digs a pit or a ditch in the ground removes what was previously there so that someone will fall into it, so they have done to me: they have dug in your Torah—the level ground—and made a pit in it so that I might fall

---

44. Cf. the repetition of this passage in the *Pinḥas* sermon translated below, pp. 436–37, recapitulating the Christian falsifications and distortions and citing the same three examples of phrases taken out of context. The first of these was one of the most fiercely disputed verses in Jewish-Christian polemical literature, starting from its use in the birth narrative of Matthew 1:23. In addition to the lexical dispute over the meaning of the noun *'almah*, a characteristic Jewish response was that the Christian interpretation removed the verse from its context. See Berger, *Jewish-Christian Debate*, p. 104. On Hosea 11:1, used in Mt. 2:15 as a prophecy fulfilled by Jesus, the Son, see Machado, *The Mirror of the New Christians*, p. 65 and n. 19. On Jeremiah 31:22, see Berger, p. 152 and p. 302 n. to l. 9; Machado, *Mirror of the New Christians*, p. 143 (citing the verse in Portuguese as *femea parira ho varão*, "a woman shall bring forth a male child," which purportedly must refer to the miraculous virgin birth). In his defense of rabbinic literature against the attacks of Sixtus of Siena, Morteira similarly accuses his adversary of citing statements out of context, citing inaccurately, and even fabrication ("Declaracion de los Mahamarim del Talmud," Ets Ḥaim MS 48 c 5, fols. 143, 144, 188).

down. And this is against Your law, and "not in accordance with Your law," for when I see the matter in its proper place, it is not as they say.[45]

The illustrations in this passage presuppose specific knowledge about Christian use of three prophetic verses. While the first, used by Christians about the virgin birth, would undoubtedly have been familiar to most listeners, the second and third might not have been, and it is unlikely that even those who knew Christian polemical literature would have been able to make the associations as they were quickly cited by the preacher. The passage does not depend, however, on the listeners' internalization of the details. The preacher presents himself as an authority in his claim that Christian proof-texting falsifies by removing verses from their context. And the claim that this is done not out of ignorance but with the intent to mislead—a claim much more likely to be applied to the Catholic tradition, which discouraged the laity from reading the Bible themselves, than to the Protestants—leaves the listener with the impression of an uncompromising attack drawn from King David himself.

The polemic continues with the next verse from the same Psalm, *Help me, for they hound me with their lies, but Your commandments all stand forever* (Ps. 119:86). Morteira explains this second falsification to mean, "while they acknowledge the Torah [as God's revelation,] they claim that its time has already passed." This introduces the theme of the abrogation of the Torah, which we have seen in the *Va-Yishlah* sermon cited above, including the use of Daniel 7:25 as a prophecy of this Christian doctrine. The third type of falsification, linked with Psalm 119:87, applies to another theme in the prior sermon: the doctrine of the prophecies pertaining to the future redemption of the Jewish people. This too was removed from the Warsaw editions:

He taught by this that while they acknowledge God's promises and prophecies, they interpret them as pertaining to different times, saying that they are spiritual promises, and that they will be fulfilled at a different time, not in this world, and that they were given to the Christians themselves, for whoever wants to lie sends his witnesses far away, as is known from their words. This is why the poet says, *They had almost swept me from the earth* (Ps. 119:87).[46]

---

45. MS 1:109v, GS 1645, p. 63c, *Balaq,* Num. 22:13, 1639.

46. MS 1:110r, *GS* 1645, p. 63d–64a; cf. the translated sermon on *Pinhas*, below, pp. 436–37. For the phrase הרוצה לשקר ירחיק את עדיו, found not in the Talmud but in medieval Sephardi halakhists, see Moshe Sever, *Mikhlol ha-Ma'amarim ve-ha-Pitgamim,* 3 vols. (Jerusalem, 1961), 2:620. The precise wording is found in the *Responsa* of Tashbetz, part 3, nu. 9. Cf. Morteira, *Tratado,* p. 167–68, the passage ending with "Quem quer mentir, areda teste-

Here the verse is interpreted to mean that they almost succeeded in removing the prophetic promises of redemption from being situated in this world by recasting them as metaphoric language about a purely spiritual reward in heaven. Unlike the other passages, this one contains no explicit rebuttal by Morteira of the Christian claim; it is almost as if the Christian refusal to take the prophesies of redemption according to their simple meaning is so blatantly absurd that it requires no response.

With the fourth category, we return to concrete examples of biblical exegesis. "The poet explained a fourth falsification, saying, *Grant me life, in accordance with Your lovingkindness, that I may guard the testimony of Your mouth* (Ps. 119:88). The following passage too was removed from the Warsaw editions:

> In this he taught the fourth method of falsification: their adding and subtracting from the Holy Scriptures at will in order to sustain what they want. An example is their interpreting Isaiah 53 [as if it read] "to them" (*lamo*) instead of "to him" (*lo*).[47] And similarly, *One who is anointed shall be cut off and no one will be for him* (Dan. 9:26) they translated "One who is anointed shall be cut off and his people will not be those who did not believe in him."[48] [*Dogs have surrounded me...*]; *like a lion (ka-ari) my hands and my feet* (Ps. 22:17) [they translated] "they have dug into [karu] my hands and my feet."[49] Similarly, *A redeemer shall come to Zion* (Isa. 59:20)

---

munhas," ibid., p. 68, and Salomon, "Did Saul Levi Mortera Plagiarize Joseph Albo?" pp. 36–37, referring to the study by Nehemiah Bruell.

47. The elliptical passage is not clear even with re-reading. Reference must be to Isaiah 53:8, which reads, מפשע עמי נגע למו. The Vulgate translates, "propter scelus populi mei percussi eum," "for the wickedness of my people, I have struck him." Thus Morteira must have meant to write לו במקום למו, rather than למו במקום לו. Recapitulating this material in a later sermon (cf. above, n. 41 end), Morteira corrects the error, writing, כמו "נגע למו" העתיקו, "לו" (MS 1:93v, *Pinḥas*, Num. 26:10, below, p. 437). The 1645 edition adds another error by transcribing Isaiah 23 instead of 53, misreading Morteira's *nun* for a *kaf.* Cf. Morteira's response to the ninth question from the "Clergyman of Rouen:" "The text is in the plural, and does not allude to a single person." *www.jewish-history.com/Occident/volume3/nov1845/questions.html.*

48. Vulgate: "occidetur Christus, et non erit eius populus qui eum negaturus est;" cf. Berger, *Jewish-Christian Debate,* pp. 132 and 290 n. 4; *Kelimat ha-Goyyim* in *Kitvei Pulmus le-Profiat Duran,* ed. Frank Talmage (Jerusalem, 1981), p. 65; Yerushalmi, *From Spanish Court to Italian Ghetto,* pp. 428–29.

49. Vulgate: "foderunt manus meas et pedes meas;" cf. Berger, *Jewish-Christian Debate,* pp. 150, 301 n. 31; Frank Talmage, *David Kimḥi* (Cambridge, 1975), p. 88; Yerushalmi, *From Spanish Court to Italian Ghetto,* pp. 429–30, n. 46; Gregory Martin, *Roma Sancta* (1581), ed. George Bruner Parks (Rome, 1969), p. 81 (a report of a conversionary sermon delivered to a Jewish audience in Rome; I am grateful to James Shapiro for this reference).

[they interpret] "a redeemer shall come from Zion."[50] *The young woman is with child* (Isa. 7:14) they translated "the young woman will conceive."[51]

One wonders here how much of this highly condensed passage would have been intelligible to the listeners. Needless to say, there is just too much information expressed in too elliptical a manner to grasp at a first hearing. It is, of course, possible that Morteira expanded it a bit in his Portuguese delivery, explaining the issues that were involved so that at least some of those in the congregation could follow him. But it is also possible that this terse polemical passage, like others we have seen, was intended to be taken on faith, as if to say, "You can believe me that the Christians mistranslate and misinterpret, and I can provide you with many examples as proof."

Having classified his material and marshaled his specific evidence, Morteira now turns back to a general indictment of Gentile falsification. The underlying problem, he claims, is the failure of Christians to read the Bible in the original Hebrew. This passage too is absent from the Warsaw editions:

All this they have dared to do in their translations because the books of Torah and Prophecy do not appear before the Gentile peoples in the language in which they came from the mouth of Divine Majesty, but rather in translations to the language of each people. Therefore the translators can do whatever they want. And that is why the poet said, *Grant me life, in accordance with Your loving kindness, [that I may guard the testimony of Your mouth]* (Ps. 119:88), meaning, set out for me what I need to live, and preserve me, for I alone can guard the testimony of Your mouth in its true form as it actually came forth from Your mouth, without addition or subtraction. For through God's loving kindness, only the Jews have preserved the Holy Scriptures as they are, without translation, while the Gentiles, having seen the weakness of their faith, worked their will with the Scriptures, seeking out falsifications in order to buttress it with these changes.[52]

---

50. Vulgate: "Et venerit Sion redemptor;" cf. Berger, *Jewish-Christian Debate,* p. 116: "the heretics refer this to Jesus."

51. Vulgate: "Ecce virgo concipiet." Cf. Berger, *Jewish-Christian Debate,* p. 104; *Kelimat ha-Goyyim,* p. 49. MS 1:110r, GS 1645, p. 64a; *Tratado,* pp. 499–501: "o uerso não diz 'será prenhada,' em futuro, se não 'esfa prenhada,' em presente."

52. Ibid. Cf. Immanuel Aboab, *Nomologia, o discursos legales* (Amsterdam, 1629), pp. 214, 243-44: "y muchos passos en que claramente alteran, y contradizen a la pureza de la verdad Hebrayca ... anadiendo en algunos lugares, en otros omitiendo, y en otros alterando cosas essencialissimas" (quoted in Melnick, *From Polemics to Apologetics,* pp. 46, 78).

Of course this passage cuts in various ways. It is a strong assertion of Christian intellectual dishonesty that—like other arguments of Morteira—turns the opponent's argument on its head. Beginning in the Middle Ages, some Christian thinkers began to suggest that Jews actually knew the truth of Christianity but refused to accept it not out of blindness but out of demonic perversity. Here it is the Christian intellectuals who are fully aware of the weakness of their claims, yet they intentionally deceive the masses of believers by concealing from them the Hebrew original and exposing them only to inaccurate translations that prove their point. On the positive side, Morteira reasserts the Jews' uniqueness: they are custodians not only of the text of the Hebrew Scripture but of its authentic meaning. But he also included a message for a congregation of worshippers, some of whom still could not read the Bible in Hebrew. So long as you depend on your Spanish translation, the implication seems to be, you are no better than the Gentiles. If you want to be an authentic Jew, learn Hebrew.[53]

Near the end of the sermon, Morteira ties in the four Christian falsifications, previously related to four verses in Psalm 119, with Balaam, the subject of the Torah lesson. As with the story of Jacob and Esau, this account too is read typologically: "God has presented in the account of Balaam, occurring at the beginning, when they were in the wilderness, an analogy and a prototype of what would occur to them among the nations during the long period of exile. For while these nations acknowledge prophecy, they seek to falsify in four ways, just as Balaam did, but it was of no avail to him." After correlating the four Christian distortions with references to the Balaam narrative, he concludes, "If so, we can truly and properly say that Balaam was a prototype for the fourth kingdom and its scholars." In his final moments he turns to a verse from *Ha'azinu* (Deuteronomy 32:21) that he would use as the basis of a full-length sermon for the Sabbath of Repentance two years later:

---

53. Morteira emphasized the importance of Hebrew for an understanding of the Bible in an early sermon on *Toledot*, delivered ca. 1622: "With great wisdom God arranged to hint the secrets of the Torah in the holy language, the language unique to the people of Israel. Even when the other nations study it and try to translate the Torah, they cannot convey in their language even one percent of its allusions and mysteries, for these are bound up with the numerical equivalents of the letters and their forms. Words may be written sometimes *plene* and sometimes not, a distinction that always conveys some special esoteric significance. Sometimes there are dots over the letters. Sometimes the word is written one way but pronounced a different way. Thus when a person tries to translate it, he immediately loses the esoteric meaning of these passages" (MS 3:247a, *Toledot*, Gen. 25:23). In this passage, Morteira speaks of a genuine though futile effort to translate the Torah accurately, while in our sermon he proposes a conscious intent to defraud. With this passage, compare Isaac Cardoso, cited by Yerushalmi, *From Spanish Court to Italian Ghetto*, pp. 426–27.

They provoked My jealousy with a non-god, by saying "You are my God" to one who is not divine, "*so I'll provoke their jealousy with a non-people*" (Deut. 32:21), for others will say to the Jews that *they* are God's people, *they* are Israel, while the Jews are not. This truly incenses. *They vexed Me with their false gods,* their foolishness, their lies; *with a foolish nation I'll vex them* (Deut. 32:21), a nation that will utter a thousand inanities and lies against the Torah, but they will not be able to deny that the Torah of the Jews is from God and that the Jews have the covenant of salvation.[54]

As with so many of Morteira's sermons, all the strands are woven together at the end. The polemic is given an exegetical texture; the verses from Psalms and the Torah lesson are shown to pertain not only to the distant past but to the ongoing struggle with a powerful rival faith.

In addition to matters of doctrine, Morteira criticizes aspects of Roman Catholic spirituality and practice. The following example, from a sermon on *Va-Yiqra* (Lev. 1:6) delivered in 1629, is a polemical response to a challenge by Christian polemicists. The introduction to the sermon begins with a statement from the Talmud (b. *Qiddushin* 70a) that he says is confirmed by common experience: "Whoever declares others unfit... stigmatizes with his own blemish." This is the case with "the fourth kingdom, namely Edom," the common reference to Christianity centered in Rome.

Thus some of them cynically and falsely rebuke us for what is in truth and by nature in them. Among the other things of this category—some of which are *words against the Most High* (Dan. 7:25)—one of them pertains to our theme-verse . It is something I have seen in their books, and also something cited by [Rabbi Joseph Albo], the author of *Sefer ha-'Iqqarim,* in the 25th chapter of part 3 of his book. This is a challenge brought against him by one of their mouth-gaping scholars, saying that the divine service of sacrifices in the Torah is not pure, but rather filthy because of blood and skins and fats and the killing of animals, all of

---

54. MS 1:110r, *GS* 1645, p. 64c–d; cf. above, p. 257. The Warsaw edition (1912, p. 240) not only removes the anti-Christian barbs, but substitutes the editor's own statement reflecting a different agenda: "*so I'll provoke their jealousy with [being considered a] 'non-people' (be-lo 'am)*" (Deut. 32:21), that people will say to them that Israel has ceased to be a nation, that they are no longer a people like other peoples, but only a group of certain individuals." This seems to be directed against opponents to Zionism who denied Jewish peoplehood and national aspirations; the editor thus—without any indication—shifts Morteira's polemic from the religious to the national level. Yet amazingly, the editor hit upon one of four interpretations of the phrase that Morteira incorporated into his long manuscript sermon on this verse, to which the editor had no access. See below, pp. 508–9.

which causes defilement. They speak at length of such things, may the lying lips that speak libels about the Righteous One of the Universe be struck dumb![55]

This statement of the challenge is fairly close to that recorded in a celebrated polemical chapter from Albo's classic work. But Albo's response to this challenge is a relatively moderate defense of the Temple sacrifices, accompanied by a critique of the Christian "sacrifice" as having no empirically verifiable efficacy and entailing a doctrine (transubstantiation) that conflicts with reason.[56] Morteira's pugilistic response is much more highly charged with indignant emotion:

> They have not seen that they try to disqualify us with their own blemish! For none of the forms of idolatrous worship that preceded them was as steeped in impurity and squalor as their own worship. Even the worship of Peor [Num. 25:1–5], which was so despised, was not nearly as despicable as their impurity. This can be seen first from the burial of the dead in their churches. It is God's command that the body of the dead is the most severe source of impurity, and God prohibited allowing it to remain overnight within the city (Deut. 21:23). Wherever Jews dwelled, their cemeteries were outside the city domain.
>
> Furthermore, look at the power of their veneration of bones and skulls of the dead. To them they burn incense, to them they bow down, before them they fall and prostrate themselves. The extensive use of bones of the dead by those who summoned up ghosts and spirits (Lev. 20:27) has not dried up.... They filled many large houses with bones that were worshipped, until God made this public through His prophet, proclaiming the destruction of this impurity with the words, *I will remove the spirit of impurity from the land* (Zech. 13:2). For this impurity passes every border and boundary; it is therefore called the "spirit of impurity" because of its powerful prevalence. I do not mention the impurity of those who serve [this religion?], for that is a lengthy matter.
>
> Yet with all this, they have the gall to criticize us for the very things that are decisively found in themselves![57]

---

55. MS 22:37r, *Va-Yiqra*, Lev. 1:6, 1629.

56. Joseph Albo, *Sefer ha-'Iqqarim*, book 3, chap. 25. Morteira refers to this chapter again in MS 5:62r, *Va-Yishlaḥ*, Gen. 32:19, 1639, citing the Christian claims that the Torah is imperfect, as reported by Albo. For other examples of Morteira's use of Albo, see H. P. Salomon, "Did Saul Levi Mortera Plagiarize Joseph Albo?" *StRos* 23 (1989): 28–37.

57. MS 2:37r, *Va-Yiqra*, Lev. 1:6, 1629.

In this passage, Morteira does not even bother to defend the sacrificial cult. That will come later in the sermon. Instead, he moves directly to the attack. The association of Christianity with pagan idolatry is pronounced. He no longer portrays Christianity as an imitation of Jewish practices and institutions; rather, he presents it in continuity with the forms of pagan worship described in the Bible. Pouncing on practices he considers particularly repugnant—the veneration of bones of the saints and the use of the church as a place of burial—the preacher describes Christianity as worse—more impure—than any of its predecessors, even the sexual licentiousness associated with the worship of the Moabite Baal-Peor.[58] As important as the cult of the saints was for medieval Christian popular piety,[59] Morteira undoubtedly knew that many would not describe it as central to Christianity, and that Protestants (who made the same argument against Jewish sacrifices) also attacked the veneration of relics.[60] It is another debater's trick: to defend one's position by attacking at the weakest point of the opponent.[61] The

---

58. Pagan writers such as Julian "the Apostate" and Eunapius of Sardis expressed similar abhorrence for these Christian practices: "they collected the bones and skulls of criminals who had been put to death for numerous crimes ... made them out to be gods, and thought that they became better by defiling themselves at their graves." See Peter Brown, *The Cult of the Saints: Its Rise and Function in Latin Christianity* (Chicago, 1981), p. 7. Brown presents the Christian veneration of relics as a "rapid and flagrant departure from pagan and Jewish practice" (p. 78). Christian apologists, both in antiquity and in the Counter-Reformation period, tried to defend the practice through purported precedents in the Hebrew Bible; see Jerome, cited by Caroline Bynum, *The Resurrection of the Body in Western Christianity, 200–1336* (New York, 1995), p. 93, and the 1564 sermon of Martin Eisengrein, cited in Philip Soergel, *Wondrous in His Saints: Counter-Reformation Propaganda in Bavaria* (Berkeley, 1993), p. 110.

59. There is an enormous literature on this; see the annotated bibliography in Stephen Wilson, *Saints and Their Cults* (Cambridge, 1983), and the fine recent treatment by Bynum, *The Resurrection of the Body*, esp. pp. 104–8, 200–25, 320–28. For a 1616 decision in Flanders to venerate publicly the bones of Catholic martyrs killed in a massacre by Dutch soldiers in 1572, see Craig Harline and Eddy Put, *A Bishop's Tale: Mathias Hovius Among his Flock in Seventeenth-Century Flanders* (New Haven, 2000), pp. 168–69.

60. E.g., John Calvin: "When supplication is made to the images of saints, and divine honours paid to dead men's bones ... we call them abominations as they are"—*Theological Treatises*, ed. J.K.S. Reid (Philadelphia, 1954), p. 188; Calvin published an entire *Traité des réliques* on this issue in 1543. See, in general, Carlos Eire, *War Against the Idols: The Reform of Worship from Erasmus to Calvin* (Cambridge, 1972). The repudiation in principle of burial in the church as contrary to the dignity of religion apparently did not come until the eighteenth century, when it was linked with arguments from hygiene and public health. Philippe Ariès, *The Hour of Our Death* (New York, 1982), p. 479.

61. Cf. the similar attack on the practice of taking the bones of the dead as holy relics in *Sefer Nitsaḥon Yashan*: Berger, *The Jewish-Christian Debate*, p. 225. Morteira was apparently

preacher's vehement diction is buttressed by the claim that this is only one example of Christian weakness. The others, pertaining to theology and "the impurity of those who serve"—apparently an allusion to immorality among the celibate clergy—are introduced in passing, suggesting that an even stronger attack could be mounted, but this is not the time.[62]

"New Christians" in Portugal

Among the subjects of contemporary significance treated by Morteira, none appears in passages more probing and powerful than the subject of the New Christians—those who were returning to the Jewish community and, even more, those who failed to return. Virtually every family in the Portuguese community of Amsterdam during the first decades of its existence had relatives, associates, and friends living in what were frequently called "the lands of idolatry," Portugal and Spain, or in cities such as Bordeaux and Antwerp. Why did these Jews not leave their oppressive Christian environments and join their people? Did their refusal to come to a Jewish community such as Amsterdam cast doubt upon the wisdom of those who had uprooted themselves, broken their ties with the Iberian peninsula, left their native land and their familiar surroundings behind? These were questions that apparently troubled many in the congregation, and Morteira provided a whole range of answers for them on various occasions.[63]

One explanation he proposes is that those who chose to remain in the "lands of idolatry" were not of pure Jewish descent to begin with. In a sermon delivered in 1622 or 1623 and published in *Giv'at Sha'ul,* Morteira refers to this idea in passing: "Those who are truly of Jewish descent never cease, day or night, from trying to return to the estate they inherited from their ancestors, paying no heed to the dangers or the perils that might befall them. And those

---

so proud of his argument that he referred back to it a little more than a year later in a sermon on the lesson *Ḥuqqat* (MS 2:123r, Num 19:9, 1630): "For already in our sermon on the lesson *Va-Yiqra* we shut the mouths of those who claim that the worship in the Temple did not have the proper level of cleanliness. For it is not right to look at the matters pertaining to that Temple with eyes of flesh, but rather with eyes of the intellect." For a later attack on the cult of sacred bones and burial in churches in a different polemical context, see *Tratado,* p. 249 (end of chap. 49).

62. See the sermon on *Va-Etḥanan* from the 1645 *Giv'at Sha'ul,* which does indeed raise the common charge of rampant licentiousness among the purportedly celibate Catholic priests (below, p. 421).

63. On the actual reasons why many New Christians did not leave the Iberian peninsula when they had the opportunity to do so, see Yerushalmi, *From Spanish Court to Italian Ghetto,* pp. 29–31. It is interesting to compare the modern historian's assessment of the factors with those presented by the contemporary preacher.

who have been forgotten, why they are from that element mixed into [the Jewish people]. For God, who knows all hidden things, purifies our dross and removes our slag (cf. Isa. 1:25), so that we might return to our original condition."[64] This passage served two functions. First, it validated the decisions of those who sat before the preacher. Their willingness to take risks and make sacrifices proved not only their Jewish loyalty but also their genuine descent from biblical Israel. Second, it minimized the significance of those who remained behind by suggesting that they were never fully Jewish.[65] The "Marrano" experience ensuing from the forced conversions of 1497 is thereby presented as one of God's providential techniques for separating the true Jews from the bad seed among the Jewish people.

In a later sermon for the Sabbath of Repentance, delivered in 1645, Morteira is clearer about the historical setting of this foreign element that was mixed in with the true Israel. Discussing the agents of destruction withstood by the Jewish people, Morteira mentions the large number of proselytes from Edom who joined the Jews as a result of the forced conversions in the time of John Hyrcanus.[66] These outsiders endangered the people of Israel; it was to them that the Sages referred in comparing proselytes to a boil on the skin (b. *Yebamot* 47b). Yet their negative influence was not decisive.

> For God separated out all those who became assimilated among them during the Second Temple period, in that they were the Jews who accepted the new religion [Christianity] and were removed from the rest. Therefore, this is one of the reasons why this nation is called Edom, as R. Isaac Abravanel explained in chapter 34 of Isaiah. And those who were assimilated among the Gentiles in their exile became estranged from their brothers and alien to their mothers' children, so that they were set aside for evil from all the tribes of Israel (cf. Deut. 29:20).[67]

Juxtaposing this passage with the previous one, we get a clear picture of

---

64. *GS* 1645, p. 92a–b, 1912, p. 308. Morteira's reference to "dangers and tribulations" is confirmed by contemporary sources cited by Yerushalmi, p. 29 n. 42.

65. Compare the earlier claim, attributed to Crescas, that those who converted to Christianity in 1391 rather than dying as martyrs demonstrated that they were not truly "of the seed of Abraham;" Saperstein, "*Your Voice Like a Ram's Horn,*" p. 261, and the reaction to this on pp. 263–64.

66. MS 3:162r, *Ve-Zot ha-Berakhah*, Deut. 33:3, Shabbat Teshuvah, 1645. On the forced circumcisions, see *Sefer Yosippon*. ed. David Flusser, 2 vols. (Jerusalem, 1978), 1:116.

67. MS 3:162r, *Ve-Zot ha-Berakhah*, Deut. 33:3, Shabbat Teshuvah, 1645. For Abravanel's explanation of the continuity between Edom and Rome, see Netanyahu, *Don Isaac Abravanel*, pp. 233–34.

Morteira's claim. The Edomites were victims of a forced conversion to Judaism. Because this kind of compulsion never works, the weakness of their Jewish loyalties was no surprise; therefore, they and their descendants were susceptible to the heretical teachings of Jesus and his followers that eventually became the Christian religion. But not all the former Edomites left the Jewish people in antiquity. Later there was another forced conversion, this time to Christianity. The descendants of the Edomites, then, are those who have tried to assimilate among the Gentiles. There is, of course, no way to prove their lineage, except by their behavior. We see here a kind of genetic determinism not dissimilar to that used by many Christians to attack the *conversos*.[68]

Material considerations were a second reason suggested by the preacher for the unwillingness of Portuguese New Christians to leave their Iberian homes. Portuguese Christians who suspected they might be investigated by the Inquisition and thus thought of fleeing were not permitted to liquidate their assets and take their money out of the country. For most of them, the decision to return to Judaism entailed a considerable financial loss.[69] Morteira noted more than once that this was a powerful, though unacceptable, inducement to remain. In a sermon delivered in early 1621, he argues that the sons of Jacob sinned by not remaining in the land of Canaan when they went there to bury their father. There was no need for them to return to Egypt; they did so only because of the comfortable circumstances in which they found themselves.[70] The moral is then applied to the present.

> We have seen this very same phenomenon, because of our sins, in those who, thinking of their need for sustenance, assimilate in a land that is not theirs and worship idols. They make vows to God that as soon as they accumulate a little wealth, they will leave that land and go to serve

---

68. See B. Netanyahu, *The Origins of the Inquisition in Fifteenth Century Spain* (New York, 1995), index, s.v. "racism" (terminology which is often quite problematic in context); Glaser, "Invitation to Intolerance," pp. 364–67. As H. P. Salomon has shown, Ferñao Alvares Melo (1659–1632) also maintained that exiled New Christians who remained faithful to Catholicism in Flanders or France revealed by their choice both their materialistic values and that they had an admixture of non-Jewish blood in their lineage. Salomon, *Portrait of a New Christian*, p. 179.

69. See Cecil Roth, "Immanuel Aboab's Proselytization of the Marranos," *JQR* n.s. 23 (1932–1933): 130, 145 ; I. S. Révah, "La religion d'Uriel da Costa, Marrane de Porto," *Revue de l'Histoire des Religions* 161 (1962): 49. According to a decree of March 13, 1610, the property of any New Christian who left Portugal without royal authorization would be forfeit to the Crown, a premium being deducted from it to pay informants (H. P. Salomon and I. S. D. Sassoon, Introduction to Uriel da Costa, *Examination of Pharisaic Traditions* [Leiden, 1993], p. 7).

70. A similar idea can be found in Solomon Levi's *Divrei Shelomoh*, pp. 173a–b.

the true God. But when wealth comes to them, they forget their vows, and their good fortune makes them rebellious. So it has always been.[71]

The following year, in his sermon on the same scriptural lesson, he made a similar point, arguing that Jews living in exile should not purchase real property—houses or vineyards—for these "keep Jews from going with their brothers and promote assimilation with the Gentiles."[72]

In the mid-1630s, Morteira returned to this theme in a different biblical context. The sermon, on the lesson *Toledot,* is entitled "the Sins of Edom." Drawing on the familiar typology of Esau-Edom-Christian, the preacher discusses the sins attributed to Esau in the midrashic literature. Their significance is presented typologically, applied not to the Christians themselves but to the "New Christians," Jews who sell their birthright by remaining in a Christian land. The rabbis recount the "sins of Edom,"

> to teach all those who are similar to Esau, those who, because of physical sustenance and bodily pleasures spurn the Eternal and His service, make their offspring assimilate among the Gentiles, destroy their souls and lose their portion in the resurrection of the dead. They do not trust that God will provide them with food without transgressing His word. Yet this is all done to no avail, for they spurn their birthright after experiencing wealth and tranquility, and they are embarrassed over it, although it is the highest birthright of all. In this regard they are similar to Esau, and their inheritance will be like his, as the Bible says, *I hate Esau* (Mal. 1:3).[73]

Contemporary evidence confirms the preacher's claim that New Christians did indeed often delay their decision to leave Portugal in order to amass and transfer sufficient capital to their new destination.[74] Morteira was not the only religious leader to conclude that those who did not come revealed an excessive preoccupation with material concerns.[75] But few integrated this

---

71. MS 3:108r, *Shemot,* Exod. 1:6, 1621.

72. Saperstein, *Jewish Preaching,* p. 278 (paperbound edition; the freer translation in the original edition reveals my failure to appreciate in this sentence an allusion to the New Christians who remained in Portugal, an allusion that became clear only because of the manuscript sermons). Cf. MS 3:307r, *Ha'azinu,* Deut. 32:21, 1641 (below, p. 520): "Because of their money they exchange their God, and they remain in the lands of their enemies serving a different God, in order to tend to their wealth, their fields, and their houses."

73. MS 5:32r, *Toledot,* Gen. 25:32, mid-1630s.

74. Roth, "Immanuel Aboab's Proselytization," pp. 131, 147–48; Yerushalmi, *From Spanish Court to Italian Ghetto,* p. 30.

75. Cf. Abraham Israel Pereyra, criticizing in 1671 those who remain because of "financial

theme as consistently into the texture of biblical sources. The message to his listeners was clear: if they had made financial sacrifices to leave Portugal, they had demonstrated the proper hierarchy of values, abandoning temporal wealth for the worship of the true God.[76]

Another reason the New Christians were reluctant to leave the Iberian peninsula was fear that any expression of commitment to Judaism would get them into serious trouble with the authorities. Morteira touches upon this fear in a sermon from 1630 on the lesson *Mi-Qets*. The passage begins with a verse from Ezekiel (5:7): *Because you have outdone* (hamonkhem) *the nations that are round about you—you have not obeyed My laws or followed My rules, nor have you observed the rules of the nations round about you.* His application of this verse is drawn from one of the great figures of the Sephardi tradition:

> It is as Rabbi Isaac Abravanel interpreted: it speaks about the *conversos*, who have become like the masses (*hamon*) of the Gentiles. They do not observe God's Law because of fear, and they do not observe the idolatrous law because they do not believe in it. Their portion is worse than that of the original idolaters, for they merely remained the same as believers in their idols. But those who believe in God and know him: their sin is too great to bear (cf. Gen. 4:13).
>
> About them, God said that he would do something He had never done, the like of which He would never do again (cf. Ezek. 5:9). That is the judgment of the Inquisition, something unprecedented, and never to be replicated, as the experts know. What will result from it? *Assuredly fathers shall devour their children* (Ezek. 5:10), meaning not the devouring of food in hunger but as in the verse, *They have devoured Jacob* (Ps. 79:7), referring to destruction. Thus the fathers, in order to appear like the others before the Gentiles, will destroy their children by making them priests and nuns, cutting off their line of descent, destroying and anni-

interest, or fearfulness for losing our wealth" (cited in Kaplan, *From Christianity to Judaism*, p. 337), and, from an earlier period, Isaac Karo, cited in B. Netanyahu, *The Marranos of Spain* (New York, 1966), p. 160. Ironically, Portuguese preachers at the autos-da-fé agreed that the New Christians in Portugal were preoccupied with a desire for wealth, but they argued that this thwarted their acceptance of Christianity. See Glaser, "Invitation to Intolerance," pp. 362–63.

76. Cf. also Morteira's vehement condemnation in his manuscript "Responses to the Questions of a Priest from Rouen" (Ets Ḥaim MS EN48 D38, fol. 105v), question 21, referring to New Christians as "truly worshippers of gold (*adoradores del oro*)" who try to deceive God "for the sole purpose of accumulating wealth" (*por puro interes de acomular hazienda*). H. P. Salomon, "Haham Saul Levi Morteira en de Portugese Nieuw-Christenen," *StRos* 10 (1976): 137 n. 50, *http://www.jewish-history.com/Occident/volume3/jan1846/questions.html*.

hilating them. *And children will devour* and destroy *their parents* (Ezek. 5:10), by informing upon them before the judges, as has occurred in many cases, so that the fire devoured them. And because of this fear, they will be dispersed in every direction. That is why the prophet concluded, *I will scatter all your survivors in every direction* (ibid.).[77]

Morteira follows Abravanel in the interpretation of Ezekiel 5:7 as applying to the New Christians, caught between two worlds, unwilling to observe Judaism because of their fear, yet incapable of sincere observance of Christian practices in which they do not really believe.[78] But he finds his own way with Ezekiel 5:10, which Abravanel interpreted literally, applying it to the conditions of starvation during the Roman siege of Jerusalem. Morteira's metaphoric interpretation of that verse removes it from the distant historical past and relates it to the desolate experience known by many in the congregation: parents trying to prove their *bona fides* as Christians by pressuring their children to become priests and nuns, and children informing on their parents out of fear that the Inquisition authorities might otherwise prosecute them.[79] It is a devastating picture of New Christian life that could only reaffirm the decision made by those in the audience. We shall return to the Inquisition later in the chapter in discussing how Morteira sees the future destiny of the New Christians.

Attributing financial interest and fear to the New Christians in Portugal, Morteira implies that they were insincere in their profession of Christianity. On the whole, he believes that the New Christian community managed to remain endogamous, as he notes in a sermon from early 1624:

How God warned us against intermarriage, for this causes a blurring of

---

77. MS 2:153r, *Mi-Qets,* Gen. 41:6, 1630.

78. Cf. also Menasseh ben Israel: "Or it may be said, the prophet here [Ezek. 5:7] speaks of those wicked Israelites who separate from the flock, and neither observe the law of Moses, nor that of the Gentiles they had been converted to and which they do not believe, living like Atheists without any religion; for it is better to profess one, even if erroneous, than none whatever" (*Conciliator* 2:210).

79. On the difficulties encountered by New Christians trying to enter the Church because of "purity of blood" legislation, see Kaplan, "R. Sha'ul Levi Morteira ve-Ḥibburo," pp. 22–23; English version: "Rabbi Saul Levi Morteira's Treatise," pp. 103–4. Morteira wrote a responsum about a Jew asked to use his contacts to intercede with the Pope on behalf of Portuguese New Christians who are "requesting permission from the Pope to allow their sons to become priests and their daughters nuns" (ibid., Hebrew version, p. 24, English, p. 106). He may well have been thinking of this when he wrote this passage for his sermon. On *conversos* informing against each other, "the young against the old," cf. Joseph ha-Kohen, *Emeq ha-Bakha* (Cracow, 1895), pp. 99–100.

the identity of peoples. Even today we have seen God's gracious love
in this matter. What has enabled the last remnant of *the exile of Jerusalem
which is in Sefarad* (Obad. 20) to preserve its identity is their refusal to
intermarry with the Gentiles of that land. This has preserved their
lineage and their identity, so that they are not lost to the community of
the Eternal.[80]

On occasion, however, Morteira recognizes that some of those who remained
did so from a genuine desire to live as Portuguese Christians. In the very same
sermon, he concedes that there were those who married and bore children in
the Christian faith. Such an individual could now claim that "he actually loves
the qualities of the people where he has been exiled and his Gentile wife, or
the new religion and his children who are devoted to idolatry."[81] Motivated
by more than economic self-interest, these Jews approached full assimilation
into the Portuguese Christian ethos, accompanied by genuine commitment
to the new faith. We shall see later what Morteira claimed was in store for
these individuals.

Particularly striking are those occasions when Morteira refers to various
rationales used by New Christians to justify their clinging to the status quo.
One such passage comes in a sermon on the lesson *Mattot* delivered very early
in Morteira's preaching career. Discussing the various types of oaths in what
might have seemed at first to be a rather dry halakhic sermon, Morteira turns
to verses from the twentieth chapter of Ezekiel, a passage that had a long
history of application to the New Christians.[82] After raising several problems
in the verses, he introduces his own interpretation as follows:

> The prophet's intention was to rebuke Israel because of the evil of a false
> opinion that is prevalent among us and some of the descendants of our
> people. This is that God demands what is in the heart and is concerned
> only about inwardness, caring not about external actions performed in
> contradiction to the inner truth. For "the Merciful One desires the
> heart."[83]
>
> Therefore the prophet said, *What has come upon your mind,* and upon
> your thought and your intellect, meaning *in opposition to* your mind and

---

80. MS 3:345v, *Mishpatim,* Exod. 21:6, 1624. On endogamy among the Portuguese New
Christians, see above, p. 199.

81. Ibid., 346r.

82. See Abravanel's commentary on this passage (*Nevi'im Aharonim,* p. 519b–520a) and the
discussion by Netanyahu, *The Marranos of Spain,* pp. 181–90. Cf. also Yerushalmi, *From
Spanish Court to Italian Ghetto,* p. 377.

83. B. *Sanhedrin* 106b.

the truth that you possess, *it shall never, never be, when you say* alone, without doing it,[84] *"We will be like the nations, in order to live among them, like the families of the lands"* (Ezek. 20:32). This means, "Let us become like the family in whose midst we live, following their religion and their way of thinking, for since it is all nonsense to us and our only intention is to live among them, we may act in accordance with the place and the family in whose midst we find ourselves." You also say, "What difference does it make to God that we have become like them, *worshiping wood and stone* (ibid.), for this is nonsense, and we recognize and say in their presence that they are wood and stone. What is the problem with being like them in this matter?"[85]

Nor was this the only time Morteira emphasized this aspect of New Christian ideology from the pulpit. In the sermon on *Mattot*, he continued to relate this rationalization based on inwardness to a passage from the lesson *Nitsavim*; a few years later he referred back to this interpretation, recapitulating its application to the New Christians:

We have interpreted this matter of *the moist and dry alike* (Deut. 29:18) in a different context, as pertaining to those who say that "The Merciful One desires the heart," and He is not strict about actions, and therefore it is permissible to worship idols and to act as a Gentile together with those who worship them, while worshiping God in one's heart alone, for *the Eternal examines the hearts* (Prov. 17:3). That is why [Moses] said, *Perchance there is among you some man or woman, or some clan or tribe, whose heart is even now turning away from the Eternal our God to go and worship the gods of those nations* [...],*fancying himself immune, thinking "I shall be safe,"* and these curses do not pertain to me, *for I follow the dominance of my heart* (Deut. 29:17–18), meaning, so long as I follow the dictates of my heart, believing in God, even though in my actions I follow a different path. He does this *in order to share the moist and dry alike* (Deut. 29:18). He labeled the true faith in God *the moist*, for it satisfies and quenches the thirst of those who follow it. *The dry* is a label for idolatry, which causes thirst and does not suffice to quench the thirst of those who pursue it. He does this in order to hold on to both of them, to share and cleave to the moist and the dry, continuing to make one adhere to the other. *The Eternal will never forgive him; rather will God's anger rage* ... (Deut.

---

84. This is a possible but not certain reading of the words אתם אומרים לבד לא עושים, which are not entirely clear in context. The implication would be that they are not successful in carrying out their plan.

85. MS 3:66v, *Mattot*, Num. 30:3, early 1620s.

29:19).[86]

Morteira's exegetical twist here applies to the Hebrew conjunction *ki* in Deuteronomy 29:18. It is usually understood to have the force of "although": "I shall be safe although I follow the dominance of my heart." By using its more common meaning, "because," the preacher is able to make the next phrase an expression of the ideology of inwardness: the reason the sinner mistakenly believes that all will be well.[87]

Of course, sermons by a preacher in Amsterdam cannot be assumed to constitute reliable evidence for the thinking of New Christians in Portugal. The above passage certainly should not be used to establish that New Christians knew and cited the the Talmudic phrase "The Merciful One desires the heart,"[88] for this may be the preacher's own addition. Yet the argument attributed to them—that God does not care about external actions so long as the heart is pure—seems to have been a genuine aspect of "Marrano" ideology. There is a certain plausibility about it; it is the kind of rationalization that people in that situation desiring to justify their behavior would be likely to generate. The question "Why should a purely spiritual God care about external acts?" was a powerful challenge for all streams of medieval Jewish thought,[89] and the leap from the insistence that God requires *also* the heart to the claim that God requires *only* the heart was occasionally made by Jews in less dangerous circumstances than the men and women who were threatened by the Inquisition.[90]

---

86. MS 2:46r, *Be-Midbar,* Num. 1:16, mid 1620s. Cf. MS 2:66v, *Mattot,* Num. 30:3, early 1620s, the continuation of the passage cited in the previous note. I have quoted the recapitulation from the later sermon because some aspects of Morteira's homiletical exegesis are clearer here than in the original.

87. Nahmanides suggested this meaning of *ki* as an alternative interpretation, although his reading of the verse is different: the sinner believes he will be safe because, following the dominance of his heart, he never accepts the oath to begin with. Abravanel, with the same meaning of *ki,* also has a different reading, relating to philosophically driven heresy: "I shall be safe because I act in accordance with my mind, my intellect, and God has given the intellect to man that he might follow its light." A similar view is cited by Abraham Saba ("there are those who say"), who is more specific than Abravanel: it is the view of those who believe that the essence of the commandments is to know their inner content, not actually to perform them—yet Saba apparently links this with radical philosophy, not with *converso* ideology (*Tseror ha-Mor,* Deuteronomy, 26a).

88. רחמנא לבא בעי; this is the way it is popularly cited in the Middle Ages, although the original Talmudic source is הקב"ה ליבא בעי (b. *Sanhedrin* 106b).

89. For a summary see Joseph Dan, *Sifrut ha-Musar ve-ha-Derush* (Jerusalem, 1975), pp. 47–68.

90. For example, the view cited by Abraham Saba, above, n. 87. This issue was also a matter of internal Christian debate over the position called "Nicodemism": that it was per-

There is also external corroboration of Morteira's statement of Marrano doctrine.[91] Immanuel Aboab's *Nomologia*, published at Amsterdam in 1629, contains both a statement and a refutation of the claim, attributed to the Portuguese Marranos, that God had given permission to worship false gods in case of necessity so long as the heart remained committed to the true God. The same idea is cited in a responsum of Samuel Aboab: The New Christians believe that "the prohibition of idolatry applies to the 'service of the heart' when external actions are consistent with it. However, so long as there is no inward sincerity, and the deeds [of idolatry] are performed out of fear of the Gentiles, there is no guilt in God's sight."[92] Morteira's sermon, which pre-dates both of these texts, would therefore appear to articulate a genuine aspect of "the religion of the Marranos."

In a different sermon on *Mattot*, delivered about a decade after the one cited, Morteira returns to the New Christians who remained in Portugal. Here too, he claims to reveal something of their thinking:

---

missible to dissemble acceptance of a persecuting majority church in order to avoid persecution and save life, so long as the heart remains committed to the truth faith. Calvin, responding to this view, insisted that it was not enough to acknowledge God in the heart; the believer must do so publicly, in true worship and "exterior profession." See Brad S. Gregory, *Salvation at Stake* (Cambridge, 1999), pp. 155–56, and cf. p. 173 bottom.

91. Note that Morteira himself refers to this rationale in a totally different context: his "Responses to the Questions of a Priest from Rouen": "y piensan estos que teniendo el coraçon bueno con el Señor, tienen satisfecho a su obligacion" (Salomon, "Haham Saul Levi Morteira," p. 137, n. 50).

92. Immanuel Aboab, *Nomologia* (Amsterdam, 1629), Pt. 2, chap. 18, pp. 213–17; Samuel Aboab, *Devar Shemu'el* (Venice, 1720), nu. 45. Cf. Roth, "The Religion of the Marranos," p. 5, and "Immanuel Aboab's Proselytization," pp. 130–44; Yerushalmi, *From Spanish Court to Italian Ghetto,* pp. 38–39. In both texts, the belief is said to be supported by a passage from the apocryphal "Letter of Baruch," in which Jeremiah says to the Babylonian exiles, "When you see a multitude before you and behind bowing down, you shall say in your hearts: You alone are to be praised, O Lord." Cf. "The Epistle of Jeremy," vv. 5–6, in R. H. Charles, *The Apocrypha and Pseudepigrapha of the Old Testament* 2 vols. (Oxford, 1913) 1: 600. Morteira's sermon does not have this reference, which may indicate an independent source of information. In the Portuguese *auto-da-fé* sermons, Christian preachers attacked the idea that one can be a Jew in the heart and a Christian in the mouth (Glaser, "Invitation to Intolerance," pp. 357–58). For an early expression of this ideology reported in a rabbinic source, see the responsa of Simeon ben Tsemaḥ Duran (*Teshuvot Tashbets*, Part 3, nu. 47: "A *converso* may ask you whether he is defective or worthy (*pasul o kasher*) [in God's sight]. If he is told that he is defective, he will no longer pay attention to you; rather he will say, 'You are the one who is defective and I am worthy,' because his heart is devoted to God." And compare the sources (including Inquisitional documents) and discussion in Gitlitz, *Secrecy and Deceit,* (Philadelphia, 1966), pp. 41, 83, 124 n. 2, 335; Bodian, *Hebrew of the Portuguese Nation,* pp. 100–101 and 145.

Neither the wicked of Israel nor the other peoples should think that the ugly vows and the sordid oaths that the Israelites sought to fulfill while living on the land, and that were frustrated by God in His zeal, may be put into effect during the period of exile, for having left the land [of Israel], we are no longer subject to the original covenant but are like a widow, God forbid!... Those cursed vows that were made to Baal while they were still in their land, they think that they may fulfill them in their exile, and that although God frustrated them by meting out severe punishment in their land, He will not be strict about them now that the people are outside the land.... God is always our King, watching over us.[93]

Although there is less external corroborating evidence for this view than for the previous one, this too is a plausible expression of "Marrano" rationalization.

Just as the appeal to the supremacy of the inner religious life takes a principle with a strong foundation in internal Jewish thought and pushes it to a radical conclusion, so the claim that God is less strict about idolatry outside the land of Israel has a recognizable background. That the land of Israel has higher standards concerning ethical and religious behavior is indeed a doctrine with biblical roots; one of the most highly respected and influential medieval thinkers, Nahmanides, made it a focal point of his commentary.[94] There is also some evidence of heretical counter-currents among Jews who questioned whether the commandments as a whole were binding outside the land, arguing on biblical grounds in ways that—as we have seen Morteira report—were used by Christians to attack the viability of Diaspora Judaism.[95] Such a thesis might well have been useful to New Christians who could not observe the commandments, yet who continued to believe that they would be included in the messianic ingathering of the exiles, when the full array of commandments could once again be observed in the land.[96] It is therefore possible that this passage too draws from some genuine themes of "Marrano ideology," which may some day be corroborated by further evidence.

Morteira's refutation of this view is based on Jeremiah's message, addressed after the destruction of Jerusalem, to Judeans living in Egypt and

---

93. MS 3:154r, *Mattot,* Num. 30:11, early 1630s.

94. See, e.g., Nahmanides, Commentary on Genesis 1:1 and 19:5, Leviticus 18:25.

95. See above, pp. 262–63.

96. For other Jewish references to the *converso* use of the claim that the obligation to perform the commandments applies only to the land of Israel, see the sources cited by Ravitzky, *"'Hatzivu Lekha Tziyunim' le-Tziyon,"* pp. 20–25.

worshipping alien gods there. This passage contains one of the few explicit defenses of idolatry attributed to Israelites in the Bible. It is an argument from history: things began to deteriorate in Judea and Jerusalem when we *stopped* offering sacrifices to the Queen of Heaven (Jer. 44:17–18). Therefore, the Judeans reportedly say, *"We will do everything that we have vowed—to make offerings to the Queen of Heaven and to pour libations to her"*(Jer. 44:17). Jeremiah replies, *You said, "we will fulfill the vows which we made, to burn incense to the Queen of Heaven and to pour libations to her." So fulfill your vows; perform your vows! But listen to the word of the Eternal...*(Jer. 44:25–26). There follows a prophecy of punishment by God for all the Judeans dwelling on Egyptian soil. This is the precedent for Morteira's insistence that God's providence extends throughout the world, and that idolatry committed by Jews outside the land of Israel will be punished no less vehemently than the sins of their ancestors in the holy land.

Whatever the reasons so many of the New Christian chose to remain in Portugal or in other lands where they could not live as Jews, Morteira shows little doubt about their ultimate fate. Try as they may, they cannot escape their Jewish identity. They remain Jews, and they will ultimately be punished as Jews. This message is asserted on many occasions in some of the most powerful passages of Morteira's preaching, and in order to convey something of their impact, it is worth citing several of these passages at length. For example, in early 1624, speaking on the lesson *Mishpatim,* Morteira raised the question: Why do the first biblical chapters devoted entirely to legal matters begin with the apparently minor case of the Hebrew slave? The answer, coming at the conclusion of the sermon, is that the passage should be read as a warning about issues of contemporary significance. Here is the rather impressive and apparently original interpretation:

> *If his master gives him a wife* (Exod. 21:4) means, if his masters compel him to take another wife and a new religion, as occurred to many of our people because of our sins, *and she bears him sons or daughters* who are devoted to it, despite it all they [i.e., the masters] will not extinguish the love nor will they remove him from the Jewish people, for "even though he sins he remains a Jew."[97] *The wife and her children will belong to her master, and he will go forth alone* (Exod. 21:4). Since the wife belongs to an alien faith, they are not truly his children. *The scepter of the wicked surely*

---

97. B. *Sanhedrin* 44a. On the emergence of this statement as basis for the principle that even the apostate Jew remains a Jew, see Jacob Katz, "Af al pi she-Ḥata Yisrael Hu," in *Halakhah ve-Qabbalah* (Jerusalem, 1984), pp. 255–69; *Exclusiveness and Tolerance* (New York, 1962), pp. 70–73.

will not rest over the portion allotted to the just (Ps. 125:3); *may God lead them away with the evildoers, and may peace be upon Israel* (Ps. 125:5). He will go forth alone, and be counted with his people.

But *if the slave should say, "I love my master and my wife and my children, I will not go forth to freedom"* (Exod. 21:5), meaning, if this slave should be one of those Jews who sin by defiling their bodies,[98] saying that he actually loves the qualities of the people where he has been exiled, and his Gentile wife, or the new religion and his children who are devoted to idolatry, and will therefore not go forth to freedom, *his master,* namely, his original Master *will bring him to judgment* (Exod. 21:6), removing him from the exile to pass sentence against him....

He will remove him from his home, *and bring him before the door or the doorpost* (Exod. 21:6), meaning close to the entrance or the door to the land of Israel, as in "you shall see it but you shall not eat of it,"[99] and there *he shall pierce his ear with a bore,* an implement of iron, wreaking vengeance against them [sic]. *He shall serve him forever* (Exod. 21:6), cleaving to his master and his accursed wife, as in the verse, *Go down and be laid to rest with the uncircumcised* (Ezek. 32:19), for *Their worm will never die and their fire will never be extinguished* (Isa. 66:24).

This is why the section begins with the law of the slave: ...to teach that if they fail to uphold the terms of the covenant, *These are the judgments* (ha-mishpatim) *which He will place before them* (Exod. 21:1).[100]

Morteira's typological approach to the biblical laws concerning the Hebrew slave enables him to take a passage of merely theoretical interest, with absolutely no relevance to the realities of seventeenth-century Jewish life, and unpack a message that speaks directly to the concerns of many of his listeners.[101] The two categories of slaves allude to two categories of New

---

98. See b. *Rosh Hashanah* 17a, where the phrase refers to the category of those *not* condemned to eternal punishment. Cf. Altmann, "Eternality of Punishment," p. 44 (Morteira's citation of R. Asher ben Yehiel). In the present passage, Morteira seems to be using the phrase in a new way.

99. This appears to be a quotation, but I cannot identify it. It may be a slip of the pen, conflating Deut. 34:4 and Gen. 2:17.

100. MS 3:346r, *Mishpatim,* Exod. 21:6, 162. I omitted from the translation the citation of Ezekiel 20:32–33, which is used by the preacher with explication in other passages cited (above, p. 285; below, p. 291).

101. This interpretation of the Hebrew slave passage was adumbrated by Morteira in his sermon on the second verse in *Mishpatim,* delivered in 1620 or 1621 (MS 3:29v, Exod. 21:2): "It is like this slave, who does not want to leave when the time of his manumission arrives and says, *I love my master and my wife and my children, I will not go forth to freedom* (Exod. 21:5). This refers to those people who at the time of redemption, at the end of six [millennia] will

Christians. The slave that goes free in the seventh year represents those who have left the enslavement of enforced Christianity and who sit before him as free Jews in Amsterdam. The slave who chooses to remain with his master represents those who are still in Portugal, living as Christians. The ceremonial humiliation of the slave who renounces the opportunity for freedom prefigures the punishment ordained by God at the beginning of the messianic age. In addition to validating the choice made by his listeners, this interpretation explains the purpose of the seemingly anticlimactic legal material fthat follows the revelation at Sinai. The content is not insignificant at all: it deals with the crucial issue of Jewish identity. The word *mishpatim* in the first verse of the lesson is not just "laws"; it is the "judgments" that God wanted to be set out clearly for all Jews who seek to abandon their people.

We have already cited a passage from the early sermon on *Mattot* in which Morteira, drawing from Ezekiel 20:32, articulated the Marrano belief that God would overlook their outward display of Christian worship because of the inner purity of their hearts. After stating how the New Christians purportedly rationalized their behavior, the preacher continues with the message he derives from the Bible:

> To this, seeing that they violated the oath they had sworn [at Sinai: see below], God replied with an oath of His own: *As I live, declares the Eternal God, I will reign over you with a strong hand* (Ezek. 20:33). This means, I will see to it that you who want to be just like them will keep your oath against your will. You will confess to them in humiliation and disgrace what you did not want to affirm with honor and joy in other places. And this in three ways. *With a strong hand,* namely, through the power of a strong Inquisition investigating all the laws of the realm. *And with an outstretched arm:* an arm extended and stretched for a long, long time, a period of imprisonment and punishment lasting many years. *And with overflowing fury* (Ezek. 20:33), which they pour out to each other, by calling each other to pay their debts to this punishment.[102] All of this is

---

remain bound with strong love for their masters, namely the Gentiles among whom they have assimilated and taken Canaanite wives, and they love their servant wives and their children, the fruits of their lust, and do not await God's salvation. The waters of salvation will not fall upon them; they will serve their masters forever, as a perpetual reproach and abhorrence (cf. Dan. 12:2)." This sermon interprets the laws of the Hebrew slave as a hint about the exile and redemption of the Jewish people, with the six and seven years referring to the messianic advent by the end of the sixth millennium. For another later use by a Jewish writer of Exod. 21:5 to express the unwillingness of a Portuguese New Christian to leave the Iberian peninsula, see Yerushalmi, *From Spanish Court to Italian Ghetto*, p. 30.

102. לפרוע חובותיהם אל בעונש ההוא. This phrase is not entirely clear to me; it may refer to the

the result of the violation of their oath, for God wants them to fulfill it [even?] against their will, and not to their good.[103]

This passage shifts the punishment from an eschatological setting to the familiar experience of the present. The Inquisition is God's instrument, which He uses to punish those who seek to escape from their true identity.[104]

Morteira then turns to the theological basis for the punishment—the original oath of the covenant—moving to a homiletical explication, with contemporary relevance, of verses we have already encountered from the lesson *Nitsavim*:

> For this hypocrisy and this concealing of their true faith in God is detested by Him. It is truly a violation of their oath, which our ancestors explicitly accepted, making it a futile oath. After the statement, *Cursed be the one who will not uphold the terms of this Torah and observe them—all the people shall say, Amen* (Deut. 27:36). Now the words "uphold" and "observe" clearly entail the obligation of actual performance, to which they explicitly responded, "Amen." The divine Torah did not fail to speak prophetically about these people and inform them how they were violating the oath, and how God would become furious with them.[105]

There follows an interpretation of Deut. 29:18–19, which we have cited above as it was recapitulated in a later sermon on the same scriptural lesson. After presenting the rationale of those who think they will be safe despite their idolatry because they believe in God in their hearts, Morteira moves on to the sanction in the Deuteronomy passage:

> But *the Eternal will never forgive him* [...] *Every sanction... will come down upon him* (Deut. 29:19), meaning that he casts his oath to the ground, yet despite it all, he will not accomplish what he wants, for *The Eternal will single him out from all the tribes of Israel for misfortune* (Deut. 29:20), single him out not for good but for evil, so that he too will admit being of the

pressure imposed upon the New Christians by the Inquisition to turn against each other by denouncing their neighbors and, as we have seen above, even their own family members.

103. MS 3:66v, *Mattot*, Num. 30:3, early 1620s.

104. With this providential explanation of the Inquisition, cf. Abravanel, discussed in Netanyahu, *The Marranos of Spain*, pp. 187–89; Usque, *Consolation for the Tribulations of Israel*, Third Dialogue, chaps. 25, 30–31, pp. 198–99, 206–209; Salomon, *Portrait of a New Christian*, pp. 167–69, 180. Salomon refers there to Morteira's use of this argument in his "Responses to the Questions of a Priest from Rouen," see Salomon, "Haham Saul Levi Morteira," p. 137, n. 51. Quoting Ezekiel 20:32–33 in Spanish, Morteira interprets: "estos son los que *con mano fuerte* del tormento, *y con braço tendido* de priçiones, *y con sana derramada* de reçelos de la vida, confiessan ser Judios" (vol. 106r–v).

105. MS 3:66v, *Mattot*, Num. 30:3, early 1620s.

tribes of Israel, admitting against his will what he wanted to conceal.[106]

Again, it is the sufferings imposed by the Inquisition that foster an identification with the Jewish people—an identification that had not previously been overtly manifest, and that confounds the efforts of this group of New Christians to hide it.

The final passage to be cited in this context is taken from the later sermon on *Mattot.* The climactic moment depends on an application of the rabbinic dictum, taken from the Tannaitic Midrash *Sifra,* containing a dialogue that must have been rendered by the preacher in a highly theatrical manner:[107]

> *I will heap your carcasses upon your lifeless fetishes* (Lev. 26:30). What do carcasses have to do with fetishes? Once Elijah was conversing about those swollen with hunger. He found a man swollen and prostrated with hunger. He asked, "From which family are you?"
>
> "From such and such."
>
> "How many are left of you?"
>
> "I alone."
>
> "Would you say one thing to save your life?"
>
> "Yes."
>
> "Say, *Hear, O Israel, the Eternal our God, the Eternal is one* (Deut. 6:4), and you shall live."
>
> He shouted at him, "I will not mention the name of God, for my father did not teach me to do so."
>
> What did he do? He took his fetish and placed it upon his heart and hugged and kissed it until his body split, and he fell together with his idol to the ground. Therefore it was said, *I will heap your carcasses upon your lifeless fetishes* (Lev. 26:30).

Morteira's application of the passage follows the purported rationale justifying the fulfillment of idolatrous vows cited above. Those who may have known that God punished their ancestors in biblical times thought they were safe because God did not care about such behavior outside the land of Israel:

> No, the same punitive vengeance that God wrought upon them then He wreaks now.... As God refused to renounce the honor due Him, as He frustrated their oaths to other gods in antiquity, so does He frustrate them in our exile.... Do we not see it in the experience of all those

---

106. Ibid.

107. Compare the discussion of preaching and dramatic performance in chap. 4, above, and the eulogy by Leon Modena cited in Saperstein, *Jewish Preaching,* pp. 99–100.

households that wanted to be like the Gentiles—how precisely upon them God's wrath abided, manifesting itself in punishments and suffering, so that they were lost, body and soul? But those who believed in God and did not abandon Him, He supported and helped to leave the environment of calamity.

This is precisely the simple meaning that emerges from the rabbinic dictum read at the beginning of my sermon. We see with our own eyes today among those descendants of Israel who are devoted to idolatry in the Iberian peninsula that they are "swollen with hunger," puffed up and filled with the wind of imaginary glory, rising in status according to the values of the Gentiles. But they are actually "swollen with hunger," for all their status is devoid of substance. It vanishes in the twinkling of an eye. We see this day after day.

God metes out His punishment through "Elijah," referring to the events and developments that impel them to return to the God of their ancestors. One of these, the most important, is their realization that though they were many, now they are few. Some of them have died horrible deaths, the traces of some have been lost in the priesthood of idolatry, some have been burned for religious reasons. That is why Elijah asked how many were in that family and how many remained: so that the man would take God's judgment to heart and realize how few had flourished in this worship. But even though he responded that he alone remained, he did not take the lesson to heart.

Therefore Elijah spoke more explicitly to him, telling him to say one thing (*Hear, O Israel*), and thereby save his life. It is exactly what happens with them, when they are approached by someone who wants to teach them. When they hear the name of God, they become angry, responding that he should not mention that name, for they did not learn it from their fathers. Thus the man in the rabbinic statement is split and dies in his swollen state, with his fetish in his hand, fulfilling the verse, *I will heap your carcasses upon your lifeless fetishes, and I will detest you*" (Lev. 26:30). This destroys him, body and soul.[108]

In this final, dramatic statement of Morteira's message to his congregants about the fate of the New Christians, several important motifs are accentuated. The New Christians may have achieved superficial success in Portuguese society, but their numbers were actually diminishing through assimilation, persecution, and entrance of some into the priesthood. The only hope for them was a return to an affirmation of their Jewish identity, yet they

---

108. MS 3:154r, *Mattot,* Num. 30:11, early 1630s.

are unable to recognize this. Moreover, even when they are offered the opportunity through "one who wants to teach them"—an apparent reference to the underground "proselytizing" activity among the New Christians—there is deep resistance to the Hebrew "name of God." Their fate is therefore sealed. From the other sermons it is quite clear: devastation in this world, eternal damnation in the next.

This is, to be sure, a bleakly pessimistic outlook on the feasibility of successful "outreach" to the New Christians. Passages in earlier sermons present a rather different picture. Preaching on the lesson *Shemot* in early 1620, Morteira speaks of the natural affinity between the soul of the Jew and the Torah, as proven by the openness of the New Christians to the study of Torah, the eagerness with which they study it, the aptitude they display in mastering its teachings once they are exposed to it. He cites empirical confirmation that this aptitude is related to a genetic predisposition:

> This is the meaning of *God's Torah is perfect, restoring the soul* (Ps. 19:8), namely that the soul of the Israelite and the Torah dwell serenely and peacefully together, but not with any other religious teaching.... Thus we have seen that the *conversos* of Jewish descent immediately embrace the Torah when they hear something from it, for there is a close affinity between them. By contrast, it is extremely difficult for Gentile proselytes to understand it, with the rare exception of those who devote enormous energy and intense prayer.[109]

This observation is undoubtedly based on a Kabbalistic doctrine about the souls of Jews—even those forced to abandon their religion—and the Torah as manifestations of the Godhead.[110] A similar statement is made in a sermon on *Be-Ha'alotekha* delivered perhaps a year later: "Thus experience proves that when one speaks about Torah matters to a Jew who is from the seed of Israel, he embraces it willingly and accepts it as if it were something he had already seen and heard, which is not true for the Gentiles."[111] Both of these passages indicate what appear to be ongoing efforts to expose New Christians to the Torah, with encouraging results.

Perhaps the frustration, discouragement, and apparent anger of the later *Matot* sermon can be explained by a very different outcome in Morteira's own experience. Several scholars have recently written about an Inquisitional re-

---

109. MS 3:20r, *Shemot,* Exod. 1:5, 1620.

110. On the metaphysically different souls of Jews, see Zohar I, 13a–b, II, 95b; Johanan Wijnhoven, "The Zohar and the Proselyte," in *Texts and Responses: Studies Presented to N. N. Glatzer* (Leiden, 1959), pp. 120–40.

111. MS 3:140v, GS 1645, p. 57a, 1912, p. 216, *Be-Ha'alotkha,* Num. 8:4, ca. 1621.

cord dated May 15, 1635, in which a New Christian named Esteban de Ares de Fonseca recounted his experience of the previous years. He came to Amsterdam from Lisbon, by way of Bayonne. In Amsterdam, his relatives tried to convince him to be circumcised and to live as a Jew. When he informed them he had no interest in doing so, "they introduced him into the company of a certain rabbi, whose name was Morteira, a preacher in the Torah of Moses, so as to convince him to practice [Judaism]. After he stayed with [Morteira] for more than six months, and after they realized that they did not have the power to persuade him, they had a ban placed on him in the synagogue."[112] It cannot be demonstrated that these events occurred before the above-cited sermon on *Mattot,* which dates from the early 1630s, but that chronology is certainly possible. The exasperation of failing to convince a New Christian to accept Judaism despite six months of effort may well be expressed through the figure of Elijah—representing "someone who wants to teach them"—patiently using different arguments in an ultimately futile effort.

Why did Morteira continue to emphasize his uncompromising message of divine retribution against those Jews who remained in the "lands of idolatry"? He may have believed that it was possible, even from Amsterdam, to motivate Portuguese New Christians to make the right decision by threatening dire consequences if they persisted in renouncing their Jewish identity. In the letter he wrote to defend the traditional doctrine of eternal punishment against the strictures of Isaac Aboab da Fonseca, he argued that were it not for this severe doctrine, none of the New Christians living peacefully "in the lands of their enemies" would ever decide to leave.[113] Homiletical-exegetical passages and refutations of Christian claims such as those cited above might conceivably have been useful to congregants who would encounter New Christians, whether on Portuguese soil or abroad, and try to convince them to return to their people.

On the other hand, good preachers do not frequently bombard their listeners with a message that is of relevance only to people living somewhere else. These powerful passages, coming at climactic points in his sermons, indicate that the subject must have been of importance to the listeners as well. Presumably, it was not just that they would have derived some sadistic pleasure from contemplating the eventual suffering of others, though this element can-

---

112. Kaplan, "Wayward New Christians and Stubborn New Jews," 27–28; Gitlitz, *Secrecy and Deceit,* pp. 234–35. The original text was transcribed by Julio Caro Baroja, *Los judíos en la España moderna y contemporánea* (Madrid, 1961), 3:332–36. H. P. Salomon believes that the entire account of the experience in Amsterdam may have been an invention of Ares de Fonseca (personal communication).

113. Altmann, "Eternality of Punishment," pp. 18, 50. See above, pp. 25–26.

not be entirely discounted. More important, those in the congregation who had made the decision to leave Portugal for Amsterdam experienced a major rupture in their lives. Even those whom the Inquisition had robbed of any potential future in Portugal must have felt something of a loss. Amsterdam, with all its attractions, was not a paradise, and not all were successfully integrated into the community. Many experienced severe economic hardship, others spiritual and intellectual dislocation. Lingering doubts as to whether they had made the right decision would have been normal. To such listeners, these passages would have provided reassurance that they had done the right thing, and that whatever difficulties they might be experiencing at present, their decision to cast their lot with the Jewish people would be decisively vindicated.

"New Christians" in Amsterdam

Some of these issues can be sensed as we turn to passages where Morteira refers not to those New Christians who stayed behind but to those who have chosen to leave Portuguese soil. The decision to leave Portugal and join a Jewish community was, of course, welcomed, but Morteira notes that there were different motivations for this decision, not all of which are equally acceptable in God's sight.[114] Discussing the doctrine of repentance in a sermon delivered in 1625, he reflects on those who have come for the wrong reasons. The passage begins with an evocation of the economic well-being of New Christians in Portugal, unexpectedly interrupted by "disaster" when the Inquisition intrudes into their lives:

> There are those who dwell at ease in the lands of God's enemies. Their children are with them, and their houses are filled with possessions. Feeling secure and serene, as if they lack nothing, they do not remember God or ever call Him to mind. Then, suddenly, when disaster strikes, they flee for their lives from the oppressor's wrath. They arrive in these lands and return to Judaism, thinking that God owes them much because they have done a great deed. This is not the repentance that God wants. It is rather repentance that occurs "in the very context in which they sinned" (cf. b. *Yoma* 86b), while they are living in peace and

---

114. The variety of motivation among those who left Portugal is noted by Rehuel Jessurun in his *Dialogo dos montes*: "Some with holy zeal alone imbued, Others driven by ignoble terror, Still others tortures suffering in horror... ." Jessurun, *Dialogo dos montes,* p. 131; cf. also Yerushalmi, *From Spanish Court to Italian Ghetto,* p. 40.

quiet and contentment: to leave it all—wealth, honors, even family—
and return to God. Then He will have mercy upon them.[115]

This passage presumably would have had resonance for many in the
congregation. If they themselves did not identify with the people being
described, they might well have reacted, "Why, that applies to so-and-so."
Those who could think of themselves as having left Portugal before they
actually got in trouble with the Inquisition would conclude that their
"repentance" was the kind the preacher was praising; those who left to flee
from the Inquisition would be pushed to recognize with contrition that their
motivations were not entirely pure. We also sense here an expression of the
preacher's distaste for what he presents as a kind of spiritual arrogance in
some of the new arrivals, who think they have done God a great favor by
coming when they actually had little choice.

On the other hand, some of those who may have come for the right reasons
lose sight of their purpose after their arrival. Here the rhetoric of rebuke is
directed against those in the preacher's own congregation for their behavior
in the present. In an early sermon on *Shemot,* Morteira grafts this theme onto
a biblical passage in which Saul, seeking Samuel and David, comes upon a
band of prophets speaking in ecstasy, forgets his purpose, strips off his clothes,
and lies naked all that day and all night (1 Sam. 19:18–24):

> From this we may derive a lesson in the opposite direction, pertaining
> to people in this world. While it is true that they may come from great
> distances to gain salvation for their souls, to acquaint themselves with
> their Creator and come to know His works and study His Torah, for
> that is why they [?], yet when they are here, an *evil* spirit rests upon them.
> They forget what they came to do, which is of fundamental importance,
> and they cling to the ethos of the group that they find. Worldly things
> seem good to them, they forget the essentials for which they came, and
> they do not remember their own essence. Rather, they "lie naked" of
> Torah and commandments all the days and all the nights of their
> lives.[116]

The preacher seems aware that his biblical grounding is rather forced. Saul is
distracted by something good ("the spirit of God") while the people Morteira
is criticizing are distracted by something bad; Saul stripped off the externals
of clothing, while the worldly "new Jews" strip off the essentials of Torah and

---

115. MS 3:355v, *Va-Yiqra,* Lev. 1:5, 1625.

116. MS 3:108r, *Shemot,* Exod. 1:6, early 1621 (some words illegible because of damage
to the page).

commandments. It is the theme of forgetting one's purpose in an important venture that Morteira hopes will remain with the listeners and that they will apply to their own lives.

The most significant sign of good intent on the part of the male new arrivals was the ceremony of circumcision. Even in Portugal, this ritual took on immense symbolic significance as an expression of the commitment to bind one's life with the destiny of the Jewish people. It was not feasible on Portuguese soil, for its discovery was tantamount to a death sentence both for the individual circumcised and the one who performed the operation.[117] But for male New Christians who decided to join a Jewish community such as Amsterdam, this became the initiation ritual par excellence. Even so, there were some who resisted the pressures for immediate circumcision.[118] Their hesitation went beyond a reasonable reluctance to undergo major surgery, with its concomitant pain and danger of infection. So long as the male remained uncircumcised, his options remained open. He could return to Portugal, claim he had been abroad on business, hope that no one would denounce him to the Inquisition, deny that he had ever lived as a Jew. Circumcision ended any such deniability; it was a burning of bridges with the past, a repudiation of any possibility of changing one's mind and returning to a familiar if precarious Christian identity. The leaders of the Amsterdam community had no interest in allowing this kind of hedging, and they insisted that circumcision be performed immediately.[119]

Many of Morteira's sermons touch upon the nature and importance of circumcision in general. I shall cite a few passages that deal with the specific issue of delaying the operation once it is feasible. In a sermon delivered early in 1619 and repeated on several later occasions, the preacher discusses the significance of circumcision as the first commandment addressed to the people of Israel, the first observed following the Exodus, and the first observed upon entrance into the land of Canaan. He mentions the seriousness of the punishment for transgressing the commandment: excision of the soul (*karet*).[120] He

---

117. For the significance of circumcision in "Marrano" consciousness, see Roth, "The Religion of the Marranos," p. 11; Yerushalmi, *From Spanish Court to Italian Ghetto,* pp. 37, 378; Gitlitz, *Secrecy and Deceit,* pp. 202–7; Bodian, *Hebrews of the Portuguese Nation,* p. 97.

118. See Kaplan, "Wayward New Christians," pp. 28–31.

119. For example, the Beth Israel congregation passed an ordinance in 1620 stating that anyone who was not circumcised by the coming New Year would be excluded from the synagogue after that date. Kaplan, "Wayward New Christians," p. 31; Bodian, *Hebrews of the Portuguese Nation,* p. 113. This emphasis on the importance of circumcision for Jewish identity undoubtedly underlies the highlighting of the ritual by Spinoza, who grew up in Morteira's congregation (*Theological-Political Treatise,* end of chapter 3, p. 46).

120. A detailed discussion of the halakhic debate over the nature of the *karet* associated

notes a parallel between circumcision and the commandment concerning the paschal lamb, both performed with blood, both entailing the punishment of *karet.* And then, probably emphasizing the point with increased volume and perhaps with a glance around the congregation, he concludes, "One who is able to be circumcised and is not circumcised is guilty every passing moment of a new punishment of *karet,* making for infinite punishment, and he cannot be saved. However, one who is circumcised and circumcises his sons at this time when there is no longer a paschal sacrifice—the Bible speaks of him [in Ps. 50:5] as if he had offered the paschal sacrifice as well."[121]

A more extensive discussion of the same message, derived from the biblical context, can be found in the sermon on the lesson *Yitro* from 1623. Addressing a classical crux in Exodus 4:24–26—on their way back to Egypt from Midian, God tries to kill Moses, and Zipporah prevents this by circumcising their son—Morteira presents a narrative reconstruction of Moses' life in Midian. Jethro, having no sons, insisted that he be allowed to educate the first son born to Zipporah for the Midianite priesthood. He therefore did not allow the first-born to be circumcised. As Jethro did not care about Eliezer, the second son, Moses had him circumcised.[122] Then Moses decided to return to Egypt:

> When Moses set out on the road, *God found him and sought to kill him* (Exod. 4:24). It is unlikely that this pertains to Eliezer. The Bible does not say that he was born eight days before they set out. If he was born prior to this, why would Moses have refrained from circumcising him? Yet the verse says that there was only one uncircumcised son. Therefore, it must pertain to Gershom, who was not circumcised because of the aforementioned reason: that Jethro prevented it. When

---

with the failure to circumcise—whether it is a spiritual punishment or early death—appears in a sermon on *Be-Midbar* from 1622 or 1623: MS 136v.

121. MS 3:115v, *Be-Shallah,* Exod. 13:19, Jan. 26, 1619, repeated in 1626 and 1650. With Morteira's use of Psalm 50:5 in this context, compare Bahya ben Asher on Genesis 17:13. A sermon on *Tazri'a,* probably delivered on the Sabbath preceding Pesach a year or two after the first, similarly emphasizes the importance of circumcision and the analogies between this commandment and the paschal sacrifice, expressed through all ten of the Aristotelian categories. It ends with the assertion that the merit of these two commandments brought about the liberation from Egypt and will bring about the "destruction of the fourth kingdom" and the end of the present exile. MS 3:46v, *Tazri'a,* Lev. 12:3, early 1620s.

122. This is based on a midrashic tradition, preserved in *Mekilta* (ed. Lauterbach, 2: 168–69), that Jethro's condition for allowing Moses to marry his daughter was that the first son would be raised as a Gentile, a condition that Moses accepted by an oath. Cf. Louis Ginzberg, *Legends of the Jews,* 7 vols. (Philadelphia, 1912) 2: 294–95, 328, 5:92, 423. Morteira expands upon this tradition, and ignores others in the rabbinic literature, for the purposes of the point he will make.

he [Jethro] heard from Moses that God sent him, he gave Moses his two sons. Once Moses was outside his father-in-law's house, he decided to wait for the circumcision until he reached Egypt. But as "God deals strictly with His pious ones, to a hair's breadth" (b. *Yebamot* 121b), He met Moses and sought to kill him, until Zipporah circumcised their son. She called him *a bridegroom of blood* (Exod. 4:26), meaning that on the day of his wedding, because of his oath, he was obligated about this blood without knowing what he had sworn. From this we learn how God pardons the sin of those who dwell among the Gentiles and are not able to be circumcised because their lives would be endangered. However, *once they have the opportunity [and neglect it], God punishes them immediately.*[123]

Just as Moses was not punished for failing to defy his father-in-law by circumcising Gershom in Midian, so the failure to undergo circumcision, or to perform it on one's sons, in Portugal itself is not held by God against the New Christians. But if the life of Moses could be imperiled by the delay in circumcising once he left Midian, even though he intended to do so as soon as he reached civilization in Egypt, it is obvious that any delay by those who reached Amsterdam would entail serious danger, and could not be tolerated.

How did the members of the Portuguese community in Amsterdam think of their former homes, the country they abandoned? Several passages in the sermons reflect upon Morteira's understanding of the complex emotions associated with this rupture. One major problem encountered by many of the new arrivals was economic hardship, the result, as we have seen, of the difficulty in transferring wealth to the new environment. Their ambivalent feelings about this hardship can be seen in two sermons, using different biblical models. The first is the sermon on *Yitro* that we have just cited, delivered in the late winter of 1623. In the above passage, Midian serves as a type for life in exile; here, Egypt represents the full harshness of exile and Midian the relative freedom of Amsterdam. The preacher focuses on Moses' mental outlook in the house of Jethro:

When people who find themselves in a difficult situation remember a far more serious one from which they have been saved and enabled to escape, the current problem seems like nothing to them, and they are thankful to God that they have escaped from the other. For example, the "children of Israel" who have left Portugal, though they live here in conditions of severe economic hardship that make even the provision

123. MS 3:270r, *Yitro,* Exod. 18:4, 1623, emphasis added.

of food a burden, nevertheless accept it all cheerfully, giving thanks to God for having saved them from the terrible suffering and the fearful oppression they experienced in the place they left. For when they were back there, they used to say, "If only we could escape from this place, we would be content to eat grass." So it was with Moses: though he was living in the house of his father-in-law, dependent on others, earning his keep with difficulty as a shepherd, when he thought of the place from which God had saved him he rendered praise and thanks.[124]

This may indeed be an idealized portrayal of the mentality of the recent arrivals, as other passages will indicate. But the terrors of Portugal and the economic hardships of Holland seemed familiar enough to be used to explain a biblical situation: the relationship between the life-threatening danger of Egypt and the difficult but secure existence in Midian. The preacher's purpose would be defeated unless the listeners recognized his description of current circumstances as valid.

A very different psychological outlook is depicted in a sermon delivered some fifteen years later. The point of departure is the astonishing characterization of Egypt made by Dathan and Abiram in the lesson *Korah: Is it not enough that you brought us from a land flowing with milk and honey to have us die in the wilderness?*(Num. 16:13). Morteira takes the common reaction to this verse and uses it to drive home his message:

Now when we hear what happened in those days, we ask about it [in amazement], considering these people to be inordinately evil. Yet every day our ears hear similar things, and we are not amazed! For what difference is there between these [Dathan and Abiram] and those whom God has brought out with great strength and a strong arm from the Iberian peninsula—a place where death is present at every moment, where terror and fury never cease—and brought them to a peaceful land, where they can save their bodies and their souls from death. Yet day after day, when they "remember the fish" (cf. Num. 11:5), they praise that land and sigh over it, showing contempt for the land in which they now live. Do they not transform God's mercies into evil? There is no difference between these people and those in the Bible, for they are already prefigured in Scripture.... Therefore, just as the punishment of [the biblical rebels] was extraordinary, so will be the punishment of all who are similar to them, Heaven help them![125]

---

124. MS 3:269v.
125. MS 1:83v, *Korah*, Num. 16:14, 1638.

As in the previous passage, biblical Egypt serves as a type for the Iberian peninsula with its terrors. But unlike Moses, whose life in Midian provided a proper model for the Jews in Amsterdam, those who idealize Egypt in their memories because of the difficulties of life in the wilderness pervert the entire order of God's plan. The rhetorical power of the passage derives from the expected assent among the listeners that the villainous view recorded in the biblical lesson is indeed to be found at present.

In this *Koraḥ* sermon, Morteira speaks of those who think longingly of Portugal and show contempt for their new surroundings. Related to this inversion of values, but more extreme in its challenge to the community, was the decision actually to return to the Iberian peninsula. We have already encountered one individual who claimed to have resisted the arguments of Morteira and, after more than six months in Amsterdam, returned to make a full deposition before the Portuguese Inquisition. Several scholars have drawn attention to various kinds of source material indicating that the return to Spain or Portugal, whether permanently or on a limited journey, was by no means exceptional during our period. A communal ordinance from the year 1644 reflects the extreme disfavor with which the Amsterdam leadership viewed such behavior by members of their community.[126] Morteira's sermons show that he was scandalized by the idea of returning and spoke out forcefully against it long before the ordinance was passed.

Early in 1622, in a sermon filled with social criticism, Morteira commented on the rabbinic statement, "Whoever feasts excessively anywhere will eventually destroy his household, make his wife a widow and his fledglings orphans, and forget what he has learned" (b. *Pesaḥim* 49a). His explication of the final phrase is, "'He will forget what he has learned,' for this often requires one to forget God by going to a land of idolatry. This causes the fear of God he had learned to be forgotten."[127] Travel to the "lands of idolatry" was com-

---

126. On the return to the Iberian peninsula, see Cecil Roth, "The Strange Case of Hector Mendes Bravo," *HUCA* 18 (1944): 221–45; Simha Assaf, "Anusei Sefarad u-Fortugal be-Sifrut ha-Teshuvot," *Me'assef Tziyon* 5 (1933): 22–23; Yerushalmi, *From Spanish Court to Italian Ghetto,* pp. 34–35; idem., "Professing Jews in Post-Expulsion Spain and Portugal," in *Salo W. Baron Jubilee Volume* 3 vols. (Jerusalem, 1974) 2:1023–58; Jonathan Israel, "Manuel Lopez Pereira of Amsterdam, Antwerp and Madrid," *StRos* 19 1985): 109; Joseph Kaplan, "Pesaqim mi-Beit ha-Din shel ha-Qehillah ha-Sefaradit-ha-Portugalit be-Amsterdam," in *Meḥqarim al Toledot Yahadut Holland* 5 (1988): 28–30; idem, "The Travels of Portuguese Jews from Amsterdam to the 'Lands of Idolatry,'" in *Jews and Conversos,* ed. Joseph Kaplan (Jerusalem, 1985), 197–224; Bodian, *Hebrews of the Portuguese Nation,* pp. 24, 77. The text of the regulation is given in Kaplan, "Travels," pp. 205–6.

127. *GS* 1645, p. 24d, 1912, p. 114; cf. Saperstein, *Jewish Preaching,* p. 283 (see above, n. 72).

monly understood terminology for the return to the Iberian peninsula. Economic distress in Amsterdam often impelled such journeys by individuals who may still have retained assets or business connections in their former homes and hoped to return briefly without being denounced to the Inquisition. The brief phrase thus alluded to a real issue in the community. Less than a year later, Morteira discussed at length, using biblical examples, the pattern by which children are punished in the place where their parents were punished, concluding, "Therefore one should stay far away from the places where harm occurred to one's parents."[128] There is no explicit reference here to the Iberian peninsula, but it stands to reason that this was the message that would have been heard by the listeners.

Some fifteen years later, in the context of the public dispute over eternal punishment in hell, Morteira argued that the denial of the traditional doctrine would remove an important deterrent from one "whose heart impelled him to return to the land of impurity."[129] And a few years after that, in a sermon for the Sabbath of Repentance, he waxed eloquent on this issue. The first sentence reiterates a theme we have seen above: the economic inducement of Iberian New Christians to remain where they are. But then he moves on to the matter at hand, choosing his biblical model with precision:

> Because of their money they abandon God, remaining in the lands of their enemies and worshipping another god in order to care for their wealth, their lands, and their houses. Worse than this: some of them return there, like Lot's wife, who *looked behind her and turned into a pillar of salt* (Gen. 19:26). She did not understand the great act of kindness God had performed for her in saving her from that conflagration, but looked behind her, in defiance of God's command. Her concern was for her property rather than for God's act of kindness; therefore she became a pillar of salt. This will be the fate of those who have escaped from the conflagration yet return there to take out their property: they will remain a useless pillar of salt burnt by brimstone. We see examples of this every day.[130]

The biblical narrative, of course, is not explicit about the reason for Lot's wife turning back in violation of the instructions. Concern for her wealth is only

---

128. MS 3:258r, *Va-Yiggash,* Gen. 44:22, 1622.

129. Altmann, "Eternality of Punishment," p. 50.

130. MS 3:310r, *Ha'azinu,* Deut. 32:21, 1641. For the full context, see below, p. 520. Cf. the use of Lot's wife in this context in the reply to the twenty-first question of the Priest of Rouen: *http://www.jewish-history.com/Occident/volume3/jan1846/questions.html* .

one proposal in the exegetical tradition.[131] It is the one that fits Morteira's purpose in condemning the return to Iberia out of material interests.

The preacher then shifts to different biblical precedents, moving from the biblical laws of kingship and the history of the return from Babylonian exile to an explicit application to the Iberian émigrés:

> God commanded that they not buy horses from that first evil and sin-inducing land from which He had brought out the Israelites, lest he send the people back there (Deut. 17:16), for it is against God's will for the people to return to that wicked land. From that model we learn a lesson that applies to other cases.
>
> When God brought the Jews out of Babylonia, some of them brought from there forbidden wives—Sidonian, Moabite, Hittite—as is written in the Book of Ezra. When they divorced them, following Ezra's counsel, it is obvious that these women returned to their fathers' homes in their own countries. It was forbidden for the Jews to return to those countries, lest they take up again with these women. Similarly, God has brought out a great number of the "children of Israel" from the sin-inducing land of Spain; beyond a doubt, the person who returns there to make more money is an abomination to God. God has said to you, *You must not go back that way again* (Deut. 17:16), for this is like Egypt, nay, even worse in its sins. Whoever pays no heed to this *vexes God with his trivialities* (Deut. 32:21).[132]

In this passage, we sense the preacher drawing from biblical literature to make the strongest possible emotional appeal. He tarnishes Spain and Portugal with the most negative associations of biblical geography—Sodom, Egypt—and those who endanger their physical and spiritual lives for business interests are branded as violating a divine prohibition. This is rhetoric reserved for attacking serious communal problems, and it may well have been this kind of preaching that created the atmosphere for the communal ordinance, which followed not long after. Yet the logic of Morteira's position should have produced an ordinance that prohibited even the temporary visit for business purposes, to which the enactment of 1644 does not apply. It is also possible, therefore, that Morteira, pushing for something stronger, lost this battle, overruled by the lay leaders of the community, who had their own

---

131. That of Abravanel, *Perush al ha-Torah, Bereshit,* p. 251a. Other proposals were that she was a skeptic and turned to see if it was really being destroyed (David Kimhi), and that she looked back out of compassion for her married daughters to see if they were coming (*Pirqei de-R. Eliezer,* chap. 25).

132. MS 3:310r, *Ha'azinu,* Deut. 32:21, 1641.

reasons for keeping open the option of a commercial trip to Iberia. Powerful preaching may be moving and inspiring, but it does not always determine communal policy.

Any emphasis on a single theme in a monumental body of work such as the extant sermons by Morteira is bound to mislead. While Christianity and the New Christians are a significant focus of this preacher's homiletical efforts, they were by no means the central concern. As should be evident from the other material in this study, the fundamental purposes of the sermons were to provide a sustained program of sophisticated yet accessible adult education that would anchor his congregants in the tradition they were constantly discovering; to defend that tradition against internal challenges by validating those aspects of rabbinic literature that seemed arbitrary, foolish or incomprehensible to inquiring minds or restless souls in the pews; to define and defend the boundaries of acceptable doctrine and behavior for a community seeking to construct its identity and establish its reputation within the context of world Jewry. The evidence reviewed in this chapter suggests that in Morteira's judgment, in order to help his congregants build up a new identity as Jews, it was necessary to tear down their former identity as Iberian Catholics. Despite the risks of offending Dutch neighbors, this end was pursued as vigorously and as passionately as the other, more constructive goals of his preaching.

9

Exile and Its Culmination

As Isadore Twersky *z"l* showed from the writings of Maimonides, conscious-ness of the geographical and psychological dislocations of exile have had a significant impact on Jewish creativity. The RaMBaM describes R. Judah the Patriarch's awareness that "the Roman empire was expanding and growing stronger, and Jews were wandering away to the ends of the earth" as a major impulse behind the compilation of the Mishnah. Similar upheavals in the RaMBaM's lifetime may have impelled him to his own monumental halakhic achievements, attained despite his claim that his mind was "frequently trou-bled by the calamities of our times and God's decree that we should suffer exile and wandering in the world from one end of the heavens to the other."[1] For the towering twelfth-century scholar, the personal experience of exile was both a cause for pessimism about the possibilities for contemporary scholar-ship and an impetus for unparalleled intellectual accomplishment.

Despite its own geographical mobility, the Portuguese Jewish community in seventeenth-century Amsterdam would appear to have enjoyed an envi-ronment far removed from the negative experiences associated with *galut*. Here Jews were tolerated, permitted to worship freely, allowed to prosper, rarely humiliated or harmed by their neighbors. One might assume that the theme of exile would not be a major preoccupation of the community or its rabbinic leadership. In fact, however, we encounter *galut* as a powerful pres-ence in many of Morteira's sermons, especially in his unpublished manu-scripts. Regular listeners could not avoid hearing about it for very long. As we have seen in chapter four, occasionally Morteira emphasized the uniqueness of Amsterdam and highlighted the absence there of the oppressive conditions

---

1. *Mishneh Torah, introduction; Commentary on the Mishnah: Uqtsin*, postscript; both cited by Isadore Twersky, "The Mishneh Torah of Maimonides," in *Proceedings of the Israel Academy of Sciences and Humanities* 5:10 (Jerusalem, 1976): 276–77 (reprinted in *Studies in Jewish Law and Philosophy* (New York, 1982), pp. 87–88; *Introduction to the Code of Maimonides (Mishneh Torah)* (New Haven, 1980), pp. 63–64. Cf. Joseph Garçon's sermon, translated in Saperstein, *Jewish Preaching*, pp. 202–3.

suffered by Jews in every other community throughout the world,[2] but this was unusual. The main thrust of his message—reiterated month after month and year after year—was to remind his listeners that they were living in a prolonged and bitter exile under the power of a people that hated them, the descendants of the biblical Edom, and at the same time to reassure his listeners that this exile did not invalidate their relationship with God and to explain how God's providential protection continued even at the present time. The many complex aspects of this theme, and the ways in which they are integrated into the homiletical fabric of the sermons, are the subjects of the present chapter.

It is important to emphasize that we are not analyzing here a systematic treatise on a specific topic in Jewish religious thought. The internal consistency one looks for in a unified speculative work is not to be expected in sermons delivered over a period of more than thirty years. The exegetical issues presented by the verse from the Torah lesson, the occasion in the liturgical calendar, and the preacher's perception of the needs of the moment all colored his decisions about what to emphasize in any particular sermon. We are on firmest ground analyzing a specific sermon as a discrete literary text produced at an identifiable historical moment; our standing is more tenuous when we try to reconstruct a doctrine by weaving together passages from many different sources. Nevertheless, we can indeed find certain themes highlighted and frequently reiterated in the corpus of Morteira's preaching; together those themes enable us to understand the aspects of this doctrine he wanted to communicate to his congregation.

Several sermons are particularly important in presenting Morteira's outlook on exile, and I shall refer to them in detail. Among them are three that undertake to explicate different biblical similes used in divine promises for the future of the Jewish people. The first, delivered in 1622 or 1623, is on God's pledge to Jacob in Genesis 28:14: *Your descendants shall be as the dust of the earth; you shall spread out to the west and to the east, to the north and to the south; all the families of the earth shall bless themselves by you and your descendants.*[3] The second, delivered in late 1631, is on Jacob's report of God's promise in Genesis 32:13, *You have said, "I will deal bountifully with you and make your offspring as the sands of the sea, which are too numerous to count."* The third, dating from a year or two later, is on Moses' description of the Israelites in Deuteronomy 1:10 (which echoes God's promise to Abraham in Genesis 15:5), *The Eternal your God has multiplied you until you are today as numerous as the stars in the sky.*

---

2. See above, pp. 135–36, and the full text below, pp. 402–4.

3. Translated below, beginning p. 380.

It would appear that these verses should serve better as cornerstones for a discussion of redemption than of exile. While the specific context of Moses' statement applies to his own lifetime, each of the three phrases resonates as a blessing for a glorious future, in two cases (sand, stars) suggesting a population beyond counting, in the third case (dust), geographical expansion to the point of filling the world. The predictable reaction of Jews after hearing each of these phrases read from the Bible is that its promise has not yet been fulfilled. Morteira, following the direction pointed by rabbinic midrash, transmutes the images to make them apply to the current condition of exile. The glory of the future vision is certainly diminished as the promise is shown to apply to the present; yet at the same time, something of the luster of eschatological assurance serves to illuminate the darker aspects of life in *galut*.

"Exile, which is a type of death"

A good example of this transforming process can be seen in a general statement on exile from the sermon on the lesson *Devarim,* selected for inclusion in the 1645 edition of *Giv'at Sha'ul.* The theme-verse for the sermon, Deuteronomy 1:10, compares the Jews to stars, denoting abundant population and connoting exalted stature. But the preaching occasion for this lesson is the Sabbath preceding the Ninth Day of Ab, the paradigmatic day of mourning associated with destruction and expulsion in the Jewish past. The mood in which the verse was to be discussed is therefore not celebratory but somber. The sermon's introduction is already in a minor key, starting with a treatment of the suffering of Job and proceeding to compare it with the suffering of the Jewish people in exile, both of which illustrate the claim that the greater the stature of the individual who is afflicted, the greater will be his distress. At this point the theme-verse is unexpectedly adduced, with the assurance that "the Jews are like the stars in every respect." But "in accordance with the mood of this Sabbath today, the Sabbath of Lamentations," the issue to be explored will be not the radiant light of the stars but the reasons the light from the eternal stars is sometimes concealed from human sight. This serves as an emblem for the Jewish people in exile, Israel in eclipse—still eternal, its luminous quality no longer readily visible.

The first reason Morteira offers for the concealment of the stars relies upon the ancient model of the universe: the stars regularly descend beneath the horizon. "From our perspective, there is no greater abasement and descent than this," for the lofty stars are removed from their proper place, covered by the mundane element of earth.

A similar descent and fall occurred to the Jewish people when they were removed from their land and went into exile, in which aspects of sword, famine, and disease are to be found, as I have explained in another sermon of mine on this scriptural lesson, which I entitled *From Heaven to Earth* (Lam. 2:1). My purpose there was to teach that just as human councilors and judges have a kind of punishment that is somewhat unusual, not death, which they use to punish those deserving of the death penalty, substituting this punishment for death when for whatever reason they do not want to take the person's life, so God has this punishment of exile. As God took an oath to the Jewish people that He would not utterly destroy them, He cannot exterminate them. He therefore substitutes for their death this punishment of exile, which is a kind, a type, of death. For in it are to be found aspects of sword, disease, and famine, as the Sages said, noting that a life of wandering diminishes three things: fame, offspring, and fortune [Gen. Rabbah 39,11]. There we explained at length and in detail how these three tribulations are present in exile. And especially in *our* exile, which is not similar to someone who travels from place to place on earth, but rather similar to someone who falls from the heavens to the very lowest place on earth.[4]

It is indeed unfortunate that the sermon to which Morteira refers, "From Heaven to Earth," is no longer extant among the manuscripts; it would undoubtedly have provided us with a detailed presentation of *galut* as Morteira considered it to be relevant to the experience of his listeners.[5] Even from this brief summary, the bleakness of the presentation is apparent. Reaffirming the traditional doctrine of exile as divine punishment,[6] Morteira

---

4. *GS, Devarim,* Deut. 1:10, (1645, p. 68a–b, 1912, p. 253); the concluding phrase (*taḥtiyot ha-arets*) echoes Isa. 44:23 and Ezek. 26:20 (it is unclear to me whether these verses were ever used to refer to the "Low Countries" or the "Netherlands"). On this concept of *galut,* cf. Joseph Hayyun, on the "descent from their stature and their possessions [in *galut*]... punishments worse to the Jews than death" (cited in Haim Hillel Ben-Sasson, "Galut u-Ge'ulah be-Einav shel Dor Golei Sefarad," in *Sefer Yovel le-Yitshaq Baer* [Jerusalem, 1960], p. 217). Philo described exile, which perpetuates misery rather than ending it, as equivalent to a thousand deaths (*Abraham* 64, cited in Erich S. Gruen, *Diaspora* [Cambridge, 2002], pp. 233–34). The beginning and end of the passage cited from Morteira (omitting the references to a previous sermon), together with substantial additional material from the sermon, was appropriated without attribution by Moses Edrehi and published under his name in *Yad Mosheh* (Amsterdam, 1809); see p. 13b–c there. See p. 31, above.

5. The summary of the sermon's content in *GS* 1645, p. 111a, is less detailed than the passage here. That summary reveals that its theme-verse was Deuteronomy 1:8, and that it was therefore delivered two or three years previously.

6. Note the statement by Miriam Bodian that the Portuguese émigrés were "not inclined to content themselves with traditional notions of exile as punishment:" "Biblical Hebrews

presents the experience of *galut* not just as geographical displacement but also as metaphysical plummet; the preacher's formulation must have resonated with the motif of fallen angels and, for those brought up in a Christian environment, the myth of Lucifer.[7] It is not actual death—that would be a violation of the covenant—but a type of death, entailing both profound suffering (sword, disease, famine) and the loss of sources of fulfillment and pleasure (fame, offspring, fortune).[8] The melancholy picture is certainly in keeping with the mood of the "Sabbath of Lamentations."

The explication of the rabbinic statement that a life of wandering diminishes fortune, which Morteira says he discussed at length in the lost sermon "From Heaven to Earth," can be reconstructed from passages in other homilies. Preaching on the first two lessons in the book of Exodus, Morteira frequently presented the enslavement of the Israelites in Egypt as a paradigm, type, or prefiguration of subsequent exiles. This homiletical strategy for connecting the biblical past with the present informs a powerful sermon called "The People's Envy," delivered early in 1622: God used the "Egyptian exile" to teach the Jewish people "lessons of great import, extremely beneficial to us in this current exile. These lessons might even alleviate the misfortunes that weigh upon us."[9] The following week, in his sermon on *Va-Era,* he returned to this motif. The experience in Egypt prefigures all subsequent exiles,[10] but especially the current exile, which is unique. "In no other exile were

and the Rhetoric of Republicanism: Seventeenth-Century Portuguese Jews on the Jewish Community," *AJS Review* 22:2 (1997): 203. This raises the methodological problem of the relationship between the sermon and the beliefs and ideas of the listeners (discussed above, p. 143). Morteira certainly does maintain the traditional view, although he expands it as noted below; was he representing the beliefs of the audience or speaking against them?

7. The continuation of the passage links the precipitous decline of the Jews with the statement in b. *Ḥagigah* 5b: "Rabbi [Judah] was once holding the Book of Lamentations and reading therein: when he came to the verse, *He has cast down from heaven to earth* (Lam. 2:1), it fell from his hands. He said, 'From a roof so high to a pit so deep!'" (*GS* 1645, p. 68b, 1912, p. 253).

8. Cf. the formulation of Joseph Hayyun, in his commentary on Ps. 59:12: "He punished them with two punishments: first, uprootedness and dislocation ... and second, He brought them down from their stature and their possessions, for these punishments are more severe to them than death." Quoted in Abraham Gross, *R. Yosef ben Avraham Ḥayyun* (Ramat Gan, 1993), p. 40.

9. Saperstein, *Jewish Preaching*, p. 273; MS 3:187r, *GS* 1645, p. 23c, 1912, p. 109. The entire sermon expresses important aspects of Morteira's view of *galut* and the appropriate behavior of Jews living in exile.

10. This central idea in Morteira's sermons is linked here with an acrostic interpretation in which the letter *tsaddi* in *Mitsrayim* stands for Nebuchadnezzer (representing Babylonia, the linguistic connection is with the element *tsar*, enemy), the *mem* for Medea, the *yod* for

the Jews dispersed and isolated throughout the entire world.... Furthermore, in this exile we have always been going from one reversal to the next; throughout its duration, none of us has ever owned enough land for a foot to tread on (cf. Deut. 2:5). These are distinctive elements not present in any other exile." The connection is then made with the biblical model:

> All this the Israelites tasted in Egypt. The dispersal we see in the verse, *The people scattered throughout the land of Egypt* (Exod. 5:12).... And the lack of ownership in Pharaoh's command, *No straw shall be issued to you, but you must produce your quota of bricks* (Exod. 5:18), so that they had to go and gather stubble for straw (Exod. 5:12). This is a prefiguration of the Jews at this time, who have to go out each morning, day after day, to gather stubble as they can find it, or as God provides for them.[11]

This is a rather surprising characterization of contemporary Jewish life, coming from a preacher in Amsterdam whose congregants included some extremely wealthy men. Indeed, it presents a stark contrast with the previous week's sermon, which lambasted the congregation for their ostentatious display of wealth in excessively large homes, ornate dress, and lavish banquets.[12] The biblical language generates a rhetoric of hyperbole in describing the current conditions of exile, but this characterization could not be unrecognizable to the listeners. The passage is a reminder that many in the community did indeed suffer economic hardship, and that the wealthy merchants whose behavior had been criticized the previous week represented only a part of the Portuguese nation in Amsterdam.[13]

For those who were more prosperous, the preacher provided reminders that exile was a reality from which there was no simple escape. In "The People's Envy," he insisted that ostentatious behavior inappropriate for outsiders

Yavan (Greece) and the *resh* for Rome. Morteira cited this acrostic numerous times; cf. *GS* 1645, p. 28d, 1912, p. 126 (*Bo*, Exod. 10:1, one of his earliest sermons, ca. 1619); MS 2:19r, *Shemot,* Exod. 1:10, mid-1620s. And cf. the similar acrostic attributed to his "teacher," Elijah Montalto, MS 3:321b, *Toledot,* Gen. 25:25, mid-1620s.

11. MS 3:189r, *Va-Era,* Exod. 6:6, 1622.

12. Saperstein, *Jewish Preaching,* pp. 276–85.

13. A report by an economic advisor in Madrid made in 1619, based on his experience as a merchant visiting Amsterdam, stated that most of the 600 Jewish heads of families in Amsterdam and Rotterdam were poor, there being only about a dozen Dutch Jews who could be considered substantial international merchants. See Jonathan Israel, *Empires and Entrepots* (London, 1990), p. 359. For the problems raised by the immigration of impoverished Jews to Amsterdam, and the efforts of the Portuguese community's leadership to induce them to travel elsewhere, see Bartal and Kaplan, "'Aliyat 'Aniyim me-Amsterdam le-Erets Yisra'el, esp. pp. 175–79.

in a land where they were tolerated as guests set into motion forces that produced resentment, hostility, and expulsion. This had been the pattern of Jewish communities in the past; by implication it was the danger for the Jews in Amsterdam as well.[14] The wealthy were also subject to "the taxes and levies and confiscations of money that the nations impose upon us in this long exile."[15] And in an early sermon, delivered on Shavu'ot 1619, Morteira emphasized the uncertainties and insecurities of the commercial life upon which the Portuguese community's economic well-being was based:

> We are as despised and vile as [the enslaved Israelites] are. This is because one of the curses is, *Your life shall hang in doubt before you . . . and you shall have no assurance of survival* (Deut. 28:66), which the Sages interpreted to apply to one who buys wheat for a year (Esth. Rab. Proem 1). This refers to their not allowing us to own fields and vineyards. In this way, our lives hang in doubt before us—regarding commercial ventures and opportunities—as is well known to this distinguished audience.[16]

To counteract their insecure status, Jewish leaders appealed to the Christian power structure, arguing for toleration and emphasizing the economic value to the host country of Jewish involvement in international commerce. A letter that may have been written just a year or two before this sermon was delivered stated that "since the Portuguese nation came to this country with their trade and shipping, the country has enjoyed large profits.... [The Jews] carry to other countries products of this country.... Many poor people here earn their livelihood through them, such as laborers, artisans, skippers, and

---

14. Saperstein, *Jewish Preaching*, pp. 273–74.

15. MS 2:58r, *Va-Yetse*, Gen. 32:21.

16. MS 2:223r, Deut. 16:10, Shavu'ot 1619. It is unclear whether Morteira is speaking of a prohibition against Jewish purchase of land in Holland or generalizing about European practice in the late Middle Ages. For the background of medieval restrictions against Jewish ownership of land, see Baron, *SRHJ*, 12:29–31. The Jews of Amerstam were not prevented from owning houses; see Herbert Bloom, *The Economic Activities of the Jews of Amsterdam in the Seventeenth and Eighteenth Centuries* (Williamsport, 1937), pp. 64–65. Occasionally, Jews did purchase other pieces of land; for a later example (1659), see Bloom, p. 66. As for international commerce, the uncertainties were often of a political nature. Merchants in the audience would have known that the truce between Spain and Holland, which made commerce possible, was due to expire in 1621. Indeed, with the expiration of the truce, merchants who traded with Spain and Portugal were deemed to be aiding the enemy, and cargos on ships belonging to members of the community were confiscated. See Vlessing, "New Light on the Earliest History of the Amsterdam Portuguese Jews," p. 71 n. 84.

other occupations."[17] This positive spin notwithstanding, the message to the Jews was otherwise: in the internal context of the sermon, the restrictions against owning real estate and the need to rely on the instabilities and vagaries of trade were perceived and presented as a negative aspect of *galut* quite familiar even to the wealthiest of the listeners.[18]

Another negative aspect was humiliation. The Sephardi community of Jews was fiercely proud of its status within the Jewish people. They thought of themselves as the aristocracy of Israel, descended from its royal leadership, *the exiles of Jerusalem that are in Sepharad* (Obad. 20). For these Jews, conceptions of honor, reinforced by attitudes and values of the Iberian peninsula, were of paramount importance. Morteira frequently discussed the importance of honor, as in yet another sermon for the "Sabbath of Lamentations" that has been lost. The description in the 1645 edition of *Giv'at Sha'ul* states, "Its content is to explain how the most exalted possession a man can have is his true honor, and no greater evil can befall him than when this is lost, and this is the essence of our punishment in exile."[19] Athough the disappearance of the manuscript containing detailed discussion is indeed unfortunate, we can see from other passages that one of the most painful aspects of life in exile is the humiliation endured by the Jews.

As we have seen in the previous chapter, Morteira's mode of typological interpretation led him to read accounts of Jacob's relationship with Esau as a prototype for Jewish exile under Christianity. In one of his first sermons on the lesson *Va-Yishlaḥ*, delivered ca. 1620, he maintains that the Jewish people was given over into the power of Esau (namely, Edom, Rome, Christianity) five times because of the five times Jacob referred to himself as a "servant."

---

17. Cited in Vlessing, "New Light," p. 58. Note also the very different valence later given to the absence of Jewish landholding by Menasseh ben Israel in his letter to Oliver Cromwell: "The Jews have no opportunity to live in their own Country, to till the Lands or other like employments, give themselves wholy unto merchandizing, and for contriving new Inventions, no Nation almost going beyond them. And so 'tis observed, that wheresoever they go to dwell, there presently the Traficq begins to florish" (Paul Mendes-Flohr and Jehuda Reinharz, eds., *The Jew in the Modern World* [Oxford, 1995], p. 10).

18. Several years later, Morteira returned to this theme in a discussion generated by Pharaoh's dream but bearing undeniable resonance for the merchants in the audience. The first condition of true abundance, he maintains, is that a population does not depend on "ships and caravans" for what it needs to eat. "For the expectation of waiting for these ships and caravans, the anxiety and uncertainty that are obvious from the misadventures of travel—for all roads are presumed to be dangerous (Eccles. Rabbah 3,2)—these considerably diminish the excellence of abundance" (MS 5:111r, *Mi-Qets*, Gen. 41:2, 1625. Cf. b. *Menaḥot* 103b and above, n. 16.

19. *GS* 1645, p. 99b.

The final time was in Genesis 33:14, *Let my lord go ahead of his servant.* For this unnecessary expression of self-abasement, God punished the Jewish people with the present exile under the children of Edom, an exile that "exceeds all its predecessors both in length and in harshness:"

> No earlier exile was as long as this, nor were the Jews as despised and debased in the eyes of the Gentile nations as they are today: a proverb and a byword. All this is hinted in these two formulations. He said, *Let [my lord] pass before* (Gen. 33:14), teaching about the extreme length that would pass before him before sovereignty would come to him. And he said, *[pass before] his servant* (Gen. 33:14), [referring to him] in the third person, teaching about the contempt and debasement in one who speaks without using the second person, who is afraid to use the second person when he addresses his master. So this very day, many nobles consider it contemptible to speak with a single Jew.[20]

It is not easy to assess the resonance of this reference to humiliating treatment of Jews by Christian notables, for it does not seem to reflect the realities of contemporary Amsterdam. Was it intended to elicit an experience familiar to the Portuguese New Christians on the Iberian peninsula? Or was it perhaps an allusion to Morteira's own experience with Dr. Elijah Montalto in the court of France?[21] In either case, it is presented as one of the defining characteristics of life in exile for the contemporary Jew.

An even more graphic depiction of Jewish degradation is given in a sermon from ca. 1640 on the lesson *Balaq.* The preacher begins with an evocation of the inherent honor of the Jewish people, a quality which persists even in the period of exile.

> All these are signs, unambiguous and obvious for anyone who cares to look at them, of the natural honor that God has established in this nation. For even in its abasement and its exile, it displays its strength and its true nature. And especially this nation, *the exiles of Jerusalem who*

---

20. MS 3:10r, *Va-Yishlah,* Gen. 32:5, ca. 1620. The point is that it was bad enough for Jacob to refer to himself as a "servant," but using the expression "his servant" rather than "your servant" when addressing Esau was a further means of self-abasement. The claim that the Jews were the most vilified and despised nation on earth and that the greatest possible insult was to call somebody a Jew was used for polemical purposes in Portuguese *auto-da-fé* sermons; see Glaser, "Invitation to Intolerance," p. 361. Cf. also MS 3:307v, *Ha'azinu,* Deut. 32:21, 1641, on the devastating impact of relatively insignificant affronts such as not permitting Jews to sit in the presence of a Gentile or speaking contemptuously of Jews (translated below, p. 514.

21. On Elijah Montalto and the period with Morteira in Paris, see above, chap. 1, n. 4.

are in Sepharad (Obad. 20). For because they were from the tribe of royalty, God exiled them among peoples in whose midst they would more easily preserve the rules of their honor, because of patterns of honor those peoples practiced among themselves. About them, the Bible said, *Even if He were to banish you to the ends of the heavens [from there the Eternal your God will gather you]* (Deut. 30:4).[22]

This is indeed an upbeat, positive message. But then, after turning to criticize the excessive pursuit of vainglory, Morteira portrays the experience of Jews in more somber hues:

Now when the persecutors of the Jews recognized the honor naturally implanted in their stock, they tortured and afflicted them by removing this honor, in order to make their name synonymous with absolute disgrace, humiliating them in every possible way. They portrayed the faces of the Jews in bizarre caricatures, setting up their portraits as a permanent symbol to scandalize all who come by, for they know that in an honorable soul, these forms of degradation have a powerful effect.[23]

This passage too seems to evoke something familiar to the audience that we cannot easily identify. Certainly the depiction of Jews in bizarre caricatures intended for public humiliation does not reflect the sympathetic portraits in Amsterdam by Rembrandt and his colleagues. Nor was there an established tradition of caricature on the Iberian peninsula or in Italy at this time; even in blatantly hostile portrayals of ritual murder or desecration of the host, the Jews are generally depicted as human beings, often with a rather noble visage.[24] The tradition of caricature with its bizarre exaggeration of Jewish features, which later became a staple of modern antisemitism, seems to have taken root in sixteenth-century Germany.[25] The extent to which this would have been

---

22. MS 1:103v, *Balaq*, Num. 22:14, early 1640s.

23. MS 1:104r, as in previous note.

24. See, for example, the picture of "Jews desecrating a Host," included by B. Netanyahu in *The Origins of the Inquisition,* following p. 810. For a more extended treatment, see Bernhard Blumenkranz, *Le juif médiéval au miroir de l'art chrétien* (Paris, 1966), pp. 23–28, for portrayal of Jews engaged in "wicked" activities, but without caricature of their appearance, and pp. 29–33 for the beginnings of caricature.

25. See Eduard Fuchs, *Die Juden in der Karikatur* (Munich, 1921); a clear example from the early seventeenth century is on p. 22. Cf. Joshua Trachtenberg, *The Devil and the Jews* (Philadelphia, 1983), frontispiece, p. 195; Isaiah Shachar, *The Judensau* (London, 1974), passim; Nadler, *Rembrandt's Jews,* pp. 62–63 (emphasizing the novelty of seventeenth-century Dutch art).

familiar to Morteira's Portuguese audience remains to be established. Yet the impression left by this passage is that the preacher is exposing a raw and sensitive nerve.

In addition to humiliation, Morteira speaks of hatred for the Jews as endemic to their situation in exile. Sometimes this hatred is attributed to Jewish behavior. In the 1622 sermon "The People's Envy," mentioned above, the arrogant conduct of the Israelites in Egypt inspired envy and contempt, which led in turn to persecution. And the same pattern is reenacted in the current exile: "God despises [the behavior of the Jews], and He makes the Gentiles among whom they are exiled despise them."[26] Indeed, he argues in a different sermon from about the same time, if Pharaoh tried to kill the Jews because he was threatened by their numbers, "all the more would they try to do this today because of their great hate for us."[27] Elsewhere Morteira explains the hatred of Jews in a manner that does not suggest Jewish shortcomings or sinfulness. It is rather attributed to divine providence, and it serves not to punish Jews but to preserve their identity. This point is made in a 1621 sermon on the lesson *Bo:*

> It is well known how intense love is generated among friends by eating and drinking together. Therefore, in order to keep us at a distance and separate from the other nations, God commanded us not to eat with them, for eating together leads easily to close attachments. From this matter is derived the hatred of the nations for us.[28]

In this passage, the dietary laws are explained as fulfilling God's intention to guarantee a measure of social segregation between Jews and Gentiles under conditions of exile. The inability to eat together not only prevents the development of bonds of friendship but engenders the antithetical emotion of hatred.

In a later sermon, hatred is presented not as a natural byproduct of either inappropriate Jewish behavior or of the regimen imposed by the commandments, but as the direct providential creation of God, in deliberate violation of the natural order. The preacher outlines in detail those aspects of Jewish character and lineage that would naturally be expected to arouse admiration and love. Such feelings among the Gentile neighbors would lead to intimate relations that would threaten Jewish identity and survival as a distinct group.

---

26. *Jewish Preaching,* p. 284.

27. MS 3:249v, *Va-Yetse*, Gen. 29:14, 1622 or 1623.

28. MS 3:112r *Bo*, Exod. 10:3, 1621. For the impact of dietary regulations on social interaction between Jews and Gentiles, see Jacob Katz, *Tradition and Crisis* (New York, 1993), p. 20.

However, foreseeing this natural danger, God removed it from us and generated in the hearts of these nations, a great unnatural hatred, totally unprecedented, so that they would despise us and set us at a distance from them. Lest they seduce us with their honors, God ensured that they would set us aside like a menstruous woman in her impurity—all for our own benefit and to ensure our survival up to this day.[29]

The idea that it is hatred of the Jews, engendered by their separatist religious rites, that makes possible their survival would appear again two generations later, freed from its providential context, in the work of the student whom Morteira ultimately joined in banning from the community, Benedict Spinoza.[30] In its original homiletical context, the doctrine is rather more complex than Spinoza's presentation of it. Morteira insists that according to nature, Jews would inspire the utmost esteem and affection, a claim that would hearten listeners harboring doubts about the value of Jewish identity. But the impact of the assertion that hatred for the Jews is endemic to exile because it is part of God's plan is harder to assess. Did it fit the experience of the listeners in Portugal, or in Holland? Were they more comforted by the assurance that God looked out for the well-being of the Jews, or disturbed by the claim that nothing they could do would alleviate the hostility of their neighbors? The impact of these words might have varied with the experience of each individual.

Whatever effect the preacher was attempting to produce in this passage, in others he articulates the impact of the exile experience in unambiguously devastating terms. The combination of its length and severity have produced demoralization, despondency, even despair in the hearts of many Jews, who wonder whether it is worth the price of maintaining a separate existence. One expression of such despair is in our sermon for the "Sabbath of Lamentation," on Deuteronomy 1:10, called "The Stars of Heaven:"

So with the Jewish people: the multitude of their afflictions, the length of their exile, the enormity of their distress leads them to say, "Would that we had never been," or "If only we could be like one of the Gentile

---

29. *GS* 1645, p. 90a, *Ha'azinu,* Deut. 32:12, early 1630s; see below, p. 481.

30. "They [the Jews] have separated themselves from other nations to such a degree as to incur the hatred of all... through external rites alien to the rites of other nations..." Note that God is removed as the agent in this formulation. He goes on to say, in agreement with Morteira, "That they are preserved largely through the hatred of other nations is demonstrated by historical fact." Spinoza, *Theological-Political Treatise,* p. 45. See the full sermon below, pp. 481–82, n. 83.

nations, like the other peoples on earth, for whom divine punishment never lasts so long." They are at such point that they would, with little exaggeration, choose absolute annihilation over the suffering of all the great afflictions they have experienced, and their continuing to experience every disease and plague which is (not) written in the Torah, as is known from previous generations, and as has been experienced by our brothers in our own time.[31]

The reference to "our brothers" as the contemporary proof for the disastrous consequences of the exile suggests that he is referring to the experience of other Jews, not those in the congregation. Yet he expresses a reaction with which the listeners were expected to empathize.

Morteira presents other negative effects of exile more moderately, describing them not as a direct but as an indirect consequence, an incidental harm. This distinction is central to a sermon on the lesson *Mattot* from the summer of 1630 or shortly thereafter. The essential impairments that come from Jewish exile are connected with a rabbinic interpretation of a verse from Jeremiah: "*Give honor to the Eternal your God, before it grows dark* (Jer. 13:16): before it becomes dark to you for lack of words of Torah, before it becomes dark to you for lack of words of prophecy" (Lam. Rabbah, Proem 25). The preacher unpacks each of these phrases: "lack of words of Torah" refers to the loss of Jewish government and self-determination, "the absence of the Sanhedrin, the subjection to an exile of captivity, the loss of wealth, and all the misfortunes that beset the exile;" "lack of words of prophecy" encompasses "all aspects of sanctity and godliness that have been lost to us because of the exile."[32] But in addition to these essential characteristics of exile, there are subsidiary repercussions. Jews suffer in exile not only because they must be punished to atone for their sins, but because, by being away from their proper

---

31. *GS* 1645, p. 68a, 1912, p. 252, *Devarim*, Deut. 1:10. I read the negative *lo* before "written in the Torah" as a euphemistic avoidance of saying something that might arouse the "evil eye." This passage is incorporated almost verbatim, without attribution in a sermon for the "Sabbath of Lamentations" by Moses Edrehi, *Darash Mosheh* (Amsterdam, 1809), p. 10c, section starting *e-me-'atah*. On this theme of despair about redemption, see Joseph Hacker, "Ha-Ye'ush min ha-Ge'ulah ve-ha-Tiqvah ha-Meshiḥit be-Khitvei R. Shelomoh le-Veit ha-Levi mi-Saloniqah," *Tarbiẓ* 39 (1969–70): 195–213.

32. MS 2:200r–200v, *Mattot*, Num. 30:10, ca. 1630. Of course this includes the loss of prophecy itself. In a sermon on *Balaq* delivered a few years later than this, Morteira explained that God ended prophecy during the period of exile in order to protect the Jewish people from being deceived in their hope for redemption by false prophets who could not be distinguished from those with an authentic message: MS 2:262v, *Balaq*, Num 22:10, early 1630s.

home, they are ineluctably bound up with the fate and fortunes of their host nation:

> In addition to the essential pain, the punishments that come to us because of our sins, we are to suffer . . . the damage deriving from the people and the state under which we are subjected, for their misfortune intensifies our own punishment beyond its essential nature. For example, if (heaven forbid!) war or pestilence is decreed upon the inhabitants of a certain land because of their sin, the Jews who are in their midst will be harmed with them, because we are there among them, just as a plague caused by stagnant air will harm whoever is there, which would not occur if he were somewhere else. This would not happen to us if we were in our own land.[33]

Exile thus subjects the Jewish people to a double indemnity. Jews suffer the punishment they deserve, imposed upon them by divine providence, but they also suffer incidentally because they happen to be in lands that are being afflicted. Jewish destiny in exile is determined not only by the behavior of Jews, but by forces totally beyond their control.

Up to this point we have noted aspects of exile as experienced by the masses of Jews. Other passages in the sermons reflect the perspective of the religious leader on contemporary Jewish behavior. Like most preachers, Morteira occasionally criticizes the members of his congregation for their failure to observe all the requirements imposed by Jewish law; here we shall refer to only a few passages in which the connection with exile is explicit. The problem is one of influence: living in a Gentile environment, the Jews adopt behavioral patterns that make them similar to their neighbors in undesirable ways—despite God's commandments intended to preserve their distinctiveness. Morteira introduces this theme in an early sermon on *Va-Yetse,* in which

---

33. MS 2:200v, *Mattot,* Num. 30:10, ca. 1630. Morteira continues by applying to this the rabbinic statement, "Whoever lives outside the land [of Israel] is similar to one who has no God" (B. *Ketubot* 110b). His interpretation defuses the radical theological import of this perennially problematic hyperbole: since the fate of Jews in exile is bound up with the fate of their host nations, "it seems as if they are governed by the gods of the nations, and have no private God of their own, heaven forbid!" There is an interplay, perhaps not worked out in a fully consistent manner, between providential punishment of the nations (war or plague is decreed because of their sins) and natural causality (anyone living in a place where the air is bad will suffer). It is not impossible that Morteira's reference to plague in this passage alluded to the plague that devastated Venice around the time this sermon was delivered; Morteira refers explicitly to this plague and its impact on him personally in a note dated 18 Kislev 5391 [November 24, 1630]: MS 3:178b, *Va-Yishlah,* Gen. 32:7 (cited above, p. 70, n. 4).

he establishes the principle that the patriarchal narratives are typological pre-figurations of subsequent Jewish history. Genesis 26:15 is interpreted to hint of a cultural malaise: "*For all the wells dug by the servants of Abraham,* namely, the fine qualities of character and intellect, *the Philistines stopped up,* meaning, exile did not allow the Jews to cultivate fine qualities, *and filled them with earth* (Gen. 26:15), referring to the destruction of books, and [the development of] repugnant traits, for they assimilated with the Gentiles and learned their ways."[34] This pattern is explained in detail some ten years later in a climactic passage with considerable rhetorical power from the sermon "Like the Stars of Heaven." Morteira reuses the phrase from his earlier typological exegesis, "the exile did not allow the Jews to cultivate fine qualities," but here he adds an ironic twist, "and those fine qualities and character traits that were appropriate for the Jews we now find, to our disgrace, among the most ordinary Gentiles among whom we live."[35] The preacher then proceeds to specify the negative qualities that Jews have learned from their Gentile neighbors, and the positive qualities which they have failed to learn.[36] Exile exposes the Jews to both good and bad models of behavior, but it apparently predisposes them to imitate only the bad.

Even Jews with the best of intentions are hindered by living in Gentile lands; this is another important example of the indirect consequences of exile. Morteira begins by noting that there are some Christian countries where Jews are prevented from observing their faith, forced to transgress the commandments, a reality quite familiar to many in the audience.[37] He then turns to Amsterdam, with its toleration and relative religious freedom:

> Even in a place where they give us permission to keep [our religion] and do not prevent us, unintentionally, accidentally, our weakness becomes

---

34. MS 3:7v *Va-Yetse,* Gen. 28:11, ca. 1620. The phrase *meḥiqat sefarim* might refer to the destruction of Jewish books or to the censoring of passages in them.

35. *GS* 1645, p. 109d, 1912, p. 256: even Gentiles upon whom many Jews would look with disdain have superior moral qualities. On other occasions, Morteira complimented his people for the qualities they preserved despite the harshness of exile. For example, in a sermon on the Sabbath honoring the *Biqqur Ḥolim* Society in 1644, he noted (MS 5:110v, *Mi-Qets,* Gen. 41:17): "Experience proves, for although they are in exile and do not have their own city or state, their charitableness in comparison with their position exceeds that of all other nations. We see this especially with regard to the absolute consistency of this sacred society in fulfilling so many of its religious acts."

36. The passage is cited above, pp. 190–91.

37. For another allusion to this, see MS 3:111r, *Va-Era,* Exod. 6:5, 1621, interpreting *Our hope is lost; we are doomed* (Ezek. 37:11): "*Our hope is lost* because *we are doomed,* meaning because they want to wipe us out not in our bodies but in our souls; this is like the verse, *Waters flowed over my head; I am doomed* (Lam. 3:54)."

apparent when various situations arise before us. It is like an injured limb, the weakness of which becomes apparent when an occasion for use arises, while without such an occasion the damage that has occurred is not even discerned. For example, as much as we are careful about our eating and drinking, we cannot avoid certain forms of improper behavior brought about by the Gentiles in whose midst we live. This is what the prophet said, *So shall the people of Israel eat their bread, unclean, among the nations* (Ezek 4:13). If we go on a journey, the conditions of exile make it burdensome for us, and we fall into several kinds of traps that we do not know how to avoid. And so in the matter of the levirate marriage and similar issues pertaining to marriage: the exile causes us various forms of torment and sorrow because of the near impossibility of observing these properly, which is due not to the nature of the laws but to the persecution and dispersal that has occurred to us.[38]

Here the emphasis is quite different from Morteira's occasional rebukes of his listeners for their religious and ethical shortcomings. Rather than condemning the failings of the people he highlights the constraints imposed by the realities of *galut* even on those who want to be faithful.

Talmudic legislation prohibited Jews from eating bread baked by a Gentile, but conditions of the medieval and early modern Jewish community often made it unfeasible for Jews to maintain their own bakeries. Rabbinical authorities tended toward a lenient stance, providing a legal fiction (by throwing a wooden chip into the oven, a Jewish woman would be considered to be baking bread jointly with the Gentile baker), but the boundary lines were often difficult to enforce, and there was a tacit acknowledgment that the law could not be properly observed.[39] Traveling often entailed the need to stay and eat at inns owned by Gentiles, and it was not a simple matter to negotiate the complex rules governing a journey that included a Sabbath.[40] The problems for the observance of marital law, including the law of levirate marriage, pervade

---

38. MS 2:200v–201r, *Mattot*, Num. 30:10, ca. 1630.

39. M. *'Avodah Zarah* 2,6, b. *'Avodah Zarah* 38b, Tosafot there, *va'ata*; Maimonides, *Code, Hilkhot Ma'akalot Asurot* 17:12–13; R. Asher on b. *'Avodah Zarah*, chap. 2, sect. 33; Judah ben Asher, *Zikhron Yehudah* (Berlin, 1846), p. 45b (the sermon at Toledo by Todros ha-Levi Abulafia; see Saperstein, "The Preaching of Repentance," p. 164); Katz, *Exclusiveness and Tolerance*, p. 40.

40. See Jacob Katz, *The "Shabbes Goy"* (Philadelphia, 1989), pp. 35–48 on travel and the Sabbath (with sources from the medieval period); idem, *Tradition and Crisis*, p. 280 n. 8. For a later example of the dangers encountered by Jews interrupting their journey for the Sabbath, see Dan Manor, *Galut u-Ge'ulah be-Hagut Ḥakhmei Maroqoh ba-Me'ot ha-Yod-Zayin–Yod-Ḥet* (Lod, 1988), p. 104.

the responsa literature that pertains to the *conversos:* What was to be done with a couple in Amsterdam if the husband died without a son, and his brother—required by law to marry the woman or to free her through a ri tual to marry someone else—was living as a Christian back in Portugal? [41] These were problems that taxed the ingenuity of rabbinic leaders and engendered the frustrating awareness that even under optimal conditions—such as pertained in Amsterdam—Jewish life in exile was highly problematic.

Providential Protection

The material presented to this point presents a bleak picture of Jewish life over a period of more than 1500 years. Morteira maintains that even under the best of circumstances, such as prevailed in Amsterdam, the conditions of exile ineluctably produce severe problems. Permitted to prosper, the Jews' behavior arouses the envy and anger of their neighbors, leading to hostility and expulsion. Allowed to observe their religion freely, they are unable to avoid transgression of its norms. And Amsterdam is the fortunate exception. In most Jewish communities, Jews are subjected to physical persecution, material impoverishment, psychological humiliation. The roles attributed to God in these passages are punisher of sin, source of the commandments that guarantee distance and conflict between Jews and their neighbors, and implanter of an unnatural hatred of Jews in the hearts of the Gentiles to prevent any possibility of social bonding. The unprecedented and inordinate length of the exile blunts the hope that these circumstances will soon change. Hearing this message time and again, what listeners could escape becoming discouraged and despondent about their decision to bind up their personal future with the destiny of the Jewish people? That was not a result any preacher wanted.

Therefore, other elements in the sermons provide a different perspective on exile. Alongside the emphasis on exile as punishment, positive functions appear as an integral part of Morteira's message. These may not change the bleak reality of the experience, but they alter its valence and its psychological significance. Suffering as punishment has little constructive impact, except as an affirmation of divine power and justice. Suffering as atonement and puri-

---

41. There is a huge literature reviewing the responsa on marital problems pertaining to the *conversos.* For the earlier period, see Netanyahu, *The Marranos of Spain,* chap. 2. For a recent review of the legal problems of levirate marriage in the sixteenth and early seventeenth centuries, including the inability of rabbinic leaders to reach a consensus about whether *yibbum* or *ḥalitsah* was preferable, see Howard Adelman, "Custom, Law, and Gender: Levirate Union among Ashkenazim and Sephardim in Italy after the Expulsion from Spain," in *The Expulsion of the Jews: 1492 and After,* ed. Raymond Waddington and Arthur Williamson (New York, 1994), pp. 107–25.

fication, however, may be perceived as having value and serving as a basis for hope. This is the context in which Morteira discusses the financial burdens imposed upon the Jews by the rulers of their host countries. As in many other cases, his point is derived from a typological interpretation of the narrative in *Va-Yishlah* discussing the relationship between Jacob and Esau:

> Throughout the length of our exile, we make an effort to cleanse our sins. For even one quarter of these sins, Israel would deserve destruction; and if they had been committed by the other nations, not even a fugitive remnant would survive. Yet God has converted absolute and sudden destruction into a prolonged punishment, thereby leaving us a surviving remnant. About this, the Bible says, *[Jacob] said, "I will propitiate Him with an offering in advance"*(Gen. 32:21). He was referring in this to God, mentioned above in the phrase, *and He Himself is right behind us* (Gen. 32:19), as we have explained. The phrase *an offering in advance* (Gen. 32:21) refers to the taxes and levies and confiscations of money that the nations impose upon us in this long exile; as a result of these, sins are cleansed and devastation diminished. This is the meaning of *"I will propitiate Him with an offering in advance"*(Gen. 32:21).[42]

There are indeed harsh elements in this passage, particularly the striking (and rather unusual) insistence that the Gentile nations are far *less* sinful than the Jews, and that the commutation of destruction into exile was an act of divine favor that the Jewish people did not really deserve.[43] But the main force of the passage is to present economic oppression, including confiscatory taxes, in a positive light—part of God's plan, encoded in the biblical narrative—to cleanse the sins that require the exile to continue. The money may be paid to Esau, but the one propitiated is God.

A second interpretation of the verse applies it to a different form of suffering: the loss not of property but of life:

> Or it may be that he said, *"I will propitiate Him with an offering in advance"* (Gen. 32:21) in allusion to those who die in every generation as martyrs, sacrificing themselves as an offering to God for the glory of His name, and in this way propitiating the divine anger. This in truth is called a

---

42. MS 5:58r, *Va-Yishlah*, Gen 32:21, mid 1640s. Morteira reprises this passage in his sermon on the following verse (MS 5:59v, *Va-Yishlah*, Gen. 32:22), mid 1640s. Morteira actually wrote "those who hate Israel would deserve destruction," a euphemism to avert misfortune, following one rescension of b. *Sanhedrin* 63a; cf. below, translations of "The Land Shudders," n. 28, and "They Provoked My Jealousy," nn. 41 and 46.

43. Cf. the passage cited above, p. 310.

sacrifice, as we see in the verse, *Bring in my devotees, who made a covenant with Me over sacrifice* (Ps. 50:5), which the Sages interpreted with respect to those killed by the Romans.[44]

Since many in the audience had lost members of their own families to the Portuguese Inquisition, this evocation of martyrdom as a sacrifice to God, cleansing the sins of the people, making possible the end of the tribulations in exile, would have had more than merely theological resonance.

A dominant metaphor for this conception of exile as purification and refinement is the biblical phrase used for Egypt, *an iron blast furnace* (Deut. 4:20). This image is explicated in the 1622 sermon called "The People's Envy": "It affected us the way a blast furnace works upon silver or gold placed within it. These are refined by the removal of all dross, prepared to withstand fire, strengthened for the touchstone and the blows of the hammer. So the calamities of Egypt taught Israel to endure as slaves, thereby preparing her to endure the calamities of later exiles."[45] Part of this process of purification—"the removal of all dross"—pertains not just to the character of the individual Jew but to the ethnic purity of the nation. As we have seen, Morteira believed that those who have assimilated into the Gentile nations during the long exile were descendants of the Edomites forcibly converted to Judaism by John Hyrcanus. The exile thus provides a process of selection, removing from the people those who do not really belong, leaving those who are strongest in their faith. [46]

One of the most important themes, recurring in many different contexts, is

---

44. MS 5:58r, *Va-Yishlah*, Gen 32:21, early 1640s. For the rabbinic interpretation of Ps. 50:5, see Maimonides, *Code, Hilkhot Yesodei ha-Torah* 5:1.

45. *Jewish Preaching*, p. 275; *GS* 1645 p. 23c, 1912 p. 109. Cf. the reiteration of this idea in a sermon delivered more than 20 years later, MS 5:48r, *Va-Yetse*, Gen. 29:7, mid-1640s: "The Egyptian exile was only for the benefit of Israel, purifying them and preparing them to receive the Torah. That is what it was called an *iron blast furnace* (Deut. 4:20), in which [metals] are purified."

46. MS 3:162r, *Ve-Zot ha-Berakhah*, Deut. 33:3. Sabbath of Repentance, 1645. For a similar conception of the purifying function of exile, accomplished through the apostasy of those weaker in faith, see Mordecai Dato, cited in Yoram Jacobson, *Bi-Netivei Galuyot u-Ge'ulot* (Jerusalem, 1996), p. 121. Cf. Morteira's use of the mystery of the "red heifer" as a symbolic expression of the experience of exile (*GS* 1645, p. 62b, 1912, p. 234): "This is also why God commanded that the clothing of all who have contact with the red heifer becomes impure, while it has the capacity to purify clothing. This may allude to the dispersion of the Jews as a consequence of their sins, and to their suffering and their exiles and their loss of numbers, a result of their cleaving to the dross of the Gentiles who resemble them while they are dispersed among them.... Yet those who remain [Jews} will be called 'holy.'"

the insistence that God's providential relationship with the Jewish people has not ended in *galut*. Morteira did not endorse the view that with the exile of the Jews from the land of Israel, their fate was no longer under the control of divine providence but had been abandoned to chance, the ethically neutral forces of nature, the determinism of the stars.[47] God continued to provide for the wellbeing of the Jewish people. The period of open miracles might have ended with the Second Commonwealth, but even though the Jewish people was no longer worthy of such public demonstrations of divine power, "God has not removed from us His great miracles, hidden from the sight of the masses but revealed to the sight of all who are wise in heart."[48] Indeed, the very survival of the Jewish people in exile throughout the centuries is a miraculous sign of God's providence. For it is indeed a great miracle "to sustain the Jewish people among a nation which is so antithetical to it that according to nature it could not endure for even a single hour."[49]

A fundamental expression of God's providential protection, in Morteira's view, is in the realm of material sustenance. Despite the insecurities of life in exile, despite the prohibition against Jews purchasing fields and vineyards, as noted above in the Shavu'ot sermon from 1619, "God has not caused us to want, nor will He do so, forever." And this is a "great wonder": that a people considered so lowly and despicable are sustained in their external needs— eating and drinking and clean clothing.[50] Speaking to a congregation that contained some extremely successful Jews, Morteira thought it important to convince them that their ability to prosper under conditions of exile was the result not of their own ingenuity or efforts, but rather of God's providence. "Expelled from certain countries, we have arrived in others totally destitute," he

---

47. On astral determinism of Jewish destiny in *galut*, see Shalom Rosenberg, "Exile and Redemption in Jewish Thought in the Sixteenth Century: Contending Conceptions," in *Jewish Thought in the Sixteenth Century*, ed. Bernard Cooperman (Cambridge, 1983), pp. 406–7, including statements by Abraham ibn Migash: the Jewish people has been abandoned to their "patrons and their decrees," and to the "accidents of time." Cf. also Ben-Sasson, "Galut u-Ge'ulah," p. 217.

48. *GS* 1645, p. 63b; 1912, p. 238, *Balaq*, Num. 22:13, 1639. Cf. Dato in Jacobson, *Bi-Netivei Galuyot*, p. 128.

49. MS 1:64r, *Be-Midbar*, Num. 1:30, early 1640s. On the idea that the survival of the Jews throughout the centuries of a harsh exile is itself a proof of wondrous providence, cf. Ben-Sasson, "Galut u-Ge'ulah," p. 222, citing Joseph Hayyun, and Joseph Hacker, "Yisra'el ba-Goyyim be-Te'uro shel R. Shelomoh le-Veit ha-Levi," *Zion* 34 (1969): 55.

50. MS 2:223r, Deut. 16:10, Shavu'ot 1619. Morteira may have been influenced in this and other similar passages cited below by Jacob ibn Habib's comment in *'Ein Ya'aqov* on b. *Berakhot* 3a: "Our survival among the seventy nations and our having sufficient food… and clothing… are marvels as great as the splitting of the Red Sea, though they are hidden miracles" (cited by Ben-Sasson, "Galut u-Ge'ulah," p. 222).

reminded them early in 1622, "and God has graciously enabled us to acquire new wealth and possessions."[51] This statement is for the preacher not merely a platitude but a profound religious truth, and Jews ignore it—forgetting they are in exile, assuming they can use their wealth as they please—at their peril.

These points are reiterated in a sermon on *Va-Yishlaḥ,* from the early 1630s, which brings together a number of important themes and demonstrates Morteira's masterful manner of moving from an exegetical problem to a homiletical message. The theme-verse is Genesis 32:14, which I shall translate literally: *He spent the night there, and he took from what came into his hand as an offering to his brother Esau.* As we have seen in chapter three, the central exegetical problem is the ambiguous phrase *from what came into his hand,* and Morteira reviews a dozen earlier interpretations before suggesting his own:

> One might also say that this verse alludes to the way in which this wealth came into the possession of our ancestor Jacob: miraculously, not as a result of his own efforts. For in the natural order, there would have been no way for him to enrich himself. Look at the reasons. He was in a land that was not his. He came there without any funds that could serve as the beginning of successful economic endeavors, as he himself said, *With my staff alone I crossed the Jordan* (Gen. 32:11). The evil inhabitants of that place became envious of him, as we see from the verse, *He heard that Laban's sons were saying, ["Jacob has taken all that was our father's, and all his wealth has come from our father's property"]*(Gen. 31:1). Laban, his father-in-law, treated him with deception and trickery, changing his wages ten times over: *If he said thus,* etc. (cf. Gen. 31:7–8). Yet despite all this, through God's providential lovingkindness, he became wealthy and increased beyond measure. Therefore his wealth was as if it had fallen from heaven, as if it had come to his hand by having found it, not by his own strength or industriousness (cf. Deut. 8:17). That is the meaning of *He took from what had come into his hand as an offering to Esau* (Gen. 32.14).[52]

To be sure, this passage is not fully convincing as an interpretation of the simple meaning of the passage in *Va-Yetse.* One might indeed find in the biblical narrative testimony to precisely those qualities that Morteira dismisses: Jacob's industriousness, perseverance, and ingenuity.[53] The

---

51. "The People's Envy," in Saperstein, *Jewish Preaching,* p. 274.

52. MS 5:51v, *Va-Yishlaḥ,* Gen. 32:14, early 1630s.

53. This is indeed a point made in a different typological reading of the Jacob story by Solomon Levi (Shelomoh le-Bet ha-Levi): "We learn also that the industriousness of our people to earn money and acquire wealth is similar to that found in our father Jacob. But

preacher takes Jacob's highly rhetorical apologia before Laban (Gen. 31:36–42) as an objective statement of fact. As with the classical rabbinic comments, Morteira is interested not in a dispassionate evaluation of Jacob's conduct, but rather in presenting Jacob as a model of something beyond himself. His portrayal of Jacob's economic prosperity in exile is determined by the point he wants to make about the present.

This connection is made explicit in the continuation of the passage: "The Bible mentioned this matter so it would serve as a lesson for Jacob's descendants." Jacob's spending the night is an allusion to Jewish life in exile ("for exile and its sorrows are compared to night, as in the biblical verse, *Watchman, what is left of the night?* [Isa. 21:11])."[54] The application to Jewish experience becomes clear:

> He took from what had come to hand, in a miraculous manner, for indeed our profits and our sustenance this day are all achieved in a miraculous manner, due to the small size of the funds we brought out of our land,[55] because of the large number of obstacles inherent in exile, which prevent us from engaging in many areas of business or trades, due to the envy of the Gentiles and their hatred toward us. All of these are hindrances and major causes of our impoverishment. Yet despite it all, we have not lacked and we will never lack sustenance, without our being dependent upon another people. All of this is certainly a prodigious miracle, about which it is appropriate to say *from what had*

---

his industriousness was rooted in justice and truth.... The meaning [of this passage] is that our people should not be blamed because they are so energetic and devote such effort to acquire wealth and capital in a land not their own, so long as they amass it justly and equitably, for this is what our father Jacob did, and this is what has preserved us among the Gentiles." *Divrei Shelomoh* (Venice, 1596), p. 231a; cf. the discussion in Saperstein, *"Your Voice,"* pp. 29–30.

54. Another connection with the current exile is made through a second exegetical crux in the verse: *He spent the night there* (Gen. 32:14), but there is no obvious referent for the word *there*. Morteira maintains that it refers back to the word *sea* in the previous verse (*I will make your offspring as the sands of the sea, too numerous to count* [Gen. 32:13]). Reminding the listeners of his sermon from the previous year, he recapitulates that "the great, turbulent sea" refers to Christendom, the waves of which threaten to inundate the Jewish people, but are blocked by the sand on its shores, which create "a barrier its waves can never pass." See the discussion below.

55. It is not clear whether "our land" here refers back to the exile from the land of Israel, or to more recent experience of departure from the Iberian peninsula. Note that Jacob left home "without any funds," where here it is "the small size of the funds we brought out." Some of the members of the audience were indeed able to bring substantial resources as the basis for their enrichment in their new homes.

come into his hand (Gen. 32:14). From this He [God] lays upon us various taxes and imposts to give to Esau.[56]

Various motifs of Morteira's preaching and his doctrine of exile are beautifully exemplified in this passage. Typological exegesis serves the preacher's purpose by enabling him to move from a Biblical narrative to contemporary realities. The conditions of exile, experienced paradigmatically by Jacob in the alien and hostile environment of the evil Laban, are not conducive to economic prosperity. Gentiles envy Jews and hate them, energetically resisting Jewish progress. In the natural order of things, nothing Jews could achieve through their own efforts would overcome the obstacles they encounter. Whatever wealth they manage to accrue is a result of divine providence expressed not through open miracles but through the hidden miracles that look as if they might be part of nature.[57] All of this is encapsulated in the phrase, *what had come into his hand.* An exegetical curiosity is turned by the preacher into an emblem for an entire outlook on the economic and religious life of a potentially thriving community.

One of Morteira's major sermons for the Sabbath of Repentance, printed in the 1645 edition of *Giv'at Sha'ul* (and translated below), argues that providential protection guards the Jewish people in their exile against the danger of forgetting their noble origins, their ancient history, and the Torah that records this past. Powerful forces press the Jewish people to abandon its roots: the unprecedented length of the exile, the triumphalist claims of the rival religions, the worldly success and the material prosperity of the nations contrasted with the impoverishment and oppression suffered by the Jews. "These are compelling reasons for accepting the Gentile claims." Coercion and duress are imposed upon the Jews, including "the destruction and loss of Jewish books."[58] Had the long exile occurred in the midst of prosperous idolaters who forcefully removed Jewish books and pressured Jews to adopt their pagan rites throughout the centuries, the Jews would not have been able to perpetuate the memories that sustain them. In order to avoid this danger, God provided that the long exile would be not among idolaters but among the Christians, who have a fundamentally different relationship to the Hebrew Scriptures:

56. MS 5:51v–52r, *Va-Yishlaḥ,* Gen. 32:14.

57. Cf. also Morteira's formulation in a Sabbath of Repentance sermon (*GS* 1645, p. 89c, below, p. 478): because poverty threatens to extinguish what is good in people, God has provided wealth for the Jews in all their exiles in order to preserve some of their fine ethical qualities, "as we ourselves see this day through wondrous and miraculous individual providence." And cf. the formulation in *Tratado,* p. 81.

58. *GS* 1645, p. 88c, *Ha'azinu,* Deut. 32:12, early 1630s; see below, p. 471.

God exiled His children in their midst. He wanted them all [the Christians] to accept the Torah of Moses, to believe in its words, to seek it out and print it and bear witness to its truth. In this way, despite the length of the exile, the wardens of the prison would remind the prisoner each day of his lineage, his origins, his crime and its consequences, and the faith of his Torah, so that he and his offspring would never forget. This is an act of divine love surpassing our imagination.[59]

This idea was apparently quite appealing to Morteira, as we encounter it several times in his sermons. Prior to the long sermon for the Sabbath of Repentance discussed above, he had noted in a sermon for Hanukkah, 1627 that "it was an aspect of divine wisdom in this long exile that the peoples among whom we were exiled would confess our sacred Torah, so that despite the weight of our sorrows we would be able to persist in the worship it entails, as even our enemies admit its truth."[60] Then in the early 1640s, he returned to this theme by means of a lengthy citation from Isaac Arama's *'Aqedat Yitshaq* that expresses a very similar idea, followed by a passage from Maimonides' *Mishneh Torah* (the uncensored version, for, Morteira notes, "these words are not in all the printed editions"), about the role of Christianity in spreading knowledge of the Torah throughout the world.[61]

-----

59. Ibid., p 88d, below, p. 471. This proposition that the Christians, through their commitment to and interest in the Bible, make it impossible for the Jews to forget their Sacred Scripture has ironic overtones in that one of St. Augustine's arguments to support his claim that God wanted the Jewish people to remain in Christian society was that the Jews served as "guardians of the Scriptures." They testified to the authenticity of the Old Testament before anyone who might deny it and served as a constant reminder of the validity of its message. If the Jews were to disappear, Augustine suggests, Christians themselves might forget the divine revelation; in this sense he cites the verse from Psalms, *Do not kill them, lest My people forget* (Ps. 59:12). Morteira stands this doctrine on its head, making the Christians the unwitting guardians of Scripture, who ensure that the Jewish people will not forget. Their belief in the Bible, indeed their desire to "seek it out and print it," serves an unintended role in God's providential plan, strengthening the Jewish identity that some of them wanted to eradicate.

60. MS 2:15r, *Va-Yeshev*, Gen. 37:7, Hanukkah 1627.

61. Following these long quotations, he refers his listeners back to the Sabbath of Repentance sermon we have been discussing: "Before I saw the words of these scholars, I too was able to comprehend this great wonder in a sermon I composed on the verse, *The Eternal alone did guide him, no alien god was with Him* (Deut. 32:12), which I called 'Guarded him as the Pupil of His Eye.' Its content was to show how divine wisdom was perspicacious to fix in this long exile everything that harmed us in previous exiles" (MS 2:15r, *Va-Yeshev*, Gen. 37:7, Hanukkah, 1627). Despite perhaps a little disappointment in discovering that he was not the first to formulate this idea, there is a certain amount of pride that he was anticipated by two of the great figures of the Sephardi tradition. It may seem surprising that a celebrated

One of the dominant characteristics of the Jewish experience in exile is the scattering of the people among the nations. In its biblical context, this is part of the punishment, the curse that is a consequence of failing to abide by the covenant: *And I will scatter you among the nations* (Lev. 26:33), *The Eternal will scatter you among all the peoples from one end of the earth to the other* (Deut. 28:64). Medieval Jews also tended to view the scattering of the Jews as a disadvantage.[62] Yet, following a pointer in the rabbinic literature, Morteira transvaluates the dispersal of the Jewish people and makes this too a sign of divine providential protection and of benefit to the Jews. This is the central theme of his sermon, delivered in 1622 or 1623, called "Dust of the Earth" (translated below); its theme-verse is Genesis 28:14: *Your descendants shall be as the dust of the earth; you shall spread out to the west and the east, to the north and to the south; all the families of the earth shall bless themselves by you and your descendants.*

Following a rabbinic dictum that explicates the simile of dust, Morteira gives seven different explanations of the advantages of being scattered throughout the world rather than concentrated in a single foreign country. Three of them are connected with Jewish self-preservation. First, given the large numbers of Jews—a claim he substantiates (without an actual number) by appealing to the "Travels of Benjamin of Tudela"—the concentration of the entire population would inevitably be seen as a threat to the local ruler. The experience in ancient Egypt provides an example; if Pharaoh wanted to kill the male Israelites because he feared their numbers (Exod. 1:8–9), "how much more would this be so today, because of their great hate for us. Therefore in order to conceal us from their evil eye, God scattered us a few here and a few there, so that our true population would not be recognized."[63] The emphasis on the vastness of the world Jewish population, and the acceptance of Benjamin's numbers for distant Jewish communities, strikes us as rather

---

passage from Maimonides' *Mishneh Torah* was not known to Morteira for many years, but this passage had been removed from the printed editions since the time of the Counter-Reformation, and it is possible that he got access to the earlier edition (Constantinople, 1509) only later. Morteira also had access to an uncensored text of Arama's *Aqedat Yitshaq*, as key phrases in the passage he cites were inked out by censors: see, e.g., the Venice, 1545 edition at the Center for Judaic Studies Library, Philadelphia, p. 253a. This work was published again at Venice in 1565 and 1573.

62. E.g. Nahmanides: "And we remain a few among each nation, even though together we are many," "Ma'amar ha-Ge'ulah," in *Kitvei RaMBaN,* 2 vols., 1:263, cited by Rosenberg, "Exile and Redemption," p. 426, n. 34; Joseph Hayyun and Isaac Arama, cited by Ben-Sasson, "Galut u-Ge'ulah," pp. 218, 223.

63. MS 3:249v, *Va-Yetse,* Gen. 28:14, 1622 or 1623, see below, p. 386. Cf. Dato's similar formulation, cited by Jacobson, p. 130: "So that the nations would not cast their eyes upon the multitude of Jews."

naive, but it was not unusual for a time when many Christians as well as Jews believed in the continued existence of the ten "lost tribes."[64]

If the first benefit relates to the motivation for genocide, the second pertains to its feasibility. There have indeed been governments that wanted to destroy the Jews under their control. The scattering of the Jews makes it impossible for this plan to be fulfilled:

> The Sages of sacred memory interpreted the scriptural phrase, *His gracious deliverance [pirzono] of Israel* (Jud. 5:11), "God acted graciously with Israel by scattering them (*pizaram*) among the nations" (b. *Pesaḥim* 87b). If they should kill us, they would be designated a "barbarous kingdom" (b. *Pesaḥim* 87b, b. *Avodah Zarah* 10b). But since we are dispersed, they cannot annihilate us, for one abandons us and another takes us in. In this we are saved from them, and God *has not let us be ripped apart* (Ps. 124:6).[65]

The rabbinic interpretation of Judges 5:11 will recur frequently as a proof text for the benefits of dispersion as they are concretized by our preacher in different ways.

When Jews are subjected not to murderous but to oppressive policies, relocation from one country to another—either voluntary or compulsory—becomes an important option. Many of those in the audience would have identified with this theme of geographical mobility from their own experience:

> In this exile, Israel endures under pressure and pain, toiling to eke out a livelihood, experiencing afflictions and terrible diseases that come upon them. Now on many occasions it has become necessary to change

---

64. The impact of the belief in the survival of the tribes, and therefore the potential large number of Israelites in the world, can be seen in the writings of Menasseh ben Israel and in the messianic propaganda of Nathan of Gaza. Morteira believed that the tribes had not been dispersed throughout the world but were all in one place and would play an active role in the scenario of redemption (MS 5:47v, *Va-Yetse*, Gen. 29:7, ca. 1645). See the fuller discussion later in this chapter.

65. MS 3:249v, below, p. 387. Morteira returned to this idea at the end of his Sabbath of Repentance sermon on Deut. 32:12, mentioned above. Referring back to his discussion in "Dust of the Earth," he claims that this consideration is "the most important of all." "God acted providentially in scattering us among the nations as a remedy for their great hatred, so that they would not annihilate us; He therefore placed us in the power of many rulers, so they would not all agree on one plan [of destruction]." Cf. Usque, *Consolation for the Tribulations of Israel*, p. 227: "By scattering you among all peoples, He made it impossible for the world to destroy you, for if one kingdom rises against you in Europe to inflict death upon you, another in Asia allows you to live." Also Dato, cited in Jacobson, p. 144, and Samuel Saul Siriro, *Derushei Maharashash Siriro*, 2 vols. (Jerusalem, 1989-1991), 1: 122.

their country, to travel *from nation to nation, from one kingdom to another* (1 Chron. 16:20), to change climate whether for reasons of health or sustenance. If the Jewish people were in one place, when a Jew wanted to move from his home and depart for a different land, [the inhabitants of the new land] would drive him away, for not knowing him they would be astonished at him. That is why God scattered his people to the four corners of the earth: so that wherever one Jew goes to change his residence, he will find his fellow Jews established. This will make his journey easier, for all will help each other, thereby facilitating their survival in their exile.[66]

The contrast drawn in this description between local inhabitants refusing to accept Jews because of their unfamiliarity with a living Jewish people, and an established Jewish community that can welcome newcomers, may well reflect the different stages in the experience of the Jews in Amsterdam. By the time Morteira came, the community was sufficiently entrenched to make the acceptance of new arrivals almost routine, but many would have remembered the earliest years when the status of the Portuguese Jews in Holland was being fiercely contested.[67] A few years later, in a sermon for Hanukkah of 1627, Morteira reiterated this aspect of the benefits of geographical dispersion:

Without real estate or patrimonies, God blesses them and preserves them and makes them grow numerous, so that in every place there can be found *His gracious deliverance [pirzono] of Israel* (Jud. 5:11), [which the Sages interpreted], "God acted graciously with Israel by scattering them (*pizaram*) among the nations" (b. *Pesahim* 87b). For wherever a Jew may go, there he finds some of his brothers, who have mercy on him, for that is how they are.[68]

There is, to be sure, a hortatory element in these passages. The description of more established Jews reaching out to help needy newcomers because it is their nature to be merciful contains beneath its surface an appeal to his listeners to continue acting in this manner. But the force of the argument relies upon the claim that by this behavior, the Jews of Amsterdam are not only fulfilling their own self-conception as a compassionate people, but also

---

66. MS 3:250r, below, p. 390.

67. On this early period, see Huussen, "The Legal Position of Sephardi Jews in Holland," and Vlessing, "New Light on the Earliest History of the Amsterdam Portuguese Jews," Daniel Swetschinski, *Reluctant Cosmopolitans*, pp. 8–53; Swetschinski, "From the Middle Ages to the Golden Age," esp. pp. 59–81.

68. MS 2:16r. *Va-Yeshev*, Gen 37:7, 1627.

playing their role in God's providential plan of exilic experience.

Another passage in "Dust of the Earth" is based on the economics of *galut*. As we have seen, Morteira claims that the prohibition against Jews owning land is a major difference between exile and normal life, producing impoverishment and uncertainty. Against this background, geographical dispersal provides an important measure of economic diversity:

> God has decreed upon the Jewish people in this exile that in the land of our enemies we would not own *so much as a foot can tread on* (Deut. 2:5), so that we would recognize that we are exiled from our land and constantly raise our hearts to God to beseech food for our sustenance, and benefit from our own physical labor. He has scattered us among the nations, to the four corners of the earth, so that each one of us may find what is necessary for a livelihood, sustain himself from the work of his hands, figure out a way to provide food for his house and to graze his kids until the time of anger has passed. If we were all in the same land, each person would eat his neighbor up alive. But being scattered, each one can engage in matters appropriate to his own country—some as sellers of clothing and others as merchants on the sea, some as moneylenders at interest, and others as craftsmen, some as purchasers of livestock and others as brokers for merchandise—so that everyone can find what he needs for a livelihood.[69]

In this passage, a contrast is drawn between an agrarian economy based on land-holding, in which a nobility lives as a leisured class from the toil of others, and an economy in which labor, effort, initiative and ingenuity are necessary to provide basic sustenance. The first may have prevailed in the land of Israel; the second, characteristic of Jewish life in exile, produces a deeper sense of dependence upon God, and is therefore an appropriate mode for a life of atonement. Whereas the sermon on the verse *he took from what came into his hand as an offering to his brother Esau* (Gen. 32:14), discussed above, minimizes the importance of Jewish efforts, here they are emphasized as a necessary means for survival alongside the providential provisions from God.

Second, a clustering of Jews in one country is undesirable not only because large numbers of Jews arouse the suspicion of Gentile rulers, as explained earlier in the sermon, but also because no one country can support the entire Jewish people economically. The resulting competition among Jews to sustain themselves would be destructive. Hence the benefit of dispersion. Different countries provide different economic opportunities. Being situated in many

---

69. MS 3:249v, below, p. 388.

countries therefore enables the Jewish people to diversify and take full advantage of the various options available for sustaining themselves. Although this passage was intended to represent the range of Jewish economic activity throughout the world, there is in this list of occupations something with which virtually every member of the congregation could identify.[70]

All of the above passages present the exile in a negative way. Its defining characteristics remain insecurity and danger for the Jewish people, even if geographical dispersion serves to mitigate these dangers. But other explanations provided by Morteira present the scattering of the Jews in a way that serves some purpose or accomplishes some task that could not be fulfilled if they remained in the land of Israel. One such explanation is given in a 1631 sermon called "Like the Sand of the Sea" (on Genesis 32:13). Morteira interprets this simile in a manner that apparently reflects one of the distinctive realities of life in the Netherlands: "*I will make your offspring like the sand* and the wall *of the sea,* for since the sand is the sea wall, He used the word *sand* in place of *wall.*"[71] This becomes the basis for a statement about the nature of the exile:

> If so, [Jews] are frequently like the sand of the sea in relation to the states where they are scattered, so that the sea of Edom will not sweep over [them?] and bring them under their control. [The Jews] prevent this, thereby serving for the benefit of all the nations of the earth... by serving as a barrier to this raging sea, which is Esau, Jacob's brother, the father of Edom.[72]

This is one of the relatively few comments in Morteira's sermons that refer, though indirectly, to Jews living in Islamic lands (Jews who are not under the power of Edom). The precise force of the assertion that these Jews serve as a barrier to the raging sea of Christendom is not fully clear. Apparently he is implying that the Jews of the Ottoman Empire strengthen their host countries

---

70. See Bloom, *The Economic Activities of the Jews of Amsterdam.* Jews in Amsterdam were not permitted to carry on retail trade ("sellers of clothing"), for example (p. 23 n. 106, cf. p. 66), while they did so in other countries. On Jewish involvement in livestock trade in a slightly later period (including the importing of horses from New England to Curaçao and Surinam, see pp. 146, 156. Cf. also Blom et al., eds., *The History of the Jews in the Netherlands,* entries listed pp. 494–95 s.v. "economic activity."

71. MS 2:214v, *Va-Yishlah,* Gen. 32:13, 1631. Compare Solomon Levi, cited in Hacker, "Yisra'el ba-Goyyim," pp. 45–46.

72. MS 2:214v, *Va-Yishlah,* Gen 32:13, 1631. The interpretation is based on a reading of *the sea, too abundant to count* (Gen. 32:13) as an allegorical representation of Edom–Rome–Christianity, whose rule seems interminable. Note that Morteira interprets the phrase *too abundant to count* as referring not to "sand" but to "sea," the nearest possible noun in the verse.

and thereby prevent the expansion of Christian power into the Middle East.[73] What cannot be mistaken, however, is the assertion that the dispersal of the Jews serves not only internal Jewish interests but, in accordance with the blessing of Jacob, "the benefit of all the nations of the world."

An even more striking, though somewhat ambivalent, exemplification of this principle is made in our sermon "Dust of the Earth." Sometimes, the preacher maintains, the entire world deserves destruction because of its evil deeds. While the Temple was still in existence, there were sacrifices to atone for the Gentile nations, but these are no longer possible. The dispersal of the Jewish people anomg the nations, studying the record of God's revelation, serves as a substitute for these sacrifices, guaranteeing the preservation of the entire world:

> Therefore God has scattered us among them as one who sprinkles salt over meat, so that our presence everywhere enables us to preserve the world from destruction. This is because of the Torah, which is studied wherever we are found. It is for our benefit, for "why should the world be destroyed because of those who stray"—why should the world, which be ours, be destroyed because of the Gentiles? That is why in our dispersal, we are a "covenant of salt" for the world.[74]

This is a deceptively complex passage. The image of the Jews as salt is derived from two sources: the common usage of salt as a preservative for meat, and the biblical phrase "covenant of salt" used to characterize a divine commitment to the descendants of Aaron (Num. 18:19) and of David (2 Chron. 13:5). Indeed, the end of the passage is an untranslatable play on the phrase from Numbers: a "covenant of salt forever" (*berit melaḥ 'olam*) becomes a "covenant of salt for the world" (*berit melaḥ le-'olam*), introducing a universalistic dimension that is absent from the biblical context. Yet, as if embarrassed by the suggestion of universalism, Morteira immediately recasts the assertion in narrowly Judeocentric terms. Alluding to a rabbinic response to the question "Why does God not destroy the idols in the world?"—since even the heavenly bodies have been made into an object of human worship, the entire universe would have to be destroyed—he recasts the rhetorical questions of the Sages ("Should God destroy the world because of the

---

73. Perhaps the strongest case for the strengthening of the Ottoman Empire by the Jews (especially those expelled from Spain) was made by Elijah Capsali: "Owing to the Jews, the Turks took over great and powerful kingdoms," as the Jews taught them about cannons (!) (cited by Ben-Sasson, "Galut u-Ge'ulah," p. 224).

74. MS 3:249v–250r, below, p. 389.

fools?"[75]) into an expression of Jewish self-interest. In the messianic age, the
world will be "ours"—under the sovereignty of the messianic king and the
Jewish people. To allow it to be destroyed because of the sins of the Gentiles
at present would be to deny the Jews part of their eventual reward in messianic
times. Therefore the Jews preserve the Gentile nations by bringing Torah
study to all lands where they are allowed to live. Yet it is not for the Gentiles
but for the Jews that God has ordained this arrangement.

Rather different is the view that the Jewish people plays a positive role in
its dispersion through its influence on the Gentile nations, teaching them religious truths that will benefit them as well as their teachers. Morteira was
certainly not the first to formulate this idea,[76] but he gives it a powerful articulation in this sermon:

> In their own land, they were *wicked sinners* (Gen. 13:13) before all the
> nations. But now in their exile, they need to proclaim and confess God's
> Torah before all. While *all the peoples walk each in the name of its god* (Mic.
> 4:5), before all of them *we will walk in the name of the Eternal our God
> forever and ever* (Mic. 4:5). If we were all in one place, our witness would
> be before only one nation. But our duty is to confess God's greatness
> before all the peoples of the earth, and before the citizens of all the
> nations. This is what the Sages said on the verse, *I will sow her on earth
> as My own* (Hos. 2:25): "The Jews were mixed among the nations only
> so that proselytes might be added to them" (cf. b. *Pesaḥim* 87b).[77]

As in the previous example, tension lies beneath the surface of these lines. In
its formulation, it appears to be a clear expression of the universalistic concept
of a Jewish mission: "Our duty is to confess God's greatness before all the
peoples of the earth." Yet the context of the passage reveals that the emphasis
is clearly on the benefit to the Jews, not to the Gentiles. It is introduced with
the statement that "by this dispersion, the sins of Israel are diminished more

---

75. M. *'Avodah Zarah* 4,7 (54b).

76. See the sources from Abraham Maimonides, Bahya ben Asher, Hasdai Crescas, and
Hayyim ben Bezalel cited by Rosenberg, "Exile and Redemption," pp. 409–10. A generation after Morteira, Josiah Pardo repeated the same idea in a sermon in Rotterdam: the
diaspora was intended "so that Jews could everywhere proclaim the truth of God and His
Torah" ("Mizbaḥ ha-Zahav," Amsterdam Ets Ḥaim Library MS 51 (47 B 21), fol. 59r. The
same doctrine is expressed by Isaac Aboab da Fonseca in his *Parafrasis* of the Pentateuch:
see Kaplan, *From Christianity to Judaism*, p. 365. Note that Portuguese Christian preachers
were aware of the Jewish (or New Christian) claim that the dispersion was intended to enable them to teach the nations among whom they reside, a claim these preachers dismissed
with contempt. See Glaser, "Invitation to Intolerance," p. 343.

77. MS 3:249v, below, pp. 386–87.

easily." And it concludes, after the sentences cited above, "In this way, from your punishment, your exile, your dispersion, great merit will accrue to you, which would not be the case if you were not like dust scattered from one end of the world to the other."[78] Essentially, this is a restatement of the classical idea that the function of exile is to atone for the sins of the Jewish people. Bringing knowledge of the true God to all the nations of the earth functions as a means to this end. Little concern for the well-being of the Gentiles is in evidence here.

More than fifteen years later, Morteira returned to this theme. He cites the same Talmudic statement, but this time with somewhat greater emphasis on a kind of Jewish mission to the unenlightened. Because of the dispersion of the Jewish people, Morteira maintains, "the belief in God and knowledge of His Torah has been spread to the four corners of the earth."

> Because of the Jews, Abraham's descendants, people speak about God and are aware of His Torah. This is what the Sages said in tractate *Pesahim*: "God exiled the Jewish people among the nations only so that proselytes would be added to them, as the Bible says, *I will sow her on earth as My own* (Hos. 2:25)." The meaning is that a person sows a bushel of seed in order to gather in from it many times the number of bushels. Now this task is great, not for a single day. For day after day people settle in previously unknown places, [where the inhabitants are?] thought to be like beasts of the fields or savages, as we ourselves can see day after day. God is completing His work, revealing the fourth region of the earth; in ways that are lofty and mysterious to us, He makes the children of Abraham, who believe in Him, settle there in order to bring knowledge to the inhabitants of what they did not know and had not yet heard of, so that they may recognize our God. Through them will be fulfilled, *He will assemble the banished of Israel, and gather the dispersed of Judah from the four corners of the earth* (Isa. 11:12). This is a great reason for the length of the exile and the delay of redemption, for this great purpose has not yet been completed.[79]

Here we find a dialectical interaction between Jews and Gentiles. The uncivilized peoples of the earth, learning about the true God, make possible the fulfillment of prophetic promises including the ingathering of the exiles. But, perhaps echoing the claims of Christian missionaries in the New World,[80]

---

78. Ibid., below, p. 387.

79. MS 1:65v, *Naso*, Num. 4:33, 1639.

80. Compare the allusion in the work of Jacob del Bene to Catholic missionaries spread-

the preacher insists that Jews in their distant settlements serve a real function as bearers of religious truth to those deprived of it. The difference between this passage and the earlier one seems to lie in the specificity of a Jewish presence in the "fourth region," the "New World"; listeners would undoubtedly have thought of their sister community in the Zur Israel congregation of Recife, established in the 1630s.[81] For Morteira, this was a powerful expression of the positive role played by the Jewish dispersion in God's universal plan. Yet awareness of a continent filled with inhabitants who had no conception of God or Torah impelled him to remind the congregation that the plan was not near its completion, the end of the exile was by no means imminent.

A sermon from the mid-1640s provides perhaps the clearest expression of a universalistic dimension for the Jewish role in exile. As we have seen, many of Morteira's sermons present the experience of enslavement in Egypt as a prototype for all later exiles, but in this sermon a contrast is drawn. The "Egyptian exile" benefited Israel alone, it brought no benefit, but only destruction, to the Egyptians. "However this [current] exile is for the benefit of the Jews—to cleanse their sins—and for the benefit of the nations, for from their midst they will be purified to the perfection hoped for at the end: *they shall all invoke the Eternal by name, and serve Him with one accord* (Zeph. 3:9)."[82] Once again the preacher cites the rabbinic interpretation of Hosea 2:5: "The Jews were mixed among the nations only so that proselytes might be added to them" (cf. b. *Pesaḥim* 87b); he seems to be implying that the end of the exile depends upon the nations coming to "know God and His Torah because of the children of Israel who are with [them]."

This introduction of the messianic moment in the experience of exile suggests two other explanations of the value of dispersal. One is in the "Dust of the Earth" sermon, the last in the list of seven benefits. The scattering of the Jews prevents them from acting on the impulse to mobilize Jewish power and throw off Gentile rule before the proper time:

> If we were all together, upon seeing our great numbers and the length of our exile, we might conceivably select a leader and rise up against

ing knowledge of Torah, cited by David Ruderman, *Jewish Thought and Scientific Discovery in Early Modern Europe* (New Haven, 1995), p. 195.

81. On this community, see the studies collected in Cohen, ed., *The Jewish Experience in Latin America*, 2:80–312.

82. MS 5:48r, *Va-Yetse*, Gen. 29:7, mid 1640s. Near the end of the sermon he returns to this theme (MS 5:48v): God "scattered the Jews among the nations to tell of His glory, so that every human being would invoke God by name." And a few lines later, "God's purpose in scattering the Jews among the nations was to inform them about the Torah."

the people in whose midst we lived, thereby seeking to speed up the end [of the exile]; this is what the children of Ephraim did in Egypt, as is known in the rabbinic tradition.[83] But that is against God's plan, as the Sages interpreted the verse, *I adjure you, O maidens of Jerusalem...: do not wake or rouse love until it please* (Song 2:7). For all of this would be to our detriment, as we see in the verse, *Do not go up [...], since I am not in your midst [else you will be routed by your enemies]* (Deut. 1:42). For *this is not the way, and this is not the town* (2 Kings 6:19). God will go before us; He will redeem us! That is why God scattered us, a few here, a few there: so that we would not set our minds to such a course. Thus, "misery is fitting for Israel like a red rose upon a white horse" (b. *Ḥagigah* 9b).[84]

This articulation of a quietistic stance, proclaiming that God scattered the Jewish people to provide a brake on messianic activism—and to ensure that incipient messianic tension would not be discharged prematurely as an actual worldwide movement—takes on an ironic dimension when one recalls that the Sabbatian movement would sweep across the entire Jewish Diaspora only a few decades later, six years after Morteira's death.

This is not to suggest that Morteira doubted that the exile would some day come to an end. Many passages in his sermons deal with eschatology in rather traditional terms. In the 1639 sermon cited above, Morteira provides yet another positive explanation for the scattering of the Jewish people. This time it is the effect they will have upon the Gentiles not during the exile itself but at the time of the messianic redemption:

At the end of days, God wants the entire world to recognize His power and greatness. If we look at all the great and marvelous deeds performed by God against the nations in ancient times, we see that they all occurred in one of the four regions into which the earth is divided.

---

83. See the sources listed in Ginzberg, *The Legends of the Jews*, 6:2–3, nn. 10–11. Cf. below, p. 362.

84. MS 3:250r, *Va-Yetse*, Gen. 28:14, 1622 or 1623. Note the level of knowledge on the part of the listeners that seems to be assumed in this passage. That the children of Ephraim tried to speed the end of the Egyptian servitude is a statement of rabbinic tradition that could be taken on faith without further explication. But the rabbinic interpretation of Song 2:7 in b. *Ketubot* 111a—the famous "oaths" of the Jews in exile—really requires some further explanation that is not forthcoming. Apparently Morteira believed it could be assumed (he discussed the three oaths at length in a later sermon on *Va-Yetse*, Gen. 29:7, delivered in the mid-1640s: MS 5:47r–48r); see the citation below, pp. 351–52. His quotation of the statement from b. *Ḥagigah* 9b follows the text of *Aggadot ha-Talmud, Ein Yaakov,* and other witnesses; see *Diqduqei Sofrim ad loc.* In context, the translation "misery" for עניותא seems better than the usual rendering "poverty."

But now, it is His desire to be glorified and sanctified in the sight of many nations in all parts of the civilized world. This will be through the war of Gog and Magog, as Ezekiel prophesied.... He mentioned Meshech and Tubal, which are Europe; Put, which is Africa; Cush, which is America; and Tugarmah, which is Asia so that all of them will say, *What is this we have done, releasing Israel* (Exod. 14:5).[85]

The horizons have expanded. Once again the presence of a Jewish community worshipping publicly in the Western Hemisphere is made to function in the providential scenario of exile and its termination. Yet the spotlight of the drama itself remains narrowly focused on the Jewish people. Ezekiel's prophecy is now read to teach that armies from all four continents will gather to make war against Jerusalem, "and God will go out to fight against these nations." The native inhabitants of the "New World" will indeed witness the miraculous ingathering of the exiles, but the result—at least in this context—is expressed not in the universalistic vision of Isaiah chapter 2, but in the apocalyptic cadences of Ezekiel chapter 38. We turn now to Morteira's understanding of this redemptive drama.

THE MESSIANIC MOMENT

In their introduction to a new edition of Menasseh ben Israel's *The Hope of Israel*, Henry Méchoulan and Gérard Nahon discuss the paucity of information about the role of messianic thought, expectation and consciousness within the Portuguese community during its first two generations. Up until 1644, when Aaron Levi de Montezinos arrived in Amsterdam and generated considerable excitement by reporting the discovery of Israelites in South America (see below), the attitude toward messianic issues, according to Méchoulan and Nahon, "remains relatively unknown. The historian may judge that this community, whose material and intellectual prosperity was obvious, would have kept the expectation of a new era under wraps or, at the least, not made it their first preoccupation.... At the present time, such texts as might enlighten us on Messianism in Amsterdam before 1644 are, in essence, certain manuscripts which set out to convince

---

85. MS 1:65v, *Naso*, Num. 4:33, 1639. For an earlier expression of this idea that the dispersal of the Jews will enable all peoples to witness God's power in the ingathering, see the passage from Anatoli cited by Rosenberg, "Exile and Redemption," p. 408 bottom. Anatoli's formulation is more universalistic conceptually (the impact of God's redemption will be to convert all the nations to the worship of God alone), if less universalistic geographically.

immigrants from the Iberian Peninsula of the truth of Judaism and the falsity of Christianity."[86] As with so many other issues, these scholars overlooked the evidence in the sermons by the leading rabbi of the community.

Given the importance of the theme of exile in Morteira's sermons, it is not surprising to find that the messianic redemption is also a recurring and significant topic. One indication of its significance is that every one of his sermons—with the exception of the eulogies, which have their own liturgical conclusion—ends with an expression of the hope for the "coming of our righteous Messiah, speedily and in our days." This, however, may be a conventional trope that does not reflect the power of the messianic dimension of the speaker's worldview, and certainly not the configurations of his messianic doctrine.[87] For these we need to look not at the final sentence but at the actual substance of the sermons.

We have seen that in the context of occasional polemical references to Christian doctrine, Morteira identified the nature of the messiah and the validity of Jewish hope for a future redemption as a crucial issue of dispute between the two faiths, alongside the doctrine of God's nature and the eternal authority of the Torah.[88] Yet at the same time, we occasionally find in the sermons a tendency to de-emphasize the centrality of the messianic belief in Judaism. This is stated briefly in a sermon for Sukkot, dated 1625:

> For this is one of the arguments used by the Gentiles against us: they say, "You have already enjoyed your greatness; you no longer have Jerusalem or sovereignty; therefore, return to us." But Israel replies to them, "*Why will you gaze at the Shulamite, like the dance of two camps?* (Song 7:1). Our perfection and our greatness does not depend upon the greatness of Jerusalem. Whether or not the Messiah comes, we are Jews! Our only concern is the observance of the Torah!"[89]

This is a strong assertion that Jewish identity is bound up with Torah, not with

---

86. Henry Méchoulan and Gérard Nahon, Introduction to Menasseh ben Israel, *The Hope of Israel* (Oxford, 1987), pp. 81–82. On Montezinos's account, see Elizabeth Levi de Montezinos, "The Narrative of Aharon Levi, alias Antonio de Montezinos," *The American Sephardi* 7–8 (1975): 62–83, and the sources cited below in n. 109 (I am grateful to H. P. Salomon for this reference).

87. According to the texts they have left, the messianic conclusion was not automatically used by all Jewish preachers. Some of them (e.g., Pseudo-Jonah Gerundi, Joshua ibn Shueib, Leon Modena) did end their sermons regularly with reference to a messianic theme, frequently citing a messianic verse, but others (Jacob Anatoli, Solomon Levi, Samuel Uceda) did not.

88. See in the previous chapter.

89. MS 2:68r, Sukkot, Lev. 23:43, 1625.

the Messiah, the rebuilding of Jerusalem, or the return to national sovereignty. But in this sermon the assertion remains on the level of an unsubstantiated claim, which must have left some in the congregation wondering. At a later occasion, Morteira returned to this point, echoing the climactic proclamation, but supporting it in a conceptual context:

This also teaches us a great, fundamental, comprehensive matter, including an answer to all of the claims that religious opponents make against us; it is a great, fundamental peg upon which hangs the entire controversy. The matter with which the nations strive against us to weaken our hearts, to dampen our hope, is the length of the exile....

Now the decisive response to this is that the essence of the covenant made with us by our God, and all that would ensue from it—that He would be our God and we would be His people and observe His commandments—does not depend upon the coming of the Messiah. Whether or not the Messiah comes, the Eternal is our God and we are His people. For the essence of the covenant is for Him to be our God, protecting us so that we will never be destroyed, and that we will cleave to Him with our souls through the Torah, and that we will never exchange Him for another god, and observe His commandments, so that our souls may find pleasure in His light. We see this in the verse, *You shall be holy, as I the Eternal your God am holy* (Lev. 19:2).

All of the temporal goods promised in the Torah are nothing but preparation and training for this ultimate end. If, as a result of our sins, we are unable to attain this end in the context of these [worldly] goods, then we shall attain it in the context of afflictions and exile. The Sages said that Abraham chose oppression by the kingdoms in order to save his descendants from the judgment of hell;[90] thus if we are afflicted in exile, it is to cleanse our sins, so that our end will be in God's light, finding pleasure in His rest. This is the ultimate purpose of the Torah, for "the reward of the commandments is not in this world,"[91] which is a preparation to attain the spiritual reward.

This being so, whether the Messiah comes and we attain this ultimate goal in the context of temporal goods, or he does not come and we attain it in the context of afflictions, we are Jews, God's people, and there is no doubt that we shall attain the ultimate purpose of the Torah. Therefore, what is the point of their vilifying us with the delay in the coming of the Messiah? It is not the essence of our covenant with God. Their

90. Gen. Rabbah 44, 21 and parallels.
91. B. *Qiddushin* 39b and parallels.

purpose is only to weaken our hearts entirely from [devotion to] His Torah.[92]

Although the only authorities cited to buttress this declaration are the rabbinic Sages, two monumentally influential medieval Jewish thinkers provide the intellectual context for the position that Morteira communicates to his congregation. The first is Maimonides. At the end of his classic formulation of a rationalistic Jewish eschatology concluding his *Code of Jewish Law*, he wrote that "the Sages and Prophets did not long for the days of the Messiah that Israel might exercise dominion over the world, or rule the heathens, or be exalted by the nations, or that it might eat and drink and rejoice. Their aspiration was that Israel be free to devote itself to the Torah and its wisdom, with no one to oppress or disturb it, and thus be worthy of life in the world to come."[93] Elsewhere in his *Code*, he makes it clear that "life in the world to come" refers to eternal existence of the soul in a purely spiritual, incorporeal realm.[94] Thus Maimonides clearly defines the relationship between these two central concepts of Jewish eschatology—the messianic age and the world to come—hierarchically and instrumentally. Since the messianic age provides temporal, material good—independence and prosperity— for the Jewish people, the "world to come," which provides permanent, spiritual good, is of incomparably greater importance. Furthermore, the messianic age is a means to achieving the ultimate end. The freedom from political oppression and economic hardship will provide an environment in which all Jews will be able to do what is necessary to earn the ultimate reward free of the obstacles that life in exile creates.

This is clearly the background for Morteira's insistence that the temporal goods promised in the Torah are not its ultimate purpose, but only a means for preparing the people to attain the final, spiritual reward. Maimonides, however, defined the belief in the coming of the Messiah as one of the thirteen fundamental principles of Jewish faith. He did not raise in writing, as Morteira does here, the possibility that the Messiah will never come. For this we need to turn to a second major influence, Moses ben Nahman or Nahmanides.

At a tense moment in his public disputation with Paul Christian (1263), when pressed by his opponent's citation of rabbinic statements indicating that the Messiah had come centuries before (and by implication, that the Jews had

---

92. MS 5:66r, *Va-Yishlaḥ*, Gen. 32:20 (ca. 1640). Yet one paragraph later, he ends the sermon in his characteristic manner, "May it be God's will that the coming of our righteous Messiah will be quickly and in our days. Amen."

93. Maimonides, *Code, Hilkhot Melakhim* 14,4.

94. Ibid., *Hilkhot Teshuvah* 8,2.

nothing to look forward to), Nahmanides turned to the king and (according to his later account) said,

> My lord king, bear with me [a little]. The essence of our judgment, truth, and justice does not depend upon the Messiah.... The Messiah is but a king of flesh and blood like you. When I worship my Creator in your dominion, exiled, suffering, and under subjugation, *the reproach of the nations* (Ezek. 36:15), who taunt me always, my reward is abundant, for I bring a whole offering to God from my physical being. Because of that, I shall increasingly merit life in the world to come. However, when a king of Israel, of my own faith, will rule over all the nations, and I have no choice but to abide the law of the Jews, my reward will not be as abundant.[95]

While the language about the "ultimate" purpose or reward (*takhlit*) comes from Maimonides, the language about the "essence" (*'iqar*) of the covenant seems to be taken from this passage of Nahmanides. Accepting Maimonides' premise that the spiritual reward in eternity is greater than the material benefits of the messianic age, he considers two alternative ways of attaining the ultimate reward, as Morteira does. In fact, he goes further than Morteira, arguing that the reward for observing the commandments in exile is greater than the reward will be for doing the same thing in the messianic age, precisely because it is more difficult now. Morteira's emphasis is different here: it does not matter whether the Messiah comes or not. We remain Jews one way or another; the essence of the covenant with God is not affected. One way or another we will attain the reward that is the ultimate purpose of the Torah.

Evidence from the rest of the sermons makes it difficult to judge whether this stance reflected an actual indifference toward messianism or was just an easy way for Morteira to escape from the arguments of religious opponents and the doubts in the hearts of listeners raised by the length of an oppressive exile.[96] Many passages would appear to mitigate against a devalorization of

---

95. The Hebrew text is in *Kitvei Rabbenu Moshe ben Naḥman*, 1:310. There are many translations and many discussions of the Disputation; for a fuller treatment of this passage, see Marc Saperstein and Nancy Berg, "'Arab Chains' and 'the Good Things of Sepharad': Aspects of Jewish Exile," *AJS Review* 26:2 (2002): 307–11.

96. There is a similar ambiguity in evaluating Nahmanides' statement; see Saperstein and Berg, p. 309, and n. 21, for other medieval Jewish formulations similar to that of Morteira. Note, however, that in Morteira's response to the second question from the "Priest of Rouen," he asserts that "those who do not believe that God will send the Messiah to redeem

the messianic dimension. Let us survey some of the elements of traditional Jewish eschatology as they appear in the sermons.

1. Elijah

One important component of the messianic scenario is Elijah, a figure that represents continuity between past and future, the period of prophecy and sovereignty in antiquity and the restoration in the messianic age. The biblical account indicates that he did not die in the manner of other human beings, but ascended to heaven in a fiery chariot (2 Kings 2:11), and would be sent back to earth by God as an instrument of reconciliation at a preliminary stage of a final reckoning (Mal. 3:24). The rabbinic literature and folklore filled in the empty spaces with Elijah's encounters during the long interim of Jewish exile and—more important for our purpose here—precisely what role he was expected to play in an eschatological context.

Morteira devoted much of an entire sermon, which he called "Elijah the Prophet," to this theme.[97] Delivered in the early 1640s, it was included in the 1645 printing of *Giv'at Sha'ul.* Important for our purposes is his discussion of the special tasks that God appointed for Elijah to fulfill, tasks that require him to remain alive in body and soul throughout the entire period from the end of his original terrestrial career until his return. The first of these is to restore the Torah in its fullness by resolving the doubts that have arisen as a result of the suffering of exile.[98] This requires a scholar who had mastered the totality of Torah revelation during the period when it was still fresh.

The second task is directly associated with the Messiah: Elijah is to play a role analogous to that of Samuel with David:

> The second essential act that will be done by Elijah is to anoint the King Messiah. This is why God has hidden away the anointing oil with which our righteous Messiah will be anointed,[99] for the very name "Messiah" is bound up with anointing—essentially, not just metaphorically. As the

the Jews from the captivity and gather them to their land are separated from the people of Israel, and have no hope of salvation."

97. MS 2:111r–112r, *Va-Era,* Exod. 6:25; *GS, Va-Era,* 1645, pp. 25a–26d 1912, pp. 115–20.

98. For this widely-known function of Elijah in his eschatological return, see b. *Berakhot* 35b and the parallel sources listed in W. D. Davies, *The Setting of the Sermon on the Mount* (Atlanta, 1989), p. 159; Joseph Klausner, *The Messianic Idea in Israel* (London, 1956), p. 452.

99. See b. *Horayot* 11b–12a. According to the classical aggadah, Elijah is supposed to disclose where the concealed anointing oil is hidden (*Mekhilta, Va-Yassa,* chap. 6, ed. Lauterbach 2:126). Elijah's role in anointing the Messiah is apparently first attested in Justin Martyr: see Klausner, *The Messianic Idea,* pp. 455–56.

advent of the Messiah is ready and prepared to occur on any day... it is necessary to have the pure prophet who will anoint him ready and waiting, not in need of resurrection, but like a man riding on horseback, prepared at any moment to gallop along the path.

Here Morteira, implicitly rejecting the idea of an encoded future date that might preclude the messianic advent in his own generation, insists that the Messiah can indeed come at any moment. Once this occurs, once the Messiah reveals himself, it is inconceivable that there would have to be a delay in order to find a prophet suitable to anoint him.[100] Therefore Elijah is kept in readiness throughout the centuries. Nor is this the end of his responsibilities:

> We have also found a third task that Elijah will perform when he comes, and that is the resurrection of the dead, as the Sages said in the Mishnah at the end of Tractate *Sotah,* "The Holy Spirit leads to the resurrection of the dead, and the resurrection of the dead comes through Elijah."[101] This must necessarily be done by a man who exists in body and soul.

Indeed, Morteira maintains, Elijah is particularly well qualified for this task, as he had experience in effecting a restoration of life to the dead during his original earthly career (1 Kings 18:17–24). Thus Elijah, who never tasted death, is the perfect instrument for the accomplishment of this great task.

Finally, there is a responsibility that is somewhat less familiar, though necessary for the restoration of the Temple cult:

> There is also a fourth function that Elijah will perform when he comes— the refining of the Levites: *He shall act like a smelter and purger of silver; and he shall purify the descendants of Levi and refine them like gold and silver, so that they shall present offerings in righteousness* (Mal. 3:3). In this verse is also included—in addition to Elijah's separating out and demoting to the status of ordinary Jews those who are called priests and Levites but are not from the descendants of Levi[102]—what I explained about this verse in [my sermon on] the lesson *Yitro* on the verse *Jethro rejoiced* (Exod. 18:9).

---

100. A Spanish messianic personality named Moses (probably Botarel) claimed that Elijah had anointed him with the anointing oil in 1493: Aaron Zeev Aescoli, *Ha-Tenu'ot ha-Meshihiyot be-Yisra'el* (Jerusalem, 1956) p. 223. Sabbatian tradition provides a date (21 Sivan 5408=June 11, 1648) on which Sabbatai was "anointed by the prophet Elijah." See Scholem, *Sabbatai Sevi,* p. 141.

101. M. *Sotah* 9,15. Cf. Hasdai Crescas, *Or ha-Shem,* 3,4,1 end (ed. Shlomo Fisher, Jerusalem, 1990), p. 341.

102. The Talmudic basis for Elijah's role in this process is M. *'Eduyot* 8,7; see Klausner, *The Messianic Idea,* pp. 453–55.

As did many of his congregation, Morteira took matters of lineage and descent quite seriously.[103] He himself took considerable pride in his status as a Levite. Therefore the knowledge that over the course of the centuries some had come to be considered priests or Levites but did not fit the technical requirements must have been disturbing for the preacher and his listeners. Clearly, this matter would have to be straightened out before the restoration of the cult—indeed, Isaiah spoke of this (66:21)—and Elijah, who preserved in his memory the lines of descent, could demote improper individuals without revealing publicly their blemishes and humiliating them.[104]

A different sermon reports yet another function not mentioned in the *Va-Era* text. Here Morteira expounds the idea that before the crowns of royalty and Torah were lost, God sequestered the Ten Tribes and the ark so that they would be safe for their future roles. Developing this motif further, the preacher continues,

> Before the crown of priesthood was lost, God first sequestered Elijah, the High Priest, who was Phinehas, to whom was given the blessing of eternal priesthood (cf. Num. 25:13). He is the priest who will anoint King Messiah, and who will prepare the tenth heifer, and through whom the resurrection of the dead will take place.[105]

In the other sermon, Elijah would anoint in his capacity as prophet; here it is in his capacity as priest. This designation is based on the aggadic assertion—in violation of any plausible chronological considerations—that Phinehas, Aaron's grandson, was none other than Elijah.[106] In addition, we have the assertion that Elijah will "make the tenth heifer." This statement draws from another tradition: that there were only nine red heifers in antiquity. In his

---

103. See the extended discussion in the Sabbath of Repentance sermon on Deut. 32:12, below, pp. 476–81.

104. The rabbinic basis of this idea would seem to be the anonymous statement of M. *'Eduyot* 8,7; see Maimonides' Commentary *ad loc* for the application of this ambiguous statement to the priesthood. Yet in his *Code* (*Hil. Melakhim*, 12:2), Maimonides states the view of the Sages that Elijah will not disqualify those presumed to be of legitimate descent or pronounce qualified those presumed to be of illegitimate descent. Rather, this task is to be performed by the Messiah, after his kingdom is established (ibid., 12:3). Cf. Menasseh ben Israel, *Conciliator* 2:83–84.

105. MS 3:241v, *Berakhah*, Deut. 33:17, after 1641.

106. See Ginzberg, *Legends of the Jews*, 3:389, 6:316–17 (b. *Baba Metsi'a* 114b refers to Elijah as a priest, without explicitly identifying him with Phinehas); Klausner, *Messianic Idea*, p. 456: "It was the custom for high priests and prophets to anoint the kings." Elijah was both prophet and priest.

Code, Maimonides adds to this the assertion that "King Messiah will prepare the tenth, may he be quickly revealed."[107] The basis for Morteira's claim that this task would be fulfilled by Elijah is also unclear to me, as it must have been to many of the listeners.

2. The Ten Lost Tribes

Like Elijah, the tribes of the northern kingdom of Israel, conquered and deported by the Assyrians, represent continuity between glorious past and expected future, although unlike Elijah, the tribes exist as an abstract entity while the individuals in the tribes are born and die through the natural cycle of life. These tribes continued to play a significant role in Jewish (and Christian) imagination at the time when Morteira was preaching—and considerably after as well.[108] It was almost axiomatic for most Jews that these tribes had not been assimilated among the various peoples of the Assyrian empire and disappeared from the stage of history in antiquity, but that they still existed, retained their ancient Israelite traditions, and would be reunited with the Jews in messianic times. In 1644, reports of Israelite tribes in South America circulated in Amsterdam and would play an important role in the final dramatic chapter in the career of Morteira's younger rabbinic colleague, Menasseh ben Israel.[109] Morteira himself addressed this theme from the pulpit frequently, though never in more than a theoretical manner.

We have seen that the length of the exile, which took its toll on the morale of many Jews, also served as a powerful Christian polemical argument that Morteira addressed in various ways. That the Ten Tribes of Israel could have

107. M. *Parah* 3,5; Maimonides, *Code, Hilkhot Parah Adumah* 3,4. For a review of the various eschatological functions of Elijah documented in the classical literature, which does not include anything about the heifer, see Julius H. Greenstone, *The Messiah Idea in Jewish History* (Philadelphia, 1948), pp. 315–16, n. 36.

108. On Christian speculation during Morteira's lifetime, see Yerushalmi, *From Spanish Court to Italian Ghetto*, p. 306; A. J. Saraiva, "Antonio Vieira, M. Ben Israel et le Cinquième Empire," *StRos* 6 (1972): 25–56; David S. Katz, *Philo-Semitism and the Readmission of the Jews to England, 1603–1655* (Oxford, 1982), pp. 126–57; Richard Popkin, "The Rise and Fall of the Jewish Indian Theory," in Yosef Kaplan, Henry Méchoulan, and Richard Popkin, eds., *Menasseh ben Israel and His World* (Leiden, 1989), pp. 63–82; Andrew Colin Gow, *The Red Jews: Antisemitism in an Apocalyptic Age, 1200–1600* (Leiden, 1995), pp. 169–75; Hillel Halkin, *Across the Sabbath River* (Boston, 2002), pp. 166–22.

109. The story of an encounter with South American natives who claimed descent from Reuben and proclaimed *Hear, O Israel* in Hebrew, reported in Amsterdam by Aaron Levi de Montezinos, and its subsequent impact on Menasseh ben Israel's efforts on behalf of Jewish readmission to England, has been frequently recounted. See Roth, *A Life of Menasseh ben Israel*, pp. 176–93; Menasseh ben Israel, *The Hope of Israel*, introduction, pp. 60–76, text, pp. 105–11; Richard Popkin, "Rise and Fall," pp. 67–70.

retained their identity throughout a period of exile that began many centuries before the current long exile of the Jewish people might seem implausible. But Morteira, taking their continued existence as beyond question, draws from it a message of encouragement for his listeners by pointing to the tribes as a noble model. The splendor of these tribes is not the result of the early date of their punishment, he asserts;

> it derives rather from the merit of strong, trusting faith. For more than six hundred years before the Jews did, the tribes began to wait for redemption, as this is how long their exile preceded ours. This is a decisive rebuttal to those who say that the reason for the length of our exile is a specific sin, which they invented. Why, the exile of the Ten Tribes has lasted six hundred years longer than ours, and they are always strong in their trust.[110]

In addition to the positive lesson derived from the *a fortiori* argument—in well more than two millennia the tribes have not given up their trust that their redemption will come: why should you doubt?—Morteira sneaks in almost parenthetically a defensive response, what he typically calls a "decisive rebuttal," to a central Christian claim about the Jews. They maintain that the Jews' loss of sovereignty and their long exile is God's punishment for the crucifixion of Jesus. Indeed, the argument continues, no sin could justify such a long period of repudiation and suffering except for the sin of deicide. Yet the tribes have endured an even longer exile, beginning seven centuries before Jesus was born.[111] Hence, the necessary link with Deuteronomy 29:27: *He cast them into another land…* In a dramatic sermon on a great public occasion, Morteira used this verse in a very different way, deriving from it the idea of a continued Jewish presence in the land of Israel throughout the period of the current exile,[112] and indeed, Morteira refers to that interpretation here. But, following the midrashic homiletical tradition, he apparently feels no need for absolute consistency in the meaning of these verses:

> However, in accordance with our subject, since the verse refers specifically to the Ten Tribes, as they said in chapter *Ḥeleq,* as explained by Rashi, *He cast them into another land* (Deut. 29:27) means that they are all in one place, "into another land," namely, the Ten Tribes that

---

110. MS 3:241v, *Berakhah,* Deut. 33:17 (1641 or after).

111. Cf. Morteira's response to the eleventh question from the "Priest of Rouen": the exile of the Tribes was "ordered with particular and divine providence, that nobody might attribute this captivity to any sins committed during the existence of the Second Temple."

112. The sermon is translated below, p. 395.

Sennacherib exiled and settled in one place, for the tribe of Judah was scattered in many places.[113] That is why it says, *the banished of Israel . . . and the dispersed of Judah* (Isa. 11:12). Now it says, *va-yashlikhem*, derived from the root *n-sh-l*, as in *when God takes away (yeshel) his soul* (Job 27:8), which means removing and hiding, as explained by Rabbi David Kimhi.... God is preserving them and sustaining them in order to restore them.... In this manner I shall explain what the Sages said in chapter *Ḥeleq*, as I was asked about this not many days ago.[114]

The phrase *into another land* indicates that the verse cannot apply to the dispersion of the Jewish people throughout the world in the current exile. Hence the most natural referent is the tribes. This is underlined by a bit of grammatical legerdemain, reading an unsuspected root into the familiar word *va-yashlikhem*, an obscure verb from Job interpreted by Kimhi in a manner that would seem to apply to the Shi'ite doctrine of occultation: "removing and hiding." The distinction between the exile of the tribes and the exile of the Judeans is then highlighted by the difference between the two words used by Isaiah, suggesting that "dispersal" applies only to the Jews.[115]

More than a decade later, Morteira again insisted that the Ten Tribes had been exiled to a specific location, this time in the context of a verse from the Song of Songs:

> *My beloved's voice: behold he comes* (Song 2:8) means, behold God at the outset, before your exile, hid and concealed the ten banished tribes in a single place, not scattered among various peoples like the dispersion of Judah, as we explained this year on the verse, *Like a firstling bull in his majesty* (Deut. 33:17).[116] These God will arouse, *With them He will gore the peoples, the ends of the earth one and all. These are the myriads of Ephraim, those are the thousands of Manasseh* (ibid.). This is, *I will whistle to them and I will gather them* (Zech. 10:8). This behavior of the tribes is not called a

113. See Rashi on b. *Sanhedrin* 110b, beginning *va-yashlikhem*. The view that the Ten Tribes, unlike the scattered Jews, were exiled to, and have remained in, one location was not universally accepted by medieval and early modern Jews. Contrast Menasseh ben Israel, *The Hope of Israel*, pp. 102, 126, 132–33, 140.

114. MS 2:123v, *Ḥuqqat*, Num. 19:9, 1630. For Kimhi's interpretation of the root *n-sh-l* in Job 27:8, see his *Sefer ha-Shorashim*, 458; the connection with *va-yashlikhem* seems to be Morteira's own suggestion. Morteira's reference to recent conversations is not unusual in his sermons; see below his discussion of the destruction of the impulse toward evil in messianic times.

115. Abravanel makes the same point in his comment on this verse: *Perush Nevi'im Aharonim*, p. 93a.

116. This is the sermon cited below on pp. 353, 355, and 357.

"rebellion," for they are not under the government of another people. About this the Bible says, *And in that day a great ram's horn shall be sounded; and the lost ones who are in the land of Assyria and the banished who are in the land of Egypt shall come* (Isa. 27:13).... Indeed, that great day shall come, namely, the revelation of the Ten Tribes to redeem their brethren.[117]

Once more we find the motif of the tribes' concealment by God in a single location. But here we find additional themes as well, pertaining to the behavior of the tribes in the future. They will be the ones who—upon the proper signal from God—will re-emerge into the spotlight of history's center stage in other "to redeem their brothers." And this is not a "rebellion," something that would violate the famous "three oaths" that became the basis of an ideology of quietism in exile,[118] as they do not live under the jurisdiction of another government, but enjoy the autonomy of their own political leadership.[119] To look at one other formulation of this same theme, here is a passage from a sermon on the final lesson in the cycle of Torah readings from the early 1640s, from which we have already cited a passage about Elijah:

> Before the crown of royalty was lost, God sequestered a great army, a massive people, preserving them for the proper time to restore royalty to His chosen one, namely, the Ten Tribes, *the lost ones who are in the land of Assyria* (Isa. 27:13). He did not scatter and disperse them as He did to Judah; rather, *He cast them into another land, as this day* (cf. Deut. 29:27), all of them together, no aliens with them, actual hurling just like someone who hurls a stone far away.[120]

All the themes come together concisely: the antiquity of the tribes' exile, long pre-dating that of the Jews, the banishment to a single locale in contrast with the scattering of the Jews, the concealment or occultation, the invocation of

---

117. MS 5:47v, *Va-Yetse*, Gen. 29:7, 1644 or after; same year as sermon on Deut 33:17. Morteira's sermon on the following verse (5:44r, *Va-Yetse*, Gen. 29:8) refers again to sermon on Deut. 33:17 to express the same idea.

118. B. *Ketubot* 111a. On the influence of this passage in Jewish thought, see Aviezer Ravitzky, *Messianism, Zionism, and Jewish Religious Radicalism* (Chicago, 1996), pp. 211–34.

119. For the idea of descendants of the tribes living independently, not under a Gentile king, see *The Itinerary of Benjamin of Tudela* (Malibu, Ca., 1983), pp. 114–17. Morteira cites this work elsewhere (see below, p, 386) but for a different purpose.

120. MS 3:241v, *Berakhah*, Deut 33:17 (1641 or after). The idea developed in this sermon is that before the loss of the crowns of Torah, priesthood, and sovereignty, God concealed the ark, Elijah, and the Ten Tribes so that they would be safe for their future roles. See below on Elijah. As for the ark containing the original tablets, Morteira says that "when they are revealed, they will publicly testify to the Torah and its holiness in the sight of every living being" (ibid.).

Deuteronomy 29:27 as proof text. But here one final element appears explicitly: the military character of the tribes' role. They are a "great army," biding their time in isolation from their Jewish brothers, awaiting the proper historic moment to intervene mightily on their behalf. And this capacity to wait patiently, while harboring their strength for the battle to come, requires considerable discipline and fortitude.

> To Joshua, that is to say to the Messiah descended from Ephraim, the [anti]type of Joshua for reasons we have given, was given the strength of the ox to suffer and wait and be subjugated in exile until the time arrives for God to be aroused for them, as the Bible says, *I will whistle to them and gather them* (Zech. 10:8). Yet with all that he is also given the beauty of the horns of the wild-ox, for even though they have suffered in exile and not trained for many years, their heart is not weak and feeble; rather, *He has horns like the horns of the wild-ox, with them he will gore [the peoples], the ends of the earth* (Deut. 33:17).[121]

For Jews consigned to wait on the sidelines during periods of warfare between the nations of Europe and the Middle East, the idea of powerful allies, suffering in exile like their European kindred, yet confident that the time would come for their active and decisive military role of liberation and vengeance, must have been a source of significant psychological reassurance.[122]

There was an obvious question that any astute listener to these sermons could hardly fail to raise. These were, after all, not naive, provincial, unsophisticated Jews who knew nothing of the world outside their own neighborhood. Though an increasing number had been born in Amsterdam during the course of Morteira's career, most of them, especially in his early years, had made the journey from the Iberian peninsula. Some were international merchants with an entire network of contacts in various parts of the world; they knew about Africa, India, the Far East. Some had relatives who had settled in Recife and were aware of the "New World." In a sermon delivered in 1630, Morteira himself raises the question that must have occurred to them:

> Now the question "Where are they now?" seems to me to be impossible to investigate. For since the Bible says, *In that day, a great ram's horn shall be sounded, and the lost ones who are in the land of Assyria shall come* (Isa. 27:13), if their place of residence were known before this, the words of the prophet, who called them "the lost ones," would not come true. But the words of the prophet cannot turn out to be false. Therefore, it is

---

121. MS 3:242r, *Berakhah*, Deut. 33:17 (1641 or after).
122. See on this Netanyahu, *Don Isaac Abravanel*, pp. 230–32.

impossible to know where they are. And this is, in my judgment, a fully cogent proof that resolves the confusion of those who ask, "Now that almost the entire earth has been discovered, how can we not know the place where the Ten Tribes reside?" For just as Joseph was in Egypt for many years, yet in accordance with God's will . . . his father knew nothing of this . . . so, in accordance with God's will, with the sequestered Ten Tribes named after Joseph: God does not want their place to be known even though almost all inhabited places have become public knowledge.[123]

Both of Morteira's arguments are rooted not in the experience of merchants or explorers but in the Bible; the first is exegetical, the second typological. The appeal to Isaiah is almost in the form of a syllogism. Isaiah spoke of the future restoration of "the lost ones in the land of Assyria." Now if people knew precisely where the tribes were, this prophecy of restoration would not be fully true, in that they would not be "lost" (major premise). But prophetic utterances cannot be false (minor premise). Ergo.... The second appeals to a biblical model. Joseph is not only the progenitor of the largest of the tribes (Menasseh and Ephraim) but a prototype or prefiguration for them.[124] While he was in Egypt, his father and brothers were ignorant of his whereabouts, despite the importance of his role. This establishes the pattern: God can conceal the location of the tribes from the Jewish people for His own reasons until the proper time.[125]

Morteira was constantly seeking to uncover for his listeners the great pat-

---

123. MS 2:123r, *Ḥuqqat*, Num 19:9, 1630.

124. As we shall see below in discussing the Ephraimite Messiah, and as we have seen previously with many examples, Morteira took typology quite seriously. For a general programmatic statement, see MS 2:135r, at the beginning of his sermon on Deuteronomy 33:7: "We have a tradition that before any of the noteworthy and marvelous deeds that God has performed or will in the future perform in this world, He first made a limited and imperfect prototype, which teaches about the perfection of the deed which God will accomplish at the proper time."

125. Cf. Morteira's response to the twenty-second question put by the priest of Rouen: "[Isaiah] called them lost [27:30] who were carried away by the Assyrians because it was not known what had become of them, and so they will remain until the season shall be appointed by the Divine Wisdom; in the same manner as Joseph was hid in Egypt for twenty-two years, until it pleased God to discover him to his family" (*www.jewish-history.com/Occident/volume3/jan1846/questions.html*). Also Menasseh ben Israel, *The Hope of Israel*, p. 145: Joseph was "the true type of the house of Israel, in his imprisonment and future happiness. Add to this, that he was so long hid from his brethren that they did not know him; as in like manner the Ten Tribes are at this day, who are led captive but hereafter shall come to the top of felicity, in the same manner as Joseph did."

terns that unified biblical and post-biblical Jewish experience and demonstrated God's providential control over all of history. One such pattern pertains to the Ten Tribes of Israel in messianic times:

> The first king of the tribe of Judah was named David, and after him will
> be the name of the Messiah descended from him. Similarly, the first
> prince, anointed for war, was from the tribe of Ephraim, and so the
> famous leader and Messiah who will be with the Ten Tribes when they
> return will be named Joshua.[126] About this, I have a marvelous piece of
> support. This is that the first officer was named Hosea [Num. 13:8, Deut.
> 32:44=Joshua], and the first prophet who prophesied about the exile of
> the Ten Tribes and their return was named Hosea, and the [last] king
> [of Israel] who was with them during the period of their exile was named
> Hosea. All this is to hint that even though their exile will last a very long
> time, there should be no despair of deliverance, for it is always with
> them.... As Joshua was the prototype for the Ephraimite Messiah,
> Moses called Hosea son of Nun "Joshua" (Num. 13:16), adding the
> letter *yod*, to indicate that he would be the head of the Ten Tribes.[127]

In this passage, he links together thematically three separate individuals in
the Bible with the same name, Hosea, and associates them all with the tribes
at the beginning and end of their exile. The relevance of Hosea, the last king
of Israel, in the ninth year of whose reign the Assyrian king Shalmanasser
exiled the Israelites from their land (2 Kings 17:1,6; 18:10-11) is obvious. So
is the prophet Hosea, who spoke of the exile and return of the tribes (see
Hosea 10:58, 11:8–11). Hosea/Joshua obviously lived centuries before these
events. Yet Morteira makes the military leader from the tribe of Ephraim into
a prototype or prefiguration for the military Messiah from the tribe of
Ephraim, who will lead the tribes out of their exile.[128] His explanation for the

---

126. Cf. ibid., p. 144: At the time of redemption, "the Ten Tribes shall come to Jerusalem
under the leadership of a Prince, whom some rabbis in the Talmud... call Messiah the son
of Joseph, and others Messiah the son of Ephraim."

127. MS 3:242r, *Berakhah*, Deut 33:17 (1641 or after).

128. For a precedent in viewing Joshua as a prototype for the Ephraimite Messiah, see
Bahya ben Asher, near the end of his long comment on the beginning of Exodus 18 (a
passage cited by Morteira in a different context: below, n. 155. Note that in his discussion
of the Sabbatian movement, Gershom Scholem, wrote that "the idea of taking an Old Testament figure such as Moses as a type of the messiah seems to be Christian" (*Sabbatai Sevi*,
p. 586). But Morteira's ample use of typology shows that he did not need a Christian model
for this way of reading the Bible. He was undoubtedly aware that Christians from a very
early period used Joshua as a type of the Messiah, prefiguring the role to be fulfilled by Jesus
(whose name, many Christians insisted, was originally the same in Hebrew, but was short-

change of name is different from that in the classical literature, which generally associates it with the name of God (b. *Sotah* 34b and parallels, Rashi on Num. 13:16). Where the Midrash associates the additional *yod* with its numerical equivalent, ten, it is to say that Joshua's reward would be taken from that of the ten other spies (Num. Rabbah 16,9 and parallels). Morteira adds to this an esoteric hint of the future role of another Joshua as redeemer of the tribes. Finally, he provides a name for this eschatological figure generally known in Jewish lore only as the "Messiah ben Joseph" or "Messiah ben Ephraim."[129] The Ten Tribes will not merely be summoned to rejoin their brothers at the critical unfolding of redemption. They will provide their own leader as an integral part of the eschatological scenario. All of this is encoded in Scripture for the careful reader to discover and the preacher to divulge.

3. The Ephraimite Messiah (Messiah ben Joseph)

This leads us directly to a third component of Jewish eschatological speculation. The Ephraimite Messiah is a far less familiar component of Jewish messianic doctrine than his Judean, Davidic counterpart.[130] Saadia Gaon considered him to be optional, necessary only if the Jewish people failed to repent, and indeed there are some thinkers—Maimonides is a noteworthy example—in whose writings he did not appear at all. Nor does he play a central role in the extensive messianic speculation of Abravanel.[131] Yet especially in the apocalyptic strand of Jewish speculation, this figure was extremely significant. As a descendant from the largest of the Israelite tribes, he represents the expectation of their inclusion, indeed their decisive involvement in the redemptive scenario. As a military leader, he expresses the anticipation that an age of peace must be preceded by a bloodbath for the Gentiles that would avenge the historical slaughter of defenceless Jews. As a figure who, after preliminary successes, would die in battle, he made it possible for those who had bound up their hopes with a personality whose career ended in a violent

---

ened by the Jews to *Yeshu* to conceal his redemptive role). Morteira took Christian arguments and turned them on their head for his own purposes.

129. The Midrash on Psalms (60,3) gives the name "Neḥemiah ben Ḥushiel" for a leader who will be seen lying dead before the gates of Jerusalem, though not identified as the Ephraimite Messiah; *Sefer Zerubavel* and other "midrashim of redemption" apparently take this over from that source: e.g. Raphael Patai, *The Messiah Texts* (New York, 1979), p. 126; Joseph Dan, *Ha-Sippur ha-'Ivri biYmei ha-Beinayim* (Jerusalem, 1974), pp. 38–39.

130. On the origins of this figure, see Klausner, *The Messianic Idea*, pp. 483–501.

131. For an example of an incidental reference, see Abravanel's *Yeshu'ot Meshiḥo* (Koenigsberg, 1861), p. 31a; cf. Lawee, *Isaac Abarbanel's Stance Toward Tradition*, p. 165.

death to conclude that they had not been deceived, but that the death itself was an integral part of the eschatological script. All this is the background for Morteira's discussion, which suggests no hint of a doubt about the centrality of the Ephraimite Messiah's role.

Let us continue following the argument in the sermon from which the previous passage was taken, discussing Joshua as a prototype of the Ephraimite Messiah:

> To Joshua was given "majesty" through victory over enemies, but not "splendor," for he had no children, and his descendants did not inherit his position. And so with his [anti]type, the Ephraimite Messiah: even though he will defeat many peoples and he will have majesty, at the end he will be killed, as Zechariah said, *wailing over him as over a favorite son and showing bitter grief as over a firstborn* (Zech. 12:10). He will not have the splendor of leadership in peacetime with the splendor of royalty, for royalty will be given to the Messiah descended from David.[132]

This is the familiar job description for the Ephraimite Messiah: he will "defeat many peoples," as we shall soon see, and enjoy a brief period of majestic triumph. Yet this achievement will have no direct continuity. In a manner that we shall soon see, his death in battle at the hands of powerful enemies is written into the script, predicted by the prophets. The true glory—that of a royal ruler who will reign in times of peace—must be reserved for another.

Joshua, however, was not the only prototype for the Ephraimite Messiah. One of the most fruitful sources for Jewish typological interpretation were the chapters in the lessons *Toledot* and *Va-Yishlah* that narrate the relationship between the brothers Jacob and Esau, universally understood by medieval Jews as types for Jews and Christians. Using the mode of typology with unprecedented thoroughness and ingenuity, Morteira mined these chapters for information about present and future, returning to the theme in a number of different sermons, for as he said (in the passage cited below), "every incident of Jacob's interaction with Esau is an allusion for their descendants."[133] One of these is an early sermon (autumn 1621) on the third verse of *Va-Yishlah*, *I have ox and ass, a flock of sheep, male and female in servitude; I send this message to my lord, in the hope of gaining your favor* (Gen. 32:6). This passage certainly does not appear to have any messianic content. Yet Morteira moves to this subject by means of his rabbinic dictum from the Midrash Genesis Rabbah (75,6),

---

132. 3:242r, *Berakhah*, Deut 33:17 (1641 or after). For the use of the verse from Zechariah for the Ephraimite Messiah, see b. *Sukkah* 52b.

133. See on this *"Your Voice Like a Ram's Horn,"* pp. 30–33.

reporting a tradition, based on the characteristic citation of proof-texts from elsewhere in Scripture, that decodes the verse and derives from it a very different level of meaning. "*Ox* refers to the anointed for war, as we see in the verse, *A firstling ox in his majesty* (Deut. 33:17). *Ass* refers to the King Messiah, as we see in the verse, *humble, riding on an ass* (Zech. 9:9). *Flock* refers to Israel, as we see in the verse, *And you, My flock, the flock of My pasture* (Ezek. 34:31)."

Morteira begins by discussing some of the more obvious problems with the verse, especially the use of nouns in the singular where we would expect the plural, but soon moves on to its messianic content:

> When the Sages brought proof [in the dictum] from the verse *a firstling ox in his majesty* (Deut. 33:17), it became clear that this alluded to the Messiah descended from Joseph, who is mentioned in this midrashic passage.[134] We have from the tradition of our Sages in many places that he will be revealed first, then afterward our King Messiah, namely, the great and enduring Messiah. Afterward, Israel, referring to the ingathering of the exiles. For every incident of Jacob's interaction with Esau is an allusion for their descendants. That is why "ox" preceded "ass" [in Gen. 32:6], and then came "sheep." However, how this will be—how a Messiah descended from Ephraim will be revealed first, and why, and from where they derived this, and what the Sages said about him, and what we can see in this matter from their statements that contradict each other, and how after this our Messiah will appear—this will be our sermon today. We shall speak about this as best we can, even though I have not found anyone who speaks about it substantially and directly, but only indirectly. Nevertheless, we shall speak about it, as God gives us favor, for this is the theme of today's Text.[135]

The preacher does not turn immediately to this subject, however. In a leisurely manner, he discusses other issues relating to the rabbinic reading of the verse and messianic doctrine, particularly relating to the identification in contemporary terms of the people named "Paras" in certain key rabbinic statements.[136] Eventually, however, he gets to the topic he promised: "Now

---

134. The verse is part of Moses' blessing of the Joseph tribes near the end of his life; hence the proof-text signifies the warrior Messiah descended from Joseph.

135. MS 3:98r, *Va-Yishlaḥ*, Gen. 32:6, fall 1621. Cf. also *Va-Yeshev*, 3:45b, 95b.

136. Rabbinical opinion is divided about the referent of *the young of the flock* in Jeremiah 49:20 and 50:45 (see the passage cited below). One midrashic tradition, contained in Morteira's dictum for this sermon (Gen. Rabbah 75,6 and parallels), is that "Esau will fall to the descendents of Rachel" (Ephraim and Menasseh, whose father Joseph was born after the other sons). Another tradition, recorded in the Talmud (b. *Yoma* 10a), understands it to

it remains for us to explain the matter of the Messiah descended from Joseph."

This discussion introduces a dramatic scenario of world war involving the major powers of the age, bringing together the Gentile nations, the Ten Tribes, and the Ephraimite Messiah, all preceding the advent of the Davidic Messiah:

> We have a tradition from our ancestors, and we shall say that it is well known how our Sages agreed, with proofs that we have cited, that the children of Ishmael will come against Rome and besiege it. In addition to these proofs, there is the statement of R. Ishmael in *Pirqei de-R. Eliezer* [chap. 29], "The children of Ishmael are destined to wage three wars of chaos in the end of days, as the prophet says, *For they have fled before swords* (Isa. 21:15). One on land: *before the whetted sword,* one on the sea: *before the bow that was drawn,* and one at the great city of Rome, which will be more grievous than the other two: *before the grievousness of war* (ibid.).[137]

Like the Ephraimite Messiah, the destruction of Rome as an integral part of the messianic script was not clearly rooted in the Bible. For a textual basis it required applying the biblical prophecies of destruction directed toward Edom to the Christian capital far removed from the Middle East.[138] Here too there seemed to be a psychological need to wreak vengeance on the symbolic center of Christendom, even at the cost of serious logistical dislocation for the world's armies, which would have to fight their battles both on the Italian peninsula and in the Holy Land.

There is no doubt that to this war [against Rome] will be gathered all

refer to "Paras" (usually understood as "Persia"). Morteira (following Abravanel) understands "Paras" as referring to the contemporary Turks, a people who came from the east, and—as Morteira notes—have been in control of Constantinople for 168 years (98v). Morteira rarely gives such specific chronology in his sermons. For Abravanel's identification of "Paras" with the Turks, see sources cited in Netanyahu, *Don Isaac Abravanel*, pp. 216, 234. Morteira cites Abravanel in this passage (3:98r, beginning of paragraph 2).

137. MS 3:98r, *Va-Yishlah*, Gen. 32:6, fall 1621.

138. Cf. Abravanel, *Mashmi'a Yeshu'ah*, in *Perush al Nevi'im u-Khetuvim,* Ninth Announcer (Obadiah), pp. 551–57; Jean-Christophe Attias, *Isaac Abravanel* (Paris, 1992), pp. 245–76. For the background of this, see Cohen, "Esau as Symbol in Early Medieval Jewish Thought;" Netanyahu, *Abravanel*, p. 233. The Talmudic basis is the statement "Rome is destined to fall into the power of Persia" (b. *Yoma* 10a). The destruction of Rome by the Messiah became an integral part of some Protestant millenarian speculation in the seventeenth century; see Munk, *The Devil's Mousetrap*, pp. 49, 58, 66, and 67 (with Increase Mather stating that "the Jews themselves do not expect their Deliverance until Rome be first destroyed").

the inhabitants of the world to confront each other. This is because of the great and ancient reputation that Rome has throughout the world, and also because of the hatred for it, derived from the contrariness of its religion and its hegemony over all. About this gathering, the prophets [said?] that many kings would awaken (cf. Jer. 50:41), as if they were sleeping, from the corners of the earth, and that an emissary would be sent to these people (cf. Isa. 18:2). (?) the children of Ishmael, dwelling in the east against Rome.

All of the Ten Tribes will come, their king at their head, for they would not come (?) This is the Ephraimite Messiah. Then the verse, *Surely the young of the flock shall drag them away* (Jer. 49:20, 50:45) will be fulfilled for *both* of them, Joseph [i.e., "the descendants of Rachel"] and Persia, according to the words and tradition of the Sages.[139] That this is the truth, all the prophecies that spoke about the matter of the Ten Tribes have communicated clearly. Beyond this, there are many difficulties in interpreting these statements, the explanation of each one would require a sermon in itself. However, within the limits of our time, we shall pass through them to show this truth.[140]

At this point, Morteira proceeds to provide proof texts for the gathering of nations, including the Ten Tribes, drawn primarily from Isaiah at the end of chapter 17 and the beginning of chapter 18.

> This is, therefore, how the appearance of the Ten Tribes will be in the midst of many nations to wage war against Rome. Now common sense suggests, and biblical verses teach, and the Sages confirm that when the Christians see the immense horde descending upon Rome and the Pope fleeing from it, they will draw a lesson from experience, from what Scipio did to Hannibal, for he went to Carthage and caused Hannibal to abandon [his attack upon] Rome. So, by means of a great army that goes to the Holy Land and Egypt, the Christians will draw off the many Muslim nations to abandon [their attack on] Rome and to come to the aid of their own territory. Then the entire world will band together against Jerusalem, as they banded together against Rome. And then the

---

139. This scenario validates both of the rabbinic views cited in n. 136. For the war against Rome, leading to its destruction, in medieval Jewish eschatology, see Netanyahu, *Don Isaac Abravanel*, pp. 233–38; Isaiah Tishby, "Acute Apocalyptic Messianism," in Marc Saperstein, *Essential Papers on Messianic Movements and Personalities in Jewish History* (New York, 1992), pp. 259, 269–70, 281–83, n. 34. Cf. Katz, *Philo-Semitism*, pp. 91, 103 n. 44.

140. MS 3:98v, *Va-Yishlaḥ*, Gen. 32:6, fall 1621. A hole in the page at the left margin leaves lacunae at the ends of several lines.

Messiah descended from Ephraim will die in that war, for they the Christians will be victorious.... The Messiah descended from Ephraim will be killed. About him, the prophet himself said in that place, *They shall lament to Me about the one they pierced, wailing over him as over a favorite son and showing bitter grief as over a firstborn* (Zech. 12:10).[141]

In this passage, Morteira seems to be integrating two motifs of medieval Jewish apocalyptic imagination. The first is the wars of Gog and Magog, the original context for which in the prophet Ezekiel requires a setting in the land of Israel. The second is the newer motif of the apocalyptic destruction of Rome, the heart of Christendom. In order to fit both into the scenario of a world war issuing in the end of days, he appeals to a historical precedent. Once before, in ancient times, a massive army, led by Hannibal of Carthage, had threatened Rome. Scipio decided that the most effective way to defend the city against this onslaught was to launch a counterattack against the enemy's capital. Similarly in the future apocalyptic war, faced with the impending attack by the ten Israelite tribes, their Muslim allies, and various other nations—a threat that would impel the Pope once again to flee for his safety[142]—the leaders of Christendom would decide to mobilize all their forces in a new Crusade, threatening Egypt and the Holy Land. The invading armies in Italy would then need to withdraw to defend their own heartlands. Morteira's time was not a period of Ottoman advancement into Europe, so the scenario has a strong element of myth and fantasy. Following the traditional pattern, it is in this battle that the Ephraimite Messiah would be killed.

Characteristically, Morteira does not just leave this account as the fulfillment of biblical prophesy. He insists that the events of the future are not just foretold but also prefigured, encoded in biblical narratives that may seem to have no relevance to anything beyond themselves. If the prototype for exile and redemption was the Egyptian enslavement and the Exodus, there must be something in that experience that indicates the pattern of a valiant messianic figure, descendant of Ephraim, who is temporarily successful but then falls in battle. He found this prefiguration in a rabbinic narrative that is generally used to illustrate the pitfalls of premature initiative, but here serves as a model for one who points the way:

---

141. MS 3:99r. On Scipio and Hannibal, cf. *Sefer Yossipon*, pp. 1:93–95, and the discussion in chap. 7 above, p. 232.

142. This image of the Pope fleeing may be an association with the memory of Rome invaded and sacked in 1527 by imperial troops, who besieged Pope Clement VII in the Castel Sant' Angelo.

All this God hinted in the Exodus from Egypt. When the children of
Ephraim went out thirty years before, the children of Gath killed
them.[143] Afterward, the appointed redeemer came: Moses. So the
Messiah will be revealed, and God will go forth and do battle against
those nations. All this God showed us also in the narrative of Abraham,
for four kings came and defeated the five and took Lot captive, and then
Abraham arose, alone with the members of his household; he defeated
them and restored everything. So when they challenge each other in
these wars, the [Messiah] son of David will sprout forth, and he will see
the destruction of both sides.[144]

The pioneering effort of the tribe of Ephraim serves as a natural model for
the same tribe led by its king in the vanguard of the Israelite battle for
liberation in the future. The narrative of Abraham's warfare in Genesis 14
seems less promising as a source for messianic typology. Morteira takes it
simply as a paradigm for the lesson that when the great nations of the world
do battle with each other, it is a time when the Messiah may be revealed,
triumphant over all.[145]

4. Ingathering of the Exiles

The reappearance of the Ten Tribes in battle mode, led by their king, the
Ephraimite Messiah, is only part of the full ingathering of the exiles. Morteira
insists that only God can perform this act of incomparable complexity and
difficulty. Indeed, by comparison, it makes the Exodus from Egypt and the
guiding of the Israelites through the wilderness to the Promised Land seem
almost simple. In a sermon from the 1630s based on the harsh oppression
recounted in Exodus 1:14, Morteira explains the greater challenges that God
will face in the future ingathering. First, unlike the Israelites in Egypt, the Jews
are no longer a unified people sharing a common historical experience; Jews
today have become extremely diverse as a result of having lived in many
different countries.[146] Second, "many have become assimilated among the

---

143. Ginzberg, *Legends of the Jews* 3:8–9, with sources 6: 2–3; compare above nn. 83–84.
144. MS 3:99r.
145. In this context, he cites Gen. Rabbah 42,4: "If you see kingdoms combating each
other, look for the Messiah's footprint, for so it was in the time of Abraham: because the
kingdoms combated each other, redemption came for Abraham."
146. In a different sermon, for Sukkot, Morteira fleshes this out. The Bible tells us about
the divisions within the Israelites, all of whom came from the same experience of slavery.
"How much more difficult, therefore, would it be to harmonize and gather in so many Jews
born in different lands, with antithetical characteristics, who have assimilated among the
Gentiles and learned their ways. Why, certainly they would be factionalized and divided

nations and all but lost among them, and God must bring them out from there." This rather clearly alludes to the *conversos* and their descendants, who—as Morteira insists in a number of different sermons—cannot escape the destiny of the Jewish people even if they want to do so.[147] Third, God must gather those who are "concealed from human sight," referring to the "lost" tribes. And fourth is the simple logistical nightmare of gathering Jews from so many different places. Yet the biblical prophecies assure us that not a single Jew or descendent of a Jew will be left out when the ingathering occurs.[148]

Even this, however, is only one part of the process of eschatological ingathering, which, Morteira argues strongly in a different sermon, is impossible to conceive in naturalistic terms. Not only Jews but Gentiles are involved:

> The second [ingathering] is the assembling of all the Gentiles together for war, for their destruction, their crushing, and their extermination, for this is impossible without a divine act. How would all the different peoples, the separate nations, agree together, how would they compromise, to whom would they give coercive authority, so that they would not be confounded by contention and strife? Only the power of God is great enough to bring them out of their lands, to set their minds to this.... Truly this is a great miracle, to arouse the hearts of all the peoples and to gather them to one purpose.[149]

We have already seen in another sermon Morteira propose a unifying force that would inspire all of the nations to cooperate for a single goal: their hatred of Rome. Here, perhaps more realistically, he emphasizes the fissures even within, let us say, the Ottoman Empire, that would make improbable any universally coordinated effort. Finally, there is a third ingathering, pertaining to the animal world:

> The third is to arouse the hearts and the will of all living creatures to be gathered to one place, as the prophet proclaimed in the section about Gog: *And you, O mortal, say to every winged bird and to all the wild beasts.... Assemble, come and gather from all around for the sacrificial feast I am preparing for you—a great sacrificial feast—upon the mountains of Israel, and eat flesh and drink blood* (Ezek. 39:17). Who can do something like this

among themselves more than the divisiveness and splintering of the generation of the Tower of Babel. Only God can do this." MS 2:2v, Sukkot, Ezekiel 38.

147. See the texts in chap. 8, above, pp. 289–95. On the inclusion of the assimilated and intermarried in the ingathering, cf. Abravanel, *Mashmi'a Yeshu'ah*, p. 21d; Netanyahu, *Don Isaac Abravanel*, p. 238.

148. MS 4:2r, *Shemot*, Exod. 1:14.

149. Ibid.

except for God?[150]

This, to be sure, is a rather gory enterprise: the animals of the world gathered not to lie down, wolf and lamb together, in pastoral serenity, but to gorge themselves on the blood of the Gentile nations. Yet it is part of the biblical prophecy, and Morteira took this material quite seriously. It fits his passion for structure: three ingatherings, each one of them beyond the capacity of human beings to achieve through natural means, and therefore requiring divine intervention.[151] And it raises in a brutal manner the question of the fate of the Gentile nations in messianic times.

5. The Fate of the Gentile Nations

What will happen to the Gentile nations is a complicated matter in Jewish eschatological speculation. A whole range of views can be documented, from universalistic inclusiveness to xenophobic vindictiveness, from serene co-existence to apocalyptic bloodbath, all anchored in texts from the classical sources. A Jewish thinker setting out to formulate a coherent messianic doctrine needs to make choices, to privilege certain texts and overlook others, and indeed we find compelling examples of this kind of selectivity.[152] A preacher does not need to be fully consistent; sometimes he may emphasize one theme, sometimes another.

It seems clear that Morteira takes seriously the tradition of massive if not total destruction of the Gentile nations in messianic times. We have already noted his statement that the second ingathering will be the assembling of all the Gentiles together for war, for their destruction, their crushing, and their extermination (a phrase taken from Esther 9:24, referring to the annihilation of the Jews planned by Haman). In a different sermon, delivered near the

---

150. Ibid. Cf. *Midrash Alpha Betot* cited in Patai, *The Messiah Texts,* p. 155.

151. While we have seen the role played by the Ephraimite Messiah as leader of the returning tribes, the Davidic Messiah does not seem to play a central role for Morteira in the comprehensive ingathering. God's exclusive role in this enterprise is expressed in the *Amidah* liturgy ("Lift up the banner to gather our exiles, and gather us quickly from the four corners of the earth") and in various Talmudic passages, but other thinkers have given a more active role for the Messiah. See, e.g., Targum Pseudo-Jonathan on Deut. 30:4 and Jer. 33:13; Marc Saperstein, *Decoding the Rabbis* (Cambridge, 1980), pp. 103–6.

152. A striking example is Maimonides, who takes several statements attributed in the Talmud to individual rabbis ("The sole difference between the present and the Messianic days is [delivery from] servitude to foreign powers," b. *Sanhedrin* 91b), "Blasted be those who calculate the end," ibid. 97b), and presents them as authoritative formulations of rabbinic messianism (*Code, Hilkhot Melakhim* 12, 2). For a bibliography on Maimonides' messianic doctrine, see Dov Schwartz, *Ha-Ra'ayon ha-Meshiḥi ba-Hagut ha-Yehudit bi-Ymei ha-Beinayim* (Ramat-Gan, 1997), p. 70, n. 56.

beginning of his career on Shavu'ot 1619, he proposes a more contemporary model for the fate of the Gentiles. Many prophetic verses inform us that the punishment of the nations will be measure for measure (for example: *As you did, so shall it be done to you; your conduct shall be requited* (Obad. 15; he cites also Lam. 1:22 and Ps. 137:7). Therefore, Morteira suggests, it is also possible to say that "on the great and awesome day of judgment, God will make for Edom an *auto[-da-fe]*, as they do in Spain on the day they burn the *conversos*, as is known to those who have seen it, for the heart bursts over this."[153] Certainly there were those in the congregation who had witnessed such spectacular events either in Spain or in Portugal, and could respond with visceral satisfaction to the suggestion that the tables would some day be turned.

In another early sermon, delivered a few months before this, Morteira discusses a debate among the Sages not on the ultimate destiny of the Gentiles, but on the timing of this cataclysmic end (at least for those in Christendom). Interpreting an aggadic statement about the death of Esau typologically ("they spoke about the past, but hinted about the future"), he finds the Sages divided. Some hold that "the destruction and extermination of the descendants of Esau (*hashmadat u-kheliyat zera 'Esav*) would be at the time of the advent of the Messiah"; others hold that this event will be at a later stage in the Messiah's career, during the war of Gog and Magog. But lest there be any uncertainty, he insists that the eschatological destruction pertains "to all the Gentile nations, which are truly the descendants of Esau, which have no remnant or remainder, but immediately after the advent of our Messiah they will all be terminated together."[154]

On the other hand, a sermon delivered some ten years later expresses a very different view. It is on the lesson *Yitro*, which begins with Moses' Midianite father-in-law coming to praise God for the deliverance of the Israelites and making a significant contribution to the well-being of the newly liberated people. Morteira starts his discussion with a long quotation from Bahya ben Asher's commentary on this chapter, which holds that all the Gentiles will convert to Judaism in the messianic age—the antithesis of the genocidal scenario mentioned above.[155] Bahya establishes the foundation for Morteira's own reading of Jethro as a type alluding to all proselytes—a subject he has

153. MS 2:223r, *Shavu'ot* 1619, Deut 16:10.

154. MS 2:190v-191r, *Be-Ha'alotekha*, Num. 10:14, 1619 (cf. *Yalqut Shim'on, Va-Yeḥi*, end of parag. 162.

155. See Bahya ben Asher, near the end of his long comment at the beginning of Exodus 18; cf. Nissim ben Reuben Gerundi, *Derashot ha-RaN* (Jerusalem, 1973), p. 120–21, 124; Schwartz, *Ha-Ra'ayon he-Meshiḥi ba-Hagut ha-Yehudit*, p. 182. Note that in his response to the tenth question from the "Priest of Rouen," Morteira states that all of the Gentiles will

addressed in many previous sermons on the lesson whose content he briefly reviews. Jethro's coming to see Moses after the Exodus thus prefigures Gentile proselytes coming to Judaism in the messianic age, convinced of its truth by the spectacular vindication of the Jews.

The various rabbinic interpretations of the phrase "Jethro rejoiced" (Exod. 18:9) suggest to Morteira four different categories of nations with different fates. First is the category of Gentiles who will recognize the one true God and worship Him by observing the seven Noahide laws. Those in this category will abandon all beliefs that deny the unity of God, whether the dualism of "the disciples of Mani," the trinitarianism of the Christians, or the polytheism of the pagans. The second category is composed of those whom God will recognize to be part of the Jewish people by lineage—"descendants of His people and offspring of Israel's loins"—though they may not recognize this themselves: those who are "from the descendants of Israel but long ago were assimilated, or forced [to convert] or sold as male or female slaves, and do not know that they are descendants of Israel. From them, God will take some to serve as priests and Levites, revealing their family pedigree."[156] This category does not refer to "New Christians" in Portugal who know that they are of Jewish descent but who choose to remain in a Christian society, either because of materialistic considerations or sincere belief. As we have seen, they will also be selected by God, but for a devastating punishment. Here Morteira seems to be talking about the descendants of victims of past persecutions who genuinely believe that they are Christians, but who may still be by descent not just Jews but Levites or priests. As in many other places in Morteira's sermons, we see here how important was the principle of lineage for him and his community.

The third category is familiar to us from the earlier sermons:

> . . . that [whose fate is] swift annihilation. The prophetic literature is full of this, for example, *For the Eternal holds a sacrifice on Bozrah, a great slaughter in the land of Edom* (Isa. 34:6), and the wars of Gog and Magog, and the prophecy of Zechariah, *Throughout the land, declares the Eternal, two thirds shall perish, shall die* (Zech. 13:8), and the like. This destruction will begin with the descendants of Amalek, and all who associate themselves with it and intermarry with it: [God] will search after it to destroy it.[157]

---

acknowledge and obey the Messiah, who will be "revered and acknowledged in all parts of the world, and by all nations."

156. MS 2:232v, *Yitro*, Exod. 18:9.

157. Ibid.

Morteira speaks of "the descendants of Amalek and all who associate themselves with it and intermarry with it" as if he were referring to an actual group that was especially worthy of "swift annihilation" not just because of their ancestors but because of their deeds at present, though they do not seem to refer to an identifiable national group, such as the Portuguese, for then there would be no need for God's special search. Finally, the Messiah will determine a fourth category to be Gibeonites, not from the descendants of Israel. These he will place "under their burden and under their curse which [Joshua] imposed on them forever. The Bible says, *Therefore, be accursed! Never shall your descendants cease to be slaves, hewers of wood and drawers of water for the House of my God* (Josh. 9:23). Now all may be healed, but the serpent and the Gibeonites will never be healed."[158] It is difficult to know from this typology what percentage of the Gentiles Morteira assumed would fall into each of the categories. His more mature view, by contrast with the early sermons that speak of destruction for *all* the Gentiles, reveals a somewhat more nuanced approach to the world in the messianic age, reflecting the diversity of statements in the classical Jewish texts. And the very fact that he cites at length Bahya ben Asher's radically different eschatology, in which all the Gentiles are to become Jews, without polemicizing against it, shows his willingness to expose his listeners to a variety of options.

6. Davidic Messiah

As in most theoretical Jewish discussions of the messianic age, Morteira does not spend inordinate time talking about the Messiah himself. In one sermon, however, he does discuss the identity of the Messiah. The theme-verse for the sermon is Deuteronomy 33:7, beginning, *Hear, O God, the voice of Judah, and restore him to his people*; Morteira interprets the "voice of Judah" as a reference to King David, and "restore him" as a reference to the Messiah. But he then insists that "the first messiah (i.e. David, the anointed one), described as the "voice of Judah," is *himself* the one who will come to redeem Israel." This theme is later developed by discussing a passage from the extensive Talmudic treatment of messianic matters in tractate *Sanhedrin* (98b): "Rav Judah said in Rav's name, The Holy One, blessed be He, will raise up another David for us, as Scripture says, *they shall serve the Eternal their God and David, the king whom I will raise up for them* (Jer. 30:9): not 'I raised up,' but 'I will raise up.' Rav Papa said to Abaye, But it is written, *My servant David, their prince forever* (Ezek. 37:25)— like an emperor and a half-emperor." Morteira spends considerable

---

158. Ibid., 233r. The final statement is based on Gen. Rabbah 20,5, the rabbinic dictum cited at the beginning of the sermon.

time characteristically raising problems with this passage, before committing himself to his own conclusion. When the prophet spoke of "my servant David" in the context of the future redemption,

> we should not believe that *My servant David* mentioned here is another man from among his descendants who would have the same name, or one of his descendants whom the prophet would call "David" simply because he was from the line of David. This is not so. Rather, I say that the very same David who was their prince, was always their prince in the past. For the word "forever" (*le-'olam*), although it is commonly used for the future, is occasionally used for the past....
>
> Now everything is resolved quite clearly. For when Rav Judah said that in the future God would raise up for them another David, based on the word *aqim, I will raise* (Jer, 30:9), in the future tense, they challenged him by citing the verse, *and David my servant, their prince forever* (Ezek. 37:25). The answer is, the David mentioned [in Jer. 30:9] is the very same David who was their prince. How then do I fulfill *that I will raise* (ibid.)? "Like an emperor and a half-emperor." For it is known that in the days of the emperors, they would choose a "half-emperor" to reign instead of the emperor at his death. Even today, this is the practice among the emperors, with the "King of the Romans."[159] When he ascends to the status of emperor, even though he was already selected for this, it is said that he rose to royalty. That is why it says *that I will raise* (Jer. 30:9): not that it is a new person, but because of his rising in stature. That is why they called him first "king," meaning that he is the one who was their prince forever, already. And now don't raise the problem of the word "forever," for it does not speak about the future but about the past. Thus the conclusion of this matter is what we have said, namely that the Messiah is David himself. That is why David said, *I will dwell in Your tent forever* (Ps. 61:5), the Hebrew *'olamim* ("forever") referring to two periods and generations, one as king and the other as Messiah.[160]

It is not entirely clear why Morteira insisted that the Messiah would be none other than David himself (either through reincarnation or resurrection), rather than merely a descendant of David. Was it simply a matter of taking seriously

159. "King of the Romans" (*Römischerkönig*) was the technical term for Emperor Elect of Holy Roman Empire, who would become Emperor at the death of his father, with no second coronation necessary. See James Bryce, *The Holy Roman Empire* (London, 1904), pp. 472–73. (This was the status of Joseph II in the eighteenth century during the last years of his mother's reign.).

160. MS 2:135v136r, *Berakhah*, Deut. 33:7.

a rather literal reading of the prophetic verses, or was there some deeper ideological issue at stake? Certainly, if this sermon had been delivered during the frenzy of the Sabbatian movement, it would be viewed as undermining the claims of a would-be messianic figure who was manifestly not King David. But of course it is too early for this. In any case, Morteira says little about the nature of David's rule in his second, messianic, reign. The one thing he insists upon is that unlike the initial career, during which he spilled much blood in war, in David's reappearance "his hands will not be stained with the blood of his enemies, but *he shall slay the wicked with the breath of his lips* (Isa. 11:4), and God will provide him *help from his foes* (Deut. 33:7, the theme-verse), meaning, actually from his foes, for they will kill each other."[161] One warrior Messiah, apparently, was enough.

7. Conquest of the Evil Impulse

We can highlight only a few discussions of the actual nature of the messianic age in Morteira's sermons. One is a fascinating treatment of the motif of the conquest, enslavement, or even murder of the *yetser ha-ra*, which figures as a motif in some messianic speculation. Morteira introduces this motif as a report of a discussion with a Christian theologian, a discussion that does not seem to be highly polemical or hostile but rather an exploration of an issue of interest across religious lines:

> A certain scholar, not of our people, has already asked me about this, making the following point: "If it is as you say that the power of the evil impulse will be weakened in the future, then most of your reward will be annulled. For justice requires that the reward be proportional to the struggle. If so, once the struggle of overcoming the evil impulse is annulled, then correspondingly the reward of the one who conquers his impulse will be annulled, for it is so weak. Thus the loss will be greater than the gain."[162]

This is a standard issue of Jewish ethical theory: Which is a higher status, who deserves a greater reward: the person who has a strong temptation to sin and

---

161. Ibid., 136r.

162. MS 4:194r, *Pequdei*, Exod. 38:28. Note that the quotation from Morteira's interlocutor is couched in traditional Jewish terminology that a Christian probably would not have used. On this problem, cf. Judah Loew ben Bezalel of Prague, *Netsah Yisrael*, chap. 46, in *Sifrei Maharal mi-Prag.* 13 vols. (New York, 1969), 6:183. On the future uprooting of the evil impulse, see Deut. Rabbah 2,30 and parallels.

overcomes it, or the person who has no temptation at all?[163] Set in the messianic context, it raises an issue similar to that which we have encountered above in Nahmanides' statement about the Messiah: the reward for observing the commandments at present, when the pressures are so strong to desist from them, may be greater than the reward for observing them in the messianic age when a Jewish king will compel obedience.

Morteira's response is drawn not from the abstractions of theological or ethical theory, but from the realities of commercial life that must have been quite familiar most of his listeners:

> This was my reply to him: Let me give you an everyday analogy with those who provide insurance for ships in time of war and in time of peace. In time of war, the insurance rate is 10%, and from one hundred ships, ninety may be lost. In time of peace, the insurance rate is 2%, and from one hundred ships, one or two may be lost. Will the insurer say that in peacetime his reward is lost and his profit is diminished, just because the rate of insurance is diminished from 10% to 2%? This would be totally false, for in proportion to the loss of ships, he will profit more from his insurance at the lower rate when so many more return safely than he will at the higher rate when so few are safe. So it is with this matter. When the war with the evil impulse is strong, the danger is great, the reward is great, and few are saved. When its power and the war against it are weakened, the danger is less and the reward is less, but many are saved.
>
> Furthermore, the reward will not be so small because of God's kindness, since human behavior will continue to cause some difficulties. [164]

The idea of extrapolating from the upheavals in commercial life caused by war to the nature of reward in the messianic age must have struck his listeners as daring, clever, and illuminating, and may well have produced many a nod and a smile.

8. Resurrection

The final point to be treated here is Morteira's discussion of the resurrection

---

163. See, e.g., Maimonides, "Eight Chapters," chap. 6; Isadore Twersky, *A Maimonides Reader* (New York, 1972), pp. 376–79.

164. MS 4:194r, *Pequdei*, Exod. 38:28 (ca. 1630?). Amsterdam burgomasters calculated that 1,200 Dutch merchant and fishing vessels had been lost during the war with England (1652–1654); this sermon was delivered earlier than that war, and Morteira's figure of 90% may reflect losses during the Spanish embargoes beginning in 1621 and imposed through most of the 1620s. See Israel, *The Dutch Republic*, pp. 716, 478–79.

of the dead. This concept, of course, was an ongoing problem of Jewish intellectual history throughout much of the past two millennia. While defined as a central dogma of rabbinic Judaism, it was challenged from many perspectives, and it was certainly not unproblematic in Amsterdam, where questions had been raised about the far more straightforward doctrine of the immortality of the soul. In a sermon for the Sabbath of Repentance delivered in 1642, Morteira, speaking about resurrection, states that "there are many proofs for this; we have already spoken about them in various sermons on this lesson and on other scriptural lessons."[165] But even for those who accepted the doctrine in principle, there were conceptual problems. One was the timing within the eschatological scenario: Would resurrection occur near the beginning of the Messianic Age, thereby allowing Jews who lived and died in the exile to share in it? Or would it occur at the end of the Messianic Age, thereby allowing a far more naturalistic conception of messianism, without a radical intrusion of the supernatural? Who would be included in the resurrection? All Jews? Jews and Gentiles? Would it be followed by a universal final judgment? What was the purpose of the resurrection if the ultimate reward was a spiritual existence in the presence of God that was possible immediately after death? An additional problem was the philosophical challenge: a person dies, is buried, his body decomposes and its elements serve as nutrients absorbed by grass, which is eaten by cattle, which in turn are eaten by other human beings, in an ongoing cycle. How can the original body be reconstituted when its elements have been incorporated into other bodies?[166] The increasingly popular doctrine of reincarnation introduced a further set of problems: if the same soul was reborn into many different bodies, with which body would it be reunited at resurrection? Would the resurrected bodies be essentially the same as our bodies now, or different? Any seventeenth-century preacher facing an intellectually sophisticated congregation would need to address such matters.

Morteira makes one point quite clear: resurrection is not to be universal. We find this a sermon on *Va-Yishlah* from around 1640:

Jacob said, thirdly, *Perhaps he will show me favor* (Gen. 32:21), with reference to the third matter, namely, the resurrection of the dead to see

---

165. MS 3:239v, *Ha'azinu*, Deut. 32:22, ca. 1642, p. 239v.

166. This problem was raised by Saadia Gaon, *Emunot ve-De'ot* 7,1, and cf. Abravanel as cited below. It was also a problem for Christian thinkers: see Augustine, *City of God* 22,12, and Morteira's older contemporary preacher, John Donne, in a 1627 sermon published in his *Fifty Sermons* (1649), p. 3, cited in *The Complete Poetry and Selected Prose of John Donne*, pp. 433–34.

God's goodness with body and soul. He said "perhaps" because this is not for everyone. Some will be worthy of the salvation of their soul but not worthy of resurrection. The Bible says, *Many of those who sleep in the dust of the earth will awake* (Dan. 12:2), many, but not all, only those of extreme piety and those of extreme evil, *some to eternal life, others to reproaches, to everlasting abhorrence* (ibid.).[167]

Diverging from the philosophical tradition, Morteira seems to present resurrection as a higher level of reward than the "salvation of the soul." The philosophers maintain that beholding God's goodness with the intellect alone is superior to beholding it when the powers of intellect are restricted by the corporeal faculties. For Morteira the opportunity to observe God's triumph in history, on earth, is a reward limited to those of "extreme piety." Apparently part of that reward is to witness the devastating punishment not only for those alive at the time of the resurrection, but for the great villains of the historical past as well.

A more sustained discussion of the problematics of resurrection provides the content for a sermon delivered a decade earlier, in 1630. Here Morteira cites various questions raised by Abravanel in his commentary on Avot (chapter 4, 21, root 3), including the one mentioned above regarding elements from a decomposed body entering other bodies. The preacher reports Abravanel's summaries of the views of several Gentile thinkers: that the resurrected bodies are created from light, or that they are composed of the fifth elemental matter of the heavens, or that the original souls are united with newly created bodies. Then Morteira reports Abravanel's view: that God will create new bodies like the original ones, which Morteira finds as unsatisfying as the others. Finally, after referring the listeners to a fuller discussion of the topic in one of his sermons on *Ḥayyei Sarah* (unfortunately no longer extant), Morteira gives a quick statement of his own view, which is drawn from the Kabbalistic doctrine of the *ḥaluqa de-rabbanan*, a fine spiritual body created by each individual during the lifetime on earth from the commandments performed, both through action and intellect; in the Zohar, this is the garment that will clothe the soul as it enters the higher realm after death. Morteira adapts this concept to serve as his solution to the problems of resurrection.[168] Although he cannot

---

167. MS 5:58r, *Va-Yishlaḥ*, Gen. 32:21. Cf. also MS 3:239v, *Ha'azinu*, Deut. 32:22, ca. 1642, p. 239v: "God will endow the bodies *of the righteous* with the capacity to rise in resurrection" (my emphasis).

168. MS 2:123v, *Ḥuqqat*, Num 19:19, 1630. At the end of his discussion of this concept,

be described as a Kabbalist, this was a doctrine to which Morteira referred on a number of occasions in his preaching.[169]

In assessing the various discussions of messianic themes that appear in sermons delivered by Morteira over the course of his career, one obvious question is how he would have responded had he lived for six more years and retained his leadership role during the period of the Sabbatian frenzy. Needless to say, no convincing answer is possible to the question in this form. Another way of putting it, however, is whether his treatment of messianic themes from the pulpit would have predisposed the congregants to a positive or negative reaction to the claims coming from the East. Two generations ago, Ben Zion Dinur wrote that "the impassioned homilies of Rabbi Saul Morteira" were an "important factor" explaining the "wildly enthusiastic participation of the Sephardi communities in this [Sabbatian] movement."[170] I cannot reconstruct what sermons in the printed text of *Giv'at Sha'ul* accessible to Dinur at that time could have justified this description. While the manuscripts provide far more extensive discussions than the printed collection and would have led devoted listeners to a further familiarity with messianic discourse and thought, in my judgment they do not materially change the picture—that is, they would not have incited his listeners to join the messianic movement.

Morteira does insist that the Messiah can come at any time, which would seem to imply a rejection of the need to wait for a messianic date in the future:

> The advent of the Messiah is ready and prepared to occur on any day, in accordance with the verse, *Today if you would but heed His voice* (Ps. 95:7), or because he is already born, as we find in Lamentations Rabbah on the verse, *Far from me is any comforter* (Lam. 1:16), or because it may be David himself, as we have explained in [the sermon on] the lesson *Ve-Zot ha-Berakhah* on the verse *Hear, O Eternal, the voice of Judah* (Deut. 33:7).[171]

On the other hand, a statement in an earlier sermon appears to emphasize the deliberate pace of the unfolding messianic scenario, and to place the entire process in the seventh millennium, some 600 years in the future:

---

he refers the listener to the proofs cited by the author of *Ma'aseh ha-Shem*, in chapters 2 and 8. For Abravanel's discussion, see *Naḥalat Avot*, pp. 272–73.

169. E.g., below p. 405, n. 52.

170. Dinur, *Israel and the Diaspora*, p. 42.

171. MS 2:111v, *Va-Era*, Exod. 6:25; *GS* 1645, p. 26a, 1912, p. 118. The reference to the Messiah already born is in Lam. Rabbah 1,51.

For it requires an extended period of time. The advent of the redeemer will occur at one time, the resurrection of the dead at another, the wars of Gog and Magog at another, the coming of all the brothers as *an offering to God* (Isa. 66:20), the building of the Temple at another, and all this is in the seventh millennium.[172]

In addition to the formulaic endings of his sermons with their hope for a speedy redemption, occasionally Morteira incorporates the same phrase into the actual discussion ("at the time of redemption, may it come speedily in our days").[173] But there is no explicit reference to any expectation that history is drawing quickly to a *dénouement*, that the existing order is about to change very soon. The messianic scenario is laid out without communicating a sense that it has imminent relevance. These discussions of eschatology do not seem to mobilize the rhetorical power we have seen in passages of ethical rebuke or criticism of Christian doctrine. To the contrary, we have seen Morteira articulate a classical quietistic doctrine opposed to premature initiative or irresponsible activism. While it is conceivable that his imagination would have been fired by an actual messianic figure in his old age, his conservative nature and the record of his preaching makes it more likely he would have been skeptical, a potential ally for the inveterate opponent of Sabbatian messianism Rabbi Jacob Sasportas.[174]

172. MS 2:222v, Shavu'ot, 1619, Deut. 16:10.

173. MS 2:232v, *Yitro*, Exod. 18:9, top.

174. For Amsterdam during the peak of the Sabbatian movement, see Scholem, *Sabbatai Sevi*, pp. 518–45, and Yosef Kaplan, "The Attitude of the Sephardi Leadership in Amsterdam to the Sabbatian Movement, 1665–1671," in *An Alternative Path to Modernity*, pp. 211–27. On Sasportas, see Scholem, *Sabbatai Sevi*, pp. esp. 566–72, and Sasportas's *Tsitsat Novel Tsevi*, with introduction by Isaiah Tishby (Jerusalem, 1954).

The Texts

Index of Sermons

"The Dust of the Earth"

Budapest Rabbinical Seminary MS 12, vol. 3, folios 249r–250r

Va-Yetse, ca. 1623

As the main content of this sermon has been discussed above in chapter nine, I will focus on its structure. Following the standard Sephardi practice dating to the late fifteenth century, Morteira begins with a verse from the weekly lesson and a rabbinic dictum. Sometimes the verse and the dictum have no apparent connection, and the relevance of the rabbinic statement will not appear until quite late in the sermon when it is introduced for the first time. Here, however, the connection is obvious: the verse (Genesis 28:14) begins by comparing Jacob's descendants to "dust," and the dictum—taken from the Midrash on a different parasha—explains the simile through four separate analogies between dust and the Jewish people.

After citing the dictum, the preacher begins with his own words of introduction. This section often begins with a proposition: "When Israel does God's will, everything created seems to be made for its sake." The relationship between the people of Israel and the physical world is not arbitrary but organic; Israel is a microcosm, and all of the qualities of God's creation are reflected in it. That is why God chose representatives of each of the three realms—stars (heavens), dust (earth) and sand (sea)—to communicate to the Patriarchs an implicit message about the future of their descendants. The preacher reminds his audience that he has already discussed the stars and the sand in previous homilies; the verse of this pericope requires the subject of the present sermon to be the lessons derived from the comparison with dust. Characteristically, the preacher signals the end of his exordium with the words, "this will be our discourse today," and invokes God's aid with an epithet alluding to the topic: "... which we shall begin with the help of God, who shall raise us up from the dust."

In the middle of this rather conventional, Judeo-centric exposition, the preacher lets drop an autobiographical bombshell. It comes in an almost incidental citation brought to strengthen his point that even the heavens serve the Jewish people when it acts in accordance with God's will. After citing Deuteronomy 33:26 as a proof-text, Morteira continues by referring to "what my grandfather, Rabbi Judah Katzenellenbogen, may the memory of the righteous be for blessing, wrote." The passage he paraphrases is taken from Katzenellenbogen's Sheneim 'Asar Derashot, *printed at Venice in 1594, a book that was apparently in Morteira's library.[1] As we have noted above, this explicit refer-*

---

1. See Gedalyah Nigal, "Derashotav shel R. Shmuel Yehudah Katzenellenbogen," *Sinai*

ence to Rabbi Judah Katzenellenbogen as his grandfather resolves definitively a long-standing uncertainty about Morteira's family background and places him within the aristocracy of Ashknenazi Jewry.[2]

The body of the sermon can be divided into two components. The first begins by presenting a problem in the verse. The context of the divine promise is one in which Jacob, fleeing from home, needs comfort and reassurance; what sense does it make in this context for God to tell him that his descendants will be like dust: scattered and trodden upon by the other kingdoms? The answer comes through the statement of a general principle underlying divine communication in the Bible. Rational people know that there can be no permanent well-being in this world, that all success and prosperity must necessarily bring with them the fear of misfortune. Therefore, in promising good things for the future, God always includes the reassurance that the inevitable reversals will not be devastating.

This general pattern is then exemplified by recourse to specific passages from the Bible referring to Abraham and Isaac. This brings the preacher to the theme-verse of the sermon, for which, quite unceremoniously, he gives a rather startling new interpretation, unpacking it to mean that just as there will never be a time when the land of Israel will be bereft of its dust, so there will never be a time when the land will be empty of Jews, even when they are living as subjugated and humiliated aliens. History is cited as proof: never have the Jews been completely expelled from the land, and they will therefore never lose their rights to it.

Up to this point, the ideas would be appropriate for a discursive essay, with considerable focus on the land of Israel, as is appropriate to the biblical context of God's promise. At this moment, however, the preacher shifts direction and begins a new section, the main substance of his sermon, introduced with the statement that "when the Sages trod this path they interpreted the matter differently." The listener is thereby invited to file away what has come before this and prepare for something new. The rest of the sermon will be structured in accordance with the opening rabbinic dictum—an

---

70 (1971): 79–85. Generally known as Samuel Judah, he died in 1597, when Morteira would have been a toddler, and was eulogized by Leon Modena; see *Midbar Yehudah* (1602, pp. 63b–69b, 2002, pp. 231–58). There Modena's refers to the deceased's son (Saul Wahl), and "his sons-in-law, married to his daughters, and his daughters' children" (1602, p. 69a, 2002, p. 252).

2. One of Judah Katzenellenbogen's daughters married Elijah, whose father, Eliezer Ashkenazi, was the author of *Ma'aseh ha-Shem*, a work Morteira frequently cited in his sermons. A second married Joel Ashkenazi, who assumed his wife's last name. See Meyer Ellenbogen, *Hevel ha-Kesef: Toledot Mishpaḥat Katzenellenbogen* (Brooklyn, 1937), p. 28. Morteira must therefore have been the son of a Levite in Venice married to a third daughter whose descendants are not recorded in the family genealogies. It is somewhat surprising that Morteira never seems to use the name of his father; in the chart of his descendants prepared by Salomon (*Tratado*, following p. cxlvi), no names are provided for his parents.

unusual but not unprecedented pattern for Morteira's preaching. And, although the pattern of divine promises outlined above will still be continued, the focus now shifts away from the land of Israel, turning exclusively to the Diaspora. Here we enter a full homiletical mode, characteristic of Morteira, in which biblical verse, rabbinic dictum, and ideational content are integrated with significant artistry.

The dictum contains four possible explanations for the comparison between Israel and dust. However, Morteira divides the first explanation into four, thus producing a total of seven explanations. Each one of them relates to the dispersion of the Jewish people in their exile, and each one—following the pattern established earlier—provides a positive reason for that dispersion. As I have already discussed the ideas in the context of the chapter on exile above, I will note here only that each of the first four benefits of dispersion is associated with a different possible meaning of the verb u-faratsta in the theme-verse (Gen. 28:14): to increase in number, to urge or insist on their belief in the true God, to break down or destroy the plans of their would-be-oppressors, and to be strong in establishing their economic base. The association of different subsidiary ideas, and thus sections of the sermon, with various lexical meanings of a key word in the dictum or the Torah verse is also a sophisticated homiletical technique (as well as a language teaching device) that Morteira uses for special effect.[3] In distinguishing these meanings, he was undoubtedly aided not just by the classical commentators, but also by reference works such as David Kimhi's Sefer ha-Shorashim, *which he cites in other sermons.*

Characteristically, near the end Morteira recapitulates all seven factors, helping the listeners to remember a larger number of discrete points than his sermons usually contain, and signaling that the discourse is reaching its conclusion. The expected messianic coda is especially apposite here as a reminder that the entire situation being described in the sermon is temporary. Here Morteira takes a topos of ethical literature—that dust eventually rises over those who tread upon it (when they lie in their graves)—and transmutes it into an assertion of Jewish national regeneration and exaltation above the Gentiles: "May it be God's will that you shall be like the dust also in respect to what the Sages said: 'Just as dust rises above those who tread upon it, so with Israel.' May it be God's will that they will rise above those who hate them, and devour those who devour them (cf. Jer. 30:16), with the coming of our righteous Messiah, quickly and in our days. Amen."

This topic—the advantages to the Jews of being scattered in various communities during the period of their exile—is a component of a larger theme in Morteira's preaching that we have noted above: God's ongoing love and providential care for the Jewish people even during the long era of punishment. This broader theme, bearing obvious

---

3. See, for example, the eulogy in Saperstein, *"Your Voice Like a Ram's Horn,"* pp. 377, 394–97.

*relevance to Christian polemics of displacement, is central to the monumental Sabbath
of Repentance sermon on Deuteronomy 32:12, translated below. As I have indicated
in the annotation, many of the details in Morteira's explanation can be paralleled in
sources by writers who preceded him (e.g., the sixteenth-century Italian rabbi Mordecai
Dato) and by those who followed and may have been influenced by him (e.g., his
younger contemporaries in Holland, Isaac Aboab da Fonseca and Josiah Pardo,
Morteira's son-in-law), and they were recapitulated by him in the twenty-eighth chapter of his Tratado. This is clearly not an affirmation of exile as beneficial in itself, but
it is a homiletically sophisticated validation of God's concern for contemporary Jews,
revealed in a careful explication of Scripture's relevance to subsequent Jewish history.*

* * *

**Your descendants shall be as the dust of the earth; you shall spread out to the
west and to the east, to the north and to the south. All the families of the earth
shall bless themselves by you and your descendants** (Gen. 28:14).

Genesis Rabbah, chapter 41. *I will make your descendants as the dust of the earth*
(Gen. 13:16). Just as the dust of the earth is found from one end of the world
to the other, so shall your children be scattered from one end of the world to
the other. Just as the dust of the earth can be blessed only through water, so
will Israel be blessed only for the sake of Torah, which is likened to water.
And just as the dust of the earth wears out even metal utensils yet itself endures forever, so will Israel exist while the nations of the world will cease to
be. And just as the dust is downtrodden, so will your children be downtrodden under the heel of foreign kingdoms.

Exordium

In addition to what was hinted in their midrashic comment at the beginning
of our Torah on the verse *In the beginning God created* (Gen. 1:1)—on which the
Sages said, "For the sake of Torah and Israel, which are called "beginning,"
as in the verse, *Israel was holy to the Eternal, the beginning of His harvest* (Jer. 2:3)
and *The Eternal created me at the beginning of His course* (Prov. 8:22)[1]—it appears
clearly from various scriptural verses that when Israel does God's will,
everything created seems to be made for its sake. For all created things are

---

1. See Lev. Rabbah 36,4 and Gen. Rabbah 1,1 and 1,6 for the application of these verses
to this idea. Morteira is asserting that the idea hinted in homiletical interpretations of the
Sages is actually all but explicit in certain biblical verses.

everywhere divided into three categories: heavens, earth, and sea. So it says, *For in six days the Eternal made heaven and earth, the sea and all that is in them* (Exod. 20:11), and likewise in other places. Now everywhere we find that God has given them over to the service of Israel when it does His will.

As for the heavens, there is a complete verse on this: *O Jeshurun, there is none like God, riding through the heavens to help you, through the skies in His majesty* (Deut. 33:26). This means, God rides upon the heavens and stretches them out and makes them turn in accordance with His will, all in order to help you. This is consistent with what **my grandfather, the esteemed Rabbi Judah Katzenellenbogen**, wrote on the verse, *You have forgotten the Eternal Who made you, stretching out the skies and making firm the earth* (Isa. 51:13): that "Who made you" refers back to Israel, that is to say, God has made Israel capable of stretching out the skies and making the earth firm, all for its own sake.[2] As for the sea and the land, one verse includes both: *Let him rule from sea to sea, from the river to the ends of the earth* (Ps. 72:8).[3] Therefore Moses brought everything together in a single verse, saying, *Mark, the heavens to their uttermost reaches belong to the Eternal your God, the earth and all that is on it. Yet it was to your fathers that the Lord was drawn in His love for them* (Deut. 10:14–15). This means that all these belonged to the Eternal your God, yet God was drawn in love only to your ancestors to give all to them.

Not only were all these components of creation created for Israel, but within them and their activities and properties everything is hinted, as if each were a microcosm, which—as the foundation of the world—alludes to all of these component parts. Therefore, when God wanted to inform the Patriarchs of matters relating to their descendants, He compared these descendants to these three components of the realm of creation. Once he compared them to the stars, which are of the heavens, saying, [*Look toward heaven and count the stars, if you are able to count them*] *and then He said to him, So shall be your offspring* (Gen. 15:5). Once he compared them to the sand, which is from the sea, saying, *and as the sand on the shore of the sea* (Gen. 22:17). And once he compared them to the dust, saying, *I will make your offspring like the dust of the earth* (Gen. 13:16). He did not choose these things as examples of huge numbers; if He had, He would always have mentioned the example of greatest magni-

---

2. This important and previously unknown biographical detail links Morteira with the family of one of the great Ashkenazic rabbis in Italy (see introduction to the sermon). For the passage to which he was referring, see Katzenellenbogen's *Shneim 'Asar Derashot*, the fifth sermon (Warsaw, 1875, p. 13a). Morteira also cites his grandfather in the same way, this time an interpretation of Ps. 34:21, in MS 2:123v, *Ḥuqqat*, Num. 19:9, 1630.

3. Referring to the king mentioned in verse 1, and generally understood to mean that the Messiah would rule over the entire earth (cf. Zech. 9:10).

tude, namely, the stars. Rather, the reason He chose these similes was for the special characteristics of each one of them.[4]

The Sages revealed their sensitivity to the analogies with the dust in our opening dictum; they also explained this with regard to the sand,[5] and I have explained their statements about the stars in a sermon on the lesson *'Eqev*.[6] Now the analogies with dust are suggested by our Text[7] today, ***Your offspring will be like the dust of the earth*** (Gen. 28:14),[8] and our goal today will be to discover what the Sages meant in these analogies of theirs, and how they are hinted in this context, and why—given that some of them are negative—God told them to Jacob at this particular moment, which seems like a time for communicating good news, and finally how all of this is derived from the verses.[9] This will be our discourse today,[10] which we now begin with the help of God who will raise us up from the dust.

---

4. Cf. Morteira's younger colleague, Menasseh ben Israel, *Conciliator*, 1:52–53 (the book was originally printed some nine years after this sermon). Menasseh, however, states that the largest number pertains not to the stars but to the sand, and that this is therefore the simile used to refer to great multitude.

5. Morteira would discuss this in his sermon on Genesis 32:13 entitled "As the Sand of the Sea," dated 5392 (autumn 1631): MS 2:214r.

6. No sermons on this *parashah* have been preserved among the manuscripts; cf. *GS* 1645, p. 68a, 1912, p. 252.

7. I use "Text" as the translation for the technical Hebrew term *nosei* rather than "theme-verse," which have I used in all previous publication on Jewish preaching (including the first part of this book and the notes to the sermons), because I have found this to be the term used not only by such contemporary English preachers as John Donne, but also by David Aaron de Sola, one of the first Sephardic preachers in English: "Before I can proceed to explain my text..." ("A Sermon on the Excellence of the Torah," p. 1); "The words of my Text are too obvious in their meaning to require any explanation..." ("A Sermon Delivered at the Spanish and Portuguese Jews' Synagogue, Bevis Marks, on Wednesday, 7th Nisan (24th March), 5607," *www.jewish-history.com/Occident/volume5/ mar1848/sermon.html*, beginning of section 1). In this and the following sermons, the "Text" will be printed in bold italics, to distinguish it from other biblical verses and show visually the recurrence of a central motif similar to a musical theme in a symphonic composition.

8. Morteira actually wrote *I will make your offspring like the dust of the earth* (Gen. 13:16), repeating the verse he had cited a moment before rather than the verse from the current lesson.

9. This summary of the basic goals of the preacher in this sermon both sets up a rhetorical challenge in the minds of the listeners and guides them in their expectations of what they will be hearing. It also signals that the introduction to the sermon is drawing to an end.

10. Heb: *zeh yihyeh derushenu ha-yom*, a phrase used near the conclusion of the Exordium in almost every sermon. In Portuguese: *o meo discorso*; cf. the formulation by Morteira's older contemporary in France, Bishop Jean Pierre Camus: "de ces quatres vertus que nous avons marquées sera nostre Discours..." *Homélies panegyriques de Sainct Charles Borromée* (Paris,

Body of the Sermon

More than a little surprise is generated by these words of the Sages comparing Israel with the dust in this context. Jacob had left his father's house, fleeing from Esau. Yet instead of comforting him, God would seem to be distressing him by saying that his offspring will be scattered like dust, and be trodden upon by the kingdoms of the earth. Truly, this cannot be [the message] in this context. However, when we examine God's words carefully, nothing will remain difficult for us. On the contrary, we shall see how the Sages based their statements on truth and justice, all directed by the biblical verse.

Since the good things of this world are never completely good, and there is no joy not followed by sorrow,[11] when God tells people of beneficence and communicates good tidings, at the end He tells them that the cycle of reversals in this world will occur not in anger and wrath, but in compassion and kindness. This is necessary, because the rational person's mind will not be reassured by promises of the riches of this world, for as long as they increase they will bring anguish at the need to leave them. "The more possessions, the more worry."[12] Therefore, in order to allow them to rejoice even in the riches of this world, when promising something good, God also ordains that the inevitable downfall will not be great.

Thus we find with Abraham that when God brought him outside and said, *Look toward heaven and count the stars, if you are able to count them, and He said, So shall your offspring be* in multitude, exaltedness, and permanence (Gen. 15:5), immediately after this, at sunset, with the onset of darkness, God informed him that his offspring would be strangers in a land not theirs, and that they would be enslaved and oppressed for four hundred years (cf. Gen. 15:13). However, He then added that their downfall would not be total, but rather *I will execute judgment on the nation they shall serve and in the end they shall go forth with great wealth* (Gen. 15:14). And there He informed Abraham how four kingdoms would pass before them,[13] but He would save them from all four. This is God's way with words of comfort.

It was the same way with David when God promised him through Nathan that He would truly make for him a dynasty, and create for him a reputation like that of the greatest men on earth (cf. 2 Sam. 7:9), and other great benevolence that He promised him. In the middle of this God said, *I will be a father*

1623), p. 8. I am grateful to Thomas Worcester for making this text available to me (see also below, p. 409, n. 2).

11. Cf. *Tur, Oraḥ Ḥayyim* 529,4.

12. M. *Avot* 2,8.

13. See Exod. Rabbah 51,7, Mekhilta of R. Ishmael, *Ba-Ḥodesh* 9 (ed. Lauterbach, 2:268).

to him, and he shall be a son to Me. When he does wrong, I will chastise him with the rod of men and the affliction of mortals (2 Sam. 7:14), for the promise would be incomplete unless God informed him that when his descendants would sin— something so common for human beings—He would not blot them out but rather chastise them. This is the fulfillment and completion of all the blessings.

Scripture hinted of this matter also when it said regarding Isaac, *There was a famine in the land.... Isaac went to Abimelech, king of the Philistines, in Gerar. The Eternal had appeared to him and said, Do not go down to Egypt; stay in the land that I point out to you. Reside in this land, and I will be with you and bless you...*(Gen. 26:1–3). This is difficult. Why in the beginning did He say, *Stay in the land,* which is to be like a settler and a homesteader, and afterward say *Reside,* which suggests living as an alien?[14] However, in this God hinted to Isaac: Now, at this time *Stay in the land that I point out to you,* for when you shall reside there and be as an alien in that land—as the Jews are now living on the land of Israel as aliens in a land not theirs—*I will be with you and bless you,* and your name will not be erased from the land. That indeed is a great promise.

And this is exactly what God said to Jacob: **Your offspring shall be as the dust of the earth** (Gen. 28:14). This is connected with the verse immediately preceding it: *The land* (ha-arets) *on which you are lying I will assign to you and to your offspring* (Gen. 28:13). You might say, "But they will be banished from it, never again to return to it, and thus it would have been better never to have acquired it as an inheritance." Therefore God said, **Your offspring will be as the dust of the land** (*ha-arets*), namely the dust of this actual land,[15] for just as the dust will never depart from this land, which will never be without its dust, so it will never be without the Jewish people. Even though they may be living in it abased and despised like the dust, some will always remain in it, and they will never lose their claim to it. Experience shows us that the Jewish people has never been banished from it as they have been banished in other kingdoms.[16] At the time of Nebuchadnezzer, God commanded the Jews to be subjected to the land and not to leave it (cf. Jer. 42:9–19), even if they were

---

14. Cf. Ramban's commentary on Gen. 6:2 on this difficulty.

15. In a rather novel interpretation, Morteira reads the word *ha-arets* in Gen. 28:14 as referring not to the entire earth but to the land of Israel, as in the previous verse. Morteira's Portuguese, like the Latin of the Vulgate, would have used the same word (*terra*) in both verses, as we see from his rendering of the verse in the *Tratado* (p. 179): E será tua semente como o po da terra. Thus the distinction in English (v. 13: *land,* v. 14: *earth*), and in German (Luther renders v. 13 "das Land, darauf du liegst" and v. 14 "wie der Staub auf Erden") would not have existed for him. I have not seen this interpretation elsewhere.

16. Note how this point is taken up in the following sermon as well (pp. 395, 406).

to remain there despised and abased, for this was God's will: that even in their bad times, they would not leave it.

Thus within the good tidings and promises, God informed Jacob that if his descendants should sin against him, they would not lose their claim upon the land until the time when they would inherit it forever. This is the meaning of *Your offspring shall be as the dust of the land, when you shall spread out to the west and to the east...* (Gen. 28:14). This is what the Psalmist meant when he said, *Your servants take delight in its stones and its dust they cherish* (yeḥonenu) (Ps. 102:15). For this verb makes no sense when applied to dust. Rather, the meaning is that your servants will take delight in its stones and its dust, to be abased and despised with its dust; however, while in its dust, they will implore God (yithannenu) about this situation, as in the verse, *I implored* (va-ethanan) *the Eternal* (Deut. 3:23).

However, when the Sages trod this path, they interpreted the matter differently.[17] This is that among the various good tidings promised, God informed Jacob how, if his descendants should sin against Him, He would chastise them *with the rod of men and the affliction of mortals* (2 Sam. 7:14). This would however in the end be to their own advantage, and from the punishments themselves they would derive great benefit. All this is hinted in His statement, *Your offspring shall be as the dust of the earth* (Gen. 28:14). All the various analogies stated by the Sages are hinted in the verses that follow this.

They said first, "Just as the dust of the earth is found from one end of the world to the other, so shall your children be scattered from one end of the world to the other." This means, when they sin against Me, one aspect of their punishment is that they will be as the dust of the earth that is found everywhere. Yet from this punishment, great benefit will ensue for them in what God said immediately afterward, *You shall spread out to the west and to the east, to the north and to the south* (Gen. 28:14). This indicates that four great benefits come to us from this general scattering in our exile, all of which are hinted at in the phrase *U-faratsta yamah ve-qedmah* (*You shall spread out..*), according to four meanings and connotations of this verb *peh-resh-tsaddi* in Hebrew, as we shall explain.

1. The first benefit is that if God were to put us in one place in this exile of ours, because of the great multitude of our people and our nation in the

---

17. The interpretation given by Morteira, apparently as the simple meaning of the verse in context, is that the comparison of Jacob's offspring with the dust communicates a message about Jews who would be living in the land of Israel during the period of exile. The interpretation of the same verse given by the Sages, to which he now turns, and that will occupy him for the rest of the sermon, communicates a message about Jews living in the Diaspora during the period of exile.

world—for whoever reads *The Travels of Rabbi Benjamin* just on the places he visited will find the number of Jews astonishing, not to mention the places he did not visit[18]—if *a people plundered and despoiled* (Isa. 42:22) like us were to increase in population to this extent openly, so that the Gentiles would be aware of our aggregate numbers, they would certainly try any means possible to reduce our size. Experience shows this from what Pharaoh did when he said, *Let us deal shrewdly with them so that they may not increase* (Exod. 1:10), and he tried to kill the male Israelites. How much more would they try to do this today out of their great hatred for us![19] Therefore, in order to conceal us from their evil eye, God scattered us a few here and a few there, so that our large population would not be apparent. Thus He said, **Your offspring shall be as the dust of the earth**, scattered from one end of the world to the other, *u-faratsta*, meaning "so that you may expand in number." This is the first meaning of the verb *parats*, as in the phrase *ken yarbeh ve-khen yifrots* (Exod. 1:12).[20] *You shall spread out to the west and to the east, to the north and to the south* without the Gentiles becoming aware of your large total population and without their attempting to diminish it. In this way, a great benefit comes to you from this dispersion.

2. The second benefit is that in this dispersion the sins of Israel are erased more easily. In their own land, they were *wicked sinners* (Gen. 13:13) before all the nations; so now in their exile, they need to proclaim and confess God's Torah before all. While *all the peoples walk each in the name of its god*, before all of them *we will walk in the name of the Eternal our God forever and ever* (Mic. 4:5). If we were all in one place, our witness would be before only one nation. But our duty is to confess God's greatness before all the peoples of the earth, and before the citizens of all the nations.[21] This is what the Sages said on the verse, *I will sow her on earth as My own* (Hos. 2:25): "The Jews were mixed among the

---

18. This book was published several times in the sixteenth century: in Constantinople, 1543, Ferara 1556. Friburg, 1583. For other statements indicating a belief in a huge population of Jews scattered throughout the world, see Joshua ha-Lorki, cited by Benjamin Gampel in *Cultures of the Jews*, ed. David Biale, p. 413, and Menasseh ben Israel, cited by Moshe Rosman, ibid., p. 519. For a very different polemical use of the material in Benjamin's *Travels*, see Glaser, "Invitation to Intolerance," p. 342, n. 77.

19. In the twenty-eighth chapter of his *Tratado da verdade da lei de Moisés*, Morteira used material from this sermon, illustrating five reasons why God in his love for the Jews did not want his people to be in one location during their exile. For this first reason, see *Tratado*, p. 263.

20. Ibn Ezra on Gen. 28:14 interprets the word *u-faratsta* as referring to increasing in population.

21. Cf. the second reason for the dispersion in *Tratado*, pp. 265–66. In an early sermon on *Bereshit*, Morteira explained that God scattered the Jews among the nations as a device

nations only so that proselytes might be added to them."[22] In this way too they are **as the dust of the earth** because *u-faratsta to the west and to the east....* Here the meaning of *u-faratsta* is derived from the word *heftser* as in the verse *His courtiers pleaded with him* (va-yifretsu) (1 Sam. 28:23) and the verse *Absalom pleaded with him* (va-yifrots) (2 Sam. 13:27), which is like *va-yiftseru.*[23] Thus the meaning of *u-faratsta to the west and to the east* is, You shall plead and establish what they wanted to deny in you. Instead of being stubborn in your efforts to abandon Me, you shall be stubborn in your efforts to make Me known. In this way, wherever you may be—west and east, north and south—you shall plead the case that your faith is true and that your God is the true God. In this way, from your punishment, your exile, your scattering, great merit will come to you, which would not be the case were you not like the dust scattered from one end of the world to the other.

3. The third benefit is that if we were together under one government, they might decide to wipe us all out together, as indeed occurred in several kingdoms to some of us—for example in the time of Ahasuerus—*were it not for the Eternal, who was on our side* (Ps. 124:1–2). This is how the Sages interpreted the scriptural phrase, *His gracious deliverance [pirzono] of Israel* (Jud. 5:11), "God acted graciously with Israel by scattering them *(pizaram)* among the nations."[24] If they should kill us, they would be designated a "barbarous kingdom."[25] But since we are dispersed, they cannot annihilate us, for one abandons us and another takes us in. In this we are saved from them, and God *has not let us be ripped apart* (Ps. 124:6).[26] In this sense, *u-faratsta* has the meaning "breaking and destruction," as in the verse, *The Eternal has broken up your work* (2 Chron.

(*tahbulah*) to spread the light of God's truth: "so that all would know of them [the Jews] and and what they stood for": MS 3:87v, *Bereshit,* Gen. 1:3, 1621.

22. Cf. b. *Pesahim* 87b, and the discussion on pp. 337–38 above.

23. See David Kimhi's commentary on these two verses, and his *Sefer ha-Shorashim* (Berlin, 1847), p. 600.

24. B. *Pesahim* 87b.

25. B. *Pesahim* 87b, *Avodah Zarah* 10b.

26. For precedents of this idea, cf. Levi ben Abraham, "Livyat Hen," cited by Schwartz, *Ha-Ra'ayon he-Meshihi ba-Hagut ha-Yehudit,* p. 147 n. 90; Nissim Gerundi, *Derashot ha-RaN,* p. 6 (on the Tower of Babel); Isaac Abravanel, *Yeshu'ot Meshiho,* p. 11a) (the last two cited in Septimus, "Hispano-Jewish Views of Christendom and Islam," pp. 57–58; Usque, *Consolation for the Tribulations of Israel,* p. 227: "By scattering you among all peoples, He made it impossible for the world to destroy you, for if one kingdom rises against you in Europe to inflict death upon you, another in Asia allows you to live." Also Mordecai Dato, cited in Jacobson, *Bi-Netivei Galuyot u-Ge'ulot,* p. 144; Samuel Saul Siriro, *Derushei Maharshash,* 2 vols. (Jerusalem, 1989–91) 1:122. (I am grateful to Pierre Lazar for calling my attention to this older contemporary of Morteira, who preached in Fez.) Morteira returned to this idea at the end of his Sabbath of Repentance sermon on Deut. 32:12. Referring back to his

20:37).[27] Thus the meaning is, *u-faratsta*: you shall break down and destroy the thoughts of those who plan to wipe you out, whether in the west or the east, the north or the south, and when they see that they cannot succeed, their thoughts are broken up, so that in **your offspring** being *as **the dust of the earth**,* you shall break such thoughts to the west and the east, to the north and the south.

4. The fourth benefit is that since God has decreed upon the Jewish people in this exile that in the land of our enemies we would not own *so much as a foot can tread on* (Deut. 2:5), so that we would recognize that we are exiled from our land and constantly raise our hearts to God to beseech food for our sustenance, and benefit from our own physical labor. He has scattered us among the nations, to the four corners of the earth, so that each one of us may find what is necessary for a livelihood, sustain himself from the work of his hands, figure out a way to provide food for his house and to graze his goats until the time of anger has passed. If we were all in the same land, the competition between Jews would be lethal. But being scattered, each one can engage in matters appropriate to his own country—some as sellers of clothing and others as merchants on the sea, some as moneylenders at interest, and others as craftsmen, some as purchasers of livestock and others as brokers for merchandise—so that everyone can find what he needs for a livelihood.[28] That is why the Sages said, "There are three who are strong: Israel among the nations, etc."[29] This matter is well known: that the Jews have strong influence in the palaces of nobles and kings to derive sustenance from these sources. All this is derived from God's scattering us like the dust in our exile, as God said to Jacob, **Your offspring shall be as the dust of the earth**, *u-faratsta,* connected with the word *parits*, strength, as in the verse, *the slaves breaking loose (mitparretsim)* (1 Sam. 25:10). Thus the meaning of our verse in this context is, "You shall be strong and powerful,[30] wary and energetic in the lands of your enemies, *u-faratsta to the west and to the east, to the north and to the south.*"

In this way, God made Jacob a great promise in saying that when his offspring would be **as the dust of the earth**, they would not increase in population in a manner noticeable to their enemies, they would bear witness in every location to their faith in God, they would annul the plan of those who wanted

---

discussion in "Dust of the Earth," he claims that this consideration is "the most important of all" (translated below, p. 484).

27. See David Kimhi, *Sefer ha-Shorashim*, p. 599.

28. Cf. the fourth reason for the Jewish dispersion in *Tratado*, p. 269.

29. B. *Betsah* 25b.

30. See Rashi and the Targum on our verse, both giving the meaning, "you shall be strong."

to wipe them out, and all would be able to find what they needed for sustenance.[31] The reason why the Sages placed this analogy between Israel and the dust first—that the dust is from one end of the earth to the other—is because of the word *u-faratsta* that immediately follows it.

5. The Sages further said, "Just as the dust of the earth can be blessed only through water, so will Israel be blessed only for the sake of Torah, which is likened to water." Their intention in this was to express another benefit that would accrue to us as a result of God's punishing us through dispersal. This is that many times the world has deserved destruction because of its evil deeds. This occurred in the generation of the flood, and the men of Sodom and their like. Now that the sacrifices that bring atonement for the nations are lacking, God has scattered us among them as one who sprinkles salt over meat, so that our presence everywhere enables us to preserve the world from destruction.[32] This is because of the Torah, which is studied wherever we are found. It is for our benefit, for "why should the world be destroyed because of those who stray"[33]—why should the world, which will be ours, be destroyed because of the Gentiles? That is why in our dispersal, we are a "covenant of salt" for the world.[34] This is the meaning of the Sages' statement, "Just as the dust of the earth can be blessed only through water, so will Israel be blessed only for the sake of Torah, which is likened to water." And all this the Torah expressed in the phrase, *All the families of the earth shall be blessed through you and through your offspring* (Gen. 28:14), for because of you they will be blessed. It is connected to what preceded it: ***Your offspring shall be as the dust of the earth, and all the families of the earth shall be blessed through you and through your offspring.***

6. They said further, "Just as the dust of the earth wears out even metal utensils yet itself endures forever, so will Israel exist while the nations of the world will cease to be." In this they revealed to us another great benefit in

---

31. Note Morteira's characteristic recapitulation, signaling to the listeners that one section of his sermon structure is ending and helping them remember the components included within it.

32. Cf. Zohar 2,16b: "Why is Israel subjected to all nations? In order that the world may be preserved through them." And compare the statement in a sermon by John Wesley, "Ye are the salt of the earth:' it is your very nature to season whatever is round about you.... This is the great reason why the providence of God has so mingled you together with other men, that whatever grace you have received of God may through you be communicated to others." *Forty Four Sermons on Several Occasions* (Peterborough, UK, 1944), sermon 19, p. 240.

33. Cf. M. *Avodah Zarah* 4,7 and the discussion on pp. 336–37 above.

34. A play on words based on Num. 18:19, with the ambiguity of *le-'olam* (for eternity, for the world).

God's scattering us among the peoples. In this exile, Israel endures under pressure and pain, toiling to eke out a livelihood, experiencing afflictions and terrible diseases that come upon them. Now on many occasions it has become necessary to change their country, to travel *from nation to nation, from one kingdom to another* (1 Chron. 16:20), to change climate whether for reasons of health or sustenance. If the Jewish people were in one place, when a Jew wanted to move from his home and depart for a different land, [the inhabitants of the new land] would drive him away, for not knowing him they would be astonished at him. That is why God scattered his people to the four corners of the earth: so that wherever one Jew goes to change his residence, he will find his fellow Jews established. This will make his journey easier, for all will help each other, thereby facilitating their survival in their exile.[35] This is what the Sages taught in their statement, "Just as the dust of the earth wears out even metal utensils," which refer to the nations. Thus by passing from one to another, dwelling in a place where they find relief and respite, time passes, and the Jewish people does not wear out but rather endures, while the nations may be worn out and totally come to an end in some disastrous event. This too the Scripture taught by saying, **Your offspring shall be as the dust of the earth**, referring to perpetuity and endurance, for it goes on to say there, *I will bring you back to this land* (Gen. 28:15), meaning, "I will bring you back to this land after the exile: whether lowly or in honor you shall return here, for you shall not be destroyed."

7. Finally, the Sages said, "Just as the dust is downtrodden, so will your children be downtrodden under the heel of foreign kingdoms." In this they wanted to communicate a seventh benefit that comes to us out of our dispersion among the Gentiles. If we were all together, upon seeing our great numbers and the length of our exile, we might conceivably select a leader and rise up against the people in whose midst we lived, thereby seeking to speed up the end [of the exile].[36] This is what the children of Ephraim did in Egypt, as is known in the rabbinic tradition.[37] But that is against God's plan, as the Sages interpreted the verse, *I adjure you, O maidens of Jerusalem...: do not wake or rouse love until it please* (Song 2:7).[38] For all of this would be to our detriment, as we see in the verse, *Do not go up [...], since I am not in your midst [else you will be routed by your enemies]* (Deut. 1:42). For *this is not the way, and this is not the town*

---

35. Morteira returned to this point at the conclusion of a sermon on Gen. 37:7, delivered at Hanukkah 1627 (MS 2:16r), and cf. the third reason for the dispersion in *Tratado*, p. 267.

36. Compare the fifth reason for the dispersion of the Jews in *Tratado*, pp. 269–71.

37. See the sources listed in Ginzberg, *The Legends of the Jews*, 6:2–3, nn. 10–11; cf. above, p. 340, nn. 83–84.

38. B. *Ketubot* 111a.

(2 Kings 6:19). God will go before us; He will redeem us! That is why God scattered us, a few here, a few there: so that we would not set our minds to such a course. Thus, "misery is fitting for Israel like a red rose upon a white horse."[39] This is the meaning of their statement, "Just as the dust is downtrodden, so will your children be downtrodden under the heel of foreign kingdoms." And all this Scripture taught by saying, *I will not leave you until I have done what I have promised you* (Gen. 28:15). This means, **"Your offspring will be as the dust of the earth**, downtrodden and lowly. But why? So that their large numbers will not be noticeable, and they will not anticipate being saved through their own initiative. Yet with all this, God will not withhold from them His promise, for *I, I who am* the savior (cf. Deut. 32:39) *will not leave you until I have done what I have promised you* through my servants the prophets. Therefore, *The Eternal will battle for you; you hold your peace* (Exod. 14:14).

Peroration

Thus in this manner, seven great benefits accrue to us from God's punishment of casting us out and scattering us to the four corners of the earth.[40] First, that our enemies will not become aware of our large population and attempt to diminish us. Second, that we may be witnesses of the Eternal before every nation and people. Third, that we will not be under the power of a single king who might annihilate us. Fourth, so that every Jew may have what is needed for his individual sustenance correlating with the multitude of different states with their respective needs (for if they were in one place, "people would eat each other alive"). Fifth, that we might be the "salt of the world," so that it will not be destroyed because of the evil of the Gentiles. Sixth, so that wherever Jews go, they will find a place prepared for them, and *each will help the other* (Isa. 41:6). Seventh, so that they will not be aroused by the large numbers to rebel, for this redemption comes not from human initiative but God alone is the one who does what He has promised us, which we await, in accordance with the verse, *Even if it tarries, wait for it still, for it will surely come, without delay* (Hab. 2:3). All this God showed to Jacob in his promises for the future, informing him that when his descendants would sin against him, He will chastise them *with the rod of men and the affliction of mortals* (2 Sam. 7:14), but he will not annihilate them. That is one of the greatest favors given to human beings. All this is hinted in the verse, **your offspring shall be as the dust of the**

---

39. B. *Hagigah* 9b. See the annotation on p. 340, above, n. 84 end.

40. Cf. Deut. 28:64. Here Morteira beings his final recapitulation for the benefit of the listeners, signalling the peroration of the sermon.

earth (Gen. 28:14). May it be God's will that you will also be as the dust, as the Sages said, "As the dust rises over those who tread upon it, so will Israel."[41] May it be God's will that they will rise up over their enemies and consume those who consume them (cf. Jer. 30:16), with the coming of our righteous Messiah soon and in our days. Amen.

---

41. This does not seem to be a rabbinic statement. Compare Bahya ben Asher and Abraham Saba on Gen. 28:14, and Menasseh ben Israel, *The Conciliator* 1:53.

"The Land Shudders"[1]

Budapest Rabbinical Seminary MS 12, vol. 3, folios 91r–92v
Mishpatim, 1627

*For a detailed discussion of the circumstances of delivery for this sermon and its struc-
ture, see above, chapter four.*

* * *

He shall not rule over her to sell her to outsiders (Exod. 21:8).
So the Sages said, A person who is covering his house with plaster should
leave a small space uncovered. A person who is preparing what is needed for
a feast should leave out some small ingredient. A woman who is putting on
all her ornaments should omit one of them. For it is said, *If I forget you O
Jerusalem, let my right hand wither* (Ps. 137:5)" (b. *Baba Batra* 60b).

Exordium

It often happens, that because of the weakness of human reason, a person will
utter insolent words out of the great anguish of pains he cannot bear, and say
things that are not right. We see Joshua, whose face was like the face of the
moon (b. *Baba Batra* 75a), when he saw that contrary to God's promise, the
Israelites had fled from its enemies, said, *If only we had been content to remain
on the other side of the Jordan!* (Josh. 7:7). Yet while still speaking, when he had
an opportunity to contemplate the thrust of his words, he reversed himself
and said, *O God, what could I say after Israel turned tail before its enemies?* (ibid.
8); by this he meant, "I was forced to say this, it was an error, I did not really
mean it." Jeremiah thought of this common phenomenon when he saw Josiah
close to a painful death, and bent over near Josiah's lips [thinking that Josiah
might be uttering a complaint against God], for it stood to reason that this
righteous man, *unparalleled by any predecessor, a king who turned back to God with
all his heart and all his soul and all his might* (2 Kings 23:25), to whom God

---

1. The title is taken from Prov. 30:21, which will provide the structure for much of the
body of the sermon.

promised that *you will be laid in your tomb in peace* (ibid. 22:20), yet who died by being shot full of arrows,[2] might utter a complaint against God for this fate. That is why Jeremiah bent down, but he did not hear anything inappropriate from him; rather, what he heard was *God is in the right, for I have disobeyed Him* (Lam. 1:18).[3] Jeremiah then said, *The breath of our life, God's anointed* (Lam. 4:20).[4] And so Job's wife, when she was no longer able to tolerate the blows and diseases that came from God, said, *Curse God and die!* (Job 2:9).[5] However, Job, in his great power to endure these afflictions, did not lose his capacity for rational discernment and replied, *Should we accept only good from God and not accept evil?* (ibid. 10). Speaking of the good, he used the word *gam*, which generally means "also," indicating that evil may *also* be good in that it comes for a good purpose.[6]

For this reason, it is not surprising if because of the heartfelt distress of people hearing these tribulations that occurred to the inhabitants of Jerusalem, may it be speedily rebuilt, they have said, "Surely it is not God's will that our people dwell in the Holy Land, for the oppressor's rod has fallen upon them to remove them from upon it." For God has said, *And you I will scatter among the nations* (Lev. 26:33), *And He cast them into another land, as is still this day* (Deut. 29:27), and other similar verses. I myself have heard some distinguished men, because of their zeal and their pain, saying such things and expressing this idea, out of the anguish of their hearts.

However, what they say is not so, as will be evident to those who seek the truth from many proofs derived from the biblical verses. At some future time, there will be an opportunity for a leisurely discussion. However, given the limits of time at the present occasion, I shall bring one proof each from the Torah, Prophets, Writings, and the words of the Sages.

My proof from the Torah is in the verse, *All the nations will ask, Why did God do this to this land? Why that awful wrath? They will be told, Because they forsook the covenant that the Eternal God of their ancestors made with them* (Deut. 29:23–24). There is a problem here. At first the verse speaks about the blows upon the land, while the response is *Because they forsook,* without specifying who are the ones who forsook. One would have expected the verse to say,

---

2. Cf. 2 Chron. 35:23–24 and Lam. Rabbah 1,53.

3. See Lam. Rabbah, 1,53, interpreting this verse as what Jeremiah heard from Josiah before his death.

4. For this verse as Jeremiah's lament over Josiah, see Tosefta *Ta'anit* 2,10.

5. The Hebrew text of the Bible, cited by the preacher, uses the euphemism "Bless God."

6. It is not clear to me how Morteira reads this meaning into the words; one possibility is that he reads Job's response as a statement: "we shall also [some day] accept good from God, and not just [the good that comes] with the evil (*et ha-ra*)."

"They will be told, Because its inhabitants forsook." And the conclusion of the section, which says, *So God was incensed at that land and brought upon it all the curses recorded in this book* (ibid. 26): were the curses indeed proclaimed about the *land?* The answer is that "the land" includes both: the land itself and its inhabitants, as we see both included in this word in the verse, *The land became corrupt* (Gen. 6:11). This teaches that always during the period of exile, a small number of Jews will remain in the land, and about them the verse says, *Because they forsook* (Deut. 29:24). There was no need to specify "its inhabitants," because it is agreed that they are in the presence of the speaker, and that they see the blows upon the land. Scripture also hints of this in the large *lamed* of the word, *va-yashlikhem*: *He cast them out into another land, as is still the case this day* (ibid. 27). This indicates a tension between the words *va-yashlikhem, He cast them out,* and [the same word without the *lamed*:] *va-yeshkhem,* which means, "yet you are there." In other words, *The Eternal uprooted them from their soil in anger, fury, and great wrath, yet you are there* (ibid.), meaning, even though God uprooted them from there, a small number of them will remain, "and you are there," though despite this, *He cast them out into another land, as is still the case this day* (ibid.). That is why the *yod* of the *hiphil* form is missing from *va-yashlikhem*: in order to indicate the word *va-yeshkhem*.[7]

From the Prophets, consider the verse, *But I leave within you a poor, humble folk; they shall find refuge in the name of the Eternal* (Zeph. 4:12). The relevant part is *I leave within you.* This teaches what we have seen with regard to God's commanding Jeremiah after the destruction of the First Temple that the remaining Judeans should not leave the land.[8]

From the Writings: Scripture says, *Your servants take delight in its stones and cherish its dust* (Ps. 102:15), referring to the time when they are in a state of destruction, reduced to stones and dust.

From the words of the Sages: they said, "Whoever lives outside the land is as one who has no God."[9]

Thus there can be no doubt about how extremely precious to God is a continued Jewish presence in the land.[10]

If so, what is the cause of these bitter afflictions? This is not the way to

---

7. Compare the different explanations for the enlarged *lamed* in Ephraim Luntshitz, *'Ir Gibborim, Nitzavim* on this verse.

8. See Jer. 42:9–19, 43:4.

9. B. *Ketubot* 110b.

10. The claim of continual Jewish presence in the land of Israel had polemical significance, as Portuguese preachers cited Jewish exclusion from the Holy Land (especially Jerusalem), even under the Ottoman Turks, as evidence of God's rejection; see Glaser, "Invitation to Intolerance," p. 332.

answer this question; rather, *we shall follow the King's highway* (Num. 20:17).[11] We will not be able to provide a specific reason for these afflictions: God's thoughts are very profound, and His justice is like the great deep (cf. Ps. 93:6 and 36:7), and no human being can give them a specific explanation. However, those who seek out God's ways will discover that one of them will not fail to apply. No matter which one it be, we shall recognize our obligation to help the victims with every fiber of our strength.

Body of the Sermon

The first matter to bear in mind is that since all Jews are sureties for each other,[12] all of them like a single person with many limbs and organs,[13] we may learn from the analogy with the body. It is the nature of the body that all the harmful, inferior, sickly humors attack the heart, and the heart, possessing considerable strength, fights against them more than all the other organs of the body. So it is with God's patterns. When He wants to chastise, He does not chastise the weak in soul, who would kick and scream at the first afflictions. Rather, He tests the perfect vessels,[14] placing His burden on those strong enough to bear it. So the Torah says, *Through those near to Me I show Myself holy* (Lev. 10:3), and there are many similar verses.[15] We may, therefore, learn a lesson from nature, seeing that all the limbs and peripheral organs help to their utmost ability the inner organs, especially the heart, even if they may be damaged by doing so. For example, a person instinctively places his hand in front of the head to save it from injury. And if the heart is diseased, how much healing effort will be expended to save it.[16] How great is our obligation, therefore, to act to save our brothers, the inhabitants of Jerusalem, from the disaster they find themselves in right now! Scripture says

11. The meaning is apparently the need to accept God's judgments (the path of the King), or perhaps try to discover God's purpose in the afflictions.

12. B. *Sanhedrin* 27b.

13. Cf. Zohar III,218a, and the formulation closer to that of Morteira in Isaiah Horowitz's *Shnei Luḥot ha-Berit, Taʿanit* 157: "The community of Israel is like a single person. There are many organs in a person which take on a unity and become one man, and when one of these organs is afflicted, all of them suffer; so all Israel are sureties for each other."

14. Cf. Gen. Rabbah 32,3 and parallels.

15. Such as Ezek. 9:6 and 21:8, which the preacher will cite later in the sermon.

16. The analogy with the heart echoes the famous passage in the *Kuzari* 2,36, that "Israel among the nations is like the heart among the organs of the body: it is at one and the same time the most sickly and the most healthy of them." Morteira uses the analogy, however, for an internal Jewish message.

about this, *Because of this our hearts are sick, because of these our eyes are dimmed: because of Mount Zion, which lies desolate; jackals prowl over it* (Lam. 5:17–18).

These two verses show us clearly the matter we are discussing. The first shows that when the heart is in distress, all the organs are affected. Therefore, in a general punishment, the purpose is so that all will feel pain at the distress of those actually being punished. Thus the verse, *Because of this our hearts are sick,* the result being that *because of these our eyes are dimmed,* the eyes being organs far removed from the heart. The eyes were singled out because they serve their function at a greater distance than any other organ, for seeing is easier than hearing, as experience shows.[17] It is as if he said that both near and far were pained by this. He then goes on to explain what the cause of this pain is, saying, *because of Mount Zion, which lies desolate; jackals prowl over it* (Lam. 5:18). This is precisely what God ordained in the Torah: *They provoked My jealousy with a non-god, vexed Me with their trivialities; I'll provoke them with a non-people, vex them with a shameful nation [am naval]* (Deut. 32:21).[18] For the jackal is always understood to be the most shameful and lowly of creatures, and it is therefore taken as an emblem of humiliation: "When the jackal has his moment, bow to him."[19] And so all of the nations are compared to beasts, but the Egyptians are compared to the jackal.[20] *Jackals prowl over it:* a lowly, shameful people without religion or law, as we see with our own eyes this very day. *Because of this our hearts are sick.... Because of Mount Zion, which lies desolate; jackals prowl over* it (Lam. 5:17–18).

From this interpretation, I move on to say that the four things mentioned by King Solomon as reasons for the land to shudder, things it cannot bear (cf. Prov. 30:21) may suggest to us four reasons for the *diseases that the Eternal has inflicted upon that land* (Deut. 29:21). Even though the phrase "it cannot bear them" may apply to the entire earth, how much the more does it apply to the chosen land, the desirable land, the land of splendor, the land of life, the land of God, the holy land, the land of Israel!

---

17. Cf. Bahya ben Asher on Deut. 4:28, citing the "scientists" (*ḥokhmei ha-meḥqar*).

18. See the Sabbath of Repentance sermon on this verse below, especially pp. 514–15 and 523–24. "Shameful" is the first of four meanings for the word *naval* used by Morteira in the later sermon.

19. A popular adage cited in *Megillah* 16b.

20. For the association between "jackals" (or perhaps "foxes": *shu'alim*) and Egyptians, see Song of Songs Rabbah 2,42 and Rashi on Song 2:15. Morteira applies the rabbinic reference to the Egyptians of antiquity to the contemporary Muslims (apparently ignoring the fact that the Ottoman Turks were in control). Compare the statement in Zohar II (*Shemot*) 16b–17a, which applies Prov. 30:22–23 to Egypt and Ishmael: "There is no nation so lowly and disrespected and despised in God's sight as the Egyptians, yet he gave her dominion over Israel."

1. It said first, *a slave who becomes king* (Prov. 20:22). For if someone who serves royalty rises within society to stature in his conduct and prestige, even though he may retain some undesirable character traits, the fine ones will remain with him. This is not the case with a slave who seeks out the shadows (cf. Job 7:2), who has never seen any model of good, whose company is nothing but the robbery and violence that poverty has taught (as the Sages said, "The more slaves, the more robbery"[21]). Therefore, woe to those who are subjected to such a slave. The land shudders at him. About such a person Solomon cried out, *Alas for you, O land, whose king is a lackey* (na'ar).... *Happy are you, O land, whose king is a master* (ben-horin) (Eccles. 10:16–17). From the opposites in the verses, we see that the word *na'ar* (which can refer just to youthfulness) means what it does in the verse *Abraham said to* na'arav (Gen. 22:5), namely, "to his servants."[22] Because of our sins, they made Jerusalem subject to this evil, placing her under slaves lowly from their youth, hungry and thirsty, who came from far away from the King's residence to consume the lives of the destitute and the needy, to drink their blood, their funds, their honor, their very lives. Alas, the Sages taught us about this matter so well in the case of the daughter of Nakdimon ben Gorion with R. Johanan ben Zakkai. He said to her, Happy are you, O Israel: when you are doing God's will, no nation in the world can rule over you, but if you fail to do God's will, He hands you over into the power of a lowly nation,[23] namely, the Arabs.

This matter was not unknown to the prophets, as we see from the lamentation of Jeremiah. He said, *Slaves are ruling over us, with none to rescue us from their power* (Lam. 5:8). This means, since they have no redeeming character trait—no reverence for the king, no reverence for God, no ethical sense—there is *none to rescue us from their power*. If we cry out to the king, *We get our bread at the peril of our lives, because of the sword of the wilderness* (ibid. 9)—because of the distant sword, and because of the great distance between us and the king's palace, or because of the "sword of the wilderness" that the king himself raises, wreaking havoc as in a wilderness,[24] as was the case in this affair. Thus we have lost our funds, and *Our skin glows like an oven with the fever of famine* (ibid. 10). The honor of our women was in danger, and they suffered many afflictions: *They have ravished women in Zion, maidens in the towns of Judah* (ibid.

---

21. M. *Avot* 2,7.

22. This follows the midrashic understanding of *ne'arim* in Gen. 22 (e.g. Lev. Rabbah 26,7): that they were servants brought to attend to the needs of Abraham.

23. See b. *Ketubot* 66b. R. Johanan ben Zakkai had found the daughter of this formerly immensely wealthy Jew picking out barley grains from the dung of an Arab's cattle.

24. Different interpretations of the phrase "sword of the wilderness" in the Lamentations verse.

11). Finally, our very lives were taken—*Princes have been hanged by them* (ibid. 12)—as was the case now, for if it had been up to them, they would already have been hanged, were it not that God was there for the victims and for us. *No respect was shown for the elders* (ibid.), for they tortured them painfully. Why all of this? *Because of a slave who becomes king* (Prov. 30:22): because of Jeroboam who became king, under whom "the land shuddered" with his calves. *Because of a slave who becomes king,* when we—the servants and ministers of God—bestowed royalty on the Queen of Heaven. *Because of a slave who becomes king,* when some of our people bestowed divinity upon a man born to woman![25] This is measure for measure, as ordained in the poem [*Ha'azinu*], *They provoked My jealousy with non-gods* (the first "they" is in contrast with the second part of the verse, which speaks of others), *They provoked My jealousy with a non-god,* while the rest of the world *vexed Me with their trivialities; I'll provoke them with a non-people, vex them with a shameful nation* [*am naval*] (Deut. 32:21).

Since this is so, it is proper for us, whom God has placed in a land of princes,[26] of religion and law—even though we are all caught up in sin—to help and aid them, so that in their prosperity we may prosper (cf. Jer. 29:7), for whoever says, *I'll be all right,* etc. (cf. Deut. 29:18), *the Eternal will never forgive him* (Deut. 29:19).

2. Solomon said secondly, [*The land shudders at*] *a scoundrel sated with bread* (Prov. 30:22). Now this scoundrel is the source of all shameful things. It is Satan, it is the evil impulse, it is the angel of death, the accuser.[27] Alas for the Jews[28] when he is *sated with bread.* The bread of flaring vipers, the food of transgressions and sins: when he is sated, then he becomes capable of turning against us and denouncing us. Then "the land shudders." He used the metaphor of "bread" because this word, *lehem,* is connected with the word for war, *milhamah,* and this is what fights against us, for "it is not the lizard that kills, but the sin that kills."[29]

Alas, how sated he is with hatred between Jews! How sated with slanderous speech. How sated with vengeful hearts and nurturing enmities. How sated with robbery and violence. How sated with failure to study Torah. How sated with laxity in performance of the commandments. How sated with those who do them for improper reasons, *a commandment of men, learned by rote* (Isa. 29:13). [How sated with those who swear an oath falsely; with those who utter

---

25. Reviewing the most significant sins of antiquity in the land of Israel, Morteira builds to a climax with the transformation of Jesus into divinity.

26. Heb: *eretz melakhim,* contrasted with a land in which slaves rule.

27. Cf. b. *Baba Batra* 16a.

28. The Hebrew text has the euphemism, "Alas for the haters of Israel."

29. B. *Berakhot* 33a.

the Divine Name for no good purpose; with those who make vows they do not fulfill. How sated with those who have sexual relations with Gentile women.][30] How sated with the informers, and the apostates. How sated with the arrogant and the haughty. How sated with those who offer up their sons to Molech. How sated with those who mock God's words, with those who behave defiantly. How sated is this scoundrel! Divine Justice cannot annul his wish.[31]

Once permission is given (heaven forbid!), he does not distinguish. More than this: he actually begins with the righteous, as we see in the verse, *I will wipe out from you both the righteous and the wicked* (Ezek. 21:8), and the verse, *Begin here, at My sanctuary* (Ezek. 9:6). The reason is that they are the heroes, they are the walls, they are the towers for those who would not implore God's favor. Whoever pays no heed is simple, foolish, devoid of sense. Isaiah wrote, *The righteous man perishes, and no one takes it to heart* (Isa. 57:1). Be men, take it to heart, prepare, set things right, and provide help against the enemy, so that God may have mercy; be established through righteousness (cf. Isa. 54:14), and return to God, for He is gracious and compassionate, and He may renounce punishment (cf. Joel 2:13).

3. Solomon then went on to say, [The land shudders at] *a loathsome woman who gets married* (Prov. 30:23). Here too he taught us a reason—the third—for our topic [the suffering imposed on the Jewish inhabitants of the land of Israel]. It is what experience has shown us from the day when God chose us and took us as His people. *So Jeshurun grew fat and unruly, you grew fat and gross and coarse, he forsook the God who made him and spurned his supporting Rock* (Deut. 32:15). But we have not opened our eyes, nor have we learned a lesson from the many times when this was the cause that brought us so much misfortune, for when things were good, we have always turned to evil. To this very day in the long and bitter exile, we have not turned back from this way. Whenever God is generous to us, giving our remnant a respite,[32] instead of this beneficence from God leading us to cling more closely to Him and strengthening us in His service, the beneficence becomes the cause of increasing sin and transgression: conflicts and sins and battles, envy and hatred for each other, until God afflicted us, so that we sought Him in distress, and chastisement brought [us] to anguished whispered prayer (cf. Isa. 26:16).

This is the meaning of Solomon's statement, that the land shudders at *a loathsome woman who gets married*: when Israel, which in their exile is called by

---

30. The material in brackets was written by the author between the lines as an addition to what he originally wrote, though presumably part of what he intended to say.

31. On this passage, see pp. 130–31 above.

32. Perhaps alluding to Gen. Rabbah 75,13 and Ramban on Gen. 32:17.

the nations loathsome—as we see in the verse, *Where you have been forsaken and loathsome... I will make you a pride everlasting* (Isa. 60:15)—"gets married," and God through His providence treats them beneficently, and they show the signs of prosperity, then the land will shudder and it will not contain them, for their failings will proliferate. Whoever is wise would understand this and learn from earlier times: from the greatness and glory, the affluence and wisdom that were long ago in the [Jewish communities of the] kingdoms of Spain and France. Let him see now: all is destroyed and abandoned, nothing remains. One may cry out, "Aha! O Eternal our God, what is this all about? Will You totally destroy the remnant of Your estate?" (cf. Ezek. 11:13). If he had any insight, he would turn his words back against himself. *The judgments of the Eternal are true, they are just in their entirety* (Ps. 19:10). Let him read the matters in the judicial questions and responsa left by these sages: the abundance of violence, the lust, the envy, the conflicts, the informers [about Jews to the government], the most serious sexual offenses, sexual congress with Gentile women, the neglect of Torah, the eager pursuit of money, and similar things that can be found in these books by anyone who would read them.[33]

Still, we have not learned! Even today, we are worse than our ancestors. Did we not see during the good days that confronted us in this city how many conflicts occurred and how many bans were enacted, until war and loss of money and pestilence came, Heaven protect us![34] And so in Jerusalem, the holy city, may it be quickly rebuilt: for the past three years there was peace and tranquility in the land. But we knew the bewildering and chaotic conflicts among the Jews, until the anger of Satan boiled over against them and destroyed them, as our eyes see this very day. Truly, experience teaches the truthfulness of the rabbinic statement, "misery is fitting for Israel like a red rose upon a white horse."[35] Even a minor sin committed in that land is much greater than in another place, for it is done in God's presence. We see this in the verse, *The people who provoke My anger continually, in My very presence* [Isa. 65:3], and in the verse, *My eyes and My heart will be there always* [1 Kings 9:3]. How much greater is the transgression committed in the king's palace, in the king's very presence, than that committed in one's own house![36]

---

33. A striking reference to the medieval responsa as a source not for Jewish law as for Jewish social history.

34. See above, chap. 4, p. 134 and n. 41.

35. Cf. b. *Hagigah* 9b. Morteira's text is discussed at the citation of this statement on p. 340, n. 84. Note the very different attitude toward poverty expressed in the sermons on *Va-Ethanan* and *Ha'azinu* (pp. 414–20, 477–78).

36. For a discussion of the historical allusions and rhetorical strategy in this passage, see chapter 4 above, pp. 134–35.

Why then are we irresolute in our actions? Why do we undermine our preparations to accept all God's kindnesses, while we provoke Him over the good things He gives us? *I lavished silver on her, and gold, which they used for Baal* (Hos. 2:10). Indeed, how great is the obligation of the leaders of these congregations to bestir themselves to improve our way of serving God, in that He has favored us more than any other Jews in the Diaspora.[37] (Here this matter should be discussed at length.[38])

Where here are the taxes of Venice? The censorship of books that is all over Italy? The seizing of children for forced conversions? The sign of the [Jewish] hat that is there? The Ghettos? The need to receive permission [to remain] every so often? Being shut in at the evil time [Holy Week]?[39] Where is the derision shown toward the Jews of Rome, [forced to] go out naked on their holidays, forced to attend their services, forced to bow down to the

---

37. The reference to "these congregations" probably indicates that all three congregations met together for the special occasion on which this sermon was delivered. The last five Hebrew words of this section translate, "Here this matter should be developed at length;" they were probably written by Morteira when he temporarily left off writing the text of his sermon as a reminder to himself of how he intended to continue. Indeed, the following paragraph, which appears to be written with a somewhat finer pen point, goes on to specify the uniqueness of Amsterdam.

38. These five Hebrew words appearing at the end of this section were probably written by Morteira when he temporarily left off writing the text of his sermon as a reminder to himself of how he intended to continue. Indeed, the following paragraph, which appears to be written with a somewhat finer pen point, goes on to specify the uniqueness of Amsterdam.

39. On taxation in Venice, see Cecil Roth, *History of the Jews of Venice* (Philadelphia, 1930), pp. 120–22. On censorship in Venice, see Brian Pullen, *The Jews of Europe and the Inquisition of Venice, 1550–1670* (London, 1997), pp. 82–85; Modena, *The Autobiography of a Seventeenth-Century Venetian Rabbi*, p. 147, 256–57; Kenneth Stow, "The Burning of the Talmud in 1553, in Light of Sixteenth-Century Catholic Attitudes toward the Talmud," in *Essential Papers on Judaism and Christianity in Conflict*, ed. Jeremy Cohen (New York, 1991), pp. 401–28; more generally in Italy: Baron, *SRHJ* 14:52, 55–57, 63; William Popper, *The Censorship of Hebrew Books*, reprint edition: New York, 1969. On seizing of children for forced conversion (actually more of a problem in Rome than in Venice): Roth, *History of the Jews of Venice*, pp. 117–18; cf. Baron *SRHJ* 14:60.

On the Jewish hat, see Benjamin Ravid, "From Yellow to Red: On the Distinguishing Head-Covering of the Jews of Venice," *Jewish History* 6 (1992): 179–210. On the Ghettos: Benjamin Ravid, "New Light on the Ghetti of Venice," in *Shlomo Simonsohn Jubilee Volume*, ed. Daniel Carpi et al. (Tel Aviv, 1993), pp. 149–76; Donatella Calabi, in *The Jews of Early Modern Venice*, ed. Robert C. Davis and Benjamin Ravid (Baltimore, 2001), pp. 31–49. For the need to get permission to remain: Benjamin Ravid, in *The Jews of Early Modern Venice*, pp. 7–20. On Jewish seclusion in the ghetto from sunrise on Holy Thursday until the evening of Holy Saturday, see Ravid, *Economics and Toleration in Seventeenth-Century Venice* (Jerusalem, 1978), p. 176; Pullen, *The Jews of Europe*, p. 163.

Pope?[40] Where are the blood libels of Poland?[41] Where are the humiliations of Germany? Where are the hours when they prevent us from attending the [commercial] fairs? The entrances through which we may not walk, the wells from we may not drink?[42] Where is the harsh oppression of Turkey? The poll tax that is levied there? The cruelty of the Gentiles? The fire thrown into houses? The deadly tortures connected with the manufacturing of their clothes?[43] Where is the degradation of Barbary? Where is the youngster who will strike an old man? Where are the animal carcasses which they compel us to remove from their paths?[44] And much more of the like, that our brothers,

---

40. The "derision" for the Jews of Rome may refer to the *giudate*, a comic play ridiculing stock Jewish characters that, according to a recent study, by the early seventeenth century "had become a fixture in the spectrum of the Roman comic theatre and was known throughout Northern and Central Italy;" see Lynn M. Gunzberg, *Strangers at Home* (Berkeley, 1992), pp. 92–95. On the infamous footraces during Roman Carnival (held between 1466 and 1668), in which the Jews were allowed to wear only loin-cloth, see Ferdinand Gregorovius, *The Ghetto and the Jews of Rome* (New York, 1966), pp. 49–51 (a text from 1667 states that first the asses, then the Jews, then the buffaloes, then the Arab horses raced; the Jewish leaders bow before Senator, who would put his foot on their foreheads: p. 51); Hermann Vogelstein, *History of the Jews of Rome* (Philadelphia, 1940), pp. 231–33; Baron, *SRHJ* 10:260, 416 n. 50. For forced attendance at conversionist sermons, see Baron, *SRHJ* 14:50–51, 60–61; Kenneth R. Stow, *Catholic Thought and Papal Jewish Policy* (New York, 1977), pp. 19–21. Urban VIII (1623–1644) instituted the rule that at audiences, Jews may not kiss the Pope's foot as previously, but only the spot on which the Pope had stood (Vogelstein, *History of the Jews of Rome*, pp. 280–81.

41. See Bernard D. Weinryb, *The Jews of* Poland (Philadelphia, 1973), p. 152, listing 19 incidents of blood libels or charges of desecrating the host between 1551 and the date when the sermon was delivered; Baron, *SRHJ* 10:35–36, 16:101–3; Zenon Gulden and Jacek Wijaczka, "The Accusation of Ritual Murder in Poland, 1500–1800," *Polin*, 10 (1997): 139–40; Morteira's *Tratado*, pp. 69–71.

42. On the "humiliations of Germany," see Graetz, *History of the Jews*, 4:694–700, including the prohibition of purchasing food in the market at same time as Christians (pp. 695–96). Cf. Christopher Friedrichs, "Politics or Pogrom? The Fettmilch Uprising in German and Jewish History," *Central European History* 19.2 (June 1986), 186–228. Jewish attendance at and participation in the great commercial fairs was hotly contested, and economic pressures often led to permission to attend even in cities where they were not permitted to live. However, there were instances where Jews were permitted to enter only through a special gate (the *Judentor*) at fixed hours, and restricted to certain markets. (*EJ* 11:1002 on Brno).

43. On Ottoman oppression, see Baron, *SRHJ*, 18:159; for the capitation tax: Baron 18:269–71, Stanford Shaw, *The Jews of the Ottoman Empire and Turkish Republic* (New York, 1991), p. 75; for Jewish involvement in the textile industry and tailoring and problems raised by the government: Baron 18:226–31, Shaw, pp. 92–93.

44. For the humiliation of North African Jews, see H. Z. Hirschberg, *A History of the Jews in North Africa*, 2 vols. (Leiden, 1974–1981), 2:12 (Jews live in degrading conditions, even children despise and insult them: Algeria, ca 1550); 2:14 (subject to contempt and humilia-

the entire house of Israel, suffer throughout their dispersion in exile. But God has brought us out from there.[45] Why then are we ungrateful? Why do we not wake up and open our eyes [to see] that just as God has favored us more than all our brothers, so should we surpass them all in our conduct, serving as an example, a model of goodness and decency, especially by helping the Holy City at a time like this?

4. Solomon concluded, fourthly, [The land shudders at] *a slave-girl who supplants her mistress* (Prov. 30:23). Jerusalem is the *mistress of kingdoms* (Isa. 47:5), as we see in the verse, *I set Jerusalem in the midst of the nations, with countries round about her* (Ezek. 5:5). All of the other lands are called her maid-servants, or her daughters, as in the verse, *daughters of Jerusalem* (Song 1:5).[46] But it is a disgrace, which *the land ... cannot bear* (Prov. 30:21)—indeed the worst of all— when her children give all its goodness and its glory to her maid-servant. They forget the mistress, giving every kind of joy and honor to maid-servants in the land of their enemies, in their exile, in a land not theirs. They never used to adorn themselves to such an extent with so many luxuries while there were living in Jerusalem as they do when they are among her maid-servants.

This is quite different from the statement of the Sages in our opening dictum[47] about fulfilling the verse, *If I forget you, O Jerusalem* (Ps. 137:5). They said, "A person who is covering his house with plaster should leave a small space uncovered." They did not say "covering his house with paintings,"[48] but "covering his house with *plaster*," yet still a small space should be left as a reminder of the destruction. This is clear from an *a fortiori* argument. When the ark of God was in a tent, David said, *Here I am dwelling in a house of cedar, [while the Ark of God abides in a tent!]* (1 Sam. 7:2).[49] Now that the house of God is de-

tion: Algeria, 1612); 2:197–206 (a Jewish account of persecution against the Jews in Fez: 1610–1626); and, somewhat later than Morteira's sermon, 2:82 (humiliation of Jews of Tunisia by a French consul, 1665), 2: 237–43, and 2:253–54: "They are subject to suffering the blows and injuries of everyone, without daring to say a word even to a child of six who throws stones at them.... When they inter one of their own, the children harass them with blows, spit in their face, and curse them with a thousand maledictions."

45. A formulation based on the common association of the Exodus from Egypt as a model for the escape from Portugal, but here suggesting that all the rest of the world is part of the exile from which the Jews of Amsterdam have been liberated. For other aspects of Morteira's treatment of exile and Amsterdam, see above, chap. 9.

46. See Exod. Rabbah 23,10 on this verse: "Jerusalem will in the future be the mother city of all the lands."

47. B. *Baba Batra* 60b, quoted at the beginning of the sermon.

48. This is a barbed allusion to the use of artwork to decorate the homes, a practice about which Morteira seems to have felt some ambivalence. Cf. *"Your Voice Like a Ram's Horn,"* p. 416, including n. 20.

49. I.e., even though the Ark had a proper (though not magnificent) enclosure, David felt

stroyed, why do Jews of the Diaspora seek out *spacious upper chambers* (Jer. 22:14)? This is like the statement of the prophet Haggai, *Is it a time for you to dwell in your paneled houses, while this House is lying in ruins?* (Hag. 1:4).[50] Why should they seek something that is unnecessary for a life of cleanliness and modesty, while Jerusalem is destroyed? Is this not *a slave-girl who supplants her mistress?*

They further said, "A person who is preparing what is needed for a feast, should leave out some small ingredient." They said, "what is needed," yet even from these necessities one should let something remain as a reminder of the destruction. They were not talking about those banquets that destroy people's savings. Of this, the prophet said, *They lie on ivory beds, stretched upon their couches, feasting on lambs from the flock, and on calves from the stall.... They drink from the wine bowls and anoint themselves with the choicest oils, but they are not concerned about the ruin of Joseph* (Amos 6:4,6).[51]

They further said, "A woman who is putting on her ornaments should omit one of them." They specified "*her* ornaments," those ornaments appropriate to a woman in exile, who would not transgress the words of the prophet who cries out against them when in abundance. Yet "she should omit one of them" as a reminder of the destruction. But they do not act this way; rather, they see how they can outdo the ones who preceded them, so that *a slave-girl supplants her mistress* (Prov. 30:23) by acting this way in their exile.

Peroration

How good and how fine it would be for every person to take pride and to compete with his neighbor:

- not in the great size of his house but in the greatness of his soul, which is the house of ethical virtues and intellectual attainments;
- not in foods but in feeding the poor and abundant charity;
- not in clothes, but in a good name and serenity and in imitation of God's ways and in the mystical garment of good deeds.[52]

---

that his more lavish accommodations were inappropriate. How much the more should contemporary Jews in exile feel this.

50. At this point in his preparation, the preacher clearly had the text of his earlier sermon "The People's Envy" in front of him; see the similar use of this verse there, *Jewish Preaching*, p. 276.

51. Cf. the use of this verse in the same context in "The People's Envy," ibid., p. 282.

52. *Ḥaluqa de-rabbanan*, literally: "robe of the sages." This refers to the garment worn by the righteous in the world to come (see Zohar 1:66a). (Morteira referred to this kabbalistic term on other occasions in his sermons: e.g. the passage cited above, p. 95 n. 75.) In these

This would be the true "remembering of Jerusalem," this would be the shortening of our exile. But now that we fail to do this, the blows upon Jerusalem increase. Perhaps we may open our eyes from preoccupation with ourselves to see whether the way we are following is good. For these afflictions do not come upon it because God does not want us to dwell there, heaven forbid! Rather, there are many good reasons for His judgments. Among them are these five that we have mentioned: first, that it is like the heart of Israel, second because of the sins of ancient times: *They provoked My jealousy with a non-god* (Deut. 32:21), third, because of the sins of the present and the power of the prosecutor over us, fourth because of the sins of the land itself, inhabitants of which do not encompass its goodness, fifth, because the Jews living in exile, who should remember her humiliation, praise her through their luxuries, while she is in ruins.[53]

That is why the members of the *Va'ad* passed the ordinances they did to help in its redemption,[54] so that the Jewish presence will not depart from it. And that is why we began with the Text, ***He shall not have the right to sell her to an alien people*** (Exod. 21:8).[55] For this idea is also in the verse, *And which of My creditors was it to whom I sold you off?* (Isa. 50:1). For it is not sold, only given for temporary keeping, and therefore Israel will not lose her presumptive rights, she will forever remain upon it.[56] It is as I said at the beginning in my interpretation of the verse, *He cast them out into another land, as is still the case this day* (Deut. 29:27),[57] until he comes and restores it as at first, and *all who mourn over it will join in her jubilation* (Isa. 66:10), which will occur with the coming of our righteous Messiah, speedily and in our days. Amen.

---

sentences, Morteira recapitulates the three elements in the opening rabbinic dictum, which correlate to the three areas of wasteful ostentatious behavior in the sermon "The People's Envy."

53. A characteristic recapitulation of the major points of the sermon coming near the end.

54. On the decision made by fifteen lay leaders on February 7, 1627 was to borrow 1800 florins from the Dowry Fund in order to send a total of 2400 florins to "our brothers dwelling in Jerusalem," see above, p. 138, n. 49.

55. This recourse to the theme-verse at the very end of the sermon, rather than as a structuring element, seems to be characteristic especially of Morteira's eulogies. See *"Your Voice Like a Ram's Horn,"* pp. 385, 397, 433. The sermon is thus framed through the rhetorical device of *chiasmus:* theme-verse then rabbinic dictum at the beginning, dictum then theme-verse at the end.

56. The theme-verse from Exodus is thus shifted from a detail of ancient Jewish law pertaining to the Hebrew servant-woman to the historical status of the land of Israel. The Isaiah verse, a rhetorical question, indicates that there was no sale to any creditor.

57. See above, p. 395, on Morteira's discovery of the word *va-yeshkhem* concealed in this verse.

The sermon I delivered on the lesson *Mishpatim* [Exod. 21–24] at the time when written reports arrived concerning the great tribulations that were in Jerusalem, may it speedily be rebuilt, in the year 5387 [1627].

"Do Not Add To His Words"[1]

Giv'at Sha'ul (1645), pp. 69b–71b
Va-Ethanan, ca. 1630

The construction of this sermon is fairly straightforward, though by no means devoid of subtlety. The connection between the scriptural verse and the rabbinic dictum is not at all apparent. An experienced and attentive listener might have intuited that the preacher would probably link the "foolish pietist" with someone who would add or detract from God's commandments in violation of the theme-verse, but the other elements of the dictum have no such explanation; they would be stored away by the listener as the preacher begins to focus on the scriptural theme-verse.

As we have seen in our discussion of Morteira's preparation, one characteristic beginning for his sermons was to identify a significant problem in the theme-verse, and to review the attempts of his predecessors to resolve it. This is what he does at the beginning of his exordium. This problem is not intrinsic to the verse, but rather contextual: the repetition of the same verse, virtually word for word, a few chapters later in Deuteronomy. Here, however, he does not review the previous exegetical literature; he claims that despite careful research, he has found no source that addressed this problem. And a problem it is, given his assumption that there is nothing superfluous in the Torah (see below, n. 4).

Yet this is not enough: Morteira proceeds to raise a second problem, this one intrinsic to the verse, pertaining to the order of the injunctions it contains. Inherent in the axiom of nothing superfluous in Torah discourse is not just that every apparent repetition must teach something new, but also the postulate that there is nothing stated explicitly that could be logically derived from what is stated elsewhere. Now if one is commanded not to add *anything to the laws of the Torah, thereby making them more rigorous, it should be obvious that one is forbidden to remove anything and thereby make the laws more lenient. The order of the verbs should therefore have been reversed: you must not take away, and you must not even add. The way the verse is stated seems analogous to saying "You must not look at another man's wife or have sexual relations with her."*

With these two problems articulated and (the preacher must have hoped) the curiosity of the listeners aroused, Morteira offers his solutions, starting with the second,

---

1. Based on Deut. 13:1, which the preacher will quote at the beginning of his Exordium and at the end of the sermon.

easier problem. He then informs his listeners that the rest of the sermon will be devoted to the first, more difficult problem of repetition. He ends his exordium with a reference to the occasion (the Sabbath of Consolation following Tish'a be-Av) and hints that there will be a polemical response to Christianity in the words to follow.

That response comes right at the beginning of the body of the sermon, where Morteira cites a claim made in "one of the Gentiles' books that four new spiritual ideals were introduced as improvements over Judaism "when their Messiah came." These four themes—the ideals of poverty and of chastity, the love of enemy, and the active pursuit of martyrdom—provide the structure for the body of the sermon, although the four components are by no means given equal time. It is as if the preacher got carried away, refuting the claim that wealth and possession are a barrier to the ideal religious life, and then realized he had to make the other parts considerably shorter, if they were to fit into the time allotted.

(I have consulted many experts in Christian literature in the past fifteen years in an attempt to identify the obviously Catholic text that names these four ideals. The closest match is a eulogy by Morteira's older contemporary, the French preacher Jean Pierre Camus, delivered on November 4, 1616 and published in 1623. There he focuses on the four "virtues" of the apostolic man—humility, chastity, poverty, zeal—and ends his exordium with a formulation exactly parallel to the way Morteira ends his introductory sections: "Our Discourse will be about these four virtues that we have mentioned." Two of these—poverty and chastity—are identical with those Morteira discusses, and it would be possible to link "humility" with love of enemy and "zeal" with the active pursuit of martyrdom, although these connections are not in the French eulogy. Most important, however, Camus does not compare these virtues with Jewish ideals to argue a transcending of Jewish values.)[2]

After each of the new Christian values is refuted in its own terms, Morteira turns to a general principle that he claims invalidates the entire spiritual ethic of the Catholic Church. Commandments by God should apply to the entire religious community; everyone should be capable of observing them. But these four principles are by their very nature elitist. If they were observed by all believers—if everyone gave up wealth, renounced sexual relations, tried to love their enemies rather than resist them, and sought out an opportunity to die as a martyr—society would collapse. Since this cannot possibly be desired by God, the underlying assumption is impossible. Catholic spirituality fails by the standard of the categorical imperative: it cannot become universal.

At this point in the sermon the rabbinic dictum is invoked, with each of the four

---

2. On Camus, see Thomas Worcester, *Seventeenth-Century Cultural Discourse: France and the Preaching of Bishop Camus* (New York, 1997); mention of this eulogy is on p. 172. Prof. Worcester was kind enough to provide me with a reproduction of Camus's *Homélies Panegyriques de Sainct Charles Borromée* (Paris, 1623) so that I could check the full text.

elements applied to one of the four Christian values. One item on the homiletical agenda then remains: the resolution of the original problem of repetition. What may seem to be a pedantic grammatical issue becomes at the end a matter of genuine principle. The issue of supererogatory acts, standards of behavior freely chosen by elite individuals who want to go beyond the behavior of the masses, was an aspect of the Protestant critique of Catholic spirituality (see below, n. 71). On this matter debate, Morteira stood on the same side as his Protestant neighbors.

The previous sermon was intended to refute an erroneous though plausible belief about the contemporary Jewish presence in the land of Israel, to inspire moral and financial support for the hounded Jewish community of Jerusalem, and to motivate introspection and repentance among the Jews of Amsterdam. Here the purpose is totally different: it is not to change anything, but rather to reassure his congregants that they have made the correct decision in abandoning their Catholic roots, to reinforce their conclusion that the fulfillment of God's will is to be attained right where they are.

* * *

You must not add to what I command you or take away from it, but keep the commandments of the Lord your God that I enjoin upon you (Deut. 4:2).

[Tractate] Sotah, chapter 3 (20a): Rabbi Joshua said, "A foolish pietist, and a cunning knave, a secluded virgin and the blows of the secluded ones: these destroy the world."

Exordium

This commandment[3] is repeated in the lesson *Re'eh*: *All that I command you, that you shall be careful to observe; you must not add to it or take away from it* (Deut. 13:1). I have searched through the rabbinic literature, but I have not found any explanation of what the repetition in this command is intended to teach us, though they usually explain why commandments are repeated. Similarly with the commentators I have seen: I have not found a reason for it. It is indeed worth investigating, for the Torah is perfect, without anything superfluous or any defect.[4]

Since God commanded **You must not add to or take away from what I**

---

3. I.e., the theme-verse, read by the preacher at the very beginning of the sermon.

4. For a fuller statement of Morteira's position on repetition in the Bible—accepting the exegetical principle "the same content is repeated in different words" for the rhetoric of the prophets but rejecting if for the Torah—see his sermon translated in *Jewish Preaching*, pp. 274–75: "Nothing in the Torah is mere rhetoric; everything is of substantial and fundamen-

command you (Deut. 4:2), there is nothing there without a purpose, for if there were something superfluous, there would be no harm in removing it, and God would have had no reason to command us not to remove anything from it. But since He commanded ***You must not take away*** (Deut. 4:2), it follows that everything in the Torah is there because it is needed. We must therefore discover the need for the repetition of this commandment.[5]

Furthermore, we need to know about the order used by the Torah in expressing this commandment. On the surface it would appear that the opposite order is correct, namely "Do not remove anything and do not add to it." This would mean, "My intention is not only that you not remove anything, but also that you do not add." But once you say "Do not add," there is no reason to specify "Do not take away": it is obviously *a fortiori*. If an addition is forbidden, even though the divine words remain complete, then a removal of some of the divine words will certainly be forbidden![6]

This is what we find in the thirtieth chapter of Proverbs: *Every word of God is pure, a shield to those who take refuge in Him. Do not add to His words, lest He indict you and you be proved a liar* (Prov. 30:5–6). He did not say "Do not take away," for it was obvious. Why then was not the order in the two verses of Deuteronomy reversed?

The solution to the second question is simpler than the first, and we shall therefore begin with it, and afterward set our sights to see if we can arrive at a solution for the first. I would say that the warning not to take away from the commandments God has enjoined is indeed unnecessary, for it is self-evident. Who can lay hands upon the divine Torah with impunity? Such a person will have already transgressed the verse, *for he has spurned God's word* (Num. 15:31).

However, there was a need to warn about not adding, for in some of the matters about which God commanded, one might think that the more one did the better, since one would be increasing what was good, which is generally to be desired. For example, if God said to make four fringes, a person might think that he could have an even more effective reminder, which is the

---

tal significance. There is no repetition without a special purpose." There he is speaking about apparently redundant language within a single verse.

5. Thus there is a special paradox about the repetition of this specific commandment, as the prohibition against "taking away" implies that there is nothing superfluous, and thus no repetition.

6. After raising the problem of repetition, which actually belongs more to the later verse than to this, Morteira raises an additional conceptual problem intrinsic to the theme-verse. This too is related to the issue of superfluous verbiage, for what is readily deducible by the canons of logic need not be specified. For the tradition of raising problems at the beginning of a homiletical or exegetical discussion, see Saperstein, "The Method of Doubts."

reason for the commandment specified in the Torah, if he made five or six. And similarly with other matters.[7] Regarding this, God commanded *You must not add,* and gave the reason for this by saying, *for you must not take away,*[8] meaning, if you come to add and combine the commandment with details that you make up, eventually this addition will lead to a reduction and a diminution. This will certainly occur since it is a human ordinance. But people will think that everything is in the same category, so that everything will be diminished, and they will tamper with what is Mine. It is like a group of witnesses: if one of them turns out to be a relative or otherwise ineligible, all the testimony is disqualified.[9] Thus the end of the verse is the reason for the beginning: *You must not add,* and in this way, *you will not take away,* which is surely the most serious of sins.

Similar to this is *You must not steal; you must not deal deceitfully or falsely with one another. You must not swear* (Lev. 19:11–12), for one leads to the other.[10] And this is what Solomon meant when he said,[11] *Every word of God is pure, without dross; therefore, do not add to His words lest He indict you* (Prov. 30:5–6), meaning, for what you added they will indict you for a reduction and diminution; *and be proved a liar* (Prov. 30:6), meaning you will become a liar even in what God actually commanded, and you will take away from it, for all will seem to be in the same category.

The Sages expressed this idea in their statement in Genesis Rabbah, concerning Eve and the serpent. God said, *For on the day you eat of it you shall die* (Gen. 2:17), but she did not report this correctly. Instead, she said something false: *You must not eat of it or touch it* (Gen. 3:3). When the serpent saw her passing by the tree, he took her and pushed her against it and said, "See you did not die. Just as you did not die when you touched it, so you will not die when you eat it."[12] This is the explanation of that second problem.

However, the original problem pertaining to the repetition of the verses

---

7. This is the interpretation given by Rashi on Deut. 4:2 and 13:1, based on *Sifrei Re'eh* on Deut. 13:1. The "other matters" provided as examples are adding a passage to what is included in the phylacteries, or a kind of vegetation to the four kinds used on Sukkot, or a fourth blessing to the three used by the priests.

8. In this reading, *ve-lo tigra* is not a separate commandment (which could be derived by the logical argument mentioned above) but an explanation of *You must not add* drawn from human psychology—a reading syntactically plausible because of the ambiguity of the Hebrew conjunction *vav.* For a parallel rabbinic interpretation of the two clauses at the beginning of Deut. 17:17, see b. *Baba Metsi'a* 115a.

9. B. *Sanhedrin* 9a; Maimonides, *Code, Hilkhot 'Edut* 5,3.

10. See Rashi on Lev. 19:12.

11. Returning to the verse he had cited earlier.

12. Gen. Rabbah 19,3. Morteira used this midrashic passage as the rabbinic dictum at the

remains unresolved. Our message today will be devoted to a solution. For in addition to its being the theme of the verse which has come up for us according to our pattern,[13] it is extremely appropriate for the consolation of this day, the Sabbath of Comforting.[14] What greater comfort and joy can there be for a seafarer than to know that his ship is strong and will not break, and that the captain is beyond compare in expertise. The same is true for us in knowing that the Torah, the lamp for our feet and the light for our path,[15] is eternal and perfect, leaving nothing to be added to it or taken away, knowing also that all that the Gentiles have concocted is external to it.[16] How this is so will be our subject today, which we begin with the help of God, whose words are indeed pure.[17]

Body of the Sermon

Among the things spoken by the "little horn" that Daniel prophesied about, saying *There were eyes in this horn like the eyes of a man, and a mouth that spoke arrogantly* (Dan. 7:8), [is] *He will think of changing times and laws* (Dan. 7:25).[18] Now I have found in one of the Gentiles' books[19] the assertion that four things were changed when their Messiah came, bringing improvements over the

---

beginning of his Sabbath of Repentance sermon, "They Provoked Me With a Non-God" on Deut. 32:21; see below, pp. 492 and 525–26.

13. I.e., Morteira's pattern of moving systematically, verse by verse, through each biblical lesson, so that he would have reached this verse, the ninth in the lesson, after having based a sermon on each of the previous verses.

14. The Sabbath following the observance of national mourning on the Ninth Day of Ab; on this Sabbath the prophetic reading begins with Isa. 40:1, *Comfort, oh comfort My people*.

15. Cf. Ps. 119:105.

16. After discussing what appear to be totally internal Jewish issues, Morteira unexpectedly introduces an explicitly polemical statement, hinting that this may indeed be significant in the body of the sermon.

17. Cf. Ps. 12:7. This invocation of God's help after defining the subject of the sermon in language echoing the subject is Morteira's characteristic way of signaling the end of his Exordium.

18. Daniel 7:25 is part of the little horn's description of the "fourth beast" as a "fourth kingdom," universally understood by medieval Jews as referring to Christianity (or sometimes Christianity plus Islam). This verse introduces the theme of changes in the law brought about by Christianity; cf. Maimonides' "Epistle to Yemen," in *Crisis and Leadership*, pp. 100–101. Cf. also the following sermon, p. 435.

19. I have not found any instance of Morteira citing a book by a non-Jewish author by name in his sermons. This is different from his *Tratado*, in which he cites explicitly dozens of such books. Though he discusses the Christian claims to live by higher standards and reprises some of his arguments in the *Tratado* (as noted below), he does not identify his source there either.

originals. The Gentiles wax eloquent in their praise of these changes, exalting them in their sermons with parables and exempla, and thereby deceiving those who are not sufficiently alert and intelligent. We must therefore warn about them, so that all will know how to guard their hearts from being ensnared, and they will also know how our holy Torah warned about these matters to keep us from stumbling.[20]

Individual Discussion

1. The first pertains to the wealth that God has given to human beings as a gift or as a reward for observing His commandments. He has commanded us not to spurn such wealth or to fail to appreciate His gifts. Indeed, it is the means of fulfilling many of the commandments, and of preserving physical health, which is dependent upon what happens to the body. It also enables us to keep the soul free of many worries and concerns that prevent it from following God's path. That is why it was promised to our ancestors, who sought it and prayed to God for it.

We see this in Jacob's vow: *Of all that You give me, I will set aside a tithe for You* (Gen. 28:22), after specifying *If God gives me bread to eat and clothing to wear* (Gen. 28:20). Jacob called all these goods "true kindness" in the verse, *I am unworthy of all the true kindness You have shown Your servant: with my staff alone I crossed this Jordan, and now I have become two camps* (Gen. 32:11). Similarly, the promise to the stranger was of this nature: *and befriends the stranger, providing him with food and clothing* (Deut. 10:18).

God wants human beings to appreciate His gifts, not to have contempt for them. The Sages said that the righteous have compassion about their financial matters.[21] It violates God's will not only to waste one's fortune by squandering it,[22] but even to give it all to charity in the thought that one thereby shows love for God "with all one's material substance" (cf. Deut. 6:5).[23] This is not the

---

20. It is somewhat puzzling to see Morteira warn his listeners of snares in the Christian discussion of such themes as poverty and celibacy, which would have fit the context of Portugal better than Amsterdam.

21. Cf. Maimonides *Code, Hilkhot De'ot* 6,3 (part of the commandment of loving one's neighbor). Cf. also Lev. Rabbah 8,4 for God's concern for the finances of Israel.

22. For example, by spending it on ostentatious clothing and lavish banquets; see Morteira's critique of such behavior in "The People's Envy," in Saperstein, *Jewish Preaching*, pp. 272–85.

23. This is an interesting (and not implausible!) interpretation of the phrase *be-khol me'odekha*, which the Sages understood to refer to a person's wealth (b. *Berakhot* 54a). I have not found a Jewish text containing this interpretation; it seems as if it might be taken from a Christian defense of poverty written by someone familiar with rabbinic literature, perhaps even the Christian text to which Morteira was responding. Having rejected this interpreta-

intention of that commandment. It means rather that if an occasion arises which requires a choice between violating one of the divine commandments and losing one's entire fortune, one should love God and sacrifice the fortune, showing that love of God takes precedence over love of money. However, it was never intended that one should give his entire fortune to charity out of love for God.

See what the Sages taught us from the example of the patriarch Jacob. As he said, *Of all that You give me, I will set aside a tithe for You* (*'aser a'asrenu* : Gen. 28:22), they deduced that this referred to two tithes, or one-fifth of the property. Their debate concluded, "One who wants to spend liberally should not expend more than one-fifth."[24] Maimonides discussed the statement in the first chapter of *Pe'ah* that "deeds of loving kindness" are included in the category of acts that have no limitation. His conclusion was that this assertion applies to helping a person with his body, but as to helping a person with money, this does have a limitation, namely one-fifth of one's wealth.[25] A person cannot be expected to give more than one-fifth of his wealth, except out of some special kind of piety. The Sages said that in Usha it was decided that one-fifth of one's property may be set aside for the commandment of charity.[26] Even this "piety" is understood to entail just a little more than one-fifth. If one exceeds this, it is not piety but folly.

Hear what Maimonides wrote at the end of the "Laws of Valuations and Consecrations" (8,13): "A person should never consecrate or devote all of his possessions. One who does the reverse acts contrary to the intention of Scripture, for it says *of all that he has* (Lev. 27:28) and not '**all** that he has,' as the Sages made clear.[27] Such an act is not piety but folly, since he forfeits all his valuables and makes himself dependent upon other people who may show no pity toward him. Of such, and those like him, the Sages have said that the

---

tion, Morteira must continue to provide an alternative interpretation consistent with the phrase "with *all* your wealth," and indeed his explanation follows the understanding of the phrase in normative Jewish law, although there are debates over whether this phrase obligates a Jew to sacrifice all of his wealth (beyond 20%) to perform certain commandments (such as redeeming captives) or to avoid transgressing commandments short of idolatry. Cf. Jacob Weil, *She'elot u-Teshuvot* (Jerusalem, 2001), 1:203; Samuel di Medinah, *She'elot u-Teshuvot* (New York, 1959), Part 5, nu. 54. I am grateful to Rabbi Barry Freundel for these references.

24. B. *Ketubot* 50a and parallels.

25. Maimonides, *Commentary on the Mishnah, Pe'ah* 1,1, following the Sages in Y. *Pe'ah* 2,2. Examples of "helping a person with one's body" he gives are accompanying the dead to their burial and attending a wedding.

26. B. *Ketubot* 50a.

27. B. *'Arakhin* 28a.

'foolish pietist' is one of those who cause the world to perish.[28] Rather, whoever wishes to expend his money in good deeds should disburse no more than one fifth, so that he may be, as the prophets mandated, *one who conducts his affairs properly* (Ps. 112:5), whether in matters of Torah or in the business of the world. Even in respect to the sacrifices that a person is obligated to offer, Scripture has compassion upon his money, for it says that he may bring an offering in accordance with his means. How much more so in respect to those things for which he is not liable except in consequence of his own vow should he vow only what is within his means, for Scripture says, *Each with his own gift, according to the blessing that the Lord your God has bestowed upon you* (Deut. 16:17)." (Here ends the quotation from Maimonides.)

An *a fortiori* argument was already made in the Mishnah of *'Arakhin*: If, even to the Highest, no one is permitted to proscribe all his possessions, how much more should no one be excessively liberal in giving to ordinary people. For this is what is said in the sixth chapter of the Mishnah: "A person may proscribe from his flock or his herd, from his male or female Canaanite servants or from the field he possesses, but if he has proscribed the whole of them they are not considered validly proscribed. This is the view of R. Eleazar ben Azariah. If, even to the Highest, no one is permitted to consecrate all his possessions, how much more should one be sparing with regard to his property [in other matters]."[29]

All this is derived from the verse, *If anyone consecrates to the Lord from the field he possesses* (Lev. 27:16): the verse states *from* the field he possesses, not "**all** the field he possesses." Similarly, Scripture states, *But what a person has proscribed for the Lord from all that he owns* (Lev. 27:28); it does not say "**all** that he owns."[30] Even a person who gives all that he owns to his children during his lifetime is described by the Sages in the fifth chapter of *Baba Metsi'a* as being one of three in the category of those who "cry out and are not answered," because he is unworthy of pity.[31]

Now this fine doctrine has been taught by the Gentiles from the day their Messiah came: that poverty is to be desired, and blessed is the man who leaves his servants and his flocks to others and abandons all his wealth, strip-

---

28. B. *Sotah* 20a, the rabbinic dictum cited by Morteira at the beginning of the sermon. Morteira may be echoing here the use of the phrase "foolish pietists" in Jewish polemical literature to characterize the followers of Jesus who misunderstood the sermons they heard from the master. See, e.g., *Kitvei Pulmus le-Profiet Duran*, p. 49 (I am grateful to William Horbury of the University of Cambridge for this reference).

29. M. *'Arakhin* 8,4.

30. Both verses are used in *'Arakhin* 28a.

31. B. *Baba Metsi'a* 75b.

ping it away from him, so that it will not be an obstacle in his acquisition of eternal life by fostering the growth of pride in his heart, thereby driving him from the world. In this spirit they emphasize all the evils that come because of money, all of which are actually true for the person who does not know how to use it properly. They thereby entice foolish people with deceptive arguments like these to cast off all the things they love, to abandon their wealth to others, and to choose a life of poverty.[32]

They actually teach in their religion that just as it is impossible for the nautical rope to fit through the eye of a needle, so it is impossible for a wealthy man to have a share in the world to come (cf. Mk. 10:25, Mt. 19:24, Lk. 18:25).[33] They do not understand that poverty causes many times more obstacles in serving God than wealth does. I address now the specifics of this matter, postponing until the end of my sermon a general argument that deci-

---

32. The Book of Acts describes communities of early Christians that held all property in common (Acts 2:42–47, 4:32–35). Origen insisted that the Gospel commandment to sell all possessions and give the proceeds to the poor must be taken literally, as indeed it was by some of the Desert Fathers; "Christ denies that a man is his disciple," he said in a sermon, "if he sees him possessing anything." The phrase "naked to follow the naked Christ" was formulated by Jerome. The image of the naked Christ seems to have had extraordinary power over Francis of Assisi, leading him to a radical version of the ideal of poverty, a total withdrawal from the commercial system of the world including physical contact with money, a repudiation of all material goods whether held individually or in common. Whether Francis meant to exclude common property *rights* as a legal concept has remained a matter of debate from the thirteenth century to the present—and indeed, the Church considered the doctrine of *absolute* poverty to be a heresy—but the formulation used here by Morteira well reflects the accepted Franciscan ideal. See Malcolm Lambert, *Franciscan Poverty* (London, 1961), pp. 38–39, 57–65; W. A. Hinnebusch, "Poverty in the Order of Preachers," *Catholic Historical Review* 45 (1959–60): 436–53; Lester Little, *Religious Poverty and the Profit Economy in Medieval Europe* (Ithaca, 1978), pp. 81, 92–96; R. W. Southern, *Western Society and the Church in the Middle Ages* (Baltimore, 1970), pp. 252–53.

33. *Ḥevel shel sefinah,* a striking alternative to the common version ("a camel to fit through the eye of a needle"). The reading "cable" has been suggested by some Christian scholars, based on an ancient Armenian manuscript, assuming that the underlying text should be κάμιλος (cable) rather than κάμηλος (camel). Where the same phrase occurs in the *Quran* (7,38), there is a variant reading *jŭmmal* (rope), instead of *jâmal* (camel). See Paul Haupt, "Camel and Cable," *American Journal of Philology* 45 (1924): 238–41. (I am grateful to James Aitken for this reference.) Morteira's citation of the verse in *Tratado,* p. 663 l. 42: "mas liuiano trabajo es pasar un cable por el ojo de una aguja," reveals that he undoubtedly used Cipriano de Valera's revision of the Casiodoro de Reina's Spanish translation of the Bible, published at Amsterdam in 1602 (cf. Salomon's Introduction to *Tratado,* p. CXIX). I have not been able to find any explanation of continuity between the ancient attestations and the late medieval Spanish text.

sively proves that God despises such an approach, which has no merit for Him at all.[34]

Returning to the matter at hand, I say, let us concede that wealth may divert a person's heart from serenity because it requires his attention, and may stimulate desires for luxuries and foster pride, and cause other such obstacles.[35] But poverty is a grave evil preventing the fulfillment of human potential. Deprived of all good things, a person will be in danger of becoming embittered and despairing. We see this in the prophet Isaiah: *When he is hungry, he shall rage and revolt against his king and his God, turning his face upward* (Isa. 8:21). Even though a person may believe himself to be strong and courageous in his thoughts, saying *Though he slay me, still will I trust in Him* (Job 13:15) and poverty will not divert me from serving God, this is a difficult test, and few are those who are able to withstand it. That is why we always pray, "Do not put me to the test."[36] For the difference between one who says and one who does is as great as the difference between light and darkness. That is why Job said to his friends, *If you were in my place [I would also talk like you]* (Job 16:4).

Divine wisdom, knowing the impulsiveness of human thought, said, *If a man or woman explicitly* (yafli') *utters a nazirite's vow, to set himself apart for the Lord, he shall abstain from wine and any other intoxicant; he shall not drink vinegar of wine or of any other intoxicant* (Lev. 6:2–3). This means, when a man or woman to whom something extraordinarily marvelous (*pele*) occurs is moved by this to recognize the vanities and enticements of the world and vows in good faith, in the generosity felt at that moment, to abstain from the world and no longer be caught up in its affairs, thereby making an extravagant vow, God—who examines the hearts and knows what the future will bring—sees that the light of their enthusiasm will vanish like lightning and will not last, for the body has desires and necessarily wants to fulfill them. The divine law therefore set a limit to what their vow may encompass, saying, *he shall abstain from wine and any other intoxicant* and from nothing more, for God saw that more than this cannot be sustained. Therefore before the vow was made it was limited,[37] so that no transgression would occur.

The reason for this is that when the matter is carefully investigated, we

---

34. Here the preacher indicates to his listeners that, in addition to the solution to the first problem he raised (the apparent repetition of the two verses), there is something else to anticipate at the end of the sermon.

35. This theme is addressed by Morteira in other sermons; see above, pp. 196–97, and "The People's Envy" in Saperstein, *Jewish Preaching.*

36. Cf. b. *Berakhot* 60b.

37. The printed text reads *higdil et nidro,* but I can make no sense of this in context, and assume the correct reading must be *higbil et nidro* (God *limited* the vow before it was made).

discover that wealth has the positive capacity for great good, facilitating the observance of the commandments, acts of charity, the saving of life, the improvement of the welfare of others, the preparation of oneself to serve God and to promote peace between people.[38] In short, wealth creates no necessary obstacle in the path of the good. This is not true for poverty. It contains no positive good, but only the prevention of those evils that may possibly be caused by wealth. No positive good is attained by anyone through poverty; indeed, we acquire no good through poverty that wealth cannot enable us to acquire more easily if we use it properly. On the contrary, poverty necessarily raises great obstacles for the good, as was said.

In this, I am speaking about the poverty of those priests who dwell in the fields without anything or anyone to help them in time of sickness or provide for their other needs.[39] As for those who dwell in the cities, with all their needs fulfilled, I call them the true rich, for they lack nothing but the effort and thought necessary to acquire wealth.[40] In such cases, the obstacles that arise from wealth are more likely to come upon them—pride, pleasures, profligacy—as we can see for ourselves. These are the fraudulent poor, not the true poor; I am not speaking about them.

We will conclude our discussion of this matter with the verses from Proverbs (30:8–9): *Give me neither poverty nor riches, but provide me with my daily bread, lest, being sated, I renounce, saying 'Who is the Lord?' lest, being impoverished, I take to theft and profane the name of my God.* We may derive two lessons from an analysis of these verses. First, that the evil in wealth is questionable, for first one must be sated and then he may renounce and say, "Who is the Lord?" But he may be a *righteous person who eats to his heart's content* (Prov. 13:24) and attains all the benefits of wealth without any harm occurring to him. However, poverty brings certain evil, which is why the verse says, *lest, being impoverished, I take to theft and profane.* The two matters are synonymous. Therefore, the situations are not similar. The conclusion is that one who chooses poverty

---

38. Cf. Shem Tov ibn Shem Tov, in Saperstein, *Jewish Preaching,* p. 185 ("Since many things, including some of the commandments, are fulfilled through use of physical implements, wealth and glory are essential"). And compare John Wesley's Sermon on "The Use of Money:" "In the hands of His children, [money] is food for the hungry, drink for the thirsty, raiment for the naked: it gives to the traveler and the stranger where to lay his head. By it we may supply the place of an husband to the widow, and of a father to the fatherless. We may be a defence for the oppressed, a means of health to the sick, of ease to them that are in pain; it may be as eyes to the blind, as feet to the lame; yea a lifter up from the gates of death." *Forty-Four Sermons,* Sermon 44, p. 578.

39. I.e., those who live as hermits, removed from human society.

40. I.e., those monks or friars who were theoretically committed to an ideal of poverty, but who rely upon others to provide for their needs.

flees from a small evil and a questionable good, and runs toward a great evil without any hope of good.

Second, we learn that a person should not discard his wealth. For if Solomon wanted these two wishes fulfilled, he already had one available, namely not to be rich, for a person can abandon his wealth. Why then should he have asked God not to be wealthy? He should have asked only not to be given poverty, for a person cannot easily acquire wealth. However, he saw that it is forbidden and sinful for a person to discard his wealth and spurn it if God gives it to him. Nevertheless, if God bestows poverty upon a person, it is good for that person to accept it with serenity, affirming the divine decisions at whatever level it is bestowed, for God knows what is best for a person.[41] But to seek out poverty by oneself is far from God's plan. Solomon did not speak thus, nor did it occur to Him.

2. The second area is what they have said about children: that originally *children were a heritage from God* (Ps. 127:3), but after their Messiah came, the ideal became one who would die without having children, as a result of his celibacy and his being sequestered away from women.[42] In this they tried to deceive people by their vow of chastity, suggesting an exalted status in the minds of the masses because of their abstinence from worldly matters. They paid no attention to the consequence of celibacy: that they would have no children.[43] Yet all this *is base silver laid over earthenware* (Prov. 26:23). It is contrary to natural law that impels us to *be fertile and increase* (Gen. 1:28)[44] and [similar] to the curse of destruction brought by God against sinners, *they shall die child-*

41. Here, after emphasizing the negative impact of poverty, the preacher adds a few words relevant to the those members of his congregation who actually suffer from its effects. Cf. John Calvin's use of the same verses from Proverbs: *John Calvin's Sermons on the Ten Commandments*, ed. Benjamin W. Farley (Grand Rapids, 1980), p. 195.

42. This almost seems like a summary of St. Augustine's treatise *De nuptiis et concupiscentia*, which treats the mandate of procreation as having been superseded by the coming of Christ. Before the Incarnation was the "time for embracing," after it the "time to refrain from embracing" (Eccles. 3:5). Spiritual regeneration has become more important than physical procreation. *De nuptiis et concupiscentia*, Pt. 1, chap. 13, *PL* 44:422; cf. Derrick Bailey, *Sexual Relations in Christian Thought* (New York, 1959), p. 43; F. Van der Meer, *Augustine the Bishop* (London, 1961), p. 189.

43. Morteira links together two related issues pertaining to the ideal of celibacy: whether an individual lives a more spiritual life by refraining from sexual relations, and whether there is a divine mandate to procreate and continue to bring new generations into the world.

44. On the conception of Gen. 1:28 as consistent with "natural law" (in Morteira's formulation, *ha-dat ha-tiv'it*) among Christian thinkers, see Jeremy Cohen, *"Be Fertile and Increase, Fill the Earth and Master It"* (Ithaca, 1989), pp. 271–305, and especially the formulation of Melancthon cited by Cohen on p. 308.

less, they shall remain childless (Lev. 20:20–21). More than this, it paves the way to sexual immorality and all kinds of licentious fornication.[45]

We see that divine wisdom, superior to every other form of wisdom, prudence or counsel, permitted the beautiful woman captive (Deut. 21:10–13), reasoning that it is better that she be taken with permission than that she be taken despite a prohibition.[46] Similarly, the Sages interpreted the verse, *You will know that all is well in your tent; when you visit your wife you will never fail* (Job 5:24) to refer to those who marry off their sons and daughters close to the time of their reaching puberty.[47] The Bible says, *[Find joy in the wife of your youth]: a loving doe, a graceful mountain goat. Let her breasts satisfy you at all times; be infatuated with love of her always. Why be infatuated, my son, with a forbidden woman?* (Prov. 5:18–20). This means that a man's love for his wife, to whom he is married in fulfillment of God's commandment, guards him against sin. Without marriage, people would devise all kinds of stratagems to indulge in all the sexual perversions that God hates. Such acts are quite well known among those who speak of abstinence and a vow of chastity,[48] not to mention the loss of family, to which I have already referred. All this is in addition to the general refutation that applies to all four matters.

---

45. A passing allusion to a theme he will return to, also briefly, in the following paragraph.

46. Cf. b. *Qiddushin* 21b, Rashi s.v. *dibrah Torah* and comment on Deut. 21:11. As David Stern has shown, this understanding of the biblical law as a concession to sexual desire and protection of the Israelite from sin (rather than protection of the captive woman) is one of two interpretative approaches: that of R. Akiba. See "The Captive Woman: Hellenization, Greco-Roman Erotic Narrative, and Rabbinic Literature," in *Poetics Today* 19(1) (Spring 1998): 91–128, esp., pp. 100–104 and 119.

47. B. *Sanhedrin* 76b.

48. The accusation of sexual licentiousness among the purportedly celibate clergy had been a staple of Jewish polemic for centuries. This argument turns the Pauline critique of Torah on its head: it is not the Torah, but the Christian ideal, that is impossible for human beings to observe. See Joseph Kimhi, *Sefer ha-Berit* (Jerusalem, 1974), p. 28; Berger, *The Jewish-Christian Debate*, pp. 69–70, 205, 223, and 257–58. The accusation was also frequently made by Christians even in the Middle Ages, and all the more so during the Reformation, when many charged that a clergy formally committed to celibacy was scandalously notorious for its licentiousness. One critic of monastic celibacy described it as a seedbed of sexual perversions, including homosexuality and masturbation; Martin Luther, in his characteristical polemical style, claimed that no more than one in a thousand of the religious led a truly celibate life. See Steven Ozment, *The Age of Reform, 1250–1550* (New Haven, 1980), pp. 382–83. John Calvin, "The Necessity of Reforming the Church," in *Theological Treatises*, pp. 212–13, and *Sermons on the Ten Commandments*, p. 181 ("since marriage has been scorned [by them], worse than bestial abominations have emerged"). Morteira did not have to look far for ammunition against this ideal.

3. The third area is what they have said regarding hatred and vengeance: that God originally commanded *You shall not hate your brother in your heart* (Lev. 19:17), *and You shall not take vengeance or bear a grudge against your countrymen,* and *You shall love your neighbor as yourself* (Lev. 19:18). However, afterward they commanded that no person should be hated.[49] But this is unreasonable and inappropriate. How can one love those who hate God? It is considered a criminal offense for a servant of a king to love those enemies who hate the king; how much more so for a servant of God to love those who hate Him. Now all idolaters are called haters of God, as we see in the verse, *[visiting the guilt of the parents] upon the third and fourth generation of those who hate Me* (Exod. 20:5). How can a person even imagine loving those whom his Creator hates? The Psalmist said, *O Lord, You know I hate those who hate You and loathe Your adversaries; I feel a perfect hatred toward them, I count them my enemies* (Ps. 139:21).[50]

Let us assume for a moment that this quality [of loving enemies] was the ideal, but that God did not command it because He saw that most human beings could not attain it.[51] Clearly, God would not have impeded those who tried to follow this ideal. But we see just the opposite. For God rebuked Jehoshaphat through the prophet Jehu son of Hanani, saying, *Should one give aid to the wicked and befriend those who hate the Lord?* (2 Chron. 19:2). It is therefore obvious that God does not want this. Similarly, God rebuked and chastised one who did not want to marry, as the Sages said regarding Hezekiah.[52] Thus marriage is indeed what is expected, as it appears from the lives of his sons who were born during the fifteen additional years he was granted.[53] Thus it seems clear that these acts are hated by God. The cunning ones have fabri-

---

49. See Mt 5:43–44.

50. Morteira reprises this argument in *Tratado*, chap. 31, pp. 321–23. Christian writers were not unaware of this exegetical challenge. See, for example, Martin Luther: "What is to be said about the fact that the Scriptures often talk about holy men cursing their enemies, even about Christ and His apostles doing so? Would you call that blessing their enemies? Or how can I love the pope when every day I rebuke and curse him—and with good reason too?" *Luther's Works,* 21:119.

51. Following the approach of Maimonides in the *Guide for the Perplexed* 3,32 that God makes concessions to human weakness and does not command what human beings are incapable of observing.

52. See b. *Berakhot* 10a: Isaiah informs Hezekiah that he is about to die (2 Kings 20:1) because, say the Sages, he did not engage in procreation. Cf. Ginzberg, *Legends of the Jews* 4:273.

53. 2 Kings 20:6; 2 Kings 20:18 speaks of the sons that he will father during this extension of his life; cf. Ginzberg, *Legends of the Jews* 4:277 and 6:370 on the two sons, Rabshakah and Menasseh. This passage in the sermon belongs to the previous section about celibacy and childlessness; it was either added as an afterthought, or because of it fits the claim that God

cated these ideas to fight their battles and to achieve their ends deceitfully, as will be explained.[54]

4. The fourth area pertains to martyrdom. They say that one must seek it out and not be afraid of it.[55] This is the opposite of what God taught us when He commanded *You shall love the Lord your God with all your heart and with all your soul* (Deut. 6:5), intending by this "even if one takes your soul."[56] Now this means that when one is enjoined to perform a heretical act, either by transgressing one of God's commandments or by doing something that gives the appearance of renouncing God, under these terrible circumstances one

---

actually condemns these values and does not simply refrain from commanding them because they are unrealistic.

54. Here Morteira, using the word "cunning" to echo the rabbinic dictum cited at the beginning, suggests that the Christian writers and preacher are aware of the falsity of their position but take it in order to deceive their followers. See above, pp. 253–306, and below, sermon on *Pinḥas,* p. 436. This is a reversal of the common medieval Christian claim that Jews really knew the truth about Jesus as the Messiah, but perversely refused to proclaim this in public. (A classic formulation of this idea of "deliberate unbelief" is by Cecil Roth, "The Medieval Conception of the Jews," in *Personalities and Events in Jewish History* [Philadelphia, 1954], pp. 53–68).

55. Examples of voluntary martyrdom are attested at various stages of Christian history. During the period when early Christians were being persecuted by the Romans, Tertullian and Eusebius report instances of individuals who acted in a deliberately provocative manner: tearing down statues of the pagan gods, even shouting before the governor's chamber, "I want to die, I am a Christian." Robin Lane Fox, *Pagans and Christians* (New York, 1987), pp. 442–45; Arthur J. Droge and James D. Tabor, *A Noble Death* (San Francisco, 1992), esp. pp. 138–158; "I want to die" p. 154; W.H.C. Frend, *Martyrdom and Persecution in the Early Church* (Oxford, 1965). In ninth-century Cordoba, some 48 Christians in less than a decade deliberately brought about their own execution by denouncing Islam and insulting Muhammad in public with the intention of martyring themselves. Our primary source of information about these events, the works of Eulogius, provides a rationale and defense of their actions. Edward P. Colbert, *The Martyrs of Cordoba (850–859)* (Washington, 1962); Kenneth Wolf, *Christian Martyrs in Muslim Spain* (Cambridge, 1988). The theme appears again in connection with the beginnings of the Franciscan Order. In 1219, five Franciscan friars traveled to Morocco and preached to the inhabitants in such a manner as to ensure their execution; upon hearing of the deaths of his followers, Francis was reported to have envied their lot and felt humbled that God had not chosen him to share it. See Paul Sabatier, *Life of St. Francis of Assisi,* pp. 225–26, based on a document by Mark of Lisbon ("never was the mania for martyrdom better expressed than in these long pages"); Kajetan Esser, *Origins of the Franciscan Order* (Chicago, 1970), p. 222. For an example from the Reformation period, see below, n. 63.

56. B. *Berakhot* 54a: *with all your soul* is interpreted to mean, "even if He takes your soul (life)."

should allow himself to be killed rather than transgressing.[57] This is the model provided by our father Abraham when Nimrod had him thrown into the fiery furnace, enjoining him to worship his god.[58] And Hananiah, Mishael and Azariah in the fiery furnace, and Daniel in the lion's den.[59] However, for a person to go and place himself in a place of danger and to seek out death on his own initiative, claiming that in this way he fulfills God's will and achieves salvation, this is wrong, for such a person is actually guilty of a capital offense.

Although we are obligated to learn God's commandments and to guide others in the right path even if this entails danger, this applies to two situations. First, when one can save his people from death and destruction by the act that involves danger. For example, when Phinehas saw the plague threatening the people, he took his life in his hand and displayed zealous passion for his God, thereby bringing atonement for his people.[60] Second, when the danger to one's life is not immediate and certain but distant and improbable. This was the case with Abraham at the beginning of his involvement with Nimrod, when he taught his father the way of truth.[61] However, if the danger is clear and present, God does not want us to endanger our lives except in order to save the lives of many, as we said.

We see that when God sent the saintly Samuel saying, *I am sending you to Jesse the Bethlehemite* (1 Sam. 16:1), he responded, *How can I go? If Saul hears he will kill me* (1 Sam. 16:2).[62] God did not rebuke him for this; on the contrary, He taught him a subterfuge, in order to teach us that Samuel's response was

---

57. Cf. b. *Sanhedrin* 74a, b. *Yoma* 82b; Maimonides, *Code, Hilkhot Yesodei ha-Torah* 5,1–3. Maimonides continues to formulate the law, "When one is enjoined to transgress rather than be slain, and suffers death rather than transgress, he is to blame for his death" (ibid., 5,4). Morteira articulates the broader justification for martyrdom applying to royal decrees and public acts.

58. Gen. Rabbah 38,13; Rashi on Gen. 11:10.

59. Daniel 3:13–23, 6:1–25.

60. Num. 25:1–9.

61. Referring to the aggadic story of Abraham breaking the idols in his father's shop and placing the staff in the hands of the largest idol (Gen. Rabbah 38,13).

62. Cf. Morteira's use of these verses in *Tratado*, end of chap. 47, pp. 613–17, in refuting the value of voluntary martyrdom, which he describes as a *dotrina pesima e absurda* (p. 607) and *dotrina diabolica e jentilica* (p. 617). The passage was used for various purposes in Jewish ethical literature; the closest to Morteira's use is the insistence that trust in God should not lead one to place oneself in a position of danger, relying on a miracle to save one's life. Here Morteira draws a different conclusion: that one should not seek out an opportunity to die on God's behalf. See b. *Qiddushin* 39b and parallels; cf. the anonymous fifteenth-century ethical work *Orḥot Tsaddiqim*, Gate 9, "One should not say, since I am bound up with the Creator's decree, I will travel on dangerous paths and drink poison." After the verse from Samuel is cited, the author concludes, "One who places himself in danger and thereby kills

legitimate: *Take a heifer with you and say, "I have come to sacrifice to the Lord"* (1 Sam. 16:2). Thus it is foolish, ignorant behavior on the part of those who seek out death directly by speaking insults to kings and to others, which they know will provoke a death sentence.[63] God has no desire in this.

That is why when God began to speak to His prophet Jeremiah about the rebukes the prophet would be sent to deliver against the people, He said, *They will attack you, but they shall not overcome you* (Jer. 1:19). If it were good for the martyrs to die willingly for God's sake, seeking out death more than for a treasure (cf. Job 3:21), why would God say such things? It would make them sad! Now the Christians may claim to me that such was the situation originally, but after their Messiah came it was changed.[64] But in addition to this making no sense, for human beings are able to do so many more good things in the service of God while they are alive than they can by seeking an opportunity for an unnecessary and untimely death, I shall give a decisive general answer applying to all four matters.[65]

General Discussion

It is an irrefutable truth that whatever God commanded that is not specified as applying to a specific individual, such as the king, or to a family, such as the priests, or to a tribe, such as the Levites, or to a people, such as Israel, but is a categorical commandment not limited to a particular entity, it certainly applies to the entire world. No individual in the world can say that he has a

---

himself receives a greater punishment than one who kills others." This deals with recklessness, not with voluntary martyrdom.

63. Cf. Thomas Müntzer: "If you fear for your life, then heed the example of the holy martyrs. What little regard they had for their lives! And how they mocked the tyrants to their faces." *Revelation and Revolution*, ed. Michael G. Baylor (Bethlehem, Penna., 1993), p. 175. On the active yearning for martyrdom among some early modern Christians, see Gregory, *Salvation at Stake*, pp. 104, 125–26, 276–80; this was, however, accompanied by cautions against suicide and provocative courting of martyrdom (pp. 105, 286).

64. An argument that would make irrelevant Morteira's proofs from Hebrew Scripture. Note that Morteira is walking a fine line here: he repudiates strongly the active pursuit of martyrdom as a spiritual value, yet he needs to defend traditional martyrdom as a religious ideal against the attacks by Uriel da Costa (see chap. 6, above, p. 218). He wants to reassure his audience of ex-New Christian immigrants from Portugal that they did not fail by avoiding open, provocative challenges to the Inquisition that would have led to their martyrdom, while affirming the achievement of those, such as Isaac de Castro Tartas, who defied the Inquisition's appeals to repent and were executed in *autos-da-fé*. (I am grateful to Miri Rubin for this insight.)

65. As promised at the conclusion of each of the first three sections, Morteira now turns to an argument that applies to all such claims of a higher standard of religious living introduced by Christianity.

greater share in that commandment than does his neighbor. That is why the general commandments that were given to the entire people of Israel are categorical. Therefore the Sages said, "There are three crowns: of Torah, of priesthood, and of royalty."[66] The crown of priesthood is for the descendants of Aaron alone, the crown of royalty is for the house of David alone, the crown of Torah is categorical, accessible to all who will take of it.

For this reason, when God commanded *Three times a year all your males shall appear [before God]* (Exod. 34:23), the commandment was categorical. For the divine wisdom foresaw that a person would say to his neighbor, "Stay home, and I will go to appear before God," and the neighbor would say, "Why do you think you are any better than I am? You stay home and I will go." Therefore the passage continues, *No one will covet your land when you go up* (Exod. 34:24), meaning that all should go; the commandment is categorical, no one should be missing.

Now as for these four matters that we have mentioned, they claim to be ideals newly introduced when their Messiah came for the entire world, without any explicit application to a particular man or woman, family or tribe or nation.[67] Certainly then, all must be obligated by them, without exception. Why should one person reach a higher degree of perfection than another, thereby attaining a higher level of eternal bliss?[68] Why should the other not say, "I'm as good as you are; don't try to get ahead of me in your pursuit of perfection; we should both be equal"? But if this is so, then the world will necessarily go to ruin, the faith will be lost, and their religion will be cast to the ground.

If the abandoning of wealth and the election of poverty is the ideal path to be chosen, and no one can attain eternal bliss without poverty, as we said, all

---

66. M. *Avot* 4,13. See Morteira's use of this statement as the basis of his eulogy for David Masiah, below, pp. 531–34.

67. Here Morteira is taking the Christian claim of universalism and turning it against them with respect to these four principles.

68. The actual Christian claim was that such spiritual ideals as poverty, chastity, and (according to Tertullian) martyrdom were in the category of "counsels," or supererogatory acts, freely chosen by individuals aspiring to a high level of spiritual achievement, as contrasted with "precepts," which are obligatory upon all. (Love of the enemy was in a more problematic category, as its context in the Gospel makes it seem like a "precept.") These supererogatory acts of the spiritual elite do not merely raise their own level of eternal bliss; they provide capital in the spiritual treasury of the church from which others, sinners, may draw. For a recent summary, including the Scholastic defense of this principle, see David Heyd, *Supererogation* (Cambridge, 1982), pp. 16–26. Without knowledge of the specific text to which Morteira was referring, it is impossible to know whether he intentionally misrepresents the Catholic position.

should throw their money into the streets. No one will cultivate the ground, no one will weave or sew, there will be no political activity. The entire world will be ruined.

Similarly, if abstinence is the ideal and celibacy what God desires, then all will choose it, for all aspire toward the good. If so, the result is that the world will be lost in a single generation.

Similarly, if it is good to love enemies and never to be avenged of them, if when they slap you on the right cheek you should turn to offer them the left (cf. Mt. 5:39), if when those in authority make you go one mile you should run two miles before them (cf. Mt. 5:41), all in their religion will choose this way, for it is good, and no one can say "It applies only to me and not to you." But then they will very quickly be swallowed up by their enemies.

Similarly, if it is indeed the ideal to seek out death, quite soon all of them will become corpses in acquiring the supreme ideal, which they proclaim can be attained in this way. But all of this is impossible. Therefore, the assumption is impossible.

Rabbinic Dictum

Now the Sages in their exalted wisdom did not neglect to teach us in the rabbinic dictum cited at the beginning that these four principles destroy the world, as we have said. Those who toss away their possessions and opt for poverty, thinking that this is the means through which they will acquire eternal life, are called by the Sages "foolish pietist." Indeed, it is a piety of foolishness. They are like a person who thinks it is easier to save himself from a sea storm when he is in the tumultuous water, rather than when he is supported by the ship or by one of its planks.

Those who are celibate and think that they are more perfect as a result of this vow are called by the Sages "a secluded virgin." Her seclusion will surely make her promiscuous rather than a woman married with honor and dignity.

Those who say they love their enemies are called by the Sages "cunning knave." It is an appropriate epithet that reflects their nature, for their words are smoother than oil, but they are corrupt. They say "We will not shed blood; heaven forbid that we take vengeance or kill a man." But they turn him over to others, hypocritically saying, "Be careful of him, don't let a hair of his head fall to the ground," yet he has already been sentenced to a strange and cruel death by what they say.[69]

---

69. An undoubtedly clear reference to the policy of the Inquisition to turn over its convicted "heretics" to the "secular arm" for appropriate punishment, including burning at the stake.

Those who say "We seek out death," so that all will remember them, like those soldiers who undertake the most dangerous assignments for the sake of their worldly reputations, are characterized by the Sages as "blows of the secluded ones." For these secluded ones would beat themselves and gash themselves with swords, saying that they had contempt for their lives because of God.[70]

Now of all these, it is said that they destroy the world, in the manner that we explained. For if it is a perfection, everyone should seek it and find fulfillment in it. But if they do, the world will come to an end. The only alternative is for them to admit that this law is impossible for those people who accepted it to observe.[71]

Peroration

We must now come to explain the apparent redundancy in the commandment of our lead verse in accordance with what has been said. However, first we will interpret Psalm 128. *Happy are all who fear the Eternal, who follow His ways* (Ps. 128:1), teaching that God's ways are eternal and do not change. Therefore the Psalmist speaks of *the fruit of your labors* (Ps. 128:2), referring to labor and the conserving of the product of our toil, teaching that we should not despise it or pursue poverty. *Your wife shall be like a fruitful vine* (Ps. 128:3), referring to children. *May God bless you from Zion, may you see the prosperity of Jerusalem all the days of your life* (Ps. 128:4) refers to the preservation of life rather than the seeking after death, for God promises *all the days of your*

---

70. Here the reference is apparently not to self-flagellation as a public ritual (which, in addition to its famous manifestation during the Black Death, was widely practiced by Spanish confraternities in the sixteenth and seventeenth centuries: see Michael P. Carroll, *The Penitente Brotherhood* [Baltimore, 2002], pp. 80–84). Rather it is to the practice as a component of the ascetic penitential discipline of monastic life, associated especially with the hermits of Fonte-Avellana, the monks of Monte Cassino, and Peter Damian. See on this Louis Gougaud, *Devotional and Ascetic Practices of the Middle Ages* (London, 1927), pp. 184–98; Jean Leclercq et al., *The Spirituality of the Middle Ages* (London, 1968), pp. 117–18. For examples closer to Morteira's time, see Jean Delumeau, *Fear and Sin* (New York, 1990), pp. 306–7. The general practice was scourging with birch rods and leather whips, not gashing with swords.

71. The critique of supererogatory acts was a central component of the Protestant Reformers' attack on Catholic spirituality, although the strongest basis for their attack—their repudiation of justification by works—was different from Morteira's (see Heyd, *Supererogation*, pp. 26–29). An argument close to Morteira's was also occasionally used by Catholic writers; Bernardino of Siena, for example, condemned sodomy because it fails as a universal principle, resulting in no children (Franco Mormando, *The Preacher's Demons* [Chicago, 1999] p. 129).

life that have been destined for you, as in the verse, *I will let you enjoy the full count of your days* (Exod. 23:26). *And see your children's children, May peace be upon Israel* (Ps. 128:5) refers to hatred of enemies, the enemies of Israel. It says, *peace upon Israel*, not peace upon the wicked, for *There is no peace, said the Eternal, for the wicked* (Isa. 48:22). Thus the verses of this Psalm actually correspond to the four parts of this investigation.

We must now come to explain the apparent redundancy in the command-ment of our lead verse; following what has been said, it turns out to be proper and fine. Pay attention: in the place of the apparent redundancy, the warning is in the singular: *All that I command you* [pl.], *that you shall be careful to observe; you* [sing.] *must not add to it or take away from it* (Deut. 13:1). The meaning, therefore, is: in all the commandments which I have addressed to the entire people, *You shall not add ... or take away from it* (Deut. 4:2) with regard to matters possible for the entire people to observe. But in addition you must not say, "There are some other commandments and character traits that are on a higher level than those that God commanded, and the reason God did not command them is that the entire people cannot continue to perform them without destroying the world, but if a few select individuals observe them, God will deem this good"—such as the examples we discussed.

That is why God said, *you* [sing.] *must not add to it or take away from it* (Deut. 13:1) using the singular form of the imperative to indicate that even regarding a matter pertaining just to a select individual, nothing must be added or di-minished. For God's law is perfect, and what is perfect cannot be diminished or supplemented. See then how beautifully the Bible expressed it: *For I have given you a good doctrine, do not abandon my Torah* (Prov. 4:2), for it is our life, prolonging our days (cf. Deut. 30:20). Therefore the last of the prophets ended his book with the verse, *Remember the law of My servant Moses; behold I send you Elijah the prophet* (Mal. 3:22–23). May it be His will that this will occur soon, in our days, with the coming of our righteous Messiah. Amen.

"When They Agitated Against God"[1]
Budapest Rabbinical Seminary MS 12, vol. 1, folios 93r–94v
Pinḥas, mid-1640s[2]

Like so many of Morteira's sermons, this is one that insists upon the organic intercon-
nection between the biblical past and the post-biblical experience of the Jewish people.
The preacher discusses the events of the Torah narrative in their own setting, but then
he asserts that this narrative tells us something more than itself; it establishes a pattern
from which Jews are expected to learn about the present. In this case, the challenges
faced by Moses in the wilderness represent a prototype for threats to the integrity of
Torah and the well-being of the Jewish people in post-biblical times.

Morteira's presentation here is based on a verse that itself signals the theme of con-
nectedness between biblical narrative and subsequent experience. The theme-verse
(Num. 26:10), part of a three-verse historical interpolation into a genealogical listing,
rehearses the punishment meted out by those who "agitated against God" and Moses,
ending with the phrase, "they became a nes." The preacher begins with semantics,
insisting that the listeners who heard him read the Hebrew of the verse should not be
misled to think that the word in this context has its usual rabbinic meaning of "mira-
cle." The biblical meaning is "an emblem," a model, an object lesson intended to serve
as a warning for future generations. The Text thus justifies the homiletical orientation
of the sermon: typology. Referring back to an earlier sermon on the lesson Balaq, *the*
Exordium applies this approach to a series of events in the wilderness period in which
the Israelites consistently rebelled against God and Moses. By the end of the Exordium,
the preacher's approach should have been clear to every alert listener.

The body of the sermon is divided into two major components, signaled by the opening
assertion that degeneration can result from either external or internal causes. After
illustrating this commonplace with several examples familiar from general experience,
Morteira applies it to God's Torah, which may be threatened from without or from
within. The external threats are the challenges of Christianity, for which the Gentile

---

1. The title is taken from the last phrase in Num. 26:9, the verse preceding the current theme-verse.

2. The dating of this sermon is important because of a plausible allusion at the end to the death of Uriel da Costa, which occurred in 1640. For the basis of my dating, see above, p. 223, n. 100.

prophet Balaam is used as prefiguration. Four categories of such challenges are enu-
merated, each of them connected with a verse from the narrative about Balaam.

As he reminds his listeners, this entire section is a recapitulation of a sermon deliv-
ered earlier. While the congregation may have enjoyed a revisiting of the polemical
response to Christian theological claims, they would have known that the heart of the
sermon would be in the new second part, about the internal challenges. This indeed was
signaled by the preacher's selection of a rabbinic dictum read immediately after the
theme-verse: the famous passage from the Mishnah of Sanhedrin about three categories
of beliefs that exclude Jews from the eternal reward of the world to come. What Morteira
wanted his listeners to take away from this occasion was a message not about Christi-
anity, but about internal Jewish heresy.

Where the first part has four sub-sections, this second component of the body of the
sermon is sub-divided into three sections. The biblical narrative identifies three different
groups who challenged God's Torah: Korah and a group of 250 men, Dathan and
Abiram from the tribe of Reuben, and the entire community. They prefigure three dif-
ferent heretical claims, mentioned in the rabbinic ma'amar: the denial of resurrection
or spiritual rewards for the observance of Torah (the future), the denial of the divine
revelation of a complete Torah including the oral tradition (the past), and the mocking
of the authority of the rabbis devoted to the study of the Torah (the present). And each
group is punished in a different manner, by one of the three elements (other than water,
which God had promised never to re-use for this purpose) responding to the danger that
the world itself may be destroyed by the challenge to Torah: fire, earth, and air.

As this schematic summary suggests, the complex artistry in this section of the sermon
weaves together different elements woven together into a tapestry of meaning that sug-
gests a careful plan behind the Pentateuchal narrative. And this is indeed another level
of the preacher's message, consistent with a theme that pervades much of his preaching
and writing: God's providential protection of His Torah and people against all such
challenges. This is expressed early in the second part of the sermon's body, and reiterated
in the Peroration, where Morteira uses the four-word verse that follows his Text to
modulate from minor to major mode and conclude with a message of encouragement.
The children of Korah did not die *(Num. 26:11); despite the bad example of their*
father, they remained faithful. God "put the sinners to death, but He saved those who
were good, so that the Torah would always remain in its proper status." Listeners
hearing these words may well have remembered the suicide of Uriel da Costa a few
years before. They would have been warned of the dangers in espousing the views at-
tributed to the biblical figures and actually held by da Costa. But they would have been
reassured that God's providence over Israel would not permit the Torah to be captured
from without or subverted from within.

* * *

Whereupon the earth opened its mouth and swallowed them up with Koraḥ—when that cohort died, when the fire consumed the two hundred and fifty men—and they became an emblem (**nes**) (Num. 26:10).

Sanhedrin, Chapter *Ḥeleq* ("a share") (90a): All Israelites have a share in the world to come, as Scripture says, *Your people, all shall be righteous, they shall inherit the land forever; they are the shoot that I planted, My handiwork in which I glory* (Isa. 60:21). But these are the ones who have no portion in the world to come: one who says that the resurrection of the dead is not taught in the Torah, one who says that Torah is not [revealed] from Heaven, and an *Epikoros.*

Exordium

This word *nes*, which in rabbinic usage always refers to the wondrous miracles that transcend the law of nature, in biblical usage means something exalted, like this banner that is high and lofty.[3] Its meaning [in this verse] is similar to "as a sign (of)," which is how Onkelos translated it: "and they were as a sign." However, there is a difference between a sign (*ot*) and an emblem (*nes*). For a "sign" refers to something visible, as in the verses, *and they shall be as signs* (Gen. 1:14), and *they shall be as a sign upon your hand* (Exod. 13:9), *we did not see our signs* (Ps. 74:9), and so with all of them. By contrast, "emblem" refers to something present in the mind, even though it may have no visible referent, as in the verses, *The Eternal is my emblem* (Exod. 17:15), *You have given to those you fear you an emblem* (Ps. 60:6). Accordingly, the meaning in the present context of *they became an emblem* (Num. 26:10) is not what is written in the lesson *Koraḥ,*

The Eternal spoke to Moses, saying, Order Eleazar son of Aaron the priest to remove the fire pans—for they have become sacred—from among the charred

---

3. Pointing to actual banner in the synagogue? Cf. the reference to "the banner (*degel*) of our community" cited above, p. 105. Perhaps this was analogous to the banner in the old synagogue of Prague, on which see Gershom Scholem, *The Messianic Idea in Judaism* (New York, 1971), pp. 275–77; perhaps it is associated with the Torah breastplate decorated with the crown of the Amsterdam coat of arms donated by Jacob Tirado and his wife (Bodian, *Hebrews of the Portuguese Nation*, pp. 45, 178 n. 74). An emblem of the community—the phoenix rising from its ashes—appears on the title page of a 1612 printed prayer book, and this emblem might have been used on a banner (Vlessing, "New Light on the Earliest History," p. 48). I have not, however, found other confirmation for a banner in the Portuguese synagogue during Morteira's time, and both references may be metaphorical.

remains, and scatter the coals abroad. [Remove] the fire pans of those who have
sinned at the cost of their lives, and let them be made into hammered sheets as
plating for the altar—for once they have been used for offering to the Eternal,
they have become sacred—and let them serve as a sign to the people of Israel.
(Num. 17:1–3).

For there the word "sign" refers to the visible fire pans, which themselves are the sign. But here it refers to those that were mentioned—Dathan and Abiram, Korah, the community, two hundred and fifty men—the punishment of whom was engraved in the hearts of the others so that they became an emblem in the hearts of others, that is, an object lesson and reminder forever.

This meaning will be understand when we review what we said on the lesson *Balaq* when I preached on the verse *Balaam got up in the morning and said to Balak's dignitaries, Go back to your own country, for the Eternal will not let me go with you* (Num. 22:13).[4] This is that it is extremely frightening and astounding to see all that the Torah tells us in these narratives about the many sins committed by the generation of the wilderness, one after the other, and the great punishments for these sins. This is especially true because of the large number of wondrous acts and miracles that they themselves saw in Egypt, at the sea, and in the wilderness, and above all else the ineffable revelation at Mount Sinai. Yet despite all this, they sinned: those who complained to Moses, the spies, the cohort of Korah. And immediately after their death, comes the community's reproach [to Moses and Aaron], when they said, *You have killed God's people* (Num. 17: 6), speaking against God and Moses His servant. They did not listen, nor did they learn a lesson from all the great blows with which each and every one of these sinners had been punished.

Our answer to this was that it is sound political governance when kings often take some of those whose crimes have resulted in the death penalty, and use them for dangerous tasks of general and fundamental importance. The king has no regard for their lives, for they have been sentenced to death; therefore it makes no difference whether they live or die.[5] From this practice of human kings, we can draw analogies with divine governance. For having sentenced this evil generation to destruction after what it did with the golden calf, and then as a result of Moses' prayer postponed His anger with them and

---

4. MS 1:109r–110v; *GS* 1645, 62c–64d; 1912, pp. 236–40 (the polemical passages were excised from the Warsaw edition without indication by the editor).

5. In the original sermon on *Balaq* that he is summarizing here, his illustration was more specific: "For example, the king of Portugal, desirous of discovering places that were not yet settled, would send there such men, taking their lives in their hands, to scout out the unknown territory. If they died, they died." GS 1645, p. 63a, 1912, p. 237.

did not destroy them at that moment,[6] He then said, *When I make an accounting, I will bring them to account* (Exod. 32:34). Therefore, though they were sentenced to death, He preserved them in order to demonstrate through them His laws to all future human beings. They were easily drawn to further sins, for it is the nature of transgression to bring other transgressions in its wake,[7] so that God's protection had departed from them (cf. Num. 14:9), and God visited great judgments against them, openly and publicly, so that they might be a sign for the rebellious and an object lesson for future generations that this is what will happen to all who are like them. Every one of these incidents was intended as a lesson for a specific aspect of the worship of God and the observance of His Torah. And the one in our Text is the paradigm for them all, as it says, **and they became an emblem**, namely, in the hearts of those who would come after that, this is what would happen to all who misbehave as they did. However, the precise nature of the issue about which this phrase **and they became an emblem** was said, and how it was different from the phrase in the lesson *Korah* about the fire pans—*and they became a sign for the Israelites* (Num. 17:3), *so that no outsider—someone not of Aaron's offspring—should draw near* (Num. 17:5), for there the word "sign" refers to something visible and here to something intangible—this will be our discourse today, which we shall begin with the help of the Eternal, who *made everything for a purpose, even the wicked for an evil day* (Prov. 16:4).

Body of the Sermon

It is well known that those things subject to degeneration will degenerate as a result of either internal or external causes. A person may die either because his time is up due to the aging of his internal faculties, or because of pestilence or war. A city or a kingdom may be destroyed or may decline because of internal conflict among its own people, some beset against others, or because of its enemies that come against it from the outside and destroy it. And so it is with a private home, which may be destroyed because of one of these two reasons. It has already occurred that some religions have been destroyed or have degenerated, either because of the multiplicity of opinions about their fundamental principles held by the adherents of such religions, leading to disintegration and division into many factions, or because another people rose up against the first religion and forcefully suppressed and destroyed it, compelling the adherents of the first religion to accept a new one.

---

6. Exod. 32:9–14.
7. Deut. Rabbah 6,4 and parallels.

Now the entire realm of heaven and earth depends upon the fulfillment of the divine Torah, as we see in the verse, *As surely as I have established My covenant with day and night, the laws of heaven and earth* (Jer. 33:25).[8] Therefore, God has providentially guarded His Torah against these two destructive forces, from within and without, lest the pillars of heaven and earth be eroded (cf. Job 26:11), and the world return to chaos. Indeed, when Israel was in the wilderness, this too was something that God openly demonstrated in their experience, just as He demonstrated other fundamental principles through His great judgments, as mentioned before. This matter is so well known that just a few days ago I saw in one of the books of the Gentiles that the author wrote without any embarrassment that there is no other nation or state which, when its kingdom was destroyed, was able to preserve its religion and its faith except for the Jewish people–a decisive proof that the Torah of the Jewish people is divine.[9]

1. Now God showed us an object lesson of annulling the **external factors**–how they never passed from the realm of thought to reality, as we see in the verse *He will think of changing times and laws* (Dan. 7:25)[10]—in the affair of Balaam, as we explained at length with an appropriate discussion in the sermon I mentioned.[11] We shall review it now very quickly, mentioning what is necessary for our present discourse. Balaam had recognized his Master and virtually attained metaphysical knowledge of God and prophecy, as we see in the verse, *the speech of one who hears God's words* (Num. 24:4), and a knowledge of the supernal realm—*who beholds visions from the Almighty* (ibid.) and his words were true (**93v**) and firmly established as the holy spirit remained upon him. It is therefore astonishing that he had the effrontery and determination to do something that he knew was against God's will. In the sermon I mentioned, not only did I explain this important matter fully; I also

---

8. For this idea, see below, p. 441, n. 27, and see the beginning of the sermon "Dust of the Earth," above.

9. Cf. Spinoza, *Theological-Political Treatise*, near the end of chapter 3, p. 44): "It now only remains for us to answer the arguments of those who would convince themselves that the election of the Jews was not a temporal matter, concerned only with their commonwealth, but was eternal; for, they say, we see that the Jews still survive in spite of having lost their commonwealth and being scattered all over the world for so many years, separated from all nations; and that this has befallen no other nation." It is not impossible that Morteira and Spinoza were referring to the same book; alternatively, Spinoza might have remembered the argument from one of Morteira's sermons. From Morteira's passage, it is unclear whether the final phrase, drawing a conclusion about the eternity of the law of Moses, is taken from the source or is the preacher's addition to the source.

10. On Dan. 7:25, see above, p. 261, and *Va-Ethanan*, above, p. 413.

11. Above, n. 4. See the quotations from that sermon cited above, pp. 269–74.

showed that in every specific way in which Balaam sought to accomplish his purpose and to pervert God's words, others after him also sought to annul the divine Torah. Balaam was for them a sign and a model. Just as he did not succeed, so they will not succeed; to the contrary, that which God has planned will prevail. Now I have discovered four ways in which they seek to falsify the divine Torah.

a. The first is that they conceal some of the words of prophecy and disclose some of them to the masses, deriving from them a message that annuls the Torah. For example, *Behold the young woman is with child* (Isa. 7:14): they do not link it with what precedes it, *In the days of Ahaz* (Isa. 7:1), or what comes after it, *Before the lad knows [....]* (Isa. 7:16). Similarly with the verse, *From Egypt I called my son* (Hos. 11:1): they do not tell the beginning of the verse, *For Israel was a youth and I loved him* (ibid.). Similarly, *For God has created something new on earth...* (Jer. 31:22), but they do not mention the beginning of the verse, *Return, O virgin Israel...* (Jer. 31:21). And the same with many like this. This is what Balaam, in order to increase his own prestige, did to deceive the nobles and the king of Moab who sent for him, just as the Gentile scholars do before their kings and their nobles.[12] For God had said to him, *Do not go with them, do not curse the people, for it is blessed* (Num. 22:12). Yet he concealed half of this prophetic message and revealed only part of it, saying, *The Eternal has refused to allow me to go with you* (Num. 22:14), as if the matter at issue were his going with them, and not his cursing the people and becoming an impediment to them. However, he did not succeed.

b. The second falsification is that they attribute to God change and regret, claiming that He annulled his Torah, which He commanded for a fixed, short period of time, and that after this time elapsed, He gave a "new Torah" and chose a different people. Such was the intention of Balaam in going to search for omens, believing that God had regretted His love for Israel and given permission to curse them after He had decreed, *do not curse the people, for it is blessed* (Num. 22:12). However, he was compelled to say himself, *God is not a man to be capricious, or mortal to change His mind; would He speak and not act, promise and not fulfill?* (Num. 23:19).

c. The third falsification is that they claim that all the good things promised to Israel do not mean what they appear to mean; rather, they are all spiritual matters pertaining to heaven and applying to the spiritual realm alone. For

---

12. By saying *refused to allow me to go* with you," Balaam implied that he might go if the king sent a higher level of emissaries. Cf. Abravanel, *Perush al ha-Torah* ed loc. (pp. 116b–117a). I am uncertain about the precise resonance of the assertion that Gentile scholars currently maneuver this way with regard to their benefactors at the court.

"whoever wants to lie sends his witnesses far away."[13] Therefore our hope is lost, and we have nothing in which to trust. The paradigm for this was Balaam, who served as an object lesson for them when he said, *Now, as I go to my people, let me advise you of what this people will do to your people in the end of days* (Num. 24:14). These words are difficult to understand: What is the relevance of "advice" in this context of disclosing information? But the meaning is, "I will give you advice about how you can get them to sin, and consequently what this people is destined to do to your people will be in the end of days. I will set far away from them the good things intended for them, and similarly the bad things intended for you." In this way, Balaam is a paradigm for their falsification of postponing to the end of days the prophecies of present things intended for this world.

d. The fourth falsification is what they have changed in their translations. For unbenownst to the masses, the translators have revealed their evil intentions by translating as they wish, so that the masses will think it is the truth.[14] Thus *[for the sin of My people,] a blow to them* (Isa. 53:8) they translated "to him." *The anointed one will be cut off and none will be for him* (Dan. 9:26), they translated, "and his people will not be the one that did not believe in him." *Behold the young woman is with child* (Is. 7:14) they rendered, "Behold the young woman will conceive." And many like this. And so Balaam wanted to change the blessing into a curse.

And as I explained in that sermon,[15] we can see from all the conclusions of his mantic utterances what he intended to say, had not God pulled him with a rein to divert him from that path. The first he concluded, *Let my soul die the death of the righteous* (Num. 23:10), which implies the same meaning as Samson's statement, *Let my soul die with the Philistines* (Jud. 16:30). The second he concluded, *[A people that] does not lie down till it has feasted on prey and drunk the blood of the slain* (Num. 23:24), implying that it will indeed lie down. The third, *They who curse you are cursed* (Num. 24:9), ending with "cursed." The fourth, *They too shall perish forever* (Num. 24:24). For he himself always wanted to move to the curse, but God did not permit him to do evil. This is the paradigm for those who fight against the divine Torah from the outside, teaching that this is what will happen to them, and that they will not prevail.

2. Now just as God revealed an object lesson for this in the affair of Balaam, teaching about those who arise against the divine Torah and prophecies from

---

13. See above, pp. 271–72. The meaning is that it is impossible to confirm or refute their affirmations about rewards promised in Bible being fulfilled for them in heaven.

14. For annotation to a very similar passage in an earlier sermon, see above, pp. 272–73.

15. *GS* 1645, p. 64b; 1912, p. 240.

outside it, not from among the Jewish people, so He taught a different signal and paradigm pertaining to **those who arise against it from among the people of the Torah**, as did Koraḥ and all his cohort. From his affair, and our Text, its context and its component parts, we may clearly see all aspects of these factions, their strategies, and their final end; *they became an emblem*, an object lesson and a paradigm, teaching that this is what happened to them and this is what will happen to all who are like them. Therefore these two affairs occurred—that of Balaam and Koraḥ—one after the other, for they are really the same matter, but one is about the external battle and the other about the internal.

Now first we must note how the divine Torah extended its mention of Dathan and Abiram and the entire affair of Koraḥ and his cohort. It said, *These are the same Dathan and Abiram, chosen in the assembly, who agitated against Moses and Aaron* (Num. 26:9), although we already know all of this.[16] But the meaning in this context is as follows. God had taught the eternality of the name Israel in all its components—clans, tribes, and the people in its entirety—by placing His great name upon all the families of the Israelites, saying, *Enoch the clan of the Enochites; [of] Pallu the clan of the Palluites; of Hezron, the clain of the Hezronites; of Carmi, the clan of the Carmites* (Num. 26:5–6), as I explained in fine sermons on these verses.[17] He then said, *The children of [Eliab] were Nemuel and Dathan and Abiram. These are the same* (hu) *Dathan and Abiram, chosen in the assembly, who agitated against Moses and Aaron as part of Koraḥ's band when they agitated against the Eternal* (Num. 26:9). This "hu" is one of the five such examples of "hu" with a negative association counted by the Sages in Genesis Rabbah, chapter 37; they conform to the five times when God magnified His Torah as five arose against it and nefariously challenged it, but did not prevail. Corresponding to these are five who arose to defend the Torah for the good, as I explained last year in a very beautiful discussion of this verse.[18]

Now after all this, He said, *The earth opened its mouth*, etc. (Num. 26:10). This explains that the eternality of Israel depends on the eternality of the Torah, and the eternality of the Torah on the eternality of Israel, and how their punishment fit their crime and how *they became an emblem*, by which I mean an

---

16. As it was mentioned at the beginning of the *Koraḥ* lesson.

17. Morteira interprets the *heh* added at the beginning of each name and the *yod* added to the end of each name in this passage as components of the divine name, signaling the eternity of the Jewish people in all its components. Cf. Rashi on Num. 26:5. Morteira's sermons on Numbers 26:5 and 26:6 are preserved in the manuscripts (1,117r–118v and 1,45r–46v); both sermons treat the theme of the eternity of the Jewish people.

18. The sermon from the previous year on Num. 26:9 is in MS 1, 115r–116v.

object lesson to all who would arise from God's people to dispute against the Torah of Moses, or a single one of its components: that they would be like Koraḥ and his cohort. For the Torah recounted three punishments for the three separate groups involved in this affair: first Dathan and Abiram, second Koraḥ and the two hundred and fifty men, and third the entire congregation that arose against Moses and Aaron on the following day, saying, *You have killed God's people* (Num. 17:6). About the first it said, *The earth opened its mouth and swallowed them and* (ve-et) *Koraḥ* (Num. 26:10), referring to all that pertained to Koraḥ; actually Koraḥ himself was burned with those who offered incense, for he was with them.[19] About his cohort it says, *with the death of the cohort*, and about those who were burned it says, *when the fire consumed the* (**94r**) *two hundred and fifty men* (ibid.). All of them **became an emblem** and an object lesson for the future. These three groups were intended to show that in accordance with the object lesson, those who have sown confusion in matters of faith or religion from among its own adherents are in one of three categories. They may be from the elders, respected by the masses who believe what they say, or from the scholars and teachers, who "spoil their dish"[20] because of the reliance entrusted to their words, thereby introducing among the people unsound beliefs (this is the case of false prophets); or from the nobles and rulers who have the authority and power to destroy religion and sow confusion in faith.

Jeroboam used all three of these groups to sow confusion in religion and destroy the faith. This is as the Sages said in the chapter beginning "[All Israel has] a share [in the world to come]": *So the king took counsel and made two golden calves* (1 Kings 12:28). What does it mean by *So the king took counsel?* Rav Judah said, citing Rav:

> He made a righteous man sit with a wicked man and said to them, "Will you agree to whatever I say?" They answered, "Yes." He said, "That I will be king?" They said, "Yes." He said, "Even idolatrous worship?" The righteous man said, "Heaven forbid!" The wicked man said, "Could it be that a great man like Jeroboam would worship idolatrously? This must be a test." Even Ahijah the Shilonite signed in error.[21]

---

19. Morteira apparently reads *ve-et Koraḥ* as "and that which was with Koraḥ;" cf. Ibn Ezra's comment on Num. 16:35.

20. A Talmudic phrase used both literally and figuratively with regard to the expression of heretical teaching (e.g. b. *Berakhot* 17b and *Sanhedrin* 103a).

21. B. *Sanhedrin* 101b. The following discussion is based, as the preacher states, on an earlier sermon, the text of which he undoubtedly had in front of him as he prepared this

In my sermon on the verse, *Behold we were binding sheaves* (Gen. 37:7),[22] I explained that Ahijah the Shilonite could not possibly have signed this condition, heaven forbid! Rather, the meaning is that Jeroboam asked them to sign their names on a blank sheet, indicating that he would have the authority to write above their names whatever he wanted. This request to commit themselves to whatever the king desired was indeed strange to the righteous men, especially since Jeroboam pressed to the extreme—even to engage in idolatry. The righteous said "Heaven forbid!" but the wicked said that it was only a test to set up such an extreme condition, for how could it even occur to a man such as Jeroboam to engage in idolatrous worship. Therefore they signed, and even Ahijah erred and signed. Then Jeroboam wrote above the signatures the decree of the calves. This is what Jehu saw, leading him to error, as it says in this passage.[23] Thus Jeroboam used these three categories—the power of the elders, the power of the prophet, and the power of the king.

And so it was with these three factions here. Dathan and Abiram and the hundred and fifty men,[24] all were from the descendants of Reuben,[25] the elders among the people, the oldest of the tribes, for he was the first-born. Korah was the paradigm of the prophet, from the descendants of Levi, the forebear of Moses and Aaron. And his entire cohort were men of competence and power. Thus when these three factions arose to upset the stability of the Torah, *the pillars of heaven trembled in fury* (2 Sam. 22:8), for their very foundations were assaulted. They therefore reacted by arising against those who infuriated them, for it is the nature of everything to resist what opposes it. Therefore, since the fundamental elements of the world are four—water, dust, wind, and

---

one. Morteira returns to Jeroboam yet again in his later Sabbath of Repentance Sermon on Deut. 32:21, below, pp. 512–13.

22. This sermon, delivered on the Sabbath of Hanukkah 1627, is largely devoted to a discussion of Jeroboam (MS 2:15r–16v).

23. "He [Jehu] saw the signature of Ahijah the Shilonite and went astray," i.e., he assumed that Ahijah had actually signed the condition written above his signature, not realizing that he had signed a blank sheet. For the biblical basis of Jehu's error, see below, p. 512.

24. So written in the manuscript (the numerical equivalent in Hebrew letters, *kuf-nun*); this must have been a slip of the pen for "two hundred and fifty" (*resh-nun*), as in Num. 16:2, 16:35, 26:10. I know of no tradition that there were 150 men with Dathan and Abiram in addition to the 250 specified in the verses cited.

25. If indeed this refers to the 250 men as noted in the preceding note, Morteira diverges from the exegetical tradition that applies "descendants of Reuben" at the end of Num. 16:1 only to Dathan, Abiram, and On (see Rashi ad loc.), and that the 250 men were drawn from all the tribes except Levi (see Hizkuni and Sforno on Num. 16:2).

fire—and since God had sworn never again to bring the water from above,[26] the three other elements arose to implement God's vengeance against those who sought to threaten them by seeking the destruction of the Torah, upon which the continued existence of these elements depends.[27]

Now the element of dust split, *and the earth opened its mouth and swallowed them* (Num. 26:10); the element of air began to reek at the death of the cohort, as the verse states, *And those who died in the plague came to fourteen thousand [and seven hundred]* (Num. 17:14);[28] the element of fire emerged from its own domain, *as the fire consumed the two hundred and fifty men,* **and they became an emblem** (Num. 26:10) and an object lesson. For the world abides on the basis of the Torah,[29] which is its foundation, When they sought to threaten the Torah, all of its elements were stirred from their normal places, for this was an enormous danger to them, in that it was internal, coming from within the very people of God, unlike the external factor that comes from without, which is not so dangerous. It is the factional, internal war that is truly dangerous.

The Sages alluded to the seriousness of the danger of this kind of war— more than the other type—in the lofty enigma they stated in the fourth chapter of tractate *Nedarim*:

> Rava preached, What is the meaning of *Sun and moon stand still in the upper heaven* (zevul) (Hab. 3:11)? What were they doing there? Are they not affixed in the firmament (*raqi‘a*)?[30] This verse teaches that the sun and the moon ascended from the firmament to the upper heaven and exclaimed before God, "Sovereign of the Universe! If You execute judgement for Amram's son,[31] we will give forth our light; if not, we will not shine." At that moment, He shot spears and arrows at them, and said, "Every day people bow down to you, yet you give your light. You have not protested for My honor, yet you have protested for the honor

---

26. Gen. 9:15.

27. Cf. b. *Pesaḥim* 68b: "R. Eleazar said, Were it not for Torah, the heaven and earth would not endure, as it says, *As surely as I have established My covenant with day and night, the laws of heaven and earth* (Jer. 33:25)." Cf. also b. *Shabbat* 88a: "God stipulated with the works of creation: If Israel accepts the Torah, you shall exist, but if not, I will turn you back into emptiness and formlessness."

28. Apparently the preacher's own conclusion (perhaps based on experience) that with so many dead from plague, the air must have taken on a terrible stench.

29. Cf. M. *Avot* 1,2.

30. Gen. 1:17. The Sages held that there were seven heavenly spheres, of which *raqi‘ah* and *zevul* were two (b. *Ḥagigah* 12b).

31. I.e., if You vindicate Moses by punishing Koraḥ and his cohorts.

of flesh and blood!" Now every day spears and arrows are shot at them while they shine, as we see in the verse, *for light Your arrows fly* (ibid.).[32]

By this they meant that if God had not executed justice on behalf of Moses in the Koraḥ affair, and their evil had prevailed, the world would have returned to chaos because *As surely as I have established My covenant [with day and night, the laws of heaven and earth]* (Jer. 33:25). That is why the heavenly lights thundered at this, though they did not at the external threat of idolatry, which was not so dangerous.[33] Now idolatry is worse than this—for these are the arrows and spears shot and hurled against them, saying, "You have not protested on behalf of My honor, but you have protested on behalf of the honor of human beings?!"—Koraḥ and his entire cohort having challenged the tradition that comes down from person to person, which is indeed "the honor of flesh and blood." Nevertheless, though it might seem strange, God acted in accordance with their demand, [implying] that this [challenge to the tradition] is worse than the first. However, God in His loving kindness abolished it,[34] so that [only] the second [challenge] remained, and every day they shoot arrows and hurl spears at them and they shine, as if to say, "How do they shine for those who transgress His will?" For these are the arrows and spears that are shot and hurled.[35] Thus since this [challenge to the tradition] is so dangerous, God abolished it [too] from the world, and the heaven and earth were stirred up from their places to punish them, ***and they became an emblem***, demonstrating that the Torah is the foundation of the world.

This is exactly what happened to Jeroboam in his time, for these three elements were aroused to show him that in his sin he had assaulted the foundation of the world. This fits what the man of God who came from Judea said. First he mentioned the judgment of fire, saying, *O altar, altar! Thus says the Eternal: A son shall be born to the House of David, Josiah by name, and he shall slaugh-*

---

32. B. *Nedarim* 39b. This appears to be the way the Talmud interprets the verse (see Josiah Pinto [RI"F] on *'Ein Ya'aqov* ad loc), although it is not clear to me how Morteira interprets it.

33. Thus the preacher is presenting the rabbinic statement in accordance with his structure of external and (more dangerous) internal threats.

34. Apparently referring to the God's nullification of idolatry as a challenge to Jewish loyalty, a theme taken up in the Sabbath of Repentance sermon on Deut. 32:12 (below, pp. 461–66).

35. A different interpretation from Rashi's, who holds that, rebuked by God, the sun and the moon henceforth refused to shine each day because of the idolatrous worship, until spears and arrows compelled them to shine. Morteira seems to be saying that the sins of those who defy the tradition are the "spears and arrows" being shot (although the verse says, *your arrows*).

ter upon you the priests of the shrines who bring offerings upon you, and human bones shall be burned upon you (1 Kings 13:2). Then he mentioned to him the splitting of the earth, saying, *He gave a portent on that day, saying, Here is the portent that the Eternal has decreed: This altar shall break apart, and the ashes on it shall be spilled* (1 Kings 13:3). It goes on to state, *The altar broke apart and its ashes were spilled* (1 Kings 13:5). The third mentioned was the punishment by means of the air: *Jeroboam stretched out his arm above the altar and cried, "Seize him!" But the arm that he stretched out against him became rigid, and he could not draw it back* (1 Kings 13:4). This is the disease called in common language "sickness of the air."[36] Thus in this affair are mentioned the three punishments mentioned in our Text, derived from the three elements, for there had already been an oath regarding the element of water. ***And they became an emblem*** and an object lesson of general destruction in the absence of the Torah.

We see this not only from the fate of these factions, but also from those who carry forward their dissension in every generation—those who acted in ways similar to them and were punished measure for measure. And this is what will occur to *all* who are like them: ***they will become an emblem*** and a paradigm to the others.

None of those who arose from among the Jewish people to dispute the Jewish religion dared to dispute about the written Law. Had they done this, they would have left the category of the Jewish people and would no longer have been considered as part of our nation; thus no one would have paid them any heed. Rather, when they sought to introduce contention and strife, they did so regarding the words of tradition and the interpretation of the Law that was given orally, for this is the most vulnerable part, having no support in a written record. They therefore thought they could destroy the Torah through the breach in this wall, for certainly without the oral Law, the written Law would be sundered into a thousand torahs according to the large number of opinions, and everyone would make of it whatever he wanted. The breaches they wanted to make in this wall are those enumerated by the Sages in our Mishnah that mentions those who have no portion in the world to come. Such are the characteristics of these three factions [in the Koraḥ affair].

a. The first is the faction that says, "Resurrection of the dead is not (**94v**) in the Torah." This is the group that wants to confound the Torah by minimizing

---

36. I have not been able to find any reference to a disease by this name (*ḥoli ha-avir*). The traditional commentators show little interest in precisely what happened to Jeroboam. In context, it seems to be a sudden rigidity and lack of control over the arm, a kind of palsy. John Arbuthnot's "An Essay Concerning the Effects of Air on Human Bodies," records the belief that "a species of palsy invades such as incautiously expose themselves to the morning air" (see *OED*, s.v. "palsy," cited by Samuel Johnson's dictionary).

its reward. Not daring to touch it directly, they tried to weaken its power by diminishing its rewards and limiting it to perishable, destructible things, that which we can actually see. They sought to make us despair of the great eternal future rewards on the truth of which many martyrs gave up their lives for the sanctification of God's name, exchanging the perishable for the eternal.[37]

Was this not the very faction of Dathan and Abiram, who denied future things, saying, *Is it not enough that you brought us from a land flowing with milk and honey.... You have not even brought us to a land flowing with milk and honey* (Num. 16:13–14). They meant by this, "Why should we lose the benefits we can actually see for benefits promised in the future about which we know nothing?" Now just as the Sages said that whoever denies the resurrection of the dead will have no portion in the resurrection of the dead,[38] so these went down below while still alive, and were buried while living, and did not see the goodness of [the land of] Israel.

b. The second is the one that says, "Torah was not [revealed] from heaven." In my opinion, the underlying meaning is that statement denies the tradition, saying that the entire Torah is what was written and there is no other Torah given orally from heaven. For if this were not the meaning [and the statement referred to the denying the revealed character of the *written* Torah], from the statement, "Those who deny that resurrection of the dead is in the Torah have no share in the world to come" it would be obvious that "Those who say that the written Torah was not [revealed] from heaven" [would be excluded from this reward]. The doctrine of resurrection could certainly not be from the Torah, for there would be no Torah!

The Sages said there in a *beraita* explaining this mishnah, "Even if a person says that the entire Torah was revealed from heaven except for one *a fortiori* argument or one argument from analogy, he is included in the verse, *because he despised the word of the Eternal*" (Num. 15:31).[39] The nature of this second group can be seen in the entire community which rose up the following day against Moses and Aaron and said, *You two have killed God's people* (Num. 17:6): on your own initiative you placed before them the obstacle of the incense test. This was not revealed from Heaven (cf. Num. 16:17, 35).

Now their punishment was through a plague, and they saw by their own experience that without tradition the Torah cannot be sustained. For if their working assumption is that the Torah was without tradition, it would multiply into a thousand torahs, as we have said, or they would give it fabricated in-

---

37. On the importance of martyrdom in this community where many listeners had lost relatives and friends to the Inquisition, see discussion above, pp. 218, 324–25.

38. B. *Sanhedrin* 90a.

39. B. *Sanhedrin* 99a. Cf. above, p. 206.

terpretations that they had agreed upon. In this way, they learned by experience that tradition preserves the Torah. Thus they were tested through the plague that came upon them, for the incense, about which they said, *You have killed God's people* (Num. 17:6), is what saved them, as the Torah says, *Take the fire pan ... the plague stopped* (Num. 17:11, 13).

c. The third faction is the *Epikoros*, whose position is as the Sages explained there in the gemara: "*Epikoros:* Both Rav and R. Hanina said that this is the one who expresses contempt for the rabbinic scholar; R. Johanan and R. Joshua ben Levi said that this is the one who expresses contempt for his colleague in the presence of a rabbinic scholar."[40] But both are tantamount to the same thing: to teach the honor appropriate for those who study Torah, since they alone are God's domicile within the people, they are the closest to God. This sect, which would not dare to attack the Torah, shows contempt for those who study it and slander them, so that as a consequence their words will be scorned and the Torah will be scorned, for if they truly loved the Torah, they would be protective of those who study it.

This was precisely the strategy of Korah: in order to wage war against the Torah they fought against Moses and Aaron, saying, *All in the entire community are holy, and the Eternal is within them; why do you exalt yourself to rule over us?* (Num. 16:3, 13). This shows their need to degrade the tradition of these men. [We see this] also from the words of Moses, when he said, *I have not taken the ass of any one of them, nor have I wronged any one of them* (Num. 16:15). Thus we see what they said, see that they slandered Moses and Aaron, because they were materialistic,[41] with a burning passion for money. Indeed they were punished with fire (Num. 16:35), in accordance with their pride, for the highest kind of insolence of all was within them, burning feverishly with the lust for power, and so with fire they were burnt.

Peroration

These factions mentioned in our Mishnah are precisely the ones mentioned in our Text, who sought to destroy the Torah with regard to three periods of time: past, present, and future. Past, with regard to tradition; future, with regard to the spiritual reward; present in de-legitimizing the rabbinic sages. All of them were punished measure for measure; they have no share in the

---

40. B. *Sanhedrin* 99b.

41. Or "covetous." The Hebrew word looks very much like חמרנים, from *ḥomer*, "matter," but Morteira often does not clearly distinguish between *resh* and *dalet*, and it is possible that he wrote חמדנים, alluding to the commandment *lo taḥmod*, "You shall not covet."

world to come, but **they became an emblem** and an object lesson and a paradigm for all like them.

However, *the children of Korah did not die* (Num. 26:11), in order to teach that God did not allow this leprosy to spread even through one single house, for He purified it immediately. He put the sinners to death,[42] but He saved those who were good, so that the Torah would always remain in its proper status,[43] until all the peoples will acknowledge it, with the coming of our righteous Messiah, speedily and in our days. Amen.

---

42. As noted above in our discussion of heresy, references to the three challenges to Torah may well have been intended to evoke among the listeners memories of the controversial doctrines held by Uriel da Costa, and the peroration about the providential death of the sinners may have been intended as an allusion to da Costa suicide, which occurred just a few years before the sermon was delivered (see above, n. 2).

43. This is one of the subjects that Morteira would take up the following year on this lesson, when his theme-verse was Num. 26:11: since the general pattern is for youths to stray from the good paths of their elders, how is it that the sons of Korah resisted this temptation and remained faithful to the leadership of Moses? See *GS Pinhas* 1645, pp. 64d–65a; 1912, p. 242.

"Guarded Him
as the Pupil of His Eye"[1]

Giv'at Sha'ul (Amsterdam 1645), pp. 85c–90d
Nitzavim, Sabbath of Repentance, ca. 1631

*This is the first of two sermons for the Sabbath of Repentance, a special sub-genre in Morteira's homiletical oeuvre. The rabbinic dictum is certainly appropriate for this Sabbath that comes between Rosh Hashanah and Yom Kippur, a period in which the theme of individual judgment is paramount. But the theme-verse—*The Eternal did guide him alone, no alien god was with him *(Deut. 32:12)—refers to the Israelites as a people at an early stage in its history. Listeners would have been aware that Morteira's reading of the Ha'azinu poem presented it as a paradigm for all of Jewish history, but the relationship between the poem and the individual judgment mentioned in the dictum would have to be explicated.*

After introducing the central motif of love enduring and transcending a period of painful estrangement, Morteira recounts an extensive parable of estrangement between a king and his disobedient son. This seems at first to be standard midrashic fare, but the unique conditions of imprisonment arranged by the king turn out to be specially contrived to fit both the theme and the six-part structure of the ensuing sermon. At the end of the exordium, the preacher informs his listeners that "The lesson of this parable and its meaning will be our discourse today; we shall derive all of it from our Scriptural Text.... It is a subject appropriate for this Sabbath of Repentance." The alert listener would quickly grasp its relevance to the experience of Israel in exile, but how it will be derived from the theme-verse, how it can be related to the aggadic dictum, and how it is relevant to the special Sabbath during the Days of Awe, remain for the preacher to disclose.

The body of the sermon is divided into six sections, each linked with one of the narrative details in the introductory parable, with the six questions in the rabbinic dictum, and with an interpretation of one half of the theme-verse. Some of the components have sub-divisions; most of them contain a detailed discussion of a rabbinic aggadah. It is a broad canvas, but not out of control. Morteira employs several strategies

---

1. Deut. 32:10, shortly before the theme-verse for the sermon. Morteira would probably have preached on this verse a few years earlier.

to bind the parts together and to help the listener retain a conception of the sermon as a whole. The central thesis concerning God's providential care for Israel throughout the period of exile—a theme we have encountered frequently above—is stated clearly at the outset and never allowed to disappear for long. The parts of the sermon are linked together by the scriptural verse and the rabbinic dictum; each of the two parts of the theme-verse is given three different interpretations, yielding an application to each of the six sections. The dictum provides the bridge between the theoretical proposition of God's providential care for His people and the exhortation to examine specific aspects of behavior on this Sabbath of Repentance. Although this religious and ethical exhortation represents a tiny percentage of the sermon, it comes at a climactic point at the end of each section, accompanied by a stylistic leitmotif, and calculated for maximum effect. And the six components are concisely recapitulated at the end. All of these are techniques for orienting the listeners throughout the entire delivery.

One of the most striking characteristics of this (and the following) sermon to the modern reader is its length. The Hebrew text in the 1645 edition of Giv'at Sha'ul *is approximately 10,000 words long; the English rendition below runs more than 16,500 words (a number probably closer to the Portuguese version). At a normal speaking pace of 100 words per minute, this full text would take over two hours to deliver. (By contrast, the normal Shabbat sermons translated above average some 3000 words in Hebrew and 5500 words in English, lasting perhaps 45 minutes: long by contemporary standards, but consistent with attested sermon length of this era and well into the nineteenth century.)[2] Yet even the greater length for the Sabbath of Repentance sermon was not extraordinary. And Morteira himself explains why there is a significantly longer sermon on the Sabbath following Rosh Hashanah: "The New Year's Day, which has passed, and the Day of Atonement, may it come upon us in peace, are days devoted to prayer, and there is no time allotted in them to speak words of Torah; that is why this day is the best opportunity for such pulpit discourse." Morteira's disciples, who edited the 1645 collection, indicate in their introduction that a lengthy sermon was expected by the listeners on this Sabbath: The ordinary Sabbath sermons in the collection are "short, in order to make them appealing to contemporary listeners, who cannot sustain too much content...." But this is not true on the Sabbath of Repentance: "Wherever Jews dwell, it is considered appropriate to preach at length on this Sabbath, when*

---

2. See the discussion of length in Saperstein, *Jewish Preaching*, pp. 38–39. In contemporary Catholic Flanders, the time allotted for mass and sermon was an hour and a quarter: see Harline and Put, *A Bishop's Tale*, p. 155. The extraordinary record of John Calvin's daily preaching reveals an average length of 4000 words for his sermons on Jeremiah (1549), 5500 words for his sermons on Micah (1550–1551), and 7000 words for his sermons on Isaiah (1556–1557). See the Introduction to Calvin, *Sermons on the Acts of the Apostles*, ed. by Willem Balke and Wilhelmus H. Th. Moehn (Neukirchen-Bluyn, 1994), p. xxxiii.

the people tremble and go to their synagogues with trepidation, with broken and contrite heart to drink in God's word vigorously: then the words of his preaching descend upon them, his light scatters the clouds, the multitude of his words wears away sins as he chastises transgression. 'How fine is the word at the proper time' (Prov. 15:23).[3] This is not to say that no one in the congregation found the length excessive. But it was apparently not surprising, and the many aids provided by the preacher to help the listeners stay oriented and focused may have led them to conclude that this was the work of a master homiletical craftsman.

* * *

The Eternal did guide him alone, no alien god was with him (Deut. 32:12).

Shabbat, chapter 2 (31a): Rava said, Those who are brought in to judgment are asked, "Have you been faithful in your transactions? Have you fixed times for Torah? Have you engaged in procreation? Have you looked hopefully toward deliverance? Have you engaged in the dialectics of wisdom? Have you distinguished one thing from another?"

Exordium

The test of perfect love wherein its strength becomes manifest is its endurance at a time when the lover must cause harm to his beloved, yet despite this the roots of love are not torn out from the heart, for they are so deeply planted in a safe place that nothing can move them. Even when the beloved bitterly complains against the lover for the damage caused, the love still remains firm. By contrast, the love that is destroyed because of an offense against the beloved is not true love; its roots are few, and it is something different, though called by the same name by extension. The sage Solomon said in his Proverbs about this, *A friend loves at all times* (Prov. 17:17). This means that the true friend will love and endure in his love even at a time when his beloved does ill to him, and at such a time of sorrow, then he will be called not just "friend" but also "brother." That is the meaning of *a brother is born to share adversity* (ibid.).

A paradigm for this matter of perfect love being recognized at a time of anger and the experiencing of hurt is the father, the very model of perfect love in its ultimate expression. Sometimes a child infuriates the father, and he

---

3. *GS* 1625, pp. 81d, 2a; 1912, pp. 290, 38–39.

must chastise the child; his love is then expressed and revealed both in the chastisement that is motivated by love, not by hatred or revenge, and in his efforts to ensure that this chastisement will be just right to teach the proper lesson, without any cruel harm resulting. Thus we may conclude that a father's love may be recognized and revealed in its strength and intensity when he chastises (**85d**) his child through the manner in which the chastisement is accomplished.

Since this is so, in speaking of the relationship between God and the Jewish people, Scripture said, *As a father has compassion for his children, so does the Eternal have compassion for those who fear Him* (Ps. 103:13). Every person of reason and understanding will see from this teaching that God's love for the Jewish people is abundantly revealed while they are in exile, during a period of anger and chastisement, even more than it would be recognizable when He is treating them with beneficence and kindness. For kindness at a time of favor is natural, while kindness in its various expressions at a time of anger is a sign of abundant, overflowing love, the roots of which have not been severed by the sins. That is why at the end of the curses in the book of Deuteronomy,[4] God softened His message, saying *Yet, even then, when they are in the land of their enemies, I will not reject them or spurn them* (Lev. 26:44). This concluding statement is more than enough to represent all the statements of comfort and promise, revealing and informing of God's love for us, for even when we have rebelled, He has not spurned us.

Similarly, we have seen in several places of the prophetic literature God's affection and the sweetness of His words with us at a time of chastisement. An example of this are the words of Jeremiah in chapter 12: *I have abandoned My house, I have deserted My estate, I have given over My dearly beloved into the hands of her enemies* (Jer. 12:7). Now after the abandonment (**86a**) and the desertion and the giving over into the hands of the enemies, He called them His house, *bayit,* and His estate, *naḥalah,* and His dearly beloved, *yedid nefesh.* The Hebrew acronym for these three words is *banai,* "my children."[5] Now this message of consolation was known when God spoke directly to human beings, and they would be reassured by the tender sweetness of His words as expressed by the true prophets. However, now that our sins have overwhelmingly prevailed, that vision was sealed and there is no longer any voice to reassure us in the

---

4. *Be-sof ha-qelalot she-be-mishneh torah.* The author's memory or pen slipped, as the verse is from the end of the curses in Leviticus 26.

5. Compare the use of this Jeremiah verse in the *Ha'azinu* sermon on Deut. 32:21, where Morteira interprets "estate" as referring to the children, but "my dearly beloved" as referring to the wife, which together with children and husband compose the "house:" below, pp. 493–94. I have not found a source for this acrostic.

misery of our exile. For we cannot see our own signs, and there has been no prophet to speak to us in God's name. Nevertheless the enlightened may perceive God's sweet kindness from His treatment of us even at a time when He has hidden His face from us, and concealed Himself in the innermost room (cf. 1 Kings 22:25), and He no longer speaks to human beings.

To help understand this, we will propose for your consideration a parable, for this is a way to pave the path to any difficult concept, as a small lamp may help find a lost gem.[6] There was once a brave and powerful king, who ruled as sovereign over all (cf. Ps. 103:19). He was also a skilled artisan. He knew the properties of every precious stone and every kind of vegetation; nothing failed him of all he sought to accomplish in the natural sciences, performing wonders without number (cf. Job 9:10). This king had an only, beloved son, whom he guided in knowledge and the path of wisdom (cf. Isa. 40:14), and to whom he gave many gifts. But as the king grew to know his son deeply and to love him abundantly, the son burst out with rebellious behavior to the point where he made the wrath of his father the king blaze against him. The king then had him imprisoned in the royal penitentiary, where the prisoners of the king where kept, in order to see whether this rebuke of chastisement would lead him to the path of life. But it turned out to be the opposite: instead of becoming sorry for his perverse ways, he learned to be even more evil from the prisoners who were there with him and from the guards placed over them.

The king understood this, and had him removed from the prison, lest he be lost forever. He showed a double measure of kindness toward his son, as at first. Yet the son returned to his fetishes, infuriating his father with his abominable behavior. The king therefore handed him over to other officials to have him tortured. But in the misery of his torture, he denied his father, refusing to recognize him, and entering relationships with the daughters of the officials in charge of the penitentiary where he was imprisoned.

When the king saw this, he removed him once again, and turned him over to other officials who, when seeing how furious the king was at his son, sought permission to put an end to him once and for all, so that even his memory would disappear from the earth. But the king quickly removed him from their control, for he began to feel compassion for him. So he brought him back to the royal palace, and treated him extremely well. But the stubborn son would not abandon his earlier habits, making the king's wrath burn to the point where there was no assuaging it. This time he ordered that the son be imprisoned in a bleak and dismal dungeon for a long period of time. Yet, as he thought of all the unintended hardships that his son had experienced in his

6. Song of Songs Rabbah 1,8; cf. Saperstein, *Jewish Preaching*, p. 102.

earlier periods of imprisonment, he ordered that all of his remedies and secret medications be prepared in order to prevent such suffering, so that they would not cause further pain. In addition, he thought of the new tribulations that might occur in the future because of the length of the sentence which he had decreed; for these he ordered medication in anticipation so that the desired effect would be achieved and his son would not suffer harm. In addition, he had his son drink a special potion devised through the apothecary's expertise, which would give him a desire and nature different from that of all the other prisoners in the dungeon, and from all the officials in charge of him, distinguishing him from them and their way of thinking, so that he would no longer be able to learn from them and their behavior as he had done earlier. After this, he had his son drink another potion, which had the effect of calming and tempering his evil nature, the source of all his perversity, so that it would be easier for him to feel sorry and turn away from his evil ways **(86b)** and not continue them while in prison, unlike his earlier temporary relapses. Then he had him drink yet another potion, which instilled a sense of confidence and hope, so that he would not despair of liberation even though his sentence was quite long, and he would not destroy himself while in prison.

The king commanded his servants, the guards, to remind him every single day who his father was, and where he was born, and the reason for his imprisonment, so that he would not deny this because of his suffering, as he had done in the past. He implanted great hatred in the hearts of the guards, so that they would not want him to marry their daughters because of his noble lineage, as they had once done. He gave the responsibility for guarding him to a number of officials, different from each other, so that they would never get together and conspire to kill him, as had previously occurred. After all this preparation, the king had his son placed in the dungeon and went on his way, but he never stopped thinking about his beloved son, about when he would see him, and when he would return to him, and the king assisted him secretly, without revealing that he was the benefactor. Whoever is wise and remembers this will not err about the king's affection for his son and his wisdom in not openly demonstrating that his love for his son at a time of royal anger was even greater and more manifest than was publicly known during the period when he was openly favoring his son, because in the time of his son's imprisonment, he took care to remove the tribulations that might have come upon him in the future.

The lesson of this parable and its meaning will be our discourse today. We shall derive all of it from our Text, small in quantity but great in quality, *The Eternal did guide him alone, and no alien god is with him* (Deut. 32:12), for this is a subject appropriate for the Sabbath of Repentance, which we observe today.

This is the way to return to God: when we see how great is his love for us, and how consequently how great is our obligation to love Him. With this we shall begin, with the help of God, who said, *I will certainly remember him still; that is why My heart yearns for him; I will receive him back with compassion, declares the Eternal* (Jer. 31:20).

Body of the Sermon

Even though the meaning of the parable is obvious, we still need to explicate its details in order to come to an understanding of our Text, which is our goal today. I therefore say that the king mentioned is God, blessed and exalted, the King of kings of kings. His son is the people of Israel, God's firstborn son, whom He has always treated beneficently from the day He chose Abraham His servant. Yet Israel refused to observe God's commandments and sinned against Him. Therefore God first placed them in prison in the land of Egypt, handing them over to Pharaoh, so that from the suffering of affliction they might be purified there like gold in a smelting furnace, and achieve the appropriate perfection.[7] Yet Israel did not do so; rather, they added transgression to their sin, learning new perversities from the Egyptians, until, as Scripture says, [God took] *one people from the midst of another* (Deut. 4:34). The prophet Ezekiel recounted this explicitly: they contaminated themselves with the fetishes of Egypt, and learned from their ways, until God resolved to pour out His fury upon them in the land of Egypt (cf. Ezek. 20:8), yet God opened His eyes, and in order that they not be permanently destroyed, He brought them out of Egypt (cf. Ezek. 20:10), and treated them beneficently as is well known.

Yet they returned to their pattern, and infuriated God with their idols, until God handed them over to Babylonia, and to its king Nebuchadnezzar. There, when the officials of the prison saw their distinction and their noble lineage, they honored (**86c**) them greatly and sought to intermarry with them. The result of this was great perversion, for many families were assimilated in a short period of time for this reason, and when they returned to the land of Israel a sustained effort was necessary to separate them from the peoples among whom they had become mixed, as we see from the book of Ezra. Many families were disqualified from the priesthood because of this *so that a priest with the Urim and Tummim might appear* (Ezra 2:63). Finally God in His

---

7. Cf. the beginning of his sermon "The People's Envy," Saperstein, *Jewish Preaching*, p. 273.

providential care brought them out of Babylonia, so that the holy seed would not be totally mixed in with the nations of the world.

Also in this imprisonment, the beloved son was in great danger when his guarding was handed over to the kings of Medea and Persia, for they sought to destroy him. This was in opposition to God's will, for He imprisoned Israel under their power in order to afflict the people, not to kill them. For all these reasons, God redeemed them and brought them back to their land and treated them very beneficently.

Yet they returned to their perversity, and God gave them into the power of Greece. Oppressed by persecution, Jews endeavored to cleave to their oppressors and intermarry with the Gentile nations, as occurred in the time of the Hasmoneans, when many of our people apostatized voluntarily and rejected God's Torah. For this reason, in order to ensure that the remnant of His people would not be lost, God hastened their deliverance, and beneficently restored them to safety in their land. Yet with all of this, they transgressed against Him, adding new sins to old, the moist upon the dry (cf. Deut. 29:18), until God decreed upon them an extremely long exile and imprisonment, so that they might propitiate their transgressions and improve themselves in such a manner that they would never again return to a state of distress.[8]

However, God first endeavored to save them from the tribulations and misfortunes that befell them in their earlier imprisonments. He tried to ensure that they would not learn from the ways of the peoples into whose power they were handed, so that they would not continue in their original perversion, but would improve their ways over those of their ancestors. Furthermore, that they would not covet the nations of the world so as to intermarry with them, as they had previously done. And that none of the prison officials would rise up to destroy them entirely and to eradicate their memory from the earth. And that they would not seek to assimilate among the nations of the world and reject God's Torah, heaven forbid! Furthermore, because of the length of this imprisonment, there was another evil liable to befall them, and against this too God protected them, namely, ensuring that they would not despair of redemption because of the length of time in exile, saying bitterly that there is no hope for them. God implanted these marvelous qualities in the hearts

---

8. Cf. Morteira's more condensed answer to the eleventh question of the "Priest of Rouen": the redemption from Babylonia was a test to see "whether, by a restoration of the kingdom, they would repent and refrain from the heinous sins of murder, adultery, and idolatry, which they had daily committed; but instead of discharging the old debt, they contracted a new one." *www.jewish-history.com/Occident/volume3/nov1845/questions.html*

of the Jews during this long exile: in the parable, this is represented by the extraordinary potions that the king had his son drink.

All this God accomplishes wondrously for the sake of the perpetual survival of His people. Yet no one pays the least attention to this, just as no one pays attention to the course of the sun and the other heavenly bodies, or the rest of the wonders of nature intended for the perpetuation of the world. However, because the good-hearted person is astonished as he investigates this, and one who is attuned to the mysterious blesses the faithful God, who loves His people Israel deeply, and because these matters are among the marvels of God's providence, reference is not absent from this exalted poem which contains within it all of the history of the nation, with nothing missing.

1. It says first, **The Eternal did guide him alone** (Deut. 32:12). This teaches a marvelous matter. There are two ways in which a person may be in danger of learning from the ways of the wicked. The first is that his temptation may seduce him to follow these ways. The second, more dangerous than the first, is that even if he is able to overcome his temptation, he may not know how to be on guard against people who are wrapped up in the prayer shawl of concealment,[9] and he may learn from their ways, as I have already explained in several sermons, such as one for the lesson *Terumah* on the verse *Overlay it with pure gold* (Exod. 25:11), and for the lesson *Pinḥas* on the verse, *For they assailed you [by the trickery they practice against you]* (Num. 25:18).[10] This is one of the reasons explaining the rabbinic statement, "Converts are as difficult for Israel as a boil on the skin,"[11] for many of them cover themselves in the garment of conversion, but their hearts remain the same as they were, and when they participate in Jewish life, they end up teaching the Jews their own ways.[12] In any event, this path to corruption is more dangerous than the first.

We may interpret in this manner what Solomon said in Proverbs, *Foresight*

---

9. *Ba-talit ha-tsini'ut*; a bit later, Morteira uses the phrase *ba-talit ha-tsevi'ut* ("the prayer shawl of hypocrisy"), which fits the context better; the present reading therefore may be a misprint.

10. The sermon on Exodus 25:11 (*Terumah*) beginnning MS 2:236r, is entitled "*Ḥanfei Lev*" ("The Impious [or Duplicitous] of Heart," Job 36:13); the sermon on Num. 25:18 is not preserved in the manuscripts.

11. B. *Yebamot* 47b.

12. Morteira's rather negative attitude toward and suspicion of fully Gentile proselytes mirrors the Iberian Christian attitude toward the "New Christians." For the context of this in Amsterdam, see Kaplan, *From Judaism to Christianity*, pp. 324–25; idem, "Political Concepts in the World of the Portuguese Jews of Amsterdam during the Seventeenth Century," in Kaplan, Méchoulan and Popkin, eds., *Menasseh ben Israel and His World* (Leiden, 1989), pp. 54–55 (discussions that do, however, not mention this passage in Morteira's printed sermon). For the Dutch horror at the occasional phenomenon of conversion to Judaism, see

will protect you, (**86d**) *and discernment will guard you. It will save you from the way of evil men, from men who speak duplicity, who leave the paths of rectitude to follow the ways of darkness, who rejoice in doing evil and exult in the duplicity of evil men, men whose paths are crooked and who are devious in their course* (Prov. 2:11–15). He says here that wisdom and the discernment of Torah will protect you from what you do not know by your own devices how to defend yourself against, namely, flattery and hypocrisy and deceitfulness. It is easy to protect yourself against one who is publicly wicked. This is the meaning of *It will save you from the way of evil men, from men who speak duplicity,* "duplicity" meaning saying one thing while thinking another, for his words may seem pleasant and correct, while his heart runs to evil. *Who leave the paths of rectitude.* The verb *ha-'ozvim* here really means not "leave," but "strengthen" or "build" [the paths] as in the verse, *Va-ya'azvu Jerusalem as far as the Broad Wall* in Nehemiah (3:8), where the verb means strengthen and restore, as R. David Kimhi explained.[13] Thus the meaning is that these people strengthen and build paths of rectitude in order to exploit them in actually going a totally different way. And so they *rejoice in doing evil,* exulting in seeing and speaking the opposite of evil, for this is the way they implement their schemes. However, *their paths are crooked, and they are devious* and duplicitous *in their course.* This means that their paths appear as if they are leading to one place, but their actual course leads somewhere very different. From all like these, let wisdom and discernment protect us!

In this manner, an intelligent person should note how the Jewish people were dislodged from the first serious danger, to which they were liable to succumb during the period of antiquity, to the second, greater danger, to which they are liable to succumb in our own days. In the period of antiquity, God gave the Torah to Israel and chose them from the nations as His own treasure and wanted to keep them separate and distinct in every possible way. Now since the Gentile nations acted as they did, God's commandments to Israel were antithetical, so that they would not know anything about it. The rabbi and guide [Maimonides] discussed this at length when giving the reasons for the commandments, saying that God's purpose was to remove Israel far from all acts of the original Gentiles. He said this about the commandment

---

Bodian, *Hebrews of the Portuguese Nation,* p. 60, and Schama, *The Embarrassment of Riches* (Berkeley, 1988), pp. 591–92.

13. See Kimhi, *Sefer ha-Shorashim,* p. 519: *ve-yesh mefarshim....* This interpretation of *va-ya'azvu* in Nehemiah 3:8 actually appears in Jonah ibn Janah's *Sefer ha-Shorashim* (Berlin, 1896), p. 363. The same interpretation of the word is in Ibn Ezra and *Metsudat David.* I have not found elsewhere this interpretation applied to Prov. 3:13 referring, as Morteira claims, to the hypocritical and deceitful use of good for an evil purpose.

concerning mixing different fabrics in clothing: that this was the form of worship of pagan priests. Similarly about cutting the hair at the side of the head, and cooking meat with milk.[14] The Torah explicitly says, *You shall not erect for yourselves a pillar* (Deut. 16:22), for they did this for themselves, and similarly, *For those nations that you are about to dispossess do indeed resort to soothsayers and augurers; to you, however, the Eternal has not assigned the like* (Deut. 18:14).

However, at the present time, when they have set aside their idols and wrapped themselves in the prayer shawl of the hypocrisy of the pig who spreads his cloven hoofs and says, "See how I am pure,"[15] and they have abolished all the ancient forms of worship and they want to imitate God's Torah, this well-known danger is very great. For like an ape in every respect, the want to appear to be following God's Torah. This is the fourth beast, with *eyes like human eyes* (Dan. 7:8). Take the nation of Edom: they have abolished the worship of the heavenly host, and [adopted?] the faith of the Torah, and prayer taken from the words of David king of Israel, making a day of rest like the Jews, and holidays like the Jews, until they actually claim the name of Israel—and other similar things as well.[16] And the nation of Ishmael: we have seen that they have also come to resemble the truth more, in confessing the unity of God, and prohibiting pictures and statues, and prohibiting the eating of pig, and adopting circumcision, and other such matters—all these constitute an open danger to the Jewish people of learning from their ways in this exile of theirs. That is why the Sages said, "Under Edom and not under Ishmael,"[17] because of their resemblance to us, whether large or small.

This is what Moses meant when he said, *new ones, who came but recently, with whom your fathers were not acquainted* (Deut. 32:17). Everyone knows that that

---

14. Maimonides, *Guide for the Perplexed* III, 37 end (mixed fabrics), III, 48 (meat and milk); *Code, Hil. 'Aku"m* 12, 1 and 7 (cutting hair at sides of head).

15. Lev. Rabbah 13, 5, Rashi on Gen. 26:34, and elsewhere. This analogy is usually applied in the rabbinic literature to Esau and the Edomites, the model for Christianity in later Jewish literature.

16. Compare the similar passage asserting Christian imitation of Judaism in a later Sabbath of Repentance sermon by Morteira on *Ha'azinu* (on Deut. 32:21), below, p. 501, and the discussion above, pp. 255–56.

17. Cf. b. *Shabbat* 11a (*tahat Yishmael ve-lo tahat goi*); Judah Loew ben Bezalel (MaHaRaL) of Prague, *Netivot Olam, Netiv ha-Torah*, chap. 12 (in *Sifrei MaHaRaL mi-Prag* 7:52a); and the discussion by Bernard Septimus, "Tahat Edom ve-Lo Tahat Yishmael: Gilgulo shel Ma'amar," *Zion* 47 (1982): 103–11; and idem, "Hispano-Jewish Views of Christendom and Islam." Morteira's younger colleague, Menasseh ben Israel cited the statement in the common form (ibid., p. 53). The quotation implies that Jews living in the Ottoman Empire under Islam are in even greater danger of seduction and assimilation than Jews in Christian countries.

what is new comes recently, and what comes recently is new. But he was speaking about closeness in space, as in the verse, *Am I a God near at hand?* (Jer. 23:23), saying that new faiths would come into the world, not as in the time of the giving of the Torah, when (**87a**) its commandments would keep them at a distance from you and you from them. Rather, new faiths would come that would draw very near to you because people would not recognize them in their hypocrisy, and they would not clearly resemble the original pagan faiths. This is the meaning of *new ones, who came from close by,* for they never saw anything like this. Truly, the danger in this is very, very obvious, for apparently the Torah is incapable of correcting it through an effort at separation, as it made an effort to separate us from the laws of the Gentile peoples in antiquity, for "One thing God has spoken, two things we have heard,"[18] and He will not give a new Torah.

However, the severity of the danger reveals the power of God's providence in that He implanted within us in this long exile something unprecedented: an element fostering separation and distinction from those hypocritical Gentiles who draw near to us. This is what is mentioned here in the phrase, ***The Eternal did guide him alone***, namely, God will guide Israel alone, solitary, meaning that Israel is alone and solitary and separated from all the peoples.[19] This is accomplished through the potion of life that He gave us to drink, made from the words of the Sages, at whose mouths we live in isolation from these nations as we were isolated from the ancient nations by dint of the Torah.[20] Solomon taught us this at the end of Ecclesiastes, saying *The words of the wise are like goads* (Eccles. 12:11). The Sages interpreted this in the first chapter of tractate Ḥagigah (3a–b):

> Why are the words of the Torah likened to a goad? To teach you that just as the goad directs the heifer along its furrow to bring forth life to the world, so the words of the Torah direct those who study them from the paths of death to the paths of life. But [you might think that] just as the goad is movable, so the words of the Torah are mutable; therefore the text continues, *and like nails*. But [you might think that] just as the nail diminishes but does not increase, so too the words of the Torah diminish and do not increase; therefore the text continues, *well-planted*:

---

18. *Mekhilta, Shirah*, chap. 8 (Lauterbach ed., 2:62) and elsewhere, based on Ps. 62:12.

19. *Badad*, "alone" modifies not God but Israel.

20. Morteira may here be playing with and inverting Paul's statement in Eph. 2:14: *in his own body of flesh and blood he has broken down the enmity which stood like a dividing wall between [Gentiles and Jews], for he annulled the law....*

just as the plant grows and increases, so the words of the Torah grow
and increase.

Now they said first about the words of the Sages that they are like the goad
that directs the heifer: if it wants to turn to the left or the right from the furrow
being plowed for any reason whatsoever, the goad guides it in a straight path.
So with the words of the Sages, which provide direction for the words of
Scripture. Every one of their directives guides the Jews to walk in a straight
path and not to divert themselves to leave the primary and proper furrow. All
of this is accomplished through their hedges and their ordinances, inspired
by the holy spirit before we entered into this exile. When the divine wisdom
foresaw this great danger liable to confront us in this long exile, they passed
ordinances for us which preserve us among these nations: for example, the
ordinances pertaining to the Gentiles' wine, and the things that they cook, and
meat that is not properly supervised, and economic interactions on their
holidays, and the like. All of these have the function in our days that the
commandments of the Torah had in the time of the ancient peoples.

They then went on to say, "[You might think that] just as the goad is movable, so words of Torah are mutable." In other words, how can we compare
the commandments and ordinances and hedges of the Sages to the words of
Torah? The words of Torah are eternal; they cannot change for they were
given by the living God. However, the words of the Sages, uttered by human
beings, are in effect for a limited time. To this he replied, "and as nails," which
are like a peg driven through a firm base; they endure because of God who
provided their roots and underlying premises in his Torah, as is written, *They
shall keep my guard* (Lev. 22:9), meaning that they will keep a guard over my
guard,[21] and also You shall act *in accordance with the instructions that they will
teach you.... Should a man act presumptuously and disregard the the priest ... or the
magistrate* who will be in those days, [*that man shall die*] (Deut. 17:11–12). Also,
Return to your tents (Deut. 5:27). Therefore they are as nails, not movable,
because their root is God, may His name be blessed and exalted.

They said further, "Just as a nail diminishes but does not increase, so words
of Torah diminish and do not increase." This means, the hedges are often the
cause of failing to observe the essence of the commandment. We have seen
this in the case of the serpent with Eve, for when she added to (**87b**) the divine
commandment and said *And you shall not touch it* (Gen. 3:3) this became the
reason for the serpent to incite her to sin, as the Sages said.[22] To this he re-

---

21. Possibly: they will make nails for my guard, a pun on *masmerot/mishmeret.*
22. Gen. Rabbah 19,3, Avot de-R. Nathan 1,1, and parallels. Cf. the use of this aggadah

sponded, "*well-planted*: just as a plant grows and increases, so the words of Torah."

All of them *given by one shepherd* (ibid.). Indeed, God is the cause of all, and He inspired the Sages to this in order to preserve us in this long exile from learning the ways of the Gentiles, for without their teachings, the name of Israel would be mentioned no more, heaven forbid! The proof is from the seventy years of Babylonian exile, when we were not guided by this goad. Divine wisdom foresaw all of this to preserve us from the pit into which we fell in other exiles, and especially from the double danger that befalls us in this exile, as has been explained. If so, *The Eternal did guide him alone* through marvelous providence, to which every intelligent person must react with astonishment. Let those who fear God and tremble at His word learn from here how carefully we must observe the words of the Sages, how they are exalted and as necessary for the nation as the words of Torah. Woe to us when these words are insulted.[23] Were it not that I must divide my time equally among all the component parts of this discourse, I could develop this point at even greater length and breadth. But we shall bring this first part to an end, saying *The Eternal did guide him alone*.

And now, if God's love for us has become apparent to such an extent even in our exile, at a time when we have transgressed His will, how shall we approach Him, and how shall we repay even a fraction of these beneficent acts? Surely we must make an effort to do our own part regarding what is incumbent upon us. If God has separated us from the nations, we too must make an effort to fulfill His will and remain separate, recognizable, and differentiated from them in all respects, so that we may respond "Yes" when we are asked at judgment, "Have you discerned one thing from another?" This means that all who see us may recognize and know and understand the difference between us and the other peoples, since in this land we have no external sign to differentiate us as is the case in all the other lands of our exile.[24] We must therefore establish this differentiation ourselves. We must not imitate the Gentile hairstyle,[25] we must not eat of their foods or drink of their

---

in the sermon on *Va-ethanan*, above, p. 412, and in his later sermon on *Ha'azinu*, Deut. 32:21 (below, pp. 525–26).

23. Exod. Rabbah 41,7; Avot 6,2, and parallels. Compare the emphasis on the importance of rabbinic teachings in the sermon on *Pinhas*, above, pp. 444–45.

24. Based on the 1616 by-laws passed by the Amsterdam city fathers, the States of Holland and West Friesland decided in 1619 that no town council could force Jews to wear a "distinguishing mark." See Swetschinski, "From the Middle Ages to the Golden Age," p. 71.

25. On this theme, see above, pp. 190, 206–7.

wines at the time of their funerals.[26] When we travel, we must pray and bring *tefillin* with us, so that all who see us will recognize us. We must not turn back on the road on which we have come.

2. The verse ends with the phrase, ***there is no alien god with him*** (Deut. 32:12). By this it taught a second very wondrous matter: God's providential uprooting from the nation's heart a source of sickness that has been from ancient times the cause of all their rebelliousness, and that caused them in their early history, both in good times and in bad, to lash out against God. With this, He soothed and tempered their disagreeable natural disposition and prepared before them the way to return to God in the midst of their suffering. All this He showed in the phrase, ***There is no alien god with him***. However, this matter will be properly understood after we explain an exalted enigmatic dictum of the Sages; it appears in the chapter "Four deaths" of tractate *Sanhedrin* (64a) and in the chapter "[The High Priest] came" of tractate *Yoma* (69b), commenting on the verses in Nehemiah (9:1–4) *On the twenty-fourth day of this month, the Israelites assembled, fasting, in sackcloth, and with earth upon them. Those of the stock of Israel separated themselves from all foreigners, and stood and confessed their sins and the iniquities of their ancestors. Standing in their places, they read from the scroll of the Teaching of the Eternal their God. They stood on the raised platform of the Levites ... and cried in a loud voice to the Eternal their God.*

> The Sages said, What did they say? "Woe, woe! It is that [namely, idolatry] which destroyed the Sanctuary, burnt the Temple, slew the righteous, and exiled Israel from their land; and still it [the temptation to idolatry] sports amongst us. Have you not set it before us so that we might be rewarded [for overcoming it]? We want neither the temptation nor the reward!" That too was after they were seduced by it. They sat and fasted for three days, entreating for mercy. Then their sentence fell from Heaven, the word "Truth" written upon it. (R. Haninah said, This proves that the seal of the Holy One, blessed be He, is Truth.) The shape of a fiery lion's whelp then went out from the Holy of Holies, and the prophet said to Israel, "This is the evil impulse to idolatry." While they held it fast, a hair [of its body] fell out, and the roar of pain was heard for 400 parasangs. They cried, "What shall we do? May Heaven take pity upon him!" The prophet replied, (**87c**) "Cast him into a lead tub, and cover it with lead to absorb his voice," as is written, *This is*

---

26. An interesting reference to social interaction at times of funerals and accommodation in dietary practices, apparently in order not to insult Gentile hosts.

wickedness; thrusting her down into the cauldron, he pressed the leaden weight into its mouth (Zech. 5:8).

Now clearly the simple meaning of these words is not their true meaning.[27] For let us ask first[28] what brought them to this story, and how did they derive it from the biblical phrase *They cried in a loud voice to the Eternal their God?* And what did they mean by the "evil impulse to idolatry"? Is it really something that we can see and seize and shut up in a lead pot and pull out its hair? Furthermore, what is the "evil impulse" doing around the Holy of Holies: Is that where its home is, so that they could say, "The shape of a fiery lion's whelp went out from the Holy of Holies"? And why did they not compare it to a woman, seeing that this is what is written in the vision of Zechariah, which is the source of their prooftext, namely, *It was woman sitting inside the tub* (Zech. 5:7)? To sum up: this enigmatic dictum cries out for interpretation.

Now in order to arrive at the true meaning, we must first raise another problem and a few short introductory premises, from which we will be able to interpret the enigma. The problem is this. The flesh is aroused to sin by two components of the appetitive power: one of anger, the other of desire.[29] From the passion of anger one is aroused to pride, and vengeance, and spite, and other such perverted dispositions. From the passion of desire one is aroused to miserliness and sexual promiscuity and robbery and dissipation and other such behavior to which we are seduced by the pleasure and enjoyment derived from it. Now if this is so, it is very difficult to understand how Israel in its early history was so lustful after idolatry that they pursued it with unabated desire. For you see that after the death of Joshua and the elders who lived long after him—those who themselves saw God's acts—the people immediately abandoned God and worshipped all the gods of the nations around

27. *Peshatan shel devarim eilu eino ela pitronam,* literally, "the simple meaning of these words is the key to their true meaning," which does not seem to me to fit the context. My rendering requires striking the word *ela.* Cf. below at n. 53.

28. Here Morteira is following the tradition of raising a series of difficulties about a classical passage and then proceeding to resolve them in the ensuing discussion. Known especially from the generation of the Expulsion (Abravanel, Arama), this became a common pattern for preachers, and was frequently used in the sermons of Morteira's mentor, Leon Modena. On the form, see Saperstein, "The Method of Doubts,"

29. Cf. Saadia Gaon, *The Book of Beliefs and Opinions* (New Haven, 1948), 10,2, pp. 360–61; Abraham ibn Daud, *The Exalted Faith* (Rutherford, N.J., 1986), 2,6,2, p. 245 ("the evil [goes forth] either from his faculty of anger or from desire"), and Morteira's older contemporary, Robert Burton, *The Anatomy of Melancholy,* 3 vols. (London, 1932), 1:258 ("Perturbations and passions ... are commonly reduced into two inclinations, irascible and concupiscible"); for the background, see Etienne Gilson, *The Christian Philosophy of St. Thomas Aquinas* (New York, 1956), pp. 236–48.

them. All the warnings and the miracles and the prophets were insufficient to lead them back. Now what pleasure or enjoyment did either one of those capacities of arousal give to them in their sin of idolatry? Yet they lusted so much after it that the prophet Jeremiah said, *As those who remember their children [so do they yearn for] their altars [and sacred posts]* (Jer. 17:2), which R. Eleazer interpreted, "Like a man who yearns for his son."[30] And so we find in the chapter "[All Israel has a] share" of tractate *Sanhedrin*, as Manasseh said to that scholar when they asked him, "Since you are so wise, why did you worship idols?" He replied, "Had you been there, you would have pulled up the hems of your cloak and run after me."[31] All this we need to know; that is the problem I have raised.

As for the introductory premises, the first one is that the Second Temple gave to Israel through divine visitation an opportunity to prepare the way: perhaps with the restoration of their Temple and kingship it would be easier for them to return and wipe clean the sins of their ancestors, without the obstacles of subjugation to other nations. With the sacrifices they had, God could gather their dispersed brothers from the four corners of the earth, and restore the Ten Tribes and the rule of the royal house of David and all the good things that had been promised to them. But they persevered in their sinful behavior, and they were punished with this current long exile.

The second introductory premise is this: when Israel was on its land, and the full beauty of God appeared to the prophets of Israel from Zion, from between the two cherubim, in His light, prophecy, and holiness, the husks were nourished and the spirits from the side of impurity derived pleasure from the superabundant sparks of that light, for the profusion of good caused those who consumed it to flourish.[32] That is why in ancient times these spirits would appear to those among the Gentile nations who worshiped them, manifesting themselves with speeches and miraculous acts and foretelling of future events and the like among the shameful things they spoke. However, when God gathered His spirit and prophecy to Himself, these external forces were annhilated, as the Bible says, *He made all the altar-stones like shattered blocks of chalk, with no sacred post left standing,* (**87d**) *nor any incense altar* (Isa. 27:9). These are the actual idols that used to answer and give their responses.[33]

However, with regard to temporal prosperity, when divine beneficence

---

30. *Sanhedrin* 63b.

31. *Sanhedrin* 102b.

32. This is the language and imagery of Lurianic Kabbalah, used occasionally by Morteira in his sermons. Compare the analogy on the following page, and n. 35.

33. Morteira is referring here to a specific form of pagan divination, the consultation with and responses from statues of the gods. See on this James Hastings, ed., *Encyclopaedia of*

bypassed Israel it actually increased for the nations of the world. Let me give a fine analogy for this, through which the matter can be clearly understood. Think of a woman who had a son, whom she nursed and with whom she played and spoke with great joy. If that child should die, or become gravely ill, or be kidnapped, the woman might take her servant's baby in order to ease the pressure of the milk that naturally wells up in her breasts each day that she does not nurse. Thus the milk intended for her own child would be given to the child of her servant. But her playfulness in facial expression and speech, the delightful words with which she frolicked with her child, while the servant woman and her son would hear it and derive pleasure from the sound—these would be totally absent, for the woman would sit in silent anguish over the loss of her son. That is the way it is with the *Shekhinah* regarding the profusion of natural bounty: while the merit of Israel is lacking, the nations received it, but the joy and the light and the sparks of prophecy which Israel acquired as if through a mother's milk while it was on its land: this is now lacking from the nations as well.[34]

The third introductory premise is that the "hair" (*se'arot*) is an epithet for the husks and the superfluous excesses and the spirits of impurity. This is why they are called *se'irim*, "satyrs."[35] They always refer to the measure of judgment and those who serve it. No proof is needed for for what is widely known.

Now with these propositions, the enigmatic dictum of the rabbis can be quite satisfactorily explained. At first, the evil impulse to idolatry ruled so powerfully over human beings that it drew them after it with all its power and strength, as is clear from what we have said. Therefore, when the Jews returned from the Babylonian Exile in the period of the Second Temple, they perceived its power among them in matters relating to idolatry, when they stood up for their lineage and separated themselves from the Gentiles [among whom they had intermarried] and came to confess their sins and the transgressions of their ancestors, for that is why they returned at this time, as was said. But they saw that it was impossible for them to succeed if the evil impulse

---

Religion and Ethics, 13 vols. (New York, 1928), 4:793–95 (Egyptian); Fox, *Pagans and Christians*, pp. 209–10 (Roman).

34. On this striking analogy, answering the triumphalist argument of the Gentile nations through the image of God as a nursing mother, see above, pp. 109–10.

35. This negative association is linked also with the association with Esau and hair and the land of Seir (Gen. 27:11, 36:8). Cf. Joseph Gikatilla, *Sha'are Orah: Gates of Light* (San Francisco, 1994), pp. 98–99; Modena, *Midbar Yehudah*, 1602, p.15b; 2002, p. 43, linking the same root in Ps. 50:3, Isa. 13:21, and Job 9:17. A bit later in this passage, Modena refers to the Kabbalistic doctrine of the husks (*qelippot*), based on the Zoharic literature. It is significant that Morteira refers to this Kabbalistic discourse as so commonly accepted that it needs no proof.

to idolatry were to fight against them, and that they would therefore be judged deserving of annihilation—heaven forbid!—if it would remain among them. Therefore, they complained loudly to God, saying, "Woe! Woe! is this not what has caused us all the misfortunate that has come upon us from the exile and the burning of the Temple and the killing of the righteous? Yet still it sports amongst us, in that the Jews are still following the gods of the nations of the world. Is not the only reason why God gave us this belligerent antagonist so that we might be rewarded by overcoming it? We want neither the antagonist nor the reward!"[36]

Now after their outcry and their fast, God agreed to their request. This is hinted by the slip of paper that fell from the sky, on which the word "Truth" was written. Then they saw it emerge from the Holy of Holies, in the shape of a small fiery dog.[37] This is an apt representation for what we have said, for the impulse toward evil and the components of impurity are like a dog that sits under the table and eats what is left over from his master. It emerges from the Holy of Holies because from there light goes out to the world.[38] This means that it is banished, so that the demons and spirits will no longer receive the sparks of light, and they will not cause the people of Israel to go astray after them. "This is the evil impulse to idolatry." "While they held it fast, a hair [of its body] fell out" means that its hairs dropped out and fell to the ground, namely, the Asherahs and the solar columns and the demons and satyrs, which are called "hairs." "The prophet said to him"—namely, the prophet Zechariah—that he had foreseen all this in his prophetic vision. "Place him in a lead tub, close the lid and plug its mouth with a lead stone, so that its voice would not be heard," that is to say, so that the household gods would no longer speak, for the matter of the evil impulse to idolatry depends upon this.

Now everything that seemed to be unlikely and astonishing turns out to be a beautiful explanation of Zechariah's vision of a woman walking out of the Holy of Holies. The Sages called this a "fiery dog" (**88a**) for the reason we explained. The angel who spoke to him said, *"This is Wickedness,"* and *he cast her down into the tub and pressed the lead stone into its mouth* (Zech. 5:8). In this way, God uprooted from the heart of Israel the source of this fundamental illness, which caused all their suffering from antiquity, namely, the evil im-

---

36. Morteira's first citation of this Talmudic passage was in the original Aramaic; here he paraphrases it in Hebrew, presumably spoken to the congregation in Portuguese.

37. In the original, *ke-gurya de-nura*, which can refer to the cub of either a lion or a dog. Rashi explains: "a small lion," Morteira—for reasons he goes on to explain—prefers the "small dog."

38. Cf. Lev. Rabbah 31,7.

pulse to idolatry. This is what has stood by us in our exile, through marvelous providential care, so that we would not be lost among the nations if their idols should speak and foretell the future as in earlier times. Blessed is He and blessed is His name who removed this stumbling block from His people's path, treating them with beneficence that we cannot even imagine.

This is the meaning of Moses' statement here, **there is no alien god with him**, meaning that Israel no longer has the desire for alien gods as they once did: **The Eternal did guide him alone, there is no alien god with him**. And if God has uprooted the evil temptation to idolatry from us, we too must make an effort to uproot from among us everything that is similar to idolatry, and that appears like it, such as swearing for no purpose, and mentioning God's name, for this is a kind of idolatry, a sign of insufficient faith. Also, the lies. The Sages said that the liar is a kind of idolater, for the Bible says [about Jacob's deception], *I shall appear to him as a mocker* (Gen. 27:12), and [regarding idols the same word is used:] *They are a delusion, a mockery* (Jer. 10:15 or 51:18).[39] Also, spreading slander, for the Sages said that this is like denying God, [as the slanderers think] *"with lips such as ours, who can be our master?"* (Ps. 12:5).[40] If David had not listened to slander, his kingdom would not have been divided, and [the kingdom of] Israel would not have served idols, and they would not have been exiled from their land.[41] Also, spreading evil reports of something we have not seen, for this renders the supernal eye as if it cannot see.[42] We have already seen the seriousness of Israel's sin because it placed the mouth before the eye.[43] Also speaking profanity. In this way, we may respond, "Yes" when we are asked, "Have you conducted your affairs faithfully?"—for everything we have mentioned is derived from inadequate faith, and therefore is akin to idolatry.

3. Divine Wisdom made additional effort to preserve us from yet another stumbling block in this long exile, which was liable—even likely—to make us stumble. This is despair, the loss of hope because of the length of time. God implanted in our hearts hope and trust in His enormous power.[44] He said,

---

39. B. *Sanhedrin* 92a.

40. Deut. Rabbah 12,5 and parallels

41. B. *Shabbat* 56b. This refers to David's acceptance of Ziba's statement about Mephibosheth (2 Sam. 16:3–4), with consequences in 2 Sam. 19:25–30.

42. Num. Rabbah 9,44 and parallels.

43. B. *Sanhedrin* 104b: allowed themselves to say things they had not seen, thereby giving the mouth priority over the eye. Cf. Maharal of Prague, *Netsah Yisrael*, beginning of chap. 9 (New York, 1969, 6:56a).

44. The word "hope" had special resonance for this community. See the formulation of Méchoulan and Nahon: "Menasseh ben Israel knew very well the explosive charge the word *esperanza* had in Spain, as much for Judaizing New Christians as for the Old Christians

Strengthen the hands that are slack, make firm the tottering knees! (Isa. 35:3), and it was so. For they certainly could have agreed to wait a short time for Moses' descent from the mountain. Yet, *When the people saw that Moses was so long in coming down from the mountain* (Exod. 32:1), immediately they arose and rebelled. Similarly, our first king was unable to rule over his nature to wait for Samuel seven full days.[45] Samuel said to him, "Indeed we are in great trouble for *a time and times* (Dan. 7:25) and our captors are with us, saying rhetorically, 'Return, return, for how can you have the strength to continue to hope?' The people would spurn the future coming of our Messiah, *were it not for God who was with us* (Ps. 124:2)."[46] Is this hope not something great, confirmed by experience, revealing the finger of God?

The Sages taught us this through what they said in the Midrash on Psalm 40:

> *I put my hope in the Eternal; He inclined toward me, etc.* (Ps. 40:2). This is what Scripture says in the verse, *In that day they shall say, This is our God, we hoped in Him, and He delivered us; this is the Eternal, in whom we placed our hope, etc.* (Isa. 25:9). Israel has in its power only hope; let the reward for hope then be sufficient for their redemption. And so it says, *The Eternal is good to those who hope in Him* (Lam. 3:25), and it says, *Return to Bizzaron, you prisoners of hope* (Zech. 9:12). You might say, "The harvest has passed, the summer has ended, and we have not been saved." To this the Bible says, *Hope in the Eternal; be strong and of good courage! Hope in the Eternal!* (Ps. 27:14): hope and hope again. And if you should say, "How long must we hope?" to this the Scripture responds with the verse, *Let Israel wait for the Eternal* (Ps. 130:7), from now and forever. And it says, *Be strong and of good courage, all you who wait for the Eternal* (Ps. 31:25).

Now through the interpretation of this momentous dictum we may resolve several issues that can be raised about it, and our own aforementioned

---

who used to deride the Marranos' Messianic hopes. The term *esperanza* had a particular resonance for the entire population. The Spanish theatre used this word to indicate, in a satiric manner, a specifically Jewish mentality" (Introduction to *The Hope of Israel*, p. 67). Like Menasseh some years later, Morteira revalorizes the word in this section of his sermon, taking what was often a term of derision and presenting it as a special gift from God. Cf. also Kaplan, *From Christianity to Judaism*, p. 373.

45. 1 Sam. 10:8 and 13:8. The latter verse says that Saul did wait for seven days and Samuel still did not appear; the commentators say that he acted during the seventh day and therefore did not wait for seven full days. Cf. Lev. Rabbah 26,7; *Tanḥumah Emor* 2.

46. This is the most likely rendering of a rather ambiguous passage. I have not found any source that attributes such a statement to Samuel.

doctrine will emerge from it. The Sages first noted the duplication in the phrase *kavo kiviti* (Ps. 40:2). They explained this through what is written elsewhere, *In that day they shall say, This is our God, we hoped in Him, and He delivered us; this is the Eternal, in whom we placed our hope* (Isa. 25:9); there too the reference to hope is doubled (**88b**). The same meaning is in both of the verses. What then is this meaning? They explained it when they said, "Israel has in its power only hope," meaning, Israel has no other trait or virtue that is so reliable and enduring and deep-seated as hope, for God is the one who causes this. Therefore, "Israel has in its power," in its possession, under its control, "only hope." That is why the verses duplicated themselves in mentioning it: to teach us of its strength.

They also taught us something else of fundamental importance. This is that while this powerful hope comes from God, nevertheless God graciously gives a reward for it, as if it were the result of human initiative. That is what they said: "Let the reward for hope then be sufficient for their redemption." For these two matters, they cited two verses. To show that God is the cause of this hope, it says, *The Eternal is good to those who hope in Him* (Lam. 3:25), meaning that God is the helper and benefactor to those who hope in Him, giving them of His own goodness. And to show that God gives a reward for this as if they themselves were responsible for it, it says, *Return to Bizzaron, you prisoners of hope* (Zech. 9:12), meaning, return to your greatness, even though you are compelled, indeed a "prisoner of hope," which itself comes from the power on High; nevertheless, accept the reward for it as if you yourselves were responsible.

He then went back to show how this hoping is impossible without God's help, saying, "You might say, 'The harvest has passed, the summer has ended,'" namely, you might turn to despair. Therefore the Bible says, *Hope in the Eternal; be strong and of good courage! Hope in the Eternal!* (Ps. 27:14), meaning, God is the one who gives strength to hope with fervor and vigor so that you will not despair, heaven forbid! You may know how much of God's power is in this when you realize that even if this anticipation must be prolonged indefinitely, since it is from God we must indeed hope forever. That is the meaning of, "And if you say, How long must we hope? To this Scripture responds, *Let Israel wait for the Eternal* (Ps. 130:7), from now and forever." Why is this repeated so much? Because it comes from divine strength. Thus the conclusion, *Be strong and of good courage, all you who wait for the Eternal* (Ps. 31:25). Now here indeed is a precious potion, a superb remedy to guard our souls from despair in this long exile.

David taught us this true lesson in Psalm 130 when he said, *My soul is for the Eternal more than watchmen for the morning, watchmen for the morning. O Israel, wait for the Eternal, for with God is steadfast love and with Him great power to redeem. It is He who will redeem Israel from all their iniquities* (Ps. 130:6–8). This means, my soul anticipates and hopes in God with total confidence, greater than the confidence of watchmen that the morning will come, even though they are indeed absolutely certain that morning will come, since day after day they are accustomed to see morning follow the night, while for many years I have not witnessed God's beneficence. Yet despite this, my soul waits for God *more than watchmen for the morning, watchmen for the morning,* the repetition suggesting the continuous pattern, that day after day morning never fails. But who is the cause of this confidence of mine, lasting for so much time, with such strength, without weakening? It most certainly comes from God, for without divine help, naturalistically, such enduring confidence would be impossible. Therefore the Psalmist says, *O Israel, wait for the Eternal, for with Him is steadfast love* (Ps. 130:7), meaning, *if* Israel waits for God, then God will reveal the steadfast love to implant within the heart of the Jew this expectation, for his own benefit and enjoyment, so that he will not despair of the redemption. And with all this, God will reward him as if the confidence derived from his own initiative. That is the meaning of the continuation, *and with him great power to redeem* (ibid.), meaning, with *Israel,* and God will redeem Israel from all its sins with this reward.

The manner in which God through His own power implanted this confidence in the heart of Israel was explained by the prophet Isaiah when he said, *Truly, the Eternal is waiting to show you grace, truly He will arise with compassion for you, for the Eternal God is a God of justice, happy are all those who wait for Him* (Isa. 30:18). The meaning of this will become clear with something we have already explained in a different context. (**88c**) The Sages said, "All is in the hands of Heaven except for the fear of Heaven."[47] In addition to the simple meaning of these words, they also mean that we may learn all of the character traits from God, in the manner of *You shall walk in His ways* (Deut. 28:9): as God is merciful, [so you should be merciful], etc.[48] From God we can learn the perfection of these traits, by imitating Him. This is the meaning of "all is in the hands of Heaven," to learn from Him. However, fear of Heaven, which is an extremely exalted trait in the human being, indeed the source of all the other exalted traits, cannot be learned from God, for God does not fear. Therefore it said, "All is in the hands of Heaven except for the fear of Heaven."

However, we might have concluded that the same is true for trust, which

---

47. B. *Berakhot* 33b and parallels.
48. B. *Sotah* 14a, Maimonides, *Book of Commandments,* Positive 8, *Hilkhot De'ot* 1, 5–6.

is also an extremely exalted trait: that we cannot learn this from God because God does not rely upon or expect anything. Therefore the prophet said that it is not so, but rather that God attributed to Himself the quality of confident waiting so that we may learn it from Him, and so that it may appear upon us. That is why he said, *The Eternal is waiting to show you grace* (Isa. 30:18). And because this may appear so much like a liability—for trust applies only to someone who is lacking something, and it is impossible to attribute it to God (heaven forbid!)—the prophet went on to say, *He will arise in compassion for you* (ibid.), meaning, when the intention is to have compassion for you, and to implant among you the trust that is so necessary in this long exile, this is not because of any lack in God (heaven forbid!) but rather it is an expression of His greatness. Thus, *He will arise in compassion for you.* Yet despite all this, God gives you a reward, for *the Eternal is a God of justice, and happy are all who wait for Him* (ibid.). Now indeed this began to appear from on high in the time of Ezekiel, when God showed him the vision of the bones and said to him, *These bones are the whole house of Israel. They say, "Our bones are dried up, our hope is gone, we are doomed"* (Ezek. 37:11), meaning, they will say this in the future. *Therefore, prophesy* (ibid. 12), and place in them My spirit (cf. ibid. 14) and My hope, and let them never say this again.

All this Moses taught us when he said, in the verse, **The Eternal did guide them alone** (*badad*) (Deut. 32:12). Here the meaning of the word *badad* is "secure," as in the verse, *Israel dwells in safety, secure* (badad) *is Jacob's abode* (Deut. 33:28). Our verse therefore means, "The Eternal guides them full of security and hope through providential care that is marvelous to all who understand, so that they will not be lost in the exile because of its great length." And if God has made hope and security take root in our hearts, we are indeed obligated to repay Him by trusting in Him, and not despairing of His mercies in times of our suffering. We must accept His judgments as just, and know that He is able to act beneficently toward us. We must look at those who are beneath us and not at those who are above us. We must fulfill our vows and expect that they will be fulfilled for us. We must not violate the boundaries of others, or commit robbery, for we must hope in God that He will provide us with what we need and more, without delay. We must pay the wage of a hired laborer at the proper time. In this way, we may be able to answer "Yes" when we are asked at judgment, "Did you look forward to redemption?"—for all of these are tantamount to looking forward to redemption by God.

4. Divine wisdom envisioned yet another great danger that could make us stumble during this prolonged exile, and He removed this danger with marvelous providential foresight. This danger is that owing to the length of time in exile, we would forget our early history, our precious pedigree, our noble

character, and above all, our exalted God. Even though the certainty of redemption through divine power, which God has implanted in our hearts, would remain with us, we would not know what path leads to it, through which mode of service or faith we can achieve it. In this way (heaven forbid!) false beliefs could become rampant among our people, and they might deny their Torah by doubting their origins and many other similar errors that they would learn from the Gentiles in whose midst they were exiled. This would be combined with the empirical evidence of Gentile success and physical wellbeing, contrasted with the impoverishment and oppression suffered by Israel, for these are compelling reasons for accepting the Gentile claims. Add to this the hardship caused by the destruction and loss of Jewish books.[49]

As any intelligent person can easily understand, all this would be the case if the Gentiles continued in their former ways, worshipping the hosts of heaven and denying the Torah of Moses, together with the history and lineage of ancient Israel, as is known (**88d**) from the early Gentile chronicles.[50] We can also see it in our own Torah. Pharaoh said, *Who is this God, that I should hearken to his voice?* (Exod. 5:2). Even though Nebuchadnezzar and others praised God, this was only a temporary phenomenon, influenced by His awesome acts.[51] It would not have continued during the period of exile and divine anger against Israel. They would have returned to their pagan ways, and Israel would have confronted the aforementioned danger.

But the Eternal God of Hosts desired that pagan idolatry be forgotten by the nations in whose midst He exiled His children. He wanted them all to accept the Torah of Moses, to believe in its words, to seek it out and print it and bear witness to its truth. In this way, despite the length of the exile, the wardens of the prison would remind the prisoner each day of his lineage and origins, his crime and its consequences and the faith of his Torah, so that he and his offspring would never forget.[52] This is an act of divine love surpassing our imagination. In addition to this principal one, there are also other benefits

---

49. Referring probably to the burning of printed copies of the Talmud and other Jewish texts at Venice and Rome in 1553, and the subsequent suppression of Jewish books by ecclesiastical censors.

50. Perhaps referring to Roman historians, whom Morteira occasionally cited (see above, pp. 231–35), although not necessarily at first hand.

51. For Nebuchadnezzar, see Daniel 4:31–34.

52. Here is another stunning example of Morteira reversing a Christian argument. In this case it is St. Augustine's justification for toleration of the Jews as the witnesses to the authenticity of Hebrew Scripture and the consequences of rejecting the Messiah. Morteira may echo here Augustine's proof-text, *Slay them not, lest My people forget* (Ps. 59:12). Here the Christians, through their acceptance of Hebrew Scripture, serve as a reminder to keep the Jews from forgetting.

deriving from the fact that the nations recognize the truth of the Torah of Moses, but this is not the place to explore them.

This is, I believe, what the Sages wanted to teach us in one of their highly momentous enigmas, coming in the first chapter of Tractate *Yoma* (20b): "The Sages taught, Were it not for the bustle of Rome, the sound of sun in its sphere would be heard, and were it not for the sound of the sun in its sphere, the sound of the bustle of Rome would be heard." No one except for a fool who is totally ignorant of the Sages' esoteric manner of discourse could understand these words according to their simple meaning.[53] In addition to the fact that they do not conform to reality, they contradict themselves. Why should each sound drown out the other? We can say that two sounds cannot both be heard together if we are talking about speech, for two voices speaking at the same time cannot be understood; they produce only a babble of words. But two sounds that do not articulate words when added to each other make yet a louder sound; they do not drown each other out. In short, it is a waste of time to demonstrate the absurdity of these assertions according to their simple meaning.

But the true meaning is relevant to our subject. They are saying that "were it not for the bustle of Rome" in their new faith, which requires them to accept the Torah and the prophets, to preach upon them and print them,[54] to believe in the origins and history of Israel, "the sound of the sun in its sphere would be heard," meaning that Israel would, God forbid, hearken to the primal gods. For they would no longer know their true origins when their enemies challenged them, as they did in earlier times when they worshipped the sun. The Sages took the sun to represent all the heavenly bodies because it is the first, great, principal light, called the "master of the queen of heaven."[55]

Furthermore, they said, "were it not for the sound of the sun in its sphere, the sound of the bustle of Rome would be heard." This means, were it not for the fact that there was once idolatry in the world, and the manner of worship of the heavenly bodies became widely known—thereby making it clear that the faith of Rome is like the worship of the pagans except that they changed the names for new ones; the forms of worship are virtually the same, such that it is openly known that they are the pagan gods with new names[56]—"the sound

---

53. Cf. above, n. 27.

54. Note the recognition of the importance of Christian printing of Jewish texts, especially Bibles.

55. *Ba'al malkat ha-shamayim.* Although this phrase makes sense conceptually in the context of Jer. 44:17–19, I am unable to identify it in the rabbinic literature.

56. The referent of "they" in this phrase is unclear, as it implies that Christians worship a multiplicity of gods, which would most likely apply to the veneration of saints. Morteira

of the bustle of Rome would be heard," and many would follow it in error, as those who err about the pig because of its sign of purity.[57] Thus from this admirable enigma, we see an assertion of our message: that it is a sign of supreme benevolence to us that the sound of the bustle of Rome is heard in the world, so that the sound of sun worship would not be heard among us.

Along the same lines, they said, "Our Sages taught, Three sounds extend from one end of the world to another, namely, the sound of the sun in its sphere, the sound of the bustle of Rome, and the sound of the soul when it goes forth from the body; some say, also of birth; some say, also of Ridia," that is, the angel appointed over the rains. "The Rabbis sought mercy with respect to the soul when it goes forth from the body and abolished it." The bizarreness of these words (**89a**) is further indication that the previous state-ment was an enigmatic allegory. Therefore, proceeding in the same manner, we can say that these sounds are a way of expressing complaint and protest. This is similar to the rabbinic statement about the verse *Upon your belly shall you go* (Gen. 3:14): "When God said this to the serpent, the ministering angels descended and clipped its hands and its legs, and its cry went out from one end of the world to the other, as Scripture says, *its voice goes forth like the snake* (Jer. 46:22): like *the* snake."[58] Here too the Sages spoke of three things whose sound goes from one end of the world to the other, meaning that everyone throughout the entire world complains and protests about them. Yet the Holy One does not respond to their complaint, because the benefit accruing to the world exceeds the harm, and God overlooks the harm because of the benefit.

They spoke first of the sound of the sun in its sphere. This refers to the complaints deriving from idolatry. "The elders of Rome asked, If your God hates idolatry, why does He note eradicate it? They responded, Should He destroy the entire world because of the fools in it? They replied, Let Him leave the sun and the moon; what can you say about idols of wood and stone, which are not necessary to the world? They responded, If God destroyed them, people would say, These are real gods, but the others are not."[59] Thus

might be alluding shrewdly to the fact that date of the pagan festival for the birthday of Helios, December 25, was taken over by Christians for the birthday of the Christ: F. E. Peters, *The Harvest of Hellenism* (New York, 1970), p. 443; Ramsay MacMullen, *Christianity and Paganism in the Fourth to Eighth Centuries* (New Haven, 1997), p. 39. This fits beautifully with his interpretation of the "sound of the sun" in the rabbinic statement. While above he has emphasized Christian imitation of Judaism in order to entice the unwary, here he insists on the actual affinities of Christianity with paganism, a theme he would develop in his later polemical *Tratado*; see above, p. 256.

57. See above, n. 15.
58. Gen. Rabbah 20, 5.
59. M. *'Avodah Zarah* 4,7.

from one end of the world to the other, people complain that God has left the sun in its sphere as a stumbling block to those who worship it, but God overlooks their complaint—should He destroy the entire world because of the fools in it?[60]—because the benefit from the sun outweighs its potential for harm.

Similarly, the sound of the bustling of Rome goes from one end of the world to the other. This refers to the sound of protests and complaints arising from Jews wherever they are dispersed throughout the world: Why does God tolerate and permit the faith of Rome in its grandeur, with all its falsifications? They groan because of this religion and cry out, Why does God withhold His wrath with such a thing? Nevertheless, God overlooks this sound, for the benefit deriving from [Christianity] exceeds the harm, as we have stated, for "were it not for the sound of the bustling of Rome, the sound of the sun in its sphere would be heard," as explained above.

In like manner, the plaintive sound of the soul at the moment when it issues forth from the body goes from one end of the world to the other, for the entire world murmurs, why did God decree that the human being must suffer death, and the merger of soul and body be dissolved? Would it not be better if man did not die, but could live forever, never suffering the bitterness of death? Yet God did not respond to this plea because of the great benefit brought by death. For without it, men would devour each other alive, and it would be impossible to attain the enjoyment of the splendor of the Divine Presence in the manner of the incorporeal intelligences. This is why R. Meir said, "*And behold, it was very good* (tov me'od) (Gen. 1:31): and behold, death is good (*tov mot*)."[61]

There are some who say, "Even birth." For even with regard to birth, the sound of complaint spreads from one end of the world to the other. When the bitterness of this evil time is tasted, people say, "*Why did I not perish in the womb...*" (cf. Job 3:11) and other such complaints about birth. For *man is born to toil* (Job 5:7), and it would have been better for him not to have been created[62] than for him to be created to such toil and anger. Yet God does not respond to this because of the great benefit brought to man by his birth. For it would impossible for a human fetus to attain any level of merit except by living on earth as a corporeal entity. As a result of his choosing as a human being, he may become worthy through his deeds of a higher status.

Similarly, some say, "Even the rains." For there is much murmuring even about them, as the Sages taught at length in Tractate *Ta'anit*, speaking about

---

60. Cf. "Dust of the Earth," above, p. 389.

61. Gen. Rabbah 9, 5.

62. Cf. the debate between Beit Hillel and Beit Shammai, b. *'Erubin* 13b.

the harm caused by rains to travelers, to the point where they said, "Even in years like the years of Elijah, a shower descending before Shabbat is (**89b**) a sign of curse, because of the trouble it causes people."[63] Yet God did not respond to this because of the great benefit brought to men by rain, which sustains the life of all.

They further said, "The Rabbis sought mercy concerning the soul in its exit from the body and they abolished it," namely this complaint about the harm and bitterness of death. The Sages sought mercy and abolished it from their own ranks, for *The righteous man finds security in his death* (Prov. 14:32), *and she laughs at the final day* (Prov. 31:25); thus the righteous and the pious do not complain about the day of their death. This can be seen in the statement from Genesis Rabbah, chapter 92 [section 2], that I used last year as the rabbinic dictum in a sermon for the Sabbath of Repentance:

> Zabdi ben Levi, R. Joshua ben Levi, and R. Jose ben Patrus each quoted one of the following texts as he was dying. One quoted, *Therefore let every pious person pray to You* (Ps. 32:6), *For in Him our hearts rejoice* (Ps. 33:21). Another quoted, *You spread a table for me* (Ps. 23:5), *so shall all who take refuge in You rejoice* (Ps. 5:12). The third quoted, *For better one day in Your courts than a thousand [elsewhere]* (Ps. 84:11), *Truly your loving kindness is better than life* (Ps. 63:4).

Thus the complaint about death was abolished among the Sages, and consequently it is no longer included in the category "from one end of the world to the other."

In this way we can see how the Sages, through their marvelously enigmatic dictum, taught the truth of our sermon theme: how it is the result of great divine love that we find ourselves in the midst of the Gentiles among whom we are exiled at this time, Gentiles with a religion like theirs and not like that of the earlier pagans, so that they themselves sing our praises and tell us of our identity, our merits, our salvation, our Torah, and our God, rather than denying all of these as in ancient times. For that would be a major stumbling block to us. This is an act of inestimable divine love. Therefore the verse said, **There is no unknown God with him**, meaning, a god unknown to all the ordinary people, such that they might say as did Pharaoh, *"Who is this God?... I do not know this God"* (Exod. 5:2). Rather, our God is known by all peoples; all accept His divinity. *Happy is the people who have it so, happy the people whose God is the Eternal* (Ps. 144:15).

Now if God proclaimed His Torah among the peoples and they have borne

---

63. B. *Ta'anit* 8b.

witness to it, we certainly are obligated to maintain consistency in the study of Torah. This is especially important in the winter months, when the nights are long. In this way, God's Torah will be well known to all, as the Bible says, *You shall meditate upon it day and night* (Josh. 1:8). Similarly, we must make an effort to observe its commandments, especially on the Sabbath day, both regarding study on that day and observance of it in the highest manner, for it bears witness to the power of our God, as an eternal sign between God and the children of Israel.[64] Thus we will be able to answer "Yes" when we are asked, "Have you fixed times for Torah?"

5. In addition to all of this, divine wisdom foresaw yet another well-known danger that would imperil Israel in this current exile according to the natural order, to which the experts will testify, attaining the full truth. From this too, God saved Israel through His marvelous providential care. This is that, as we learn from the other exiles, when the Jews are aliens in a land not theirs, the nations of those lands will seek to marry with them, because of their noble lineage. Even kings will be honored by them. We see this with Ahasuerus and Esther. In order to avoid marrying the king, she did not disclose her nationality or the land of her birth.[65] Once the king discovered this, he honored her more than before, because of her intrinsic honor. How much more is this true in the current exile. According to proper investigation of the natural order, Jews should be highly honored by all peoples, both physically and spiritually.[66] These people should want the Jews to be nobles, to draw close to them, saying, "Bring us your abundant gifts of purity, marry with us, give us your

---

64. Cf. Exod. 31:13, and Morteira's discussion of this, above, pp. 268–69.

65. Cf. Esther 2:20. The claim that Esther concealed her identity at Mordecai's behest in order to diminish the chance that the king would marry her is unusual; contrast the interpretations cited in Barry Dov Walfish, *Esther in Medieval Garb* (Albany, 1993), pp. 66, 83.

66. Compare Menasseh ben Israel's statement in his *Conciliator* 2:185, question 29: "Among all the nations of the world, only the Israelites can be really termed noble, for the honourable titles they enjoy were conferred by [God]." Two decades later, in his "Humble Addresses" (1655), he wrote that one of the three qualities that make a foreign people "well-beloved amongst the Natives of a land where they dwell" is "the Noblenes and purity of their blood" (fol. 1); later in this work, he stated that the "Nobility of the Jews ... is enough known amongst all Christians" that there is no need to discuss it in detail, but refers the reader to two recently published English books (fol. 23, both cited by Yosef Kaplan, "Political Concepts in the World of the Portuguese Jews of Amsterdam," pp. 50–51). Kaplan's statement that this emphasis on "Nobleness and the purity of their blood" is unrelated to "any other Jewish author" (p. 51) overlooks this passage in the 1645 edition of *Giv'at Sha'ul* (which of course is used for a rather different purpose here). Cf. also Bodian, *Hebrews of the Portuguese Nation*, pp. 90–91, and (on the earlier background) David Nirenberg, "Mass Conversion and Genealogical Mentalities: Jews and Christians in Fifteenth-Century Spain," *Past and Present* 174 (2002): 3–41.

daughters and we will give our daughters to you."[67] Thus Israel would assimilate among the nations, God forbid![68]

As for physical honor and natural lineage, we have seen how this has been fully present in Israel from of old, as the nations have admitted. Therefore, they would seek it out, had not (**89c**) God removed from us this potential pitfall. The divine Torah taught us all this when it came to narrate the lines of descent of the children of Israel. There it said, *Take a census* (lit.: "lift up the head") *of the whole Israelite community by their families of their ancestral houses, listing the names, every male, head by head* (Num. 1:2). It mentioned these various categories in order to teach us in its characteristic way all of the modes of lineage. For when we look carefully at the definition of lineage, we see that it applies only to a person with a beautiful soul,[69] full of fine character traits and virtuous qualities that distinguish the person of lineage from the masses. Since the internal parts of the soul are known not to other people but only to God, people use the term "noble" for someone who has the visible external dispositions that are generally accompanied by the beautiful soul and these fine, praiseworthy character traits, for this is what the knowledge of such people can attain.[70]

Now these dispositions are specified in the various components of the verse. The first is a great and fundamental disposition for the virtue of beautiful character traits by being born into wealth and abundance, lest the character be tested by destitution and poverty, which by nature are antithetical to every good character trait,[71] as we see in the statement, "God did not leave

---

67. Echoing Gen. 34:9, where a similar proposal is made by Hamor the Hivite.

68. The view that cordial interaction with Jews by the Gentile population leads to assimilation and the disappearance of the Jewish population is reminiscent of Spinoza's claim that the population of "New Christians" in Spain "so speedily assimilated to the Spaniards that after a short while no trace of them was left" (*Theological-Political Treatise*, end of chap. 3, p. 46; see below, n. 83.

69. *Nefesh ha-yafah* is a Talmudic phrase (M. *Hullin* 4,7) referring to a person of robust temperament, not queasy about eating unusual things. But in context, the preacher seems to be referring to the Renaissance concept of the *anima bella* (e.g. Petrarch, Sonnet 305, or in the Portuguese imitations by Camões, *alma bela* or *alma gentil*). See also Joanna Weinberg, "The Beautiful Soul," pp. 115–18.

70. I have rendered the Hebrew word *meyuhas* as "noble," expressing all of the qualities Morteira is claiming for the Jewish people. Cf. Martín González de Cellorigo's 1619 "Plea in Favor of the Portuguese 'New Christians'": *la nobleza se conoce en la generosidad de animo, en la virtud, costumbres y buen proceder, ye en el aspecto y decoro de las personas.* I. S. Révah, "Le Plaidoyer en faveur des 'Nouveaux-Chrétiens' Portugais du Licencié Martín González de Cellorigo (Madrid, 1619)," *RJ* 122 (1963): 351.

71. Compare the similar position taken on the effects of wealth and poverty in the sermon on *Va-ethanan*, above, pp. 416–20.

poverty as a good quality for Israel."[72] By contrast, the wealthy person is prepared by his parents for study and generosity and largesse and others of the most praiseworthy virtues. Therefore people refer to one born into wealth as being of noble lineage, for wealth and honor generally go together. This is the meaning of the phrase, *Take a census* (se'u et rosh) *of all the whole Israelite community* (Num. 1:2); the first Hebrew words literally mean, lift up their heads and exalt their lineage, first through the circumstances of their birth, that is to say the exalted circumstances of their birth into abundance and wealth, for this is the beginning.[73] We see that when God chose Abraham and brought him out of his native land, He made this factor of his possessions fundamental, as the Torah recounts, *and all the possessions that he had acquired in Haran* (Gen. 12:5), and also, *And Abraham was very rich in cattle, silver and gold* (Gen. 13:2). And so in every generation God has watched providentially over this factor, even in times of exile, to ensure that Jews would be wealthy in order that they might have some of the noble character traits along with their noble lineage. This was the case in Egypt and in all the other exiles, and we see it ourselves today, through wondrous and miraculous individual providence.

The second disposition is having a clean and modest family,[74] without any admixture of promiscuity, for this disposes the person toward the praiseworthy traits of humility and equanimity and inner serenity. These are not to be found among those born of incest or promiscuity, who tend more toward arrogance and insolence and other such disagreeable traits that are antithetical to noble lineage. Therefore the verse went on to say, *by their families,* meaning the clean state of their families. It is obvious and well known among the Gen-

---

72. *Lo hiniaḥ oniyut midah tovah le-Yisrael.* It is hard to know what to make of this statement. The common form is the opposite: God found no good quality for Israel *except* poverty: cf. b. *Ḥagigah* 9b; Modena, *Midbar Yehudah* 1602, p. 35a, 2002, p. 122. Furthermore, elsewhere Morteira cites a companion statement from b. *Ḥagigah* 9b ("Dust of the Earth," p. 391, "The Land Shudders," p. 401) indicating that poverty (or possibly humility) befits Israel. Did he simply mis-remember the text he cites, or did he consciously invert it?

73. On the importance of Iberian conceptions of nobility in this community, see Bodian, pp. 85–92.

74. *Neqiut ha-mishpaḥah u-tseniutah.* In Morteira's Portuguese delivery, the first word ("cleanness" or "purity") would undoubtedly have been *limpeza,* despite all the associations with the Iberian "purity of blood" (Sp.: *limpieza de sangre*) legislation that made life so difficult for many New Christians. This is yet another example of Morteira appropriating a Christian claim for his own purposes. Cf. Yosef Kaplan's formulation: "When they returned to the faith of their fathers, the former secret Jews borrowed the infamous concept from their persecutors, for it now helped them define their own identity. Here we have an example of *appropriation,* as a direct result of what René Girard called *la mimesis de l'antagonisme.*" "Political Concepts," p. 53.

tiles how superior the Jews are in comparison with the other nations with regard to modesty and the clean state of their families;[75] this was the case in Egypt and in the other exiles. Regarding the verse about the Israelite who blasphemed, *he was the son of an Egyptian man* (Lev. 24:10), the Sages said, "there was only one [Israelite woman guilty of miscegenation], and the Scripture made her name public."[76] I discussed this at length on a sermon on the lesson *Tetsaveh* on the verse, *These are the vestments that they shall make* (Exod. 28:4).[77]

The third disposition is the stature of the ancestors. If they are wise and great men, their descendants will be well disposed to be schooled in every good character trait, both from the effort they devote to study and from the example they see in their ancestors, from which they may learn to do likewise. The prophet Isaiah said about Pharaoh, *How can you say to Pharaoh, "I am a scion of sages"?* (Isa. 19:11). About this our verse said, *of their ancestral homes* (Num. 1:2). Who among all the Gentiles can claim this kind of lineage like the Jews, the descendants of ancestors who are known and sacred to all the nations: Abraham, Isaac, and Jacob, and the twelve tribes, tribes of God?[78]

The fourth disposition is the intellect and the knowledge bestowed upon the human being, in addition to bravery and strength. Through these virtues a person may succeed in conducting himself (**89d**) both with wisdom and with valor. He will therefore be noble and exalted, for in general these two virtues are associated with the most praiseworthy character traits, upon which nobility and eminence depend, as we have explained earlier. Therefore, when people see the good name acquired by the wise and brave man, they will think of

---

75. Compare Isaac Cardoso, writing in Italy a generation or so after this sermon, but expressing a common conception: "Since in their lineage all are intermingled with one another, none can say that he is an Italian, Frenchman, Spaniard, German, or Greek, and so with the other peoples, because all are confused and mixed together." Cited by Yerushalmi, *From Spanish Court to Italian Ghetto*, p. 385. Similarly, Increase Mather wrote of "the secret wonderful providence of God in preserving the Jewish Nation entire from mixing with other Nations where they are dispersed. The providence of God hath suffered other Nations to have their bloud mixed very much: as you know it is with our own Nation, there is a mixture of British, Roman, Saxon, Norman bloud; but as for the body of the Jewish Nation it is far otherwise." Quoted in Munk, *The Devil's Mousetrap*, pp. 57–58.

76. Exod. Rabbah 1, 28, Lev. Rabbah 32,5 and parallels, referring to Lev. 24:10–11.

77. This sermon of Morteira, delivered in the mid-1620s, begins on MS 4:157r.

78. Cellorigo (above, n. 70) cites Friar Juan de Pineda on the Iberian New Christians who were not in Jerusalem at the time of the crucifixion: *se pueden del mejor linage del mundo, porque la nobleza de la sangre pende de las excelencias personales del fundador de la parentela, juntamente con los privilegios y honras concedidas de los Principes. Y los fundadores de la casa de Israel (Abraham, Isac, Jacob) fueron eminentissimos hombres y honrados de Dios sobre quantos en el mundo nacieron....* Révah, "Le Plaidoyer," p. 352.

him as noble and esteemed, as was said. This is what the verse meant by *listing the names* (Num. 1:2), namely, men of good name. Now it is well known how many wise and brave men are to be found among the Jews—more than the other peoples. Therefore we must be more noble, more highly esteemed.

The fifth disposition is the antiquity of the family. By this I mean that when a person can trace his lineage back from generation to generation into antiquity, this indeed makes him disposed to nobility and honor.[79] For the preservation of the names of his ancestors will result in the descendant also being mentioned by his deeds, as we see in the verse, *The wise shall inherit honor* (Prov. 3:35), like a stream, or an estate.[80] Our verse referred to this in the phrase, *every male* (Num. 1:2), for the Israelites would bring their books of lineage, containing every male, generation after generation, back to antiquity, and indeed to Adam, God's own direct creation. It is well known that there is no other nation in the world that can boast of this like the Jews.

The sixth disposition is that when a person is elevated and exalted by a king or a lord, he is thereby thought to be noble, for it appears that within him there is something good, a beautiful soul. Since the king recognized him as worthy of benevolence and honor, all others should honor him and think of him as noble. This is mentioned here in the phrase *head by head* (Num. 1:2), meaning, in the individual lifting of the head and exaltation which God bestowed upon them, He gave them a uniquely elevated status among the nations, as the Bible says, *You shall be to Me a kingdom of priests, and a holy people* (Exod. 19:6).

Thus in the matter of their numbering, God hinted by these phrases—*their [circumstances of] birth, by their families, their ancestral houses, listing the names, every male, head by head*—the various kinds of nobility and disposition, and how they were all present in Israel.

The prophet Isaiah spoke of all these when he said, *Let me sing for my beloved, a song of my lover about his vineyard. My beloved had a vineyard on a fruitful hill. He walled it in, cleared it of stones, and planted it with choice vines. He built a watchtower inside it. He even hewed a wine press in it* (Isa. 5:1–2). Now the "fruitful hill" refers to the grandeur of the ancestors, who were indeed planted on a fruitful hill, having descendants who were vigorous and replete with all the finest character traits. The word "fenced it in" alludes to these descendants being born in

---

79. For the contemporary Spanish view on the importance of antiquity, see the passage cited by Yerushalmi, *From Spanish Court to Italian Ghetto*, p. 386: "Among the Spaniards is found the most ancient nobility of any of the nations, retaining always the blood of their first progenitor, Tubal."

80. Playing with two meanings of the root *nahal*; cf. Morteira's eulogy for David Farar, in *"Your Voice Like a Ram's Horn,"* p. 396.

wealth and prosperity: the actual word refers to a ring, an encircling wall,[81] for so *the wealth of a rich man is his fortress, [a protective wall]* (Prov. 18:11). To teach of their own perfection in wisdom and valor, he said, *cleared it of stones,* meaning the stones that press down upon noble lineage, and he prepared them for himself with every kind of perfection. *He planted it with choice vines* teaches the purity of their families, as in the verse, *I planted you with choice vines, all with the finest seeds* (Jer. 2:21). *He built a watchtower inside it* shows how God exalted them with every mode of grandeur and honor, for this is truly to build a watchtower within them. *He even hewed a wine press in it* refers to the knowledge of their antiquity without compromise in their lineage, for the wine press produces a constant and abundant flow of wine: this is what they can show from their books of lineage.

Now since the lineage of Israel is so splendid and exalted, the nations would choose to draw near them, as we already said. And if this was so in the other exiles, in the present exile it would naturally be even more so, for Jews have noble lineage not only of a physical nature, but also spiritually, since they [Christians] claim that their God and savior came from the Jews.[82] Thus by law and custom, Jews should be considered by the Christians to be the most important and the noblest people conceivable, and they should therefore want to cleave to them and marry with them. However, (**90a**) foreseeing this natural danger, God removed it from us, and generated in the hearts of these nations a great unnatural hatred, totally unprecedented, so that they would despise us and set us at a distance from them. Lest they seduce us with their honors, God ensured that they would set us aside like a menstruous woman in her impurity—all for our own benefit and to ensure our survival up to this day.[83]

---

81. Morteira here follows Rashi and Kimhi, based on the Targum.

82. Morteira does not address here the claim that, as Cellorigo put it, *todos los Judíos y sus descendientes perdieron la nobleza por la muerte de nuestro Redentor* (Révah, "Le Plaidoyer," p. 351), which Cellorigo—following the Spanish-Jewish mythology—counters by insisting that the Iberian Jews had left Jerusalem centuries before the crucifixion.

83. This claim that hatred of Jews is unnatural, and the God providentially reversed the natural sociological order by making Gentiles hate Jews in order to ensure their survival, bears comparison with Spinoza's assertion that Jews are preserved in their separate identity by the hatred of the Gentiles, as historical experience shows: *Theological-Political Treatise,* end of chap. 3, p. 45 (in the original Latin: *Quod autem Nationum odium eos admodum conservet, id jam, experientia docuit*). See Yosef Hayyim Yerushalmi, "Divrei Spinoza al Qiyyum ha-'Am ha-Yehudi," *Proceedings of the Israel Academy of Sciences and Humanities (Hebrew)* 6 (1984): 171–91. Yerushalmi concludes that "Spinoza was the first to make the explicit claim that what has preserved the people of Israel is not divine providence but hatred" (p. 179). Here we find Morteira taking a middle ground: what preserves Israel is hatred, yet the

This is what our Text says, ***The Eternal did guide him alone*** (Deut. 32:12), for in addition to the other interpretations we have given—that God has separated us from them in all matters [through rabbinic law] and made us dwell alone—God has also separated them from us through the hatred and contempt He established in their hearts, so that he has made us dwell alone and apart. This is what the Lamenter said, *You have made us filth and refuse in the midst of the peoples* (Lam. 3:45), for this comes from God. For according to the ways of the world, their very own faith would lead not to this end but to the opposite. God is the one who has made us *filth and refuse*, for our own good.

From this two things are derived: we should have *fear and the pit* (Jer. 48:43), *panic and pitfall* (Lam. 3:47). By this I mean that, aware of their great contempt and hatred for us, we should fear lest we mix in with them and accompany them and participate in their affairs, for we know their great hatred for us. With all this, their hatred became so powerful that *they question me about things I do not know* (Ps. 35:11), and it has not helped me, for I have drawn apart from them and them from me, lest I fall into the evil pit that they invented for me—of which we see examples every day! This is the meaning of *calamity* (sh'et) *and destruction* (Lam. 3:47), namely, I was in their eyes like a leper, with a skin affliction (*se'et*) as regards distancing and separation. And in any evil matter, the destruction was placed upon me, as if I had done everything bad that happens among them. This is the meaning of the phrase, *the sin of the many he did bear* (Isa. 53:12).[84]

Now if God has implanted hatred in the hearts of the nations so that they will not seek to draw near to us, we are certainly obligated to distance ourselves from intermarrying with them (heaven forbid!), for this is a criminal act.[85] This is what exiled Israel from their land, and confounded their tranquility in the lands of their dispersion. In this way alone, the enemies found it possible to conquer God's people and to make strife between them and their

---

hatred is not natural but providential. As a child and young man, Spinoza would have heard Morteira preach, and perhaps the seed of this idea sprouted, fully secularized, in the mature thinker. As Yosef Kaplan has noted, Spinoza may have taken his illustrative contrast between the experience of the "New Christians" in Spain and Portugal (though not the general formulation about the role of hatred) from Cellorigo: "Political Concepts," p. 47. Compare also the formulation, quite similar to Morteira's, about the preservative role of Gentile hatred for Jews in Orobio de Castro (who arrived in Amsterdam two years after Morteira's death), cited by Kaplan, *From Christianity to Judaism*, p. 371. The difference is that Orobio claims that this hatred "corresponds to the natural order of things" (p. 366), where Morteira insists that it is a providential reversal of the natural order.

84. An articulation of the concept of sociological scapegoating.

85. For other statements in Morteira's sermons about intermarriage, see above, pp. 199–201.

God. For the closer they draw to the other peoples, the farther God draws away from them. As for the husband of the daughter of an alien god, God will cut off this man, who thereby gives from his seed to Molech,[86] and cleaves with her in this world and in the world to come—as Scripture says about Joseph: *He did not yield to her to lie with her or to be with her* (Gen. 39:10)[87] and profanes the sign of the holy covenant,[88] and the zealots may deal with him,[89] and many such statements. Thus if we distance ourselves from this, we will be able to answer "Yes" when we are asked at judgment, "Have you concerned yourself with procreation," meaning according to Jewish law and in holiness with [*the wife of your youth:*] *a loving doe, a graceful fawn* (Prov. 5:18–19), his portion, his proper wife, with fear of God on their faces, a man and woman with the divine presence between them.[90]

6. It sometimes occurs that when a physician gives a dose of medicine or a drug to a sick person for a specific purpose, the constitution and nature of the sick person is so compatible with that of the medication that its effect is stronger than anticipated; consequently, the result of the medication is not benefit but harm. Similarly, when God implanted hatred in the hearts of the Gentile nations for the reason we mentioned, He found their nature to be so well disposed to it that it spoiled the pattern and crossed the boundary line,[91] so that God thundered against them through the prophet [Isaiah], who said, *I was angry at My people, I defiled My heritage; I put them into your hands, but you showed them no mercy. Even upon the aged you made your yoke extremely heavy* (Isa. 47:6), and through Zechariah, who said, *I was angry a little, but they overdid the punishment* (Zech. 1:15). Therefore, it was necessary for God to correct this perversion and defend against this depredation through His wondrous individual providence, so that we would not be annihilated from the earth. For were it not for God's arising on our behalf, they would have swallowed us up alive.

Now the antidote and defense against this danger that is prepared and lurking around us (**90b**) was implemented by scattering us among the nations.

---

86. M. *Sanhedrin* 7,4.

87. The midrash explains that by "lying with her" in this world, Joseph would "be with her" in Gehinnom in the world to come (Gen. Rabbah 87,6 and parallels; Rashi on Gen. 39:10).

88. I.e. the mark of circumcision, profaned by allowing it to enter "alien precincts" by sexual intercourse with a Gentile woman; cf. Zohar, II,3b; Solomon Levi, *Divrei Shelomoh* (Venice, 1596), p. 230a, translated in Saperstein, *Jewish Preaching*, p. 246.

89. B. *'Avodah Zarah* 36b.

90. Cf. Gen. Rabbah 8,9.

91. I.e., God implanted an unnatural hatred of the Jews in the hearts of the Gentiles, but their hostility toward the Jews went beyond what God intended, requiring a form of providential protection against excessive danger.

God did not want us to be under one king in this exile. For in addition to the other benefits that accrue to us from this scattering—which I have explained in one of my sermons on the lesson *Va-Yetse Ya'aqov* on the verse, *Your offspring shall be as the dust of the earth* (Gen. 28:14)[92]—this is the most important of all. It is what has stood by us, enabling us to leave a remnant all over the earth. For *if Esau comes to one camp to attack it, the other camp may escape* (Gen. 32:8). This is what the Sages said in the chapter beginning "The woman" of tractate *Pesaḥim* (87b):

> *His gracious deliverance [pirzono] of Israel* (Jud. 5:11). Said R. Oshaiah, "God acted graciously with Israel by scattering them (*pizaram*) among the nations." For this is what that heretic said to R. Judah Nesi'ah: "We are better than you. Of you it is written, *For Joab and all Israel stayed there for six months until he had killed off every male in Edom* (1 Kings 11:16), while you have lived among us for many years, and we have not done anything to you." He replied, "If you agree, a disciple will debate it with you." Thereupon R. Oshaiah debated. He said, "The reason is that you do not know how to destroy us. If you wanted to kill all of us, not all are in your kingdom, and if you killed those who are among you, then you will be called a murderous kingdom!" He replied, "By the Capitol of Rome! We lie down and rise up with this in mind."

Thus God has providentially watched over us in scattering us among the nations as a great remedy for their hatred so that they would not annihilate us. He placed us under many rulers, so that they would not all agree on a single plan.

In this way we may interpret the phrase from the Haggadah, "This is what has stood by our ancestors and us." For it applies to what preceded it: "Blessed is the One who keeps His promise to Israel, blessed is He. For the Holy One calculated the end [of the bondage] in order to accomplish what He promised to our father Abraham in the 'covenant among the pieces,' when He said, *Know well that your offspring shall be strangers in a land not theirs.... But also on that nation they shall serve [I will execute judgment, and in the end they shall go free with great wealth]* (Gen. 15:13–14). And this is what has stood by our ancestors...."[93] Now the difficulty is obvious: How can the Haggadah say about the promise that was completed and fulfilled in Egypt and the redemption from that exile, "And this is what has stood by our ancestors and us, for it was

---

92. Translated above.

93. All a quotation from the Pesach Haggadah. Cf. Maimonides, *Code, Hil. Ḥametz u-Matzah* 9,12.

not only one who arose against us, but in every generation they arise us against us to destroy us"? How can that promise to Abraham be applied to every generation?

It seems to me that when God said to Abraham, *Know well that your offspring shall be strangers in a land not theirs, and they shall be enslaved and oppressed four hundred years* (Gen. 15:13), He did not give permission to the Egyptians to kill their male babies, but only to subjugate them and make them suffer through hard labor. They did the additional evil of their own accord, as we see in the verse, *I was angry*[94] *a little, but they overdid the punishment* (Zech. 1:15), by throwing their children into the Nile.[95] Because of this, God shortened the period of their subjugation in accordance with the excessive substance of their punishment, so that one compensated for the other, and started counting from the birth of Isaac, as the Sages said.[96] Thus it is perfectly appropriate to say, "Blessed is the One who keeps His promise," for even though the Egyptians exceeded what God promised in their evil against our ancestors, nevertheless God shortened the time of the oppression because of this excessive cruelty. This is the meaning of "calculating the end of the bondage in order to accomplish what He said to Abraham at the 'covenant among the pieces.'" Otherwise, what "calculation" would be necessary for this? But the term "calculation" refers to calculating the substance of the oppression against its duration, in order to compensate with one for the other, and to shorten the duration of the oppression because of its excessive character.

Therefore the Haggadah says, "This is what has stood by our ancestors and us:" "by our ancestors" in that for this reason God hastened the End, "and by us" for "it was not only one who arose against us." In other words, it shows through historical experience—not that God needed this, but in matters per-

---

94. Morteira curiously makes the same error in citing this verse that he did shortly before, substituting *amarti* (I said) for *qatsafti* (I was angry).

95. Here the preacher is following Ramban's commentary on Gen. 15:14, based on Exod. Rabbah 30:17, which cites both Zechariah 1:15 and Isa. 47:6, as Morteira cited them together a bit earlier.

96. See Gen. Rabbah 44,18 and Rashi and David Kimhi on Gen. 15:13, and above, p. 63. These commentators, however, do not speak of God's shortening the time in Egypt because of the excessive evil of the Egyptians. The closest source for Morteira's idea I have found is Gersonides on Exodus (p. 54c bottom, 54d middle, 55b bottom), where God decides to bring the Israelites out of Egypt before the appointed time because their suffering was so great that if God waited, "My covenant with the Patriarchs would almost be annulled." This interpretation was cited by Morteira's contemporary, Menasseh ben Israel in *The Conciliator*, 1:62, juxtaposed with the antithetical interpretation of Nahmanides: that the original sentence of 400 years was lengthened by God by thirty years because of the Israelites' lack of merits and repentance (1:61–62).

taining to choice, all is given over into the hands of human beings—that when (**90c**) Israel is under the power of a single ruler, there is a great danger of their name being blotted out from the earth as Pharaoh wanted to do, and so they would do in every generation. Therefore, in this exile, God wanted all of us [not] to be under one king or ruler. This is what has "stood by us," namely, Pharaoh's violation of God's promise. The reason that caused hastening the end in Egypt is what "stood by us" today, guaranteeing that we would not be under the power of one king.

This is the meaning of **and no alien God with Him**, namely that God was unwilling to extend His glory to an alien god. He alone is the director of Israel's destiny, as we see in the verse, *but you the Eternal took* (Deut. 4:20), so He was unwilling to turn the whole people of Israel over to the power of an alien god, but He alone would rule over them. This is consistent with what the Sages said in Midrash *Tanḥuma* on the verse, *I am the Eternal, that is My name; I will not yield My glory to another, nor My renown to idols* (Isa. 4:28): "That is My name that the first man called Me; that is My name that I stipulated between Myself and the supernal beings; that is my name that I stipulated between Myself and the ministering angels."[97] By this they meant that God was unwilling to hand all of Israel over to the power of one of the supernal rulers. First, because the ultimate purpose for the creation of human beings was for Israel to serve God, and furthermore, it was inconceivable for them all to be turned over to a single king. This is the meaning of "That is my name that the first man called Me," namely, the ultimate purpose for which he was created. Second, because *I will not yield My glory to another,* meaning that the Jews are God's witnesses, as in the verse, *You are my witnesses, says the Eternal, and I am God* (Isa. 43:10): this glory should not be turned over to the power of another. This is the meaning of "That is my name that I stipulated between Myself and the supernal beings," namely Israel, as in the verse, *And He will make you superior over all the nations of the earth* (Deut. 26:19). And also for a third reason: God took Israel for His own estate, and turned the other nations over to the power of the angels, as in the verse, *When the Most High gave the names their homes [... For the portion of the Eternal is His people]*(Deut. 32:8–9), and it is not appropriate to hand over His estate and His renown—namely Israel, as in the verse, *Israel, in whom I glory* (Isa. 49:3)—into the power of one ruler and one idolatrous people. This is the meaning of *nor my renown to idols.* Thus our verse, **and no alien god with Him**, meaning, with His governance

---

97. The quotation does not appear in this form in *Tanḥuma*; a similar formulation is in other Midrashim (e.g. Eccles. Rabbah 7,32, Pes. Rabbati 17,1, Pes. de Rav Kahana 7,2), but there the middle term is "that I stipulated for Myself (*beini le-vein 'atsmi*)."

and exalted stature, directing the destiny of Israel alone, to give Israel into the power of another ruler alone is impossible.

Now if God has scattered us among the nations for our own benefit, so that we would not be under the power of a single king, we in turn are obligated to make an effort to make lasting peace and unity prevail among us, and to annul all strife and contention within our people, to remove from our hearts vengeance and grudge-holding, for these are character traits of Edom, as we see from the verse, *For his anger raged unceasing, and his fury stormed unchecked* (Amos 1:11). Similarly, informing (heaven forbid!), and jealousy and baseless hatred, which caused the destruction of our Temple. And all such inferior and repugnant character traits, which are the cause of our scattering and destructive of peace. In this way, we may be able to answer "Yes" when we are asked at judgment, "Have you engaged in the dialectics of wisdom?," for this is proper discourse between human beings with wisdom and reason and balance, not like animals lacking reason, who are given over to their impulses and desires.

Peroration

These then are the six dispositions and special remedies that God ordained for us to save us from the traps spread out for us in this exile, all of them hinted in our Text.

- The first is our separation from the nations: *The Eternal did guide him alone.*
- The second is that He uprooted from us the desire for idolatry: *and there is no alien god with him* [i.e., with Israel].
- [Third], He implanted within our hearts hope and promise: *The Eternal did guide him secure.*
- Fourth, He spread our Torah and our faith among the nations, so that they would arouse us regarding them: *and there is no alien god with him,* that is, with Israel.
- Fifth, He implanted hatred in the hearts of the nations so that they would not seek to intermarry with us: *The Eternal did guide him alone.*
- Sixth, He scattered us among the nations to the four corners of the earth so that they would not be able to annihilate us: *and there is no alien god with Him,* meaning, He has not given His glory to an alien power to determine Israel's destiny alone.[98]

98. Moses Edrehi incorporated this passage of recapitulation almost verbatim, without attribution, into a sermon for the Sabbath of Repentance that he published in *Yad Moshe* (Amsterdam 1809), p. 17d. See p. 31, above.

For all these, *the fear of God is his treasure* (Isa. 33:6). How good is the portion, how pleasant the lot of the person who has all these qualities, and the fear of God upon his face, for *Happy are all who fear God* (Ps. 128:1). What does God ask from us, but to fear Him (cf. Deut. 10:12), for this is the essence of man, his ultimate purpose and his end. The prophet has already explained that this is God's tabernacle in this world, as he said, *Yet to such a one I look: to the poor and the brokenhearted who trembles at My word* (Isa. 66:2). For these the promises were said, as we see in the verse, *But for you who revere My name, a sun of victory shall rise with healing in its wings* (Mal. 3:20). May it be God's will to bring this about quickly and in our days, with the coming of our righteous Messiah. Amen.

"They Provoked My Jealousy With a Non-God"

Budapest Rabbinical Seminary MS 12, vol. 3, folios 309r–314v
Sermon for the Sabbath of Repentance, 1641

This sermon for the Sabbath of Repentance, while not quite as long as the sermon on Deuteronomy 23:12 translated above, has one of the most complex structures of any in Morteira's oeuvre. Unlike the previous sermon, in which the rabbinic dictum is a structuring element, with phrases appearing at a climactic moment at the end of each of the six sections, here the dictum appears only at the very end of the text, in a somewhat contrived manner. The biblical verse, the Text from the lesson Ha'azinu, *in its various components and shifting interpretations, shines in full glory as the cord that binds the entire sermon together. Perhaps the musical analogy is best: it is a like a musical theme, a leitmotif, that continually reappears in subtly different forms—with altered instrumentation and varied harmonies—throughout the movements of a long but fully integrated symphonic work. The bold type used for this verse is the visual equivalent of the familiar sound of the musical leitmotif recognized by the attentive ear.*

At first, however, the biblical verse like the rabbinic dictum is left in abeyance after its initial citation, as the preacher develops at a leisurely pace his introductory exordium. In the previous sermon, there was an extensive parable, which introduced the sermon's subject matter—God's providential care for the Jewish people even during the period of chastisement in exile—straightforwardly. Here the discourse is considerably more diffuse, probing the metaphorical dimensions of covenant as family. The word "house" in biblical usage is often extended beyond a physical building to refer to the family of a household: father, mother, and children. "God's house" refers to the Jewish people, the relationship of which to God metaphorically incorporates elements of both wife and children. When this "house" breaks up, when the father leaves, the impact is felt by both components of the relationship; both wife and children suffer, as can be seen in the language of the Book of Lamentations. The two related though distinct images are necessary in that they allude to two aspects of God's providential relationship: "wife" refers to the relationship with the Jewish people as an organic whole, "children" with Jews as individuals.

The preacher then applies this thesis to the earlier verses of the lesson Ha'azinu, *showing how the poem uses both metaphors—the people of Israel as wife and as children—in recounting the favors bestowed upon them by God, in the indictment of*

489

the people for their rebelliousness, and in outlining the punishment to be visited upon the people. At this point, the theme-verse is introduced, a verse that explicitly includes both sin and punishment, and—the preacher now informs his listeners—implicitly refers to the Jews first in their relationship as wife and then in their relationship as children. With this formulation of the sermon's subject matter—the Jewish people's failures and punishments as wife and as children of the Almighty—the exordium reaches its end. Some listeners might well have thought that the topic of biblical metaphors for the covenant was not exactly the most scintillating subject for the lengthy disquisition they knew would follow. And indeed, Morteira may have agreed, as this theme is not emphasized in the rest of the sermon. Instead, the components of the verse itself will dominate, and these components, dealing with sins against God and corresponding punishments by God, will generate considerable interest.

The body of the sermon is divided into two large sections, linked with the first and the second parallel halves of the theme-verse. Each of these sections in turn is divided into four sub-sections based on the preacher's ingenuity in providing four different interpretations for each half of the verse. And each of these subsections has two parts, one dealing with sin, the other with punishment. Thus the first section provides four separate interpretations of "They provoked My jealousy with a non-god," two of them applying to the false gods that the Jews worshipped, two applying to their attitude to the true God, and four interpretations of "I'll provoke their jealousy with a non-people," two of them applying to the external source of oppression, and two applying to denial of the proper status for the Jews themselves. The second section gives four different interpretations of "vexed Me with their trivialities" and "am naval" (the meaning "ignorant nation" is only one of the four). The outline would be as follows:

I. In the relationship of a **wife**

Sin (be-lo eil)	**Punishment** (be-lo 'am)
1.a. They honor a "not-god"	*1.b. "Not-God's-people" will claim to be*
2.a. source of benefits "not God"	*2.b. Jews described as "Not-God's-people"*
3.a. They consider God to be "not God"	*3.b. Jews considered as "not-a-people"*
4.a. They honor "no-single-[false] god"	*4.b. "No-single-people" will oppress them*

II. In the relationship of **children**

Sin (be-havleihem)	**Punishment** (be-'am naval)
They trivialize what is important:	
1.a. the commandments	*1.b. by a* contemptible *nation*
2.a. God's miracles	*2.b. by an* ungrateful *nation*
They make important what is trivial:	
3.a. idolatry	*3.b. by a* miserly *people*
4a. divination and witchcraft	*4.b. by a* foolish *people*

By the time the rabbinic dictum is introduced, one has the feeling that both the preacher and the congregation are ready for the end. The midrashic passage applies the first verses of Psalm 1 to the story of the serpent's enticement of Eve, the paradigmatic sin. Morteira then applies this to the four components of the second part of the sermon: the counsel of the serpent was to trivialize God's instructions in every conceivable way. In this way a homiletical connection is drawn from the very beginning of the Bible, through an overview of Jewish historical experience in biblical times, to an implied application (not nearly as explicit as in the previous sermon) to the religious life-style of the listeners, ending finally with the traditional hope for the messianic advent that will put an end to all this sinfulness and punishment.

* * *

(313r) ***They provoked My jealousy with a non-god, vexed Me with their trivialities; I'll provoke their jealousy with a non-people, with an ignorant nation I'll vex them*** (Deut. 32:21).[1]

In the Midrash: *Happy is the man who has not followed the counsel of the wicked* (Ps. 1:1): this is speaking about the First Man, [who said], "Happy am I for not having followed the counsel of the serpent." *Or taken the path of sinners* (ibid.): "Happy am I for not having taken the path of the serpent." *Or joined the company of the insolent* (ibid.): "Happy am I for not having joined the com-

---

1. Although we cannot be certain how Morteira translated this verse into Portuguese at the beginning of the sermon, we do have his translation of it in the *Tratado: Elles Me prouocaraō a zello com o que naō hera deos, Me ensanharaō com suas uanidades; e Eu os prouocarej a zello com o que naō saō pouo, com jente nescia os farej ensanhar* (*Tratado*, p. 155, l. 7–10; and [with slight differences], p. 133, l. 28–30). The Ferrara translation rendered the verse, *Ellos me hizieron zelar con el que no Dio, hizieronme ensañar con sus nadas; y yo los haré zelar con lo que no pueblo, con gente vil los haré ensañar.* Bertil Maler, *A Bíblia na Consolaçam de Samuel Usque (1553)* (Stockholm, 1974), p. 15. The Spanish and Portuguese are both quite close to the Hebrew, using the same verbs and noun constructions in both parts of the verse, and replicating the syntactic chiasmus in the second part (Usque's Portuguese is a bit freer: Maler, *Bíblia*, p. 14). Morteira's dependence on the Spanish may be seen in his use of the cognate *ensanhar* for the Hebrew words meaning to make angry, where Usque uses two different expressions (*a yra me espertarom, prejudicarey*). On the other hand, Morteira (and Usque) depart from the Spanish in their use of *vaidades* (or Morteira's Hispanicized *uanidades* for the Hebrew *hevel* in place of the Spanish *nadas*, and in the phrase *jente nescia*, an ignorant people, for Hebrew *'am naval*, rendered in Spanish *gente vil*, a vile or contemptible people. Both of these meanings are used in the course of the sermon; for his Portuguese translation at the beginning of the sermon, he had to commit to one of them. My own translation here is based on Morteira's Portuguese from the *Tratado*; versions in the continuation of the sermon will attempt to reflect how he is actually using the ambiguities of the Hebrew.

pany of the insolent serpent." R. Joshua of Sikhnin said in the name of R. Levi, "The serpent spoke slander about his Creator. He said to Eve, "Why do you not eat from this tree?" She replied, "God commanded us not to eat from it and not to touch it." He pushed her into the tree, and she did not die. Then he said, "Just as death has not befallen you for touching it, so it will not befall you for eating it."[2]

Exordium

There are places where a husband and wife acquire the name "household." For example, the rabbinic interpretation of the verse *He will make expiation for himself and for his household* (Lev. 16:6) is, "his household" means "his wife."[3] Similarly, *He shall be exempt for one year for his household* (Deut. 24:5).[4] However, a household is not termed complete and fully built without children. Proof for this is in the verse, *each coming with his household* (Exod. 1:1), for although the names of the wives of Jacob's sons are not given, the phrase *each coming with his household* refers to their children, which they brought to Egypt.[5] Similarly, the Psalmist wrote, *He sets the childless woman in her house* (Ps. 113:9), for although she was already married [???] the house is not said to be complete until she has children.[6] And thus *God restores individuals to their houses* (Ps. 68:6), [giving] them "houses." Therefore, the word for "children," *banim*, is derived from the word for "building," *binyan*,[7] for a house without children is like a house destroyed [???] upon its foundation, but with children it is built.[8] And so Rachel said, *that I may be built through her* (Gen. 30:3).[9] And also, *Thus*

---

2. Cf. Midrash Tehillim 1,9, the text in the second part of the passage is somewhat different.

3. Lev. Rabbah 5,6; cf. also M. *Yoma* 1,1.

4. The context makes it clear that the verse is referring to the man's new wife.

5. Morteira is following ibn Ezra here, who interprets the word "his household" to refer not to the wives but to the children.

6. Here too Morteira follows ibn Ezra, who writes that the word *'aqeret* ("childless woman") stands independently of *ha-bayit* ('the house') and is not in construct with it. Here and in some of the following lines, individual words are indecipherable because of damage to the page at the left margin where it is bound. Lacunae are indicated by [???].

7. Perhaps recalling the familiar statement from b. *Berakhot* 64a, "do not read *banayikh* ("your children"—in Isa. 54:13) but rather *bonayikh* ("your builders").

8. Cf. Rashi on Genesis 16:2, based on Gen. Rabbah 45,2.

9. See ibn Ezra on the similar phrase in Genesis 16:2: "*ebbaneh* is derived from *ben*, 'child,' and it is also possible that the child is the image of a building, and the father is the foundation."

shall be done to the man who will not build up his brother's household (Deut. 25:9).[10]
Thus the complete, well-established house is composed of a man, a woman,
and children. Accordingly, when God built His house in the lower realms—
He being in the lower realms because that is where His house is—the
completion of His household required these three [components]: a man, a
woman, and children.

Now indeed, we find in many places that "God's house" is the people of
Israel. First, what King David said in Psalm 52. After having proclaimed the
evil of Doeg the Edomite in his slander, and the punishment that he would
receive for this sin, David said, *So God will tear you down for good, will break you
and pluck you from your tent, and root you out of the land of the living, Selah* (Ps.
52:7). He then said the opposite about himself: *But I am like a luxuriant olive
tree in God's house* (Ps. 52:10), meaning, within the congregation of the Eternal,
which is called "God's house." Similarly, Scripture refers to the congregation
of the Eternal as "house dwellers," as in the verse, *The kings and their armies are
in headlong flight, house dwellers are sharing the spoils* (Ps. 68:13).[11] A similar
meaning is in the verse, *Your decrees are indeed enduring; holiness befits Your house,
O God, for all times* (Ps. 93:5). For after the Psalmist mentioned the multitude
of nations, metaphorically expressed by the sound of might waters, and said,
The ocean sounds, O God, the ocean sounds its thunder... (ibid. 3), *but above the
thunder of the mighty waters, more majestic than the breakers of the sea* (ibid. 4)—all
this referring to the nations that have passed[12]—he then says that the final
sovereignty will be for the people of God, and it will not be destroyed. Scripture is full of this. This therefore is the meaning of *Your decrees are indeed enduring; holiness befits Your house, O God, for all times* (ibid. 5). The prophet Jeremiah spoke of the components of the house when he said, *I have abandoned
My house, I have deserted My estate, I have given over My dearly beloved into the hands
of her enemies* (Jer. 12:7). He first mentioned the house as a whole, saying *I have
abandoned My house,* and then he went on to specify in detail. First he mentioned the children, which are called "estate"—as in the verse, *Children are the
estate of the Eternal* (Ps. 127:3), and so are the children of Israel [??? ???], *for
God's portion is His people, Jacob His own estate* (Deut. 32:9). Then Jeremiah said,

10. The context makes it clear that it is speaking about providing children in his brother's
name.

11. Cf. ibn Ezra: "the congregation that remained in Jerusalem;" Me'iri: *nevat bayit* is "the
community of Israel."

12. This interpretation of the mighty waters as referring to the nations of the world is
similar to an alternative, eschatological reading of the Psalm (*ve-yesh mefarshim..*) cited by
Menahem Me'iri, *Perush le-Sefer Tehillim,* ed. Joseph Cohn (Jerusalem, 1936), pp. 184–85.

I have given over My dearly beloved into the hands of her enemies (Jer. 12:7), referring to the wife, who is the other component that binds the house together.[13]

Regarding the breakup of this house in all its components, the prophet Isaiah provided a justification when he said, *Thus says the Eternal, Where is the bill of divorce of your mother whom I dismissed? And which of My creditors was it to whom I sold you off? You were sold off for your sins, and your mother dismissed for your crimes* (Isa. 50:1). Here the prophet divided the nation of Israel into mother and children, in addition to God. The father explains how this bond had come apart because of them, not because of Him. When sins caused a division among [the components] of this great house, the author of Lamentations constructed his work upon these components, basing the three verses that begin the series of alphabetical acrostics with the word "How"[14] upon the three components of the house. (This is in addition to another correct meaning that we explained this year on the verse *We set out from Horeb* (Deut. 1:19) from the lesson *Devarim*.[15])

The first ["How"] pertains to the wife. About her, he said, *How lonely sits the city once great with people! She that was great among the nations is become like a widow* (Lam. 1:1), for this mother is left [alone?]—not an actual widow—in that her husband has left her. The second "How" speaks of the separation between the father and [his household], saying, *How the Eternal in His wrath has beclouded fair Zion, has cast down from heaven to earth the majesty of Israel. He did not remember His footstool in the day of His wrath* (Lam. 2:1), meaning that He has placed a cloud, a kind of screen, between Himself and "fair Zion" His wife, as in the verse, *You have screened yourself off with a cloud, that no prayer may pass through* (Lam. 3:44). And if He brought with Him a picture or image of his wife, He threw it down from heaven [as He returned] to the place where He was going, as in the verse, "I will go and return to My place."[16] This is the

---

13. Compare the use of this verse from Jeremiah in the *Ha'azinu* sermon on Deut. 32:12, where Morteira makes the three elements of the verse *beiti, nahalati, yedidut* (*nafshi*) an acronym for *banai* ("my children"): above, p. 450. And cf. his use of the verse in *Tratado*, p. 131, where he speaks of four metaphorical titles for the Jewish people: wife, children, brothers (i.e., God's people), and servants.

14. I.e., Lam. 1:1, 2:1, and 4:1, each of which begins with the word *eikhah*, initiating a series of 22 verses, each beginning with a successive letter of the alphabet. Lam. 3:1, which does not begin with *eikhah*, is an alphabetical acrostic with three verses beginning with each successive letter. See Rashi on Lam. 1:1.

15. None of the sermons on the lesson *Devarim* has been preserved in the extant collection of manuscripts. Note that in the same year, Morteira preached on the 19th verse of *Devarim* and the 21st verse of *Ha'azinu*, indicating that there were two years when he either did not preach on *Devarim* or repeated a sermon.

16. *Elkhah va-ashuvah li-meqomi*. There is no such verse; cf. Hos. 2:9 and Exod. 4:18. On

meaning of *He has cast down from heaven to earth the majesty of Israel* (Lam. 2:1). And He did not remember or think about the beauty of His house, His palace where He lived with his wife: *He did not remember His footstool in the day of His wrath* (ibid.).

Above, it is relevant to note[17] that the husband is obligated to provide for his wife food, clothing, and conjugal rights (Exod. 21:10). When this husband travels away from his wife, all these are lacking to her [???]. For *How lonely sits the city* (Lam. 1:1) alludes to conjugal rights, and *she has become like a widow* (ibid.) alludes to her clothing—as we see in the verse, *So she took over her widow's clothing* (Gen. 38:14)—and *the princess among states has become a thrall* (Lam. 1:1) alludes to her food, for the enemy has consumed her sustenance.

The third component is the children. About them he said, *How the gold is dulled, debased the finest gold, the sacred gems* (avnei qodesh) *are spilled at every street corner* (Lam 4:1). The word *avnei* is actually derived from the word *banai*, "my children," and the "sacred gems" are the children of the living God, spilled and scattered.[18] Thus we see [???] here that the lamentations are constructed upon the breakup of the components of this house, the house of God.

Now we must ask the following question. In every household, these components are readily distinguishable, for there is a great [difference] between the wife and the children; The wife is not the children, and the children are not the wife; each one of them has its own distinct quality. However, in this household of God that we are discussing, the components are not separate and distinct, for the people of Israel are both the wife and the children. What then is the element that distinguishes them, that entitles us to say, this is (**313b**) the wife, and this is the children? *Where is the bill of divorce of your mother whom I dismissed? And which of My creditors was it to whom I sold you off?* (Isa. 50:1). I would say that when the people of Israel are designated by the term "wife," the meaning is the entire nation or a large group of them, but when they are designated by the term "children," this refers to specific individuals. We know

---

the casting down of the image of the beloved, cf. the aggadah about God's casting down the image of Jacob on His throne in Lam. Rabbah 2,2 and the version closer to that here cited by Samuel Uceda, *Lehem Dim'ah*, on this verse. Both, however, speak of the image of Jacob, not the image of the estranged wife.

17. *U-le-'eil shayakh lomar*: apparently the preacher's note to himself indicating that he should mention this point when he cites the first verse beginning with *Eikhah*, pertaining to the relationship with the wife.

18. Cf. Rashi ad loc.: the "sacred gems" and "children who shine like gems." Samuel Uceda on this verse cites an interpretation that *avnei* is composed of the words *av* ("father") and *ben* ("child").

that God has two kinds of providence—individual and general—and provides two kinds of guidance, one for the totality and the other for the individual.

With this distinction, we may understand a difficult verse by probing its meaning deeply. The Lamenter said, *We have become orphans, fatherless; our mothers are like widows* (Lam. 5:3). Surely it needs to be asked, who is speaking here? Is it Israel, or the young children, or the old fathers, or both of them together? If we say it is the children, this is impossible, for they are not part of the community, and it is inappropriate for the young ones to speak in the presence of their elders. And if their fathers have already died, then they are the community, but why would they say *like widows?* Their mothers would indeed be actual widows! But if it is the fathers speaking, why would they say *our mothers are like widows?* They should have said, "Our wives are like widows." And if both groups together, there is still a problem from this point.

But the meaning is that the separate individuals are speaking: *We have become orphans, fatherless.* "Fatherless" is written [despite the redundancy] to indicate that we have become orphans because of the poverty and degradation—that is what makes us seem like orphans, not because of the absence of our father, for our father still lives, but he has traveled away from us. It is as if it said, "orphans, but not from [the death of] a father." This applies to each and every individual. However, our communities are *like widows*, for they do not have the general orderliness and splendor that we have had from of old.

God commanded that His prophet Moses speak to the Israelites in his address before Mount Sinai about each of these two separate kinds of guidance and the two distinct aspects of the relationship between God and His people. Thus Moses was to inform them on the day of God's wedding and His heartfelt rejoicing that in their totality they would be betrothed to Him and accept His covenant with all the conditions that pertain to the relationship between husband and wife, while individually they would be as children to Him and He would be as their father. For such is the complete home: one wife and many children.

This is why the Torah says, *Moses went up to God, and the Eternal called to him from the mountain, saying, "Thus shall you say to the house of Jacob and declare to the children of Israel"* (Exod. 19:3). Now the duplication is obvious in this verse, and the Sages felt the need to explain it. They said, *"Thus shall you say to the house of Jacob:* these are the women, *and declare to the children of Israel:* these are the men."[19] But there is a problem: are the women so fundamental for the reception of Torah that he should begin with them? Why they are exempt

---

19. *Mekhilta Ba-Ḥodesh,* chap. 2 (ed. Lauterbach 2:201).

from some of the commandments! Rather, the Sages had a deeper meaning in mind. *Thus shall you say to the house of Jacob* alludes to the beginning of the home, the wife, namely the household of God composed of the totality of the nation; that is why it is expressed in the singular, for this is the foundation, the starting point. *And declare to the children of Israel*: this is what pertains to the separate individuals; therefore it says "to the children," plural. And the preceding verse also made this distinction: *They journeyed from Rephidim, they entered the wilderness of Sinai, and they encamped in the wilderness; Israel encamped there in front of the mountain* (Exod. 19:2). It explains that there were two [???], namely two meanings and referents, one in relationship to God like a bride, and the other like children. That is why it says "they encamped" referring to the many, and "Israel encamped," singular, referring to the individual. This is appropriate.

In the *Ha'azinu* poem, where nothing is missing, Moses did not refrain from showing us these two aspects of the relationship of God's people with their God, and all that can be derived from each one of these aspects. He said, *Remember the days of old, consider the years of ages past; ask your father, he will inform you, your elders, they will tell you: when the Most High gave nations their homes*, etc. (Deut. 32:6–7). What should you ask, and what will they tell you? *For the portion of the Eternal is His people, Jacob His own estate* (Deut. 32:9). Now the first part teaches about the relationship and the role of the totality of the nation with God as a wife to her husband, for she is called a "portion," as in the verse, *Enjoy happiness with the woman you love... for this is your portion in life,* etc. (Eccles. 9:9). The same is true of Israel, when it says, *these the Eternal your God apportioned ...*(Deut. 4:9), *but you the Eternal took ...*(Deut. 4:20). The second part teaches about the relationship of children to their father: *Jacob His own estate,* for children are called "estate," as in the verse, *Children are the estate of the Eternal* (Ps. 127:3).

Now concerning all the beneficent acts that God performed with them relating to the totality, Moses said, *He found him in a desert region, in an empty howling waste; He engirded him,* etc. (Deut. 32:10). This is in abbreviated form what Ezekiel developed at length, expressing what God did with the people of Israel through the image of a daughter, a small destitute girl lying on a heap of garbage, whom He cleaned up and took to himself, as you can find throughout chapter 16 of Ezekiel. However, what God did for them in their role as children he expressed by saying, *Like an eagle who rouses his nestlings, gliding down to his young,* etc. (Deut. 32:11). Yet they are like a wife who rebels against her husband, despite her obligation toward him regarding purity and modesty. About them he said, *They provoked Him with alien things* (Deut. 32:16), meaning that they filled Him with jealousy; *they sacrificed to demons, non-gods* (Deut. 32:17). And in their rebellion against Him in the role of children against their father, he said, *You neglected the Rock that begot you, forgot the God who brought you forth. The Eternal saw and was vexed with anger at His sons and daughters* (Deut. 32:18–19).

Keeping consistently to this order, Moses explained the punishment for both categories—the wife and the children, the totality and the individuals. Concerning the first he said, *For they are a treacherous generation* (Deut. 32:20), referring to the entire generation in the singular. Then concerning the individuals he said, *children with no loyalty in them* (ibid.). He then incorporated their sin and their punishment, measure for measure, into a single verse, which is our Text. Corresponding to the wife he said, *They provoked My jealousy with a non-god* (Deut. 32:21); concerning the children, *they vexed Me with their trivialities*; as for those who provoked Me, *I'll provoke their jealousy with a non-people*, as for those who vex Me, *with an ignorant nation I'll vex them*. How the phrase *They provoked My jealousy with a non-god* is related to the wife, namely the totality of the people, and how *they vexed Me with their trivialities* is related to the children, namely the individuals, and similarly how the punishment is related to these sins—that will be our discourse today, inasmuch as our Text fits the day, the Sabbath of Repentance. We shall now begin it with the help of God who said, *Instead of being called "You are Not-My-People," they shall be called "Children-of-the-Living God"* (Hos. 2:1).[20]

Body of the Sermon, Part I

1.a. Given that, as we have said, the people of Israel are related to God in the totality and as individuals, as a wife and as children to her husband and their father, in speaking to our community, God addresses them as a wife and as children, each in accordance with the nature of the relationship. For example, in the first two of the Ten Commandments, which are directly from the mouth of God, using the first-person, He consecrates the nation to be as a wife to Him as one who says "I will be to you and you will be to Me," as in the verse, *I am my beloved's and my beloved is mine* (Song 6:3). *I the Eternal am your God* (Exod. 20:2) refers to My relationship to you; *You shall have no other gods besides me* (Exod. 20:3) refers to your relationship with Me. This is a matter belonging entirely to the totality of the people. However, the eight succeeding commandments use the third-person [in referring to God], for the intimacy

---

20. The conclusion of the Exordium with an invocation of help from God. The phrase "not-My-people" (*lo 'ami*) in the verse from Hosea echoes the "non-people" (*lo 'am*) in the theme-verse.

with children is not as great as that with one's wife. In these He commanded reverence for the father, not swearing in vain, and recognition of His sovereignty: *Remember the Sabbath day* (Exod. 20:8), meaning that all comes from Him. The honor due to Him is derived *a fortiori* from the honor due a father and mother; this is the meaning of *Honor your father and your mother* (Exod. 20:12). The commandments also ordain peaceful relations among them, namely among the children: *You shall not murder; you shall not commit adultery; you shall not steal; you shall not covet* (Exod. 20:13–14).

Now with regard to these commandments, God gauged each one of the aforementioned categories. Regarding the wife—the totality of the people—they sinned in the matter of faith and the Godhead, for this is something that depends on the totality, like the sin of a wife against her husband. About this Moses said, **They provoked My jealousy with a non-god.** This was the primal sin: arousing God's wrath by giving the honor due Him to that which has no power or ability. This sin is intensified because what the people chose is worthless and base. We see this in the verse, *They exchanged their glory for the image of a bull that feeds on grass* (Ps. 106:20), as Rashi explains, "that has no use, for if it had a use, the jealousy would not be so compounded."[21] We have already dwelt at length with convincing proofs upon one aspect of the enormity of this sin (**314r**), namely the aspect of the laborer who exchanges something of infinite value for something incomparably more menial. This sin is greater than if it had been exchanged for something that had some use. This is in my sermon for the present Torah lesson, on the verse, *They sacrificed to demons, non-gods* (Deut. 32:17).[22]

The jealousy aroused by this is indeed intense, as in the case of a wife who causes jealousy in her husband by giving the honor due him to another who is extremely base and contemptible. This is what the Poet said in the aforementioned verse, *They exchanged their glory for the image of a bull that feeds on grass* (Ps. 106:20), which the Aramaic translation renders, "[They exchanged] the glory of their Master for the image of a bull." Thus "their glory" is an epithet for God's glory, as R. Abraham ibn Ezra explained in his commentary there. It is also possible to explain this verse according to its simple meaning. Since God ordained for His service and His glory the rituals of offering incense, sacrificing animals, making libations, and bowing down,[23] whoever worships idolatrously with one of these acts, even if this is not the normal way of worshipping the false god, is to be proscribed, in accordance with the rab-

---

21. See Rashi and Targum on Deut. 32:17.
22. This sermon has not been preserved in the extant manuscripts.
23. B. *Sanhedrin* 65a.

binic interpretation of the verse *Whoever sacrifices to a god other than the Eternal alone shall be proscribed* (Exod. 22:19).[24] It is as if they are provoking jealousy when they act this way toward any other than God.

Now with regard to the calf, the Torah says, *They have made themselves a molten calf and bowed low to it and sacrificed to it, saying, This is your god, O Israel* (Exod. 32:8). In the word "sacrificed," three acts are included, for the sacrifice entails slaughter, and incense, and the pouring of libations; bowing down is a separate act in itself.[25] Accordingly, the Psalmist said, *They exchanged their glory* (Ps. 106:20), referring to the glory that was theirs, with which they would honor God—they exchanged this *for the image of a bull,* etc. (ibid.), and they made that glory his. And there is no greater sin than this, for they did not honor the calf with other ways of expressing honor, but rather they aroused God's jealousy by honoring the calf with acts appropriate to God—and all this for something that is nothing at all! *They provoked My jealousy with a non-god.* This is what drew the rebukes of Ezekiel against the woman who took the splendid clothes and jewels that her husband had given her and honored idols with them (cf. Ezek. 16:17).[26] There is no jealousy greater than this: *They provoked My jealousy with a non-god.*

b. God punished them measure for measure: *I'll provoke their jealousy with not-the-people.* This means, I will arrange it so that a people that is not Mine[27] will arouse their jealousy in that they will attribute to themselves all the be-

---

24. B. *Sanhedrin* 60b, Maimonides, *Code, Hilkhot 'Aku "m* 3, 3.

25. Bowing down is not included under the category of "sacrificing" in Exod. 32:8 but is prohibited by a separate commandment in Exodus 34:14 (see the sources in the previous note).

26. Cf. Morteira's use of this verse at the beginning of his answer to the eleventh question of the "Priest from Rouen," *www.jewish-history.com/Occident/volume3/nov1845/questions.html.*

27. Morteira interprets *lo 'am* here to mean that the punishment is at the hands of a people that is "*not* the people" of God but that claims to be so, i.e., the Christians. It is striking that some Christian thinkers, influenced by Paul's use of this verse (Rom. 10:19), applied the phrase "non-people" to their own claim of replacing the Jews as the true Israel. Calvin, for example, insisted that Deut. 32:21 was not fulfilled during the biblical period but only after the advent of Jesus, "when the Gospel was spread throughout the whole world": "Seeing that the Jews have provoked God's wrath by refusing to embrace his only son, therefore hath He raised up a people which was nothing afore:" *The Sermons of M. John Calvin Upon the Fifth Booke of Moses called Deuteronomie* (London,, 1593; facsimile edition: Edinburgh, 1987), p. 1136b, ll. 34–35, p. 1137b ll. 51–54. Where Morteira used the verse to chastise his Jewish listeners, Calvin used this theme to promote humility among the Christians ("until such time as God hath chosen us, and drawn us to the knowledge of his truth, it is all one as if we were not at all.... Let us assure ourselves that if we provoke God to wrath, and make him as it were jealous, he will surely raise up other Nations in our stead; ... therefore let the Jews be a looking-glass for us to make us behave ourselves humbly," p. 1138b ll. 21–23, p. 1139a ll.

neficent acts and the virtues that I have bestowed upon Israel. They will claim that I have bestowed this upon them, that I have chosen them. For this is an important matter, worthy of pondering, when we see that in our exile it would have been possible to be among a people that, in its religion and its characteristics was very, very different from us, since God handed us over into its power.[28] For behold, they have divided the categories within the [Christian] nation as we do into priests and Levites with rights to tithes and a kind of High Priest patterned after us. They have invented a congregation of seventy-one, a kind of Sanhedrin.[29] Look at the holy days of the year: they have, like us, made a kind of Sabbath and Pesach and Shavuot. They have invented a "jubilee" year.[30] The structure of their communion is patterned after our prayer of sanctification (*Qiddush*) and blessing over bread (*Motsi*). The text of their liturgy is derived from our prophets. The "miracles" they placed in their books are precisely those that are written in our Sacred Scriptures—there is nothing else, as we have discussed at length in its proper place, showing one by one what corresponds to everything of theirs. Their baptism they took from our immersion of the ritually impure. And so with many of the things they boast were given them by God.[31]

Why all this? In order to provoke *us* with jealousy when, in return for our

---

9–12, 36v–38. (In the quotations, I have modernized the English spelling from the late-sixteenth-century translation by Arthur Golding.)

28. Note that in the earlier *Ha'azinu* sermon, Morteira presented the exile among Christians who accepted the Hebrew Scriptures as a beneficent act of divine providence (above, p. 471). Here he presents the similarities between Christianity and Judaism as divine punishment, intended to provoke the jealousy of the Jewish people.

29. The number of cardinals was fixed at 70 by Pope Sixtus V in his bull "Postquam verus" of December 3, 1586 (see *The Catholic Encyclopedia*, 15 vols., New York, 1908, 14:34a). The "Consistory," in which the pope met together with the cardinals, would thus have appeared as a "kind of Sanhedrin." Needless to say, the number 70 was not based on the Jewish Sanhedrin, but it may have derived from the 70 elders in biblical times.

30. The "jubilee" or Holy Year was first proclaimed by Pope Boniface VIII for the year 1300. In 1468, Pope Paul II decreed it would be observed every 25 years, and that was the practice in Morteira's time.

31. It is not clear to me to what "place" Morteira is referring when he cites his detailed discussion of the "miracles" described in the New Testament. Usually when he refers to one of his sermons, he does so more explicitly than this. It may be to one of the vernacular polemical treatises, perhaps his "Tratado das Controuersias dos Euangelios," which he cites several times in his "Treatise on the Truth of the Law of Moses" (*Tratado*, pp. 827 and 1039, cf. p. 5, and see Salomon's notes on pp. 1242 and 1249). In the large "Tratado," completed much later than this sermon, Morteira incorporated a passage quite similar to the one cited here: "Particularmente, ordenarão frades a imitação dos sacerdotes, clerigos a imitação dos leuitas, el papa a modo do Sumo Pontifice. Ordenaranlhe as dezimas como na Lej deuina se mandaua dar aos sacerdotes, as festas aos tempos e modo das antigas, a hostia e cea a

extending the honor due to God to the false gods, which are not divine, they claim the honors which are really ours, though they are not God's people. *I'll provoke their jealousy with not-the-people.* This is what the Poet spoke of in Psalm 74: *Your foes roar inside Your meeting-place; they take their signs for true signs. Till when, O God, will the foe blaspheme, will the enemy forever revile Your name?* (Ps. 74:4,10). This means that they call themselves by Your name, and though they are not-the-people, they claim to be Your people, which is a reviling of Your name. Despite it all, God is silent and consents to punish Israel with a measure of their own making. This is the meaning of *Why do You hold back Your hand, Your right hand? Draw it out of Your bosom!* (Ps. 74:11)—like a man who acquiesces and does not act, who stands by watching and does not protest, until the sin is recognized and the punishment is accepted.

2.a. There is a second meaning to the phrase *They provoked My jealousy with "not-God,"* this too relating to the rebellion of a wife against her husband, who gives her all that she needs—food and drink and clothing, everything that she needs—yet she does not recognize any of this. Rather, she says that all the wealth she has attained has nothing to do with her husband. Or when troubles come as a result of her husband's separation from her, she does not recognize that this is their cause. This is rebelliousness, a treacherous failure in the recognition that a wife owes her husband. It is the also rebuke with which Israel is criticized here: *They provoked My jealousy with "not-God."* This means that *When Jeshurun grew fat and flailed ... it forsook the God who made it* (Deut. 32:15), saying, *"My own power and the might of my own hand have won this wealth for me"*(Deut. 8:17), that all this goodness came to them independent of God. This is like the statement that those accursed women made to Jeremiah: *"Ever since we stopped making offerings to the Queen of Heaven [...] we have lacked everything"* (Jer. 44:18). This is *They provoked My jealousy with "not-God,"* meaning, when good things happened to them they said that they attained them without God.[32] Similarly in their punishment they attribute everything to chance, saying that everything occurs to them randomly, without God. This provokes intense jealousy. For when God favors them in His kindness, so that they will serve Him with joy, or when He gives them a reward for their deeds, and they, who are indebted for this goodness, attribute the good things to another cause, they provoke jealousy so that God will not continue to favor them. And when He chastises them in their sinfulness with chastisements of love intended to lead them back to what is

---

imitação do cordero pasqual. E tudo isso para pareser e representar hum nouo Jsrael:" *Tratado,* p. 129; for the lack of originality in miracles, ibid., p. 381. Cf. also *GS* 1645, p. 86d.

32. In this second reading of the phrase, *lo-el* refers not to worship of a non-god but to denial of the role of the true God in the destiny of the people.

right, and they attribute these to chance, this also provokes jealousy to increase the chastisements with blows of unusual cruelty, so that they will return. This is, ***They provoked My jealousy with "not-God."***

All I have mentioned here is the subject of the prophet's rebuke of Israel when he said, *An ox knows its owner, an ass its masters' crib; Israel does not know, My people takes no thought* (Isa. 1:3). The meaning here is not merely the *a fortiori* argument from the irrational beast to the rational human being. If that were the case, the ox or the ass alone would suffice. Furthermore, why in one instance the owner, in another the crib? Does not the ox know the crib, does not the ass know its owner? But the *a fortiori* argument applies in both directions, in the following way. The ox is a powerful animal, capable of acting destructively against man, goring with its horns. Despite this, it subjects itself to the yoke and the goad, knowing the authority its owner has over it. Yet Israel, which has absolutely no capability or power against its Maker, blessed be He, tosses off the yoke and flails at the chastisements; it does not recognize their source but attributes them to chance.

And the ass, although it works laboriously, and his master acquires him for his toil, recognizes its masters' crib. It does not say *"its* crib" but "its masters' crib," meaning that it depends upon the masters to feed it, for its labor belongs to them since its body does. But My people takes no thought of that fact that because it was created, it should serve God without reward, since it brings no benefit at all to God through its actions, for *If you are righteous, what do you give Him? If your transgressions are many, how do you affect Him?* (Job 35:6–7). Yet despite this, God graciously acts beneficently toward it, as if it deserved this. My people gives this no thought; they have not recognized God, neither in times of good nor in times of punishment. Therefore, ***They provoked My jealousy with "not-God."*** This is a great evil, for the way to sustain well-being and avoid misfortune is through recognition that when good things occur, one should thank God for them, thereby obligating Him to sustain the good as a reward for this thanksgiving. But the failure to recognize this is itself an evil that obligates God to sustain misfortune, so that one will recognize and achieve the intended purpose.

With this in mind, we may understand the interconnection of Solomon's statements in chapter 3 [of Proverbs], for they seem to be speaking about very different matters. He said, *In all your ways acknowledge Him, and He will make your paths straight. Do not be wise in your own eyes, fear God and shun evil. It will be a cure for your body, a tonic for your bones. Honor God with your wealth, with the best of all your income, and your barns will be filled with grain, your vats will burst with new wine* (Prov. 3:6–10). Says the Holy One, blessed be He: You are destined to [one of] two ways, either prosperity or its opposite. Know that neither one of them is by chance, but rather from God: *in all your ways acknowledge Him.* This is how you may attain the purpose intended, and *He will make your paths straight*, meaning that He will sustain the well-being if you find yourself in this state, and remove the misfortune from you. About the first[33] He said, *Do not be wise in your own eyes* so as to say that all this has come to me[34] from one or another accidental reason. *Fear God and shun evil*, for this is the cause. *It will be a cure for your body*, removing illness from you. About the second possibility, when you find yourself in a state of well-being, *Honor God with your wealth, with the best of all your income*, and recognize that the good comes from Him; in this way, *your barns will be filled with grain, your vats will burst with new wine.* However, this is not what Israel did. Rather, they failed to attribute any matter, whether good or bad, to God. That is, **They provoked My jealousy with "not-God."**

b. And God meted out to them measure for measure: **I'll provoke their jealousy with "not-the-people,"** meaning that the other peoples would provoke them by saying that God has abandoned them, that God does not watch providentially over them but has left them like abandoned property, and God is not with them.[35] This is in accordance with the verse, *they devour My people as they devour* (**314v**) *food, and do not invoke the Eternal* (Ps. 14:4), meaning without fear and trembling, as if they were eating bread. And this is what the author of Lamentations said, *The nations said, They shall live here no more* (Lam. 4:15), meaning, they *were* God's household,[36] and now He has banished them from His house, so that they will no longer dwell in His house. And this is what the Poet said in Psalm 69 in the name of the Israelite nation: *It is because of You that I have been reviled, that shame covers my face* (Ps. 69:8), meaning, why do they say to me that You have abandoned me and Your name is no longer invoked upon me? He then explained the nature of his shame: *I am a stranger to my brothers, an alien to my kin* (ibid. 9), meaning, the rest of the nations, who were designated as my brothers, my mother's children, have considered me to be a stranger, an alien—no longer the people of God.[37] This has provoked

---

33. From the continuation, this "first" possibility must refer to circumstances of misfortune.

34. The following two words, *me-ro'a hishtadluti*, do not make sense to me in context and seem to me to be extraneous.

35. Common assertions in Christian anti-Jewish polemics.

36. Picking up the theme from the Exordium of the Jewish people in its dual relationship of wife and children as God's "house."

37. While the first meaning of *lo am* refers to punishment at the hands of a people that is "not the people" of God, this second meaning is the punishment that others will *describe* the Jews as "not the people" of God any longer.

me to great jealousy. *For the jealousy of Your house has been my undoing; the reproaches of those who revile You have fallen upon me* (ibid. 10). It is as we explained: His "house" refers to His wife and His children, and the nations say to me that this house is destroyed, and that we will not longer live there. That is the meaning of *the jealousy of Your house has been my undoing.*

This is what the Psalmist meant when he said, *Not to us, O God, not to us but to Your name bring glory, for the sake of Your love and Your truthfulness. Why should the nations say, "Where, now, is their God?" when our God is in heaven and all that He wills He accomplishes* (Ps. 115:1-2). I find it difficult to understand how the nations would say about the God of Israel, "Where now is your God?"—as if they denied His divinity. Why the nations confess Him everywhere! The Sages said, "They call Him the God of gods" (b. *Menaḥot* 110a). This means that they have always recognized His divinity, but they thought there were many gods in the world, in accordance with the various climates.

In my view, the meaning is that when the nations saw the terrible things that occurred to the Jews, they made fun of them and used this as proof that God had abandoned them and was no longer their God. That is the meaning of "Where now is *their* God?"—speaking not about the existence of God but about His being *their* God. For our God removed His presence to the heavens because of our sins.[38] Everything that happens to us comes from Him, and *all that He wills He accomplishes.* Even the sailors in the Jonah story recognized this, saying, *For You, O God, by Your will, have brought this about* (Jonah 1:14). Therefore, *Not to us, O God, not to us but to Your name* which you have proclaimed upon us *give glory, for the sake of Your love* (Ps. 115:1), for from the beginning You have chosen us as a people through your love, *and Your truthfulness,* with which You subsequently swore to us to be our God, binding Yourself, and You keep Your word. In this regard, God promised, *Instead of being told, "Your are Not-My-People," they shall be called "Children-of-the-Living-God"* (Hos. 2:1). This is the meaning of **I'll provoke them with "not-the-people": they provoked My jealousy with "not-God,"** in failing to remember Me when they spoke, saying that God has abandoned the land (Ezek. 9:9), **and I'll provoke them with "not-the-people,"** in that the nations will say to them that they are not My people, and that I have abandoned them.

3.a. Similarly, there is a third meaning. He said, **They provoked My jealousy with "not God,"** as if to say that they provoked My jealousy by not consider-

---

38. *Tanḥuma* (Warsaw), *Naso*, chap. 16; *Pirqei de R. Eliezer*, chap. 1; Bialik and Ravnitzky, *Sefer ha-Aggadah*, p. 145.

ing Me to be God.[39] They did not even make me a partner among the false gods they chose for themselves.[40] This is in accordance with what we find in the Book of Judges, chapter 10, which the Sages interpreted beautifully in Tractate *Yom Tov*, chapter 3 (*Beitsah* 25b):

> The lupine will cut off the feet of the enemies of Israel,[41] for it is said, *The Israelites again did what was offensive to the Eternal. They served the Baalim and the Ashtaroth, and the gods of Aram, the gods of Sidon, the gods of Moab, the gods of the Ammonites, and the gods of the Philistines; they forsook the Eternal and did not serve Him* (Jud. 10:6). From the implication of *they forsook the Eternal,* do I not know that *they did not serve Him?* Then why does the text add, *and they did not serve Him?* R. Eleazar said, The Holy One, blessed be He, said, "My children have not even treated Me like the lupine, which is boiled seven times and eaten as a dessert."

Rashi, commenting on this passage, explained the phrase *they did not serve Him* as a complaint: God complained about them, saying "They made Me boil and provoked Me to anger seven times, the way one cooks the lupine, and still after all this I was not considered as anything by them."

The meaning is not—heaven forbid—that God would be satisfied if they would serve Him in partnership with the false gods. Certainly not! For the Torah states, *Whoever sacrifices to a god other than the Eternal alone shall be proscribed* (Exod. 22:19). And the Sages said, "Whoever associates the Heavenly Name in partnership with anything else will be uprooted from this world,"[42] and how much more so for idolatrous worship. Rather, the meaning is that if a person's thought moves to an extremely ugly level, we say to him, Can't you raise your thought to a level a little better, even if that too is vile? This is consistent with the statement of the Sages,[43] linking the verses *Ephraim is addicted to images—Let him be* (Hos. 4:17) and *Now that their heart is divided, they are*

---

39. The previous interpretation of "not-God" was the denial of God's responsibility for what happens to the Jewish people. Here it is the denial that He is actually God, denial that He is even one among many gods that may be worshipped.

40. This introduces the theological category of *shittuf* ("partnership'): rather than the full idolatry of worshipping only false gods, it refers to worshipping other "gods" alongside the true God. This became an important basis for medieval attempts to demark some theological legitimacy to Christianity. See Katz, *Exclusiveness and Tolerance*, pp. 35, 163; David Novak, *The Image of the Non-Jew in Judaism* (New York and Toronto, 1983), pp. 130–38. The idea of *shittuf* figured prominently in the responsa literature over the status of the *conversos*, and it undoubtedly had contemporary resonance for the listeners.

41. A euphemism for "Israel."

42. B. *Sanhedrin* 63a.

43. Gen. Rabbah 38,6; *Pesiqta Rabbati*, 4,1, and parallels.

guilty (Hos. 10:2). It is not that they give permission for idolatry, heaven forbid! Rather, when Ephraim is at peace, God holds back His anger from them for a longer time.[44] Similarly the statement in Tractate *Mo'ed Qatan* that God renounces His rights with regard to idolatry, but not with regard to profaning God's name, as is seen in the verse, *As for you, O House of Israel, thus says the Eternal God: Go, every one of you, and worship his fetishes and continue, if you will not obey Me, but do not profane My holy name any more with your idolatrous gifts* (Ezek. 20:39).[45] This means, since you have already decided not to obey My commandment, do it quietly, not publicly so as to profane My name. Similarly here: *They forsook the Eternal and did not serve Him*: even though the sin of linking the Heavenly Name in partnership with anything else is grave indeed, it is still more grave to worship false gods alone, and to forsake the true God completely. This is the meaning of *They provoked My jealousy with "not God,"* meaning that they did not include me among the "gods," even like that lupine.

Now against this complaint lodged here by the verse [Jud. 10:6] against Israel—that it worshipped false gods and did not worship God in partnership with them, for if they had worshipped Him in partnership their sin would not have been as grave—one may raise a problem from what we find in the seventh chapter of Tractate *Sanhedrin* (63a):

> R. Johanan said, "Were it not for the *vav* in the word *he'elukha*, [indicating that the verb *who brought you up* (Exod. 32:4) is plural], the haters of Israel[46] would have deserved extermination."[47] This is disputed by the Tannaim: Others say, "Were it not for the *vav* in the word *he'elukha*, the haters of Israel would have deserved extermination." Thereupon R. Simeon bar Yoḥai remarked, "But whoever links the Heavenly Name in partnership with anything else is removed from this world, for it is written, *Whoever sacrifices to a god other than the Eternal alone shall be proscribed* (Exod. 22:19).[48] What then is implied by the plural subject of *he'elukha*? That they lusted after many gods."

---

44. All the rabbinic sources use these verses to convey the message that when Jews are united (as in the time of Ephraim), God *does* allow even idolatry; the second verse applies to the time when Jews are divided, and God therefore holds them accountable. Morteira uses the passage differently, implying that idolatry is at best permitted only temporarily before the punishment that will come.

45. The statement is not in tractate *Mo'ed Qatan*; cf. b. *Qiddushin* 40a, the only place in the Talmud where the Ezekiel verse is quoted.

46. A euphemism for "Israel," as above, n. 41 and "The Land Shudders," n. 28.

47. The plural of the verb subject implies that the Israelites did not attribute the exodus to the golden calf alone, but rather to the calf and to the true God in partnership, thereby saving them from a sin punishable by annihilation.

Now R. Simeon bar Yohai has a sound argument, and in his judgment this matter of partnership is worse than lusting after many false gods, while if it is understood in accordance with the words of the "others," the "haters of Israel" would have deserved extermination. How than can the verse [in Judges 10:6] complain that the Israelites did not worship God in partnership?

To this we may reply that certainly the total abandonment of God, the failure to worship Him at all, is worse, as the verse in Judges indicates. However, [the mitigation of the sin of partnership applies] only if the worship of God is separated [from the worship of the false gods] in time and in substance. If it is done together with the worship of false gods, the evil is greater than if they had not made mention of God at all. For it is better not to make mention of the king than to mention him together with a contemptible slave. That is why R. Simeon bar Yohai raised his challenge from the verse *other than the Eternal alone.* For the verse could have said simply *other than the Eternal.* Why did it add the word "alone"? In order to teach that the worship of God must be alone. However, in the word, *he'elukha,* as R. Johanan understands the verse, they linked God together with the calf [and worshipped both together], and this is grounds for being uprooted from this world. But the verse in Judges complained that they forsook God and did not worship Him in addition to the others, for there is no graver sin than this. About this Moses said, *They provoked My jealousy with "not God."*

b. Now God meted out measure for measure, saying, *I'll provoke their jealousy with "non-people."* This means, in their depravity they chose for themselves the gods of the nations; they forsook Me and did not serve Me even in partnership [with the others]. I will also chastise them—but not on their own land, not so that they might remain a people like the other peoples within their kingdom, subject to a single king. Rather, I will scatter them among the nations, and disperse them through the lands (cf. Ezek. 36:19), so that no people will be found among them, and in their debasement they will not be considered even as a lowly people among the other peoples,[49] just as they did not consider Me to be the overlord[50] even among the false gods they worshipped. Thus it is evident that from the day when they forgot the God who saved them and said, *This is your god, O Israel* (Exod. 32:4), a decree of disper-

---

48. And therefore it does not help that they included the true God with the golden calf. This conflicts with conclusions drawn by Morteira in the preceding paragraphs.

49. In the previous interpretation, *lo 'am* referred to the claim that the Jews were no longer the people of God; here it is the claim that the Jews are no longer a people at all.

50. *Ha-marut*: see Rashi on *Elohim* in Gen. 6:2.

sion has been enacted against them, as it says in Psalm 106, *He raised His hand in oath to make them fall in the wilderness, to disperse their offspring among the nations, and scatter them through the lands* (Ps. 106:26–27). This is, *I'll provoke them with [being considered] a non-people.* For even though those who speak the same language are generally considered to be one people, this is done metaphorically. A true people must live together in a single territory. The word for people, '*am,* is derived from the word "with," '*im*: they must live together *with* each other.[51] But when God brought Israel out of its land and scattered them, it lost the name "people" in its full sense, as the Scripture says, *and in another* (**309r**) *sixty-five years, Ephraim will be shattered as a people* (Isa. 7:8).

Furthermore, we find that the prophet Ezekiel declaims in chapter 36 about this measure, namely this sin and its punishment, based on what we have said. He said, *O mortal, when the House of Israel dwelled on their own soil, they defiled it with their ways and their deeds; their ways were in My sight like the uncleanness of a menstruous woman* (Ezek. 36:17). I believe that this is a fine simile for what we are discussing. For the adulterous woman can sin at two different times: while she is ritually clean and while she is ritually unclean. During the period of her ritual cleanness, she may whore with other men and then sleep with her husband. But during the period of her uncleanness, the sin of her licentiousness is compounded, as she remains apart from her husband, who knows nothing of this. The model for this is the analogy made by Scripture between places of idolatry and prostitution.[52] So in their worshipping the false gods and forsaking the true God, not serving Him, their uncleanness is like that of a menstruous woman. Therefore their punishment was, *I scattered them among the nations, and they were dispersed through the lands; I punished them in accordance with their ways and their deeds* (ibid. 19), in accordance with what we have said: *They provoked My jealousy with "not God," I'll provoke their jealousy with "non-people,"* for they will not remain a people in their own land. This is what Ezekiel went on to say: *When they came to those nations they caused My holy name to be profaned, in that it was said of them, "These are God's people?! Yet they had to leave His land!"*(ibid. 20). This is said in amazement: "Can it be that these are God's people once they had to leave His land?"

---

51. A rather striking formulation of territoriality as an essential component of peoplehood. For Portuguese polemical invocations of the fate of Jews scattered "without even a palm of earth they can call their own," see Glaser, "Invitation to Intolerance," pp. 342–43.

52. The prophetic literature is filled with this analogy; see, e.g., Ezek. 16:15–38. This analogy picks up the theme from the Exordium of the wife metaphor for the relationship of Israel and God.

4.a. God rebuked them in this wondrous song with still another meaning of ***They provoked My jealousy with no-single-god***. This is that the sin of any adulterous wife is great, yet if she commits adultery with many lovers this sin is compounded, for she shows contempt for her husband to all of them.[53] This is what Jeremiah said in chapter 3: *Now you have whored with many lovers: can you return to Me? says the Eternal* (Jer. 3:1). This too is the content of God's rebuke in the verse we have already cited: *The Israelites continued to do what was offensive to God; they served the Baalim and the Ashtaroth* (Jud. 10:6). If they had consistently served one of them, the verse would have said only *they served the Baalim*. However, they added offense to their sin by the multiplicity of their misdeeds. The Sages were quite precise in the twentieth chapter of Numbers Rabbah, when they said,

> Come and see: I redeemed the children of Israel seven times, and they were obliged to praise Me seven times to correspond to these seven acts of redemption. This is what Scripture says: *The Eternal said to the Israelites, "[I have saved you] from the Egyptians, from the Amorites, from the Ammonites, and from the Philistines. The Sidonians, Amalek, and Maon also oppressed you; and when you cried out to Me, I saved you from them* (Jud. 10:11–12). Yet you have defied Me with seven acts of idolatry: *The Israelites continued to do what was offensive to God. [They served the Baalim and the Ashtaroth, and the gods of Aram, the gods of Sidon, the gods of Moab, the gods of the Ammonites, and the gods of the Philistines]* (ibid. 6).[54]

It is possible that these seven correspond to the others. The Baalim correspond to the Egyptians, who were indeed *ba'alim*, masters of slaves, and God liberated the Israelites from Egypt and said, *For it is to Me that the Israelites are servants; they are My servants, whom I brought out from the land of Egypt; they may not give themselves over into servitude* (Lev. 25:55 and 42). Yet the Israelites took for themselves other *ba'alim*, other masters, in order to provoke God's jealousy, *and they served the Baalim*. God redeemed them from Amalek and they served the Ashtaroth eye to eye.[55] He liberated them from the Amorites and they served the gods of Aram; from the Sidonians, and they served gods of Sidon; He liberated them from Maon, and they served the gods of Moab; He liberated them from Amon and they served the gods of Amon; He liberated them from the Philistines and they served the gods of the Philistines.

---

53. Again the wife metaphor from the Exordium.

54. Num. Rabbah 20,5.

55. I am unsure how to explain Morteira's association between Amalek and Ashtaroth. Ashtoreth (Astarte) is the goddess of the Sidonians (1 Kings 11:33).

In this manner, ***They provoked My jealousy with no-single-god***, meaning with no consistent god,[56] but rather they sought out many gods, thereby compounding their evil many times.

b. And so God, measure for measure, did not hand them over to a single people alone. That would have made their exile more moderate, for this people would have protected them as their servants. Rather, He handed them over to various overlords, *the clans of Edom and the Ishmaelites, Moab and the Hagrites [...], Assyria too joins forces with them* (Ps. 83:7, 9). *O God, my foes are so many! Many are those who attack me* (Ps. 3:2). That is the meaning of ***I'll provoke their jealousy with no-single-people***, meaning no consistent people, but rather with many different peoples.[57] *Ah, the roar of many peoples that roar as the sea roars, the rage of the nations that rage as the mighty waters rage* (Isa. 17:12). *What the cutter has left, the locust has devoured; what the locust has left, the grub has devoured; and what the grub has left, the hopper has devoured* (Joel 1:4). This is an extremely grave punishment, measure for measure. ***They provoked My jealousy with no-single-god; I'll provoke their jealousy with no-single-people***.

All this is in accordance with the first [part of the verse], which pertains to the relationship of the first component of the home, namely the wife with her husband, and the observance of the covenant made between them.[58]

Body of the Sermon, Part II

After Moses rebuked them with the first part of the verse, ***They provoked My jealousy with a non-god***, pertaining to the rebellion of the wife against her husband—the first component of the home—he rebuked them with regard to the second component: the rebellion of the children against their father. He said, ***They vexed Me with their trivialities***, and he related this to their punishment saying, ***with a foolish nation I'll vex them***.

1.a. The first meaning is that they trivialized the high seriousness of observing the divine commandments, and annulled the power of God's word: *You*

---

56. In this fourth reading of the phrase, "*lo el*" refers not to the absence of true divinity in the false gods worshiped (as in the first interpretation), but to the absence of loyalty to one false god and the succession of false gods that became the object of the Israelites' attention.

57. The fourth reading of the phrase refers not to claims made about the Jewish people itself (as in the second and third interpretations), but—as in the first—to the instruments of punishment, here to the many different peoples who have ruled over Israel in their exile. Note the contrast with the point made in "The Dust of the Earth" (above, pp. 387–88) and *Ha'azinu* GS (above, p. 484), which emphasizes the advantage of being scattered among many nations and the danger of being under the power of a single ruler.

58. A characteristic recapitulation and signal to the listeners that a major structural component of the sermon is ending and a new one beginning.

have commanded that Your precepts be kept diligently (Ps. 119:4). So the perfection
desired by God is that one should *tremble at My word* (Isa. 66:2), whatever that
word may be—that we must know that its observance is God's commandment. It is impossible to express the seriousness of the obligation placed upon
us to observe and perform what the King of the palace has said. He is the
Fashioner, the Creator, the Redeemer, the Father; who dares to be indolent
and trivialize His word? This is something that *has struck many dead, and numerous are its victims* (cf. Prov. 7:26): to trivialize the details of the commandments, to be a wise-guy and say, "What difference does it make?" This is the
first meaning of *they vexed Me with their trivialities*, meaning that they altered
My words and considered them to be trivial.

The Sages in chapter "[All Israel has] a share [in the world to come]" considered two matters together, teaching us of the need for exertion in fundamental matters, and not to trivialize them, for doing so may result in a great
mishap. On the verse, *So the king took counsel and made two golden calves* (1 Kings
2:28) they said,

> He made a righteous man sit with a wicked man and said to them, "Will
> you agree to whatever I say?" They answered, "Yes." He said, "That I
> will be king?" They said, "Yes." He said, "Even idolatrous worship?"
> The righteous man said, "Heaven forbid!" The wicked man said,
> "Could it be that a great man like Jeroboam would worship
> idolatrously? This must be a test." Even Ahijah the Shilonite signed in
> error, as the verse said, *The Eternal said to Jehu, Because you have acted well
> and done what was pleasing to Me …* (2 Kings 10:30). Yet it continues, *But
> Jehu was not careful to follow [the God's Teaching]* (ibid. 31). What was the
> cause of this? [Abaye said, A covenant is made by the lips[59]] as the verse
> says, *Ahab served Baal little; Jehu shall serve him much!* (ibid. 18). Rava said,
> He saw the signature of Ahijah the Shilonite and went astray.[60]

Now in one of my sermons for the lesson *Va-Yeshev*, on the verse, *There we
were binding sheaves* (Gen. 37:7), I investigated this matter of Jeroboam at
length, for it is a subject of fundamental importance.[61] Here I will summarize
quickly what is necessary for the matter at hand.

It is inconceivable that Ahijah the Shilonite, a holy man of God, God's

---

59. That is, words—even if spoken rhetorically—may have a binding character. This
ellipsis in the Talmudic passage was apparently copied from the text of the sermon mentioned immediately below.

60. B. *Sanhedrin* 101b–102a, with some textual variations.

61. This sermon, delivered on Hanukkah 1627, is largely devoted to a discussion of Jeroboam (MS 2:15r–16v). Morteira clearly had the text of the sermon in front of him as he

prophet, would have signed such a stipulation. What the Sages meant is that when Jeroboam realized that his ascension to kingship came from God, as Ahijah had prophesied, he wanted all Israel to come and seek his favor, so that afterward they would do whatever he asked. This is expressed in the verse, *Jeroboam and all the people came to Rehoboam* (1 Kings 12:12), followed by the verse, *When all Israel heard that Jeroboam had returned, they sent messengers and called for him* (ibid. 20). This tells us that he ignored them and hid himself until they made a request for him.[62] In this regard, Scripture says first, *[Jeroboam] came* (ibid 12), in which the word for "came" is written without an *aleph*, although it is to be read (*qeri*) as if written with an *aleph*, indicating that this coming was a chance coming,[63] in order that they would make a request for him and do their will. Now when they were satisfied as to how the prophet told them God's word—that God had chosen Jeroboam—he asked them to sign a blank sheet of paper, indicating that they would do whatever he commanded.

The righteous among them thought that such a signature would be extremely dangerous, as it could include even idolatrous worship. However, the wicked made light of the matter, not thinking—heaven forbid!—that he would explicitly demand idolatry from them. And Ahijah the Shilonite signed the paper, erring in this, for after he signed, Jeroboam wrote above the signatures the matter of the golden calves. As I explained in that sermon at length, this was under the prevaricating claim that these calves related to God, in accord-

---

wrote the current one, and copied passages directly. It begins with a lengthy discussion of Abravanel's discussion of Jeroboam. This was obviously a theme of considerable importance for Morteira; cf. also above, p. 439. The only other Jewish author I have found who gives comparable attention to the historical Jeroboam (and likewise concludes that his erection of the calves was not true idolatry) is the Karaite Jacob al-Kirkisani; see Leon Nemoy, *Karaite Anthology* (New Haven, 1952), pp. 46–48. Cf. the role of Jeroboam as arch-sinner, who transmits collective guilt to his nation, in Fernão Álavers Melo, as noted by Salomon, *Portrait of a New Christian*, pp. 180–81, 297. Kabbalistic tradition viewed the Ephraimite Messiah as a descendant or reincarnation of Jeroboam; see Arthur Green, *Tormented Master* (New York, 1981), pp. 217–18, n. 33; the theme is mentioned by Morteira's rabbinical colleague Isaac Aboab da Fonseca in his treatise *Nishmat Ḥayyim*; see Altmann, "Eternality of Punishment," 65–66. Morteira, however, seems to show no interest in this messianic dimension of Jeroboam.

62. I have not found a precedent among the commentators for this psychological-political interpretation (an ambitious man playing "hard to get"), taken from the earlier sermon.

63. Morteira's point, copied from his earlier sermon, is not clear to me. He seems to be making a play on the word *qeri* (read) and *miqrit* (chance, random), but then says it was for a purpose, as if *miqrit* had the meaning of "tactical." Among the commentators, only David Kimhi notes this spelling of the word for "came" in 1 Kings 12:12, and he says that it has no significance.

ance with His two qualities of mercy and justice. That is why he placed one in Bethel and the other in Dan (ibid. 29). He wanted to teach Israel the element of plurality and of change in God, since God rejected [the line of] David and chose him.[64] In this Jehu made a mistake; he did not discern whether the signature of Ahijah was made before or after what was written above it. In this way, because they were not careful about so grave a matter, they *vexed God with their trivialities*, for they did not deem important what they should have deemed important. Similarly, what Jehu said: he did not think of this as a fundamental matter, but considered it to be trivial, and this is what caused him to go astray, for how could a modest wife utter such words against the honor of her husband, even if for a different purpose? Therefore, **they vexed Me (309v) with their trivialities**, for they made something fundamental seem trivial. The same issue was explained by the Sages with regard to Menasseh and Ahaz, that they preached faulty teachings about the Torah verse, *Timnah was a concubine of Eliphaz* (Gen. 26:12), thereby trivializing God's words.[65] **They vexed Me with their trivialities.**

b. Now God ordained their punishment measure for measure: ***I'll vex them with a shameful nation***, according to the first meaning of the noun *naval* in the Sacred Scriptures. This is the meaning "shameful and disgraceful," as in the verse, *You talk as any shameless woman would talk* (Job 2:10).[66] This is indeed an extreme punishment: to hand over an honorable and distinguished people into the power of nation that is shameful and disgraceful, that will have contempt for them and show them no regard, as we see in the verse, *a ruthless nation that will show the old no regard and the young no mercy* (Deut. 28:50). Such a punishment is truly mortifying, for it pertains to matters of ethical and honorable behavior. Examples are that they will not allow Jews to sit in their presence, and that they will not speak to them except with terms of contempt.[67]

---

64. The point in the earlier sermon is that Jeroboam introduced these false theological claims for political purposes: in order to buttress his legitimacy and the legitimacy of a cult outside of Jerusalem. Morteira notes that the theological errors can be supported by distorted readings of biblical verses. It is hard to avoid the conclusion that, without being explicit, Morteira is setting up Jeroboam as a model for the errors of Christian theology, which posits both plurality and change in God in that He rejected Israel and chose a New Israel. See the use of this argument above, pp. 257, 275.

65. Cf. b. *Sanhedrin* 99b, about Menasseh.

66. Cf. the Targum for Job 2:10, rendering the word *ha-nevalot*, "as one of the women who does something shameful (*qelana*) in her father's house; Morteira uses the cognate "*qalon*" to express this meaning of *naval.*

67. Compare the references to humiliation of Jews in other countries in "The Land Shudders" (above, pp. 402–3). This description does not seem to pertain to the reality in Amsterdam.

Even though in itself this has no intrinsic significance, the intention behind such behavior and the shame is mortifying. Yet this punishment is appropriate for this sin, so that they might think *a fortiori* from their own experience: We feel terrible, and inwardly we weep with anguish because of the disgrace, even though the behavior itself means nothing, only the intention behind it. How then must it be for one who trivializes matters pertaining to God and says that they are not fundamental. Even though the acts may be substantially insignificant and are not fundamental,[68] as they were commanded by God, there is nothing graver than the failure to obey Him. Look how if one person behaves toward another in a manner not befitting his honor, even in a minor detail, the offended person will raise a hue and cry and strive against him even to point of depriving him of his very livelihood.[69] Yet in matters pertaining to God, every single day we see people transgressing them—acts of minor and major consequence—yet no one pays attention or protests. Is this not, *They vexed me with their trivialities*, by saying that this is *nothing*—trivial, trivial!— and their punishment, as I said, is *with a shameful nation I'll vex them*.

2.a. Moses further rebuked by saying *They vexed Me with their trivialities* for another very great evil, which itself is the cause of other great evils. This is that people fail to look constantly at God's acts and to consider them appropriately as fundamental. Rather, they trivialize these acts, thinking of them as inconsequential.[70] This was the first cause of the exile of Israel from its land and idolatrous worship: their failure to look upon the greatness of God's acts. Scripture says, *The people served the Eternal during the lifetime of Joshua and the lifetime of the older people who lived on after Joshua and who had witnessed all the marvelous deeds that the Eternal had wrought for Israel* (Jud. 21:7). *Then another generation arose after them, which had not experienced the Eternal or the deeds He had wrought for Israel* (ibid. 10). Now this second verse is problematic, for it should have expressed these elements in the reverse order: another generation arose after them which had not experienced the deeds God had wrought for Israel, and also had not experienced the Eternal, for the deeds are prior in time and cause. Without the experience of God's deeds, how could they experience God? The way to know God is through knowing His deeds, as the first verse indicates: the elders served God and knew Him because they had experienced marvelous deeds that He had wrought for Israel. However, the mean-

---

68. This statement appears to reflect an approach to the *mitzvot* different from that of both philosophers and Kabbalists: their fundamental importance is not because of the intrinsic acts themselves, but because God commanded them.

69. Exod. Rabbah 1,1, b. *Qiddushin* 28a, and parallels.

70. While the first meaning pertained to trivializing the commandments, this pertains to trivializing God's providential acts in the world.

ing is that for those who had not experienced God, when people would make mention to them of the miracles and the deeds which He had done for them, deeds which obligated them to serve Him, wicked ones would teach these people to minimize these great deeds, to trivialize them, to diminish their greatness and make them seem like other natural events that occur to the other nations.[71] Therefore the first verse said, *all the marvelous deeds*, and the second one [describing the next generation] just *or the deeds*, without saying "marvelous."

This is similar to what the Sages asserted about the generation of the flood: that they said, *What is Shaddai that we should serve Him? What will we gain by praying to him?* (Job 21:15), thus they [???] the service of God by trivializing its benefit. They said, "Do we need God for anything except for a drop of rain? We have rivers and wells."[72] This is in the category of ***They have vexed Me with their trivialities***: by trivializing My miracles.

It is the complaint made by the prophet Jeremiah in chapter two when he said, *What wrong did your fathers find in Me that they abandoned Me, and went after triviality and trivialized?* (Jer. 2:5). It does not use the reflexive form, which would mean "they became trivialized," but rather a transitive verb, meaning that they trivialized My signs and wonders. Indeed, that is what Jeremiah says right afterward: *They never asked themselves, Where is the Eternal, who brought us up from the land of Egypt, who led us through the wilderness ...* (ibid. 6). They never investigated the great deeds, the power of the miracles *in a land of deserts and pits* (ibid.). There He gave us [food?] and drink *in a land of drought and darkness* (ibid.); there He killed the fiery serpents *in a land no man had traversed* (ibid.); there He guided us with His clouds and showed us the way *where no human being had dwelt* (ibid.); there he covered us with His clouds, *shelter from rainstorm, shade from heat* (Isa. 25:4). Yet they trivialized everything, *and went after trivialities* (ibid. 5), and thus they trivialized My wonders. ***They vexed Me with their trivialities***.

King David expressed astonishment when he saw the ingratitude of some of the wicked for the abundance of good things God had done for them. Not knowing how they could possibly fail to recognize these marvelous good things, he addressed this matter and said in Psalm 36, *In my heart is what transgression says to the wicked: he has no sense of the dread of God* (Ps. 36:2). This is as if to say, "in my heart," namely, in my judgment: this is what I thought

---

71. Possibly alluding also to a younger generation of Amsterdam that did not experience deliverance from Portugal and rejected a providential interpretation of those events for a naturalistic explanation.

72. B. *Sanhedrin* 108a. Morteira's text reads *naharot ve-Ya'orim* (Isa. 33:21), where the Talmudic text reads *naharot u-ma'ayanot*.

in my heart that transgression says to the wicked: he has no sense of the fear of God, *for its speech is seductive to him, till he finds his iniquity: to hate* (ibid 3), meaning, the smooth seductiveness that sin finds to seduce him to hate the good things rather than loving them. *His words are evil and deceitful; he will not consider doing good* (ibid 4): evil and deceit tell him to minimize and to trivialize God's acts of loving kindness; he will not look carefully at their goodness, at God's abundant mercy. That is why he said, *O God, Your faithfulness reaches to heaven.... Your justice is like the high mountains* (ibid. 6–7)....*For with You is the fountain of life* ... (ibid. 10). Therefore, *bestow Your faithful care on those devoted to You, Your beneficence on upright men* (ibid. 11) who recognize these qualities and do not trivialize them, for about those it says, **They vexed me with their trivialities**. This is the accursed sect that learned this attitude from Dathan and Abiram, who trivialized God's faithful acts when they said, *Is it not enough that you brought us from a land flowing with milk and honey* (Num. 16:13). They called Egypt—the house of bondage from which God delivered them—a "land flowing with milk and honey," in order to minimize and trivialize God's faithful acts![73]

b. Now their punishment is measure for measure, **I'll vex them with an ungrateful nation**. The second meaning of the noun *naval* is "ungrateful," as in the verse, *Is this how you repay God, O ungrateful, witless people* (Deut. 32:6).[74] This punishment is that, as they minimized God's miracles and his deeds, so He will chastise them in that the nations in whose midst they feel secure—either because of the great benefit these nations receive from the Jews, the profits they receive from their commerce, and the other benefits they provide them when they come to live with them,[75] or because of their covenants and promises—these nations will change into enemies toward the Jews, and they will not remember any of these benefits. This change may occur because of various reasons that God implants their minds in order to turn their hearts against Israel, for God has many ways!

Witness and sign for us is the first exile, when Israel was banished to Egypt.

---

73. In a different sermon, Morteira applied this explicitly to the attitude of some of the immigrants from Portugal; see above, p. 302.

74. Rashi on *naval* in Deut 32:6: "they forgot what had been done for them." Sforno uses the phrase *kefui todah* ("ungrateful"), as is used by Morteira, in his comment on this word.

75. The claim that Jews brought economic benefit to countries where they were allowed to live would increasingly be used by Jewish apologists such as Menasseh ben Israel and Simone Luzzatto in the coming decades. See Mendes-Flohr and Reinharz, *The Jew in the Modern World*, pp. 10–13; Menasseh ben Israel, *The Hope of Israel*, p. 156 ("Do we not see that those republics do flourish and much increase in trade, which admit the Israelites?"). While the examples Morteira gives are from the past, there is undoubtedly resonance with more recent history, especially in Portugal, with a suggestion it could apply to Amsterdam.

There truly, because of Joseph, God kept all of them alive during the famine. Surely this people, to the very last one, owed everything they had to Him, for He had saved them all from death. The king also was deeply obligated to God. With this in mind, the Israelites assumed that their residence there would be serene and tranquil, that they would be rendered the glory and honor due to a people from which the Egyptians had benefited so much. Thinking this, they praised the deeds of the great and awesome God who, through great providential care, brought Joseph out of prison to rule. But the Israelites came to trivialize this event; they did not think rationally about it; they failed to take it to heart, but concentrated rather on reproducing in large numbers and achieving grandeur and honor.[76] *Then Joseph died, and all his brothers, and all that generation* (Exod. 1:6), as was the case with the generation that entered the land.[77] *The children of Israel were fertile, they spread out, became grandees and extremely corpulent* (ibid. 7).[78] Then God repaid measure for measure to those who trivialized the greatness of God; He raised over them a king who trivialized the benefits the Egyptians received from Israel, *and they set over them taskmasters* (ibid. 11). Since he had no other reason to mistreat them, Pharaoh seized upon the reason of their large number, the suspicion about the future based on the current situation, for *like channeled water is the mind of the king in God's hand* (Prov. 21:1). That is why one must run to seek Him. Thus, ***I'll vex them with an ungrateful nation.***

Regarding this, King David cried out in the name of the Israelite nation before God and confessed his sins. He said in Psalm 35, *They repay me evil for good, bereavement for my soul* (Ps. 35:12). Now the "children of the soul" are the thoughts and the reflections that a person thinks while pondering the constant acts of loving kindness we receive from God, how He miraculously sustains us in our exile, one lamb among seventy wolves,[79] and how according to the natural order we would have no chance to endure and survive in the world. Now when the soul is bereft of these thoughts (heaven forbid!), it will vex God with its trivialities, meaning that it trivializes God's acts of loving kindness and His great works. Then measure for measure: *they repay me evil for good,* ***I'll vex them with an ungrateful nation.*** For even though I am truly faithful to that

---

76. Compare "The People's Envy," in *Jewish Preaching*, pp. 272–85 (and the recapitulation of this sermon near the end of "The Land Shudders," above, pp. 404–5). The original sermon emphasizes recognizing the quality of being aliens, in exile; here the emphasis is on recognizing God's marvelous beneficence.

77. Cf. Jud. 2:10–14 and 21:7 and 10, cited above near the beginning of section 2.a.

78. I have translated these words as Morteira interpreted them in the aforementioned sermon.

79. Cf. *Pesiqta Rabbati* 9, 3 on Ps. 35:10.

nation in whose midst I live, and I rejoice in its well-being and am saddened by its misfortunes, and I pray for its success, if my soul is bereft of these thoughts, they will rise up against me, for God will vex me with them.[80] This is what he says afterward: *Yet when they were ill, my dress was sackcloth, I afflicted my soul with a fast; my prayer returns upon my bosom* (ibid. 13). This means, I used to pray for them as if it were something I need for myself. *I walked about as though it were my friend or my brother* (ibid. 14) (**310r**) when things were good for them; *I was bowed with gloom, like one mourning for his mother* (ibid.) when things were bad for them. Yet with all this, *When I stumble they gleefully gather* (ibid. 15), meaning, when I limp and stumble from my recognition of how I trivialized God's acts of loving kindness, *wretches gather against me*—deficient people—*I know not* (ibid.), meaning that they spread baseless libels against me without my knowing why. *They tear at me without end* (ibid.). This is a figurative way of expressing the blow given by the tongue, which does not spill blood.[81] All this is absolutely true, for as **they vexed God with their trivialities**, that is by trivializing His great deeds, so measure for measure **with an ungrateful nation** which will trivialize their contributions, **He will vex them**.

3.a. Now just as he rebuked them in the verse **They vexed Me with their trivialities** with regard to their trivializing what should be considered great and fundamental—namely God's commandments and His awe-inspiring marvelous deeds—so he rebuked them for having made what is indeed trivial and totally insignificant into something fundamental, to which they devote themselves entirely, without realizing their insignificance. This is another meaning of **They vexed Me with their trivialities**, namely that they exalt their trivialities and make them into something substantial. Look at what King Solomon said, after he had [???] from all that was before in Jerusalem, all the good things and pleasures of this world: "Again I saw, and it was all futile."[82] He called the good things of the world to come *yesh*, for in them alone there is something substantial, as we see in the verse, *I endow those who love Me with substance* [yesh] (Prov. 8:21). This means, all is futile, trivial; however, the reward for those

---

80. Here the preacher is paraphrasing David's relationship to an ungrateful people, but he seems to be invoking the position of Jews in the contemporary exile. That is how Menahem Me'iri interprets this passage: *Perush le-Sefer Tehillim* (Jerusalem, 1936), p. 76. Morteira provides a strong statement of Jewish identification with the welfare of the country of residence despite the refusal by its native inhabitants to accept the Jews.

81. Compare the popular story cited in Saperstein, *Jewish Preaching*, p. 96, ending with the words, "The wound caused by the ax has healed, the wound caused by your words has not healed." This story is brought to exemplify the Talmudic statement, "A wrong inflicted by words is worse than wrongful taking of money" (b. *Baba Metsi'a* 58b).

82. There is no verse in Ecclesiastes exactly as Morteira quotes it; cf. 1:14.

who love Me is fundamentally different from this triviality, but rather *I endow those who love Me with substance.* Now when people make this triviality into something fundamental, and ignore what is fundamental to their ultimate purpose, then God says, ***They vexed Me with their trivialities.***

This is another category of idolatry, so common that it arouses no surprise. Yet when people worship silver and gold and make them fundamental, but fail to seek God when this involves a financial sacrifice, it is just like the ancient form of idolatry. Is this not from the same pattern as the first calf, made of gold, to which its worshippers bowed down? So it is today with those who abandon the service of God and bow down to golden calves—they are the coins of currency—bow down before the image of an ox (cf. Ps. 106:20)—namely, their fields and their houses.[83] (Scripture says, *A rich harvest comes through the strength of the ox* [*shor,* Prov. 14:4], and the Sages said that this is connected with the word *shur* in the verse, *I can scale a wall* [*shur,* Ps. 18:30], alluding to their houses.)[84] They exchanged their glory for its image, and because of their money they exchange their God, remaining in the lands of their enemies and worshipping another god, in order to care for their money, their fields, and their houses.[85]

Worse than this: some of them return there, like Lot's wife, who *looked behind her, and turned into a pillar of salt* (Gen. 19:26). She did not understand the great act of kindness God had performed for her in saving her from that conflagration, but looked behind her, in defiance of God's command. Her concern was for her property rather than for God's act of kindness; therefore she became a pillar of salt.[86] This will be the fate of those who have escaped from the conflagration and return there to take out their property: they will remain a useless pillar of salt burnt by brimstone. We see examples of this

---

83. As Simon Schama has shown, contemporary Dutch preachers also used the imagery of the Golden Calf in denouncing the "lust for riches" of their congregants, as they warned about an outbreak of God's wrath as punishment: *The Embarrassment of Riches,* pp. 46–47, and the extended discussion of pulpit condemnation of conspicuous consumption, pp. 310–23. The "golden calf" as a metaphor for materialism and greed remained a *topos* of Jewish preaching at least into the nineteenth century.

84. I have not found this link between Prov. 14:4 and Ps. 18:30.

85. Materialism was one of the most important explanations for the failure of other New Christians to leave Portugal and return to Judaism. See above, pp. 195 and 280–82.

86. Cf. Morteira's answer to the twenty-first question of the "Priest of Rouen": "They ought to consider how ungrateful they are to their Creator, who hath delivered them from the flames of Sodom; and they, like Lot's wife, instead of following the path which leads to salvation, turn back and remain in the mid-way, like a pillar of salt, deceived by the apparent prosperity of riches." *www.jewish-history.com/Occident/volume3/jan1846/questions.html.*

every day![87] Concerning such things Scripture says, ***They vexed Me with their trivialities***, for by making the trivial into something fundamental, they indeed vex God.

In this they are totally different from the rock from which they were hewn—our father Abraham—for in his love of God he took no pity upon his only son, for whom he had longed for years, and who was given to him after he had given up hope.[88] How much more obvious it is that he would have had no pity upon his money! Yet *they* make the trivial into something fundamental. ***They vexed Me with their trivialities***.

We know that God prohibited excess in three things to the Jewish king: horses, wives, and silver and gold, for all of these are trivialities, lest he become haughty and his heart turn away from God (Deut. 17:16–17), and ***he vex God with his trivialities***. God commanded that the king not buy horses from that first evil and sin-inducing land from which He had removed the Israelites, lest he send the people back there, for it is against God's will for the people to return to the wicked land. From this model we learn a lesson that applies to other cases. When God brought the Jews out of Babylonia, some of them brought from there forbidden wives—Sidonian, Moabite, and Hittite—as is written in the Book of Ezra. When they divorced them, following Ezra's counsel, it is obvious that the women returned to their fathers' homes in their own countries (Ezra 9–10). It was forbidden for the Jews to return to those countries, lest they take up again with these women. Similarly, God brought out a great many of "the children of Israel" from the sin-inducing land of Spain; beyond a doubt, the person who returns there in order to make more money is an abomination to God,[89] who has said to you, *You must not go back that way again* (Deut. 17:16)—for this is like Egypt, nay, even worse than it in its sins! Whoever pays no heed to this ***vexes God with his trivialities***.

In this category of vexation are those who do not give a penny to charity. Day and night they weep if any assessment is placed upon them for a true religious or humanitarian need, but afterward they spend a fortune on superfluous jewelry and clothing.[90] These ones certainly ***vex God with their trivialities***, for they make such trivialities into the foundation of their lives. For *all*

---

87. The theme of returning to the "lands of idolatry" was important in both the sermons of Morteira and the legislation of the leadership of the Portuguese community in Amsterdam. See above, pp. 303–4.

88. Referring, of course, to Abraham's willingness to sacrifice Isaac (Gen. 22:2ff); for Abraham's having given up hope of a son through Sarah, see Gen. 17:17.

89. See above, n. 85. Morteira probably uses "Spain" here to refer to the entire Iberian peninsula.

90. Cf. "The People's Envy," in *Jewish Preaching*, pp. 279–82. On the institutions of charity

goes well with the person who lends generously, who conducts his affairs with equity (Ps. 112:5), referring to one who is balanced in his behavior and conducts his affairs with equity and proportion; as he adorns himself in his own affairs, so does he adorn himself in God's ways. However, whoever takes excessive pride in his beauty for sinful purposes, whether to associate with Gentile women or to transgress God's words in any matter because of his baubles, ***they have vexed Me with their trivialities***.

b. For all of these God ordained—measure for measure—***I'll vex them with a miserly nation***. The third meaning of the noun *naval* is "miser," as we see in the verse, *No more shall the miser be called generous* (Isa. 32:5).[91] This means that against those who made money their main object, something fundamental, God will arouse a miserly nation, which lusts for money and will take from these people all of theirs, so that they will left plucked absolutely clean.[92] This nation will take all their money, their houses, and their fields—the calf they worship—and God will heap their carcasses upon their lifeless fetishes (cf. Lev. 26:30), as we see this very day.[93] Another aspect of ***I'll vex them with a miserly nation*** in this sense is the losses that God will bring about for those who hold back from giving to the poor in accordance with their means. For as the Sages interpreted the verse *Your sons and daughters shall be delivered to another people* (Deut. 28:32) to refer to the father's [new] wife,[94] so ***I'll vex them with a miserly nation*** alludes to the person whose debtor has fled with his money, leaving the uncollectible debt in his possession; thus he gives to *a miserly nation* what he did not want to give to the poor.[95]

4.a. Moses rebuked them further in this same sense of having made fundamental something that is trivial—***they vexed Me with their trivialities***—for another great evil that has become ensconced among the people of Israel. These are the divinations and the conjurations and the other trivialities that they believe in.[96] They take these seriously for what they want to do, and are

---

in the community, see Swetschinski, *Reluctant Cosmopolitans,* pp. 199–203; for the host society, see Israel, *The Dutch Republic,* pp. 353–60.

91. In this verse, *naval* is in parallelism with *kilai,* although most commentators do not understand it as meaning a stingy person.

92. *Qereah mi-kan u-mi-kan* ("bald from both directions"), based on the parable in b. *Baba Qamma* 60b.

93. Probably referring to the confiscation of property by the Portuguese Inquisition rather than to confiscatory taxation in Amsterdam.

94. B. *Yebamot* 63b, meaning a stepmother.

95. מי שיברח בעל חובו וישאר בידו עם ממונו ויתן לגוי נבל. See the discussion of this passage in chap. 6 above, pp. 195–96.

96. It is unclear whether this theme of superstition has resonance for Morteira's own community; it is not emphasized in passages of rebuke elsewhere in his preaching. A few

afraid of things they should not fear and put their trust in this foolishness and lunacy and trivialities that vex God, who commanded, *You must be whole-hearted with the Eternal, your God* (Deut. 18:13).

The prophet Ezekiel already prophesied about this in chapter 13: *And you, O mortal, set your face against the women of your people, who prophesy out of their own imagination. Prophesy against them and say, Thus said the Eternal God: Woe to those who sew pads on all the joints of My arms and make shawls for the head of every person, in order to entrap. Can you hunt down souls among My people, while you preserve your own souls?* (Ezek. 13:17–18). These women were performing witchcraft in order to tell future events, tailoring their prophecy to the payment they received, hunting souls to believe in their lies. God rebuked them through His prophet and specified their punishment as death, showing how much **they vexed Him with trivialities**. He said, *My arms* rather than just "arms"[97] to show that He would be diligently careful with His people, the children of Israel, like a father is with his children when someone is directing them away from the paved path.[98] Instead of using the word *mitpaḥat* for the head shawls, he used the word *mispaḥat*, which can mean a rash (Lev. 13:68), for they are indeed a rash and a scaly affection on their heads. And so it is in every generation—varying in quantity place by place—these divinations and *trivialities vexing God*. The Sages spoke about this in *Sanhedrin*: *There is no divination in Jacob* (Num. 23:23): R. Joshua ben Levi said, whoever engages in divination will be harassed by divination.[99] Rashi explains that whoever pursues the diviners will always be confronted with diviners who will cause him grief. For if a person guides his life by chance, as if it were random events, then God will act toward him by chance, with random events.[100]

b. God ordained this punishment, *I'll vex them with a foolish nation*, according to the fourth meaning of the noun *naval*, which is "fool," as in the verse, *The fool thinks in his heart, "There is no God"* (Ps. 14:1).[101] For whoever

---

moments later, Morteira will attribute this kind of superstition primarily to Jews in Islamic lands (i.e., the Ottoman Empire): see below, n. 104.

97. The standard commentators on this verse (Rashi, Kimhi, *Metsudat Tsiyon*) see no significance in this formulation.

98. Picking up the motif of the relationship between father and children introduced at the beginning of the sermon.

99. The source is actually b. *Nedarim* 32a.

100. Based on Leviticus 26:27–28, as understood by Maimonides in *Guide* 3,36.

101. Cf. *Sifre Ha'azinu*, 15, juxtaposing the same two verses, and Ibn Ezra ad loc., interpreting *"naval"* as "the opposite of wise." Note the statement of the radical philosopher Levi ben Abraham (whose work, still unpublished, Morteira probably did not know): "There is no doubt that God did us a merciful favor by exiling us among peoples the falsity of whose faith is obvious, as the Scripture says, *I'll vex them with a naval people* (Deut. 32:21), which

follows these foolish trivialities will be turned over by God into the power of a foolish nation, which has neither common sense nor reason. It is a great misfortune to be under their yoke. An example is the Ishmaelites:[102] neither in matters of religion or of justice do they apply rational investigation; for them everything is a matter of arbitrary will.[103] It is possible that their folly was produced as a punishment for those who engaged in divination, for we have heard that in those places, the Jews seek out this kind of lunacy.[104]

Thus we have four meanings of *they vexed Me with their trivialities*, two in that they trivialize what is fundamental—first (**310v**) by minimizing the observance of the commandments, and *I'll vex them with a contemptible nation* that will have contempt for them, and second by minimizing God's marvelous miracles, and *I'll vex them with an ungrateful nation*. The second set pertains to their making what is trivial and inconsequential into something fundamental—first in making various forms of idolatry fundamental, and for this *I'll vex them with a miserly nation*, and second in making something

---

the Targum renders *be-'ama tafsha*, "a foolish people": Schwartz, *Ha-Ra'ayon he-Meshiḥi ba-Hagut ha-Yehudit*, p. 147 n. 90. Levi ben Abraham presents this as an act of beneficence, Morteira as a humiliating punishment.

102. Universally used by medieval Jews as an epithet for Muslims. On Morteira's contempt for Islam, cf. above, p. 129, and "The Land Shudders," p. 397. This convention of applying "a foolish people" to the Muslims continued into the nineteenth century, as can be seen in a sermon by Isaac Leeser delivered on July 24, 1840: "in Jerusalem, on Zion, on Moriah, the rightful possessors are strangers, aliens, oppressed, outcasts, slaves! And a foolish people, a nation that has no wisdom, revels in its invented rites on the spot where once was the glory of Israel." *Discourses on the Jewish Religion*, vol. 3 (Philadelphia, 1867), p. 154.

103. Perhaps referring to the Ashariyah school of Islamic theology; see Majid Fakhry, *A History of Islamic Philosophy* (New York, 1970), pp. 235–43, esp. p. 238: "They were reluctant to admit that any merit attached to that type of rational knowledge which is attainable through unaided reason. God's power and sovereignty are such that the very meaning of justice and injustice is bound up with His arbitrary decrees." If Morteira knew about Islamic theology, it would probably have been through the works of Jewish philosophers such as Maimonides. Occasionally, Morteira expressed the Maimonidean view that Islam as a religion was preferable to Christianity as its errors did not pertain to the Godhead but only to the claim of prophecy for Muhammad (MS 3:87r, *Bereshit*, Gen. 1:3).

104. Cf. Abraham Danan, "Les superstitions des Juifs Ottomans," in *Actes du Onzième Congrès Internationale des Orientalistes* (Paris, 1898–1899), section 7; Isaac Jack Lévy and Rosemary Lévy Zumwalt, *Ritual Medical Lore of Sephardic Women* (Urbana, 2002), pp. 16–17 on memories of consulting Turkish women for cures and p. 21 on the seventeenth-century Rabbi Judah Lerma of Belgrade's objection to "the superstitious practice called 'Indulcho.'"

fundamental out of the trivial lunacy of divination and witchcraft, and therefore *I'll vex them with a foolish nation.*[105]

Peroration

The Sages alluded to all of these themes in our opening dictum, for all of them are the work of the primal serpent, in whose words we find these four matters. First the Midrash said, "Happy am I for not having followed the counsel of the serpent," for the counsel of the serpent was to make something fundamental from what is inconsequential, to exalt what has no real substance, and to ignore what is indeed fundamental. The serpent said, *Your eyes will be opened and you will be like divine beings, who know good and bad* (Gen. 3:5). For so indeed the counsels of the wicked make trivialities seem beautiful and anger God by exalting their trivialities, so that the good will be abandoned. This is the meaning of *Happy is the man who has not followed the counsel of the wicked* (Ps. 1:1)

Secondly, it said, *Or taken the path of sinners* (ibid.): "Happy am I for not having taken the path of the serpent." Now the "path of the serpent," indeed the path of all the wicked, is to minimize and trivialize God's beneficent acts of loving kindness. This is as the serpent said, *For God knows that on the day you eat of it, your eyes will be opened* (Gen. 3:5). It was not enough for the serpent to say in his wickedness, *your eyes will be opened,* enticing them to the imaginary good, but he also said, *For God knows.* What God did for the benefit of the human beings, and to safeguard them from great damage, the serpent attributed to a self-centered destructive impulse in God! This **vexed God by trivializing** His beneficent acts; that is why it is called "the path of the sinners."

Furthermore he said, *Or joined the company of the insolent* (ibid.): "Happy am I for not having joined the company of the insolent serpent." Now the "company of the serpent" is the company of the insolent who deride the divine commandments, minimizing and trivializing them, and **vexing God with their trivialities.** They say in a mocking manner, "What difference does it make, what difference does it make?" and they invent arguments to be derisive. This is what the serpent did at the beginning of his conversation with the woman: *Did God really say, You shall not eat of any tree of the garden?* (Gen. 3:1). He said this derisively, for God prohibited only the tree of the knowledge of good and bad (Gen. 2:17), not every tree in the garden. But the serpent acted as if he were surprised, as if he did not know, in order to say to her afterward, *You will not die* (Gen. 3:4).

---

105. A characteristic recapitulation of the second part of the sermon.

Finally, when the woman said *or touch it* (ibid. 3), he pushed her [against the tree], and **vexed God with his trivialities** by employing divination and enchantment to entrap the woman, saying, "Just as death has not befallen you for touching it, so it will not befall you for eating it."

Happy are all those who do not listen to him, but *who take delight in God's teaching, and study that teaching day and night. They will be like a tree planted beside streams of water* (Ps. 1:2–3); no evil shall occur to them, *but whatever they produce will succeed* (ibid. 3), and they will see God's deliverance. May it be God's will to bring this about through the coming of our righteous Messiah, quickly and in our days. Amen.

Eulogy for David Masiah
Budapest Rabbinical Seminary MS 12, vol. 1, fols. 78rv, 81rv
Tetsavveh, February 22, 1652

As biographical aspects of this eulogy have already been discussed in chapter 5 (see above, pp. 157–61), I will concentrate here on the structural components. The scriptural theme-verse is the first verse of the lesson, and the rabbinic dictum is a highly influential formulation of the nature of existence after death, and therefore obviously relevant to the situation. Morteira begins in a familiar manner, raising problems with one of the two building blocks for his sermon, in this case the dictum. The first problem focuses on the relationship between the full content of the statement and the proof text used to support it. In this introductory section of the eulogy, Morteira discusses the proof text in its completeness, touching upon a classical conundrum of medieval Jewish exegesis, the vision of God by the elders of Israel near the time of the revelation at Mount Sinai.[1] He first reiterates a reading that he gave in an earlier sermon, drawing from Abravanel's interpretation of the verse that the elders apprehended a doctrine about God's special providential association in each of the three realms of being. He then suggests a different interpretation appropriate to the dictum, in which the unique characteristics of the elders in this epiphany teaches us about the nature of life after death.

The second question, about the "diadems" ['atarot] in the rabbinic dictum, introduces the body of the sermon. This is structured by a delicate counterpoint between two additional well-known dicta from Tractate Avot: one about four crowns [ketarim] (royalty, priesthood, Torah learning, and a good name), the other about the qualities of wisdom, heroism, wealth, and honor. Each of these "crowns" is associated with one of the personal qualities, and then applied to the deceased. Morteira's review of Masiah's chartacter is not at all stereotypical; rather, it provides a considerable amount of information about the deceased, although of course not quite as much as the historian would like to know. Finally, as is characteristic of his eulogies, the scriptural verse is introduced at the very end, its four elements also juxtaposed with the four crowns. The doctrinal point is that each person is rewarded in the future world with the crown that has been figuratively created from worthy personal qualities; the homiletical point is that each of these crowns applies to the person being mourned.

---

1. On various interpretations, see Shaul Regev, "Re'iyat Atsilei B'nei Yisrael (Shemot 24:9–11) be-Filosofiyah ha-Yehudit Bi-Ymei ha-Beinayim," *Meḥqerei Yerushalayim ba-Maḥshevet Yisrael* 4 (1985): 281–302.

* * *

(78r)*Pure olive oil, beaten for the light, to make a light flame continually* (Exod. 27:20).

Berakhot, chapter 2 (17a): A favorite saying of Rab was: In the future world, there is no eating, no drinking, no procreation, no commercial activity, no jealousy, no hatred, no competition. Rather, the righteous sit with their diadems on their heads, delighting in the radiance of the divine presence, as the Torah says, *They beheld God, and they ate and drank* (Exod. 24:11).

Exordium

Two questions occur to me now regarding this weighty dictum. The first: How does Rab derive all this from the biblical verse? It provides proof only for the assertion that in the future world there is no eating or drinking, for he cites the verse, *They beheld God, and they ate and drank* (Exod. 24:11), which means, as Rashi explained, that their enjoyment was as if they ate and drank.[2] However, all the other characteristics of the future world—how are these derived from the verse? Second, why "with *their* diadems on their heads"? That implies that he was speaking about specific, familiar diadems. One would have expected simply, "with diadems on their heads."

To answer the first question: it seems to me that Rav cited the end of the verse to illuminate the beginning,[3] deriving his message from the entire verse,[4] which states, *They saw the God of Israel: under His feet there was something like a pavement of sapphire, like the essence of the heavens in purity. Yet He did not raise a hand against the leaders of the Israelites; they beheld God, and they ate and drank* (Exod. 24:10–11). Now in a different context I explained this verse to mean[5] that the leaders of Israel apprehended through this vision that while

---

2. Rashi's position on this verse is not so clear: he says that they envisioned God with "coarse heart," while eating and drinking, a reading he attributes to Midrash *Tanḥuma*; then he continues, "But the Aramaic Targum did not translate it in this way." Indeed, the phrase "as if they ate and drank" comes from the Targum and is not cited by Rashi.

3. A Talmudic principle of interpretation (b. *Gittin* 42a, b. *Baba Qamma* 98a, b. *Baba Metsi'a* 10a, etc.): something explicit at the end of a textual passage (usually of Mishnah) illuminates something less clear at the beginning of that passage.

4. The following two paragraphs, as well as most of the second page, are illegible from the microfilm because of the heavy ink that shows through from the second side of the page. I was able to decipher most of the text from the actual manuscript.

5. Morteira characteristically refers to his discussion of the verse in a different sermon, focusing on a cosmological and metaphysical doctrine, wherein the unique relationship of

the universe is divided into three components, in each of them there is one individual closer to God than the other beings in that realm, related to God in a special manner, even though everything receives providential direction from Him.[6] In the sub-lunar realm, even though God is called *the God of the entire earth* (Isa. 54:5), He is specifically called *the God of Israel* (Exod. 24:10). In the realm of the spheres, even though all of them are governed by Him, the sphere *'Aravot* is uniquely related to God through the divine chariot, as we see in the verse, *Extol Him who rides the heavens ('aravot)* (Ps. 68:5).[7] And so in the realm of the angels: even though all of them are governed by Him, the supreme angel, the *sar ha-penim*, is called *the angel of His countenance* (Is. 63:9), whose name is like that of his Master, and he is uniquely close to God.[8] About the first the verse says, *They saw the God of Israel.* About the second, *under His feet there was something like a pavement of sapphire,* meaning, under His feet and His specific governance and related to His chariot *like the pavement of sapphire,* which is an emblem for something extremely precious. And about the third, which is spiritual, essential, without any material component, it says, *like the essence of the heavens in purity.*

However, for our subject[9] we might say that it is not just the intellectual apprehension they achieved but also the quality of the condition in which they found themselves at the moment they attained this apprehension. First,

the Jewish people to God in the sublunar realm is parallel to the structure of the higher realms of being. The sermon he refers to appears to be a discourse delivered at the meeting of a study group (see above, p. 173), which discusses this verse at some length; unfortunately, the text is largely illegible from the microfilm.

6. This passage, summarized quite briefly from the earlier sermon, is apparently derived from Abravanel's treatment of these verses, based on the same assertion that in each of the three realms there is one being that is uniquely related to God and is caused, moved, or guided directly by God without intermediaries. See Abravanel, *Perush al ha-Torah* 3:271b–273b and *'Ateret Zekenim,* chapter 12, and the discussion by Regev, "Re'iyat Atsilei Benei Yisra'el," pp. 295–97. Cf. also Lieberman, "Sermons and the Construct of a Jewish Identity," p. 56, on a similar theme in a Portuguese sermon printed at Hamburg in 1629.

7. See b. *Hagigah* 12b on the seven firmaments, the highest of which is *'aravot.* Maimonides (*Guide* 1,70) identified *'aravot* with the all-encompassing celestial sphere (cf. beginning of 1, 72); God's "riding" on it (Ps. 68:5) means that He governs it but exists beyond it, separate from it. In Morteira's sermon on Genesis 1:6 (MS 3:316r), he discusses *'aravot* as one of the four biblical words for "heavens" (see above, p. 113), suggesting that this refers to the ultimate purpose of creation.

8. On the supreme angel (frequently called "Metatron," see Gershom Scholem, *Kabbalah* (New York, 1974), pp. 377–81; Scholem, *The Origins of the Kabbalah* (Princeton, 1987), pp. 212–16); Saperstein, *Decoding the Rabbis,* pp. 79–89.

9. I.e., for the present context of the eulogy and the interpretation of the rabbinic dictum relating to the future world.

they were without any envy or hatred or competition or any of the other affective responses that depend upon the body, for their spirits and souls were so exalted it was as if they had forgotten all that affected their bodies. That is the meaning of *They saw the God of Israel,* for *in the light of the king's face there is life* (Prov. 16:15), and there is perfect joy, as the Psalmist said, *Teach me the path of life. In Your presence is perfect joy, delights are ever in Your right hand* (Ps. 16:11). Therefore, if their experience was a taste of the future world, as *they saw the God of Israel,* it necessarily follows that in the future world there is no envy, or hatred, or competition, for all of these are affective responses that produce sadness and anxiety, and there can be no sadness or anxiety in God's presence.[10]

It says further, *under His feet there was something like a pavement of sapphire.* This means that in this vision all the precious things in the world seemed trivial to them, all the precious stones and jewels seemed to them like vanity and emptiness in comparison with that beauty. That is the meaning of *under His feet there was something like a pavement of sapphire*: like something that a person steps on and tramples under foot. From this we learn that the future world has no commercial activity, for how could people crave and desire such base implements when they behold such splendor? It says further, *like the essence of the heavens in purity.* This means that at that moment they became like supernal angels [??] the arousal and desire for anything corporeal, but rather like the essence of the angels in immaculate purity. If so, the world to come has no procreation or any corporeal activity. They approached on high through the soul, although their souls did not separate from their bodies. *He did not raise a hand against the leaders of the Israelites,* rather, their bodies and souls co-existed, and they were nourished as if they were eating and drinking.[11] *They beheld* (**78v**) *God and they ate and they drank.* If so, the future world has no eating or drinking, but the righteous sit, their diadems upon their heads, and delighting in the radiance of the divine presence, from which they are nourished.

---

10. Cf. b. *Shabbat* 30b, Maimonides, *Code, Hilkhot Yesodei ha-Torah,* 7,4. Cf. also Morteira's discussion of this theme in *Tratado,* p. 655, citing 1 Samuel 10:5 and Deut. 28:47 as proof that "prophecy and the spirit of God requires joy and contentment;" Méchoulan, "Morteira et Spinoza au carrefour du Socianisme," p. 62, and idem, "La mort comme enjeu théologique, philosophique et politique à Amsterdam au XVIIe siècle," *XVII Siècle,* 46 (1994): 342–43.

11. In denying literal eating and drinking, Morteira follows the interpretation of Gersonides on this verse; cf. Regev, "Re'iyat Atsilei Benei Yisra'el," p. 290.

Body of the Eulogy

But what are these diadems that are called "*their* diadems," rather than just "diadems"? They are the ones a person acquires in this world, the ones mentioned in the rabbinic statement, "There are three crowns (*ketarim*): the crown of Torah, the crown of priesthood, and the crown of royalty, but the crown of a good name is superior to them all."[12] The meaning of this statement is more than meets the eye. For the crown of royalty is restricted to the descendents of David, the crown of priesthood is restricted to the descendents of Aaron, and the crown of Torah is restricted to the scholars who have achieved much in the discipline of advanced Torah study. Nevertheless, every single Jew—even if he is not a descendent of David, or of Aaron, and even if he is unable to attain advanced knowledge of the Torah—is capable of acquiring these crowns. This is the meaning of "the crown of a good name is superior to them all": through a good name and the good deeds that bring this about, every single Jew is capable of being a king, a priest, a wise scholar.

Proof of this is in the rabbinic statement, "Who is wise? One who learns from every person."[13] Thus the crown of Torah is acquired by one who thinks of himself as devoid of knowledge and wants to learn from everyone, who looks not at the teacher but at what is taught, *whose delight is God's teaching, on which he meditates day and night* (Ps. 1:2), who always thinks of himself as if he knows nothing.

The statement continues, "Who is heroic? One who conquers his impulses." Thus the crown of priesthood is acquired by such a person even if he is not a descendent of Aaron. For what is the essential quality of the priest if not to be separated and distinguished from the rest of the people through holiness, including renunciation of those things permitted to others, whether relating to women, or food, or the other things that human desire is attracted to? This is especially true when they see the rest of the people deriving pleasure from those things permitted to them, yet because of their holiness and priestly status they conquer their impulses.

They went on to say, "Who is rich? One who is content with his lot." Such a person acquires the crown of royalty. One of the characteristics of the king—indeed an essential attribute—is that he has acquired much gold and silver. So Scripture says, *Don't revile a king even among your intimates; don't revile a rich man even in your bed-chamber* (Eccles. 10:20).[14] Now the person who is

---

12. M. *Avot* 4,13.

13. M. *Avot* 4,1.

14. Since "king" and "rich man" are in parallelism, they are taken to be synonymous.

content with his lot has acquired the crown of royalty by being as content and satisfied with the little he has as a king would be with all his wealth, indeed, with many times more than that.

About the crown of a good name, "Who is honored? One who honors everyone," with humility and satisfaction and congeniality, showing respect for every single person. In this way, he will acquire a good name in the conversation of all, and "anyone from whom their fellow human beings take pleasure, from such a person the Omnipresent takes pleasure."[15]

This is the meaning of Rav's phrase, "their diadems on their heads"—namely the diadems they themselves acquired, the familiar diadems, the three crowns of the rabbinic statement, with the crown of a good name superior to them all—"delighting in the radiance of the divine presence." Who is it, and where is the one (cf. Esth. 7:5), of all the members of our sacred community, from the smallest to the greatest (cf. Jer. 6:13), who can fail to see with his spirit and intellect this humble, pious man, the honorable David Masiah (may the memory of the righteous be for blessing), sitting before God, adorned with all of these crowns, delighting in the radiance of the divine presence?

Behold the "crown of Torah," as we said: "Who is wise? One who learns from every person." Everyone knows how much he labored and toiled to learn all he was capable of attaining. All night long, his diligence was manifest in all the *yeshivot*, as he went from one to another, and from that to yet another, to the very last of them. Even in the Morning Yeshivah,[16] before the first rays of the dawn could be seen, he was among the ten first men [in the synagogue]. This is not to mention his efforts in the Gentile lands to learn by heart several

---

15. M. *Avot* 3,10. Morteira used this statement in both of his eulogies for Dr. David Farar: *"Your Voice Like a Ram's Horn,"* pp. 385, 394.

16. Reading: ואף בישיבת הבקר. No yeshivah by this name is listed among the well-known yeshivot or voluntary societies of Amsterdam; see Kenneth R. Scholberg, "Miguel de Barrios and the Amsterdam Sephardic Community," *JQR* 53 (1962–63): 128–41; Swetschinski, *Reluctant Cosmopolitans*, pp. 210–11; Kaplan in Blom, Fuks-Manfeld and Schöffer, *The History of the Jews in the Netherlands*, p. 147. The name, if such an institution did briefly exist, may reflect continuity from the Iberian experience, where there was a society called *Ashmoret ha-Boqer* (*confradria de la Maytinal*), the members of which undertook to rise before dawn for prayer: see Assis, "Welfare and Mutual Aid," 1:339 and Saperstein, *"Your Voice Like a Ram's Horn,"* p. 191 n. 8. On contemporary confraternities for the recitation of predawn prayers, called "Shomrim la-Boqer," see Elliott Horowitz, "Coffee, Coffeehouses, and the Nocturnal Rituals of Early Modern Jewry," *AJS Review* 14 (1989): 30–33, and Rivlin, "*'Arevim Zeh la-Zeh*," pp. 152–54 and passim. According to Rivlin, the *ḥazzan* of the *Shomrim la-Boqer* Society at Venice in 1607 was Joseph Morteira, quite possibly a relative of our preacher, and Leon Modena had many contacts with this Society (*The Autobiography of a Seventh-Century Venetian Rabbi*, p. 229).

of the divine commandments.[17] He [?] spirits[18]; all who heard him would rejoice to hear him speak these words without hesitation or stumbling. And the crown of Torah was glorified not only in his great desire to learn, but also in his desire to teach others, as is known to many of our people.[19] He learned God's way in his own manner, and when there was something he could not understand, he sought from all who were near him books or shorter written expositions ... in order to teach sinners God's way and bring them close to Torah. And so, this crown is certainly upon his head, as he delights in the radiance of the divine presence.

(**81r**) As for the crown of priesthood, [he wears this as well,] for he was a hero, conquering his impulses, and sanctifying himself in what is permitted to him. Did he not, in the sight of everyone, set aside his own affairs and tend to the poor? He did not refrain even from matters that arouse disgust in most people. He was thoughtful toward the wretched (cf. Ps. 41:2), both emotionally and physically. Those in pain, suffering from ringworm[20]—he would wash them himself and cut their hair. Every Friday he would leave aside his own work and go to the jail to bring the prisoners' meat, so that no work would be done on the Sabbath.[21] He would take the bread from his own mouth, being himself poor and hard pressed, and divide it among the poor, as I myself have seen on a number of occasions. Once arrested because some accused him of speaking against their beliefs,[22] when Friday came he would banish from his heart all sadness and worry, adorning himself and cutting his own hair in

---

17. A tantalizing allusion to Masiah's crypto-Jewish life on the Iberian peninsula. See above, pp. 158–59.

18. One Hebrew word in the manuscript is indecipherable.

19. The phrase לכמה מבני עמנו, rather than a simple reference to members of the community, suggests that Morteira is speaking here too about relations with "New Christians" during the period before Masiah left Portugal.

20. Hebrew: אנשי מכאובים וידועי חולי הנתק, echoing Isa. 53:3. I have not found the phrase *ḥoli ha-neteq* as a technical medical term in any of the standard Hebrew dictionaries. My rendering is based on the translation of *neteq* in Lev. 13:30 as *tiña* in Spanish and *tinha* in Portuguese, a cognate of "tinea," the technical name for ringworm.

21. The meaning would seem to be that if he neglected to bring meat for the prisoners on Friday, Jewish relatives of the prisoners might violate the Sabbath by preparing or carrying meat on Saturday. For the problem of Jewish prisoners in the Rasphuis of Amsterdam, see chap. 5, above, p. 159. Cf. the special efforts on behalf of prisoners attributed to his father by Elijah ha-Kohen of Izmir, Saperstein *Jewish Preaching*, p. 323.

22. This might refer to an experience with the Inquisition in Portugal. However, Jews in Amsterdam could be imprisoned for blasphemy, as Uriel da Costa discovered and recounted in his memoir (see Leo W. Schwarz, ed., *Memoirs of My People* [Philadelphia, 1960], p. 88), and it is possible that an anti-Christian animus might have led him to statements that caused problems with the Dutch authorities.

order to receive the Sabbath with joy, for he always conquered his impulses and his emotions for the love of his Creator. How he afflicted himself here among us with fasts and ascetic discipline! And even in Portugal, for many years no meat crossed his lips, so as not to defile himself with something forbidden.[23] Is he not a hero who conquers his impulse? He is a priest of the most high God,[24] and he sits with this crown—the crown of priesthood—on his head, delighting in the radiance of the Divine Presence.

As for the crown of royalty, [he also wears this], for he was wealthy in being content with his lot. It is widely known how he always served his God with full-hearted joy (cf. Deut. 28:47). Though he was lacking in all material things, he never asked others for anything, neither as a gift nor as a loan, nor did he complain; it was as if he lacked nothing. He was always of good cheer; no man ever saw him angry or enraged. He always expressed gratitude [and vitality?] to others, especially to those who were kind to him.

As for the crown of a good name, [he wears this] because he was truly honored, for he honored all his fellow human beings. Who was unaware of this: that all his fulfillment and all his desire was in honoring every person, especially the destitute widows and the modest maidens, who did not have enough to get by. Why, he used to serve them joyfully, like a servant, always going to their doors to ask if they needed anything. And he used to buy them meat and bread and vegetables—whatever they needed. Is there a single person, old or young, in this sacred congregation, who ever had even a minor exchange with him that was not in love and affection? All his interactions with others were in a spirit of humility and affection. Truly in him the statement was fulfilled, "anyone from whom their fellow human beings take pleasure, from such a person the Omnipresent takes pleasure."[25] So we have seen that no one failed to volunteer to help treat him in his illness while he was alive, or to accompany him to his resting place at his death. May his merit protect

---

23. "New Christians," in Portugal were accused by the Inquisition of avoiding pork, trying to slaughter permissible animals in a kosher style, porging the sciatic vein from the hind leg, removing the fatty part of the meat, and washing and salting meat at home; see David M. Gitlitz, *Secrecy and Deceit*, pp. 533–48; Renée Levine Melammed, *Heretics or Daughters of Israel?* (Oxford, 1999), pp. 34–44; Anna Foa, "The Marrano's Kitchen," in *The Mediterranean and the Jews*, vol. 2, ed. Elliott Horowitz and Moises Orfali (Ramat-Gan, 2002), 2:13–24. I have not found reference, however, to the practice of avoiding all meat as a way of ensuring a kosher diet. Such behavior would certainly have attracted the attention of the Inquisition.

24. Gen. 14:18. Rabbi Yehuda Sarna, a student of mine, suggested that Melchizedek might serve here as a prototype for one who was not a descendent of Aaron yet a priest.

25. See above, n. 15.

us, for he is truly among those who sit before God, with their diadems on their heads, and delighting in the radiance of the divine presence.

Peroration

This is what I have taken as an emblem at the beginning of our lesson, *Pure olive oil, beaten for the light, to make a light flame daily* (Exod. 27:20).[26] For "Pure" teaches about the crown of Torah, which is a pure medication, as in the verse, *Your word is exceedingly pure* (Ps. 119:140). "Olive" teaches about the crown of royalty in its beauty and its vitality (*ra'ananuto*), as in the verse, *The Eternal named you "verdant* (ra'anan) *olive tree, fair, with fresh fruit"* (Jer. 11:16), and similarly, *His splendor shall be like the olive tree* (Hos. 4:7). "Oil" teaches about the crown of a good name, which is constantly ascending, as in the verse, *A good name is better than fragrant oil, and the day of death than the day of birth* (Eccles. 7:1). "Beaten" teaches about the crown of priesthood, the essence of which is to beat down one's body and prevail over the impulses and conquer them, as we have said. Whoever has these character traits—as this pious man did—will certainly be "for the light": to shine continually with the light of the King's countenance, as in the verse, *Only goodness and steadfast love shall pursue me all the days of my life, and I shall dwell in the house of the Eternal forever* (Ps. 23:6). But our duty is to accept this judgment, and to say, "Blessed is the Judge of Truth."[27]

(**81v**) The eulogy I delivered at the conclusion of the thirty days from the passing of the pious and humble doctor, the honorable David Masiah, may the memory of a *tsaddiq* and saint be for blessing, on Wednesday, the twelfth of Adar, 5412 [February 22, 1652]."[28]

---

26. The theme-verse, which—characteristically for his eulogies—Morteira introduces at the end.

27. This sentence appears at the end of every eulogy in Morteira's manuscript, indicating that the eulogy was delivered as an introduction to the *Tzidduq ha-Din* prayer.

28. This reading of the date, which is almost illegible from the manuscript (the two combinations of *yod-beit* could also be read as *beit* or *kaph*), is confirmed by the records of the Portuguese cemetery at Ouderkerk, according to which Dr. David Masiah died on 13 Shevat 5412 (January 23, 1652). The thirtieth day would thus be 12 Adar 5412, which did indeed fall on a Wednesday.

Eulogy for Moses de Mercado

Budapest Rabbinical Seminary MS 12, vol. 1, folios 118r–119r

Mattot, 1652

This is an unusual text, in that the Hebrew version in the manuscripts is paralleled with a Portuguese text, printed in pamphlet form. The title page reads, "הספד: Funeral Sermon Delivered in the Cemetery by Morenu ha-Rav [our Teacher the Rabbi], the Ḥ[akham] R. Saul Levi Morteira, Rosh Yeshivah and first Ḥacham of the K[ahal] K[adosh] of Amsterdam, May God make it grow, At the funeral of his worthy Talmid [student] the learned and virtuous Ḥakham Ribi [sic] Moseh de Mercado, whom God took to Himself on Shabbat 23 of the month of Tammuz, 5412 [Saturday, June 29, 1652]. May his soul be bound up in the bonds of life."[1] This and Giv'at Sha'ul *are the only publications by Morteira to appear during his lifetime. It may be the earliest example of a Jewish sermon published separately in the vernacular very soon after delivery; the practice would become common in the eighteenth and nineteenth centuries.[2] A Portuguese parallel exists for only one other of the 550 sermons in the Hebrew manuscripts.*

The structure of this eulogy is one of the simplest and most straightforward in Morteira's homiletical oeuvre; of the material I have published, only the short cemetery eulogy for David Farar is comparable.[3] The Text from the scriptural lesson has no obvious connection with the context; the dictum, by contrast, is directly linked as it recounts a model of rabbis expressing consolation to one of their own at the death of his sons. As in the first Farrar eulogy, the preacher then begins with a familiar topos, going back at least to the fifteenth century, of the reasons that would have justified him to

---

1. See H. P. Salomon, Introduction to Morteira, *Tratado,* p. xcxii. Apparently from this title page, Yosef Shein, author of the biographical sketch printed in the 1902 edition of *Giv'at Sha'ul,* was able to conclude that "on [Mercado's] grave, R. Saul Morteira shed a flood of tears in the precious eulogy he delivered there." *Giv'at Sha'ul* (Warsaw, 1902), p. 17.

2. Dan Franco Mendes wrote that Morteira "gave this sermon to the printing press in order to perpetuate the memory of the accomplishments of his disciple" (*Memorias,* p. 62; Portuguese original of the whole passage cited above, p. 163, n. 63. I am grateful to Julia Lieberman of St. Louis University for assistance with the Portuguese of this text. For later examples of such printing, mainly of occasional sermons including eulogies for royal figures, see Cecil Roth, *Magna Bibliotheca Anglo-Judaica* [London, 1937], pp. 322–28 and Saperstein, *"Your Voice Like a Ram's Horn,"* pp. 445–46.

3. Ibid., pp. 382–86.

remain silent, overcome by the reasons that impel him to speak.[4] *Silence is impelled by the precedent of Job's comforters who waited for seven days before speaking, their words stifled by the terror of the sight they see before them. Yet this impulse is overcome by others that impel him to speak.*

The body of the sermon is driven in content by the classical theological problem of the promising youth dying just at the beginning of his full flourishing. (Morteira's son-in-law, Josiah ben David Pardo, devoted a eulogy sermon to this subject, and so did many other preachers).[5] *Four explanations of this conundrum are linked with the statements of the four rabbis who came to console R. Ishmael, each one of which begins with a biblical quotation about an instance of death and then applies it* a fortiori *to the sons of Ishmael. Then all of these reasons are applied to the deceased being mourned. Morteira does not speak at length or in great detail about Mercado, but some details are provided, including his age at the time of his death and the books he had written. As with several of his other eulogies (e.g. both eulogies for David Farar and the eulogy for Menasseh ben Israel), the scriptural theme-verse is introduced only at the very end in an unexpected yet perfectly appropriate way: the female mentioned in the verse is not the young girl in her father's house, but the young soul returning to the home of its Father.*

* * *

In her youth, in her father's house (Num. 30:17).

Tractate *Mo'ed Qatan*, chapter 3 (28b): When the sons of R. Ishmael died, four elders went into his house to comfort him, R. Tarfon, R. Jose the Galilean, R. Eleazar ben Azariah, and R. Akiba. [...] R. Ishmael opened and said, "His sins were many, his sorrowful bereavements came in close succession, he troubled his masters more than once."

R. Tarfon responded and said, "*But your brothers, all the house of Israel, shall bewail the burning [that the Eternal has wrought]* (Lev. 10:6). If with Nadab and Abihu, who had performed only one office—as it is written, *Aaron's sons brought the blood to him* (Lev. 9:9)—how much more is due to the sons of R. Ishmael!"

R. Jose the Galilean responded and said, "*And all Israel shall lament over him and bury him* (1 Kings 14:13). If with Abijah, who had done only one good thing—as it is written, *for in him there was something good* (ibid.)—how much more is due to the sons of R. Ishmael!"

---

4. On this topos, see Saperstein, *Jewish Preaching*, pp. 76–77, and *"Your Voice Like a Ram's Horn,"* index, s.v. "Silence, reasons for."

5. Pardo, "Mizbaḥ ha-Zahav," Amsterdam Ets Ḥaim MS 51 (47B21), sermon 16, fol. 34.

R. Eleazar ben Azariah responded and said, *"You will die a peaceful death, and as incense was burned for your ancestors who preceded you, so shall it be burned for you* (Jer. 34:5). If with Zedekiah, king of Judah, who had performed only one office—in having lifted up Jeremiah from the mire[6]—how much more is due to the sons of R. Ishmael!"

R. Akiba responded and said, *In that day the wailing in Jerusalem shall be as great as the wailing of Hadadrimmon ... (son of Tabrimmon)* (cf. Zech. 12:11).[7] The Aramaic translation says, 'As the wailing of Ahab son of Omri, who was killed by Hadadrimmon son of Tabrimmon.' If with Ahab, king of Israel, who had done only one [good] thing—as it is written, *the king remained propped up in the chariot facing Aram ... and at dusk he died* (1 Kings 22:35)—how much more is due to the sons of R. Ishmael!"

Exordium

The Bible tells us that when Job's friends heard about all the misfortune that had come upon him, they came, *each one from his home; they met together to go and console and comfort him* (Job 2:11). When they saw him, *they sat with him on the ground seven days and seven nights; none spoke a word to him, for they saw how very great was his suffering* (Job 2:13). Indeed, that is the nature of a vessel that is crammed so completely full that nothing can spill out of it.[8] No less than this is the spectacle that is before us.[9] When we see this flower, *who bloomed like a blossom and then withered* (Job 14:2), perfect in his character, perfect in his learning, *bright-eyed and handsome* (1 Sam. 16:12) at the time of his wedding, beloved on High and esteemed here below[10]—truly "the suffering is very great," and it would be fitting not to say a word until seven days and seven nights have passed. However, *the spirit in my gut presses me* (Job 32:18), and my

---

6. See Jeremiah 38:10–13.

7. The phrase "son of Tabrimmon" is not in the biblical text or in the standard versions of the Talmudic passage.

8. This is a rather dramatic physical illustration of a psychological phenomenon: a person too overcome by emotion to express anything articulately, and therefore remains silent. The Hebrew suggests a vessel crammed so full of objects (e.g. apples, or walnuts) that you can turn it over and nothing will fall out. The Portuguese, however, specifies a liquid content (*o licor*), perhaps a narrow-mouthed bottle filled with liquid turned over vertically, with the liquid held in place by the air pressure outside.

9. The printed Portuguese text states that the eulogy was delivered "in the cemetery" (like the first eulogy for David Farar), at the time of burial. Morteira was therefore probably gesturing toward the coffin when he said these words. The Hebrew is *ha-nosei* (literally: the subject), but the Portuguese reads *o espectaculó*.

10. Cf. b. *Berakhot* 17a.

great love for the injunction "Let the honor of your disciple be as precious to you as your own."[11] Therefore, even though I am in need of comfort, however inadequately, I shall express some of the things that have come into my heart as I looked upon this terrifying sight.

Body of the Eulogy

I would say that even though we know that God's judgments are *like the great deep* (Ps. 36:7), and *who has stood in the council of the Eternal* (Jer. 23:18), nevertheless we know from His Torah and the words of his prophets the way of God's actions in general, even though we cannot attain the insight to apply these to any specific case. Therefore, when we see such a foreshortened life in such an outstanding person [lit: subject], we can be certain that it is for one of four reasons. Indeed, the four leaders of the Jewish people extended their comfort on the basis of these reasons, when they came together to console R. Ishmael at the death of his youthful sons, full to the brim with knowledge of Torah and good deeds; this is the idea they expressed in their arguments from the weaker case to the stronger.

1. R. Tarfon comforted him first, demonstrating their obligation to mourn from the case of Nadab and Abihu. In this he taught him that sometimes God takes to Himself a righteous person who is still young for His own glory, because the person was worthy. This is as the Sages said about the verse, *You are awesome, O God, through Your holy ones* (Ps. 68:36).[12] For then everyone will think, "If the flame has fallen upon the cedars, what can the moss upon the wall do?"[13] It is as the Bible said about the incident with Uzzah, *David was afraid that day; he thought to himself, "How can I let the ark of the Eternal come to me?"* (2 Sam. 6:9).

This is the very idea with which R. Tarfon comforted R. Ishmael, citing the verse, *all the house of Israel, shall bewail the burning that the Eternal has wrought* (Lev. 10:6), which was said about the two sons of Aaron, youthful and good. As consolation for them, they said that Moses said to Aaron, *This is what the Eternal meant when He said, "Through those near to Me I show Myself holy, and gain glory before all the people." Then Aaron was silent* (Lev. 10:3). The Sages explained this as follows: Moses said, "When God said, *it will be sanctified by My glory* (Exod. 29:43), I was under the impression that this place would be honored either by me or by you. Now I see that Nadav and Abihu were greater

---

11. M. *Avot* 4,12, *Tanḥuma Be-Shallah* 26.

12. See Rashi on Lev. 10:3 and Num. 20:13.

13. B. *Mo'ed Qatan* 25b. Note Morteira's use of this passage as a structuring element in his second eulogy for Dr. David Farar (Saperstein, *"Your Voice Like a Ram's Horn,"* pp. 387–410).

than either one of us."[14] For in this way, all the people were astonished, and dread entered their hearts, as they thought, "These were deputies to the High Priest. They achieved mastery of both fine character traits and Torah learning. The verse teaches this by saying: *This is the line of Aaron and Moses at the time when the Eternal spoke with Moses on Mount Sinai. These were the names of Aaron's sons: Nadab, the first born, and Abihu* (Num. 3:1–2)—for they were Aaron's sons by birth, and Moses' sons by the instruction he gave them concerning that which the Eternal spoke to him on Mount Sinai.[15] Now if on the day of their wedding[16] and their inauguration as priests, they died suddenly over a trivial matter, how intensely careful we need to be!"

2. R. Jose the Galilean comforted him with the case of Abijah son of Jeroboam, thereby showing him a second reason why God sometimes takes to Himself a righteous person in the midst of his life. This is that through divine wisdom, it is seen that this person is at that moment in a state of perfection, worthy of being plucked. The Sages in the Midrash Rabbah, on the verse, *Enoch walked with God; then he was no more, for God took him* (Gen. 5:24), gave an analogy with a fig farmer: the fig farmer certainly knows when the figs are ripe for plucking.[17] If we have seen this with Abijah, in whom there was [only] one thing good,[18] how much more with the sons of Ishmael should we accept God's decree and say that He certainly knows the time when they are ripe for plucking.

3. R. Eleazar ben Azariah comforted him with the case of Zedekiah, king of Judah; for having lifted up Jeremiah from the mire,[19] this message from God was proclaimed to him: *You will die a peaceful death, and as incense was burned for your ancestors who preceded you, so shall it be burned for you* (Jer. 34:5).

---

14. Cf. Lev. Rabbah 12,2, Rashi on Gen. 29:43 and Lev. 10:3. The Sages read *sanctified by My glory* (*bi-khevodi*) as "sanctified by My honored ones" (*be-mekhubadai*) (b. *Zevaḥim* 115b); thus Moses realizes at the death of Nadab and Abihu that God was hinting to him in Exodus 29:43 that on the day when God's presence would rest upon the tabernacle, it would be sanctified through the death of Aaron's sons.

15. Cf. Rashi on Num. 3:1.

16. Hebrew ביום חתונתם(?). None of the sources mentions anything about their wedding; indeed, the Midrash states that they never married because they believed that no woman was worthy of them (Lev. Rabbah 20,10, *Pesiqta de-Rav Kahana* 26,9). The Portuguese text says "e no dia que se estreyarão Sacerdotes, domesticos e validos da caza do Soberano Rey do Mundo, morẽ de supito abrazados" (on the day they became priests, servants and favorites of the house of the sovereign King of the universe, they died suddenly, burnt).

17. Cf. Eccles. Rabbah 5,14, Song Rabbah, 6,9, y. *Berakhot* 20a, all of which contain the analogy of the fig farmer to illustrate God's knowledge of when to take the righteous person, but without connecting it to Genesis 5:24.

18. See 1 Kings 14:13,

19. See Jer. 38:10–13.

In this he showed a third reason why God takes to Himself a righteous person in the midst of his life, namely, to inform and make public the principle that "the reward for the commandments is not in this world."[20] For indeed, how can the human intellect come to recognize the impact of chance when they see a righteous person who is young—full of Torah and mitzvot, good in the sight of God and of other human beings[21]—pass away in the middle of a normal life span, except by entering God's sanctuary, to reflect on their fate (cf. Ps. 73:17). This is as the poet said in Psalm 73: *Whom else have I in heaven? And having You, I want no one on earth* (Ps. 73:25). For after he showed that all the good things of this world are false by their very nature, he said to God that he does not want his [?] in this nature, but rather something worthwhile and true.

Thus he said, *Yet I was always with You; You held my right hand; You guided me by Your counsel and led me toward honor. Whom else have I in heaven? And having You, I want no one on earth. My flesh and my heart fail* (Ps. 73:23–26), referring to the vegetative and the sensate soul,[22] but *God is the rock of my heart, my portion forever* (Ps. 73:26), referring to the rational [soul], which bears and stands upon the sensate—that is why it is called *the rock of my heart*–and it cleaves to God, *the rock of my mind, my portion.* This is what he hinted at in Zedekiah's lifting of Jeremiah from the mire. It means that when he saw all the suffering that had come upon God's prophet, who went out to speak in God's name, to the point where he was sinking in the mire, he lifted him up from the mire and saw that his portion is not in this lowly, material world, but rather in *God's mountain, His holy place* (Ps. 24:3). If it was so with Zedekiah, how much more is due the sons of Ishmael.

4. However, R. Akiba comforted him with the case of Ahab's standing in the chariot, facing Aram, even though had had been fatally stricken, to the point where he died at dusk.[23] He did not [flee?], in order to prevent the enemies from pursuing the Israelites.[24] In this way, he saved many of them, and that is why they mourned him greatly, as the Bible says, *In that day the*

---

20. B. *Qiddushin* 39b and parallels.

21. Cf. b. *Qiddushin* 40a.

22. Morteira's explanation of these two terms appears to echo the commentary on Psalms of Mercado, who explained the word *sh'eri* as the "*nefesh ha-tsomaḥat*" and *levavi* as "*ha-ḥiyunit*,"—where Rashi, Ibn Ezra, Me'iri, Metsudat Tsiyon, all explain *sh'eri* as "my body," and Alsheikh explains it as the realm of human action as opposed to thought. See Mercado's *Perush Sefer Qohelet u-Tehilim,* p. 62a.

23. 1 Kings 22:35 (cited as a proof text in the dictum).

24. Cf. Rashi on 1 Kings 22:35 and b. *Mo'ed Qatan* 28b; he emphasizes more the effect of demoralization on the Israelite forces had Ahab collapsed or fled ("so that Israel would not flee and be killed while fleeing").

wailing in Jerusalem shall be as great as the wailing of Hadadrimmon ... son of Tabrimmon (cf. Zech. 12:11).[25] In this he taught a fourth reason why God takes the righteous person, namely, to stand in the breach against the angel of destruction, for one righteous person is deemed equivalent to many other Jews. Concerning [the battle at] Ai, the Bible says, *About thirty-six men from the people fell* (cf. Josh. 7:5 and Exod. 32:28).[26] The Sages said that the reason for the *kaf* of comparison [*dimyon*: "approximation"?], rather than the precise number intended, is that the verse refers to Jair ben Manasseh, who was deemed equivalent to a majority of the Sanhedrin.[27] If they made great wailing for Ahab, because he stood in the breach, how much more is due the sons of Ishmael.

Coda

From all of these examples, who would not know how all of us should bewail and feel pain over the loss of this wise and intelligent young man, may the memory of the righteous be for blessing, the esteemed R. Moses de Mercado. By his Torah learning, his perfection, his youthfulness, and his noble character traits, God is honored through him.[28] God found him in a state of perfection,[29] for when he was less than twenty years old he had already written a commentary on Psalms and had almost completed his commentary on Ecclesiastes,[30] not to mention his fine, highly rhetorical poems. From him we see and know clearly that there is a time of doom for everything that occurs (cf. Eccles. 8:5 and 3:17), and the reward for the commandments is not in this world.[31] Commenting on the verse, *that you may fare well and have a long*

---

25. See above, n. 7.

26. Morteira seems to have conflated the two verses. The Portuguese version contains the same error, identifying the verse as Joshua 7:5, but rendering it, *E cahio de povo como trinta e seis homẽs*.

27. B. *Sanhedrin* 44b, b. *Baba Batra* 121b.

28. Echoing the statement about Nadab and Abihu.

29. Echoing the statement about Enoch and the analogy with the fig farmer.

30. The two works were published together by the press of Immanuel Benveniste at Amsterdam. The year of publication on the title page is 5413 (1652–1653), some time within two to fourteen months after the author's death. The introductory section contains a preface by Morteira, four memorial poems (Samuel de Cassires, Isaac Nahar, Solomon de Olivera, Samuel Valverde), and an introduction by Jacob Sasportas, who is identified as the editor of the book. Sasportas may have been responsible for completing what the author did not quite finish in the commentary on Qohelet, which appears in print to be complete.

31. Echoing the statement cited above in the comfort by R. Eleazar ben Azariah (above, n. 20).

life (Deut. 22:7), the Sages told of a youth who climbed a ladder [in order to honor his father's instruction to fulfill the commandment by sending away the mother bird; the young men fell and died], asking, "Where is the long life of this one? Rather, the verse refers to a world that is entirely good, a world that is entirely long."[32] Finally, God wanted to make atonement for our remnant, making him into a sacrifice before God to remove from us all misfortunes.[33] God will *give him a portion with the multitude, he shall receive his spoil with the mighty* (Isa. 53:12).

This fits our Text, ***in her youth, in her father's house*** (Num. 30:17). For this pure soul returned in her youth, at the beginning of his life, to her heavenly Father, as the Bible says, *The dust returns to the ground as it was, the spirit returns to God who gave it* (Eccles. 12:7). As for us, we must accept the divine judgment and say, "Blessed is the Judge of Truth."

---

32. B. *Qiddushin* 39b and parallels.

33. Literally: "all happy things," a euphemism, as in the title of the rabbinic treatise on mourning. Although the echo is not as clear as in the previous cases, this must allude to Akiba's reason for the death of the young, "to stand in the breach against the angel of destruction." Thus, characteristically (although less explicitly than usually), Morteira recapitulates the major substantive points of his discourse near the end.

Epilogue

Concluding this survey of the records of Morteira's homiletical output, it seems appropriate to summarize its content and significance. I begin with what is missing, what I have not discovered in these texts: First of all, personal glimpses of the speaker. Some modern preachers regularly introduce themselves into their sermons, using their own experiences, spiritual struggles, intellectual perplexities and triumphs, whether recent or early in their lives, as a basis for the message directed to others. Like most pre-twentieth-century Jewish preachers, however, Morteira rarely speaks about himself. Occasionally, especially in the eulogies, he will mention his own relationship with the deceased. Sometimes he will talk about his difficulties in deriving an appropriate message from the biblical verse at hand. If the sermon was delivered in conjunction with a life cycle event of a family member (e.g. the betrothal or wedding of one of his daughters), this will be noted at the end. The first-person singular pronoun appears when he is referring the listeners to a sermon he delivered in the past, or a book he has read, a conversation with a Christian thinker, or an interpretation by his distinguished grandfather (Judah Katzenellenbogen) or his mentor Elijah Montalto. But the personal voice of the preacher is difficult to hear in these texts. One reads through hundreds of pages without learning anything about his biography (his parents and siblings, childhood, his education in Venice or the years spent with Montalto in France), or even his personality. For this we need the archival records of the Amsterdam community. The sermons reveal his mind and his aesthetic sense, but not his life or his emotions.

Many names from the community appear in the texts, especially in the postscripts that provide information about the circumstances of delivery. These details complement the archival records about individuals and institutions. Several of the eulogies poignantly illuminate personal qualities and experiences of such important community figures as Abraham and Sarah Farar and David their son, as well as David Masiah and Rabbi Menasseh ben Israel. But we look in vain for explicit mention of the most famous "heretics" of the time: Uriel da Costa, Juan de Prado, Baruch Spinoza. I have found no mention of the Venetian rabbi assumed to be Morteira's primary teacher, Leon Modena—no reference to a personal relationship, no citation of Modena's works—or of Morteira's colleague in Amsterdam, Isaac Aboab da Fonseca, with whom he engaged in a vehement intellectual polemic over the ultimate punishment for unrepentant sinners. While he refers occasionally to "the books of the Gentiles," he does not appear to cite by name any Christian thinker. Where exempla are introduced for a homiletical purpose, they are of nameless types (a nursing mother, a person attempting to study alchemy, a printer, a master artist and his school of disciples), not of real individuals.

Moreover, if we did not know where Morteira was delivering the sermons, it would be difficult to identify the unique environment of Amsterdam from internal evidence. The one dramatic survey of the discrimination and oppression suffered by Jews in the other great contemporary communities (see above, pp. 402–4), and a reference to the absence of any requirement for distinctive clothing (above, p. 460, n. 24) would be the best clues. But the sermons appear to contain no explicit reflection on the civic government of Amsterdam (or of his native city, Venice); indeed, the various discussions of political theory in the texts seem to be based on the monarchy of the biblical sources. While Morteira speaks about the uncertainties of wealth, I have found no reference to the celebrated tulip craze of 1636–1637. I have found no reference to the princes of the House of Orange who reigned during Morteira's tenure; no specific mention of (though a probable allusion to) the lapse of the Twelve-Years' Truce with Spain in 1621 (above, p. 134); no reference to the Thirty Years' War or the dramatic Treaty of Münster that ended it in 1648, or to the Anglo-Dutch War of 1652–54. While Morteira uses history—mainly ancient history—for homiletical purposes, with rare exceptions these sermons are not texts from which to learn about contemporary events. Nor is there evidence of intellectual confrontation with the challenges of contemporary science. Like many of his rabbinic colleagues, scientifically his horizons remained confined by a medieval worldview, his cosmology rooted in the Bible and the Talmud, with no hint of the dramatically expanding Copernican Universe.

Despite these lacunae, I hope to have succeeded in convincing readers of the many levels of importance in the manuscripts of Morteira's sermons. First, they are uniquely abundant documents for the history of Jewish preaching, reflecting its homiletical and exegetical art at a consummate level. The canon of medieval and early modern Jewish preachers, as it had been established by the few scholars who have investigated the field, consisted almost exclusively of individuals whose written legacy was limited to a single book of sermons (occasionally supplemented by exegetical works), analogous to Morteira's *Giv'at Sha'ul*, with one sermon for each biblical lesson. The 550 manuscript sermons, a unique corpus for the period, enable us to evaluate a preacher's productivity week after week for an entire career. Although he re-used some of his material, especially during the last two decades of his life, he continued to deliver carefully crafted and intellectually stimulating sermons for more than four decades. The quality of the printed sermons is not noticeably higher than that in the manuscripts; they were not selected because of their special brilliance, nor were they (with rare exceptions) extensively re-worked and polished for publication. The entire corpus of texts in manuscript and in print represents a consistently high level of creativity under the pressure of time, sustained by their author throughout much of his life.

In addition to their importance for the history of Jewish preaching, the sermons are windows into one of the most fascinating and dynamic Jewish communities of the early modern period. Abundant evidence about this Portuguese community, preserved in various archives and in the writings of some of its members, has been mined by scholars whose conclusions have appeared in a spate of recent articles and books. Until now, Morteira's sermons were the largest untapped body of primary source material for this community. Even if the information they provided pertained only to its leading rabbi, they would be valuable for this reason. But as I have shown above, they illuminate aspects of the community as well: in eulogies about some of its leading figures, in names of individuals designated for special honors or terms of office, in references to institutions and events and special occasions, in criticisms of behavior that the preacher denounced as incompatible with proper Jewish life. The other rabbis of the community during this period—Isaac Aboab da Fonseca, Menasseh ben Israel, David Pardo—preached regularly as well, perhaps as impressively as Morteira, but as no collections of their sermons have been preserved, Morteira's texts become the more significant.

Finally, viewed as a whole, these texts represent a sophisticated articulation of many aspects of Jewish tradition and Jewish historical experience, presented to intelligent laymen engaged in the process of discovering the meaning of being Jewish. They are creations of a highly talented and respected seventeenth-century rabbi—not a profoundly original thinker, but an undeniably gifted communicator and interpreter of traditional texts. Imagine a typical new member of the community. Arriving from Portugal in 1620 with only the most rudimentary knowledge of Judaism and almost no comprehension of Hebrew, he sits in the congregation on the Sabbath morning trying to follow the service. As he gradually becomes more familiar with the prayer book, he still listens to the required Hebrew readings from the Pentateuch and Prophets without understanding what they mean beyond the lingering memories from a Christian education. For such a congregant, it is not far-fetched to conclude that the sermon delivered in Portuguese by a young rabbi exploring one of the biblical verses in conjunction with a passage from rabbinic literature and a conceptual religious problem, might well be one of the highlights of the morning. Furthermore, that the hypothetical listener not only would have been impressed by the clarity of the preacher's presentation and the elegance of his delivery, but that he would also have learned something about that biblical verse, or about the rabbinic text, or about the problem that the preacher raised and explored, something that would remain with him.

As the weeks and years elapsed the listener would find himself, while becoming more familiar with the liturgy and the rituals, also accumulating a wealth of such insights and integrating them in his mind, so that new information acquired from the weekly pulpit discourse would begin to fit into a pattern. Occasionally, he would hear the vaguely troubling Christian arguments he remembered from his childhood education in Portugal rehearsed and rebutted. He would hear a cogent defense of Jewish teachings about the tradition of Torah that the Christians had derided. From time to time he would be informed that certain patterns of behavior, though familiar and perhaps even prevalent, were unacceptable to the rabbi and should be improved. Frequently he would be reminded that he and his family and friends were protagonists in a great drama of a noble people exiled from its land, buffeted by many nations, uprooted from newer homes, but destined for ultimate vindication: events that were the result neither of the vagaries of chance nor of the brutality of power politics, but were rather encoded in the Bible and remained under the direct providential supervision of the Master of the Universe. Gradually, through the ongoing educational program of the sermons, the listener might begin to feel comfortable in his new identity and in the tradition that, though new to him, was presented from the pulpit as something ancient, venerable, and precious. Through the sermons, alongside the other instruments of acculturation mobilized by the community, the "New Jew" would begin to feel rooted.

I conclude with a special plea. This source material should not remain unpublished, accessible only to those who visit the Library of the Rabbinical Seminary in Budapest or the Institute for Microfilmed Hebrew Manuscripts in Jerusalem. Many Hebrew texts of far less literary and historical significance are available in multi-volume printed editions. The entire corpus of Morteira's manuscript sermons deserves to be published, in an edition that will identify texts cited by Morteira (biblical verses, rabbinic passages, quotations from or allusions to medieval writers), note the cross-references to other sermons delivered earlier, include some discursive annotation where the content requires explanation for the non-specialist reader, and highlight points of comparisons with Morteira's other works (especially the *Tratado*). A comprehensive cumulative index for the entire corpus will be invaluable.

This will not be a simple publishing task. While many of the sermons are fully legible from the microfilm to those who have mastered the author's script, many others contain passages legible only from the original manuscripts. The task of transcription will be extremely demanding. Publication is too large a project for any one person; rather, a team of scholars with different areas of expertise would need to cooperate. The finished project would be a monumental contribution to Jewish scholarship.

Those who are interested in the history of Jewish preaching look with envy at the splendid multi-volume annotated editions of sermons by such Christian preachers as John Donne, Jonathan Edwards, and John Wesley. Morteira's homiletical oeuvre is worthy of a comparable treatment.

Bibliography

Primary Sources

Aboab, Immanuel. *Nomologia.* In *Be-Ma'avaq al 'Erkah shel Torah: Ha-Nomologia le-R. Immanuel Aboab,* transl. and ed. Moises Orfali. Jerusalem: Ben Zvi Institute, 1997.

Aboab, Isaac. *Luaḥ sefarim: Catalogus variorum … librorum, praecipue theologicorum … clarissimi doctissimique viri D. Jsaaci Abuab….* Amsterdam: David Tartas, 1693.

Aboab, Samuel. *Devar Shemu'el: She'elot u-Teshuvot.* Venice, 1720.

Abravanel, Isaac. *Naḥalat Avot.* New York: Hubert Printing, 1953.

———. *Perush al Nevi'im Aharonim.* Jaffa: Torah ve-Da'at, n.d.

———. *Perush al Nevi'im u-Khetuvim.* Tel Aviv: Elisha, 1970.

———. *Perush al ha-Torah.* 3 vols. Jerusalem: B'nei Arbel, 1964.

———. *Yeshu'ot Meshiho.* Koenigsberg, 1861.

Albo, Joseph. *Sefer ha-'Ikkarim,* ed. Isaac Husik. 3 vols. Philadelphia: JPS, 1930.

Alfalas, Moses. *Va-Yaqhel Moshe.* Venice, 1597, reprint edition Brooklyn, 1992.

Andrewes, Lancelot. *Sermons,* ed. with an Introduction by G. M. Story. Oxford: Clarendon Press, 1967.

Arama, Isaac. *'Aqedat Yitshaq.* 3 vols. Warsaw, 1883,

Ashkenazi, Eliezer Elijah. *Ma'aseh ha-Shem.* New York: Grosman, 1962.

Azulai, Ḥayyim Joseph David. *Sefer Ma'agal Tov ha-Shalem.* Berlin: Mekiẓe Nirdamim, 1921.

Basnage, Jacques. *Histoire du peuple Juif depuis Jésus Christ jusquà présent, pour servir de continuation à l'histoire de Joseph.* 9 vols. in 15 pts. The Hague, 1716–1721.

Bossuet, Jacques Bénigne. *Ouevres de Bossuet.* 4 vols. Paris: Chez Firmin Didot, 1862.

Burton, Robert. *The Anatomy of Melancholy.* 2 vols. London: Dent, 1932.

Calvin, John. *Institutes of the Christian Religion.* 2 vols. Philadelphia: Presbyterian Board of Christian Education, 1936.

John Calvin's Sermons on the Ten Commandments, ed. Benjamin W. Farley. Grand Rapids: Baker Books, 1980.

———. *The Sermons of M. John Calvin Upon the Fifth Booke of Moses called Deuteronomie.* London: Henry Middleton, 1593; facsimile edition, Edinburgh: Banner of Truth Trust, 1987.

———. *Sermons on the Acts of the Apostles,* ed. Willem Balke and Wilhelmus H. Th. Moehn. Neukirchen-Bluyn: Neukirchener Verlag des Erzhiehungs- vereins, 1994.

———. *Theological Treatises,* ed. J.K.S. Reid. Philadelphia: Westminster Press, 1954.

Camus, Jean-Pierre. *Homélies panegyriques de Sainct Charles Borromée.* Paris, 1623.

Carpov, Paul Theodor. *Animadversiones philologico-critico-sacrae.* Leipzig, 1740.

da Costa [Acosta], Uriel. *Examination of Pharisaic Traditions,* ed. H. P. Salomon and I. S. D. Sasson. Leiden: Brill, 1993.

Crescas, Ḥasdai. *Or ha-Shem,* ed. Shlomo Fisher. Jerusalem: Sifrei Ramot, 1990.

———. *The Refutation of the Christian Principles by Ḥasdai Crescas,* tr. Daniel Lasker. Albany: SUNY Press, 1992.

Donne, John. *The Complete Poetry and Selected Prose of John Donne.* New York: Modern Library, 1941,

———. *John Donne's Sermons on the Psalms and Gospels,* ed. Evelyn Simpson. Berkeley: University of California Press, 1963.

549

Duran, Profiat. *Kelimat ha-Goyyim* in *Kitvei Pulmus le-Profiat Duran*, ed. Frank Talmage. Jerusalem: Zalman Shazar Center, 1981.

Duran, Simeon ben Tsemaḥ. *Teshuvot Tashbets.* Amsterdam, 1738.

Edrehi, Moses. *Yad Mosheh.* Amsterdam, 1809.

Franco Mendes, David. *Memorias do estabelecimento e progresso dos judeos portuguezes e espanhoes nesta famosa citade de Amsterdam*, ed. L. Fuks and R. G. Fuks-Mansfeld. Assen: van Gorcum, 1975.

Gans, David. *Tsemaḥ David le-Rabbi David Gans*, ed. Mordecai Breuer. Jerusalem: The Magnes Press, 1983.

Gikatilla, Joseph. *Sha'are Orah: Gates of Light*, transl. Ari Weinstein. San Francisco: HarperCollins, 1994.

Ḥagiz, Moses. *Sefat Emet.* Jerusalem: Yo'el Mosheh, 1881; Jerusalem: Hotsa'at Sha'ar, 1986.

Ha-Kohen, Joseph. *Emeq ha-Bakha*, ed. M. Letteris. Cracow: Faust's Buchhandlung, 1895.

Ḥayyot, Isaac. *Paḥad Yitsḥaq.* Lublin, 1573.

Ibn Daud, Abraham. *The Exalted Faith*, translated with commentary by Norbert M. Samuelson. Rutherford, N.J.: Fairleigh Dickinson University Press, 1986.

Ibn Janaḥ, Jonah. *Sefer ha-Shorashim.* Berlin: Mekiẓe Nirdamim, 1896.

Ibn Shu'eib, Joel. '*Olat Shabbat.* Venice, 1577, offset edition Jerusalem, 1973.

Ibn Shu'eib, Solomon. *Derashot R. Yehoshu'ah ibn Shu'eib*, 2 vols. Jerusalem: Makhon Lev Sameaḥ, 1992.

Ibn Verga, Solomon. *Shevet Yehudah.* Jerusalem: Mosad Bialik, 1947.

Ibn Yaḥya, Gedaliah. *Shalshelet ha-Qabbalah.* Warsaw: P. Levenzohn, 1877.

Israel ben Benjamin of Belzyce. "Tiferet Yisra'el." Oxford Bodleian Hebrew MS 989.

Jaffe, Samuel. *Sefer Yefeh To'ar.* 8 vols. Jerusalem: H. Wagschal, 1989.

Jessurun, Rehuel. *Dialogo dos Montes*, ed. Philip Polack. London: Tamesis, 1975.

Judah Loew ben Bezalel (Maharal). *Sifrei Maharal mi-Prag.* 13 vols. New York: Hebraica Press, 1969.

Kasher, Menaḥem, ed. *Torah Shelemah.* 35 vols. New York: American Biblical Encyclopedia Society, 1949.

Katzenellenbogen, Samuel Judah. *Shneim 'Asar Derashot.* Warsaw, 1875.

Kimḥi, David. *Sefer ha-Shorashim.* Berlin: G. Bethge, 1847.

Kimḥi, Joseph and David. *Sefer ha-Berit u-Vikkuḥei RaDaK im ha-Natsrut*, ed. Frank Ephraim Talmage. Jerusalem: Mosad Bialik, 1974.

Levi ben Gershom (RaLBaG), *Perush al ha-Torah.* Venice, 1547, reprint edition New York, 1958.

Levi, Solomon. *Divrei Shelomoh.* Venice, 1596.

Lucas, Jean-Maximilien (supposed author). *La Vie de Spinosa*, in *The Oldest Biography Of Spinoza*, ed. A. Wolf. London: Allen & Unwin, 1927.

Luther Martin. *Luther's Works.* 55 vols. St. Louis: Concordia Publishing House, 1955–1967.

Machado, Francisco. *The Mirror of the New Christians of Francisco Machado*, ed. Mildred Vieira and Frank Talmage. Toronto: Pontifical Institute of Mediaeval Studies, 1977.

Maimonides, Moses. *Code (Mishneh Torah).* 14 books in 5 volumes. Jerusalem: Pardes, 1955.

———. *Crisis and Leadership: Epistles of Maimonides.* Translations and notes by Abraham Halkin, discussions by David Hartman. Philadelphia: JPS, 1985.

———. *Guide for the Perplexed*, translated and annotated by M. Friedländer. 3 vols. in 1. New York: Hebrew Publishing Company, 1946.

Medinah, Samuel de. *She'elot u-Teshuvot.* New York: Polak, 1959.

Me'iri, Menaḥem. *Perush le-Sefer Tehillim.* Jerusalem: Mekize Nirdamim, 1936.

Menasseh ben Israel. *Conciliator: A Reconcilement of the Apparent Contradictions in Holy Scripture.* 2 vols. London: Duncan and Malcolm, 1842; reprint edition, Brooklyn: Sepher Hermon Press, 2000.

——. *De la fragilité humaine et de l'inclination de l'homme au péché,* transl. and ed. Henry Méchoulan. Paris: Cerf, 1996.

——. *The Hope of Israel,* ed. Henry Méchoulan and Gérard Nahon. Oxford: Oxford University Press for the Littman Library, 1987.

Mercado, Moses Israel. *Perush Sefer Qohelet u-Tehillim.* Amsterdam: Immanuel Benveniste, 1652–1653.

Messer Leon, Judah. *The Book of the Honeycomb's Flow,* transl. and ed. by Isaac Rabinowitz. Ithaca: Cornell University Press, 1983.

Modena, Leon. *The Autobiography of a Seventeenth-Century Venetian Rabbi: Leon Modena's Life of Judah,* ed. Mark Cohen. Princeton: Princeton University Press, 1988.

——. *Iggerot R. Yehudah Aryeh mi-Modena,* ed. Jacob Boksenboim. Tel Aviv: Tel Aviv University, 1984.

——. *Midbar Yehudah.* Venice, 1602.

——. *Midbar Yehudah.* B'nei B'rak: Sifrei Qodesh Mishor, 2002.

——. *Ziqnei Yehudah,* ed. Shlomo Simonsohn. Jerusalem: Mosad ha-Rav Kook, 1956.

Morteira, Saul Levi. "Declaracíon de los Mahamarim del Talmud contra las calumnias del Seniense," Ets Ḥaim MS 48 c 5 (= "Respuesta a los objeciones con que el Sinenese injustamente calunia al Talmud").

——. *Giv'at Sha'ul.* Amsterdam: Imanoel Benveniste, 1645.

——. *Giv'at Sha'ul,* with biographical introduction by the publisher. Warsaw: Joseph Shein, 1902.

——. *Giv'at Sha'ul.* Warsaw, 1912.

——. *Giv'at Sha'ul.* Brooklyn: Moriah Offset, 1992.

——. "Giv'at Sha'ul." Budapest Rabbinical Seminary Hebrew MS 12. 5 vols.

——. "Responses to the Questions of a Priest from Rouen," translated by J. R. Paynado.
{*http://www.jewish-history.com/Occident/volume3/jun1845/questions.html*}
{*http://www.jewish-history.com/Occident/volume3/nov1845/questions.html*}
{*http://www.jewish-history.com/Occident/volume3/dec1845/questions.html*}
{*http://www.jewish-history.com/Occident/volume3/jan1846/questions.html*}

——. "Sete Derashot compostos pelo doctissimo è carissimo Senhor Haham asalem Morenu a Rab Saul Levi Morteira," Ets Ḥaim MS 48 C 7.

——. "Sermão funeral feito em bet aḤaim pelo excelentissimo Moreno Arab o H. r. Saul Levi Morteyra." Amsterdam, 5412 [1652].

——. *Traktaat betreffende de waarheid van de wet van Mozes,* transl. and ed. H. P. Salomon. Braga: Barbosa & Xavier, 1988.

——. *Tratado da verdade da lei de Moisés,* transcribed and ed. H. P. Salomon. Coimbra: Por Ordem da Universidade, 1988.

Moses ben Naḥman (RaMBaN). *Kitvei Rabbenu Mosheh ben Naḥman,* ed. Ḥayyim (Charles) Chavel. 2 vols. Jerusalem: Mosad ha-Rav Kook, 1971.

Müntzer, Thomas. *Revelation and Revolution: Basic Writings of Thomas Müntzer,* ed. Michael G. Baylor. Bethlehem, Penna.: Lehigh University Press, 1993.

Nissim ben Reuben Gerundi. *Derashot ha-RaN,* ed. Leon A. Feldman. Jerusalem: Shalem Institute, 1973.

Pardo, Josiah. "Mizbaḥ ha-Zahav." Amsterdam Ets Ḥaim Library MS 51 (47 B 21).

de' Rossi, Azariah. *Kitvei Azariah min ha-Adumim,* ed. Robert Bonfil. Jerusalem: Mosad Bialik, 1991.

_____. *The Light of the Eyes,* translated and annotated by Joanna Weinberg. New Haven: Yale University Press, 2001.

_____. *Me'or 'Einayim.* Vilna, 1866.

Saadia Gaon. *The Book of Beliefs and Opinions.* New Haven: Yale University Press, 1948.

Saba, Abraham. *Tseror ha-Mor.* Tel Aviv: Offset Brodi-Katz, 1975.

Sasportas, Jacob. *She'elot u-Teshuvot Ohel Ya'aqov.* B'nai B'rak: Yosef Heilperin, 1985.

_____. *Tsitsat Novel Tsevi,* ed. and introd. by Isaiah Tishby. Jerusalem: Mosad Bialik, 1954.

Schapiro, Tuviah Pesach. *Beit ha-Otsar: Sippurim.* Warsaw, 1876, pp. 50–61.

Siriro, Samuel Saul. *Derushei Maharshash Siriro,* ed. David Ovadyah. 2 vols. Jerusalem: David Ovadyah, 1989–1991.

Sobol, Yehoshu'a. *Solo.* Tel Aviv: Or Am, 1991.

Sola, David Aaron de. "A Sermon on the Excellence of the Holy Law." London: H. Barnett, 1831.

Spinoza, Baruch. *Theological-Political Treatise.* Second edition, transl. Samuel Shirley, introd. and annot. Seymour Feldman. Indianapolis: Hackett Publishing Co., 1998.

Usque, Samuel. *Consolation for the Tribulations of Israel,* transl. and ed. Martin A. Cohen. Philadelphia, JPS, 1965.

Vital, Benjamin ben Eliezer ha-Kohen. *Gevul Binyamin.* Amsterdam, 1727.

Weil, Jacob. *She'elot u-Teshuvot.* Jerusalem: Makhon Yerushalyim, 2001.

Wesley, John. *Forty-Four Sermons on Several Occasions.* Peterborough, UK: Epworth Press, 1944.

Yosippon. *Sefer Yosippon,* ed. David Flusser. 2 vols. Jerusalem: Mosad Bialik, 1978.

Zacuto, Abraham. *Sefer Yuhasin ha-Shalem,* ed. H. Filipowski. London: Me'orerei Yeshenim, 1857.

Zahalon, Jacob. *A Guide for Preachers on Composing and Delivering Sermons: The OR HA-DARSHANIM of Jacob Zahalon,* transl. and ed. Henry Sosland. New York: JTSA, 1987.

Zangwill, Israel. *Dreamers of the Ghetto.* Philadelphia: JPS, 1898.

Secondary Works

Adelman, Howard. "Custom, Law, and Gender: Levirate Union among Ashkenazim and Sephardim in Italy after the Expulsion from Spain," in *The Expulsion of the Jews: 1492 and After,* ed. Raymond Waddington and Arthur Williamson. New York: Garland Publishing, 1994, pp. 107–25.

_____. "Success and Failure in the Seventeenth-Century Ghetto of Venice: The Life and Thought of Leon Modena, 1571–1648." Brandeis University Ph.D. Dissertation, 1985.

Aescoli, Aaron Zeev. *Ha-Tenu'ot ha-Meshihiyot be-Yisra'el.* Jerusalem: Mosad Bialik, 1956.

Altmann, Alexander. "Eternality of Punishment: A Theological Controversy Within the Amsterdam Rabbinate in the Thirties of the Seventeenth Century." *PAAJR* 40 (1973): 1–88.

Ancona, J. d'. "Komst der Marranen in Noord-Nederland: De Portugese Gemeenten te Amsterdam tot de Vereneging 1639," in *Geschiedenis der Joden in Nederland*, ed. H. Brugmans and A. Frank. Amsterdam: Van Holkema & Warendorf, 1940, pp. 201–69.

Ariès, Philippe. *The Hour of Our Death*. New York: Vintage Books, 1982.

Assaf, Simha. "Anusei Sefarad u-Fortugal be-Sifrut ha-Teshuvot." *Me'assef Tziyon* 5 (1933): 19–61.

Assis, Yom Tov. "Welfare and Mutual Aid in the Spanish Jewish Communities," in *Moreshet Sefarad: The Sephardi Legacy*, ed. Ḥaim Beinart. 2 vols. Jerusalem: Magnes Press, 1992, 1: 318–45.

Attias, Jean-Christophe. *Isaac Abravanel: La mémoire et l'espérance*. Paris: Cerf, 1992.

Bailey, Derrick. *Sexual Relations in Christian Thought*. New York: Harper, 1959.

Baldwin, C. S. *Ancient Rhetoric and Poetic*. Gloucestor, Mass.: Peter Smith, 1959.

Baron, Salo W. *SRHJ*. 18 vols. Philadelphia and New York: JPS and Columbia University Press, 19521983.

Bartal, Israel and Yosef Kaplan, "'Aliyat 'Aniyyim me-Amsterdam le-Eretz Yisra'el Be-Reshit ha-Me'ah ha-Sheva-'Esreh." *Shalem* 6 (1992): 175–93.

Baruchson, Shifra. *Sefarim ve-Qor'im*. Ramat-Gan: Bar-Ilan University Press, 1993.

Barukh, Y. L. *Sefer ha-Mo'adim*, 8 vols. Tel Aviv: Dvir, 1946–1965.

Bashan, Eliezer. "Ḥevrot *Biqqur Ḥolim* ba-Qehillot ha-Mizraḥ ha-Tikhon." *Daf le-Tarbut Yehudit* 213 (Sivan 5755): 8.

Benayahu, Meir. "Rabbi Avraham Skandari," in *Sefer Zikkaron le-ha-Rav Yitshaq Nissim*, ed. Meir Benayahu. 2 vols. Jerusalem: Yad ha-Rav Nissim, 1984, 2:291–314.

Ben-Sasson, Ḥaim Hillel. "Galut u-Ge'ulah be-Einav shel Dor Golei Sefarad," in *Sefer Yovel le-Yitshaq Baer*. Jerusalem: Israel Historical Society, 1960, pp. 216–27.

———. "The Reformation in Contemporary Jewish Eyes." *Proceedings of the Israel Academy of Sciences and Humanities*, 4:12 (1970): 239–326.

Ben-Zvi, Yitzhak. *Eretz Yisra'el ve-Yishuvah bi-Ymei ha-Shilton ha-Ottomanit*. Jerusalem: Yad Yitzhak Ben-Zvi, 1975.

Berger, David. *The Jewish-Christian Debate in the High Middle Ages*. Philadelphia: JPS, 1979.

Berger, Shlomo. "Codices Gentium: Rabbi Isaac Aboab's Collection of Classical Literature." *StRos* 29 (1995): 5–13.

———. "Remus, Romulus and Sephardi Jews in Amsterdam." *StRos* 26 (1992): 38–45.

Biale, David, ed. *Cultures of the Jews*. New York: Schocken, 2002.

Blom, J. C. H., R. G. Fuks-Mansfeld, and I. Schöffer, eds. *The History of the Jews in the Netherlands*. Oxford: Littman Library of Jewish Civilization, 2002.

Bloom, Herbert. *The Economic Activities of the Jews of Amsterdam in the Seventeenth and Eighteenth Centuries*. Williamsport, Penna.: Bayard Press, 1937.

Blumenkranz, Bernhard. *Le juif médiéval au miroir de l'art chrétien*. Paris: Études augustiniennes, 1966.

Bodian, Miriam. "Amsterdam, Venice, and the Marrano Diaspora." *Dutch Jewish History* 2 (1989): 47–65.

———. "Biblical Hebrews and the Rhetoric of Republicanism: Seventeenth-Century Portuguese Jews on the Jewish Community." *AJS Review* 22:2 (1997): 199–221.

———. *Hebrews of the Portuguese Nation: Conversos and Community in Early Modern Amsterdam*. Bloomington: Indiana University Press, 1997.

———. "In the Cross-Currents of the Reformation: Crypto-Jewish Martyrs of the Inquisition, 1570–1670." *Past and Present* 176 (2002): 66–104.

_____. "'Men of the Nation': The Shaping of *Converso* Identity in Early Modern Europe." *Past and Present* 143 (1994): 48–76.

_____. "The 'Portuguese' Dowry Societies in Venice and Amsterdam: A Case Study in Communal Differentiation within the Marrano Diaspora." *Italia* 6 (1987): 30–61.

den Boer, Harm, and H. P. Salomon, "Another 'Lost' Book Found: The Melo Haggadah, Amsterdam 1622." *StRos* 29 (1995): 119–34.

Böhm, Günter. *Los sefardíes en los dominios holandeses de América del Sur y del Caribe, 1630–1750*. Frankfurt am-Main: Vervuert, 1992.

Braun, Joachim. *Music in Ancient Israel/Palestine*. Grand Rapids: Eerdmans, 2002.

Brody, Saul. *The Disease of the Soul: Leprosy in Medieval Literature*. Ithaca: Cornell University Press, 1974.

Brown, Peter. *The Cult of the Saints: Its Rise and Function in Latin Christianity*. Chicago: University of Chicago Press, 1981.

Bryce, James. *The Holy Roman Empire*. London: Macmillan, 1904.

Bynum, Caroline. *The Resurrection of the Body in Western Christianity, 200–1336*. New York: Columbia University Press, 1995.

Calabi, Donatella. "The 'City of the Jews,'" in *The Jews of Early Modern Venice*, ed. Robert C. Davis and Benjamin Ravid. Baltimore: Johns Hopkins University Press, 2001, pp. 31–49.

Carlebach, Elisheva. *Divided Souls: Converts from Judaism in Germany, 1500–1750*. New Haven: Yale University Press, 2001.

_____. *The Pursuit of Heresy: Rabbi Moses Ḥagiz and the Sabbatian Controversies*. New York: Columbia University Press, 1990.

Carlson, Marvin. *Performance: A Critical Introduction*. London: Routledge, 1996.

Carroll, Michael P. *The Penitente Brotherhood: Patriarchy and Hispano-Catholicism in New Mexico*. Baltimore: Johns Hopkins University Press, 2002.

Carruthers, Gale. *Donne at Sermons: A Christian Existential World*. Albany: SUNY Press, 1972.

Castro, David Henriques de. *Keur van grafsteenen op de Nederl.-Portug.-Isral.begraafplats te Ouderkerk aan de Amstel (Selected Gravestones from the Dutch-Portuguese Jewish Cemetery)*. Reprint of 1883 edition with English translation. Ouderkerk aan de Amstel, 1999.

Chamberlain, John. *Increase and Multiply: Arts-of-Discourse Procedure in the Preaching of Donne*. Chapel Hill: University of North Carolina Press, 1976.

Chandos, John, ed. *In God's Name: Examples of Preaching in England 1534–1662*. Indianapolis: Bobbs-Merrill, 1971.

Charland, Th.- M. *Artes praedicandi*. Publications de l'Institute d'Etudes Médiévales d'Ottawa 7 (1936).

Chartier, Roger. *Forms and Meanings: Texts, Performances and Audiences from Codex to Computer*. Philadelphia: University of Pennsylvania Press, 1995.

_____. *The Order of Books: Readers, Authors, and Libraries in Europe Between the Fourteenth and Eighteenth Centuries*. Stanford: Stanford University Press, 1994.

Cohen, Gerson. "Esau as Symbol in Early Medieval Thought," in *Jewish Medieval and Renaissance Studies*, ed. Alexander Altmann. Cambridge: Harvard University Press, 1967.

Cohen, Jeremy. *"Be Fertile and Increase, Fill the Earth and Master It."* Ithaca: Cornell University Press, 1989.

Cohen, Martin, ed. *The Jewish Experience in Latin America*, 2 vols. Waltham: American Jewish Historical Society, 1971.

Cohen, Pieter. "Saul Levi Mortera's historische opvattingen in zijn 'Traktaat Betreffende de Waarheid van de Wet van Mozes,'" in *Een gulden Kleinood*, ed. H. den Boer, J. Brombacher, and P. Cohen. Appeldoorn: Garant, 1991, pp. 106–20.

Colbert, Edward P. *The Martyrs of Cordoba (850–859): A Study of the Sources*. Washington: Catholic University of America Press, 1962.

Cooperman, Bernard. "Eliahu Montalto's 'Suitable and Incontrovertible Propositions': A Seventeenth-Century Anti-Christian Polemic," in *Jewish Thought in the Seventeenth Century*, ed. I. Twersky and B. Septimus. Cambridge: Harvard University Press, 1987, pp. 469–97.

Dan, Joseph. *Sifrut ha-Musar ve-ha-Derush*. Jerusalem: Keter, 1975.

——. *Ha-Sippur ha-'Ivri bi-Ymei ha-Beinayim*. Jerusalem: Keter, 1974.

Dan, Robert and Antal Pernat, eds. *Antitrinitarianism in the Second Half of the Sixteenth Century*. Leiden: Brill, 1982.

Davies, W. D. *The Setting of the Sermon on the Mount*. Atlanta: Scholars Press, 1989.

Davis, Joseph. "The *Ten Questions* of Eliezer Eilburg and the Problem of Jewish Unbelief in the 16th Century." *JQR* 91 (2001): 293–336.

Delumeau, Jean. *Fear and Sin: The Emergence of a Western Guilt Culture, 13th–18th Centuries*. New York: St. Martin's Press, 1990.

Dinur, B. Z. *Israel and the Diaspora*. Philadelphia: JPS, 1969.

Dorman, Menahem. *Menasheh Ben-Yisra'el*. Tel Aviv: Hakibbuz Hameuchad, 1989.

Droge, Arthur J. and James D. Tabor. *A Noble Death: Suicide and Martyrdom Among Christians and Jews in Antiquity*. San Francisco: HarperSanFrancisco, 1992.

Dubnov, Simon. *History of the Jews From the Later Middle Ages to the Renaissance*, 5 vols. South Brunswick, N.J.: Thomas Yoseloff, 1967–1973.

Eire, Carlos. *War Against the Idols: The Reform of Worship from Erasmus to Calvin*. Cambridge: Cambridge University Press, 1972.

Elbaum, Jacob. *Petihut ve-Histagrut*. Jerusalem: Magnes Press, 1990.

Ellenbogen, Meyer. *Hevel ha-Kesef: Toledot Mishpahat Katzenellenbogen*. Brooklyn: Moyneshter, 1937.

Emmanuel, Isaac. "Siyyu'an shel Qehillot ha-Sefaradim be-Amsterdam u-ve-Curaçao la-Aretz ha-Qedoshah u-li-Tsefat." *Sefunot* 6 (1962): 399–424.

——. "Yedi'ot Hadashot al ha-Qehilah ha-Portugezit me-Amsterdam." *Otsar Yehudei Sefarad* 6 (1963): 160–82.

Esser, Kajetan. *Origins of the Franciscan Order*. Chicago: Franciscan Herald Press, 1970.

Fakhry, Majid. *A History of Islamic Philosophy*. New York: Columbia University Press, 1970.

Farine, Avigdor. "Charity and Study Societies in Europe of the Sixteenth–Eighteenth Centuries." *JQR* 64 (1973): 16–47.

Feiner, Shmuel. *Haskalah and History: The Emergence of a Modern Jewish Historical Consciousness*. Oxford: Littman Library, 2002.

Fish, Stanely. *Is There A Text in the Class?* Cambridge: Harvard University Press, 1980.

Fishman, Talya. *Shaking the Pillars of Exile: 'Voice of a Fool,' an Early Modern Jewish Critique of Rabbinic Culture*. Stanford: Stanford University Press, 1997.

Fleischer, Ezra. *Shirat ha-Qodesh ha-Ivrit bi-Ymei ha-Beinayim*. Jerusalem: Keter, 1975.

Foa, Anna. "The Marrano's Kitchen," in *The Mediterranean and the Jews*, ed. Elliott Horowitz and Moises Orfali. 2 vols. Ramat-Gan: Bar-Ilan University Press, 2002.

Fox, Robin Lane. *Pagans and Christians*. New York: Knopf, 1987.

Frend, W. H. C. *Martyrdom and Persecution in the Early Church: A Study of a Conflict from the Maccabees to Donatus.* Oxford: Blackwell, 1965.

Friedrichs, Christopher. "Politics or Pogrom? The Fettmilch Uprising in German and Jewish History." *Central European History* 19.2 (June 1986): 186–228.

Fuchs, Eduard. *Die Juden in der Karikatur.* Munich: Albert Langen,1921.

Fuks, Leo and Rena. "The First Hebrew Types of Menasseh Ben Israel." *Studies in Bibliography and Booklore* 12 (1979): 3–8.

Gilson, Etienne. *The Christian Philosophy of St. Thomas Aquinas.* New York: Random House, 1956.

Ginzberg, Louis. *Legends of the Jews.* 7 vols. Philadelphia: JPS, 1912.

Ginzburg, Carlo. *The Cheese and the Worm: The Cosmos of a Sixteenth-Century Miller.* New York: Penguin Books, 1982.

Gitlitz, *Secrecy and Deceit: The Religion of the Crypto-Jews.* Philadelphia: JPS, 1996.

Glaser, Edward. "Invitation to Intolerance: A Study of the Portuguese Sermons Preached at Autos-da-fé." *HUCA* 27 (1956): 327–85.

Goldberg, RoseLee. *Performance Art: From Futurism to the Present.* New York: H. N. Abrams, 1988.

———. *Performance: Live Art, 1909 to the Present.* New York: H. N. Abrams, 1979.

Gougaud, Louis. *Devotional and Ascetic Practices in the Middle Ages.* London: Burns, Oates and Washbourne, 1927.

Gow, Andrew Colin. *The Red Jews: Antisemitism in an Apocalyptic Age, 1200–1600.* Leiden: Brill, 1995.

Graetz, Heinrich. *Divrei Yemei Yisrael.* 8 vols. Warsaw, 1890–1899.

———. *History of the Jews.* 6 vols. Philadelphia: JPS, 1891–1898.

Green, Arthur. *Tormented Master: A Life of Rabbi Naḥman of Bratslav.* New York: Schocken, 1981.

Greenstone, Julius H. *The Messiah Idea in Jewish History.* Philadelphia: JPS, 1948.

Gregorovius, Ferdinand. *The Ghetto and the Jews of Rome.* New York: Schocken, 1966.

Gregory, Brad S. *Salvation at Stake: Christian Martyrdom in Early Modern Europe.* Cambridge: Harvard University Press, 1999.

Gross, Abraham. "Demuto shel Rabbi Ya'aqov Sasportas Mi-Tokh Sefer ha-She'elot u-Teshuvot *Ohel Ya'aqov*." *Sinai* 97 (1983), pp. 132–41.

———. *R. Yosef ben Avraham Ḥayyun: Manhig Qehillat Lisbon vi-Ytsirato.* Ramat Gan: Bar-Ilan University Press, 1993.

Gruen, Erich S. *Diaspora: Jews Amidst Greeks and Romans.* Cambridge: Harvard University Press, 2002.

Gulden, Zenon and Jacek Wijaczka. "The Accusation of Ritual Murder in Poland, 1500–1800." *Polin,* 10 (1997): 99–140.

Gunzberg, Lynn M. *Strangers at Home: Jews in the Italian Literary Imagination.* Berkeley: University of California Press, 1992.

Hacker, Joseph. "Ha-Ye'ush min ha-Ge'ulah ve-ha-Tiqvah ha-Meshiḥit be-Khitvei R. Shelomoh le-Veit ha-Levi mi-Saloniqah." *Tarbiz* 39 (1969–70): 195–213.

———. "Yisra'el ba-Goyyim be-Te'uro shel R. Shelomoh le-Veit ha-Levi." *Zion* 34 (1969): 43–89.

Hallamish, Moshe. *Ha-Qabbalah bi-Tsefon Afriqah le-min ha-Me'ah ha-Tet Zayin.* Tel Aviv: Hakibbuz Hameuchad, 2001.

Halkin, Hillel. *Across the Sabbath River: In Search of a Lost Tribe of Israel.* Boston: Houghton Mifflin, 2002.

Harline, Craig and Eddy Put. *A Bishop's Tale: Mathias Hovius Among His Flock in Seventeenth-Century Flanders.* New Haven: Yale University Press, 2000.

Hastings, James, ed. *Encyclopaedia of Religion and Ethics.* 13 vols. New York: Scribner's Sons, 1928.

Haupt, Paul. "Camel and Cable." *American Journal of Philology* 45 (1924): 238–41.

van der Heide, Albert. "Banner, Miracle, Trial? Medieval Hebrew Lexicography Between Facts and Faith," in *Hebrew Scholarship and the Medieval World*, ed. Nicholas de Lange. Cambridge: Cambridge University Press, 2001, pp. 92–106.

Heyd, David. *Supererogation: Its Status in Ethical Theory.* Cambridge: Cambridge University Press, 1982.

Hinnebusch, W. A. "Poverty in the Order of Preachers." *Catholic Historical Review* 45 (1959–60): 436–53;

Horowitz, Elliott. "Coffee, Coffeehouses, and the Nocturnal Rituals of Early Modern Jewry." *AJS Review* 14 (1989): 17–46.

———. "Membership and Its Rewards: The Emergence and Decline of Farrara's *Gemilut Hasadim* Society (1515–1603)," in *The Mediterranean and the Jews: Society, Culture, and Economy in Early Modern Times*, ed. Elliott Horowitz and Moises Orfali. 2 vols. Ramat-Gan: Bar-Ilan University Press, 2002, 2:27–65.

———. "Speaking of the Dead: The Emergence of the Eulogy Among Italian Jewry of the Sixteenth Century," in *Preachers of the Italian Ghetto*, ed. David Ruderman. Berkeley: University of California Press, 1992, pp. 129–62.

Houlbrooke, Ralph. *Death, Religion, and the Family in England, 1480–1750.* Oxford: Clarendon Press, 1998.

Huussen, Arend H. Jr., "The Legal Position of Sephardi Jews in Holland, *circa* 1600." *Dutch Jewish History* 3 (1993): 19–41.

Idel, Moshe. "The Attitude to Christianity in *Sefer ha-Meshiv.*" *Immanuel* 12 (1981): 77–95.

Israel, Jonathan. "The Changing Role of the Dutch Sephardim in International Trade, 1595–1715." *Dutch Jewish History* 1 (1984): 31–51.

———. *The Dutch Republic: Its Rise, Greatness, and Fall, 1477–1806.* Oxford: Clarendon Press, 1995.

———. *Empires and Entrepots: The Dutch, the Spanish Monarchy, and the Jews, 1585–1713.* London: Hambledon Press, 1990.

———. *European Jewry in the Age of Mercantilism, 1550–1750.* Oxford: Clarendon Press, 1985.

———. "Manuel Lopez Pereira of Amsterdam, Antwerp and Madrid." *StRos* 19 (1985): 109–26.

———. *Radical Enlightenment: Philosophy and the Making of Modernity, 1650–1750.* Oxford: Oxford University Press, 2001.

Jacobs, Louis. *Theology in the Responsa.* London: Routledge, 1975.

Jacobson, Yoram. *Bi-Netivei Galuyot u-Ge'ulot: Torat ha-Ge'ulah shel R. Mordekai Data.* Jerusalem: Mosad Bialik, 1996.

Jansen, Katherine. *The Making of the Magdalen: Preaching and Popular Devotion in the Later Middle Ages.* Princeton: Princeton University Press, 2000.

Jones, Phyllis M. and Nicholas R. Jones, eds. *Salvation in New England: Selections from the Sermons of the First Preachers.* Austin: University of Texas Press, 1977.

Kaplan, Yosef. *An Alternative Path to Modernity: The Sephardi Diaspora in Western Europe.* Leiden: Brill, 2002.

———. *From Christianity to Judaism: The Story of Isaac Orobio de Castro.* Oxford: Oxford University Press, 1989.

———. "'Karaites' in Early-Eighteenth-Century Amsterdam," in *Sceptics, Millenarians and Jews*, ed. David S. Katz and Jonathan I. Israel. Leiden: Brill, 1990, pp. 196–236.

———. "Maslulei Hitbolelut u-Temi'ah be-Qerev Anusei Sefarad ba-Me'ot ha-Tet-Vav–Yod-Zayin," in *Hitbolelut u-Temi'ah*, ed. Yosef Kaplan and Menaḥem Stern. Jerusalem: Merkaz Zalman Shazar, 1988–1989, pp. 157–72.

———. *Les nouveaux-Juifs d'Amsterdam: Essais sur l'histoire sociale et intellectuelle du judaïsme séfarade au XVIIe siècle.* Paris: Chandeigne, 1999.

———. "Pesaqim mi-Beit ha-Din shel ha-Qehillah ha-Sefaradit-ha-Portugalit be-Amsterdam." *Meḥqarim al Toledot Yahadut Holland* 5 (1988): 1–54.

———. "Political Concepts in the World of the Portuguese Jews of Amsterdam during the Seventeenth Century," in *Menasseh ben Israel and His World*, ed. Y. Kaplan, H. Méchoulan, and R. Popkin. Leiden: Brill, 1989, pp. 45–62.

———. "The Portuguese Community in 17th-Century Amsterdam and the Ashkenazi World." *Dutch Jewish History* 2 (1989): 23–45.

———. "Rabbi Saul Levi Morteira's Treatise 'Arguments Against the Christian Religion.'" *Immanuel* 11 (1980): 95–112.

———. "R. Sha'ul Levi Morteira ve-Ḥibburo 'Ta'anot ve-Hasagot Neged ha-Dat na-Notsrit.'" *Meḥqarim al Toledot Yahadut Holland* 1 (1975): 9–31.

———. "The Social Functions of the Ḥerem in the Portuguese Jewish Community of Amsterdam in the Seventeenth Century." *Dutch Jewish History* 1 (1984): 111–55.

———. "The Travels of Portuguese Jews from Amsterdam to the 'Lands of Idolatry,'" in *Jews and Conversos*, ed. Yosef Kaplan. Jerusalem: Magnes Press, 1985, pp. 197–224.

———. "Wayward New Christians and Stubborn New Jews: The Shaping of a Jewish Identity." *Jewish History* 8 (1994): 27–41.

Katchen, Aaron L. *Christian Hebraists and Dutch Rabbis.* Cambridge: Harvard University Press, 1984.

Katz, David S. *Philo-Semitism and the Readmission of the Jews to England, 1603–1655.* Oxford: Clarendon Press, 1982.

Katz, Jacob. "Af al pi she-Ḥata Yisra'el Hu," in *Halakhah ve-Qabbalah.* Jerusalem: Magnes Press, 1984, pp. 255–69.

———. *Exclusiveness and Tolerance: Jewish-Christian Relations in Medieval and Modern Times.* New York: Schocken, 1962.

———. *The "Shabbes Goy": A Study in Halakhic Flexbility.* Philadelphia: JPS, 1989.

———. *Tradition and Crisis: Jewish Society at the End of the Middle Ages*, transl. Bernard Cooperman. New York: NYU Press, 1993.

Katz, Shmuel. *Lone Wolf: A Biography of Vladimir Jabotinsky.* 2 vols. New York: Barricade Books, 1996.

Kaufmann, David. "L'élégie de Mose Zacout sur Saul Levi Morteira." *REJ* 37 (1898): 111–19.

Kayser, Rudolph. *Spinoza: Portrait of a Spiritual Hero.* New York: Philosophical Library 1946.

Kayserling, Mayer. *Biblioteca Española-Portugueza-Judaica.* Reprint edition with Prolegomenon by Yosef Yerushalmi. New York: Ktav, 1971.

_____. "Isaac Aboab, The First Jewish Author in America," in *The Jewish Experience in Latin America*, ed. Martin A. Cohen. 2 vols. New York: Ktav, 1971, 2:193–204.

Kienzle, Beverly Mayne. *Cistercians, Heresy and Crusade in Occitania, 1145–1229*. York: York Medieval Press, 2001.

_____. "Medieval Sermons and Their Performance," in *Preacher, Sermon, and Audience in the Middle Ages*, ed. Carolyn Muessig. Leiden: Brill, 2002, pp. 89–124.

_____, ed. *The Sermon*. Turnhout-Belgium: Brepols, 2000.

Klausner, Joseph. *The Messianic Idea in Israel*. London: George Allen and Unwin, 1956.

Koen, E. M. "The Earliest Sources Relating to the Portuguese Jews in the Municipal Archives of Amsterdam up to 1620." *StRos* 4 (1970): 25–42.

Lambert, Malcolm D. *Franciscan Poverty: The Doctrine of the Absolute Poverty of Christ and the Apostles in the Franciscan Order, 1210–1323*. London: S. P. C. K., 1961.

Landsberger, Franz. *Rembrandt, The Jews and the Bible*. Philadelphia: JPS, 1972.

Lawee, Eric. *Isaac Abarbanel's Stance Toward Tradition: Defense, Dissent, and Dialogue*. Albany: SUNY Press, 2001.

_____. "On the Threshold of the Renaissance: New Methods and Sensibilities in the Biblical Commentaries of Isaac Abarbanel." *Viator* 26 (1995): 283–319.

Leclercq, Jean, François Vandenbroucke, and Louis Bouyer. *The Spirituality of the Middle Ages*. London: Burnes & Oates, 1968.

Leiman, Sid (Shnayer). "'Al Diyuqano shel R. Sha'ul Levi Morteira(?)," in Daniel Sperber, *Minhagei Yisra'el*. 7 vols. Jerusalem: Mosad ha-Rav Kook, 1989–2003, 6:רן‎-רם‎.

_____. "Temunato shel Rabbi Sha'ul Ha-Levi Morteira." *'Alei Sefer* 10 (1982): 153–55.

Lerner, Robert E. "Refreshment of the Saints: The Time after Antichrist as a Station for Earthly Progress in Medieval Thought." *Traditio* 32 (1976): 97–144.

Levi de Montezinos, Elizabeth. "The Narrative of Aharon Levi, alias Antonio de Montezinos." *The American Sephardi* 78 (1975): 62–83.

Levin, Hirschel. "The Sermons of Saul Levi Morteira." Rabbinical and MHL Thesis submitted to Hebrew Union College, February 1942.

Lévy, Isaac Jack and Rosemary Lévy Zumwalt. *Ritual Medical Lore of Sephardic Women*. Urbana: University of Illinois Press, 2002.

Lieberman, Julia R. "Sermons and the Construct of a Jewish Identity: The Hamburg Sephardic Community in the 1620s." *Jewish Studies Quarterly* 10 (2003): 49–72.

Little, Lester. *Religious Poverty and the Profit Economy in Medieval Europe*. Ithaca: Cornell University Press, 1978.

MacMullen, Ramsay. *Christianity and Paganism in the Fourth to Eighth Centuries*. New Haven: Yale University Press, 1997.

Mak, Geert. *Amsterdam*. Cambridge: Harvard University Press, 2000.

Maler, Bertil. *A Bíblia na Consolaçam de Samuel Usque (1553)*. Stockholm: Almqvist & Viksell, 1974.

Mann, Jacob. "An Early Theologico-Polemical Work." *HUCA* 12–13 (1937–1938): 411–59.

Manor, Dan. *Galut u-Ge'ulah be-Hagut Ḥakhmei Maroqoh ba-Me'ot ha-Yod-Zayin–Yod-Ḥet*. Lod: Makhon Haberman, 1988.

Marx, Alexander. *Studies in Jewish History and Booklore*. New York: JTSA, 1944.

Méchoulan, Henry. *Être juif à Amsterdam au temps de Spinoza*. Paris: Albin Michel, 1991.

_____. "Hispanicity in Seventeenth-Century Amsterdam," in *In Iberia and Beyond*, ed. Bernard Dov Cooperman. Newark: University of Delaware Press, 1998, pp. 353–72.

———. "La mort comme enjeu théologique, philosophique et politique `a Amsterdam au XVIIe siècle." *XVII Siècle*, 46 (1994): 337–48.

———. "Morteira et Spinoza au carrefour du Socianisme." *REJ* 135 (1976): 51–65.

Meeks, Wayne and Robert Wilken. *Jews and Christians in Antioch in the First Centuries of the Common Era.* Missoula: Scholars Press, 1978.

van der Meer, Frederik. *Augustine the Bishop: The Life and Work of a Father of the Church.* London: Sheed and Ward, 1961.

Melammed, Renée Levine. *Heretics or Daughters of Israel? The Crypto-Jewish Women of Castile.* Oxford: Oxford University Press, 1999.

Melnick, Ralph. *From Polemics to Apologetics: Jewish-Christian Rapprochement in Seventeenth-Century Amsterdam.* Assen: van Gorcum, 1981.

Mendes-Flohr, Paul and Jehuda Reinharz, eds. *The Jew in the Modern World.* Oxford: Oxford University Press, 1995.

Menocal, Maria Rosa, *Shards of Love: Exile and the Origins of the Lyric.* Durham: Duke University Press, 1994.

Meyer, Michael A. *Ideas of Jewish History.* Detroit: Wayne State University Press, 1987.

Michman, Jozeph. "Introduction," in *Pinqas ha-Qehillot: Holland.* Jerusalem: Yad Va-Shem, 1985.

Mormando, Franco. *The Preacher's Demons: Bernardino of Siena and the Social Underworld of Early Renaissance Italy.* Chicago: University of Chicago Press, 1999.

Munk, Linda. *The Devil's Mousetrap: Redemption and Colonial American Literature.* Oxford: Oxford University Press, 1997.

Nadler, Steven. *Rembrandt's Jews.* Chicago: University of Chicago Press, 2003.

———. *Spinoza: A Life.* Cambridge: Cambridge University Press, 1999.

———. *Spinoza's Heresy: Immortality and the Jewish Mind.* Oxford: Clarendon Press, 2002.

Neher, André. *Jewish Thought and the Scientific Revolution of the Sixteenth Century.* New York: Oxford University Press, 1986.

Nemoy, Leon. *Karaite Anthology.* New Haven: Yale University Press, 1952.

Netanyahu, B. (Benzion). *Don Isaac Abravanel.* Philadelphia: JPS, 1968.

———. *The Marranos of Spain.* New York: American Academy for Jewish Research, 1966

———. *The Origins of the Inquisition in Fifteenth Century Spain.* New York: Random House, 1995.

Nigal, Gedalyah. "Derashotav shel R. Shmuel Yehudah Katzenellenbogen." *Sinai* 70 (1971): 79–85.

Nirenberg, David. "Mass Conversion and Genealogical Mentalities: Jews and Christians in Fifteenth-Century Spain." *Past and Present* 174 (2002): 3–41.

Novak, David. *The Image of the Non-Jew in Judaism.* New York and Toronto: Edwin Mellen Press, 1983.

O'Connell, John. *The Eschatology of Saint Jerome.* Mundelein, Il.: Seminary of Sancta Maria ad Lacum, 1948.

Ong, Walter. *Rhetoric, Romance, and Technology.* Ithaca: Cornell University Press, 1971.

Ozment, Steven. *The Age of Reform, 1250–1550.* New Haven: Yale University Press, 1980.

Parker, T. H. L. *Calvin's Preaching.* Louisville: Westminster/John Knox Press, 1992.

Patai, Raphael. *The Jewish Alchemists.* Princeton: Princeton University Press, 1994.

———. *The Messiah Texts.* New York: Avon Books, 1979.

Peters, F. E. *The Harvest of Hellenism.* New York: Simon and Schuster, 1970.

Pieterse, Wilhelmina C. *Daniel Levi de Barrios als geschiedschrijver van de Portugees-Israelietische Gemeente te Amsterdam in zijn "Triumpho del govierno popular."* Amsterdam: Scheltema and Holkema, 1968.

———. *Livro de Bet Ḥaim do Kahal Kados de Bet Yahacob.* Assen: van Gorcum, 1970.

——— and E. M. Koen. "Notarial Records Relating to the Portuguese Jews in Amsterdam up to 1639." *StRos* 5 (1971): 219–45; 15 (1981): 143–54; 19 (1985): 79–90.

Poliakov, Léon. *Jewish Bankers and the Holy See.* London: Routledge, 1977.

Popkin, Richard H. "The Historical Significance of Sephardic Judaism in 17th-Century Amsterdam." *The American Sephardi* 5 (1971): 18–27.

———. "Jewish Anti-Christian Arguments As A Source Of Irreligion From The Seventeenth To The Early Nineteenth Century," in *Atheism from the Reformation to the Enlightenment,* ed. Michael Hunter and David Wooten. Oxford: Clarendon Press, 1992, pp. 159–81.

———. "Rabbi Nathan Shapira's Visit to Amsterdam in 1657." *Dutch Jewish History* 1 (1984): 185–205.

———. "The Rise and Fall of the Jewish Indian Theory," in *Menasseh ben Israel and His World,* ed. Y. Kaplan, H. Méchoulan, and R. Popkin. Leiden: Brill, 1989, pp. 63–82.

———. "Skepticism About Religion and Millenarian Dogmatism: Two Sources of Toleration in the Seventeenth Century," in *Beyond the Persecuting Society,* ed. John Christian Laursen and Cary J. Nederman. Philadelphia: Pennsylvania University Press, 1998, pp. 232–50.

———. "Spinoza's Excommunication," in *Jewish Themes in Spinoza's Philosophy,* ed. Heidi M. Ravven and Lenn E. Goodman. Albany: SUNY Press, 2002, pp. 263–79.

Popper, William, *The Censorship of Hebrew Books.* Reprint edition. New York: Ktav, 1969.

Prawer, Joshua. *The History of the Jews in the Latin Kingdom of Jerusalem.* Oxford: Clarendon Press, 1988.

Pullan, Brian. *The Jews of Europe and the Inquisition of Venice, 1550–1670.* London: I.B. Tauris, 1997.

———. *Rich and Poor in Renaissance Venice.* Cambridge: Harvard University Press, 1971.

Raba, Joel. *Between Remembrance and Denial.* Boulder, Colorado: East European Monographs, No. 178, 1995.

Rabinowitz, Hyman Reuven. *Diyokna'ot shel Darshanim.* Jerusalem: Reuven Mass, 1967.

Ravid, Benjamin. *Economics and Toleration in Seventeenth-Century Venice.* Jerusalem: American Academy for Jewish Research, 1978.

———. "From Yellow to Red: On the Distinguishing Head-Covering of the Jews of Venice." *Jewish History* 6 (1992): 179–210.

———. "New Light on the Ghetti of Venice," in *Shlomo Simonsohn Jubilee Volume,* ed. Daniel Carpi et al. Tel Aviv: Tel Aviv University, 1993, pp. 149–76.

———. "The Venetian Government and the Jews," in *The Jews of Early Modern Venice,* ed. Robert C. Davis and Benjamin Ravid. Baltimore: Johns Hopkins University Press, 2001, pp. 7–20.

Ravitzky, Aviezer. "'Hatzivu Lekha Tziyunim' le-Tziyon: Gilgulah shel Ra'ayon," in *Eretz Yisrael ba-Hagut ha-Yehudit Bi-Ymei ha-Beinayim,* ed. Moshe Hallamish and Aviezer Ravitzky. Jerusalem: Yad Ben-Zvi, 1991, pp. 1–39.

———. *Messianism, Zionism, and Jewish Religious Radicalism.* Chicago: University of Chicago Press, 1996.

Regev, Shaul. "Re'iyat Atsilei B'nei Yisra'el (Shemot 24:911) be-Filosofiyah ha-Yehudit Bi-Ymei ha-Beinayim." *Meḥqerei Yerushalyim ba-Mahshevet Yisrael* 4 (1985): 281–302.

Révah, I. S. "Fragments retrouvés de quelques éditions amstelodamoises de la version espagnole du rituel juif." *StRos* 2 (1968): 108–10.

——. "L'hérésie marrane dans l'Europe catholique du 15e au 18e sïecle," in *Hérésies et sociétés dan l'Europe pre-industrielle,* ed. Jacques le-Goff. Paris: Mouton, 1968, pp. 327–37.

——. "Le Plaidoyer en faveur des 'Nouveaux-Chrétiens' Portugais du Licencié Martín González de Cellorigo (Madrid, 1619)." *REJ* 162 (1963): 279–398.

——. "Le premier règlement imprimé de la 'Santa Companhia de dotar orfans de donzelas pobres.'" *Boletim internacional de bibliografia luso-brasileira* 4 (1963): 650–91.

——. "La religion d'Uriel da Costa, Marrane de Porto." *Revue de l'Histoire des Religions* 161 (1962): 44–76.

——. *Spinoza et Dr Juan de Prado.* Paris: Mouton, 1959.

Rivlin, Bracha (Arlos). '*Arevim Zeh la-Zeh ba-Getto ha-Italqi: Ḥevrot GM"Ḥ 1516–1789.* Jerusalem: Magnes Press, 1991.

Rosenberg, Shalom. "Emunat Ḥakhamim," in *Jewish Thought in the Seventeenth Century,* ed. Isadore Twersky and Bernard Cooperman. Cambridge: Harvard University Press, 1987, pp. 285–341.

——. "Exile and Redemption in Jewish Thought in the Sixteenth Century: Contending Conceptions," in *Jewish Thought in the Sixteenth Century,* ed. Bernard Cooperman. Cambridge: Harvard University Press, 1983, pp. 399–430.

Roth, Cecil. *A History of the Jews in Italy.* Philadelphia: JPS, 1946,

——. *History of the Jews of Venice.* Philadelphia: JPS, 1930.

——. *A History of the Marranos.* Philadelphia: JPS, 1959.

——. "Immanuel Aboab's Proselytization of the Marranos." *JQR* n.s. 23 (1932–1933): 121–62.

——. *A Life of Menasseh ben Israel: Rabbi, Printer, and Diplomat.* Philadelphia: JPS, 1934.

——. *Magna Bibliotheca Anglo-Judaica.* London: Jewish Historical Society of England, 1937.

——. *Personalities and Events in Jewish History.* Philadelphia: JPS, 1954.

——. "Rabbanei Ancona." *Sinai* 11 (1947): 323–26.

——. "The Religion of the Marranos." *JQR,* n.s. 22 (1931): 1–33.

——. "The Strange Case of Hector Mendes Bravo." *HUCA* 18 (1944): 221–45.

Ruderman, David. "The Founding of a *Gemilut Ḥasadim* Society in Ferrara in 1515." *AJS Review* 1 (1976): 233–67.

——. *Jewish Thought and Scientific Discovery in Early Modern Europe.* New Haven: Yale University Press, 1995.

——. *The World of a Renaissance Jew: The Life and Thought of Abraham ben Mordecai Farissol.* Cincinnati: HUC Press, 1981.

Sabatier, Paul. *Life of St. Francis of Assisi.* New York: Charles Scribner's Sons, 1906.

Salomon, H. P. "Did Saul Levi Mortera Plagiarize Joseph Albo?" *StRos* 23 (1989): 28–37.

——. "Ḥaham Saul Levi Morteira en de Portugese Nieuw-Christenen." *StRos* 10 (1976): 127–41.

——. "Une lettre inédite du Docteur Felipe Rodrigues Montalto," in *Les rapports culturels et littéraries entre le Portugal et la France.* Paris: Centre Culturel Portugais, 1983.

——. "Menasseh ben Israel, Saul Levi Mortera et le 'Testimonium Flavianum.'" *StRos* 25 (1991): 31–41.

——. "Myth or Anti-Myth?: The Oldest Account Concerning the Origin of Portuguese Judaism at Amsterdam." *LIAS* 16 (1989): 275–316.

_____. *Portrait of a New Christian: Fernão Álvares Melo, 1569–1622*. Paris: Gulbenkian Foundation, 1982.

_____. *Os primeiros Portugueses de Amesterdão: documentos do Arquivo Nacional da Torre do Tombo*. Braga: Barbosa & Xavier, 1983.

_____. "La vraie excommunication de Spinoza," in *Forum Litterarum*, ed. Hans Bots and Maxim Kerkhof. Amsterdam: Holland University Press, 1984, pp. 181–99.

Saperstein, Marc. *Decoding the Rabbis: A Thirteenth-Century Commentary on the Aggadah*. Cambridge: Harvard University Press, 1980.

_____, ed. *Essential Papers on Messianic Movements and Personalities in Jewish History*. New York: NYU Press, 1992.

_____. *Jewish Preaching 1200–1800*. New Haven: Yale University Press, 1989.

_____. "The Method of Doubts: The Problematizing of Scripture in Late Medieval Jewish Culture," in *With Reverence for the Word*, ed. Jane Dammen McAuliffe, Barry D. Walfish, and Joseph W. Goering. New York: Oxford University Press, 2003, pp. 133–56.

_____. "The Preaching of Repentance and the Reforms in Toledo of 1281," in *Models of Holiness in Medieval Preaching*, ed. Beverly Kienzle et al. Louvain-la-Neuve: F.I.D.E.M., 1996, pp. 155–72.

_____. "Saul Levi Morteira's Treatise on the Immortality of the Soul." *StRos* 25 (1991): 131–48.

_____. "The Sermon as Art Form: Structure in Morteira's *Giv'at Sha'ul*. *Prooftexts* 3 [1981]: 243–61.

_____. "*Your Voice Like a Ram's Horn*': Themes and Texts in Traditional Jewish Preaching*. Cincinnati: Hebrew Union College Press, 1996.

_____ and Nancy E. Berg. "'Arab Chains' and 'the Good Things of Sepharad': Aspects of Jewish Exile." *AJS Review* 26:2 (2002): 301–26.

Saraiva, A. J. "Antonio Vieira, M. Ben Israel et le Cinquième Empire." *StRos* 6 (1972): 25–56.

Schama, Simon. *The Embarrassment of Riches*. Berkeley: University of California Press, 1988.

Schappes, Morris U., ed. *A Documentary History of the Jews in the United States, 1645–1875*. New York: Citadel Press, 1950.

Scholberg, Kenneth R. "Miguel de Barrios and the Amsterdam Sephardic Community." *JQR* 53 (1962–63): 120–56.

Scholem, Gershom. *Kabbalah*. New York: Quadrangle, 1974.

_____. *The Messianic Idea in Judaism*. New York: Schocken, 1971.

_____. *The Origins of the Kabbalah*. Princeton: Princeton University Press, 1987.

_____. *Sabbatai Sevi: The Mystical Messiah*. Princeton: Princeton University Press, 1973.

Schroeter, Daniel J. *The Sultan's Jew*. Stanford: Stanford University Press, 2002.

Schwartz, Dov. *Ha-Ra'ayon ha-Meshiḥi ba-Hagut ha-Yehudit bi-Ymei ha-Beinayim*. Ramat-Gan: Bar-Ilan University Press, 1997.

Schwarz, Leo W., ed. *Memoirs of My People*. Philadelphia: JPS, 1960.

Schweinburg-Eibenschitz, S. "*Une confiscation des livres hébreux à Prague*." *REJ* 29 (1894): 266–71,

Segal, Lester A. "Jacques Basnage de Beauval's *L'Histoire des Juifs*: Christian Historiographical Perception of Jewry and Judaism on the Eve of the Enlightenment." *HUCA* 54 (1983): 303–324.

Septimus, Bernard. "Hispano-Jewish Views of Christendom and Islam," in *In Iberia and Beyond*, ed. Bernard Dov Cooperman. Newark: University of Delaware Press, 1998, pp. 43–65.

———. "Taḥat Edom ve-Lo Taḥat Yishmael: Gilgulo shel Ma'amar." *Zion* 47 (1982): 103–11.

Sever, Moshe. *Mikhlol ha-Ma'amarim ve-ha-Pitgamim.* 3 vols. Jerusalem: Mosad ha-Rav Kook, 1961–1962.

Shachar, Isaiah. *The Judensau: A Medieval Anti-Jewish Motif and Its History.* London: Warburg Institute, 1974.

Shaw, Stanford. *The Jews of the Ottoman Empire and Turkish Republic.* New York: NYU Press, 1991.

Shazar, Zalman. *Morning Stars.* Philadelphia: JPS, 1967.

Smith, Hilary Dansey. *Preaching in the Spanish Golden Age.* Oxford: Oxford University Press, 1978.

Soergel, Philip. *Wondrous in His Saints: Counter-Reformation Propaganda in Bavaria.* Berkeley: University of California Press, 1993.

Sola, Abraham de. *Biography of David Aaron de Sola.* Philadelphia: Wm. H. Jones & Sons, 1864.

Southern, R. W. *Western Society and the Church in the Middle Ages.* Baltimore: Penguin Books, 1970.

Stanislawski, Michael. "The Yiddish *Shevet Yehudah*: A Study in the 'Ashkenization' of a Spanish-Jewish Classic," in *Jewish History and Jewish Memory*, ed. Elisheva Carlebach, John M. Efron, and David N. Myers. Hanover: University Press of New England for Brandeis University Press, 1998.

Stern, David. "The Captive Woman: Hellenization, Greco-Roman Erotic Narrative, and Rabbinic Literature." *Poetics Today* 19(1) (Spring 1998): 91–128.

Stout, Harry. *The Divine Dramatist: George Whitefield and the Rise of Modern Evangelism.* Grand Rapids: W. B. Eerdmans, 1991

———. *The New England Soul: Preaching and Religious Culture in Colonial New England.* New York: Oxford University Press, 1986.

Stow, Kenneth R. "The Burning of the Talmud in 1553, in Light of Sixteenth-Century Catholic Attitudes toward the Talmud," in *Essential Papers on Judaism and Christianity in Conflict*, ed. Jeremy Cohen. New York: NYU Press, 1991, pp. 401–28.

———. *Catholic Thought and Papal Jewish Policy, 1555–1593.* New York: JTSA, 1977.

Strayer, Joseph Reese, ed. *Dictionary of the Middle Ages.* 13 vols. New York: Scribner, 1982–1989.

Studemund-Halévy, Michael. *Biographisches Lexikon der Hamburger Sefarden.* Hamburg: Hans Christians Verlag 2000.

Sutcliffe, Adam. *Judaism and Enlightenment.* Cambridge: Cambridge University Press, 2003.

Swetschinski, Daniel M. "From the Middle Ages to the Golden Age, 1516–1621," in *The History of the Jews in the Netherlands*, ed. J. C. H. Blom, R. G. Fuks-Mansfeld, and I. Schöffer. Oxford: Littman Library of Jewish Civilization, 2002, pp. 44–84.

———. "The Portuguese Jews of Seventeenth-Century Amsterdam: Cultural Continuity and Adaptation," in *Essays in Modern Jewish History*, ed. Frances Malino and Phyllis Albert. Rutherford, N.J.: Fairleigh Dickinson University Press, 1982, pp. 56–80.

———. *Reluctant Cosmopolitans: The Portuguese Jews of Seventeenth-Century Amsterdam.* London: Littman Library of Jewish Civilization, 2000.

Talmage, Frank. *David Kimḥi: The Man and His Commentaries.* Cambridge: Harvard University Press, 1975.

Taylor, Larissa. *Soldiers of Christ: Preaching in Late Medieval and Reformation France.* New York: Oxford University Press, 1992.

Thorndike, Lynn. *A History of Magic and Experimental Science.* 8 vols. New York: Macmillan, 1929–1958.

Trachtenberg, Joshua. *The Devil and the Jews: The Medieval Conception of the Jew and Its Relation to Modern Anti-Semitism.* Philadelphia: JPS, 1983.

Tracy, Patricia. *Jonathan Edwards, Pastor.* New York: Hill and Wang, 1979.

Twersky, Isadore. *Introduction to the Code of Maimonides (Mishneh Torah).* New Haven: Yale University Press, 1980.

———, ed. *A Maimonides Reader.* New York: Berhman House, 1972.

———. "The Mishneh Torah of Maimonides." *Proceedings of the Israel Academy of Sciences and Humanities* 5:10 (Jerusalem, 1976): 265–96.

———. *Studies in Jewish Law and Philosophy.* New York: Ktav, 1982.

Ullmann, Salomon. "Geschichte der spanisch-portugiesischen Juden in Amsterdam im XVII Jahrhundert." *Jahrbuch der Jüdisch-Literarischen Gesellshaft* 5 (1907): 1–74.

Vickers, Brian. *In Defence of Rhetoric.* Oxford: Clarendon Press, 1988.

Vlessing, Odette. "New Light on the Earliest History of the Amsterdam Portuguese Jews." *Dutch Jewish History* 3 (1993): 43–75.

Vogelstein, Hermann. *History of the Jews of Rome.* Philadelphia: JPS, 1940.

Walfish, Barry Dov. *Esther in Medieval Garb: Jewish Interpretation of the Book of Esther in the Middle Ages.* Albany: SUNY Press, 1993.

Weinberg, Joanna. "The Beautiful Soul: Azariah de' Rossi's Search for Truth," in *Cultural Intermediaries: Jewish Intellectuals in Early Modern Italy,* ed. David B. Ruderman and Giuseppe Veltri. Philadelphia: University of Pennsylvania Press, 2004, pp. 109–48.

Weinryb, Bernard. *The Jews of Poland.* Philadelphia: JPS, 1973.

Wesselius, J. W. "Herman P. Salomon on Saul Levi Mortera" [review of the Dutch edition of the *Tratado*]. *StRos* 23 (1989): 93–98.

Wijnhoven, Johanan. "The Zohar and the Proselyte," in *Texts and Responses: Studies Presented to N. N. Glatzer,* ed. Michael A. Fishbane and Paul R. Flohr. Leiden: Brill, 1959, pp. 120–40.

Wilbur, Earl. *A History of Unitarianism.* Cambridge: Harvard University Press, 1946, pp. 535–70.

Wilensky, Mordecai. "Al Rabbanei Ancona." *Sinai* 13 (1949): 64–82.

———. *Ḥasidim u-Mitnagdim.* 2 vols. Jerusalem: Mosad Bialik, 1970.

Williams, George Huntston. *The Polish Brethren: Documentation of the History and Thought of Unitarianism in the Polish-Lithuanian Commonwealth and in the Diaspora, 1601–1685.* 2 vols. Missoula, Mont.: Scholars Press, 1980.

Wilson, Stephen. *Saints and Their Cults.* Cambridge: Cambridge University Press, 1983.

Wiznitzer, Arnold. "The Exodus from Brazil and Arrival in New Amsterdam of the Jewish Pilgrim Fathers, 1654," in *The Jewish Experience in Latin America,* ed. Martin A. Cohen. 2 vols. New York: Ktav, 1971, 2:313–30,

———. "The Merger Agreement and Regulations of Congregation Talmud Torah of Amsterdam (1638–39)." *Historia Judaica* 20 (1958): 109–32.

———. "The Minute Book of Congregations Zur Israel of Recife and Magen Abraham of Mauricia, Brazil," in *The Jewish Experience in Latin America*, ed. Martin A. Cohen. 2 vols. New York: Ktav, 1971, 2:227–312.

———. "The Number of Jews in Dutch Brazil, 1630–1654." *JSS* 16 (1954): 112–114.

Wolf, A. *The Oldest Biography of Spinoza.* London: Allen and Unwin, 1927.

Wolf, Kenneth Baxter. *Christian Martyrs in Muslim Spain.* Cambridge: Cambridge University Press, 1988.

Wolfson, Harry. *The Philosophy of Spinoza.* 2 vols. in 1. New York: Meridian Books, 1958.

Worcester, Thomas. *Seventeenth-Century Cultural Discourse: France and the Preaching of Bishop Camus.* New York: Mouton de Gruyter, 1997.

Yaari, Avraham. *The Goodly Heritage.* Jerusalem: Youth and Hechalutz Department of the Zionist Organization, 1958.

———. "R. Moshe Edrehi u-Sefarav." *Qiryat Sefer* 33 (1957–58): 521–28.

———. *Sheluḥei Erets Yisra'el.* Jerusalem: Mosad ha-Rav Kook, 1977.

Yerushalmi, Yosef Hayyim. "Divrei Spinoza al Qiyyum ha-'Am ha-Yehudi." *Proceedings of the Israel Academy of Sciences and Humanities (Hebrew)* 6 (1984): 171–91.

———. *From Spanish Court to Italian Ghetto: Isaac Cardoso, A Study in Seventeenth-Century Marranism and Jewish Apologetics.* New York: Columbia University Press, 1971.

———. *The Lisbon Massacre of 1506 and the Royal Image in the "Shevet Yehudah."* Cincinnati: Hebrew Union College Press, 1976.

———. "Professing Jews in Post-Expulsion Spain and Portugal," in *Salo W. Baron Jubilee Volume.* 3 vols. Jerusalem: American Academy for Jewish Research, 1974, 2:1023–58.

———. "The Re-Education of Marranos in the Seventeenth Century." Rabbi Louis Feinberg Memorial Lecture in Judaic Studies. University of Cincinnati, March 26, 1980.

———. *Zakhor: Jewish History and Jewish Memory.* Philadelphia: JPS, 1982.

Yovel, Yirmiyahu. *Spinoza and Other Heretics: The Marrano of Reason.* Princeton: Princeton University Press, 1989.

Zell, Michael. *Reframing Rembrandt: Jews and the Christian Image in Seventeenth-Century Amsterdam.* Berkeley: University of California Press, 2002.

Zunz, Leopold. *Ha-Derashot Be-Yisra'el.* Jerusalem: Mosad Bialik, 1974.

Index of Passages Cited

General Index